HAND  ESEARCH

An Interdisciplinary Survey and Introduction

International Handbook Series on Entrepreneurship

VOLUME 1

Series Editors

Zoltan J. Acs, *University of Baltimore, U.S.A.*

David B. Audretsch, *Indiana University, U.S.A.*

SERIES FOREWORD

Interest in entrepreneurship has surged in the last decade. Scholars across a broad spectrum of fields and disciplines have responded by generating new research approaches uncovering a wealth of new findings and insights about entrepreneurship. This new research spans not just a diverse set of fields, such as management, finance, psychology, economics, sociology, and geography but also a wide range of countries reflecting the fact that entrepreneurship is a global phenomenon. The exceptionally cross-disciplinary nature of entrepreneurship has made it difficult for scholars in any one particular field to become aware of and understand the leading contributions and insights emerging in other disciplines. The purpose of this series is to compile a series of handbooks, each devoted to a particular issue in the entrepreneurship field. Each handbook will draw upon the leading international scholars from the entire range of disciplines contributing to entrepreneurship to articulate the state of knowledge about a particular topic. The contribution should identify the fundamental questions which are being posed, the methodological approaches, types of data bases used for empirical analyses, the most important empirical regularities to emerge in the literature, major policy conclusions, and the most promising research direction. Thus, each handbook will reflect the interdisciplinary nature of entrepreneurship that has proven to be elusive to discipline-based scholars. A goal of the Handbook Series is not only to provide a state-of-the-art coverage of what has been learned about entrepreneurship, but that when viewed in its entirety, entrepreneurship is emerging as a bona fide academic discipline.

The particular topics in the Series will be drawn from discussions with the leading scholars. Each handbook will be directed and compiled by a Handbook Editor. (S)he will work closely with the Series Editor to ensure that the contents and contributions are appropriate, and that there is consistency with the other volumes in the Series.

The titles published in this series are listed at the end of this volume.

HANDBOOK OF ENTREPRENEURSHIP RESEARCH

An Interdisciplinary Survey and Introduction

Edited by

ZOLTAN J. ACS
University of Baltimore, U.S.A.

and

DAVID B. AUDRETSCH
Indiana University, U.S.A.

 Springer

Library of Congress Cataloging-in-Publication Data

A C.I.P. Catalogue record for this book is available
from the Library of Congress.

ISBN 1-4020-7358-5 (HC)   ISBN 0-387-24080-2 (SC)   E-book ISBN 0-387-24519-7

Printed on acid-free paper.

First softcover printing, 2005

Printed in the United States of America.

9 8 7 6 5 4 3 2 1   SPIN 11313915

springeronline.com

"Research and theory on entrepreneurial phenomena is advancing rapidly in scope and quality. The year 2003 is an excellent time for a comprehensive status report by the best scholars in the field. Acs and Audretsch have clearly organized such a statement – it will be a boon to all those seeking an authoritative overview of the current status of entrepreneurial research. The focus on advanced economies or the advanced sectors of developing countries reflects the emphasis in the extant research and theory. This new *Handbook* sets the framework for an expansion of attention to the vast majority of entrepreneurs – who are operating in the third world."

Paul D Reynolds, London Business School, UK and Babson College, USA

"In the Kluwer *Handbook of Entrepreneurship Research*, Acs and Audretsch have complied an impressive collection of contemporary contributions from many of the very best scholars in entrepreneurship across disciplines. It provides doctoral students with a broad yet solid introduction to the field, and established scholars with an overview that is otherwise very hard to obtain. It is a must read for every academic who is serious about entrepreneurship."

Per Davidsson, The Jönköping International Business School, Sweden

"Acs and Audretsch have assembled a virtual who's who list of researchers in the fledgling field of entrepreneurship. Even more usefully, the *Handbook* also includes reviews of the vast array of work closely related to entrepreneurship that has appeared primarily in economics, psychology and sociology journals; despite their relevance, locating these studies can prove difficult as their authors frequently do not focus on the implications for their research for entrepreneurship. As its 'Handbook' label implies, it should be a valuable reference tool for those in the area for years to come."

Olav Sorenson, Anderson School of Business, University of California at Los Angeles (UCLA), USA

Table of Contents

Preface

The purpose of the *Handbook of Entrepreneurship Research* is to provide a distinctive multidisciplinary, starting point for entrepreneurship research as defined by leading scholars. The chapters are carefully written reviews of the literature focusing on current research problems and future research directions. They are written by leading disciplinary scholars that have made a major impact on entrepreneurial thinking in economics, finance, psychology, management, strategy and sociology.

The first edition of the *Handbook of Entrepreneurship Research* has been very well received. Indeed, it far exceeded our expectation. The reason for this we believe is that there was a real need for a handbook of entrepreneurship. While entrepreneurship is not a field of research in any major discipline (certainly not in economics, if judged by the JEL classification) it is, in fact, a blossoming field of study that cuts across several disciplines.

The *Handbook of Entrepreneurship Research* provides a high quality introduction to and synthesis of the field of entrepreneurship research under one cover. It is not a collection of existing articles, but a carefully crafted "roadmap" through the emerging literature on entrepreneurship. Answers to many research questions can easily be found in the Handbook. Therefore, we have achieved our main objective with this book, that is, creating a reader friendly but still, valuable resource for the entrepreneurship community.

Of course there was one problem with the original idea. While the Handbook was written primarily with graduate students in mind, it was priced for professors of entrepreneurship with endowed chairs! We hope that this paperback edition remedies that problem. Enjoy.

Zoltan J. Acs
David B. Audretsch

.

List of Contributors

ZOLTAN J. ACS
Doris and Robert McCurdy
    Distinguished Professor of
    Entrepreneurship
Robert G. Merrick School of Business
University of Baltimore
1420 North Charles Street
Baltimore, MD 21201, USA

HOWARD E. ALDRICH
Sociology Department
The University of North Carolina at
    Chapel Hill
202 Hamilton Hall
Campus Box 3210
Chapel Hill, NC 27599, USA

SHARON A. ALVAREZ
The Ohio State University
850 Fisher Hall
2100 Neil Ave
Columbus, OH 43210, USA

DAVID B. AUDRETSCH
Ameritech Chair of Economic
    Development
Director, Institute for Development
    Strategies
Indiana University
School of Public & Environmental
    Affairs
1315 East 10th Street, Room 201
Bloomington, IN 47405, USA

ALLEN N. BERGER
Federal Reserve Board
Mail Stop 153
20th and C Streets NW
Washington, DC 20551, USA

MARTIN CARREE
Erasmus University Rotterdam
CASBEC
NL-3000 DR Rotterdam
The Netherlands

NANCY CARTER
University of St. Thomas
Mail TMH 470 1000 La Salle Avenue
Minneapolis, MN 55403, USA

MARK CASSON
The University of Reading
Department of Economics
Whiteknights, P.O. Box 218
Reading RG6 6AA, United Kingdom

ARNOLD COOPER
Krannert Graduate School of
    Management
Purdue University
West Lafayette, IN 02157, USA

NICK DEW
Darden Graduate School of Business
University of Virginia
P.O. Box 6550, Office 288
Charlottesville, VA 22906, USA

JONATHAN T. ECKHARDT
Weinert Center for Entrepreneurship
Department of Management and
   Human Resources
University of Wisconsin
5252 Grainger Hall
975 University Avenue
Madison, WI 53706

WILLIAM B. GARTNER
Marshall School of Business
University of Southern California
Bridge Hall One
Los Angeles, CA 90089, USA

SHARON GIFFORD
Rutgers University
180 University Avenue
Newark, NJ 07102, USA

PAUL GOMPERS
School of Business Administration
Harvard University
Morgan Hall, Room #481
Soldiers Field
Boston, MA 02163, USA

ROGER KOPPL
Department of Economics and
   Finance
Fairleigh Dickinson University
Madison, NJ 07940, USA

NORRIS KRUEGER
Department of Management
College of Business and Economics
Boise State University
1910 University Drive
Boise, ID 83725, USA

JOSHUA LERNER
School of Business Administration
Harvard University
Morgan Hall, Room 395
Soldiers Field
Boston, MA 02163, USA

MARTHA MARTINEZ
Sociology Department
The University of North Carolina at
   Chapel Hill
Chapel Hill, NC 27599, USA

RITA GUNTHER McGRATH
Columbia University
Business School
406 Armstrong Hall, 2880 Broadway
New York, NY 10025, USA

MARIA MINNITI
Department of Entrepreneurship
Babson College
Babson, MA, USA

SARAS SARASVATHY
Darden Graduate School of Business
University of Virginia
P.O. Box 6550, Office 288
Charlottesville, VA 22906, USA

SCOTT SHANE
Robert H. Smith School of Business
University of Maryland
Van Munching Hall
College Park, MD 20742, USA

KELLY G. SHAVER
Professor of Psychology
College of William & Mary
217 Millington Hall
P.O. Box 8795
Williamsburg, VA 23187, USA

DAVID J. STOREY
SME Centre
Warwick Business School
University of Warwick
Coventry CV4 7AL
United Kingdom

PATRICIA THORNTON
Fugua School of Business
Duke University
P.O. Box 90120
Durham, NC 27708, USA

A. ROY THURIK
Erasmus University Rotterdam
CASBEC, Room H8-24
P.O. Box 1738
NL-3000 DR Rotterdam
The Netherlands

GREGORY F. UDELL
Kelley School of Business
Room 370
Indiana University
10th & Fee Lane
Bloomington, IN 47405
USA

RAMA VELAMARI
Darden Graduate School of Business
University of Virginia
P.O. Box 6550, Office 288
Charlottesville, VA 22906, USA

SANKARAN VENKATARAMAN
Darden Graduate School of Business
University of Virginia
P.O. Box 6550, Office 288
Charlottesville, VA 22906, USA

The International Award for Entrepreneurship and Small Business Research

BACKGROUND

In 1996, The Swedish Foundation for Small Business Research (FSF) and NUTEK (The Swedish National Board for Industrial and Technical Development), together with the Swedish telecommunications company Telia Företag AB, founded the International Award for Entrepreneurship and Small Business Research.

The ambition behind the Award was, and still is, threefold: to highlight the importance of the research that is being produced in the areas of entrepreneurship and small business, to further stimulate and promote scholarly work within these fields of research and to spread the research among scholars, practitioners and people involved in small business development.

In line with the last of these three ambitions, the Award winner is invited to give seminars in a yearly seminar tour held in Sweden. The tour, organized jointly by FSF and Nutek, who today are the two organizations behind the award, covers 10 cities yearly and has been running since 1998. The Award winner is also invited as keynote speaker at the yearly World Congress of the International Council for Small Business (ICSB).

The Award is given annually to a person who has produced scholarly work of outstanding quality and importance, thereby giving a significant contribution to theory-building concerning entrepreneurship and small business development, and the importance of new firm formation and/or small and medium sized enterprises' role in economic development. The research results for which the Award is presented should lead to an increased understanding of the conditions under which small business operates.

The Scientific Council of FSF is responsible for the evaluation on candidates and the final selection of the annual winner.

NOMINATION PROCESS

An independent award committee appointed by the Swedish Foundation for Small Business Research annually appoints the winner. This committee reviews nominations from 250 qualified researchers globally who are invited to nominate candidates for the Award on a yearly basis. This procedure is unique and a way of ensuring the academic quality and relevance of the Award winner.

This nomination- and decision-making process, together with its USD 50 000 prize sum, gives the Award a unique position, making it the most prestigious award of its kind. Besides the honour and the prize sum, the Award consists of the statuette "God's Hand" created by the famous Swedish sculptor Carl Milles (1875–1955).

PREVIOUS AWARD-WINNERS:

2003   Dr William Baumol
2002   Dr Giacomo Becattini and Dr Charles Sabel
2001   Dr Zoltan J. Acs and Dr David B. Audretsch
2000   Dr Howard E. Aldrich, USA
1999   Dr Ian C. MacMillan, USA
1998   Dr David J. Storey, UK
1997   Dr Arnold C. Cooper, USA
1996   Dr David Birch

To learn more about the award and for more information on all award winners, please visit our website: www.fsf.se. For more information on ICSB, please visit: www.icsb.org

Anders Lundstrom
Swedish Foundation for Small Business Research (FSF)

PART ONE

Introduction to Entrepreneurship

ZOLTAN J. ACS[1] and DAVID B. AUDRETSCH[2]

[1]*University of Baltimore*, [2]*Indiana University*

1. Introduction to the Handbook of Entrepreneurship Research

The role of entrepreneurship in society has changed drastically over the last half century. During the immediate post-World War II period the importance of entrepreneurship seemed to be fading away. When J.J. Servan Schreiber (1968) warned Europeans of *Le Defi American,* or the American Challenge in 1968, it was not from small entrepreneurial firms, but exactly the opposite from the "dynamism, organizational, innovation, and boldness that characterized the giant American corporations."

By that time, a generation of scholars had systematically documented and supported the conclusion of Joseph A. Schumpeter (1942, p. 106): "What we have got to accept is that the large-scale establishment or unit of control has come to be the most powerful engine of progress and in particular of the long-run expansion of output ..." John Kenneth Galbraith (1956, p. 86), put it this way: "There is no more pleasant fiction than that technological change is the product of the matchless ingenuity of the small man forced by competition to employ his wit to better his neighbor."

This situation has been reversed completely in recent years (Acs and Audretsch, 2001). Entrepreneurship has come to be perceived as an engine of economic and social development throughout the world. According to Edward Lazear at Stanford University (2002, p. 1), "The entrepreneur is the single most important player in a modern economy." David Hart at the Kennedy School of Government at Harvard University discussing the dot-com bubble in the late 1990s wrote, "The entrepreneurship fad rested on a foundation of fact. New companies made significant contributions to economic growth in the past decade, both directly and by stimulating their more established competitors, as they indeed had in the decades before that. If the fad exaggerated these contributions, its fading should not obscure them entirely. Entrepreneurship is an economic phenomenon worthy of attention from those who worry about economic growth and particularly from those charged with sustaining that growth" (Hart, 2003, p. 1).

The focus of entrepreneurship research over the past decade has also changed significantly. Today, entrepreneurship, and the impacts of entrepreneurship on society are the subject of a growing body of research primarily in the disciplines of economics, geography, management, finance, strategy, psychology and sociology. Entrepreneurship is a subfield in most of the above disciplines. While the

Z.J. Acs and D.B. Audretsch (eds.), Handbook of Entrepreneurship Research, 3–20
© 2003 *Kluwer Academic Publishers. Printed in Great Britain.*

literature before the 1980s was mostly fragmented, during the 1980s several journals specific to entrepreneurship were started and the non disciplinary literature expanded greatly: *Journal of Business Venturing, Small Business Economics, Entrepreneurship Theory and Practice,* and *Entrepreneurship and Regional Development.*[1] However, this stream of literature has not developed the theoretical foundations to create a field of entrepreneurship research (Christensen, Carlile, and Sundahl, 2002).

In 1988 Low and MacMillan published an article in the *Journal of Management* on "Past Research and Future Challenges." Several observations were made in the article including the eclectic nature of entrepreneurship research, the need for theory driven research, and the fact that much of the research in the field was done by scholars in different disciplines. If research remained contained within the traditional discipline boundaries, how will a field of entrepreneurship be created? These questions were recently revisited in a special issue of *Entrepreneurship Theory and Practice* (Davidson et al., 2001) on Low and MacMillan Ten Years On. The field of entrepreneurship in the early 21st century is a catchall. It included such a wide-ranging set of topics that it is impossible to include them all under the umbrella of entrepreneurship (see, for example, Westhead and Wright, 2000). This has led to an exciting field where sometimes passion for the subject was sufficient for entry. According to Low (2001, p. 20), "One can argue in favor of a field that is inclusive and eclectic. In many ways, the broad range of subjects is the strength of the field. ... However, this inclusiveness and eclecticism is not free of cost ... I think this is partly because of lack of focus, and partly because entrepreneurship researchers are less steeped in the rigors of traditional disciplines." One thing is clear. There is a tension between those who would like to see entrepreneurship develop as a distinctive domain and those that think it should cast a very wide net. Of course this leads to the question, "What is the distinctive domain of entrepreneurship?"

There have been several important developments in entrepreneurship research over the past decade that call for a distinctive domain. First, while traditional research in entrepreneurship focused on the study of the entrepreneur herself, today there is a shift away from research on "traits" and personality. The study of individuals with an emphasis on behavior and cognitive issues and the recognized need to focus on the discovery and exploitation of opportunity (Shane and Venkataraman, 2000). The same is true in economics where there has been a shift to entrepreneurial choice models (Evans and Jovanovic, 1989). The focus has shifted from the study of firms to the study of individual

---

[1] Most of the early literature appeared in two places. First, the *Frontiers of Entrepreneurship Research* collected the papers from the Babson Conferences starting in 1980. Second, for twenty years Donald Sexton has been a keen observer and expert synthesizer of the latest scholarship and emerging trends. Sexton's determination to periodically bring together influential scholars in the field to take stock of the "state-of-art" of entrepreneurship and package the outcome of those meetings has done much for advancing the distinctiveness and legitimacy of the entrepreneurship domain (Powers and McDougall, 2000).

entrepreneurs as agents of change (Audretsch, 1995). This renewed focus on the individual brings into sharp focus the need to examine the environment and environmental factors that affect firm formation (Thornton, 1999).

The second development involves the study of the nascent entrepreneur. The concept of the nascent entrepreneur captures the flavor of the chaotic and disorderly founding process. A nascent entrepreneur is defined as someone who initiates serious activities that are intended to culminate in a viable business start-up (Reynolds, 1994). Each year between four and six percent of the working age population in the United States takes action to start a new venture, and about 40 percent of American adults experience bouts of self employment in their lifetime. The relationship between nascent entrepreneurs, organization/ firm births, and economic growth is a vital area of research.

The third development is that research on economic growth has shifted to the study of the new growth theory with an emphasis on endogenous technical change (Romer, 1990). In technological change and economic growth, there has been a shift towards the importance of space, especially at the regional level with a focus on R&D spillovers (Acs, 2002). There is a recognition to study the impact of new firm formation, and firm dynamics on economic and social variables, for example, economic development, technological change, economic growth, productivity, wealth creation and inequality.

Finally, it is important to keep in mind that much of the best research in entrepreneurship has been, and continues to be, in the disciplinary journals, like *the American Economic Review, American Sociological Review, Administrative Science Quarterly, Journal of Financial Economics, Strategic Management Journal*. This brings us back to the issue of a distinctive domain of entrepreneurship research or discipline based research. We believe that this distinction is not as valid as one might think. While discipline based research is needed to advance the field of entrepreneurship, a community of scholars is also needed with a common interest. One cannot advance without the other. Without a community of scholars, research in one field will not become familiar with other researchers and entrepreneurship will not develop as a field of study. An example of this kind of cross-fertilization is a recent article by Paul Geroski (2001) that compares the literature in Organizational Ecology and Industrial Economics, and Barnett and Sorenson (2002) look at the difference between Organizational Ecology and Organizational Sociology.

We would suggest at this juncture that there are many research questions that are discussed in the disciplines that are marginal to the discipline but are central to entrepreneurship research. Bringing these topics into entrepreneurship would greatly strengthen the field. There are many examples. In the discipline of Economics the field of Industrial Organization offers an excellent example. Industrial organization economists have for years studied the role of entry and the determinants of entry (Acs and Audretsch, chapter 5, 1990). Their conclusion was that entry was not very important. (This is in part because they only looked at manufacturing.) So the study of entry has received less and less attention over the years. In entrepreneurship research, the topic of entry (entering an industry with a new venture) plays a central role. It is one of the vehicles by which opportunity is exploited. Therefore, borrowing from this literature, would build a bridge between the two fields and strengthen both of them.

This refocusing of entrepreneurship research involves a parallel process of both broadening and narrowing down. In a fashion we suggest a pruning of the branches. The narrowing of the field involves less of an emphasis on different samples of small firms, for example, small business, family business, self employed, international entrepreneurship etc. Our definition of entrepreneurship embraces all businesses that are new and dynamic, regardless of size or line of business, while excluding businesses that are neither new nor dynamic as well as all non-business organizations. This leaves the entrepreneurial process, opportunity and the nature of exploitation, the emergence of new ventures, and entrepreneurship and organizational interaction as core topics. The broadening brings in questions of entrepreneurial dynamics. The issues of economic growth, economic development, regional growth bring into sharp focus both economics and sociology research, evolutionary economics and population ecology. According to Schoonhoven and Romanelli (2002, p. 401), "We begin with contexts, communities and populations as the settings from which the entrepreneurship dynamic emerges. For scholars of entrepreneurship, to stop short of addressing the impact of new firms on the evolution of industries is to miss what we argue is one of the most important questions to be resolved among the mass effects of the entrepreneurship dynamic."

The current developments in entrepreneurship research suggest the need for a handbook of entrepreneurship. While entrepreneurship is not a field of research in any discipline, it is, in fact, a blossoming field that cuts across several disciplines. In fact, some of the most interesting fields of research today are those that cut across several or many fields (de Solla Price, 1986). Herein lies the need for a handbook. In anticipation of this need, over the last few years, several authors have edited collections of existing articles in an attempt to pull together research on the subject. These collections have been useful in that they pull together a literature that is spread out over many journals and books some of them difficult to find. They also pointed to an interesting problem. That is, the subject matter of these collections has very little overlap. In other words, one does not know where to go for a comprehensive overview of the subject matter on entrepreneurship research.

An early attempt was *Entrepreneurship* by Mark Casson (1990) concentrating on the entrepreneurial process, empirical studies, and culture and development. This was an excellent start. *Small Business and Economic Growth* by Zoltan J. Acs (1996) focused on a broader set of topics including theories of the firm, finance, technological change, self-employment, clusters, job creation and industrial districts. The focus was more on samples of small firms and less on entrepreneurship but the question that motivated the collection was, "Do small firms and entrepreneurship have any relationship to economic growth?" David Storey (2000), in *Small Business: Critical Perspectives on Business and*

Management, also took a broad approach with an emphasis on the process of firm formation, firm exit, firm survival and firm growth. In the above collections, the topic selections were more economic and there was less of a focus on management and organization processes.

Two more collections followed. *Advances in Entrepreneurship* (2000) by Paul Westhead and Mike Wright, as the title indicates, pulled together a very large collection of articles from entrepreneurship and management with a focus on the literature from entrepreneurship journals over the past decade. This clearly accepted the broadening view of entrepreneurship research as the excellent introduction by the authors tried to cover most of the advances in the literature. Finally, Scott Shane (2000) in *The Foundations of Entrepreneurship*, pulled together the foundations of entrepreneurship research with a focus on the major disciplines. Clearly here the focus was on the foundations with an emphasis on narrowing the field. The topics covered the entrepreneurial process, technology, opportunity and finance with a call for focusing entrepreneurship on the exploitation of opportunity.

These collections of the literature raise two important questions. First, since the coverage in these different collections does not significantly overlap, which literature reflects the field of entrepreneurship? Second, how is one to interpret the different collections about where the field of entrepreneurship is going? In order to understand how the field is evolving we need a handbook that can serve as a reference source for current and future researchers.

At this juncture, it is fair to offer our vision of the field that in part guides this volume. We view entrepreneurship as what happens at the intersection of history and technology. History is the written record of everything that has happened in the past, and technology is a way we view the future. This leads to two concepts. First, is the stock of knowledge or the technology set. This is a part of history, the codification of language and knowledge (van Doren, 1991). Second, is the technology opportunity set. It consists of all the opportunities that have not been exploited. Investment in new knowledge increases the technology opportunity set and sharpens our ability to gaze into the future. It is this intersection of history as a guide, and technology as a way to look forward at a point in time that creates the window of opportunities. Recently, Olsson and Frey (2002) building on Schumpeter (1934) formally examine this intersection and discuss the constraints on economic growth. It is here that entrepreneurship resides, and where individuals play a crucial role. As G.L.S. Shackle wrote, "*The entrepreneur is a maker of history, but his guide in making it is his judgement of possibilities and not a calculation of certainties*" (Hebert and Link, 1982, p. viii.). Finally, the intersection of history and technology exists in space. This spatial dimension has institutional and structural characteristics that influence social and economic outcomes (Oinas and Malecki, 2002). As Baumol (1990) pointed out, entrepreneurship has always existed and its outcomes can be productive, unproductive or destructive depending on the incentive that exists in the system. How those structures and institutions interact is crucial. For example, in his book *Against the Gods*, Peter L. Bernstein, asks the question "What distinguished the thousands of years of history from what we think of as modern times? The answer goes way beyond the progress of science, technology, capitalism, and democracy ... The revolutionary idea that defines the boundary between modern times and the past is the mastery of risk: the notion that the future is more than a whim of the gods and that men and women are not passive before nature" (Bernstein, 1996, p. 1).

The purpose of the *Handbook of Entrepreneurship Research* is to provide a distinctive, multidisciplinary, starting point for entrepreneurship research as defined by leading scholars. It is not a practical guide for practitioners. We focus on entrepreneurship from a disciplinary perspective. The papers are carefully written reviews of the literature focusing on current research and future research directions. They are written by leading disciplinary scholars that have made a major impact on entrepreneurial thinking in economics, finance, psychology, management, and sociology. Five are recipients of the International Award for Entrepreneurship and Small Business Research, awarded on behalf of the *Swedish Foundation for Small Business Research* and *The Swedish National Board of Industrial and Technical Development*. Arnold Cooper the author of Chapter 2 was the recipient in 1997. David Storey the author of Chapter 18 was the recipient in 1998. Howard Aldrich the author of Chapter 15 was the recipient in 2000. Zoltan J. Acs and David B. Audretsch were the recipients in 2001. Four have edited previous handbooks. Most are distinguished research professors at major research universities. They are also members of a community of scholars that have tried to translate that research into the field of entrepreneurship through specialty journals. In fact, one of the reasons for creating this volume is to strengthen the community of scholarship in entrepreneurship.

The 19 chapters, including this introduction, are organized into eight sections with several papers in each section including two introductory chapters and an epilogue. The topics are organized by three units of analysis, the individual, the firm and the larger society and economy. The material is organized in such a way as to make it easy to follow by building up from the individual to the firm and finally to larger social units.

Part One, "Introduction to Entrepreneurship," has two chapters. These two chapters – "Editors' Introduction," by Zoltan J. Acs and David B. Audretsch and "The Past, the Present, the Future," by Arnold Cooper – present an introduction to this volume by discussing the need for the present project and putting that need into a larger context in the development of entrepreneurship research.

Chapter 1 provides an introduction to the Handbook. The editors discuss the current state of entrepreneurship research, they examine recent developments in the field of entrepreneurship, discuss the justification for the Handbook of Entrepreneurship Research, and reasons for the selections included and omitted. In Chapter 2, Cooper reviews the past, present and future of entrepreneurship research mostly in the United States. *The purpose of his chapter is to reflect on half a century of teaching research and community building in the field of entrepreneurship.* In some sense it is from this background that advances in the 1990s were made in the budding field. Cooper documents the early development of small firms and entrepreneurship teaching, the role of the U.S. Small Business Administration, the role of Babson College, and the community of scholars that laid the early foundations for the field. Cooper, one of the giants in both strategy and entrepreneurship, is optimistic about the future developments of a field of study. While entrepreneurship is as old as human history, entrepreneurship research is relatively new, and the field of entrepreneurship is only in its infancy.

Part Two, "The Entrepreneurial Process," discusses the topic of risk and uncertainty, innovation and technological change and market processes as they relate to entrepreneurship. While these topics are not necessarily only about entrepreneurship, they all have something to offer in understanding the entrepreneurial process. These traditional economic topics are identified at least to some extent in the literature with the works of Frank Knight (1921), Joseph Schumpeter (1911[1934]) and Frederick Hayek (1937) respectively.

For Knight profit is defined as the surplus, which remains once wages of labor, the rent of land and the interest on capital have been paid out of revenue. In a static competitive economy anyone can purchase factors and combine them to generate output. With free entry and exit, and no economies of scale, competition between producers maintains long run economic profit at zero. There is simply no need for an entrepreneur. If we relax the assumption of a static environment and the environment is unpredictable, we introduce the element of risk and uncertainty. Knight refined this idea by distinguishing between risk and uncertainty. Risk, according to Knight, relates to recurrent situations in which, by repeated observation, it is possible to estimate the relative frequencies with which different outcomes will arise. Knight argued that it is not measurable risk but unmeasurable uncertainty that constitutes the basis for pure profit.

Schumpeter's view of the entrepreneur as innovator has widespread appeal. His early work, which highlighted the romantic and visionary aspects of business, appeals to artists and individuals (Schumpeter, 1934 [1911]), whilst his later work appeals to scientists and collectivists because of his claim that innovation can be effectively programmed and coordinated within large organizations (Schumpeter, 1942). Because of its visionary nature it is difficult to model. Several writers have attempted this within an evolutionary perspective. From a Darwinian perspective, innovation is a source of potential diversity analogous to genetic variation. In one version of this analogy, the variation occurs within a population of firms when one of them adopts a new technology. The innovative firm then competes with established firms in a competitive survival (Nelson and Winter, 1982).

The three chapters in Part Two – "Risk and Uncertainty," by Sharon Gifford, "Innovation and Technological Change," by Zoltan J. Acs and David B. Audretsch, and "Market Processes and Entrepreneurial Studies," by Roger

Koppl and Maria Minniti – all directly address aspects of the entrepreneurial process. All three chapters are written from an economic perspective.

In Chapter 3, Gifford illustrates an elementary element of most economic theories of the entrepreneur, uncertainty and the accompanying risk. The entrepreneur functions in the economic environment only if the environment is uncertain. If all individuals in the economy had perfect information, then all profitable opportunities would be exploited instantaneously and there would be no further entrepreneurial role. Equilibrium is a set of prices at which there are no profit opportunities. Thus, uncertainty and risk, as well as a disequilibrium economy, as opposed to equilibrium, are necessary elements for any economic analysis that explicitly addresses the role of the entrepreneur. *The purpose of her chapter is to propose an approach to decision making under uncertainty that, instead of assuming that individuals are risk averse, derives risk averse behavior as a result of limited attention.* If we understand the sources of risk averse behavior, we would be better able to predict entrepreneurial behavior. According to Gifford there is no need to rely on assumptions about unavoidable risk behavior or animal spirits. The question of how entrepreneurs overcome the problem of asymmetric information about their experiences, knowledge and skills and subsequent effort can be advanced by the implications of the economics of asymmetric information.

In Chapter 4, Acs and Audretsch show that the innovative potential of small firms was burdened with the view that large firms had the innovative advantage. *The purpose of this chapter is to suggest that a much wider spectrum of enterprises contributing to innovative activity, and that, in particular, small entrepreneurial firms as well as large established incumbents play an important role in the innovation and technological change process* (Acs and Audretsch, 1990). These studies comprise a new understanding about the links between the individual entrepreneur, firm size and innovative activity. The chapter begins with the knowledge production function where the firm is exogenous and technology is endogenous. A key finding is that the conventional wisdom regarding the process of innovation and technological change is generally inconsistent with the new understanding about the role of entrepreneurship and innovative activity. The empirical evidence strongly suggests that small entrepreneurial firms play a key role in generating innovations, at least in some industries. Recent evidence suggests that scale economies bestowed through geographic proximity facilitated by spatial clusters seem to be more important than those for large enterprises in producing innovative output. Because of the appropriability problem they propose shifting the unit of observation away from exogenously assumed firms to individuals, agents with endowments of new economic knowledge. When the lens is shifted away from the firm to the individual as the relevant unit of observation, the knowledge is exogenous and embodied in a worker. The firm is created endogenously in the agents' effort to appropriate the value of her knowledge through innovative activity (Audretsch, 1995).

Koppl and Minniti, in Chapter 5, examine the role of entrepreneurship from an Austrian perspective. *The purpose of this chapter is to show how the Austrian approach helps to integrate and organize much of the entrepreneurship literature and how it may be used to create a common theoretical framework for entrepreneurial studies in a disequilibrium analysis.* Their concern is the lack of a definition for entrepreneurship that captures both aspects of entrepreneurship and the entrepreneur. For them entrepreneurship is alertness to new opportunities. Second, entrepreneurship is seizing an opportunity by taking innovative action. Alertness leads to the discovery of new opportunities. The chapter explains Kirzner's theory and the contribution of more recent Austrians in their proper context. They suggest an Austrian definition of entrepreneurship that addresses the concerns of Shane and Venkataraman (2000).

Part Three, "Opportunity and the Nature of Exploitation," examines opportunity from a psychological and management perspective. These chapters build on some of the issues discussed in the previous section including disequilibrium and uncertainty. While opportunity recognition and information search are often considered to be the first critical steps in the entrepreneurial process, limited empirical research has been conducted about this process. Venkataraman (1997) argues that one of the most neglected questions in entrepreneurship research is where opportunities come from. Why, when and how certain individuals exploit opportunities appear to be a function of the joint characteristics of the opportunity and the nature of the individual. There are three main areas where certain individuals recognize opportunities while others do not: knowledge differences, cognition differences and behavioral differences.

The three chapters in this Part – "The Cognitive Psychology of Entrepreneurship," by Norris Krueger, Jr. "Three Views of Entrepreneurial Opportunity," by Saras Sarasvathy, Nick Dew, Sankaran Venkataraman and Ramakrishna Velamuri, and "The Individual-Opportunity Nexus" by Scott Shane and Jonathan Eckhardt – all address the question of opportunity in entrepreneurship research: existence, discovery and exploitation. These chapters are written from the perspective of psychology and management.

In Chapter 6, Krueger examines entrepreneurial cognition. *The purpose of this chapter is to focus on a key issue, "What cognitive phenomenon is associated with seeing and acting on opportunities?"* According to Krueger, understanding entrepreneurial cognition is imperative to understanding the essence of entrepreneurship. This is especially true if we wish to move from descriptive research to theory-driven research. Cognition research offers rich theory and well-developed methods. What is unique about entrepreneurial thinking? Krueger focuses on the most critical distinction between entrepreneurs and non-entrepreneurs, the intentional pursuit of opportunity. As Stevenson and Gumpert (1985) pointed out long ago, the "heart" of entrepreneurship is the seeking of and acting upon opportunities. To understand entrepreneurship requires understanding of how we learn to see opportunity and decide to pursue them.

In Chapter 7, Dew, Sarasvathy, Velamuri and Venkataraman present three views of entrepreneurial opportunity. *The purpose of this chapter is to challenge the assumption underlying current theories of innovation that if a market can be created it will.* Instead, the chapter focuses on Arrow's exhortation to researchers to tackle one of the central problems in economics today, uncertainty. They begin with a definition of entrepreneurial opportunity. Then they delineate its elements and examine it within three views of the market process: the market as an allocative process; as a discovery process; and as a creative process. Within each literature they examine the assumptions about the knowledge of the decision marker regarding the future, and the implications of those assumptions for strategies to recognize, discover, and create entrepreneurial opportunities. The chapter concludes with a set of conjectures that challenge the inevitability of technological commercialization and argue for a more contingent approach to the study of the central phenomenon of entrepreneurship.

Shane and Eckhardt, in Chapter 8, examine the relationship between the individual agent and opportunity. *The purpose of this chapter is to build on Shane and Venkataraman (2000), first by broadening the treatment of the topic, second, by clarifying the dimensions of the organizing framework and third by updating the research with the latest findings.* They start with a discussion of disequilibrium to show why it is necessary for entrepreneurship. Their model consists of a two by two matrix that identifies entrepreneurial discovery and exploitation. The four possibilities are, first, independent discovery and startup. The second possibility is individual discovery with corporate exploitation resulting in an acquisition. Third is a corporate discovery and individual exploitation, which calls forth a spin-off. Finally, a corporate discovery and exploitation is corporate venturing. The chapter discusses what modes of exploitation will be used to exploit entrepreneurial opportunities. Because only individuals are capable of discovering opportunities, the locus of decision making about exploitation of discovered opportunities lies with people. Two dimensions of this choice appear to be important. First, can the opportunity be effectively pursued through markets? Second, are new or established firms better entities for undertaking the opportunity exploitation process?

Part Four, "The Emergence of New Ventures" follows from the previous section. If new firms are important in the mix of market exploitation how firms emerge, how we think about them from a theoretical perspective and what strategies they pursue are important questions. Perhaps one of the most important developments in entrepreneurship research over the past decade has been the concept of nascency by Reynolds, as we mentioned above. This concept has opened up several research areas and greatly increased our understanding of where firms come from and how opportunities are pursued.

The three chapters – "Entrepreneurial Behavior and Firm Organizing Processes," by William B. Gartner and Nancy M. Carter, "Entrepreneurship, Business Culture and the Theory of the Firm," by Mark Casson and "Resources and Hierarchies: Intersections between Entrepreneurship and Business Strategy," by Sharon A. Alvarez – all directly address the question of the role of the firm as a unit of analysis in entrepreneurship research. These chapters are written from the perspectives of organization theorists, economists and business strategists.

In Chapter 9, Gartner and Carter offer some insights and evidence about the process of organization formation. They examine the founding of independent for profit business for insights into the nature of organization formation. *The purpose of this chapter is to focus research on entrepreneurial behavior that involves activities of individuals who are creating new organizations, rather than the activities of individuals who are involved with maintaining or changing the operations of on-going established organizations.* They view entrepreneurship as an organizational phenomenon and as an organizing process and posit that the roots of entrepreneurship are embedded in social processes and consider the process of organizational formation to be the core characteristic of entrepreneurship. They also view entrepreneurial behavior as an individual level phenomenon, which occurs over time, and results in an organization as the primary outcome of these activities by drawing a sharp distinction between new organizations and emerging organizations. The study of a new organization is not the same as the study of emerging organizations.

In Chapter 10, Casson examines the relationship between entrepreneurship and the theory of the firm. According to Casson, there is a gulf between economic theories of entrepreneurship, which tend to be abstract, and studies of entrepreneurial behavior, which tend to be more about individual behavior. *The purpose of this chapter is to bridge this gap by developing a mutually consistent set of hypotheses about entrepreneurial behavior from a parsimonious set of assumptions.* The key to bridging the gap according to Casson is to relax some of the very restrictive assumptions about human motivation and decision making that underpin conventional economic theory. The main assumptions that need to be relaxed concern the objectivity of information, autonomy of preferences and cost-less optimization. Relaxing these assumptions makes it possible to accommodate theoretical insights derived from other social sciences. Once these assumptions are relaxed, it becomes evident that theories of entrepreneurship are closely related to modern theories of the firm, such as transaction cost theories and resource-based theories. The theory of entrepreneurship emerges as a powerful mechanism for synthesizing the insights of these modern theories of the firm.

Alvarez, in Chapter 11, examines the relationship between entrepreneurship and strategy. *The purpose of this chapter is to examine the intersection of entrepreneurship and strategic management as rent seeking behavior through entrepreneurship in either established firms or in newly forming firms with the recognition that entrepreneurship is intimately connected with the appearance and adjustment of unique and idiosyncratic resources.* For years there has been a cozy relationship between these two fields of research. In fact many have viewed entrepreneurship as simply an extension of strategy, and have called for closer work between the two. These two fields developed independently of each other and strategy has focused on helping existing firms develop alternatives for competitive advantage. Alvarez defines strategic management as the process an existing firm goes through to achieve competitive advantage. Strategy and entrepreneurship come into close contact when we are dealing with an innovation that the firm is trying to develop internally, or corporate venturing. It builds on the previous chapters in this section and integrates ideas about entrepreneurship, the firm and strategy.

Section Five, "Financing the New Venture," is included because finance is such an important function in new firm formation that leaving it out would leave our understanding of the subject incomplete. Moreover, research on the financing of the emerging organizations has made great strides in the past decade in the field of finance. While we do not discuss other issues of resource acquisition, for example, team building, etc., the financial acquisition question is important, in part, because venture capital is central to the management of risk and the financing of high growth firms. Finally, venture capital is also part of the networking of regional growth and development.

Finally, equity financing cannot be fully understood without a discussion of debt. The research on small business debt is older and more firmly established in the banking literature (Berger and Udell, 1998). The research on equity is newer and is part of an active research agenda in the field of finance. This literature is important for several reasons. First, much of venture capital is used to finance new technology-based firms. Second, this is a good example of research on entrepreneurship at the highest level in peer reviewed disciplinary journals. It sets an example for how disciplinary research and community building can progress hand in hand. However, much of this research has not filtered down to the entrepreneurship journals.

The two papers in Part Five – "Equity Financing," by Paul Gompers and Joshua Lerner and "Small Business and Debt Finance," by Allen Berger and Gregory Udell – present a comprehensive survey of the subject of financing small and emerging organizations. This section does not cover a related topic on whether small and emerging organizations are debt rationed (Evans and Jovanovic, 1989). While entrepreneurship scholars have written much about venture capital, both of these chapters are written from the discipline of finance.

In Chapter 12, Gompers and Lerner explore venture capital and private equity. *The purpose of this chapter is to summarize and synthesize what we do know about equity finance from recent research, and to indicate the important questions that we cannot yet answer.* The starting point of their chapter is what constitutes venture capital and angel financing. They define venture capital as independently managed, dedicated pools of capital that focus on equity or equity-linked investments in privately held, high growth companies. The primary focus of the chapter is on drawing together the empirical academic research on venture capital and angel financing. The chapter is also important because it raises important public policy issues about what is and should be the role of government in the financing of new ventures. Has venture capital and a robust IPO market been a source of U.S. competitive advantage? This institutional arrangement is unavailable in countries dominated by banks like

Germany and Japan. It is often unclear at what point countries should start duplicating the United States.

In Chapter 13, Berger and Udell examine the role of debt, the less glamorous side of entrepreneurial finance. *The purpose of this chapter is to put into perspective the vital role played by debt in entrepreneurial finance.* The proportion of debt in the capital structure of small business in the U.S. is similar to the 50 percent overall proportion of debt in the capital structure of all U.S. business. This holds true for the youngest firms and even high growth firms before initial pubic offering has a debt equity ratio of 33 percent. While the proportion of debt in the capital structure of small firms is similar to that of large firms, the debt financing itself is quite different in terms of type of debt issued, the contracting tools used, the lending technologies employed, and the role of intermediaries in the process. For large firms the majority of debt is in the form of traded instruments, such as commercial paper, syndicated bank loans and public bond issues. For small firms, in contrast, virtually all of the debt is non-traded – the biggest portion of which is in non-syndicated commercial loans. Moreover, the typical terms of small firm debt contracts are significantly different than those in large firm's debt contracts because of informational opacity often associated with small businesses. Another striking difference between small and large firms is found in their governance. The chapter concludes with some of the key factors that affect the supply of small business credit, including global consolidation of the banking industry, credit crunches, discrimination in lending, and the impact of technological innovation.

Part Six, "The Social Context," looks at social outcomes that are larger than individuals: organizations, populations and communities. If entrepreneurship is important, and one of the outcomes of entrepreneurial behavior is new organization, then how these organizations relate to each other in the formation of larger social groups is important to study. These larger organizations also have an impact on firm formation.

The three papers in this section – "The Social Psychology of Entrepreneurial Behavior," by Kelly G. Shaver, "Entrepreneurship as Social Construction: A Multi-level Evolutionary Approach," by Howard Aldrich and Martha Martinez and "Entrepreneurship, Networks and Geographies," by Patricia Thornton and Katherine Flynn – all directly address issues of larger units of analysis and the simultaneous interaction between the impact of new organization on this environment and the impact of the environment on organization creation. A social psychologist and four sociologists wrote the chapters.

In Chapter 14, Shaver suggests that social psychology is important for the study of entrepreneurship because the creation of a new venture is a truly social enterprise. Social psychology is the scientific study of the personal and situational factors that affect individual social behavior. As psychology concentrates on dependent variables smaller than the individual person, sociology concentrates on structures and processes that are larger than any particular individual. Social psychology investigates the socially meaningful actions of individuals. *The purpose of this chapter is to examine four major areas of theory and research in social psychology and indicates how each has found its place in the study of entrepreneurial activity: cognition, attribution, attitudes and the self.* These specific topics are included because they are traditional concerns of social psychologists and have all been the subject of numerous articles in entrepreneurship. The self, "who are you?" and "how did you get that way?," both "is' and "does". In the development of our social selves, we must often choose between accuracy and distortion. We need to know our capabilities, but we would like them to be more extensive than they are. This has application when considering if we have the right stuff to start new venture, and in networking from the standpoint of social comparison, among others. Specifically, self-efficacy in the entrepreneurial domain is a replacement for the "perceived behavioral control" that is part of the theory of planned behavior.

In Chapter 15, Aldrich and Martinez review and analyze the multi-level selection processes that apply across three different levels of entrepreneurial social construction: organizations, populations and communities. *The purpose of this chapter is to emphasize the inexorable tension between selection forces at the three levels that affect variations generated by entrepreneurs.* Sometimes these forces work in concert and sometimes they do not. Two concepts are important in their analysis. First, the concept of a "nascent entrepreneur" captures the flavor of the chaotic and disorderly process driving the creation of new firms, and second the distinction between an innovator and a replicator. Most new ventures are replications. Reproducing organizational forms constitutes the norm, rather than the exception. A franchise is a classic example of a replication, because from the very beginning new establishments are intended to be identical. Their main goal is to describe the entrepreneurial process as a form of social construction that goes beyond the firm itself to the creation of populations and communities. In contrast to the view that the best companies will prevail in the economy, they present evidence that collective action early in the life of a population affects which firms prosper and which do not. Following an evolutionary argument, the survival of a firm, population or community depends as much on the existence of favorable environmental forces as on the effectiveness of individual entrepreneurs. This is especially important for entrepreneurs that are innovators creating new organizations, populations and communities. They emphasize the importance of collective action, which depends on social psychology, in providing entrepreneurs with the capacity to shape their environments.

Thornton and Flynn in Chapter 16, build on the previous chapter by examining entrepreneurship and networks, as an example of a population. However, their theoretical perspective is not so much population ecology as geography, economics and sociology. *The purpose of this chapter is to argue that entrepreneurship is increasingly the domain of organizations and regions, not individuals.* These organizations and regions are environments rich in entrepreneurial opportunities and resources and they have been increasing in numbers and in varieties. These environments influence individuals and they also influence new ventures. However, how these environments spawn new entrepreneurs and create new business remains relatively understudied. Although these organizations and regional environments have been described as network structures and geographic clusters, research that links the spatial and relational aspects of these larger contexts to the micro process of entrepreneurship is relatively underdeveloped. They review the literatures on networks and geographies to examine how these environments affect the ability of entrepreneurs to garner scarce resources. They seek to address questions of how individuals are likely to become entrepreneurs within the context of why and where entrepreneurship is likely to occur. They define entrepreneurship as both the discovery and exploitation of entrepreneurial opportunities, and the creation of new organizations, which occur as a context-dependent social and economic process.

Part Seven, "Entrepreneurship, Economic Growth and Policy," examines the question, "What are the consequences of entrepreneurial activity for economic growth and can public policy affect the outcome?" These are important questions, and, as we have hinted in the opening paragraphs of this introduction, the conventional wisdom today is that the formation of new organizations does lead to economic growth and public policies aimed at individuals may increase the flow of new organizations in societies. Lundstrom and Stevenson (2002a, 2002b) make a distinction between small business policies and entrepreneurship policies. They view small business policies as focused upon existing enterprises, whereas entrepreneurship policies are directed towards individuals. These individuals are considering, or have recently started a new business. However, they only play a modest role in the policy armory of developed economies.

The two papers in this section – "The Impact of Entrepreneurship on Economic Growth," by Martin Carree and Roy Thurik and "Entrepreneurship, Small and Medium Sized Enterprises and Public Policies" by David J. Storey – both address the relationship between entrepreneurial activity and economic growth. The paper by Storey while acknowledging the difference between entrepreneurship policy and SME policy is more about the latter and less about the former. This is because SME policy aimed at small and medium-sized firms is now a well-established area of study and experimentation. Entrepreneurial policy directed at individuals is more or less new. Economists have written both of these chapters.[2]

In Chapter 17, Carree and Thurik observe that the last two decades have witnessed a wealth of studies analyzing the determinants of entrepreneurship, and the decision to go into business. The consequences of this behavior have also been studied extensively in the literature, for example, there is a large literature on firm survival. However, this literature has generally been restricted to two units of observation – that of the firm and the region. When it comes

---

[2] For those interested in the subject we refer you to the forthcoming book by David M. Hart, ed., *The Emergence of Entrepreneurship Policy: Governance, Start-ups, and Growth in the Knowledge Economy.* Two volumes on the subject are also available from Anders Lundstrom and Lois Stevenson (2002a, 2002b).

to linking entrepreneurship to growth at the national level, there is a relative void despite the recent efforts of the Global Entrepreneurship Monitor (GEM) research program (Reynolds et al., 2001). *The purpose of this chapter is to review the theoretical and empirical literature linking entrepreneurship and economic growth.* Explanations for economic growth have generally been restricted to the realm of macroeconomics. A different scholarly tradition linking growth to industrial organization dates back to at least Schumpeter (1934[1911]). According to this tradition, performance measured in terms of economic growth, is shaped by the degree to which the industry structure utilize scarce resources most efficiently (Schoonhoven and Romanelli, 2001).

Storey, in Chapter 18 reviews the rational and the consequences of small business policy in OECD countries. *The purpose of this chapter is to review the contribution that such policies and programs have made in those countries with a key focus on methodologies for assessing the impact of policies.* Storey starts out by pointing out that over the past forty years there has been a striking change in the perception of small firms, especially in the United States and in the United Kingdom. In the 1960s small-scale enterprise was equated with technological backwardness, managerial conservatism and modest economic contribution. This contrasts with the current view that, whilst many small firms do fit the 1960s stereotype, the sector also contains dynamic and innovative enterprises that collectively make a considerable contribution to economic well-being (Acs, Karlsson, Carlsson, 1999). Governments can facilitate or impede this contribution, and this chapter reviews public polices towards small firms in OECD countries.

Part Eight, "Epilogue," provides a roadmap for a future research direction. The purpose of the *Handbook* is to provide a starting point for entrepreneurship research. Given the many different directions and approaches, there is a need to provide a reference work for this emerging field. Each chapter offers a carefully presented summary of the field and discusses future research needs for different topics. While we do not summarize these, the final chapter offers a perspective on future research needs.

In Chapter 19, "Connecting the Study of Entrepreneurship and Theories of Capitalist Progress. An Epilogue," Rita McGrath discusses future research needs of the field. *The purpose of the chapter is to argue that there is now a significant body of research on entrepreneurship, as is evident in this Handbook, and now we should reach out to other fields and tackle even bigger questions.* The field of entrepreneurship offers a useful vantage point from which to tackle some of the more pressing issues of today's business organizations and the institutions in which they exist. McGrath concludes that the insights gained by entrepreneurship scholars through their study of often small, fragile, new entities can be a powerfully leverage to improve our understandings of the workings of the capitalism system.

REFERENCES

Acs, Zoltan J. (ed.) (1996). *Small Business and Economic Growth.* Cheltenham: Edward Elgar, 2 volumes.

Acs, Zoltan J. (ed.) (2002). *Innovation and the Growth of Cities.* Cheltenham: Edward Elgar.

Acs, Zoltan J. and David B. Audretsch (1990). *Innovation and Small Firms.* Cambridge: The MIT Press.

Acs, Zoltan J. and David B. Audretsch (2001). The emergence of the entrepreneurial society. Stockholm, Sweden, Swedish Foundation for Small Business Research, May 2001.

Acs, Zoltan J., Bo Carlsson and Charlie Carlsson (eds.) (1999). *Entrepreneurship, Small and Medium-Sized Enterprises and the Macroeconomy.* New York: Cambridge University Press.

Audretsch, David B. (1995). *Innovation and Industry Evolution.* Cambridge: The MIT Press.

Barnett, William P. and Olav Sorenson (2002). The red queen in organizational creation and development. *Industrial and Corporate Change,* 11(2), 289–325.

Baumol, William, J. (1990). Entrepreneurship: Productive, unproductive and destructive. *Journal of Political Economy,* **98**, 893–921.

Berger, Allen N. and Gregory F. Udell (1998). Special issue on "The economics of small business finance." *Journal of Banking and Finance,* **22**(6–8), 613–616.

Bernstein, Peter L. (1996). *Against the Gods: The Remarkable Story of Risk.* New York: John Wiley and Sons.

Casson, Mark (ed.) (1990). *Entrepreneurship.* Cheltenham: Edward Elgar.

Christensen, Clayton, Paul Carlile and David M. Sundahl (2002). The process of theory-building. Harvard University.

Davidson, Per, Murray B. Low and Mike Wright (2001). Editor's Introduction: Low and MacMillan ten years on: Achievements and future directions for entrepreneurship research. *Entrepreneurship Theory and Practice,* 25(4), 5–16.

De Solla Price, Derek J. (1986). *Little Science, Big Science – and Beyond.* New York: Columbia University Press.

Evans, David and Boyan Jovanovic (1989). Estimates of a model of entrepreneurial choice under liquidity constraints. *Journal of Political Economy,* 97, 808–827.

Galbraith, John K. (1956). *American Capitalism: The Concept of Countervailing Power.* Boston: Houghton Mifflin.

Geroski, Paul (2001). Exploring the niche overlaps between organizational economy and industrial economics. *Industrial and Corporate Change,* 10(2), 507–540.

Hart, David, (ed.) (2003). *The Emergence of Entrepreneurship Policy: Governance, Start-ups and Growth in Knowledge.* New York: Cambridge University Press.

Hayek, Frederick A. von (1937). Economics and knowledge. *Economica,* 4, 33–54.

Hebert, Robert F. and Albert N. Link (1982). *The Entrepreneur.* New York: Praeger.

Knight, Frank (1921). *Risk, Uncertainty and Profit.* Chicago: University of Chicago Press.

Lazear, Edward P. (2002). Entrepreneurship. National Bureau of Economic Research, working paper 9109, August 2002.

Low, Murray B. (2001). The adolescence of entrepreneurship research: Specification of purpose. *Entrepreneurship Theory and Practice,* 25(4), 17–27.

Low, Murray and Ian MacMillan (1988). Past research and future challenges. *Journal of Management,* 14, 149–162.

Lundstrom, Anders and Lois Stevenson (2002a). *On the Road to Entrepreneurship Policy,* Volume 1. Orebro, Sweden: Swedish Foundation for Small Business Research.

Nelson, Richard and Sydney Winter (1982). *An Evolutionary Theory of Economic Growth.* Cambridge: Harvard University Press.

Oinas, Paivi and Edward J. Malecki (2002). The evolution of technologies in time and space: From national and regional to spatial innovation systems. In Zoltan J. Acs and Attila Varga (eds.), special issue on Regional Innovation Systems. *International Regional Science Review,* 24(1), 102–130.

Olsson, Ola and Bruno S. Frey (2002). Entrepreneurship as recombinant growth. *Small Business Economics*, 19(2), 69–80.

Powers, Joshua B. and Patricia P. McDougall (2000). A review of the *Blackwell Handbook of Entrepreneurship*, Donald Sexton and Hans Lundstrom (eds.). *Small Business Economics*, 15(4), 321–328.

Reynolds, Paul (1994). Reducing barriers to understanding new firm gestation: Prevalence and success of nascent entrepreneurs. Paper presented at the annual meeting of the Academy of Management, Dallas.

Reynolds, Paul D., Michael Camp, William D. Bygrave, Erko Audio, and Michael Hay (2001). *Global Entrepreneurship Monitor*, 2001 Executive Report.

Romer, Paul (1990). Endogenous technical change. *Journal of Political Economy*, 98, S71–S102.

Schoonhoven, Claudia B. and Elaine Romanelli (eds.) (2001). *The Entrepreneurship Dynamic*, Stanford: Stanford University Press.

Schumpeter, Joseph A. (1934 [1911]). *The Theory of Economic Development*. Cambridge: Harvard University Press.

Schumpeter, Joseph A. (1942). *Capitalism, Socialism and Democracy*. New York: Harper and Row.

Servan Schreiber, J.J. (1968). *The American Challenge*. London: Hamish Hamilton.

Shane, Scott (ed.) (2000). *The Foundations of Entrepreneurship*. Cheltenham: Edward Elgar, 2 volumes.

Shane, Scott and Sankaran Venkataraman (2000). The distinctive domain of entrepreneurship research. *Academy of Management Review*, 25, 217–221.

Stevenson, Howard H. and David E. Gumpert (1985). The heart of entrepreneurship. *Harvard Business Review*, March–April, 85–94.

Stevenson, Lois and Lundstrom, Anders (2002b). *Patterns and Trends in Entrepreneurship/SME Policy and Practice in Ten Economies*, Volume 3. Orebro, Sweden: Swedish Foundation for Small Business Research.

Storey, David (ed.) (2000). *Small Business: Critical Perspectives on Business and Management*. London: Routledge, 2 volumes.

Thornton, Patricia H. (1999). The sociology of entrepreneurship. *Annual Review of Sociology*, 25, 19–46.

Van Doren (1991). *A History of Knowledge*. New York: Ballantine Books.

Venkataraman, Sankaran (1997). The distinctive domain of entrepreneurship research. In *Advances in Entrepreneurship, Firm Emergence and Growth*, 3, 119–38. Greenwich, Conn.: JAI Press.

Westhead, Paul and Mike Wright (eds.) (2000). *Advances in Entrepreneurship*. Cheltenham: Edward Elgar, 3 volumes.

ARNOLD COOPER
Purdue University

2.   Entrepreneurship: The Past, the Present, the Future

INTRODUCTION

This chapter considers entrepreneurship as an academic field of study, looking at its past, its present, and its future. It is primarily a consideration of events in academia in the United States. However, what happens inside universities is clearly a reflection of what happens outside. Furthermore, research and teaching in American universities are linked to activities in universities outside the United States and to events around the world. Thus, even though our primary emphasis is upon teaching, research, and outreach programs in the United States, we shall consider the broader context which influences these developments.

ENTREPRENEURSHIP: THE PAST

It is important to remember that entrepreneurship, as an academic field of study, is quite young. The first course in entrepreneurship was apparently offered at the Harvard Business School in 1947 by Myles Mace. Peter Drucker started a course in entrepreneurship and innovation at New York University in 1953. Early courses often dealt primarily with small business management. However, it was many years before most business schools began to offer courses focusing upon entrepreneurship.

The first conference on small businesses and their problems was held at St. Gallen University in Switzerland in 1948. This biennial conference had its 51st anniversary in the fall of 2000. The predecessor organization of the International Council for Small Business (ICSB), the National Council for Small Business Management Development, grew from a conference on small business management development held at the University of Colorado in 1956. Many of the early leaders were with the Small Business Administration, such as Wilford White and Wendell Metcalf. The organization had a strong orientation toward small business education and included many university educators involved in service or outreach programs. Starting in 1962 the Council presented its first Outstanding Businessman Award. The name of the organization

Z.J. Acs and D.B. Audretsch (eds.), Handbook of Entrepreneurship Research, 21–34

was changed to the International Council for Small Business (ICSB) in 1977. Subsequently, international affiliates were formed, with the Canadian division starting about 1979.

The first academic conference on entrepreneurship research was at Purdue in the fall of 1970. It was co-sponsored by The Center for Venture Management, a recently established foundation headed by John Komives. It brought together 12 researchers to report upon their studies of technical entrepreneurship in various parts of the country. Some of those involved who continued to be active in entrepreneurship research were Al Shapero, Ed Roberts, Karl Vesper, Jeffrey Susbauer, and Arnold Cooper. This was the first time in the United States that a group of active researchers had been able to get together to present their findings and to question one another about their work.

The Entrepreneurship Division of the Academy of Management is another organization that began quite recently. At the annual meeting of the Academy in 1974, Karl Vesper held an organizational meeting for those interested in forming an Interest Group on Entrepreneurship. He did not know whether anyone would show up, but the room was full. The Interest Group was formed as a part of the Division of Business Policy and Planning. However, it remained rather small throughout the 1970s. For instance, in 1977 there were only 12 papers submitted for the program on entrepreneurship. The Entrepreneurship Interest Group did not achieve full status as the Entrepreneurship Division of the Academy of Management until 1987.

There were several early conferences in the 1970s. What was termed the "First International Conference on Entrepreneurship Research" was held in Toronto in 1973; it brought together primarily Canadian and American researchers. At that time there was an effort to organize a new professional organization of professors interested in the field. It was called SERA, The Society for Entrepreneurship Research and Application. There was a mailing list of 42 members. However, it never progressed very far. Possibly the name, SERA, was too suggestive of the then popular song, "Que sera, sera, whatever will be, will be."

A major meeting occurred in Cincinnati in 1975, the "International Symposium of Entrepreneurship and Enterprise Development" (ISEED). This was a very ambitious undertaking, with an international steering committee and many sponsors and cooperating agencies. It involved more than 230 participants from all over the world who gathered for the four-day conference. Many were with government agencies that sponsored programs to encourage entrepreneurship, and they reported about what had worked and had not worked in their countries. Planners of the Symposium were James Schreier, Jeffrey Susbauer, Robert Baker, William McCrea, Albert Shapero, and John Komives.

A number of interesting developments occurred at Babson College. The Academy of Distinguished Entrepreneurs was established in 1978 to recognize "world-class" entrepreneurs. This became the prototype for other programs to recognize entrepreneurs, including the Ernst and Young "Entrepreneur of the

Year Awards," the National Federation of Independent Business "Best in America" contest, and a number of local and regional programs intended to celebrate entrepreneurs and their achievements. The Babson Research Conference was started in 1981. Karl Vesper and Jack Hornaday organized the first conference which involved the presentation of 39 papers. It was established from the beginning as a working conference, with all of the participants having to write a paper as the ticket for admission. The organizers recalled that, after that first conference, they were unsure whether there would be enough new work to justify a conference for the second year. In the spring of 2000 the twentieth annual conference was held, with 139 papers presented. After the first few conferences, other universities became co-sponsors, including Georgia Tech, the Wharton School, Pepperdine University, the University of Calgary, St. Louis University, the University of Pittsburgh, INSEAD, the University of Houston, the London Business School, the University of Washington, University of Gent in Belgium, University of South Carolina, Jönköping International Business School in Sweden, and University of Colorado. Another development at Babson was the Price-Babson Fellows program. Under the leadership of Jeff Timmons and the sponsorship of The Price Foundation, this program brought to the Babson campus experienced entrepreneurs who were interested in teaching entrepreneurship. They were joined by faculty sponsors from their home campuses as they worked to develop their teaching skills.

Another important development was the Small Business Institute Program (SBI), first started in 1972 at Texas Tech University. This program, sponsored by the Small Business Administration (SBA), provided support to universities that set up courses in which students consulted with small businesses. This program got off to a fast start; by 1976, 398 universities were participating. The professional organization, Small Business Institute Director's Association (SBIDA) was organized to bring involved faculty together. Although SBA no longer funds this program, variations of it can be found on many campuses and SBIDA continues as an organization binding together faculty who share interests in students learning through being involved with businesses.

The first of the "State of the Art" conferences was held at Baylor University in 1980. A number of researchers were asked to summarize what was known and not known on particular topics. The resulting book, *Encyclopedia of Entrepreneurship*, edited by Calvin Kent, Don Sexton, and Karl Vesper (1982), was the first of what have become six such volumes. The subsequent conferences were organized primarily by Don Sexton and were held about every five years, with the later locations being Austin, Chapel Hill, Kansas City, Fort Lauderdale, and Kansas City again.

When scholars first began to try to publish articles on entrepreneurship there were few outlets. The *Journal of Small Business Management* had been started in 1963 under the auspices of the National Council for Small Business and became the official publication of the successor organization, ICSB, in 1977. The *American Journal of Small Business* was started about 1975; later, under the leadership of Ray Bagby, its name was changed to *Entrepreneurship Theory and Practice* in 1988. The *Journal of Business Venturing* was started in 1985 by Ian MacMillan with the sponsorship of New York University and the Wharton School.

There also have been a number of journals in related fields or on specialized topics in entrepreneurship or small business. The earliest was *Explorations in Entrepreneurial History*; it was published at Harvard from 1949 to 1958 and later at the University of Wisconsin from 1963 to 1969. The name was subsequently changed to *Explorations in Economic History*. The journal *Small Business Economics* was started in 1989 by Zoltan Acs and David Audretsch. A number of specialized journals also were introduced, including *Small Business Strategy* (started in 1990), *Family Business Review* (founded in 1988), and *Entrepreneurship and Regional Development* (started in 1989).

In reviewing these developments, one thing stands out. Most of the journals we read and most of the conferences we attend were started in the last 20 to 25 years, a little more than half of a professional's working life. Ours is indeed a young field.

Not only is our field young, but it also has been relatively small, particularly in numbers of full-time faculty doing research. Although there has been a great growth in total courses, the number of people able to devote their full energies to teaching and research in the area has continued to be limited. Many of the courses are taught by non-tenure track faculty, often on a part-time basis. These are often fine teachers, but their other commitments are such that they are usually not involved in developing the intellectual capital of the field. I recall a conversation with a Department Head at one major university which has been recognized for its entrepreneurship program; they had 14 courses, but no tenure-track faculty.

Even where tenure track faculty are involved, they often teach and do work in other areas in addition to entrepreneurship. Furthermore, many entrepreneurship faculty are of an applied bent, good at relating to practicing managers, but sometimes less inclined toward research. The upshot of all of this is that our field has been relatively small, in terms of full time faculty involved in research.

THE CONCEPTUAL DEVELOPMENT OF THE FIELD

The conceptual development of the field of entrepreneurship has followed a number of paths, often not connected to each other.

Knight (1921) examined factors bearing upon profits realized by entrepreneurs. Schumpeter (1936), an economist, emphasized the central role of entrepreneurially driven innovation in economic development. Kirzner (1973) described how subsets of the population may be alert to opportunities and, in pursuing these, realize entrepreneurial profits. In this vein, Shane and Venkataraman (2000) see the heart of entrepreneurship research as being the study of the development and exploitation of opportunities. Some people may perceive opportunities when others do not because of prior information which they possess or because of their cognitive abilities. Consistent with this view, a study by Palich and Bagby (1995) compared entrepreneurs and managers as they reacted to ambiguous business situations presented to them. The entrepreneurs were more likely to perceive opportunities and less likely to perceive problems.

There has been a long tradition of work seeking to determine whether entrepreneurs are distinctive in particular ways. McClelland (1961), a psychologist, examined the motivations of people who act in entrepreneurial ways, whether they are starting new ventures or are within established organizations. He reported that entrepreneurs are characterized by "high needs for achievement." An early study by Collins and Moore (1964) examined the personal histories and psychological makeup of entrepreneurs who founded small manufacturing firms in the Detroit area. Those entrepreneurs had personal histories of poor relationships with their fathers and authority figures and seemed driven to entrepreneurship in order to realize their needs for independence. Not all studies have found that entrepreneurs are distinctive. For instance, Brockhaus (1980) found that the risk-taking propensity of entrepreneurs was about the same as for managers or the population as a whole.

The stream of research which examines characteristics of entrepreneurs has sometimes been described as "trait" research. Often utilizing demographic and work experience data, it has compared particular groups of entrepreneurs with each other or with the larger population. Many of the papers presented at the first Babson Research Conference in 1981 were of this sort.

However, this kind of research has come under sharp criticism. Gartner (1988) argued that the focus should be upon behaviors, not traits. He noted that many who start businesses do so only once in their lives and may subsequently not exhibit entrepreneurial behaviors.

Organizational sociologists have focused upon populations of firms in considering organizational births and deaths. This large literature has considered such factors as organizational legitimacy, the carrying capacity of environments, and competition for resources. Firms are seen as having limited ability to transform themselves and populations evolve as some organizations are better able to compete than others (Hannan and Freeman, 1984; Aldrich, 1999).

A number of research streams have developed which examine processes of venture formation, including opportunity identification, information search, team formation, resource assembly, and strategy formulation. Three areas which have received particular emphasis are new venture financing, the role of networks in entrepreneurship, and the role of new and small firms in innovation. Bygrave and Timmons (1992) described in detail the operating practices and the returns realized by the venture capital industry. The ways in which venture capital firms analyze ventures and structure investments have been examined (MacMillan et al., 1987; Sahlman, 1992). A number of scholars have considered how entrepreneurs develop and utilize networks to access information, raise capital, and add to credibility (Larson, 1992). Network ties with reputable parties, such as highly-regarded alliance partners, have been shown to increase legitimacy and lead to higher sales growth (Stuart, 2000). In regard to technological innovation, there has been a long tradition of studying the extent to which small firms play important roles. Acs and Audretsch (1990) reported that small firms account for a substantial percentage of major innovations, much more than their relative employment would lead one to expect, in many industries.

From the earliest days of research in entrepreneurship, there has been interest in predictors of performance. This work examines the extent to which characteristics of entrepreneurs, the processes of starting, the nature of the new firms, and environmental characteristics bear upon later success. One of the earliest studies examined the performance of 81 firms during their first two years (Mayer and Goldstein, 1961). Later work utilized much larger samples, more theoretically derived variables, a variety of performance measures, and multivariate methods of analysis. Thus, Bruderl *et al.* (1992), studying 1849 startups, found that there was greater likelihood of survival if there were more employees, greater initial capital, greater human capital, and strategies directed at national markets.

Although discontinuance has often been equated with failure, one study found that each entrepreneur appeared to have a "threshold level" of required performance in order to stay in business. The threshold level was a function of the entrepreneur's opportunity costs, switching costs, and personal values (Gimeno, Folta, Cooper, and Woo, 1997).

Corporate entrepreneurship has been concerned with how new ventures can be developed in existing firms or, more broadly, with making existing organizations more innovative. An early study examined the rise and fall of new venture departments (Fast, 1978). Much of this work has involved clinical studies which examine the organizational and administrative approaches used by particular organizations to nurture internal entrepreneurship (Kanter, 1983). The processes by which venture ideas are developed through experimentation and selection within large organizations have been described (Burgelman, 1983). An entrepreneurial posture was found to be related to higher performance for small firms which operated in hostile environments (Covin and Slevin, 1989).

Public policy-makers have become interested in entrepreneurship and small business, in part, because of its role in job creation. The seminal work by Birch (1987), showing that growth-oriented firms, which he called "gazelles," accounted for much of the job growth in the United States has sparked worldwide interest.

The field of entrepreneurship has always asked interesting questions, including "What are the processes by which new ventures are formed?" and "What factors influence the development of new firms?" These and other questions have been explored with increasing sophistication. However, there are critics of scholarship in our field. They say that we lack a central research paradigm, that we devote inadequate attention to issues of validity and reliability, and that our analytical methods have often been crude. They say, "You don't even agree on definitions." However, we might note that some of these critics calling for increasing rigor, are themselves in fields characterized not only by increasing rigor, but also by increasing mortis.

ENTREPRENEURSHIP: THE PRESENT

The current condition of entrepreneurship reflects tremendous growth in almost all dimensions of the field. The number of universities with entrepreneurship courses (according to the periodic surveys by Karl Vesper) has increased from fewer than 10 in 1967, to 105 in 1975, to 173 in 1980, to 250 in 1984, to 370 in 1993 (Vesper, 1993). (George Solomon estimates the total number of courses in entrepreneurship and small business, counting those at junior colleges, to be 1064.)

There are now many schools with sets of courses and majors. Furthermore, many of these courses and programs are very popular. When *Success* magazine gave annual ratings of entrepreneurship programs, it required a minimum of three courses at the graduate level even to be considered in the ratings.

Jerry Katz of St. Louis University has tracked the growing infrastructure in the field. According to his website (http://eweb.slu.edu/Default.htm), the number of journals has grown to 41, not counting these in languages other than English. Conferences are now so numerous that it is difficult to keep track of them. Chaired professorships have been added at many schools, 271 in entrepreneurship and related fields. In addition, more than 100 universities have established Entrepreneurship Centers. These serve as focal points for research, for outreach, for student enrichment, and for fund-raising.

Similar developments are occurring in Europe and elsewhere. Entrepreneurship courses and doctoral programs have been growing rapidly. The number of conferences has multiplied. Entrepreneurship research has been growing with investigation of such topics as novice, portfolio, and serial founders (Westhead and Wright, 1998) and entrepreneurial networks (Birley, 1985).

Public interest in entrepreneurship has never been higher. Magazines such as *INC* (started in 1979), *Entrepreneur* (started in 1977), *In Business* (started in 1979), *Success* (since discontinued), and *Business 2.0* (started in 1998) attract both subscribers and advertisers. Articles in the general business press attract widespread readership. Not only are there articles about how to be an entrepreneur, there are articles "about" entrepreneurs, presumably because this is of interest to the general public. The evolution of entrepreneurs to the role of folk heroes is a remarkable development. The extent to which entrepreneurship has captured the public imagination is illustrated in that well-known academic publication, *USA Today*. It surveyed young people, asking if they could devote one year to any occupation, what would they choose? For the women, 47% chose entrepreneur, more than tour guide or novelist. For the young men, 38% chose entrepreneur, even more than professional athlete. Increasingly, in many countries entrepreneurs are becoming "folk heroes." A recent Gallup poll reported that more than 90% of Americans would approve if either a daughter or son attempted to start a small business (Dennis, 1997a).

This widespread interest in entrepreneurship reflects what is happening in society. A few years ago, *Fortune* magazine estimated that the average young person entering the job market would have ten different jobs with five different organizations before retirement. Old industries decline and well-known corporate names disappear. Many young people recognize that they must take responsibility for their own careers. Even if they expect to start with larger firms and hope to stay with them, conditions can change. Those who have developed entrepreneurial skills will be better prepared for a constantly changing world, and they may also have more interesting options in the future. In addition, it is increasingly clear that many of the careers offering the greatest rewards and excitement are in entrepreneurial firms.

All of this is very different from 25 to 30 years ago. At that time entrepreneurship as an academic field of study was just starting. There were few courses and student interest was limited. The popular view was that large firms were increasingly likely to dominate the economy. In 1969, only 274,000 new corporations were started per year; in 1998, the annual number had reached 761,000. Furthermore, recent data suggest that, when all organizational forms and part-time and home-based businesses are counted, the total number of startups seems to be on the order of 4.5 million per year, far higher than anyone had suspected (Dennis, 1997b). In the early 1970s, the *Fortune 500* seemed increasingly likely to dominate the economy. In 1972, those firms accounted for 19.9% of the nonfarm employment, and the trend had been upward. However, since then the share of employment accounted for by the *Fortune 500* has declined steadily; in 1991, it was down to 10.9%. In the United States, the *Fortune 1000* lost 3.5 million jobs during the decade of the 1980s. During that same period, firms with fewer than 500 employees added 10 million jobs. Today, both within universities and the larger society, it is increasingly recognized that new and small firms are a vital part of our economy.

ENTREPRENEURSHIP: THE FUTURE

What does the future hold for entrepreneurship as a field of academic study? Will the growth trends of the last 30 years continue or will this later be viewed as a field which was popular for a time and then was replaced by other "hot" topics? On this and other matters, I tend to be an optimist. My friends tell me that, had I been on the Titanic, I would merely have assumed that the ship was stopping to take on more ice.

What are the drivers of future development for the entrepreneurship field? Much will depend upon whether the environmental trends leading to increased entrepreneurship continue. A number of factors seem to favor continued high rates of new firm formation. They suggest that the wealth and job creation associated with new firms in recent years is likely to continue.

(1) High rates of change create opportunities for new firms. New firms do not have a stake in the status quo. If the world were stable, then eventually all of the opportunities would be met and there would be few possibilities for new firms. However, we live in a world characterized by enormous change, and much of that change is driven by innovative small firms. Although the small firm segment of the economy spends only a fraction of what large firms spend on R&D, small firms, in the aggregate, account for more than half of all major product innovations in the United States. Many industries characterized by high rates of innovation also have high rates of new venture creation. This manuscript was written on a computer that was installed in my office less than three years ago. Yet, our computer support people have persuaded me to order a replacement because the old one is so ancient.

(2) Another characteristic of our economy is the continued growth of the service sector of our economy, a sector where the rate of new firm formation is high. For instance, when jobs generated by sector from 1991 to 1996 are considered, the annual growth in jobs in services was 3.4%, far higher than for other sectors. This growth was concentrated in small service firms. Service firms with more than 100 employees added jobs at a rate of only 0.8% per year. Those with fewer than 100 employees grew at 7.2% per year (*Who's Creating Jobs?* and *Corporate Almanac*, 1996). For the 1997 INC 500, 59% of those high growth firms were in the service sector (INC 500, October 1997, p. 26).

(3) The concept of the virtual corporation, in which firms increasingly outsource not only support functions, but also basic activities such as producing and selling, also creates opportunities for entrepreneurs. One reason why employment in the Fortune 500 has been declining has been the increased emphasis upon downsizing and outsourcing, as corporations re-examine everything they do to consider what should be retained and what should be farmed out to others. Virtual corporations also make it possible for new firms to get established without large investments while relying upon others to make, sell, and finance their products.

(4) Attitudes toward small business have never been more favorable. A recent survey sponsored by NFIB indicated that 85% of the American public believes that small business is primarily a positive influence on the way things are going in this country. Furthermore, 70% think that owning a small business is one of the best ways to "get ahead" in this country (Dennis, 1997a).

(5) Not only are there opportunities for local entrepreneurs within a growing number of countries, there also are opportunities for American entrepreneurs to do business overseas. Global trade is growing at 6% per year, more than twice as fast as the world GNP is growing (INC 500, October

1997, p. 59). Historically, American entrepreneurs have been less internationally minded than their counterparts in many other countries, but this may be beginning to change. Certainly, there are opportunities. Within the former Soviet Empire, it is indeed remarkable that an activity formerly considered to be criminal behavior – entrepreneurship – is now positively encouraged.

(6) Within the United States tremendous numbers of jobs and great amounts of wealth have been created through entrepreneurship. However, the benefits have not been equally distributed. Some minority groups, such as African Americans, American Indians, and some groups of Hispanics have been handicapped by lower levels of human and financial capital. This has led to lower, and on the whole, less successful rates of entrepreneurship (Bates, 1997). Whether this will change will depend upon whether many challenges are overcome – some economic, some psychological, and some sociological. The geographic distribution of entrepreneurial activity, particularly the establishment of growth-oriented firms, has also not been equal. David Birch, in his studies of job creation, tells us that much of the entrepreneurial activity has been in the counties around metropolitan areas. The growth of telecommunications capabilities makes it possible for some entrepreneurs to locate wherever they want. It will be interesting to see whether this has a substantial impact on the future geographic locations of entrepreneurial activity.

This is not to say that all new ventures will prosper. High rates of change and high rates of entry into developing industries can create enormous competitive pressures. Of the firms listed in the *INC 500* in 1985, 19% had failed or disappeared by 1995, ten years later (INC 500, October 1995, p. 76). However, the trends noted in our economy are likely to result in continued high rates of new firm formation, and with that, high levels of interest in entrepreneurship within universities.

Within our universities, student interest will be a primary driver. If our courses are popular and viewed as making solid contributions, then it is more likely that growth in entrepreneurship courses, majors, and centers will continue. It is also necessary to have the support of our colleagues in other fields. Here, lest we get carried away by all of the favorable trends, we should recognize that some of the strongest universities, where there are the resources to provide substantial support, have met their teaching needs primarily with adjunct faculty. In addition, some of the most selective journals have not published much to date on entrepreneurship. For entrepreneurship to be fully accepted in these settings, it will be necessary to develop useful conceptual frameworks, well-grounded in theory. For our courses to be successful, the continued development of good teaching materials is necessary. The deepening and broadening of the intellectual foundations of our field will depend upon successful research and course development. Ours is a young field and there is still much to be done.

The role of entrepreneurship teaching and research as a contributor to economic development will be an important driver at some universities. If it can be shown that our efforts contribute to new firm formation, to technology transfer, and to the strengthening of existing small firms, this can help to attract resources from central administrations and from legislatures. To achieve this, we will need effective outreach programs and better understanding of how to transfer and commercialize technology.

The development of our field to date has been significantly impacted by support from wealthy alumni and from foundations. This has led to chaired professorships, to centers, and to novel courses and outreach programs. It has also led to a curious development in regard to opportunities within the field. In most academic fields, the job opportunities in any given year might be represented by a pyramid on its base, with more opportunities at the assistant professor level, followed by somewhat less at the associate level, and with relatively few opportunities at the full professor and chaired professor levels. In entrepreneurship, the pyramid historically has been upside down, with relatively few full-time opportunities for assistant professors, but with many chairs unfilled. I have talked to deans who had funding for new chairs in entrepreneurship, but who were concerned that they could not find anyone with the required credentials to fill those chairs. Sometimes this has led to chairs being filled by professors with good academic credentials, but with little previous involvement in entrepreneurship.

In every university, deans are under pressure to raise money. As they talk to constituents, they discover that their wealthier alumni often have made their money in entrepreneurship. What do these successful alumni get excited about? Often, it is programs related to entrepreneurship. The development of entrepreneurship as a field has also been tremendously stimulated and supported by the foundations that have channeled funds to chairs, centers, awards, and special conferences. The Coleman Foundation, the Price Foundation, the NFIB Foundation, and the Kauffman Foundation have all sponsored an impressive number of initiatives to encourage and support entrepreneurship research and education. There is probably no other field of management that has been so supported and influenced by foundations. Will this outside support continue? Much will depend upon whether deans and fund-raisers understand the opportunities associated with the field. Much will also depend upon whether faculty develop effective teaching, research, and outreach programs that generate excitement. Students, foundations, government, and donors – all see entrepreneurship as promising and important. However, for support to continue, we have to deliver. We have to develop the theoretical and empirical base of the field so that students, entrepreneurs, and policy makers consistently conclude that there is real benefit from taking our courses, studying our writings, and considering our advice.

As we consider the future development of the field, it is important to bear in mind that entrepreneurship as a field of study is really quite young. Its progress depends upon a continuing development of the intellectual base of the field and the ongoing creation of effective teaching materials. Many of these contributions will come from the young faculty entering the field, who are well trained and motivated to "make a career" in entrepreneurship. There will be limited progress if the reliance is primarily upon individuals who move into the field in mid-career and who lack the motivation to devote their full energies to trying to develop the field.

This means that there must be career opportunities for young faculty. If entrepreneurship is only "in addition to other duties" and if most of the energy is devoted to the other fields, then progress will be slow. Young faculty must be supported, mentored, and encouraged. To create a flow of young faculty, doctoral programs must be developed and supported. Some of the best doctoral students must be exposed to the excitement of the field. Trained in the latest techniques, they will provide the energy that drives the field forward. In this connection, it is encouraging to note that an increasing number of schools seem interested in hiring young people who have entrepreneurship as a primary interest.

How will the field develop in regard to kinds of research and writing? Howard Aldrich, writing in *Entrepreneurship 2000*, noted three views of entrepreneurship research, each of which implies different paths of development (Aldrich and Baker, 1997). One path is that of a "normal science," with an accumulation of empirically tested hypotheses and well-grounded generalizations in what might increasingly be viewed as a specialized field. A second pattern is a multiple paradigm view, in which research frameworks from a variety of disciplines, such as economics, sociology, and psychology, might be applied, as well as work in related functional areas, such as finance and marketing. In this view, theories might be borrowed from relevant fields, and much of the research might be published in the journals of those fields. A third approach is more pragmatic and less theory driven; it considers topicality, data availability, and perceived usefulness.

In the future, concern for "academic respectability" and the near universal concern about getting tenure may promote the first two patterns of development. However, the field of entrepreneurship attracts a variety of kinds of faculty. Many are adjunct professors or lecturers, with extensive real world experience as entrepreneurs or venture capitalists. Others are full-time academics of a practical bent, particularly concerned with making their courses and writing relevant and immediately useful. The wide variety of individuals in the field may mean that it will continue to be eclectic and open to a variety of theoretical frameworks and research methodologies and will continue to speak to a variety of audiences.

It seems likely that the trend toward specialization will continue, as researchers concentrate on particular sub-topics, such as international entrepreneurship, the role of networks, or informal venture capital. This has been a field characterized by eclectic research methods, with a variety of approaches being used. I see no reason why this will change, nor do I foresee a single dominant research paradigm emerging. The field has also been noted for many large sample studies. This is exemplified by the Entrepreneurial Research Consortium project, the multiyear, multi-university study being led by Paul Reynolds. The

Dun and Bradstreet/Kauffman Foundation database of 1.2 million firms is another example. However, as Howard Stevenson has noted, entrepreneurship might be viewed as particularly concerned with innovative behavior and unusual achievements. Thus, small-scale studies of unusually interesting or innovative new ventures will undoubtedly continue to be of interest. All of this suggests that multiple patterns of development will occur.

Entrepreneurship is as old as human history. Some of the cuneiform tablets in Babylon record commercial transactions involving entrepreneurs. Queen Isabella functioned as a venture capitalist when Columbus sought capital to support his entrepreneurial vision. However, as a field of academic study, entrepreneurship is very young. Some compare it with older fields, which represent the fruits of decades of scholarship. I would suggest that comparing the older fields with entrepreneurship is somewhat like comparing a train station with an airport. The train station was built long ago. The schedules are well-established; things are clear-cut and not very confusing. However, there may be some dust here and there. The airport, by contrast, is under continuous reconstruction, with temporary signs, and changes from week to week. There is confusion and there may seem to be a lack of clear organization. But, there is also energy and dynamism and change. I would suggest that entrepreneurship is like that airport. It is still under construction and the best is yet to come.

By any measures, there has been tremendous growth in the academic field of entrepreneurship. This includes courses, programs, conferences, journals, and centers. Accompanying and driving these developments have been the growing interest and commitment of students and foundations. Acceptance and legitimacy in the larger academic community has developed more slowly, but will grow as the intellectual foundations of the field are strengthened. Future developments will depend upon whether entrepreneurship continues to be a vital part of the economies of the world and whether it seems to offer career prospects which are interesting and rewarding.

REFERENCES

Acs, Z.J. and D.B. Audretsch (1990). *Innovation and Small Firms.* Cambridge, MA: MIT Press.

Aldrich, H. (1999). *Organizations Evolving.* Thousand Oaks, CA: Sage Publications.

Aldrich, H.E. and T. Baker (1997). Blinded by the cites? Has there been progress in entrepreneurship research? In Sexton, D.L. and R.W. Smilor (eds.), *Entrepreneurship, 2000.* Chicago, IL: Upstart Publishing Company, pp. 377–400.

Bates, T. (1997). *Race, Self-employment and Upward Mobility.* Baltimore, MD: Johns Hopkins University Press.

Birch, D.L. (1987). *Job Creation in America: How our Smallest Companies Put the Most People to Work.* New York: Free Press.

Birley, S. (1985). The role of networks in the entrepreneurial process. *Journal of Business Venturing,* 1(1), 107–118.

Brockhaus, R. (1980). Risk taking propensity of entrepreneurs. *Academy of Management Journal,* 23(3), 509–520.

Bruderl, J., P. Preisendaorfer and R. Ziegler (1992). Survival chances of newly founded business organizations. *American Sociological Review*, **57**(2), 227–242.

Burgelman, R.A. (1983). A process model of internal corporate venturing in the diversified major firm. *Administrative Science Quarterly*, **28**, 223–244.

Bygrave, W.D. and J.A. Timmons (1992). *Venture Capital at the Crossroads*. Boston, MA: Harvard Business School Press.

Collins, O.F. and D.G. Moore (1964). *The Enterprising Man*. East Lansing, MI: Michigan State University.

Covin, J. and D. Slevin (1989). Strategic management of small firms in hostile and benign environments. *Strategic Management Journal*, **10**, 75–87.

Dennis, W.J. Jr. (1997a). *The Public Reviews Small Business*. Washington, DC: NFIB Education Foundation.

Dennis, W.J. Jr. (1997b). More than you think: An inclusive estimate of business entries. *Journal of Business Venturing*, **12**(3), 175–196.

Fast, N. (1978). *The Rise and Fall of Corporate New Venture Divisions*. Ann Arbor, MI: UMI Research Press.

Gartner, W. (1988). Who is an entrepreneur? Is the wrong question. *Entrepreneurship Theory and Practice*, **13**(4), 47–68.

Gimeno, J., T. Folta, A. Cooper and C. Woo (1997). Survival of the fittest? Entrepreneurial human capital and the persistence of underperforming firms. *Administrative Science Quarterly*, **42**(4), 750–783.

Hannan, M. and J. Freeman (1984). Structural inertia and organizational change. *American Sociological Review*, **49**, 149–164.

INC 500, October 1995.

INC 500, October 1997.

Kanter, R.M. (1983). *Change Masters: Innovation for Productivity in the American Corporation*. New York: Simon and Schuster.

Kent, C.A., D.L. Sexton and K.H. Vesper (1982). *Encyclopedia of Entrepreneurship*. Englewood Cliffs, NJ: Prentice-Hall, Inc.

Kirzner, I.M. (1973). *Competition and Entrepreneurship*. Chicago, IL: University of Chicago Press.

Knight, Frank H. (1921). *Risk, Uncertainty and Profit*. Boston, MA: Houghton Mifflin Company.

Larson, A. (1992). Network dyads in entrepreneurial settings: A study of the governance of exchange relationships. *Administrative Science Quarterly*, **37**, 76–104.

McClelland, D. (1961). *The Achieving Society*. Princeton, NJ: Van Nostrand.

MacMillan, I., L. Zeman and P. Subbamarasimha (1987). Criteria distinguishing unsuccessful ventures in the venture screening process. *Journal of Business Venturing*, **2**, 123–137.

Mayer, K.B. and S. Goldstein (1961). *The First Two Years: Problems of Small Firms Growth and Survival*. Washington, DC: H.S. Government Printing Office.

Palich, L. and R. Bagby (1995). Using cognitive theory to explain entrepreneurial risk-taking: Challenging conventional wisdom. *Journal of Business Venturing*, **10**, 425–438.

Sahlman, W.A. (1992). Aspects of financial contracting in venture capital. In W.A. Sahlman and H.H. Stevenson (eds.), *The Entrepreneurial Venture*. Boston, MA: Harvard Business School Publications, pp. 222–242.

Schumpeter, J.A. (1936). *Theory of Economic Development*. Cambridge, MA: Harvard University Press.

Shane, S. and S. Venkataraman (2000). The promise of entrepreneurship as a field of research. *Academy of Management Review*, **25**, 217–221.

Stuart, T.E. (2000). Interorganizational alliances and the performance of firms: A study of growth and innovation rates in high-technology industries. *Strategic Management Journal*, **21**(8), 791–811.

Vesper, K.H. (1993). *Entrepreneurship Education*. Los Angeles, CA: Entrepreneurial Studies Center, University of California, Los Angeles.

Westhead, P. and M. Wright (1998). Novice, portfolio, and serial founders in rural and urban areas. *Entrepreneurship: Theory and Practice*, **22**(4), 63–100.

Who's Creating Jobs? and *Corporate Almanac*. Cambridge, MA: Cognetic, 1996.

PART TWO

The Entrepreneurial Process

Entrepreneurship is a process. This section focuses directly on this process of entrepreneurship. In particular, the entrepreneurial process is examined from three distinct perspectives. The first, in Chapter 3, "Risk and Uncertainty," by Sharon Gifford, is from the perspective of the individual, who engages in activities that are inherently risky and uncertain. This view dates back to Frank Knight, and analyzes an approach to decision making under uncertainty that, instead of assuming that individuals are risk averse, derives risk averse behavior as a result of limited attention. The key to understanding and predicting entrepreneurial behavior is to understand the sources of risk averse behavior.

Gifford extends Israel Kirzner's observation that alertness and attention to opportunities are crucial attributes of the entrepreneurial process. She emphasizes the limits upon the entrepreneurial endowment available, raises issues of the allocation of attention between the management of the established enterprises, and the formation of new enterprises. An important implication derived from the assumption of limited attention for a theory of risk taking is that investment in knowledge, either in the form of information or human capital, is a primary determinant of risk taking behavior. Gifford shows that investments in human capital can generate an apparent increase or decrease in risk aversion, depending on the type of investment made. In either case, those with more knowledge may be apparently willing to take more risk, not because they are less risk averse, but because they have better information.

The second contribution, "Entrepreneurship, Innovation and Technological Change," by Zoltan J. Acs and David B. Audretsch examines the entrepreneurial process from a very different perspective – the relationship between firm size and innovative activity. There are two important ways that the role of firm size and innovation intersects with entrepreneurship. The first is more direct and obvious. Systematic research has used a static framework, which takes the firms as exogenous, and identified small firms as making an important contribution to innovative activity, which is shaped by factors specific to the firm, the industry, and the region. Firms are viewed as undertaking knowledge-creating activities in order to generate innovative activity. The second way is more subtle and involves a dynamic or evolutionary framework. From this view, knowledge is viewed as being embedded in individual agents or groups of agents in an exogenous manner. New firms are then created, at least in some cases, in the entrepreneurial process of the agent appropriating the returns from her knowledge endowment. Seen through this dynamic lens, the creation of a new firm is the entrepreneurial process by which individuals seek to equilibrate the expected value of their knowledge endowment with their expected income from employment in different organizations.

This dynamic view of the entrepreneurial process in small-firm innovation is the starting point for the third chapter in this section, "Market Processes and Entrepreneurial Studies," by Roger Koppl and Maria Minniti. Entrepreneurship is the mechanism by which markets and industries change and evolve over time. In Chapter 5, Koppl and Minniti connect the entrepreneurial process in market processes to the intellectual tradition of the Austrian School. Entrepreneurship emerges as the driving engine of growth and economic development from this analysis.

SHARON GIFFORD

Rutgers University

3. Risk and Uncertainty

INTRODUCTION

Imagine that you have a brilliant idea for a new business. In fact, your experience and expertise lead you to believe that this is a sure-fire winner. You approach the bank with your idea and they only laugh. You also discover that venture capitalists require a very high interest rate (or equity stake) in order to fund your venture. What's going on here? One explanation is that, because you are an entrepreneur, you are more willing to undertake risk, that is, you are less risk averse, than investors are. This is a long-standing argument in the literature on what makes an entrepreneur (Brockhaus, 1980).[1] An alternative explanation is that entrepreneurs seeking funding think they are selling U.S. Treasury bills while investors think they are buying pre-Castro government bonds.[2]

This example illustrates an underlying element of most economic theories of the entrepreneur: Uncertainty and the accompanying risk. The entrepreneur functions in the economy only if the environment is uncertain. If all individuals in the economy had perfect information, then all profit opportunities would be exploited instantaneously and there would be no further entrepreneurial role. This is the reason for the absence of the entrepreneur in much economic analysis, which focuses on an equilibrium framework.[3] An equilibrium is a set of prices at which there are no profit opportunities.

Thus, uncertainty and risk, as well as a dynamic, as opposed to equilibrium, perspective, are necessary elements for any economic analysis that explicitly addresses the role of the entrepreneur. In an uncertain, dynamic world, the entrepreneur is often seen as bearing the risks implied by the uncertainty of the future outcomes of his or her decisions.

It has been suggested that one of the roles of the entrepreneur is to bear the risks that others avoid because entrepreneurs are less averse to risk (Kihlstrom and Laffont, 1979; Knight, 1921). Although this assumption is

---

[1] See also Stewart et al. (1999), and references therein. Empirical studies include Rees and Shah (1986) and Jennings, Cox and Cooper (1994).
[2] Fernando Alvarez, private communication.
[3] See Casson (1982), Hebert and Link (1988) and Barreto (1989).

Z.J. Acs and D.B. Audretsch (eds.), Handbook of Entrepreneurship Research, 37–53
© 2003 *Kluwer Academic Publishers. Printed in Great Britain.*

borne out by empirical research (Cramer et al., 2002), it leaves us with no explanation of why entrepreneurs should be less risk averse than other individuals (Scholtens, 1999). The purpose of this chapter is to propose an approach to decision making under uncertainty that, instead of assuming that individuals are risk averse, derives risk averse behavior as a result of limited attention. If we understood the sources of risk averse behavior, we would be better able to predict entrepreneurial behavior.

The immediate implication of assuming limited attention is that, as a scarce resource, it must be allocated among alternative uses. Thus, at any point in time attention can be allocated to one of any number of currently known targets (Becker, 1965). However, for the purposes of analyzing the effect of limited attention on entrepreneurial behavior, we need to allow the entrepreneur to create new activities. For example, an entrepreneur may be the founder of a number of enterprises and still have the ability to found additional ones. Therefore, the number of activities that an entrepreneur allocates attention among is endogenous.

In this chapter we are concerned with how this ability to be innovative (start new activities) affects the willingness of the entrepreneur to do so. However, the willingness to innovate also depends on the ability to manage current operations. We expect such an effect because limited attention implies an opportunity cost of starting new activities embodied in the neglect of current activities. We will see that this endogenous opportunity cost of innovation generates what appears to be risk averse behavior but is only the result of limited attention. By explicitly modeling this relationship we can deduce how changes in the environment that decrease the opportunity cost of attention generate behavior which appears to be the result of lower risk aversion.

The primary result of the assumption of limited attention for a theory of risk taking is that investment in knowledge, either in the form of information or human capital, is a primary determinant of risk taking behavior. We will see that investments in human capital can generate an apparent increase or decrease in risk aversion, depending on the type of investment made. In either case, those with more knowledge may be apparently willing to take more risk, not because they are less risk averse, but because they have better information.

The next section of this chapter provides a brief review of the research on the role of risk-taking in theories of entrepreneurship. This is followed by a simple analogy illustrating the relationship between the accumulation of human capital and apparent risk aversion behavior. The theory of limited attention and its implications for risk taking behavior is then described. Concluding remarks follow.

A Brief Review of the Literature

Before offering a theory of the source of risk averse behavior, this section briefly reviews the importance of this behavior for theories of entrepreneurial decision making. This literature appears in a number of disciplines including economics, finance and management. Because of the extent of this literate, this review can offer only a general description of the main issues.

There are many possible explanations for why individuals might be averse to risk. Some economists have suggested that less risk averse individuals become entrepreneurs (Kihlstrom and Laffont, 1979), implying that risk aversion is critical to the understanding of entrepreneurial behavior. Others have suggested that liquidity constraints are a significant hindrance to entrepreneurship (Evans and Jovanovic, 1989). Kihlstrom and Laffont point out that these two assumptions are related, in that those with greater wealth will also be less risk averse. But the assumption of different liquidity constraints begs the question of why some decision makers have more wealth than others do if their abilities are the same. There may be a feedback mechanism at play here. Those who are successful at perceiving and exploiting profit opportunities will have more wealth in the future, reducing their future liquidity constraints. These successful entrepreneurs with more wealth may be willing to take on risk projects because they have a high probability of success.

The argument that entrepreneurs are more willing to take risks than others are is intuitively appealing. After all, entrepreneurs are those who undertake risky decisions. Some empirical studies have borne out this conjecture (Hyrsky and Tuunanen, 1999; Pattillo, 1998) while others have found mixed results (Schiller and Crewson, 1997). However, using a measure of risk aversion as a criterion to identify entrepreneurs is quite difficult since it is widely believed that a person's attitude toward risk depends upon wealth, among other things. Kahneman and Tversky (1991) provide evidence that attitudes toward risk depend on the status quo and on whether outcomes are gains or losses. Their "prospect theory" approach to the analysis of behavior towards risk is one of several approaches that challenge Expected Utility Theory (EUT). EUT suffers from a number of well-documented problems. This is significant, since our views of risk aversion and its relationship to the shape of the utility function come from EUT. Starmer (2000) summarizes the problems inherent in the theory and a number of conventional and unconventional challenges to EUT.

The economics of limited attention is not a challenge to EUT. In fact, it is based on EUT. The difference is how each theory explains risk taking, or averting, behavior. The primary difficulty with the risk preference approach of EUT is that risk aversion cannot be observed separate from other influences on choice. For example, the assumed dependence of risk aversion on wealth makes it difficult to separate a greater willingness to take risks, as a motivation for taking them, from the opportunities created by wealth. For example, Blanchflower and Oswald (1998) find that the probability of self-employment depends positively on whether the individual ever received an inheritance or gift. Having that wealth eliminates financial barriers to innovative activity, but it also reduces risk aversion.

The liquidity assumption also has significant implications for the role of risk aversion in entrepreneurial activities. Since many entrepreneurs do not have the necessary wealth to pursue perceived profit opportunities, they are dependent on others for financial backing. But the perception of risk is also assumed to play a critical role, or roles, in the relationship between an entrepreneur and lender. Differences in risk perceptions have been found between bankers and entrepreneurs (Sarasvathy, Simon and Lave, 1998). Hillier (1998) finds evidence that entrepreneurs are biased in their perceptions of risks and opportunities. This optimism, if known to lenders, can lead to credit rationing. On the other hand, entrepreneurs may practice self-restraint as a signal of their realistic perceptions of risks (Manove and Padilla, 1999). Coco (1999) argues that the use of collateral by lenders as a screen to identify safer entrepreneurial investments may prove impossible.

Palich and Bagby (1995) provide evidence that entrepreneurs are more optimistic than non-entrepreneurs but did not differ in their risk propensity. In addition, the optimism of entrepreneurs may be partly due to their ability to walk away from some debts. As pointed out in Hart and Moore (1994), investors cannot prevent an entrepreneur from withdrawing his human capital from the funded project. This possibility of default further reduces the availability of financing for risky ventures. Therefore, the questions about the accuracy of the perceptions of risk by entrepreneurs create significant problems in obtaining financing.

All of this interest in risk perceptions indicates that it is extremely difficult to determine the actual riskiness of a venture. Cheung (1999) provides a "rule-of-thumb" that might be used by entrepreneurs and bankers alike to ascertain the riskiness of a venture from data on similar businesses. Sykes and Dunham (1995) develop a process for risk management based on learning. But the decision to undertake risk has many components. Hai and See (1997) offer evidence that a tolerance for ambiguity and risk alleviates the stress due to the strains of the conflicting roles of the entrepreneur and thus improves the performance of the venture. Witt (1998) describes a theory of the firm in which "business conceptions" play a key role. A successful venture requires the coordination and motivation of the firm members through the "cognitive leadership" of the entrepreneur in implementing and defending the business conception. Khalil (1997) associates entrepreneurship with "self-competition", or the desire to achieve ever-greater goals over time. However, this quest can lead to either immobilizing anxiety or entrepreneurial action. Van Praag and van Ophem (1995) find that willingness and opportunity are both necessary for entrepreneurial behavior, but that opportunity, especially financial, is usually lacking.

So far we have considered arguments that entrepreneurs are those with less risk aversion, and that this leads to problems obtaining financing. However, greater risk aversion can also provide an incentive to engage in self-employment, or ownership of a small firm. Firm ownership allows for greater control over decision making and thus less moral hazard. Wiggins (1995) argues that risky activities are difficult to undertake in a large enterprise because of incentive problems due to risk aversion on the part of employees. Therefore, many risky ventures are carried out in small firms, where these incentive problems do not exist. This argument implies that entrepreneurs choose to own their own businesses to avoid the risks of moral hazard in larger firms.

Observations of apparent willingness to take risks may have other explanations.

Cooper and Artz (1995) suggest that job satisfaction plays a critical role in the decision to start and maintain entrepreneurial ventures. Baron (2000) presents evidence that entrepreneurs' lower perceptions of risk are due in part to a lower ability to engage in counterfactual thinking; that is, how past events might have turned out differently. Baron (1998) suggests a number of cognitive tools for determining who will behave entrepreneurially, based on these sources of entrepreneurial errors. Empirical research by Simon, Haughton and Aquino (2000) suggests that risk taking is not due to differences in risk aversion but to cognitive biases other than risk aversion, such as overconfidence in their knowledge or skills, or to the law of small numbers according to which individuals extrapolate from small samples of information.

Keynes and Schumpeter identified the entrepreneur with "animal spirits", or irrationality. Marchionatti (1999) argues that these animal spirits have had no place in mainstream economics, which relies on assumptions of rationality. In a bounded rationality approach, Marchionatti treats animal spirits as an entrepreneurial impulse that depends on many elements of the entrepreneur's environment. However, this seems no firmer a foundation on which to build a theory of entrepreneurship than willingness to take risks. In either case, the source of the differences between those who appear to be entrepreneurial and those who do not also require explanation.

An alternative explanation of apparent risk-taking is that entrepreneurs are more optimistic about the outcome of the venture because they have more knowledge in their abilities to bring about a profitable result (Hayek, 1945). This explanation does not require the irrationality, or differences in innate preferences, such as risk aversion and animal spirits. Clearly, inborn talents can be very useful to the entrepreneur and much time and effort has been spent trying to determine what these innate characteristics might be (Brandstätter, 1997). However, we can say something about the sources of *acquired* abilities. For example, Fiet (1996) argues that entrepreneurs engage in information acquisition in order to reduce the uncertainty and risks of a venture. Greater information gives the entrepreneur a greater ability to make good choices. This, and other, acquired abilities may lead the entrepreneur to be more optimistic about the outcome of the venture and make the entrepreneur appear to view the venture as less risky. Efforts to acquire abilities are essentially a form of human capital investment. The possession of these abilities may not be easily observable, say to the lender, and so the optimism that they engender might be interpreted as lower risk aversion or greater animal spirits. However, for the purposes of economic analysis, efforts to invest in human capital can be observed, from schooling and job experience to information acquisition. Thus, the question of the role of uncertainty and risk in the entrepreneurial process suggests that we consider the role of human capital investment as an alternative hypothesis for the entrepreneur's apparent willingness to take risks.

An Analogy

In this analogy, the role of the entrepreneur is played by you the aspiring magician. The entrepreneurial activity is the effort to launch a new career. The role of the lenders is played by your sister and other relatives. The role of a venture capitalist is played by the established magician.

Assume that you want to start a career as a magician who "saws people in half". You have seen others do this successfully and know that people are willing to pay to watch this amazing feat (as economists, we do not question why people might want to do this). You even have experience since you have been a butcher for many years, a job in which you "saw" with great precision. However, you have no experience sawing people in half. You approach your younger sister to "loan" you her body to be sawn in half. However, she is not as confident as you are in your skills and is concerned about being injured. Your optimism here may be perceived as low risk aversion, or plain foolishness, but, in fact, it is your sister, like any lender, who is bearing much of the risk in this situation. Unfortunately, or fortunately, your sister, like a local banker, is aware of your inexperience and so refuses (local bankers are often in a much better position to assess the profit potential of a local venture because of their knowledge of the applicant and the situation).

After getting similar responses from the rest of your family members and close friends, you decide to read some books on the practice. Here you are endeavoring to invest in human capital by acquiring greater ability or at least the evidence of ability. Your confidence may even have been shaken (lenders' questioning of the soundness of the proposed venture can often lead to improving the proposal). However, without any practice, you are still unable to instill confidence in your potential victims. Your investment in human capital alone is not sufficient. Others must perceive your newly acquired skills.

To establish a track record, you next apprentice yourself to a well-known magician for several years in order to learn his skills. This was not an easy decision. You have to allocate time away from other activities to do this and if you fail on your first public effort, the value of your investment in this human capital is diminished. After much practice you become very proficient in sawing the magician's assistant in half and so you again ask for volunteers. However, your friends and loved ones are still reluctant to go under the knife with you. They have never seen evidence of your abilities and so are reluctant to take the risk.

Finally, you are allowed to perform in public using the magician's experienced assistant (the magician has seen how skilled you are). You are a great success. Now your family and friends can't wait to be relieved of their lower extremities (why they want to, even with the lack of risk, is not questioned).

Your demonstrable abilities solve the problem of getting the loan of enthusiastic assistance and you career is launched. In addition, your success has enriched the magician, since he will be able to attract new apprentices.

This silly analogy has many of the elements of risk, information and ability that are present in the entrepreneur's problem of starting a new venture. An inexperienced entrepreneur will, perhaps justifiably, not be able to get financing. This entrepreneur may, in fact, be suffering from animal spirits, or delusions, and the lack of financing is appropriate. However, the desire to start this venture is not evidence of a greater willingness to take risks if the entrepreneur can walk away from the debt, and so bears little risk. This is the source of the lender's reluctance to back the venture.

However, the entrepreneur's optimism may be based on investments in private but unverifiable information about the highly likely success of the venture. This private nature of the information makes this a problem of asymmetric information: The entrepreneur knows more about what he knows than the lender does. This investment was costly and was undertaken with the expectation of future success. If future efforts fail, then the value of this investment may be worthless. Therefore, the entrepreneur has a reputation at stake. Failure of the venture will reduce the entrepreneur's future "bankability". Now the entrepreneur still appears to be optimistic and willing to take risks, but in fact the entrepreneur is justifiably confident in the outcome of the venture. If the entrepreneur has enough at stake, such as collateral, the bank may take that as a signal of the good prospects of the venture.[4]

The apprentice needs the magician to vouch for his abilities. This role is often played by venture capitalists, who become closely involved in managing and controlling the venture in return for equity (Amit, Brander and Zott, 1998). A successful venture not only yields equity value for the venture capitalist, but also reputational capital, which attracts additional investors to the fund. Our parable ends with a successful outcome if the entrepreneur acquires the human capital and credentials that generate the confidence of investors.

To treat the problem as one of an innate willingness to take given but unknowable risks would leave us with little understanding of how these problems are resolved. Rather than analyzing the problem as a decision to take on risks, we see that it can be understood as a need for an investment in human capital.[5] The problem is solved if the investment is in information, knowledge, skills and experience that increase the expected value of the venture for all concerned. This may require bringing in a third party between the entrepreneur and the ultimate investors (banks, stockholders). This party (the magician, the venture capitalist) serves the role of certification, or verification, of the profit-

---

[4] See Bates (1990) for an empirical investigation of the effect of investment in human capital on the willingness of investors to invest.

[5] See Chandler and Hanks (1998) for evidence that human capital and financial capital are partly substitutable.

ability of the venture. The quality of the reputation of the venture capitalist is reflected in the IPO market through less underpricing (Lin, 1996).

One thing that we have glossed over in our analysis of entrepreneurial risk-taking is the cost of the investment in human capital. As we saw in the magician analogy, in order to become more competent, you, the budding magician, apprenticed yourself to a professional magician for some time. The cost of acquiring the necessary skills was the opportunity cost of the time spent paying attention to the magician's instructions and practicing them. Economists have considered the opportunity cost of time since the seminal work of Gary Becker (Becker, 1965). Amit, Muller and Cockburn (1995) provide evidence that those engaging in entrepreneurial activities have lower opportunity costs in terms of forgone wages. Cooper, Folta and Woo (1995) provide evidence that entrepreneurs with less experience search for more information, those with greater confidence search less. However, interaction effects indicate that less experienced entrepreneurs search less in unfamiliar domains than in familiar ones, suggesting a form of bounded rationality. More experienced entrepreneurs did not vary their search efforts.

More recently the opportunity cost of time, or attention, has been analyzed in a series of studies on the implications of limited attention when the number of targets of attention is endogenous. (Gifford, 1998, and references therein). This work considers the opportunity cost of allocating attention to adopting a new project (in this case, skill, knowledge, expertise) which is embodied in the neglect of ongoing current projects. The main insight of this work is that the opportunity cost of time is partly determined by how it is allocated. That is, the opportunity costs of acquiring new skills depends on how valuable the old ones are, which in turn depends on how much time was spent developing them.[6]

For example, instead of learning how to saw a person in half, you could have spent that time at your occupation as a butcher. You are quite skilled as a butcher because you have been doing it for a number of years. You could even have gotten better and perhaps eventually have your own slaughterhouse. All of that, however, was forgone, at least temporarily, when you decided to study magic. The economic, and psychic, value of those forgone activities is the opportunity cost of acquiring your new skills as a magician.

When this endogenous opportunity cost is taken into account we will see that a risk neutral individual will behave as though they are risk averse. This apparent risk aversion is seen in the fact that the entrepreneur does not take on projects with a positive "expected value". The issue is how this expected value is calculated.

---

[6]The relationship between attention and risk preferences has also been addressed in March and Shapira (1987 and 1992). Their analysis concerns how the focus of attention on aspects of the risky venture affect risk perceptions. Here, I suggest that the allocation of attention affects only the expected value of the venture.

LIMITED ATTENTION

The model of limited attention shows how entrepreneurs can *display* a different degree of risk aversion although they are all risk neutral. The term "risk neutral" means that entrepreneurs care only about the expected value of their prospects. The riskiness of a new venture is irrelevant. We will see that entrepreneurs who have made human capital investments in the past to increase their ability to recognize a profit opportunity will behave as if they are less risk averse than entrepreneurs who have made less investment in human capital.

In the analysis of the allocation of limited attention, the entrepreneur chooses to either consider a new venture or to pay attention to one of an endogenous number of current ventures.[7] The reward to considering a new venture is the expected value of that venture. The reward to attending to a current venture is an increase in the profitability of the venture, which is stochastic. Therefore, the entrepreneur faces an uncertain environment. The relative value of these two choices depends on the abilities of the entrepreneur. These abilities are of two types: The ability to recognize a profitable new venture and the ability to improve a current venture. The first we will refer to as entrepreneurial ability and the latter managerial ability.[8]

In addition to allocating attention each period, the entrepreneur also chooses which venture to shut down. This action requires no attention. The entrepreneur always has the option of evaluating a venture and then choosing whether to shut it down or not. The entrepreneur receives a return from each of the retained current ventures.[9]

After the entrepreneur has made these two decisions, the next period starts. If a new venture was evaluated, then the entrepreneur may have an addition venture in her "portfolio." This depends on her entrepreneurial ability. Alternatively, if a current venture has been evaluated, then this venture's performance may have been improved. This depends on her managerial ability. The goal of the entrepreneur is to maximize the discounted *expected value* of all ventures over time. Therefore, the entrepreneur is assumed to be risk neutral.[10]

The optimal course of action takes the forms of one of two rules. In the first, current projects are discarded, unevaluated, upon reaching a critical age and a new project is evaluated every period. In the second, each current venture

---

[7]Another useful analogy is to imagine a juggler who is rewarded according to the number of plates he can spin on the tips of long sticks. As soon as one plate is spinning, he can set up another one. However, as he continues to set up additional spinning plates, the first one starts to wobble, threatening to fall. The choice the juggler faces is to either continue to set up new plates or to go back and try to respin old plates. New plates may or may not be balanced and current plates that have fallen may be broken.

[8]For a more detailed description of these abilities see Gifford (1998).

[9]In some cases, the returns to the venture are received only when it is liquidated (Gifford, 1997).

[10]This problem is solvable as long as the one-period return to any venture is bounded. The number of projects is not bounded.

is evaluated periodically and a new venture is evaluated if no current project requires evaluation. The first rule, which we will refer to as the innovation rule, is best if the entrepreneurial ability of the entrepreneur is sufficiently high. The second rule, which we call the managerial rule, is best if the managerial ability is sufficiently high. Therefore, we will consider these two alternative situations.

In the first, entrepreneurial ability is high relative to managerial ability and the entrepreneur does not try to improve the profitability of current ventures. Instead, the entrepreneur considers a new venture every period and current ventures are liquidated when their current returns fall to zero. In this case, the rate of innovation is constant and equal to entrepreneurial ability.

In the second case, entrepreneurial ability is low relative to managerial ability. The entrepreneur will evaluate each current project when its profitability is sufficiently low, but before it has fallen to zero. The entrepreneur will still consider new ventures, but only when there is no current venture that warrants attention. Therefore, in this case the entrepreneur is less innovative. For simplicity, we will first consider two types of entrepreneur, one that has high entrepreneurial ability and so follows the innovation rule and one that has high managerial ability and so follows the managerial rule. The first will be called the innovative entrepreneur and the latter the managerial entrepreneur. Nevertheless, it is important to keep in mind that these entrepreneurs choose these different behaviors because of their different abilities.

Another implication concerning the frequency with which ventures are evaluated is that each venture will be evaluated before its expected returns fall to zero. An innovative entrepreneur will retain each venture until its current returns fall to zero. Therefore, the innovative entrepreneur is willing to take on more ventures than the managerial entrepreneur, making the former appear to be less risk averse than the latter. However, the actual distinction between the two is in the differences in their innovative and managerial abilities. Both are risk neutral. The prediction that a managerial entrepreneur evaluates current ventures before their current returns fall to zero also implies that this entrepreneur will appear not to be maximizing expected value, and so appear to be risk averse.

When two managerial entrepreneurs are compared, we see another indication that they appear to differ in risk aversion, even though they are both risk neutral. Of these two managerial entrepreneurs, the one with higher entrepreneurial ability will evaluate each current venture less frequently than the other. Therefore, this entrepreneur will innovate more frequently and be willing to maintain more current ventures. Both of these behaviors seem to imply that this entrepreneur is less risk averse. However, these behaviors are due only to the fact that this entrepreneur has higher innovative ability. Therefore, the managerial entrepreneur with higher innovative ability will appear to be less risk averse.

Two managerial entrepreneurs appear to have different degrees of risk aversion for another reason. This is because the optimal frequency with which a managerial entrepreneur evaluates each current venture is independent of the riskiness of the venture. Assume that two managerial entrepreneurs face environments that are the same in every respect except for the riskiness of the ventures.[11] Then the entrepreneur facing greater risk will evaluate each current project with the same frequency as an entrepreneur facing less risky ventures. This means that this entrepreneur will be equally as innovative and willing to take on as many ventures as the second will. This appears to be the result of lower risk aversion. However, both entrepreneurs are risk neutral.

These implications of the allocation of limited attention for a risk neutral entrepreneur give us an alternative theory for observations of apparent risk aversion. Although the model assumes that the entrepreneur is risk neutral, in that she cares only about expected returns, not the variance in these returns, the model generates commonly observed behaviors that others have attributed to risk aversion.

Thus, the theory can explain observed behavior, but more importantly, it does not depend on an exogenous assumption about preferences, such as risk aversion, to generate these predictions. Instead, these behaviors are due to differences in entrepreneurial and managerial abilities. The question then remains, how are these different abilities in individuals explained? To address this question we turn next to consideration of the role of investments in human capital.

INVESTING IN HUMAN CAPITAL

From the analysis of the last section, we have seen that limited attention and risk neutrality can generate different behaviors in uncertain environments, depending on the entrepreneur's abilities to innovate new ventures and to manage current ventures. Differences in these abilities are critical to generating apparent differences in attitudes towards risk, even though the individuals are assumed to be risk neutral. Therefore, it is important to consider what affects these abilities.

From earlier research on the allocation of limited attention, we can draw a few conjectures about the implications of limited attention for the problem of investing in human capital. Investing in human capital requires attention to be allocated to learning new things. We will see that limited attention limits the amount of learning we will optimally do. The more valuable the skills we have already learned, the less willing we will be to allocating attention away from using those skills in order to learn new ones. In addition, greater opportunities for learning will increase human capital investment. Therefore, those who have few, or less valuable, current skills will be more inclined to invest in human

---

[11] Assuming that all else is equal, if one distribution $F(x)$ of a random variable x is a mean preserving spread of another distribution $G(x)$, then these two distributions have the same expected value but F has a greater variance and so is more risky.

capital. Those who have greater opportunities for acquiring new skills will invest more in human capital.[12]

This can lead to a variety of outcomes. We do not expect those with low skills to invest in human capital if the opportunities for doing so are low. Those who are highly skilled do not necessarily cease to invest in human capital if the opportunity for acquiring additional skills is high. Therefore, the decision to invest in human capital is a complex one. However, *all else equal*, a person with fewer skills will be inclined to invest more in human capital. A person with higher skills will use those skills and invest less in human capital. Those with higher opportunities for learning will invest more in human capital. These are intuitively clear. The contribution of limited attention is to recognize that the investment in human capital depends on the *relative values* of the ability to use current skills and the ability to obtain new skills.

The implications for entrepreneurial behavior of investments in human capital depend on what kind of investments is made. If someone focuses his or her attention on developing managerial skills by obtaining an MBA, and getting managerial experience, then this would imply that this person would not be very innovative. If someone decided to focus their attention on developing their innovative ability by acquiring better information about market or production conditions, then this person would tend to be more innovative. This decision depends on the person's perceived expected value of these two activities, without appealing to risk aversion.

There are social benefits from investments in human capital, as well. If others benefit from what we know, we will not know enough to satisfy them. This is due to the fact that we bear all of the costs of the investment in human capital but not the entire benefit. This is a form of moral hazard. However, the analysis of limited attention implies that this moral hazard can be efficient (Gifford, 1999). This is because the costs of investment in human capital are real costs, not only to the would-be entrepreneur making the investment, but to society as well. While learning new skills (being a magician), the entrepreneur is not engaged in other activities (being a butcher).

So how does this explain the difficulty entrepreneurs have in getting financial backing? If entrepreneurial behavior is motivated by a high ability to be successfully innovative, then why wouldn't an investor be willing to back this entrepreneur? The reason is that entrepreneurial ability is not directly observable to the investor. The entrepreneur may want to undertake a new venture not because of a high probability of success, but because of a low opportunity cost.

For example, individuals with lucrative employment that consumes most of their working time should be less inclined to undertake entrepreneurial activities than those who are not gainfully employed, all else equal. Even if a 100% sure profit opportunity is serendipitously discovered (Kirzner, 1997), the entrepre-

---

[12] See Iyigun and Owen (1997) for a macroeconomic analysis of the effects on the economy of investments in human capital.

neur may still be unable to verify this to a financial backer. Therefore, the investor does not know the true expected value of the venture. The investor must go by the average expected value. This results in a higher interest rate required to compensate the investor for the low average expected value that results from the asymmetric information.

However, things get worse. The investor may be even more skeptical because this pre-contractual asymmetric information leads to the problem of adverse selection. In this example, adverse selection occurs when the lender charges a high interest rate, which is required to compensate for a lower average expected value. Then only the entrepreneurs with a lower intent to pay back the loan will apply for it. These are not the borrowers that the lender wants to attract; thus, the adverse selection. This in turn further reduces the average expected value for the lender, requiring an even higher interest rate. The end result is a missing market for ventures with high expected values.

One way to resolve the adverse selection problem is for entrepreneurs with ventures that have a high expected value to provide a credible signal of this, such as collateral or other personal commitments that increase the cost of default to the entrepreneur.[13] This, however, does not resolve the problem of moral hazard. If an investor does finance a venture with an entrepreneur, then the investor is affected by how much investment of time the entrepreneur has made, and continues to make, in the venture. The model of limited attention implies that the investor would like for the entrepreneur to allocate more attention to the venture than the entrepreneur is willing to and more than is optimal.[14] This moral hazard reduces the expected value of the venture to the investor and so reduces the availability of funds.

Therefore we see that risk aversion is not required to derive the adverse selection that leads to missing capital markets. Nor is it required to explain the moral hazard that occurs between the investor and the entrepreneur. Both of these problems contribute to capital constraints. A model of risk neutral entrepreneurs and investors can generate apparent risk averse behavior because of asymmetric information concerning the entrepreneur's abilities.

However, from a research perspective, the fact that the entrepreneurial and managerial abilities of a particular entrepreneur are not observable to an investor does not generate the same concerns as unobservable risk aversion. This is because risk aversion is an assumption about preferences, which cannot be explained. Entrepreneurial and managerial abilities are the result of investments in human capital, which are partially observable through activities such as schooling, training, and experience. Therefore, we can test the hypothesis that entrepreneurial activities depend on investments in human capital, whereas we cannot test whether it is due to lower risk aversion (Cramer et al., 2002).

---

[13]See Levy and Lazarovich-Porat (1995) for an empirical test of the effectiveness of such a "revelation mechanism".

[14]See Gifford (1997).

CONCLUSION

The assumption of limited attention made in this chapter is a natural one, although some may feel that they can attend to many things at once – multitasking (say driving, talking on the phone and reading a map). The implications of limited attention are not affected by increasing the number of things that can be attended to at once, as long as this is a finite number. Efforts to increase attention require the delegation of decision making to others, which is captured by the principal–agent model (Jensen and Meckling, 1976). Assuming that the entrepreneur has delegated decisions to others also does not change the implications of limited attention. The assumption of limited attention leads naturally to a theory of organizations and the existence of principal–agent relationships. A common explanation for the delegation of decision making in organizations is the desire to make use of the expertise of others (Holmstrom, 1984). Limited attention implies another reason to delegate decision-making: To free up the principal's time in order to allocate attention to the most import targets. Therefore, this research program also addresses the reasons for *why* organizations exist, in contrast to Gartner and Carter (this volume).

This chapter has presented the argument that explanations of entrepreneurial behavior based on risk aversion are inherently flawed by the fact that we cannot observe or explain risk aversion. Animal spirits and irrationality suffer from the same shortcoming. However, we can analyze the entrepreneur's decisions under uncertainty as a problem of allocating limited attention among activities, depending upon the entrepreneur's managerial and entrepreneurial abilities. These abilities in turn depend on the allocation of attention to investments in human capital. The difficulty for entrepreneurs of obtaining financing is due to asymmetric information concerning these abilities (adverse selection) and to the difficulty of enforcing effort by the entrepreneur after the investment (moral hazard). That is, we can analyze entrepreneurial behavior as a rational solution to a series of allocation problems. There is no need to rely on assumptions about unobservable risk aversion or animal spirits. The question of how entrepreneurs overcome the problem of asymmetric information about their experience, knowledge and skills and subsequent effort can be advanced by the implications of the economics of asymmetric information.[15]

REFERENCES

Amit, R., J. Brander and C. Zott (1998). Why do venture capital firms exist? Theory and Canadian evidence – an essay on the economics of imperfect information. *Journal of Business Venturing,* 13, 441–466.
Amit, R., E. Muller and L. Cockburn (1995). Opportunity costs and entrepreneurial activity. *Journal of Business Venturing,* 10, 95–106.

[15] See Bester (1987) for an early paper explaining credit rationing with asymmetric information.

Baron, R.A. (1998). Cognitive mechanisms in entrepreneurship – entrepreneurship in the 1990s. *Journal of Business Venturing,* 13, 275–294.

Baron, R.A. (2000). Counterfactual thinking and venture formation – the psychology of new venture creation. *Journal of Business Venturing,* 15, 79–91.

Barreto, H. (1989). *The Entrepreneur in Microeconomic Theory: Disappearance and Explanation.* New York: Routledge.

Bates, Timothy (1990). Entrepreneur human capital inputs and small business longevity. *Review of Economics and Statistics,* 72, 551–559.

Becker, Gary S. (1965). A theory of the allocation of time. *Economic Journal,* 75, 493–517.

Bester, Helmut (1987). The role of collateral in credit markets with imperfect information. *European Economic Review,* 31, 887–899.

Blanchflower, D.G. and A.J. Oswald (1998). What makes an entrepreneur? *Journal of Labor Economics,* 16, 26–60.

Brandstätter, H. (1997). Becoming an entrepreneur – a question of personality structure? *Journal of Economic Psychology,* 18, 157–177.

Brockhaus, R.H. Sr. (1980). Risk taking propensity of entrepreneurs. *Academy of Management Journal,* 23, 509–520.

Casson, M. (1982). *The Entrepreneur: An Economic Theory.* Totowa, NJ: Barnes and Noble Books.

Chandler, Gaylen N. and Steven H. Hanks (1998). An examination of the substitutability of founders' human and financial capital in emerging business ventures. *Journal of Business Venturing,* 13, 353–370.

Cheung, J. A. (1999). Probability based approach to estimating costs of capital for small business. *Small Business Economics,* 12, 331–336.

Coco, G. (1999). Collateral, heterogeneity in risk attitude and the credit market equilibrium. *European Economic Review,* 43, 559–574.

Cooper, A.C. and K.W. Artz (1995). Determinants of satisfaction for entrepreneurs. *Journal of Business Venturing,* 10, 439–457.

Cooper, A.C., T.B. Folta and C. Woo (1995). Entrepreneurial information search. *Journal of Business Venturing,* 10, 107–120.

Cramer, J.S., J. Hartog, N. Jonker and C.M. Van Praag (2002). Low risk version encourages the choice for entrepreneurship: An empirical test of a truism. *Journal of Economic Behavior and Organization,* 48, 29–36.

Evans, D.S. and B. Jovanovic (1989). An estimated model of entrepreneurial choice under liquidity constraints. *Journal of Political Economy,* 97, 808–827.

Fiet, James O. (1996). The informational basis of entrepreneurial discovery. *Small Business Economics,* 8, 419–430.

Gifford, S. (1997). Limited attention and the role of the venture capitalist. *Journal of Business Venturing,* 12, 459–482.

Gifford, S. (1998). *The Allocation of Limited Entrepreneurial Attention.* Kluwer Academic Publishers.

Gifford, S. (1999). Efficient moral hazard. *Journal of Economic Behavior and Organizations,* 40, 427–442.

Hai, Y.T. and L.F. See (1997). Moderating effects of tolerance for ambiguity and risk-taking propensity on the role conflict-perceived performance relationship: Evidence from Singaporean entrepreneurs. *Journal of Business Venturing,* 12, 67–81.

Hart, O. and Moore, J. (1994). A theory of debt based on the inalienability of human capital. *Quarterly Journal of Economics,* 109, 841–879.

Hayek, F.A. (1945). The use of knowledge in society. *American Economic Review,* 35, 519–530.

Hebert, R.F. and A.N. Link (1988). *The Entrepreneur: Mainstream Views and Radical Critiques.* New York: Praeger.

Hillier, B. (1998). The borrower's curse: Comment. *Economic Journal,* 108, 1772–1774.

Holmstrom, Bengt (1984). On the theory of delegation. In M. Boyer and R. Kihlstrom (eds.), *Bayesian Models of Economic Theory,* 115–141 (Amsterdam: North-Holland).

Hyrsky, K. and Tuunanen, M. (1999). Innovativeness and risk-taking propensity: A cross-cultural study of Finnish and U.S. entrepreneurs and small business owners. *Liiketaloudellinen Aikakauskirja,* 48, 238–256.

Iyigun, Murat and Ann L. Owen (1997). Risk, entrepreneurship, and human capital accumulation. Board of Governors of the Federal Reserve System.

Jennings, Reg, Charles Cox and Cary L. Cooper (1994). *Business Elites: The Psychology of Entrepreneurs and Intrapreneurs.* London and New York: Routledge.

Jensen, M.C. and W.H. Meckling (1976). Theory of the firm: Managerial behavior, agency costs and ownership structure. *Journal of Financial Economics*, 3, 305–360.

Kahneman, Daniel, and Amos Tversky (1991). Loss aversion in riskless choice: A reference dependent model. *Quarterly Journal of Economics*, 106, 1039–1061.

Khalil, Elias L. (1997). Buridan's Ass, Risk, Uncertainty, and Self-Competition: A Theory of Entrepreneurship. *Kyklos.* Vol. 50(2), pp. 147–63.

Kihlstrom, R.E. and J.J. Laffont (1979). A general equilibrium theory of firm formation based on risk aversion. *Journal of Political Economy*, 87, 719–748.

Kirzner, I.M. (1997). Entrepreneurial discovery and the competitive market process: An Austrian approach. *Journal of Economic Literature*, 35, 60–85.

Knight, F. (1921). *Risk, Uncertainty and Profit.* New York: Houghton Miffin.

Levy, Haim and Esther Lazarovich-Porat (1995). Signaling theory and risk perception: An experimental study. *Journal of Economics and Business*, 47, 39–56.

Lin, Timothy H. (1996). The certification role of large block shareholders in initial public offerings: The case of venture capitalists. *Quarterly Journal of Business and Economics*, 35, 55–65.

Manove, M. and A.J. Padilla (1999). Banking (conservatively) with optimists. *RAND Journal of Economics*, 30, 324–350.

March, James G. and Zur Shapira (1987). Managerial perspectives on risk and risk-taking. *Management Science*, 33, 1404–1418.

March, James G. and Zur Shapira (1992). Variable risk preferences and the focus of attention. *Psychological Review*, 99, 172–183.

Marchionatti, Roberto (1999). On Keynes' Animal Spirits. *Kyklos.* Vol. 52(3), pp. 415–39.

Palich, L.E. and D.R. Bagby (1995). Using cognitive theory to explain entrepreneurial risk-taking: Challenging conventional wisdom. *Journal of Business Venturing*, 10, 425–438.

Pattillo, C. (1998). Investment, uncertainty, and irreversibility in Ghana. *International Monetary Fund Staff Paper*, 45, 522–553.

Rees, H. and A. Shah (1986). An empirical analysis of self-employment in the U.K. *Journal of Applied Econometrics*, 1, 95–108.

Sarasvathy, D.K., H.A. Simon and L. Lave (1998). Perceiving and managing business risks: Differences between entrepreneurs and bankers. *Journal of Economic Behavior and Organization*, 33, 207–225.

Schiller, B.R. and P.E. Crewson (1997). Entrepreneurial origins: A longitudinal inquiry. *Economic Inquiry*, 35, 523–531.

Scholtens, B. (1999). Analytical issues in external financing alternatives for SBEs. *Small Business Economics*, 12, 137–148.

Simon, M., S.M. Houghton and K. Aquino (2000). Cognitive biases, risk perception, and venture formation – implications of interfirm (mis)perceptions for strategic decisions. *Journal of Business Venturing*, 15, 113–134.

Starmer, Chris (2000). Developments in non-expected utility theory: The hunt for a descriptive theory of choice under risk. *Journal of Economics Literature*, 38, 332–382.

Stewart, Wayne H. Jr., Warren E. Watson, Joann C. Carland and James W. Carland (1999). A proclivity for entrepreneurship: A comparison of entrepreneurs, small business owners, and corporate managers. *Journal of Business Venturing*, 14, 189–214.

Sykes, H.B. and D. Dunham (1995). Critical assumption planning: A practical tool for managing business development risk. *Journal of Business Venturing*, 10, 413–424.

Van Praag, C.M. and H. van Ophem (1995). Determinants of willingness and opportunity to start as an entrepreneur. *Kyklos*, 48, 513–540.

Wiggins, S.N. (1995). Entrepreneurial enterprises, endogenous ownership, and the limits to firm size. *Economic Inquiry*, **33**, 54–69.

Witt, U. (1998). Imagination and leadership – the neglected dimension of an evolutionary theory of the firm. *Journal of Economic Behavior and Organization*, **35**(2), 161–177.

ZOLTAN J. ACS[1] and DAVID B. AUDRETSCH[2]

[1]*University of Baltimore*, [2]*Indiana University*

4.   Innovation and Technological Change

INTRODUCTION

Just as the economy has been besieged by a wave of technological change that has left virtually no sector of the economy untouched, scientific understanding of the innovative process – that is, the manner by which firms innovate, and the impact such technological change has, in turn, on enterprises and markets – has also undergone a revolution, which, if somewhat quieter, has been no less fundamental. Well into the 1970s, a conventional wisdom about the nature of technological change generally pervaded. This conventional wisdom had been shaped largely by scholars such as Alfred Chandler (1977), Joseph Schumpeter (1942) and John Kenneth Galbraith (1956) who had convinced a generation of scholars and policy makers that innovation and technological change lie in the domain of large corporations and that small business would fade away as the victim of its own inefficiencies.

At the heart of this conventional wisdom was the belief that monolithic enterprises exploiting market power were the driving engine of innovative activity. Schumpeter had declared the debate closed, with his proclamation in 1942 (p. 106) that, "What we have got to accept is that (the large-scale establishment) has come to be the most powerful engine of progress." Galbraith (1956, p. 86) echoed Schumpeter's sentiment, "There is no more pleasant fiction than that technological change is the product of the matchless ingenuity of the small man forced by competition to employ his wits to better his neighbor. Unhappily, it is a fiction."

At the same time, the conventional wisdom about small and new firms was that they were burdened with a size inherent handicap in terms of innovative activity. Because they had a deficit of resources required to generate and commercialize ideas, this conventional wisdom viewed small enterprises as being largely outside of the domain of innovative activity and technological change. Thus, even after David Birch (1981) revealed the startling findings from his study that small firms provided the engine of job creation in the U.S., most scholars still assumed that, while small businesses may create the bulk of new jobs, innovation and technological change remained beyond their sphere.

While this conventional wisdom about the singular role played by large enterprises with market power prevailed during the first three decades subse-

Z.J. Acs and D.B. Audretsch (eds.), Handbook of Entrepreneurship Research, 55–79
© 2003 *Kluwer Academic Publishers. Printed in Great Britain.*

quent to the close of the Second World War, more recently a wave of new studies has challenged this conventional wisdom. Most importantly, these studies have identified a much wider spectrum of enterprises contributing to innovative activity, and that, in particular, small entrepreneurial firms as well as large established incumbents play an important role in the innovation and process of technological change.

Taken together, these studies comprise a new understanding about the links between entrepreneurship, firm size and innovative activity. The purpose of this chapter is to identify this new understanding about the role that entrepreneurship and small firms play with respect to technological change and innovation and to contrast it with the previous conventional wisdom. This chapter begins with the most prevalent theory about innovation and technological change – the model of the knowledge production function. Just as the conventional wisdom was shaped largely by the available empirical data and analyses, so it is with the newer view. Thus, in the following section of this chapter, issues arising when trying to measure innovative activity are discussed.

The debate and the evidence regarding the relationship between innovative activity and firm size is examined in the third section. In the fourth section, the impact that the external industry environment exerts on technological change is identified. The role that knowledge spillovers and geographic location plays in innovative activity is explained in the fifth section. This leads to a re-interpretation of the knowledge production function when entrepreneurial activity is considered in the sixth section.

Finally, a summary and conclusions are provided in the last section. A key finding is that the conventional wisdom regarding the process of innovation and technological change is generally inconsistent with the new understanding about the role of entrepreneurship in innovative activity. The empirical evidence strongly suggests that small entrepreneurial firms play a key role in generating innovations, at least in certain industries. While the conventional wisdom is derived from the Schumpeterian Hypothesis and assumption that scale economies exist in R&D effort, for which there is considerable empirical evidence, more recent evidence suggests that scale economies bestowed through the geographic proximity facilitated by spatial clusters seems to be more important than those for large enterprises in producing innovative output.

THE KNOWLEDGE PRODUCTION FUNCTION

The starting post for most theories of innovation is the firm (Baldwin and Scott, 1987; Cohen and Levin, 1989; Scherer, 1984, 1991; Dosi, 1988). In such theories the firms are exogenous and their performance in generating technological change is endogenous (Scherer, 1984, 1991; Cohen and Klepper, 1991, 1992; Arrow, 1962).

For example, in the most prevalent model found in the literature of technological change, the model of the *knowledge production function*, formalized by

Zvi Griliches (1979), firms exist exogenously and then engage in the pursuit of new economic knowledge as an input into the process of generating innovative activity.

The most decisive input in the knowledge production function is new economic knowledge. As Cohen and Klepper conclude, the greatest source generating new economic knowledge is generally considered to be R&D (Cohen and Klepper, 1991, 1992).

When it came to empirical estimation of the knowledge production function, it became clear that measurement issues played a major role. The state of knowledge regarding innovation and technological change has generally been shaped by the nature of the data which were available to scholars for analyses. Such data have always been incomplete and, at best, represented only a proxy measure reflecting some aspect of the process of technological change. Simon Kuznets observed in 1962 that the greatest obstacle to understanding the economic role of technological change was a clear inability of scholars to measure it. More recently, Cohen and Levin (1989) warned, "A fundamental problem in the study of innovation and technical change in industry is the absence of satisfactory measures of new knowledge and its contribution to technological progress. There exists no measure of innovation that permits readily interpretable cross-industry comparisons."

Measures of technological change have typically involved one of the three major aspects of the innovative process: (1) a measure of the inputs into the innovative process, such as R&D expenditures, or else the share of the labor force accounted for by employees involved in R&D activities; (2) an intermediate output, such as the number of inventions which have been patented; or (3) a direct measure of innovative output.

These three levels of measuring technological change have not been developed and analyzed simultaneously, but have evolved over time, roughly in the order of their presentation. That is, the first attempts to quantify technological change at all generally involved measuring some aspects of inputs into the innovative process (Scherer, 1965a, 1965b, 1967; Grabowski, 1968; Mueller, 1967; Mansfield, 1968). Measures of R&D inputs – first in terms of employment and later in terms of expenditures – were only introduced on a meaningful basis enabling inter-industry and inter-firm comparisons in the late 1950s and early 1960s.

A clear limitation in using R&D activity as a proxy measure for technological change is that R&D reflects only the resources devoted to producing innovative output, but not the amount of innovative activity actually realized. That is, R&D is an input and not an output in the innovation process. In addition, Kleinknecht (1987 and 1989), Kleinknecht and Verspagen (1989), and Kleinknecht et al. (1991) have systematically shown that R&D measures incorporate only efforts made to generate innovative activity that are undertaken within formal R&D budgets and within formal R&D laboratories. They find that the extent of informal R&D is considerable, particularly in smaller enterprises.[1] And, as Mansfield (1984) points out, not all efforts within a formal R&D laboratory are directed towards generating innovative output in any case. Rather, other types of output, such as imitation and technology transfer, are also common goals in R&D laboratories.

As systematic data measuring the number of inventions patented were made publiclcy available in the mid-1960s, many scholars interpreted this new measure not only as being superior to R&D, but also as reflecting innovative output. In fact, the use of patented inventions is not a measure of innovative output, but is rather a type of intermediate output measure. A patent reflects new technical knowledge, but it does not indicate whether this knowledge has a positive economic value. Only those inventions which have been successfully introduced in the market can claim that they are innovations as well. While innovations and inventions are related, they are not identical. The distinction is that an innovation is "... a process that begins with an invention, proceeds with the development of the invention, and results in the introduction of a new product, process or service to the marketplace" (Edwards and Gordon, 1984, p. 1).

Besides the fact that many, if not most, patented inventions do not result in an innovation, a second important limitation of patent measures as an indicator of innovative activity is that they do not capture all of the innovations actually made. In fact, many inventions which result in innovations are not patented. The tendency of patented inventions to result in innovations and of innovations to be the result of inventions which were patented combine into what F.M. Scherer (1983a) has termed as the propensity to patent. It is the uncertainty about the stability of the propensity to patent across enterprises and across industries that casts doubt upon the reliability of patent measures.[2] According to Scherer (1983a, pp. 107–108), "The quantity and quality of industry patenting may depend upon chance, how readily a technology lends itself to patent protection, and business decision-makers' varying perceptions of how much advantage they will derive from patent rights. Not much of a systematic nature is known about these phenomena, which can be characterized as differences in the propensity to patent."

Mansfield (1984, p. 462) has explained why the propensity to patent may vary so much across markets: "The value and cost of individual patents vary enormously within and across industries ... Many inventions are not patented. And in some industries, like electronics, there is considerable speculation that the patent system is being bypassed to a greater extent than in the past. Some types of technologies are more likely to be patented than others." The implications are that comparisons between enterprises and across industries may be

---

[1] Similar results emphasizing the importance of informal R&D have been found by Santarelli and Sterlachinni (1990).

[2] For example, Shepherd (1979, p. 40) has concluded that, "Patents are a notoriously weak measure. Most of the eighty thousand patents issued each year are worthless and are never used. Still others have negative social value. They are used as 'blocking' patents to stop innovation, or they simply are developed to keep competition out."

misleading. According to Cohen and Levin (1989), "There are significant problems with patent counts as a measure of innovation, some of which affect both within-industry and between-industry comparisons."

Thus, even as new and superior sources of patent data have been introduced, such as the new measure of patented inventions from the computerization by the U.S. Patent Office (Hall et al., 1986; Jaffe, 1986; Pakes and Griliches, 1980, 1984), as well as in Europe (Schwalbach and Zimmermann, 1991; Greif, 1989; Greif and Potkowik, 1990), the reliability of these data as measures of innovative activity has been severely challenged. For example, Pakes and Griliches (1980, p. 378) warn that "patents are a flawed measure (of innovative output); particularly since not all new innovations are patented and since patents differ greatly in their economic impact." And in addressing the question, "Patents as indicators of what?", Griliches (1990, p. 1669) concludes that, "Ideally, we might hope that patent statistics would provide a measure of the (innovative) output ... The reality, however, is very far from it. The dream of getting hold of an output indicator of inventive activity is one of the strong motivating forces for economic research in this area."[3]

It was not before well into the 1970s that systematic attempts were made to provide a direct measure of the innovative output. Thus, it should be emphasized that the conventional wisdom regarding innovation and technological change was based primarily upon the evidence derived from analysing R&D data, which essentially measure inputs into the process of technological change, and patented inventions, which are a measure of intermediate output at best.

The first serious attempt to directly measure innovative output was by the Gellman Research Associates (1976) for the National Science Foundation. Gellman identified 500 major innovations that were introduced into the market between 1953 and 1973 in the United States, the United Kingdom, Japan, West Germany, France, and Canada. The data base was compiled by an international panel of experts, who identified those innovations representing the "most significant new industrial products and processes, in terms of their technological importance and economic and social impact" (National Science Board, 1975, p. 100).

A second and comparable data base once again involved the Gellman Research Associates (1982), this time for the U.S. Small Business Administration. In their second study, Gellman compiled a total of 635 U.S. innovations, including 45 from the earlier study for the National Science Foundation. The additional 590 innovations were selected from fourteen indus-

---

[3] Chakrabarti and Halperin (1990) use a fairly standard source of data for U.S. patents issued by the U.S. Office of Patents and Trademarks, the BRS/PATSEARCH online database, to identify the number of inventions patented by over 470 enterprises between 1975 and 1986. Of particular interest is their comparison between the propensity of firms to patent and company R&D expenditures, and a measure not often found in the economics literature, the number of published papers and publications contributed by employees of each firm. Not only do they bring together data from a number of rich sources, but they compare how the relationships between the various measures of innovative activity vary across firm size.

try trade journals for the period 1970–1979. About 43 percent of the sample was selected from the award winning innovations described in the Industrial Research and Development magazine.

The third data source that has attempted to directly measure innovation activity was compiled at the Science Policy Research Unit (SPRU) at the University of Sussex in the United Kingdom.[4] The SPRU data consist of a survey of 4,378 innovations that were identified over a period of fifteen years. The survey was compiled by writing to experts in each industry and requesting them to identify "significant technical innovations that had been successfully commercialized in the United Kingdom since 1945, and to name the firm responsible" (Pavitt et al., 1987, p. 299).

The most recent and most ambitious major data base providing a direct measure of innovative activity is the U.S. Small Business Administration's Innovation Data Base (SBIDB). The data base consists of 8,074 innovations commercially introduced in the U.S. in 1982. A private firm, The Futures Group, compiled the data and performed quality-control analyses for the U.S. Small Business Administration by examining over one hundred technology, engineering, and trade journals, spanning every industry in manufacturing. From the sections in each trade journal listing innovations and new products, a data base consisting of the innovations by four-digit standard industrial classification (SIC) industries was formed.[5] These data were implemented by Acs and Audretsch (1987, 1988b, 1990) to analyze the relationships between firm size and technological change and market structure and technological change, where a direct rather than indirect measure of innovative activity is used.

In their 1990 study (chapter 2), Acs and Audretsch directly compare these four data bases directly measuring innovative activity and find that they generally provide similar qualitative results. For example, while the Gellman data base identified small firms as contributing 2.45 times more innovations per employee than do large firms, the U.S. Small Business Administration's Innovation Data Base finds that small firms introduce 2.38 more innovations per employee than do their larger counterparts. In general, these four data bases reveal similar patterns with respect to the distribution of innovations across manufacturing industries and between large and small enterprises. These similarities emerge, despite the obviously different methods used to compile the data, especially in terms of sampling and standard of significance.

Just as for the more traditional measures of technological change, there are also certain limitations associated with the direct measure of innovative activity. In fact, one of the main qualifications is common among all three measures – the implicit assumption of homogeneity of units. That is, just as it is implicitly

---

[4] The SPRU innovation data are explained in considerable detail in Pavitt et al. (1987), Townsend et al. (1981), Robson and Townsend (1984), and Rothwell (1989).

[5] A detailed description of the U.S. Small Business Administration's Innovation Data Base can be found in chapter 2 of Acs and Audretsch (1990a).

assumed that each dollar of R&D makes the same contribution to technological change, and that each invention which is patented is equally valuable, the output measure implicitly assumes that innovations are of equal importance.[6] As Cohen and Levin (1989) observe, "In most studies, process innovation is not distinguished from product innovation; basic and applied research are not distinguished from development." Thus, the increase in the firm's market value resulting from each innovation, dollar expended on R&D, and patent, is implicitly assumed to be homogeneous – an assumption which clearly violates real world observation.

In order to at least approximate the market value associated with innovative activity, FitzRoy and Kraft (1990, 1991) follow the example of Pakes (1985), Connolly et al. (1986), and Connolly and Hirschey (1984). Based on data for 57 West German firms in the metalworking sector, FitzRoy and Kraft (1990, 1991) measure innovation as the "proportion of sales consisting of products introduced within the last five years." Presumably the greater the market value of a given product innovation, the higher would be the proportion of sales accounted for by new products.

Similarly, Graf von der Schulenburg and Wagner (1991, 1992) are able to provide one of the first applications of a direct measure of innovative activity in West Germany. Their measure is from the IFO Institute and is defined as the "percentage of shipments of those products which were introduced recently into the market and are still in the entry phase."[7] Like the measure of innovative activity used by FitzRoy and Kraft (1990, 1991), the Graf von der Schulenburg and Wagner measure reflects the market value of the innovation and therefore attempts to overcome one of the major weaknesses in most of the other direct and indirect measures of innovative activity.

The knowledge production function has been found to hold most strongly at broader levels of aggregation. The most innovative countries are those with the greatest investments to R&D. Little innovative output is associated with less developed countries, which are characterized by a paucity of production of new economic knowledge. Similarly, the most innovative industries, also tend to be characterized by considerable investments in R&D and new economic knowledge. Not only are industries such as computers, pharmaceuticals and instruments high in R&D inputs that generate new economic knowledge, but also in terms of innovative outputs (Audretsch, 1995). By contrast, industries with little R&D, such as wood products, textiles and paper, also tend to produce only a negligible amount of innovative output. Thus, the knowledge production model linking knowledge generating inputs to outputs certainly holds at the more aggregated levels of economic activity.

---

[6] It should be emphasized, however, that Acs and Audretsch (1990, chapter 2) perform a careful analysis of the significance of the innovations based on four broad categories ranking the importance of each innovation.

[7] The data based used by Graf von der Schulenburg and Wagner (1991) is the IFO-Innovations-Test and is explained in greater detail in Oppenlander (1990), and Konig and Zimmermann (1986).

Where the relationship becomes less compelling is at the disaggregated microeconomic level of the enterprise, establishment, or even line of business. For example, While Acs and Audretsch (1990) found that the simple correlation between R&D inputs and innovative output was 0.84 for four-digit standard industrial classification (SIC) manufacturing industries in the United States, it was only about half, 0.40, among the largest U.S. corporations.

The model of the knowledge production function becomes even less compelling in view of the recent wave of studies revealing that small enterprises serve as the engine of innovative activity in certain industries. These results are startling, because as Scherer (1991) observes, the bulk of industrial R&D is undertaken in the largest corporations; small enterprises account only for a minor share of R&D inputs.

THE ROLE OF FIRM SIZE

At the heart of the conventional wisdom has been the belief that large enterprises able to exploit at least some market power are the engine of technological change. This view dates back at least to Schumpeter, who in *Capitalism, Socialism and Democracy* (1942, p. 101) argued that, "The monopolist firm will generate a larger supply of innovations because there are advantages which, though not strictly unattainable on the competitive level of enterprise, are as a matter of fact secured only on the monopoly level." The Schumpeterian thesis, then, is that large enterprises are uniquely endowed to exploit innovative opportunities. That is, market dominance is a prerequisite to undertaking the risks and uncertainties associated with innovation. It is the possibility of acquiring quasi-rents that serves as the catalyst for large-firm innovation.

Five factors favoring the innovative advantage of large enterprises have been identified in the literature. First is the argument that innovative activity requires a high fixed cost. As Comanor (1967) observes, R&D typically involves a "lumpy" process that yields scale economies. Similarly, Galbraith (1956, p. 87) argues, "Because development is costly, it follows that it can be carried on only by a firm that has the resources which are associated with considerable size."

Second, only firms that are large enough to attain at least temporary market power will choose innovation as a means for maximization (Kamien and Schwartz, 1975). This is because the ability of firms to appropriate the economic returns accruing from R&D and other knowledge-generating investments is directly related to the extent of that enterprise's market power (Cohen and Klepper, 1991, 1992; Levin et al., 1985, 1987; Cohen et al., 1987). Third, R&D is a risky investment; small firms engaging in R&D make themselves vulnerable by investing a large proportion of their resources in a single project. However, their larger counterparts can reduce the risk accompanying innovation through diversification into simultaneous research projects. The larger firm is also more likely to find an economic application of the uncertain outcomes resulting from innovative activity (Nelson, 1959).

Fourth, scale economies in production may also provide scope economies for R&D. Scherer (1991) notes that economies of scale in promotion and in distribution facilitate the penetration of new products, thus enabling larger firms to enjoy a greater profit potential from innovation. Finally, an innovation yielding cost reductions of a given percentage results in higher profit margins for larger firms than for smaller firms.

There is also substantial evidence that technological change – or rather, one aspect of technological change reflected by one of the three measures discussed in the previous section, R&D – is, in fact, positively related to firm size.[8] The plethora of empirical studies relating R&D to firm size is most thoroughly reviewed in Acs and Audretsch (1990, chapter 3), Baldwin and Scott (1987), and Cohen and Levin (1989). The empirical evidence generally seems to confirm Scherer's (1982, pp. 234–235) conclusion that the results "tilt on the side of supporting the Schumpeterian Hypothesis that size is conducive to vigorous conduct of R&D".

In one of the most important studies, Scherer (1984) used the U.S. Federal Trade Commission's Line of Business Data to estimate the elasticity of R&D spending with respect to firm sales for 196 industries. He found evidence of increasing returns to scale (an elasticity exceeding unity) for about twenty percent of the industries, constant returns to scale for a little less than three-quarters of the industries, and diminishing returns (an elasticity less than unity) in less than ten percent of the industries. These results were consistent with the findings of Soete (1979) that R&D intensity increases along with firm size, at least for a sample of the largest U.S. corporations.

While the Scherer (1984) and Soete (1979) studies were restricted to relatively large enterprises, Bound et al. (1984) included a much wider spectrum of firm sizes in their sample of 1,492 firms from the 1976 COMPUSTAT data. They found that R&D increases more than proportionately along with firm size for the smaller firms, but that a fairly linear relationship exists for larger firms. Despite the somewhat more ambiguous findings in still other studies (Comanor, 1967; Mansfield, 1981, 1983; Mansfield et al., 1982), the empirical evidence seems to generally support the Schumpeterian hypothesis that research effort is positively associated with firm size.

The studies relating patents to firm size are considerably less ambiguous. Here the findings unequivocally suggest that "the evidence leans weakly against the Schumpeterian conjecture that the largest sellers are especially fecund sources of patented inventions" (Scherer, 1982, p. 235). In one of the most important studies, Scherer (1965b) used the Fortune annual survey of the 500 largest U.S. industrial corporations. He related the 1955 firm sales to the

---

[8] Fisher and Temin (1973) demonstrated that the Schumpeterian Hypothesis could not be substantiated unless it was established that the elasticity of innovative output with respect to firm size exceeds one. They pointed out that if scale economies in R&D do exist, a firm's size may grow faster than its R&D activities. Kohn and Scott (1982) later showed that if the elasticity of R&D input with respect to firm size is greater than unity, then the elasticity of R&D output with respect to firm size must also be greater than one.

number of patents in 1959 for 448 firms. Scherer found that the number of patented inventions increases less than proportionately along with firm size. Scherer's results were later confirmed by Bound et al. (1984) in the study mentioned above. Basing their study on 2,852 companies and 4,553 patenting entities, they determined that the small firms (with less than $10 million in sales) accounted for 4.3 percent of the sales from the entire sample, but 5.7 percent of the patents.

Such results are not limited to the U.S. Schwalbach and Zimmermann (1991) find that the propensity to patent is less for the largest firms in West Germany than for the medium-sized enterprises included in their sample.

A number of explanations have emerged why smaller enterprises may, in fact, tend to have an innovative advantage, at least in certain industries. Rothwell (1989) suggests that the factors yielding small firms with the innovative advantage generally emanate from the difference in management structures between large and small firms. For example, Scherer (1991) argues that the bureaucratic organization of large firms is not conducive to undertaking risky R&D. The decision to innovate must survive layers of bureaucratic resistance, where an inertia regarding risk results in a bias against undertaking new projects. However, in the small firm the decision to innovate is made by relatively few people.

Second, innovative activity may flourish the most in environments free of bureaucratic constraints (Link and Bozeman, 1991). That is, a number of small-firm ventures have benefited from the exodus of researchers who felt thwarted by the managerial restraints in a larger firm. Finally, it has been argued that while the larger firms reward the best researchers by promoting them out of research to management positions, the smaller firms place innovative activity at the center of their competitive strategy (Scherer, 1991).

Scherer (1988, pp. 4–5) has summarized the advantages small firms may have in innovative activity: "Smaller enterprises make their impressive contributions to innovation because of several advantages they possess compared to large-size corporations. One important strength is that they are less bureaucratic, without layers of 'abominable no-men' who block daring ventures in a more highly structured organization. Second, and something that is often overlooked, many advances in technology accumulate upon a myriad of detailed inventions involving individual components, materials, and fabrication techniques. The sales possibilities for making such narrow, detailed advances are often too modest to interest giant corporations. An individual entrepreneur's juices will flow over a new product or process with sales prospects in the millions of dollars per year, whereas few large corporations can work up much excitement over such small fish, nor can they accommodate small ventures easily into their organizational structures. Third, it is easier to sustain a fever pitch of excitement in small organizations, where the links between challenges, staff, and potential rewards are tight. 'All-nighters' through which tough technical problems are solved expeditiously are common."

Two other ways that small enterprises can compensate for their lack of R&D is through spillovers and spin-offs. Typically an employee from an established large corporation, often a scientist or engineer working in a research laboratory, will have an idea for an invention and ultimately for an innovation. Accompanying this potential innovation is an expected net return from the new product. The inventor would expect to be compensated for his/her potential innovation accordingly. If the company has a different, presumably lower, valuation of the potential innovation, it may decide either not to pursue its development, or that it merits a lower level of compensation than that expected by the employee.

In either case, the employee will weigh the alternative of starting his/her own firm. If the gap in the expected return accruing from the potential innovation between the inventor and the corporate decision maker is sufficiently large, and if the cost of starting a new firm is sufficiently low, the employee may decide to leave the large corporation and establish a new enterprise. Since the knowledge was generated in the established corporation, the new start-up is considered to be a spin-off from the existing firm. Such start-ups typically do not have direct access to a large R&D laboratory. Rather, these small firms succeed in exploiting the knowledge and experience accrued from the R&D laboratories with their previous employers.

The research laboratories of universities provide a source of innovation-generating knowledge that is available to private enterprises for commercial exploitation. Jaffe (1989) and Acs, Audretsch, and Feldman (1992), for example, found that the knowledge created in university laboratories "spills over" to contribute to the generation of commercial innovations by private enterprises. Acs, Audretsch, and Feldman (1994) found persuasive evidence that spillovers from university research contribute more to the innovative activity of small firms than to the innovative activity of large corporations. Similarly, Link and Rees (1990) surveyed 209 innovating firms to examine the relationship between firm size and university research. They found that, in fact, large firms are more active in university-based research. However, small- and medium-sized enterprises apparently are better able to exploit their university-based associations and generate innovations. Link and Rees (1990) conclude that, contrary to the conventional wisdom, diseconomies of scale in producing innovations exist in large firms. They attribute these diseconomies of scale to the "inherent bureaucratization process which inhibits both innovative activity and the speed with which new inventions move through the corporate system towards the market" (Link and Rees, 1990, p. 25).

Thus, just as there are persuasive theories defending the original Schumpeterian Hypothesis that large corporations are a prerequisite for technological change, there are also substantial theories predicting that small enterprises should have the innovative advantage, at least in certain industries. As described above, the empirical evidence based on the input measure of technological change, R&D, tilts decidedly in favor of the Schumpeterian Hypothesis. However, as also described above, the empirical results are somewhat more ambiguous for the measure of intermediate output – the number of patented inventions. It was not until direct measures of innovative output became available that the full picture of the process of technological change could be obtained.

Using this new measure of innovative output from the U.S. Small Business Administration's Innovation Data Base, Acs and Audretsch (1990) shows that, in fact, the most innovative U.S. firms are large corporations. Further, the most innovative American corporations also tended to have large R&D laboratories and be R&D intensive. At first glance, these findings based on direct measures of innovative activity seem to confirm the conventional wisdom. However, in the most innovative four-digit standard industrial classification (SIC) industries, large firms, defined as enterprises with at least 500 employees, contributed more innovations in some instances, while in other industries small firms produced more innovations. For example, in computers and process control instruments small firms contributed the bulk of the innovations. By contrast in the pharmaceutical preparation and aircraft industries the large firms were much more innovative.

Probably their best measure of innovative activity is the total innovation rate, which is defined as the total number of innovations per one thousand employees in each industry. The large-firm innovation rate is defined as the number of innovations made by firms with at least 500 employees, divided by the number of employees (thousands) in large firms. The small-firm innovation rate is analogously defined as the number of innovations contributed by firms with fewer than 500 employees, divided by the number of employees (thousands) in small firms.

The innovation rates, or the number of innovations per thousand employees, have the advantage in that they measure large- and small-firm innovative activity relative to the presence of large and small firms in any given industry. That is, in making a direct comparison between large- and small-firm innovative activity, the absolute number of innovations contributed by large firms and small enterprises is somewhat misleading, since these measures are not standardized by the relative presence of large and small firms in each industry. When a direct comparison is made between the innovative activity of large and small firms, the innovation rates are presumably a more reliable measure of innovative intensity because they are weighted by the relative presence of small and large enterprises in any given industry. Thus, while large firms in manufacturing introduced 2,445 innovations in 1982, and small firms contributed slightly fewer, 1,954, small-firm employment was only half as great as large-firm employment, yielding an average small-firm innovation rate in manufacturing of 0.309, compared to a large-firm innovation rate of 0.202 (Acs and Audretsch, 1988, 1990).

The most important and careful study to date documenting the role of German SMEs (enterprises with fewer than 500 employees) in innovative activity was undertaken by a team of researchers at the Zentrum für Europaeische Wirtschaftsforschung (ZEW) led by Dietmar Harhoff and Georg Licht (1996).

They analyzed the findings made possible by the Mannheim Innovation Data Base. This data base measures the extent of innovative activity in German firms between 1990 and 1992. Harhoff and Licht (1996) use the data base to identify that 12 percent of the research and development expenditures in (West) German firms comes from SMEs (defined as having fewer than 500 employees).

Harhoff and Licht show that the likelihood of a firm not innovating decreases with firm size. For example, 52 percent of firms with fewer than 50 employees were not innovative. By contrast, only 15 percent of the firms with at least 1,000 employees were not innovative. More striking is that the smallest firms that do innovate have a greater propensity to be innovative without undertaking formal research and development. While only 3 percent of the largest corporations in Germany are innovative without undertaking formal R&D, one-quarter of the innovative firms with fewer than 50 employees are innovative without formal R&D.

The study also shows that even fewer SMEs in the five new German Laender are innovative than is the case in West Germany. Over two-thirds of the smallest SMEs in East Germany are not innovative, and they are less than half as likely to undertake R&D as are their Western counterparts.

Systematic empirical evidence also suggests that the German *Mittelstand* is confronted by considerable barriers to innovative activity. Beise and Licht (1996) analyzed the *Mannheimer Innovationspanel* consisting of 43,300 innovating firms to identify the main barriers to innovative activity confronting German small- and medium-sized enterprises. The major barrier to innovation listed in both 1992 and 1994 was too high of a gestation period required for innovative activity. In 1994 nearly 60 percent of German SMEs reported that too long of a high gestation period required to innovate was a very important barrier to innovative activity. Other major barriers to innovative activity include legal restrictions and restrictive government policies, too long of duration required to obtain government approval for a new product, a shortage of finance capital, a lack of competent employees, and too high of a risk.

Thus, there is considerable evidence suggesting that, in contrast to the findings for R&D inputs and patented inventions, small enterprises apparently play an important generating innovative activity, at least in certain industries. By relating the innovative output of each firm to its size, it is also possible to shed new light on the Schumpeterian Hypothesis. In their 1991a study, Acs and Audretsch find that there is no evidence that increasing returns to R&D expenditures exist in producing innovative output. In fact, with just several exceptions, diminishing returns to R&D are the rule. This study made it possible to resolve the apparent paradox in the literature that R&D inputs increase at more than a proportional rate along with firm size, while the generation of patented inventions does not. That is, while larger firms are observed to undertake a greater effort towards R&D, each additional dollar of R&D is found to yield less in terms of innovative output.

THE INDUSTRY CONTEXT

In comparison to the number of studies investigating the relationship between firm size and technological change, those examining the relationship between innovation and the external industry structure or environment are what Baldwin and Scott (1987, p. 89) term "miniscule" in number. In fact, the most comprehensive and insightful evidence has been made possible by utilizing the Federal Trade Commission's Line of Business Data. Using 236 manufacturing industry categories, which are defined at both the three- and four-digit SIC level, Scherer (1983a) found that 1974 company R&D expenditures divided by sales was positively related to the 1974 four-firm concentration ratio. Scherer (1983a, p. 225) concluded that, "although one cannot be certain, it appears that the advantages a high market share confers in appropriating R&D benefits provide the most likely explanation of the observed R&D-concentrator associations."

Scott (1984) also used the FTC Line of Business Survey Data and found the U-shaped relationship between market concentration and R&D. However, when he controlled for the fixed effects for two-digit SIC industries, no significant relationship could be found between concentration and R&D. These results are consistent with a series of studies by Levin et al. (1985, 1987), Levin and Reiss (1984), and Cohen et al. (1987). Using data from a survey of R&D executives in 130 industries, which were matched with FTC Line of Business Industry Groups, Cohen et al. (1987) and Levin et al. (1987) found little support for the contention that industrial concentration is a significant and systematic determinant of R&D effort.

While it has been hypothesized that firms in concentrated industries are better able to capture the rents accruing from an innovation, and therefore have a greater incentive to undertake innovative activity, there are other market structure variables that also influence the ease with which economic rents can be appropriated. For example, Comanor (1967) argued and found that, based on a measure of minimum efficient scale, there is less R&D effort (average number of research personnel divided by total employment) in industries with very low scale economies. However, he also found that in industries with a high minimum efficient scale, R&D effort was also relatively low. Comanor interpreted his results to suggest that, where entry barriers are relatively low, there is little incentive to innovate, since the entry subsequent to innovation would quickly erode any economic rents. At the same time, in industries with high entry barriers, the absence of potential entry may reduce the incentives to innovate.

Because many studies have generally found positive relationships between market concentration and R&D, and between the extent of barriers to entry and R&D, it would seem that the conventional wisdom built around the Schumpeterian Hypothesis has been confirmed. However, when the direct measure of innovative output is related to market concentration, Acs and Audretsch (1988b, 1990) find a pointedly different relationship emerges. In fact, there appears to be unequivocal evidence that concentration exerts a negative influence on the number of innovations being made in an industry.

Acs and Audretsch (1987, 1988b, 1990) found that not only does market structure influence the total amount of innovative activity, but also the relative innovative advantage between large and small enterprises. The differences between the innovation rates of large and small firms examined in the previous section can generally be explained by (1) the degree of capital intensity, (2) the extent to which an industry is concentrated, (3) the total innovative intensity, and (4) the extent to which an industry is comprised of small firms. In particular, the relative innovative advantage of large firms tends to be promoted in industries that are capital-intensive, advertising intensive, concentrated, and highly unionized. By contrast, in industries that are highly innovative and composed predominantly of large firms, the relative innovative advantage is held by small enterprises.

THE GEOGRAPHIC CONTEXT

The evidence revealing small enterprises to be the engine of innovative activity in certain industries, despite an obvious lack of formal R&D activities, raises the question about the source of knowledge inputs for small enterprises. The answer emerging from a series of studies (Jaffe, 1990) is from other, third-party, firms or research institutions, such as universities. Economic knowledge may *spill over* from the firm or research institution creating it for application by other firms.

That knowledge spills over is barely disputed. However, the geographic range of such knowledge spillovers is greatly contested. In disputing the importance of knowledge externalities in explaining the geographic concentration of economic activity, Krugman (1991) and others do not question the existence or importance of such knowledge spillovers. In fact, they argue that such knowledge externalities are so important and forceful that there is no compelling reason for a geographic boundary to limit the spatial extent of the spillover. According to this line of thinking, the concern is not that knowledge does not spill over but that it should stop spilling over just because it hits a geographic border, such as a city limit, state line, or national boundary.

A recent body of empirical evidence clearly suggests that R&D and other sources of knowledge not only generate externalities, but studies by Audretsch and Feldman (1996), Jaffe (1989), Audretsch and Stephan (1996), Anselin, Varga and Acs (1997, 2000), and Jaffe, Trajtenberg and Henderson (1993) suggest that such knowledge spillovers tend to be geographically bounded within the region where the new economic knowledge was created. That is, new economic knowledge may spill-over but the geographic extent of such knowledge spillovers is limited.

Krugman (1991, p. 53) has argued that economists should abandon any attempts at measuring knowledge spillovers because "... knowledge flows are

invisible, they leave no paper trail by which they may be measured and tracked."
But as Jaffe, Trajtenberg and Henderson (1991, p. 578) point out, "knowledge
flows do sometimes leave a paper trail" – in particular in the form of patented
inventions and new product introductions.

Studies identifying the extent of knowledge spillovers are based on the
knowledge production function. Jaffe (1989) modified the knowledge production function approach to a model specified for spatial and product dimensions:

$$I_{si} = IRD^{\beta_1} * UR_{si}^{\beta_2} * (UR_{si} * GC_{si}^{\beta_3}) * \varepsilon_{si} \tag{1}$$

where I is innovative output, IRD is private corporate expenditures on R&D,
UR is the research expenditures undertaken at universities, and GC measures
the geographic coincidence of university and corporate research. The unit of
observation for estimation was at the spatial level, s, at state, and industry
level, i. Estimation of equation (1) essentially shifted the knowledge production
function from the unit of observation of a firm to that of a geographic unit.

Implicitly contained within the knowledge production function model is the
assumption that innovative activity should take place in those regions, s, where
the direct knowledge-generating inputs are the greatest, and where knowledge
spillovers are the most prevalent. Audretsch and Feldman (1996), Anselin, Acs
and Varga (1997, 2000) and Audretsch and Stephan (1996) link the propensity
for innovative activity to cluster together to industry specific characteristics,
most notably the relative importance of knowledge spillovers.

The Knowledge Production Function Reconsidered

The model of the knowledge production function becomes even less compelling
in view of the evidence documented in section 3 that entrepreneurial small
firms are the engine of innovative activity in some industries, which raises the
question, "Where do new and small firms get the innovation producing inputs,
that is the knowledge?"

The appropriability problem, or the ability to capture the revenues accruing
from investments in new knowledge, confronting the individual may converge
with that confronting the firm. Economic agents can and do work for firms,
and even if they do not, they can potentially be employed by an incumbent
firm. In fact, in a model of perfect information with no agency costs, any
positive economies of scale or scope will ensure that the appropriability problems of the firm and individual converge. If an agent has an idea for doing
something different than is currently being practiced by the incumbent enterprises – both in terms of a new product or process and in terms of organization
– the idea, which can be termed as an innovation, will be presented to the
incumbent enterprise. Because of the assumption of perfect knowledge, both
the firm and the agent would agree upon the expected value of the innovation.
But to the degree that any economies of scale or scope exist, the expected value

of implementing the innovation within the incumbent enterprise will exceed that of taking the innovation outside of the incumbent firm to start a new enterprise. Thus, the incumbent firm and the inventor of the idea would be expected to reach a bargain splitting the value added to the firm contributed by the innovation. The payment to the inventor – either in terms of a higher wage or some other means of remuneration – would be bounded between the expected value of the innovation if it implemented by the incumbent enterprise on the upper end, and by the return that the agent could expect to earn if he used it to launch a new enterprise on the lower end.

A different model refocuses the unit of observation away from firms deciding whether to increase their output from a level of zero to some positive amount in a new industry, to individual agents in possession of new knowledge that, due to uncertainty, may or may not have some positive economic value. It is the uncertainty inherent in new economic knowledge, combined with asymmetries between the agent possessing that knowledge and the decision making vertical hierarchy of the incumbent organization with respect to its expected value that potentially leads to a gap between the valuation of that knowledge.

Divergences in the expected value regarding new knowledge will, under certain conditions, lead an agent to exercise what Albert O. Hirschman (1970) has termed as *exit* rather than *voice*, and depart from an incumbent enterprise to launch a new firm. But who is right, the departing agents or those agents remaining in the organizational decision making hierarchy who, by assigning the new idea a relatively low value, have effectively driven the agent with the potential innovation away? *Ex post* the answer may not be too difficult. But given the uncertainty inherent in new knowledge, the answer is anything but trivial *a priori*.

This initial condition of not just uncertainty, but greater degree of uncertainty *vis-à-vis* incumbent enterprises in the industry is captured in the theory of firm selection and industry evolution proposed by Boyan Jovanovic (1982). The theory of firm selection is particularly appealing in view of the rather startling size of most new firms. For example, the mean size of more than 11,000 new-firm startups in the manufacturing sector in the United States was found to be fewer than eight workers per firm.[5] While the minimum efficient scale (MES) varies substantially across industries, and even to some degree across various product classes within any given industry, the observed size of most new firms is sufficiently small to ensure that the bulk of new firms will be operating at a suboptimal scale of output. Why would an entrepreneur start a new firm that would immediately be confronted by scale disadvantages?

An implication of the theory of firm selection is that new firms may begin at a small, even suboptimal, scale of output, and then if merited by subsequent performance expand. Those new firms that are successful will grow, whereas those that are not successful will remain small and may ultimately be forced to exit from the industry if they are operating at a suboptimal scale of output.

An important finding of Audretsch (1995) verified in a systematic and comprehensive series of studies contained in the reviews by Caves (1998),

Sutton (1997) and Geroski (1995) is that although entry may still occur in industries characterized by a high degree of scale economies, the likelihood of survival is considerably less. People will start new firms in an attempt to appropriate the expected value of their new ideas, or potential innovations, particularly under the entrepreneurial regime. As entrepreneurs gain experience in the market they learn in at least two ways. First, they discover whether they possess *the right stuff,* in terms of producing goods and offering services for which sufficient demand exists, as well as whether they can product that good more efficiently than their rivals. Second, they learn whether they can adapt to market conditions as well as to strategies engaged in by rival firms. In terms of the first type of learning, entrepreneurs who discover that they have a viable firm will tend to expand and ultimately survive. But what about those entrepreneurs who discover that they are either not efficient or not offering a product for which there is a viable demand? The answer is, *It depends – on the extent of scale economies as well as on conditions of demand.* The consequences of not being able to grow will depend, to a large degree, on the extent of scale economies. Thus, in markets with only negligible scale economies, firms have a considerably greater likelihood of survival. However, where scale economies play an important role the consequences of not growing are substantially more severe, as evidenced by a lower likelihood of survival.

What emerges from the new evolutionary theories and empirical evidence on the role of small firms is that markets are in motion, with a lot of new firms entering the industry and a lot of firms exiting out of the industry. The evolutionary view of the process of industry evolution is that new firms typically start at a very small scale of output. They are motivated by the desire to appropriate the expected value of new economic knowledge. But, depending upon the extent of scale economies in the industry, the firm may not be able to remain viable indefinitely at its startup size. Rather, if scale economies are anything other than negligible, the new firm is likely to have to grow to survival. The temporary survival of new firms is presumably supported through the deployment of a strategy of compensating factor differentials that enables the firm to discover whether or not it has a viable product.

The empirical evidence (Caves, 1998; Sutton, 1997; Geroski, 1995) supports such an evolutionary view of the role of new firms in manufacturing, because the post-entry growth of firms that survive tends to be spurred by the extent to which there is a gap between the MES level of output and the size of the firm. However, the likelihood of any particular new firm surviving tends to decrease as this gap increases. Such new suboptimal scale firms are apparently engaged in the selection process. Only those firms offering a viable product that can be produced efficiently will grow and ultimately approach or attain the MES level of output. The remainder will stagnate, and depending upon the severity of the other selection mechanism – the extent of scale economies – may ultimately be forced to exit out of the industry. Thus, the persistence of an asymmetric firm-size distribution biased towards small-scale enterprise reflects the continuing process of the entry of new firms into industries and not necessarily the permanence of such small and sub-optimal enterprises over the long run. Although the skewed size distribution of firms persists with remarkable stability over long periods of time, a constant set of small and suboptimal scale firms does not appear to be responsible for this skewed distribution. Rather, by serving as agents of change, entrepreneurial firms provide an essential source of new ideas and experimentation that otherwise would remain untapped in the economy.

CONCLUSIONS

Within a generation, scholarship has produced theories, evidence and new insights that have dramatically changed the prevalent view about the role of entrepreneurship in innovation and technological change. The conventional wisdom held that small firms inherently have a deficit of knowledge assets, burdening them with a clear and distinct disadvantage in generating innovative output. This view was certainly consistent with the early interpretation of the knowledge production function. As Chandler (1990) concluded, "to compete globally you have to be big."

More recent scholarship has produced a revised view that identifies entrepreneurial small firms as making a crucial contribution to innovative activity and technological change. There are two hypotheses why scholarship about the role of small firms has evolved so drastically within such a short period. This first is that, as explained in this chapter, the measurement of innovative output and technological change has greatly improved. As long as the main instruments to measuring innovative activity were restricted to inputs into the innovative process, such as expenditures on formal R&D, many or even most of the innovative activities by smaller enterprises simply remained hidden from the radar screen of researchers. With the development of measures focusing on measures of innovative output, the vital contribution of small firms became prominent, resulting in the emergence of not just the recognition that small firms provide an engine of innovative activity, at least in some industry contexts, but also of new theories to explain and understand how and why small firms access knowledge and new ideas. This first hypothesis would suggest that, in fact, small firms have always made these types of innovative contributions, but they remained hidden and mostly unobserved to scholars and policy makers.

The alternative hypothesis is that, in fact, the new view towards the innovative capacity of small firms emerged not because of measurement improvements, but because the economic and social environment actually changed in such a way as to shift the innovative advantage more towards smaller enterprises. This hypothesis would say that the conventional wisdom about the relative inability of small firms to innovate was essentially correct – at least for a historical period of time. Rather, the new view of small firms as engines of innovative activity reflect changes in technology, globalization and other factors that have fundamentally altered the importance and process of innovation and technological change. As Jovanovic (2001, pp. 54–55) concludes, "The new economy is one in which technologies and products become obsolete at a much faster rate than a few decades ago ... It is clear that we are entering the era of the young firm. The small firm will thus resume a role that, in its importance, is greater than it has been at any time in the last seventy years or so."

Future research may sort out which of these two hypotheses carries more weight. However, one important conclusion will remain. Scholarship has clearly changed in its assessment of the role of small firms in the process of innovation and technological change from being mostly unimportant to carrying a central role.

REFERENCES

Acs, Zoltan J. (1984). *The Changing Structure of the U.S. Economy: Lessons from the Steel Industry.* New York: Praeger.

Acs, Zoltan J. (ed.) (1995). *Small Firms and Economic Development.* Northampton, MA: Edward Elgar.

Acs, Zoltan J. and Catherine Armington (1999). Job flow dynamics in the service sector. Discussion Paper 99-14, Center for Economic Studies, Bureau of the Census, Washington, D.C.

Acs, Zoltan J. and David B. Audretsch (1988a). Innovation in large and small firms: An empirical analysis. *American Economic Review,* 78(4), September, 678–690.

Acs, Zoltan J. and David B. Audretsch (1988b). R&D and small firms. Testimony before the Subcommittee on Monopolies and Commercial Law, Committee on the Judiciary, U.S. House of Representatives, February 24.

Acs, Zoltan J. and David B. Audretsch (1989). Patents as a measure of innovative activity. *Kyklos,* 42(2), 171–180.

Acs, Zoltan J. and David B. Audretsch (1990). *Innovation and Small Firms.* Cambridge, MA: MIT Press.

Acs, Zoltan J. and David B. Audretsch (eds.) (1991). *Innovation and Technological Change: An International Comparison.* Ann Arbor, MI: University of Michigan Press.

Acs, Zoltan J. and David B. Audretsch (eds.) (1993). *Small Firms and Entrepreneurship: An East–West Perspective.* Cambridge: Cambridge University Press.

Acs, Zoltan J. and David B. Audretsch (1987). Innovation, market structure and firm size. *Review of Economics and Statistics,* 69(4), 567–575.

Acs, Zoltan J., Catherine Armington and Alicia Robb (1999). Gross Job Flows in the U.S. Economy. Discussion Paper 99-01, Center for Economic Studies, Bureau of the Census, Washington, D.C.

Acs, Zoltan J., David B. Audretsch (1987). Innovation, market structure and firm size. *Review of Economics and Statistics,* 69(4), 567–575.

Acs, Zoltan J., David B. Audretsch and Maryann P. Feldman (1992). Real effects of academic research. *American Economic Review,* 82(1), 363–367.

Acs, Zoltan J., David B. Audretsch and Maryann P. Feldman (1994). R&D spillovers and recipient firm size. *Review of Economics and Statistics,* 100(2), 336–367.

Almeida, P. and B. Kogut (1997). The exploration of technological diversity and the geographic localization of innovation. *Small Business Economics,* 9(1), 21–31.

Anselin, L., A. Varga and Zoltan J. Acs (1997). Local geographic spillovers between university research and high technology innovations. *Journal of Urban Economics,* 42, 422–448.

Anselin, L., A. Varga and Zoltan J. Acs (2000). Geographic and sectoral characteristics of academic knowledge externalities. *Papers in Regional Science,* 79(4), 435–443.

Arrow, K.J. (1962). Economic Welfare and the Allocation of Resources for Invention, in R.R. Nelson (ed.), *The Rate and Direction of Inventive Activity,* pp. 609–626. Princeton University Press: Princeton, NJ.

Arvanitis, Spyros (1997). The impact of firm size on innovative activity – an empirical analysis based on Swiss firm data. *Small Business Economics*, 9(6), 473–490.

Audretsch, David B. (1995). *Innovation and Industry Evolution.* Cambridge, MA: MIT Press.

Audretsch, David B. and Maryann P. Feldman (1996). R&D spillovers and the geography of innovation and production. *American Economic Review*, 86(3), June, 630–640.

Audretsch, David B. and Paula E. Stephan (1996). Company-scientist locational links: The case of biotechnology. *American Economic Review*, 86(3), June, 641–652.

Baldwin, John R. (1995). *The Dynamics of Industrial Competition.* Cambridge: Cambridge University Press.

Baldwin, William L. and John T. Scott (1987). *Market Structure and Technological Change.* London and New York: Harwood Academic Publishers.

Beise, Marian and Georg Licht (1996). Innovationsverhalten der deutschen Wirtschaft. Unpublished manuscript, Zentrum für Europaeische Wirtschaftsforschung (ZEW), Mannheim, January.

Berger, Georg and Eric Nerlinger (1997). Regionale Verteilung von Unternehmensgruendungen in der Informationstechnik: Empirische Ergebnisse fuer Westdeutschland. In Dietmar Harhoff (ed.), *Unternehmensgruendungen: Empirische Analysen fuer die alten und neuen Bundeslaender.* Baden-Baden: Nomos, pp. 151–186.

Birch, D.L. (1981). Who Creates Jobs? *The Public Interest*, 65, 3–14.

Bound, John, Clint Cummins, Zvi Griliches, Bronwyn H. Hall and Adam Jaffe (1984). Who does R&D and who patents? In Z. Griliches (ed.), *R&D, Patents, and Productivity.* Chicago, IL: University of Chicago Press, pp. 21–54.

Braunerhjelm, Pontus and Bo Carlsson (1999). Industry clusters in Ohio and Sweden 1975–1995. *Small Business Economics*, 12(4), 279–293.

Caves, Richard E. (1998). Industrial organization and new findings on the turnover and mobility of firms. *Journal of Economic Literature*, 36(4), December, 1947–1982.

Chakrabarti, Alok K. and Michael R. Halperin (1990). Technical performance and firm size: Analysis of patents and publications of U.S. firms. *Small Business Economics*, 2(3), 183–190.

Chandler, A.D. Jr (1997). *The Visible Hand: The Managerial Revolution in American Business.* Harvard University Press: Cambridge, MA.

Cohen, Wesley M. and Steven Klepper (1991). Firm size versus diversity in the achievement of technological advance. In *Handbook of Industrial Organization*, Vol. 2, eds. R. Schmalansee and R. Willig, 1059–1107. Amsterdam: North-Holland.

Cohen, Wesley M. and Steven Klepper (1992). The tradeoff between firm size and diversity in the pursuit of technological progress. *Small Business Economics*, 4(1), 1–14.

Cohen, Wesley M. and Richard C. Levin (1989). Empirical studies of innovation and market structure. In Richard Schmalensee and Robert Willig (eds.), *Handbook of Industrial Organization*, Volume II, Amsterdam: North-Holland, pp. 1059–1107.

Cohen, Wesley M., Richard C. Levin and David C. Mowery (1987). Firm size and R&D intensity: A reexamination. *Journal of Industrial Economics*, 35, June, 543–565.

Comanor, William S. (1967). Market structure, product differentiation and industrial research. *Quarterly Journal of Economics*, 81, 639–657.

Connolly, Robert A. and Mark Hirschey (1984). R&D, market structure and profits: A value based approach. *Review of Economics and Statistics*, 66, November, 682–686.

Connolly, Robert A., Barry T. Hirsch and Mark Hirschey (1986). Union rent seeking, intangible capital, and the market value of the firm. *Review of Economics and Statistics*, 68, November, 567–577.

Dosi, G. (1988). Sources, Procedures, and Microeconomic Effects of Innovation. *Journal of Economic Literature*, 26, 1120–1171.

Edwards, Keith L. and Theodore J. Gordon (1984). Characterization of innovations introduced on the U.S. market in 1982. The Futures Group, prepared for the U.S. Small Business Administration under Contract No. SBA-6050-OA82.

Fisher, Franklin M. and Peter Temin (1973). Returns to scale in research and development: What does the Schumpeterian hypothesis imply? *Journal of Political Economy*, 81, 56–70.

FitzRoy, Felix R. and Kornelius Kraft (1990). Innovation, rent-sharing and the organization of labour in the Federal Republic of Germany. *Small Business Economics*, 2(2), 95–104.

FitzRoy, Felix R. and Kornelius Kraft (1991). Firm size, growth and innovation: Some evidence from West Germany. In Zoltan J. Acs and David B. Audretsch (eds.), *Innovation and Technological Change: An International Comparison*. Ann Arbor, MI: University of Michigan Press, pp. 152–159.

Galbraith, John K. (1956). *American Capitalism: The Concept of Countervailing Power*, revised edition. Boston, MA: Houghton Mifflin.

Gellman Research Associates (1976). Indicators of international trends in technological innovation. Prepared for the National Science Foundation.

Gellman Research Associates (1982). The relationship between industrial concentration, firm size, and technological innovation. Prepared for the Office of Advocacy, U.S. Small Business Administration under award no. SBA-2633-OA-79.

Geroski, Paul A. (1995). What do we know about entry. *International Journal of Industrial Organization*, 13(4), December.

Glaeser, E., H. Kallal, J. Scheinkman and A. Shleife (1992). Growth of cities. *Journal of Political Economy*, 100, 1126–1152.

Grabowski, Henry G. (1968). The determinants of industrial research and development: A study of the chemical, drug, and petroleum industries. *Journal of Political Economy*, 76(4), 292–306.

Greif, Siegfried (1989). Zur Erfassung von Forschungs- and Entwicklungstatigkeit durch Patente. *Naturwissenschaften*, 76(4), 156–159.

Greif, Siegfried and Georg Potkowik (1990). *Patente und Wirtschaftszweige: Zusammenfiihrung der Internationalen Patentklassifikation und der Systematik der Wirtschaftszweige*. Cologne: Carl Heymanns Verlag.

Griliches, Zvi (1979). Issues in assessing the contribution of R&D to productivity growth. *Bell Journal of Economics*, 10(Spring), 92–116.

Griliches, Zvi (1990). Patent statistics as economic indicators: A survey. *Journal of Economic Literature*, 28(4), 1661–1707.

Hall, Bronwyn H., Zvi Griliches and Jerry A. Hausman (1986). Patents and R&D: Is there a lag? *International Economic Review*, 27, 265–302.

Harhoff, Dietmar and Georg Licht (1996). *Innovationsaktivitaeten kleiner und mittlerer Unternehmen*. Baden-Baden: Nomos Verlagsgesellschaft.

Hirschman, Albert O. (1970). *Exit, Voice, and Loyalty*. Cambridge, MA: Harvard University Press.

Jaffe, Adam B. (1986). Technological opportunity and spillovers of R&D: Evidence from firms' patents, profits and market value. *American Economic Review*, 76, 984–1001.

Jaffe, Adam B. (1989). Real effects of academic research. *American Economic Review*, 79(5), 957–970.

Jaffe, A.B., M. Trajtenberg and R. Henderson (1993). Geographic Localization of Knowledge Spillovers as Evidenced by Patent Citations. *Quarterly Journal of Economics*, 63, 577–598.

Jovanovic, Boyan (1982). Selection and evolution of industry. *Econometrica*, 50(2), 649–670.

Jovanovic, Boyan (2001). New technology and the small firm. *Small Business Economics*, 16(1), 53–55.

Kamien, Morton I. and Nancy L. Schwartz (1975). Market structure and innovation: A survey. *Journal of Economic Literature*, 13, 1–37.

Karlsson, Charlie and Ola Olsson (1998). Product innovation in small and large enterprises. *Small Business Economics*, 10(1), 31–46.

Kleinknecht, Alfred (1987). Measuring R&D in small firms: How much are we missing? *Journal of Industrial Economics*, 36(2), 253–256.

Kleinknecht, Alfred (1991). Firm size and innovation: Reply to Scheirer. *Small Business Economics*, 3(2), 157–158.

Kleinknecht, Alfred, Tom P. Poot and Jeroen O.N. Reijnen (1991). Technical performance and firm size: Survey results from the Netherlands. In Zoltan J. Acs and David B. Audretsch (eds.), *Innovation and Technological Change: An International Comparison*. Ann Arbor, MI: University of Michigan Press, pp. 84–108.

Kleinknecht, Alfred and Bart Verspagen (1989). R&D and market structure: The impact of measurement and aggregation problems. *Small Business Economics*, 1(4), 297–302.

Kohn, Meier and John T. Scott (1982). Scale economies in research and development: The Schumpeterian Hypothesis. *Journal of Industrial Economics*, 30, 239–249.

Konig, Heinz and Klaus F. Zimmermann (1986). Innovations, market structure and market dynamics. *Journal of Institutional and Theoretical Economics*, 142(1), 184–199.

Krugman, Paul (1991). *Geography and Trade*. Cambridge, MA: MIT Press.

Kuznets, Simon (1962). Inventive activity: Problems of definition and measurement. In R.R. Nelson (ed.), *The Rate and Direction of Inventive Activity*. National Bureau of Economic Research Conference Report, Princeton, NJ, pp. 19–43.

Levin, Richard C., Wesley M. Cohen and David C. Mowery (1985). R&D appropriability opportunity and market structure: New evidence on the Schumpeterian hypothesis. *American Economic Review*, 15, 20–24.

Levin, Richard C., Alvin K. Klevorick, Richard R. Nelson and Sydney G. Winter (1987). Appropriating the returns from industrial research and development. *Brookings Papers on Economic Activity*, 3, 783–820.

Levin, Richard C. and Peter C. Reiss (1984). Tests of a Schumpeterian model of R&D and market structure. In Zvi Griliches (ed.), *R&D, Patents, and Productivity*. Chicago, IL: University of Chicago, pp. 175–208.

Licht, Georg and Eric Nerlinger (1997). Junge innovative Unterhemmen in Europa: Ein internationaler Vergleich. In Dietmar Harhoff (ed.), *Unternehmensgruendungen: Empirische Analysen fuer die alten und neuen Bundeslaender*. Baden-Baden: Nomos, pp. 187–208.

Licht, Georg, Erik Nerlinger and G. Berger (1995). Germany: NTBF literature review. Mannheim: ZEW.

Link, Albert N. (1995). The use of literature-based innovation output indicators for research evaluation. *Small Business Economics*, 7(6), 451–455.

Link, Albert N. and Barry Bozeman (1991). Innovative behavior in small-sized firms. *Small Business Economics*, 3(3), 179–184.

Link, Albert N. and John Rees (1990). Firm size, university based research, and the returns to R&D. *Small Business Economics*, 2(1), 25–32.

Mansfield, Edwin (1968). *Industrial Research and Technological Change*. New York, NY: W.W. Norton, for the Cowles Foundation for Research Economics at Yale University, pp. 83–108.

Mansfield, Edwin (1981). Composition of R&D expenditures: Relationship to size of firm, concentration, and innovative output. *Review of Economics and Statistics*, 63, November, 610–615.

Mansfield, Edwin (1983). Industrial organization and technological change: Recent empirical findings. In John V. Craven (ed.), *Industrial Organization, Antitrust, and Public Policy*. The Hague: Kluwer-Nijhoff, pp. 129–143.

Mansfield, Edwin (1984). Comment on using linked patent and R&D data to measure interindustry technology flows. In Z. Griliches (ed.), *R&D, Patents, and Productivity*. Chicago, IL: University of Chicago Press, pp. 462–464.

Mansfield, Edwin, A. Romeo, M. Schwartz, D. Teece, S. Wagner and P. Brach (1982). *Technology Transfer, Productivity, and Economic Policy*. New York: W.W. Norton.

Mueller, Dennis C. (1967). The firm decision process: An econometric investigation. *Journal of Political Economy*, 81(1), 58–87.

National Science Board (1975). *Science Indicators 1974*. Washington, D.C.: Government Printing Office.

National Science Foundation (1986). *National Patterns of Science and Technology Resources 1986*. Washington, D.C.: Government Printing Office.

Nelson, Richard R. (1959). The simple economics of basic scientific research. *Journal of Political Economy*, 67(2), 297–306.

Nerlinger, Erik (1998). *Standorte und Entwicklung junger innovativer Unterhehmen: Empirische Ergebnisse fuer West-Deutschland* [*Location and the Development of Young, Innovative Firms: Empirical Evidence for West Germany*]. Baden-Baden: Nomos.

Oppenlander, Karl Heinz (1990). Investitionsverhalten and Marktstruktur – Empirische Ergebnisse für die Bundesrepublik Deutschland. In B. Gahlen (ed.), *Marktstruktur and gesamtwirtschaftliche Entwicklung*. Berlin: Springer-Verlag, pp. 253–266.

Pakes, Ariel (1985). On patents, R&D, and the stock market rate of return. *Journal of Political Economy*, **93**, 390–409.

Pakes, Ariel and Zvi Griliches (1980). Patents and R&D at the firm level: A first report. *Economics Letters*, **5**, 377–381.

Pakes, Ariel and Zvi Griliches (1984). Patents and R&D at the firm level: A first look. In Z. Griliches (ed.), *R&D, Patents, and Productivity*. Chicago, IL: University of Chicago, pp. 55–72.

Pavitt, Keith, M. Robson and J. Townsend (1987). The size dstribution of innovating firms in the U.K.: 1945–1983. *Journal of Industrial Economics*, **55**, 291–316.

Roper, Stephen (1999). Under-reporting of R&D in small firms: The impact on international R&D comparisons. *Small Business Economics*, **12**(2), 131–135.

Rothwell, Roy (1989). Small firms, innovation and industrial change. *Small Business Economics*, **1**(1), 51–64.

Santarelli, E. and A. Sterlachinni (1990). Innovation, formal vs. informal R&D, and firm size: Some evidence from Italian manufacturing firms. *Small Business Economics*, **2**(2), 223–228.

Saxenian, A. (1990). Regional networks and the resurgence of Silicon Valley. *California Management Review*, **33**, 89–111.

Scherer, Frederic M. (1965a). Firm size, market structure, opportunity, and the output of patented inventions. *American Economic Review*, **55**, 1097–1125.

Scherer, Frederic M. (1965b). Size of firm, oligopoly and research: A comment. *Canadian Journal of Economics and Political Science*, **31**, 256–266.

Scherer, Frederic M. (1967). Market structure and the employment of scientists and engineers. *American Economic Review*, **57**, 524–530.

Scherer, Frederic, M. (1982). Inter-industry technology flows in the United States. *Research Policy*, **11**, 227–245.

Scherer, Frederic M. (1983a). Concentration, R&D, and productivity change. *Southern Economic Journal*, **50**, 221–225.

Scherer, Frederic M. (1983b). The propensity to patent. *International Journal of Industrial Organization*, **1**, 107–128.

Scherer, Frederic M. (1984). *Innovation and Growth: Schumpeterian Perspectives*. Cambridge, MA: MIT Press.

Scherer, Frederic, M. (1988). Testimony before the subcommittee on monopolies and commercial law. Committee on the Judiciary, U.S. House of Representatives, February 24.

Scherer, Frederic M. (1991). Changing perspectives on the firm size problem. In *Innovation and Technological Change: An International Comparison*, edited by Z.J. Acs and D.B. Audretsch. Ann Arbor, MI: University of Michigan Press, pp. 24–38.

Schulenburg, J.-Matthias Graf von der and Joachim Wagner (1991). Advertising, innovation and market structure: A comparison of the United States of America and the Federal Republic of Germany. In Zoltan J. Acs and David B. Audretsch (eds.), *Innovation and Technological Change: An International Comparison*. Ann Arbor, MI: University of Michigan Press, pp. 160–182.

Schulenburg, J.-Matthias Graf von der and Joachim Wagner (1992). Unobservable industry characteristics and the innovation-concentration-advertising maze: Evidence from an econometric study using panel data for manufacturing industries in the FRG 1979–1986. *Small Business Economics*, **4**(3), 210–19.

Schumpeter, Joseph A. (1942). *Capitalism, Socialism and Democracy*. New York, NY: Harper and Row.

Schwalbach, Joachim and Klaus F. Zimmermann (1991). A Poisson model of patenting and firm structure in Germany. In Zoltan J. Acs and David B. Audretsch (eds.), *Innovation and Technological Change: An International Comparison*. Ann Arbor, MI: University of Michigan Press, pp. 109–120.

Scott, John T. (1984). Firm versus industry variability in R&D intensity. In Z. Griliches (ed.), *R&D, Patents and Productivity*. Chicago, IL: University of Chicago Press, pp. 233–248.

Soete, Luc L.G. (1979). Firm size and inventive activity: The evidence reconsidered. *European Economic Review*, **12**, 319–340.

Sutton, John (1997). Gibrat's legacy. *Journal of Economic Literature*, **35**, 40–59.

Van Dijk, Bob, Rene den Hertog, Bert Menkveld and Roy Thurik (1997). Some new evidence on the determinants of large- and small-firm innovation. *Small Business Economics*, **9**(4), 335–343.

Wagner Joachim (1994). Small firm entry in manufacturing industries: Lower Saxony 1979–1989. *Small Business Economics*, **6**(3), 211–224.

Wagner, Joachim (1995). Firm size and job creation in Germany. *Small Business Economics*, **7**(6), 469–474.

ROGER KOPPL[1] and MARIA MINNITI[2]

[1]*Fairleigh Dickinson University*, [2]*Babson College*

5. Market Processes and Entrepreneurial Studies*

INTRODUCTION

Recent years have witnessed a proliferation of research on entrepreneurship and the development of an entire field of inquiry. Yet, the central concept and boundaries of entrepreneurial studies are not well defined. In particular, the concept of "entrepreneurship" has been given different meanings. Shane and Venkataraman (2000) argue, "Perhaps the largest obstacle in creating a conceptual framework for the entrepreneurship field has been its definition" (p. 218). In entrepreneurial studies, entrepreneurship sometimes refers to the founding of a new venture, and sometimes to one or more special characteristics of the founder.

In 1988, Low and MacMillan suggested that entrepreneurship research should focus on new enterprise and its role in economic progress. But, already in 1990, Gartner's survey of business and academic professionals revealed a diversity of concepts falling under the label "entrepreneurship." Gartner's cluster analysis showed that the professionals in his survey fell into two groups, each with a different basic concept of entrepreneurship. The first group thought of the "*characteristics of entrepreneurship*"; the second group thought of the "*outcomes of entrepreneurship*" such as creating value or owning an ongoing business (p. 27, emphasis in original). We can express this difference in a simple formula. Sometimes entrepreneurship means what the actor is like; sometimes it means what the actor does.

In principle, this diversity is not necessarily a problem, as Gartner noted. In practice, however, the result has been that much research on entrepreneurship has weak theoretical foundations. We are getting more pieces of the puzzle, but no picture is emerging. Today, scholars of entrepreneurship still find themselves in the awkward position of using the same word to identify very different things. We believe this unnecessary diversity of meanings for "entrepreneurship" has frustrated progress in the field. We would benefit from a definition that captured both aspects of entrepreneurship, but in a coherent and consistent

* For helpful comments and discussion, we thank David Deeds, Alice deKoning, an anonymous referee, and participants in the Austrian Economics Colloquium of New York University. All errors are ours.

Z.J. Acs and D.B. Audretsch (eds.), Handbook of Entrepreneurship Research, 81–102 way. We seek a definition in which what the entrepreneur is like determines necessarily what the entrepreneur does. The Austrian school of economics has produced just such a definition in the work of Israel Kirzner. In his work, entrepreneurship has two aspects. First, entrepreneurship is the "alertness" to new opportunities. Entrepreneurs are alert; this is what they are like. Second, entrepreneurship is seizing an opportunity by taking innovative actions. Entrepreneurs innovate; this is what they do. In Kirzner's theory, what the entrepreneur is like determines necessarily what the entrepreneur does. Alertness leads to the discovery of new opportunities. If the opportunity discovered is a real one, the entrepreneur will act on it. Thus, as we will explain more carefully below, alertness necessarily leads to innovative actions such as founding a new venture.

It is difficult to appreciate the value, indeed the nature, of Kirzner's contribution, however, if it is not set in the larger context of the Austrian theory of markets. Kirzner may seem to neglect the entrepreneurial process, to view profit opportunities as external to the entrepreneur, and to restrict entrepreneurship to simultaneous arbitrage. These limits to Kirzner's analysis, however, are more apparent than real. Placing Kirzner's work in the context of the Austrian school reveals his theory to be much less static and narrow than it often appears to critical observers. In addition, more recent writers in the Austrian tradition have produced much work on entrepreneurship, which completes and expands his vision. This chapter explains Kirzner's theory and the contributions of more recent Austrians in their proper context.

A solid comprehension of the Austrian definition of entrepreneurship requires scholars to familiarize themselves with the elements of Austrian economics. One could almost define the Austrian theory as entrepreneurial economics. Thus, the Austrian school addresses the concern of Shane and Venkataraman (2000) that, "the absence of entrepreneurship from our theories of markets, firms, organizations, and change makes our understanding of the business landscape incomplete" (p. 219).

The rest of this chapter is organized as follows. The section entitled "The Austrian theory of markets" provides the context and background for Kirzner's theory. The section entitled "Kirzner's Theory of Entrepreneurship" discusses Kizrner's theory in detail. The section entitled "Recent Developments in the Austrian Theory of Entrepreneurship" surveys several authors working under Kirzner's influence. Finally, the conclusion explains how the Austrian approach helps to integrate and organize much of the entrepreneurship literature and how it may be used to create a common theoretical framework for entrepreneurial studies.

THE AUSTRIAN THEORY OF MARKETS

The Disequilibrium Economics of Menger

The Austrian school of economic thought began with Carl Menger's 1871 classic, *Principles of Economics*. Menger was an Austrian who taught at the

University of Vienna. With Jevons and Walras, he was one of the three creators of marginal utility theory and neoclassical economics. Unlike the other two founders of neoclassical economics, however, Menger did not use equations or mathematical notation.

While Jevons and Walras simply posited the utility curves of economic actors, Menger developed an economics of the planning mind. He imagined an "economizer" who is conscious of his various "needs." Menger's economizer uses his limited knowledge to determine what things are "goods." For a thing to be a "good," four conditions must hold. There must be a "human need," a "causal connection" between the thing and the need, "knowledge of this causal connection," and "command of the thing sufficient to direct it to the satisfaction of the need" (Menger, 1871, p. 52). Once the economizer has determined which things are "goods," he decides how much of each good he needs. Then Menger's economizer determines the available quantities for each good. He discovers that for some goods the available quantities are smaller than his requirements. These are "economic goods." The economizer then imputes value to the economic goods. For Menger, marginal utility is "the importance that individual goods or quantities of goods attain for us because we are conscious of being dependent on command of them for the satisfaction of our needs" (p. 115). Thus, Menger emphasizes the "subjective" nature of marginal utility. Value emerges from an act of evaluation. Exchange takes place when evaluations differ. When two parties trade, each individual values the goods of the other more highly than the goods he has control of. Thus, for Menger, exchange is always exchange of *unequal* values and always, therefore, a disequilibrium phenomenon. Because exchange can occur only in disequilibrium, it is the process that matters, not any imaginary equilibrium that a process might lead to. Austrian scholars continue Menger's tradition of process analysis. Although equilibrium plays an honored role in the Austrian theory of markets, that role is subsidiary to their analysis of economic processes.

Menger does not address the role of entrepreneurs explicitly, his economizer, however, is "entrepreneurial" because he possesses an active mind and seeks out new knowledge with which to improve his situation. He learns and grows and changes. Thus, Menger's work lays the foundation for the methodological subjectivism of the Austrian school and, especially, for the Kirznerian approach to the entrepreneur as an agent of change.

Mises and the Austrian Logic of Choice

In the twentieth century, Ludwig von Mises (1949) and F.A. Hayek (1973–1979) became the leading advocates of the Mengerian tradition.[1] Mises developed

---

[1] Friedrich Weiser and Eugen von Böhm-Bawerk were early followers of Menger. Frederick A. Hayek and Ludwig von Mises were their students. Mises was an important influence on Hayek and the leader of the Austrian school from about 1920 to his death in 1973.

the pure logic of choice originally outlined by Menger. Hayek emphasized the role of knowledge and its dispersion amongst economic actors.

In Menger's description of "economizing," Mises saw the elements of a universal logic of all human action. He developed this "logic of choice" and made it the foundation for economic theory. Modern "neoclassical" microeconomics does the same thing. Neoclassical microeconomics uses, however, a mathematical and somewhat stylized picture of choice. Mises, instead, continued Menger's tradition and used words rather than equations. To describe his version of the logic of choice, Mises invented the unfortunate word "praxeology." Specifically, "praxeology" is the economic theory of human action. The Austrian microeconomics of Mises and others follows Menger by viewing the chooser as an active mind trying to improve its situation.

Mises's microeconomics integrated Menger's market process theory with the general equilibrium theory of Walras and the partial equilibrium theory of Jevons and Marshall. Like Menger, Mises emphasized the thought behind the action. This view led him to preserve Menger's emphasis on process. In Mises, as in Menger, the process is more important than the imaginary endpoint. Indeed, Mises emphasized that all action occurs in disequilibrium. The equilibria of economic theory are entirely imaginary; they are aids to reasoning, not realistic descriptions of the world. By definition, as we shall see, entrepreneurship occurs in disequilibrium.[2]

Hayek and the Austrian Knowledge Problem

Early in his career Hayek came under the influence of Mises. Hayek analyzed a problem raised by Mises, namely, the economic role of knowledge in society. Menger, too, had placed great emphasis on the role of knowledge. But Menger was considering mostly theoretical knowledge generally available to all "economizers." Hayek recognized that the division of labor produces a division of knowledge. Different people know different things. Thus, the knowledge that guides economic decision-making is dispersed among many independently acting economic agents, such as individuals, families, and firms. Hayek was the leading theorist of the Austrian "knowledge problem."

---

[2]In addition to his contribution to the Austrian theory, Mises is also the defining figure of the migration of the Austrian school from Europe to the U.S. Inter-war Vienna saw the flourishing of intellectual circles, which were groups of scholars meeting regularly to discuss common interests. The Mises circle was an important one attracting economists, philosophers and social scientists. Among them were Oskar Morgenstern, Alfred Schutz, Felix Kaufmann, Frederick von Hayek, Erich Voegelin, and Gottfried von Haberler. Another member of this illustrious group, Fritz Machlup, once mused, "I wonder whether there has ever existed anywhere a group from which so large a percentage of members became internationally recognized scholars" (Machlup as quoted in Mises, 1984, p. 203). The group was eventually dispersed by the dramatic events surrounding the rise of Nazism. One after the other, Voegelin, Morgenstern, Haberler, Schutz and many others fled to the United States. Finally, in 1940, Mises too arrived in New York. In the following years, a group of American students fell under his influence (see Vaughn 1994).

The knowledge of what to produce, how to produce it, and so on is scattered in bits and pieces across many different economic actors. The Austrian knowledge problem is that of coordinating this dispersed knowledge. Hayek and the Austrians arrived at their argument about knowledge during a debate on socialism. Hayek and Mises maintained that socialism was not a feasible system because socialist planners would not have access to all relevant knowledge in society, which is always dispersed though the system as noted earlier. Significantly, Joseph Schumpeter was among those who rejected this argument and saw no economic objections to socialism.

Hayek showed how the market process solves the knowledge problem through decentralized decision-making. The gist of his position is conveyed by his famous tin example.[3] Tin may grow scarcer because of a new opportunity for its use or because of the loss of a source of supply. "It does not matter for our purpose – and it is significant that it does not matter – which of these two causes has made tin more scarce" (Hayek, 1948, p. 85). All that is needed is that those on the spot recognize the need to economize on its use. Individuals in markets that use tin will be induced to economize on tin by the increase in its price. Increases of demand will induce suppliers of substitute goods to expand their outputs. Such changes "will rapidly spread throughout the whole economic system and influence not only all the uses of tin but also those of its substitutes and the substitutes of these substitutes, and so on; and all this without the great majority of those instrumental in bringing about these substitutions knowing anything at all about the original cause of these changes" (1948, p. 86).

Each actor knows only a few things; no one has a synoptic view of the whole. In spite of this widespread ignorance, the market acts as an integrated whole. The individual spheres of knowledge and action overlap, producing a system-wide chain of adjustments to a change of knowledge occurring in any part of the system.

The market process is the leading example of Hayek's concept of "spontaneous order." A spontaneous order is one that emerges as a "result of human action, but not of human design" (Hayek, 1967a). Examples include the development of social institutions such as money and language, the growth of great cities, and, as we have seen, the emergence of order out of the potential chaos of market exchange.

If the market is a spontaneous order in Hayek's sense, then market participants can have only partial understandings of it. No one knows in detail how the whole system works. A spontaneous order hangs together and follows its own laws of operation even if no one has a theoretical understanding of it. Participants can always hope to profit from the discovery of new opportunities within the system. This is why Hayek was led to describe the market competition as a "discovery procedure" (Hayek, 1978).

[3] This paragraph is lifted from Minniti and Koppl (1999).

Hayek's idea of competition as a discovery procedure (1978) is quite different from the neoclassical notion of allocation. In a model of general equilibrium, tastes and technology are known; prices allocate known resources to their highest valued uses. Known methods are applied to known resources to best satisfy known preferences. In Hayek's vision of the market process, by contrast, knowledge of resources, tastes, and technology is dispersed. No one person, firm, or government agency possesses all the knowledge required to allocate resources optimally. Resources can always be allocated more satisfactorily. Thus, anyone in the system may chance upon new knowledge or information that allows him to reallocate resources profitably. Such acts of discovery are characteristic of the market process.

For understanding Kirzner's theory, it is important to include creative acts among such scenes of "discovery". The creator brings something to the scene that was not already implied in the problem situation he faced. But if his innovation is to make a profit, it must fit the existing realities of the market. If it does, the innovating entrepreneur may reasonably be said to have "discovered" an opportunity.

Discovery is not only possible in the market; it is necessary. Consider Hayek's earlier example of an increase in tin prices. Firms that use tin have an incentive to cast about for new ways to reduce their tin inputs. Those who discover such new techniques will enjoy profits. Those sticking to the old ways of doing things will suffer losses. Hayek's theory of the market as a discovery procedure forms an essential part of Kirzner's notion of entrepreneurial discovery.

Schumpeter versus the Austrian Tradition

The tradition of Austrian economics as described here does not include the great theorist of entrepreneurship, Joseph Schumpeter. Schumpeter was an Austrian national and a student of Menger's great disciple, Böhm-Bawerk. He was thus an "Austrian economist" by both national origin and intellectual heritage. He was not, however, an "Austrian economist" in the most current sense of the term. First, Schumpeter put Walras's system of general equilibrium at the center of modern economics and denied to Menger the central role that modern Austrians attribute to him. Second, Schumpeter predicted the collapse of capitalism from within and its replacement by socialism. This argument contradicted Austrian arguments for the impossibility of a workable socialism. Finally, Schumpeter's theory of market process was quite different from that of modern Austrians. He had a theory of disruptive innovations (Schumpeter, 1934). For modern Austrians, however, the core of market process theory explains how individual adjustments to changing circumstances tend to produce market equilibrium and to restore it when equilibrium is disrupted. (Objecting to the term "equilibrium," some Austrians would substitute the word "coordination.") In this sense of the term, Schumpeter did not have a theory of the market process. Schumpeter's importance to entrepreneurial studies is hardly subject to doubt. His theory of innovation is a permanent contribution to the field. But it is a contribution that is not "Austrian" in the modern sense.

KIRZNER'S THEORY OF ENTREPRENEURSHIP

Israel Kirzner was a student of Mises; he was also influenced by Hayek, especially Hayek's theory of competition as a discovery procedure. Kirzner's theory of entrepreneurship is a part of the Austrian theory of markets and, like all contemporary Austrian theory, bears the imprint of its founder, Carl Menger. Kirzner developed his theory in a long series of writings beginning with his 1973 classic, *Competition and Entrepreneurship*. (See also Kirzner, 1979, 1992.)

What is Entrepreneurship?

Kirzner gives the word "entrepreneurship" a precise meaning. First, entrepreneurship is the "alertness" to new opportunities. This is what entrepreneurs are like. Second, entrepreneurship is the sequence of innovative actions following from the "discovery" of such an opportunity. This is what entrepreneurs do. In Kirzner's theory, what the entrepreneur is like determines necessarily what the entrepreneur does. A simple example illustrates.

A professor walks the same route to class every day. His path is optimal given his knowledge; it gets him there in the least time. One day he discovers that a slightly roundabout route allows him to avoid his dean, who usually pesters him along his accustomed path. He takes the new route and avoids the dean. Our professor has found a new ends–means framework. He had been minimizing travel time; he now minimizes the bother of getting to class, considering both travel time and obnoxious deans. Thus, his ends have changed. The means have changed too; he takes a different route. Our professor could have made this change only by being "alert" to the opportunity to improve his situation by changing his route. The new, roundabout route was a profit opportunity; he could profit by switching to the new route. When he discovered it, his actions changed. His actions had to change if the new route was truly a profit opportunity. For him this is an innovation. If he had considered the new route but found it to be too long, then it would not have been a true profit opportunity and he would not have taken it. Of course, the dean may find the professor along the new route too and the new plan may fail. It is not *profit* that drives the professor to the new route, but the *expectation* of profit.

Traditional neoclassical microeconomics can explain our professor's old route assuming his goal of minimizing time. It can explain his new route assuming his new goal of minimizing bother. But it cannot explain the movement from the old route to the new route. Being alert to the opportunity for such a movement is what the entrepreneur is like. Making the move is what the entrepreneur does.

It is important to recognize the necessary link between these two aspects of entrepreneurship. If there is innovative action, it is because there was discovery, which cannot occur without alertness. Therefore, innovative action necessarily emerges from alertness. Also, if the actor is truly alert, he discovers profit opportunities and acts on them. (If he does not, it is because it was not worth doing in the first place and what he discovered were not true profit opportunities.) Thus, alertness necessarily leads to innovative action.

To summarize, Kirzner's definition of entrepreneurship has two aspects. First, entrepreneurship is the "alertness" to new opportunities. Entrepreneurs are alert; this is what they are like. Second, entrepreneurship is seizing an opportunity by taking innovative actions. Entrepreneurs innovate; this is what they do. Within this context, what the entrepreneur is like determines necessarily what the entrepreneur does. Alertness leads to the discovery of new opportunities. If the opportunity discovered is a real one, the entrepreneur will act on it.

Entrepreneurship is Alertness

In its first meaning, entrepreneurship is an aspect of action. It is the element in the Austrian logic of choice that is missing from the traditional neoclassical logic of choice. Thus, entrepreneurship is present in Austrian microeconomics, but not in neoclassical microeconomics. In both versions of the logic of choice, every human action entails the allocation of scarce resources across competing uses. The chooser must allocate his time and attention across different possible activities, even when no other resources are involved. The agent allocates resources to maximize some end, perhaps utility, perhaps net revenue. In the neoclassical version, however, the agent's framework of ends and means is simply given. This model of action has proved useful in many scientific contexts. But, it cannot account for change in the agent's framework of ends and means.

According to Kirzner, entrepreneurship is a change in the ends–means framework of the chooser. Such change can happen because the entrepreneur is "alert" to new possibilities for action. If the entrepreneur were not alert, he would never adopt a new ends–means framework, and change in economic life would be impossible. But change is a necessary feature of human action because the passage of time subjects us all to change and uncertainty. Time and chance happen to us all. Thus, alertness is a necessary feature of all human action. Because we cannot step into the same river twice, all our actions contain an element of improvisation. Such improvisation would be impossible without alertness to new opportunities.

Entrepreneurs are alert to new opportunities. When one is found, Kirzner says the entrepreneur has "discovered" it. The word "discovery" may suggest to some readers that the opportunity the entrepreneur acts upon was "already out there," whereas an entrepreneur may create such opportunities. Any opportunity he "creates," however, must fit external reality. It must conform to external constraints. Thus, as we argued when discussing Hayek, it is reasonable to use the word "discovery" even when the entrepreneur exercises his creativity.

Entrepreneurship is Action

In its second meaning, entrepreneurship is the series of actions that follow from the alert discovery of an opportunity. These actions follow necessarily from the discovery. If the entrepreneur does not act on an opportunity, he has not "discovered" it at all. Imagine someone noticing a price discrepancy, but not acting on it. Why was there no action? Perhaps he could not imagine how to coordinate the required resources; perhaps he is uninterested in money profits. In any case, the failure to act shows that the price discrepancy did not correspond to any imagined change in plans that the individual really preferred to his pre-existing course of action. If he did not do it, he did not want to, whether for lack of know-how, lack of will, or other causes. If he did not want to, it was no opportunity. It was no opportunity *for him.*

Just as the entrepreneurial role in individual action produces change in the agent's ends–means framework, the entrepreneurial role in the market produces change there. This is what Kirzner means when he says entrepreneurship "occupies precisely the same logical relationship to the more narrow 'economizing' elements in the market that, in individual action, is occupied by the entrepreneurial elements in relation to the efficiency aspects of decision-making" (Kirzner, 1973, p. 32).

The market process cannot emerge, Kirzner argues, unless entrepreneurship operates. This statement has an important implication: To some degree all market participants are entrepreneurs. We are all alert, though in different degrees. We all innovate, though in different degrees. Entrepreneurship is sometimes taken to be a property of a few special individuals. Sometimes the property is even viewed as a mystery, to be admired and revered. Kirzner encourages us to the more scientific view of entrepreneurship as a universal characteristic of human action, though a characteristic more pronounced in some cases than in others.

In Kirzner's theory, arbitrage is the fundamental form of entrepreneurship. This stipulation seems to reduce entrepreneurship to something very narrow. But Kirzner gives arbitrage an enlarged meaning that includes even the most elaborate entrepreneurial ventures. Thus, we should not imagine that Kirzner's theory is limited or inapplicable because he represents entrepreneurs as arbitrageurs. His arbitrageur is a highly creative and innovative individual or organization with significant managerial abilities. A business plan may be very complex. No matter how complex it is, however, the plan requires the purchase of inputs and the sale of output. If we consider the plan from a sufficiently distant and abstract perspective, we may always see in it buying in one set of markets and selling in another. The plan calls for arbitrage between the two sets of markets. Even when I sell today where I bought yesterday, there are two distinct markets, namely, yesterday's market and today's market. If the plan is a success, the value of sales will exceed the value of purchases. In that case, we may say that the inputs came cheap and the output sold dear. Consider, for example, Henry Ford's assembly line. Ford's innovation consisted in a new method of production. The assembly line was a business success, however, only because it increased the difference between input prices and output prices. In this sense, the assembly line represented an arbitrage opportunity for Henry Ford. Thus, his achievement was at the same time a creative act and the discovery of an arbitrage opportunity.

Entrepreneurship Produces Market Order

In Kirzner's theory, market order is produced by entrepreneurship. Without acts of entrepreneurial alertness, our never-changing actions would gradually fall further and further away from consistency with the underlying scarcities. In Kirzner's vision, the "constant market agitation" caused by "jostling competitors and innovative entrepreneurial upstarts" is "not chaotic at all." Rather, it is here, "in this apparently chaotic sequence of market events that the market's orderliness resides" (1992, p. 49). The market process is a dynamic process of change driven by alert entrepreneurs who discover new profit opportunities. Throughout the market process, economic incentives exist for people to reallocate resources. People respond to such incentives, but the ability of individuals to recognize incentives and reallocate resources varies. Individuals with superior alertness to changes and to the state of disequilibrium move to exploit opportunities and earn economic profits. Thus, the role of the entrepreneur is to discover and seize market opportunities through the re-allocation of productive resources.

Market order is where the difference and complementarity between Kirzner and Schumpeter are revealed. Kirzner provides a theory of equilibration. The entrepreneur coordinates the plans of other economic actors. Schumpeter's entrepreneur disrupts the plans of other economic actors. This difference is a substantive one. Without the equilibrating entrepreneur Schumpeter cannot explain the existence of the order disrupted by his disequilibrating entrepreneur. Thus, as we said earlier, there is a sense in which Schumpeter has no theory of the market process. (See Kirzner, 1999.)

Entrepreneurship Involves Calculation

In Kirzner's sense, an opportunity is "seen" if and only if it is acted on. It entails no opportunity cost. Essential to the process is the non-deliberative discovery of an unexpected opportunity. This statement must not be taken to imply, however, that the discovery of an entrepreneurial opportunity entails no calculations of money costs and revenues. Kirzner recognizes that to "see" an opportunity requires planning and calculation (Kirzner, 1973, pp. 74–75).[4]

Consider the simplest case of Kirznerian entrepreneurship, namely, instantaneous arbitrage. There is no true opportunity cost associated with the discovery of a price differential. But before the arbitrageur elects to buy here

---

[4]This paragraph and the next come from Minniti and Koppl (1999).

and sell there he does calculate costs and revenues. He adds to his prospective purchase price any transaction costs that he now expects – now that his costless discovery has put the arbitrage opportunity on his list of possible actions. Once the possibility of arbitrage is on his menu of choice, the potential entrepreneur employs the usual economic calculus of maximization. If the costs of the arbitrage are sufficiently low, then the discovery was indeed a real, entrepreneurial discovery and the arbitrage will occur. (None of this goes to deny, of course, that the entrepreneur's calculations may have been mistaken. He may suffer losses.) Thus, while the entrepreneurial discovery is, as such, costless, the entrepreneur does calculate his costs when deciding whether to act on what he has noticed.

Entrepreneurship is a Process

Entrepreneurship is a process involving many stages of action. If we look at the process from a sufficiently distant and abstract perspective, however, the particulars fall out of view. This perspective is the one Kirzner has adopted. In his theory, the stages of the discovery process fall out of view. But if we look closely, we can notice separate stages occurring at different times. Kirzner's lack of interest in the stages of the entrepreneurial discovery process should not be taken to imply that they do not exist or that his theory denies that they exist. Harper's theory discussed below provides an Austrian approach to the stages of action involved in the entrepreneurial process (Harper, 1994, 1996, 1998).

RECENT DEVELOPMENTS IN THE AUSTRIAN THEORY OF ENTREPRENEURSHIP

Theories of Entrepreneurial Learning

In 1985, O'Driscoll and Rizzo published *The Economics of Time and Ignorance* (O'Driscoll and Rizzo, 1985). After this classic work, it was "impossible to think of Austrian economics as anything but the economics of time and ignorance" (Vaughn, 1994, p. 134). O'Driscoll and Rizzo made Austrian theory "the economics of *coping* with the problems posed by real time and radical ignorance" (Rizzo, 1995, p. xiv). The term "real time" refers to the subjective experience of time and change. It contrasts with clock time, which leaves out of consideration the inner experiences of memory, expectation, and surprise (O'Driscoll and Rizzo, 1985, pp. 52–70).

The Economics of Time and Ignorance includes an important section on "The Nature and Process of Learning." For O'Driscoll and Rizzo "learning" is moving from one interpretative framework to another (p. 37). When the book was published in 1985, they could say, "At present we do not have a theory that enables us to say something significant about the move from one problem context to another" (p. 37). But they did say something "about how such a theory might look" (p. 37). Their emphasis on real time and learning encouraged Austrian economists to develop theories of entrepreneurial learning.

For O'Driscoll and Rizzo, "The *process* of entrepreneurial learning is neither determinate nor random" (p. 38). Thus, it has two important features. "First, although what individuals will learn is not determinate, that they will learn something may well be." Second, each interpretive framework will have a "loose dependency" on its predecessor. Given the entrepreneur's initial framework, we can rule out many frameworks as possible successors. The succeeding framework must not be one of the ones ruled out (p. 38).

Complementary considerations also favor the construction of a theory of entrepreneurial learning. Entrepreneurship is a part of the Austrian logic of choice. Thus, it is a universally applicable theory. Anything that happens fits the theory. Like any pure theory, the pure theory of entrepreneurship cannot give us testable knowledge of the world. It cannot tell us how entrepreneurship unfolds in real markets. To produce such testable results, the theory must be combined with a theory of entrepreneurial learning. A theory of learning adds empirical content. Several figures within the Austrian tradition have attempted to provide such a theory.

Harper

As we have seen, "entrepreneurship" is both "alertness" to new opportunities and the actions following the "discovery" of an opportunity. Learning is involved in both aspects. When the entrepreneur's alertness produces a discovery, he learns about an opportunity. As he attempts to act on his new knowledge he acquires still more knowledge; he learns. Kirzner's theory is silent on learning. It isolates the "category" of alertness, but does not provide a theory thereof. It further identifies entrepreneurship with acting on the discovered opportunities, but, as mentioned earlier, does not elaborate upon the process of doing so. Kirzner does not provide a theory of alertness or a theory of the entrepreneurial process. David Harper's theory of entrepreneurial learning provides both.

Among self-consciously "Austrian" economists since Kirzner, Harper (1994, 1996, 1998) has offered the most extensive discussions of the theory of entrepreneurship. His basic theoretical framework can be divided into two parts. His discussion of "locus of control" provides a theory of alertness. His discussion of "growth of knowledge" provides a theory of entrepreneurial learning.

Harper draws on Gilad (1982) to argue that a person's "locus of control" (LOC) influences his degree of alertness. A person with an "internal" locus of control tends to believe that events are "contingent upon his own behavior or his own relatively permanent characteristics" (Rotter, 1966, p. 1 as cited in Harper, 1998, p. 248). People with "external" locus of control tend to see their actions as less effective in producing outcomes. They see events "as under the control of powerful others, or as unpredictable because of the great complexity of the forces surrounding" them (Rotter, 1966, p. 1 as cited in Harper, 1998,

p. 249). Harper cites evidence that entrepreneurs tend to have internal locus of control.

In Harper's theory, an internal locus of control increases entrepreneurial alertness. This increased alertness leads to more incidental learning and, therefore, to more entrepreneurship. On this view of things, it is important to know what, if any, social conditions promote alertness. Following Gilad, Harper argues that the nature of our political and economic institutions influences alertness. Those institutions and policies that increase the objective link between action and outcome tend to increase the subjective perception of such a link. They increase, therefore, the number of persons who have an internal locus of control. Harper's "central hypothesis" is that "an environment of freedom is more likely than other environments to generate internal LOC beliefs and acute entrepreneurial alertness" (1998, p. 253). He discusses this and other institutional factors at some length.

Harper's theory of the entrepreneurial process draws on the "growth of knowledge" literature. It thus borrows heavily from twentieth-century philosophy of science. Karl Popper (1959) and Imre Lakatos (1970) are the leading figures in this group. Citing Boland (1982, 1986), Loasby (1976), and others, Harper compares entrepreneurs to scientists. His theory enjoins us to "Explicitly ascribe Popperian theories of learning to the economic agents in economic theories" (1994, p. 53).

In the philosophy of Karl Popper, scientists are problem solvers. The scientific process of discovery begins with a scientific problem. The scientist applies his mind to the problem and generates competing hypotheses as potential solutions to that problem. Each solution is always a guess, a conjecture. Scientists engage in testing and experimentation in order to find the best solution to the problem. As a result of these tests, they might even redefine the problem or obtain a deeper understanding of it. To solve the new problem, the scientist makes a new guess and tests it, thus arriving at yet another problem to be solved. It is also important to note that there is no "logic of induction" that carries scientists from particular observations of hard facts to general hypothesis. All conjectures are theory-laden and tentative. New evidence may always turn up that refutes or "falsifies" conjectures that have until then been reliable. Thus, science is an ongoing process of trial and error-elimination or, in Popper's words, an endless process of conjecture and refutation.

Harper suggests that the entrepreneurial process is similar to the scientific process of conjecture and refutation. Entrepreneurship begins with the alert discovery of an opportunity. The discovery is like the scientist's conjecture. It is a prediction (of success in the marketplace) that must be tested. The entrepreneur tests the conjecture by, say, conducting market research or talking to a trusted advisor. He will learn from these tests. (Nothing guarantees, however, that he will learn something true or useful. Entrepreneurs make mistakes.) The entrepreneur will apply what he learns to modify the original business conception. He will amend his entrepreneurial conjecture. The process may repeat any number of times. Eventually, the repeatedly amended conjecture that got the process started will meet with a market test. The entrepreneur will learn from this test, too. Thus, he will amend his entrepreneurial conjecture yet again and adjust his business plan accordingly.

The two central aspects of Harper's theory are the testing of conjectures and endogenous change. If entrepreneurs are like Popperian scientists, then the entrepreneurial process is, indeed, a process with identifiable stages. The movement from alert discovery to market action is not automatic or instantaneous. It is a fallible error-elimination process. If entrepreneurs are like Popperian scientists, then the market process is driven by endogenous change. The ceaseless learning of entrepreneurs implies ceaseless change in their plans. In Harper's entrepreneurial vision, the market process does not wind down to some grand equilibrium. It is an open-ended process of change and discovery. This point is consistent with Hayek's vision of the market as a "discovery procedure."

Choi

Choi (1993a, 1993b, 1999) proposes a theory of decision making as a learning process that has direct relevance to entrepreneurship and the market process. Choi argues that the process of coming to an understanding of one's environment is an inferential process. In this process the entrepreneur marshals his information to make sense of things. He tries to see how things hang together. The understanding he arrives at is a guess, though it is his best guess. The entrepreneur can find out whether his understanding is sound only by observing the consequence of his actions. In this sense, human decision making is experimental and can be likened to the process of science – proposing conjectures and testing them. Choi calls the understanding by which a person resolves uncertainty a "paradigm." He uses this word to indicate that the decision-making process rests heavily on the entrepreneur's prior experiences and his understanding of other things.

When faced with uncertainty, people do not know how to act. Since this state is intolerable, they try to identify usable paradigms. The process ends when the decision maker identifies a usable paradigm to act on. This process of identifying usable paradigms is the process of learning. Because paradigms are best guesses, they may or may not bring the expected results. If they do not, the decision maker has an incentive to look for new paradigms. If they bring satisfactory results, then they are reused. The paradigms proven to be usable repeatedly are retained and become parts of the entrepreneur's "tool box". They become behavioral regularities and, over time, each individual comes to have a set of serviceable habits and routines that make his life easier.

In society, people have the possibility of learning from others' practices. Trial and error processes in society generate conventions. That is, people identify mutually compatible paradigms. These conventions make social life possible. Their stability, however, makes innovation difficult. Social and economic practices, therefore, tend to continue through time, even as experiences of different individuals might suggest (to some) that by adopting alternative paradigms, profit is possible. With the stability of conventions, therefore, the size of neglected opportunities (and the possibility of profitable exploitation), grows over time. In this way, Choi accounts for the existence of neglected opportunities, and their eventual exploitation; he accounts for entrepreneurship.

The entrepreneur discovers the neglected opportunities and tries to capture them. He is going against the "conventional" crowd. If he fails, others will ignore him. If he succeeds, then, others will try to imitate him. In the process, the prevailing practices are transformed. Choi calls the process of entrepreneurial discoveries and their eventual adoption by the rest of the society a "social learning process".

Butos and Koppl

Butos and Koppl (1999) view Kirznerian entrepreneurs as Hayekian learners. They rely on Hayek's classic work of 1952, *The Sensory Order*. In this work, Hayek developed an evolutionary theory of mind. Hayek's theory bears many striking similarities to the work of complexity theorists such as Holland et al. (1986). (See Koppl, 2000a, 2000b.) Several of Hayek's conclusions are relevant to a theory of entrepreneurial learning.

Butos and Koppl rely on Hayek's theory, to argue that entrepreneurial knowledge is always an interpretation. The entrepreneur does not so much "see" as "interpret." Thus, each entrepreneur's mental model is unique in some degree. Two entrepreneurs will interpret any situation differently. The entrepreneur's interpretations are expressed in his habits of action and reaction to market events. They are expressed in the rules entrepreneurs follow. Following Hayek, Butos and Koppl point out that the entrepreneur's habits are subject to a market test. Some habits produce profits; others produce losses. Thus, the market system of profit and loss shapes the interpretations of entrepreneurs. They tend to fit the market because they will be weeded out if they do not.

Butos and Koppl point out that Hayek's discussion of "attention" in *The Sensory Order* fits nicely with Kirzner's notion of "alertness." Attention, Hayek notes, is always directed to things "we are on the look-out" for and can perceive, therefore, more clearly when they happen (Hayek, 1952, p. 139). Thus, entrepreneurs tend to learn only what they are prepared to learn. Entrepreneurial discovery is not a pure bolt from the blue.

By relying on Hayek's theory of mind, Butos and Koppl view learning from a relatively objective and external perspective. Koppl (2002a, 2002b) adds a more subjective and internal perspective by bringing in the "phenomenological psychology" of Alfred Schutz. In Schutz's system, our knowledge is a system of typifications, a system of stereotypes and recipes guiding us through our daily activities. The entrepreneur's knowledge, too, is such a structure. The entrepreneur organizes his collection of typifications through a "system of relevancies" (Schutz, 1951, p. 76). This system of relevancies guides the entrepreneur and influences the sorts of discoveries he can make. (Koppl, 2002b, attempts to refine and clarify the idea of alertness with the aid of concepts from phenomenological psychology.)

Any act of entrepreneurship has its meaning for the entrepreneur within his system of relevancy even as it transforms that system. Kirzner's pure arbitrageur discovers apples selling for one price on one side of the street and another price on the other side. This discovery has meaning only within the entrepreneur's existing system of relevancy. The entrepreneur knows already what apples are and recognizes the apples on each side of the street to be "the same." He knows what buying and selling are. He knows how to make a purchase, carry inventory, and make a sale. Without this pre-existing body of knowledge, he cannot make his discovery. We see again from this relatively subjective angle that entrepreneurs tend to learn only what they are prepared to learn.

The entrepreneur's discovery depends on his pre-existing knowledge. At the same time, the entrepreneur's discovery transforms that knowledge. He looks at apples or, say, automobile assembly differently after the discovery. The actions following from the initial discovery induce further change in his knowledge. The entrepreneur learns by exploiting his discovery.

The writings of Butos and Koppl help us unite relatively subjective and objective perspectives on entrepreneurial learning. Therefore, they help us to move from close descriptions of how entrepreneurs think of things to larger perspectives on the role of entrepreneurial learning in producing economic growth and change.

THE MACRO-ECONOMIC IMPLICATIONS OF ENTREPRENEURSHIP

Several empirical studies have shown that the amount of entrepreneurial activity (in the sense of new ventures) differs significantly across countries and across different regions of the same country (Reynolds, et al., 2001). Indeed, entrepreneurship may have significant growth implications. Chamlee-Wright and Holcombe provide contributions in this direction.

In her work on development, Emily Chamlee-Wright takes an Austrian approach and explains how cultural meanings and government policies influence entrepreneurs (Chamlee-Wright, 1997). She shows the need to study culture if we hope to have a satisfactory theory of economic development. Chamlee-Wright provides useful case studies illustrating the importance of trust, reputation, and personal relationships in regulating the supposedly anonymous forces of the market. Close studies such as hers reveal the cultural underpinnings of market relations. Each culture and each market has its own mechanisms for producing trust. Thus, Chamlee-Wright shows that entrepreneurs are cultural figures. On the one hand, their actions reflect the cultural environment in which they act. On the other hand, their actions are an important influence on the culture in which they operate. Development theory should take account of the role of entrepreneurs as cultural figures.

Holcombe (forthcoming) provides a complementary contribution. He argues that every time an entrepreneur seizes a new opportunity, the possibility for new markets is created. When an entrepreneur fills a niche in his market, resources are mobilized, the possibility of complementary products or services is created and, as a result, new entrepreneurial opportunities exist. Thus, the entrepreneur is an equilibrator within his market and, simultaneously, a catalyst of activity for the economy as a whole.

The works of Holcombe and Chamlee-Wright both complement Minniti (1999, 2001, forthcoming). Minniti links complexity theory to the study of entrepreneurship. Her work provides a model of the possible relationship between entrepreneurial behavior and aggregate entrepreneurial activity in which non-pecuniary externalities and embeddedness take center stage. These dimensions are consistent with Hayek's notion of spontaneous order in the sense that, as in many complex phenomena, the aggregate outcome "cannot be reduced to the regularities of the parts" (Hayek, 1967b, p. 74). In particular, Minniti (forthcoming) shows that, when information is evenly distributed, the number of entrepreneurs remains low even when agents are highly alert, whereas, when information is asymmetrically distributed, entrepreneurship increases and concentrates geographically. Her results are consistent with observed clustering of entrepreneurial activity in otherwise similar regions. Also, Minniti (2001) shows that if the entrepreneur is a catalyst of further economic activity then entrepreneurship breeds entrepreneurship, the aggregate level of entrepreneurial activity within an economy is uncertain, and that the level of entrepreneurship is determined through a path dependent process.

CONCLUSION

An entire field of inquiry centering on the entrepreneurial process has developed in recent years. The domain and boundaries of the field, however, are not well defined. As a result, much of the literature in the area has produced results based on narrow empirical studies and often lacks a robust theoretical foundation. And yet, the questions and issues surrounding entrepreneurship concern important components of human action and integral aspects of psychological, social, and economic phenomena. The Austrian approach provides a methodological and theoretical context that may help ground the field of entrepreneurial study in a sound disciplinary tradition.

If we define entrepreneurial studies to be the study of "(1) why, when, and how opportunities for the creation of goods and services come into existence; (2) why, when, and how some people and not others discover and exploit these opportunities; and (3) why, when, and how different modes of action are used to exploit entrepreneurial opportunities" (Shane and Venkataraman, 2000, p. 218), an Austrian approach to entrepreneurship seems appropriate. In addition to a clearly defined body of entrepreneurial theory grounded in a complete theory of markets, Austrian methodological subjectivism and focus on process rather than equilibrium are particularly well suited for the study of entrepreneurial behavior. Several points illustrate our claim.

First, we noted that, at the highest level of abstraction, the Austrian concept of entrepreneurship is an intrinsic aspect of human action, a dynamic process centered on the existence, discovery and exploitation of opportunities. The Austrian approach studies the interdependence between individuals and opportunities and is thus well suited to the organizational approach of Shane and Venkataraman (2000).[5] The Austrian approach is nevertheless suited to issues neglected by Shane and Venkataraman such as the environmental antecedents of entrepreneurship and its consequences in the form of growth and cultural change. Indeed, the flexibility of the Austrian approach allows studies of the characteristics of the individual entrepreneur, studies of organizations, and studies of the macroeconomic implications of entrepreneurship all under the same theoretical umbrella.

Second, scholars of entrepreneurship and organizations are often frustrated with economic approaches that focus on equilibrium outcomes rather than the dynamics tending toward such equilibria. As Baumol (1983, 1993) has lamented, mainstream economists working with analytical models have neglected entrepreneurship and simply treated it as a residual that cannot be attributed to any measurable productive input. Some scholars have introduced entrepreneurship in an equilibrium context (Bates, 1990; Gifford, 1998; Iyigun and Owen, 1998; Otani, 1996) and their work has made valuable contributions. Their focus on long-term equilibria, however, makes these models inappropriate for the study of the less predictable aspects of the entrepreneurial process. In contrast, the Austrian approach to entrepreneurship makes it a disequilibrium phenomenon, in which the final equilibrium is frequently not the main concern.

Third, learning and knowledge play an important role in the entrepreneurship literature. Austrian economics provides a theory of entrepreneurial learning. Menger had an evolutionary theory of change where economic growth depends on the growth of knowledge. More recently, Harper has analyzed the issue and transformed the discussion about the growth of knowledge into a theory of entrepreneurial learning. For Harper, entrepreneurship begins with the alert discovery of an opportunity about which the entrepreneur makes an inference. Then the entrepreneur tests his conjecture, learns, and revises his business plan. Harper's argument is complementary to Minniti and Bygrave (2001) who explore entrepreneurial decision making when agents choose repeatedly among actions with potentially risky consequences.

Minniti and Bygrave build on the idea that most learning takes place by filtering signals obtained by experimenting with different competing hypotheses, where some actions are reinforced and others weakened as new evidence is obtained. Over time, individuals repeat only those actions that have generated

---

[5] For an Austrian entrepreneurial treatment of organizational issues see Lewin and Phelan (2000), Yu (1999) and Sautet (2000). For related discussions see also the important work of Langlois and Robertson (1995).

better outcomes. As a result, independently of objective desirability or actual outcomes, actions whose random outcomes happened to be positive become systematic components of the knowledge stock upon which entrepreneurs form their decisions. Thus, their result is analogous to Choi's idea that paradigms proven to be usable will be retained and become parts of the entrepreneur's "tool box." Butos and Koppl develop this point too by presenting the entrepreneur as a Hayekian learner.

Indeed, for the Austrians, learning is embedded. That is, it is rooted in the specific environment of the potential entrepreneur as determined by history and institutions. As Sue Birley puts it: "There is no dichotomy between entrepreneurs and non-entrepreneurs; with the right stimulus, the most unexpected people can become entrepreneurs" (Wright, 2001, pp. 37–38). Thus, an Austrian approach to entrepreneurship complements studies of embeddedness and social networks such as those by Aldrich (1999), Aldrich and Fiol (1994), Granovetter (1985), and Uzzi (1999).

Finally, researchers in entrepreneurship have recently become fascinated with the application of complexity theory to the study of organizations [among others, Brown and Eisenhardt, 1997, and the special issue of *Organization Science* 1999, 10(3)], and, specifically, to the study of entrepreneurial dynamics (Minniti, 2001, forthcoming). Austrian explanations of entrepreneurship are consistent with the concept of emergence and with complexity theory.

In entrepreneurial studies, the study of entrepreneurship as an emergent process can be traced back to Gartner (1985). By approaching the creation of organization as an evolutionary process, entrepreneurship researchers focus on the multiple dimensions of the process necessary to create a new firm. Analogously to Hayek's concept of spontaneous order, complexity describes the formation of an order as the spontaneous and unplanned outcome of the interactions of many heterogeneous agents (Minniti and Koppl, 1999). Entrepreneurs are clearly heterogeneous agents and the level of entrepreneurial activity in a given area is the outcome of a variety of unpredictable interactions. Thus, it is an emerging unplanned order. Complex systems self-organize in hierarchical layers, react to the environment, and are adaptive and creative. These themes of modern complexity theory were explored within the Austrian tradition by Hayek and can be traced back within that tradition to the work of Carl Menger.

Our introduction noted three limits to Kirzner's theory that we consider more apparent than real. First, we noted that Kirzner may seem to neglect the entrepreneurial process. As we saw above, however, this neglect is not denial. Although Kirzner does not himself examine the entrepreneurial process, his framework is consistent with an indefinite number of theories of it. David Harper provides one example coming from within the Austrian tradition. Second, we noted that Kirzner may seem to view profit opportunities as external to the entrepreneur. As we saw above, however, we should interpret Kirzner's term "discovery" broadly so that creative acts of entrepreneurial invention are at the same time "discoveries" of profit opportunities. If the creative innovation proves profitable, it is because the entrepreneur has discovered an opportunity. Third, we noted that Kirzner may seem to restrict entrepreneurship to simultaneous arbitrage. As we noted above, however, Kirzner gives arbitrage an enlarged meaning that includes even the most elaborate entrepreneurial ventures. No matter how complex a business plan may be, it will be a success only if the end result is that inputs are bought cheap and outputs are sold dear. In that case, the entrepreneur has engaged in successful arbitrage between input markets and output markets.

The three limits to Kirzner's analysis, then, are apparent, not real. They are like optical illusions created by the relatively high level of abstraction Kirzner maintains. While this level of abstraction is a source of potential misunderstanding, it is also a great strength in his analysis and a necessary feature of any approach that might be used to unify and organize the sprawling literature in entrepreneurship.

As a field of inquiry, entrepreneurial studies has one great strength and one great weakness. Its great strength is the richness and diversity of particular studies and models. The great weakness of entrepreneurial studies is the lack of a common theoretical framework. This weakness might almost seem the flip side of its great strength, although we believe it is a weakness we can overcome. Scholars of entrepreneurial studies may lack a disciplinary core, but they share a vision of entrepreneurship. Entrepreneurship is a dynamic process of change, in which individuals having in unusual degree certain personal or psychological characteristics undertake innovative actions. The Austrian approach to entrepreneurship outlined in this chapter expresses this common vision. The Austrian framework is a broad one, uniquely suited to seize the common elements of thought uniting scholars of entrepreneurship without imposing relatively specific models or empirical hypotheses about which legitimate disagreement exists within the field.

REFERENCES

Aldrich, H. (1999). *Organizations Evolving*. London: Sage Publications.

Aldrich, H. and M. Fiol (1994). Fools rush in? The institutional context of industry creation. *Academy of Management Review*, 19(4), 645–670.

Bates, T. (1990). Entrepreneur human capital inputs and small business longevity. *Review of Economics and Statistics*, 72(4), 551–559.

Baumol, W.J. (1983). Toward operational models of entrepreneurship. In J. Ronen (ed.), *Entrepreneurship*. Lexington, MA: Lexington Books, pp. 29–48.

Baumol, W.J. (1993). Formal entrepreneurship theory in economics: Existence and bounds. *Journal of Business Venturing*, 8(3), 197–210.

Boland, L.A. (1982). *The Foundations of Economic Methodology*. London: George Allen and Unwin.

Boland, L.A. (1986). *Methodology for a New Microeconomics: The Critical Foundations*. Boston, MA: Allen and Unwin.

Brown, S. and K. Eisenhardt (1997). The art of continuous change: Linking complexity theory and time-paced evolution in relentlessly shifting organizations. *Administrative Science Quarterly*, 42(1), 1–34.

Butos, W. and R. Koppl (1999). Hayek and Kirzner at the Keynesian Beauty Contest. *Journal des Economists et des Etudes Humaines*, **9**(2/3): 257–275.

Chamlee-Wright, E. (1997). *The Cultural Foundations of Economic Development*. London and New York: Routledge.

Choi, Y.B. (1993a). *Paradigms and Conventions: Uncertainty, Decision Making and Entrepreneurship*. Ann Arbor, MI: University of Michigan Press.

Choi, Y.B. (1993b). Entrepreneurship and envy. *Constitutional Political Economy*, **4**(3), 331–347.

Choi, Y.B. (1999). Conventions and economic change: A contribution toward a theory of political economy. *Constitutional Political Economy*, **10**(3), 245–264.

Gartner, W. (1985). A conceptual framework for describing the phenomenon of new venture creation. *Academy of Management Review*, **10**(4), 696–706.

Gartner, W. (1990). What are we talking about when we talk about entrepreneurship? *Journal of Business Venturing*, **5**(1), 15–28.

Gifford, S. (1998). *The Allocation of Limited Entrepreneurial Attention*. Boston: Kluwer Academic.

Gilad, B. (1982). On encouraging entrepreneurship: An interdisciplinary approach. *Journal of Behavioral Economics*, **11**(1), 132–163.

Granovetter, M. (1985). Economic action and social structure: The problem of embeddedness. *American Journal of Sociology*, **91**(3), 480–510.

Harper, D. (1994). A new approach to modeling endogenous learning processes in economic theory. *Advances in Austrian Economics*, **1**, 49–79.

Harper, D. (1996). *Enterpreneurship and the market process: An inquiry into the growth of knowledge*. London: Routledge.

Harper, D. (1998). Institutional conditions for entrepreneurship. *Advances in Austrian Economics*, **5**, 241–275.

Hayek, F.A. (1948). The use of knowledge in society. In F.A. Hayek, *Individualism and Economic Order*. Chicago: University of Chicago Press.

Hayek, F.A. (1952). *The Sensory Order*. Chicago: University of Chicago Press.

Hayek, F.A. (1967a). The Results of Human Action but not of Human Design. In his *Studies in Philosophy, Politics, and Economics*. Chicago: The University of Chicago Press, 96–105.

Hayek, F.A. (1967b). Notes on the Evolution of Systems of Rules of Conduct. In his *Studies in Philosophy, Politics and Economics*. Chicago: The University of Chicago Press, 66–81.

Hayek, F.A. (1973–1979). *Law, Legislation and Liberty* (3 vols). Chicago: University of Chicago Press.

Hayek, F.A. (1978). Competition as a discovery procedure. In F.A. Hayek, *New Studies in Philosophy, Politics, Economics and the History of Ideas*. Chicago: University of Chicago Press, 179–190.

Holcombe, R. (forthcoming). The origins of entrepreneurial opportunities. *Review of Austrian Economics*.

Holland, J.H., K.J. Holyoak, R.E. Nisbett and P.R. Thagard (1986). *Induction: Processes of Inference, Learning, and Discovery*. Cambridge, MA: MIT Press.

Iyigun, M. and A. Owen. (1998). Risk, entrepreneurship and human capital accumulation. *American Economic Review*, **88**(2), 454–457.

Kirzner, I.M. (1973). *Competition and Entrepreneurship*. Chicago: University of Chicago Press.

Kirzner, I.M. (1979). *Perception, Opportunity, and Profit: Studies in the Theory of Entrepreneurship*. Chicago: University of Chicago Press.

Kirzner, I.M. (1992). *The Meaning of Market Process: Essays in the Development of Modern Austrian Economics*. London and New York: Routledge.

Kirzner, I.M. (1999). Creativity and/or alertness: A reconsideration of the Schumpeterian entrepreneur. *Review of Austrian Economics*, **11**(1/2), 5–17.

Koppl, R. (2000a). Policy implications of complexity: An Austrian perspective. In D. Colander, (ed.), *The Complexity Vision and the Teaching of Economics*. Cheltenham, UK: Edward Elgar, pp. 97–117.

Koppl, R. (2000b). The complexity vision and the teaching of economics. In D. Colander (ed.), *The Complexity Vision and the Teaching of Economics*. Cheltenham, UK: Edward Elgar, pp. 137–146.

Koppl, R. (2002a). *Big Players and the Economic Theory of Expectations*. New York and London: Palgrave Macmillan.

Koppl, R. (2002b). What is alertness? *Journal des Economists et des Etudes Humaines,* **12**(1), 3–13.

Lakatos, I. (1970). Falsification and the methodology of scientific research programs. In I. Lakatos, and A. Musgrave (eds.), *Criticism and the Growth of Knowledge.* Cambridge: Cambridge University Press, pp. 91–196.

Langlois, R.N. and P.L. Robertson (1995). *Firms, Markets and Economic Change.* London: Routledge.

Lewin, P. and S. Phelan (2000). An Austrian theory of the firm. *Review of Austrian Economics,* **13**(1), 59–79.

Loasby, B. (1976). *Choice, Complexity and Ignorance: An Enquiry into Economic Theory and the Practice of Decision-Making.* Cambridge: Cambridge University Press.

Low, M.B. and I.C. MacMillan (1988). Entrepreneurship: Past research and future challenges. *Journal of Management,* **14**(2), 139–161.

Menger, C. (1871 [1981]). *Principles of Economics.* New York: New York University Press.

Minniti, M. (1999). Entrepreneurship and economic growth. *Global Business and Economic Review,* **11**(1), 31–42.

Minniti, M. (2001). Entrepreneurship and network externalities. Manuscript.

Minniti, M. (forthcoming). Entrepreneurial alertness and asymmetric information in a simulated spin-glass model. *Journal of Business Venturing.*

Minniti, M. and W. Bygrave (2001). A dynamic model of entrepreneurial learning. *Entrepreneurship: Theory and Practice,* **25**(3), pp. 5–16.

Minniti, M. and R. Koppl (1999). The unintended consequence of entrepreneurship. *Journal des Economists et des Etudes Humaines,* **9**(4), 567–586.

Mises, L. von (1949). *Human Action: A Treatise on Economics.* New Haven, CT: Yale University Press.

Mises, M. von (1984). *My Years with Ludwig von Mises,* 2nd edition. Cedar Falls, Iowa: Center for Futures Education, Inc.

O'Driscoll, G. and M. Rizzo (1985). *The Economics of Time and Ignorance.* Oxford: Basil Blackwell.

Organization Science (1999). Application of complexity theory to organization science. Special Issue 10.

Otani, K. (1996). A human capital approach to entrepreneurial capacity. *Economica,* **63**(2), 273–289.

Popper, K. (1959). *The Logic of Scientific Discovery.* Hutchinson: London.

Reynolds, P., M. Camp and M. Hay (2001). *Global Entrepreneurship Monitor Report.* E.M. Kauffman Foundation, Kansas City, Missouri.

Rizzo, M. (1995). Introduction: Time and ignorance after ten years. In G. O'Driscoll and M. Rizzo (eds.), *The Economics of Time and Ignorance.* London and New York: Routledge. Reprint with a new introduction of the original 1985 edition, published by B. Blackwell, London, 1996, pp. xiii–xxxiii.

Rotter, J.B. (1966). Generalized expectancies for internal versus external control of reinforcement. *Psychological Monographs,* **80**(1), 1–28.

Sautet, F.E. (2000). *An Entrepreneurial Theory of the Firm.* London: Routledge.

Schumpeter, J. (1934). *The Theory of Economic Development.* Cambridge, MA: Harvard University Press.

Schutz, A. (1951 [1962]). Choosing among projects of action. In *Collected Papers I: The Problem of Social Reality.* The Hague: Martinus Nijhoff, pp. 67–96.

Shane, S. and S. Venkataraman (2000). The promise of entrepreneurship as a field of research. *Academy of Management Review,* **25**(1), 217–226.

Uzzi, B. (1999). Embeddedness in the Making of Financial Capital. *American Sociological Review,* **64**(4), 481–505.

Vaughn, K. (1994). *Austrian Economics in America: The Migration of a Tradition.* Cambridge, UK: Cambridge University Press.

Wright, M. (2001). Creating and growing wealth: Sue Birley on entrepreneurship and wealth creation. *Academy of Management Executive,* **15**(1), 37–39.

Yu, Tony F. (1999). Toward a praxeological theory of the firm. *Review of Austrian Economics,* **12**(1), 25–41.

PART THREE

Opportunity and the Nature of Exploitation

This section examines opportunity from a psychological and management perspective. This section focuses three related chapters. The first in Chapter 6, "The Cognitive Psychology of Entrepreneurship," by Norris Krueger focuses on a key issue, what cognitive phenomenon is associated with seeing and acting on opportunities. Understanding entrepreneurial cognition is imperative to understanding the essence of entrepreneurship. To understand entrepreneurship requires understanding of how we learn to see opportunity and decide to pursue it.

The second contribution, "Three views of Entrepreneurial Opportunity," by Saras Sarasvathy, Nick Dew, Ramakrishna Velamuri and Sankaran Venkataraman challenge the assumption underlying current theories of innovation that if a market could be created it will. They examine three theories of market processes: the market as an allocative process; as a discovery process; and as a creative process. Within each literature, they examine the assumptions about he knowledge of the decision-maker regarding the future, and the implications of these assumptions for strategies to recognize, discover and create entrepreneurial opportunities.

The relationship between the individual agent and opportunity is the starting point for the third chapter in this section, "The Individual–Opportunity Nexus," by Jonathan Eckhardt and Scott Shane. They start with a discussion of disequilibrium to show why it is necessary for entrepreneurship. Their model consists of a two by two matrix that identifies entrepreneurial discovery and exploitation. The first possibility is independent discovery and startup. The second possibility is individual discovery and corporate exploitation resulting in an acquisition. The third is a corporate discovery and individual exploitation. Finally, a corporate discovery and exploitation is corporate venturing. Two dimensions of this choice appear to be important. First, can the opportunity be effectively pursued through markets? Second, are new or established firms better entities for undertaking the opportunity exploitation process?

NORRIS F. KRUEGER, Jr.

Boise State University

6.   The Cognitive Psychology of Entrepreneurship

INTRODUCTION

If the "heart" of entrepreneurship is an orientation toward seeing opportunities (e.g. Stevenson and Jarillo, 1990), then from whence do perceptions of opportunity derive? Understanding entrepreneurial cognition is imperative to understanding the essence of entrepreneurship, how it emerges and evolves. This is especially true if we wish to move from descriptive research to theory-driven research. For example, if we wish to argue intelligently about whether entrepreneurial opportunities are "discovered" or if they are "enacted," theory is crucial. This chapter offers researchers an overview of the cognitive processes that drive "thinking entrepreneurially":

- *What is the nature of entrepreneurial thinking?*
- *What cognitive phenomena are associated with seeing and acting on opportunities?*

Research into entrepreneurial cognition offers a way to bring the entrepreneur back into entrepreneurship. While there still is little substance to the notion of a so-called "entrepreneurial personality" it always seemed counterintuitive to ignore all individual differences, especially psychological differences. Yes, entrepreneurs may not be too different in risk taking propensity, but (almost by definition) they see more opportunities. Cognition research offers us multiple mechanisms, both theory-driven and empirically-robust, to build a deeper, richer understanding of how we learn to see opportunities.

Cognitive phenomena are important throughout this process: Opportunities themselves are perceived, if not enacted, as are the critical antecedents of opportunity perceptions. Entrepreneurial activity may require a tangible infrastructure of needed resources but we neglect at our peril what I have dubbed the cognitive infrastructure (see Figure 1, p. 116) – what enables us to perceive (and learn to perceive) personally-credible opportunities. Understanding the cognitive infrastructure undergirding entrepreneurial activity also affords us richer perspectives on how to nurture entrepreneurship (Krueger and Brazeal, 1994; Krueger, 2000; Shepherd and Krueger, 2002).

If we are to better understand the entrepreneurial process, then, we need to better understand how opportunities manifest themselves as credible (Shapero,

Z.J. Acs and D.B. Audretsch (eds.), Handbook of Entrepreneurship Research, 105–140
© 2003 *Kluwer Academic Publishers. Printed in Great Britain.*

1975, 1982). However, we must first ask, "*How* do we answer that question?" As with other nascent fields, entrepreneurship studies have long had a bias toward descriptive research, grounded more in practical concerns than in theory. The cry for "more strong theory in entrepreneurship research" continues to be a loud, clarion call that still has not been heeded as enthusiastically as perhaps it should. One reason for this has been the tendency to use theory to explain one's findings retrospectively, rather than identifying a useful, appropriate theoretical base from which to work prospectively.

However, this is changing. For example, when I entered the field, there was considerable research into "budding" entrepreneurs, a rather loose definition. Today researchers talk about "entrepreneurial intentions", a more rigorous (and theory-based) focus. Similarly, most of the research on "opportunity recognition" remains highly descriptive, yet we see increasing use of theory to drive the empirical research, not just finding theory to explain the findings. The potential for continued progress lies not just in cognitive theory, but cognition research offers more than its fair share of potential for exciting, productive future research in entrepreneurship.

When we ask "Do entrepreneurs think differently?" we are thus asking, "When someone is thinking 'entrepreneurially,' what does that mean in terms of cognitive processes?" As Robert Baron would argue, we all share the same basic cognitive processes but entrepreneurs appear to face unique role demands that are accompanied by differences in the cognitive processes those role demands require.

What is unique about "entrepreneurial" thinking? We will focus here on the most critical distinction between entrepreneur and non-entrepreneur, the intentional pursuit of opportunity. As Howard Stevenson pointed out long ago, the "heart" of entrepreneurship is the seeking of and acting upon opportunities. To understand entrepreneurship, then, requires understanding how we learn to see opportunities and decide to pursue them.

For example, here is one current debate in the field of entrepreneurship studies. Are opportunities "discovered" or are they "enacted"? That is, does the pursuit of opportunity begin by a process of observation and recognition that a set of conditions constitutes a viable opportunity? Or, does the pursuit of opportunity begin with a process wherein a set of observed (and/or assumed) conditions can be constructed into a viable opportunity? Cognition research allows us to explore how both perspectives contribute to our understanding of opportunity emergence. If opportunities are enacted, then we need to explore the cognitive processes by which we take signals from the environment and construct a personally-credible opportunity. Even if opportunities are discovered, they still need to be perceived and cognition research already offers key insights into entrepreneurial perceptions.

Cognition research offers rich theory and well-developed methods. As the reader will see, it also offers considerable successes to encourage the entrepreneurship researcher. The study of human cognition has surfaced a remarkable variety of theoretical and methodological approaches to understanding how human beings apprehend data and process it. The rich variety of approaches can offer an equally rich variety of insights.

For example, entrepreneurs appear to identify opportunities based on cues or signals from the environment that they filter and process through a number of mechanisms (e.g., intentions). Cognitive psychologists would point out that entrepreneurs would likely recognize useful patterns in the myriad cues and signals we receive, patterns that suggest potential opportunities (or not). Shapero used the analogy of "antennae" – we all have our antennae tuned to certain "frequencies" (and in different directions). Entrepreneurs are no different, except in what directions, etc. their antennae are tuned. However, researching pattern recognition is not terribly simple; it requires understanding the theories behind human pattern recognition and it requires understanding the rigorous methodologies needed to research in this arena.

However, the very breadth and richness of cognitive science also reflects a heterogeneous field. As such, we must focus here in this chapter on selected topic areas that seem the most promising. Rather than pursuing one such subdomain in great depth, this chapter will take advantage of the inherent eclecticism of cognition research to offer an equally eclectic overview of the most fertile ground for future entrepreneurship research.

One way to look at the domain of cognition research would be a quick survey of leading textbooks and primers on cognitive psychology that identifies a dizzying array of highly specific topics, but we can readily combine these into several overlapping subdomains of cognition research:

- Perception (including biases, attention, consciousness)
- Decision making (problem solving, creativity, intelligences, heuristics)
- Knowledge Representation (including memory, language)
- Learning and Cognitive Development

A second way to look at cognition research is Herbert Simon's three levels of cognitive phenomena (in Sarasvathy):

- Semantic (surface level)
- Symbolic (deep structures level)
- Neurological (biological level)

This chapter will address each subdomain, but it will also be readily apparent that there are topics that entrepreneurship researchers have yet to approach, such as addressing Simon's neurological level. For example, might we research whether entrepreneurs differ in memory, perhaps having (or needing) more "chunks" in short-term memory?

Researchers face an interesting paradox: We have a very important, oft-asked question yet we have only rarely confronted it directly and with rigor. On one hand, understanding the nature of entrepreneurial thinking is central to understanding both entrepreneurs and entrepreneurship. Thus, we need to understand how we learn to see actionable opportunities. Terms such as "thinking", "perception", and "intent" suggest that cognitive psychology should naturally offer invaluable insights. But, on the other hand, research into this question has taken many different forms, using many different approaches, often *ad hoc* descriptive analyses (again, which may offer considerable grist for the research mill but also evince a glaring lack of theoretical grounding.)

As such, this chapter will emphasize existing research that was founded on well-received theory from cognitive psychology, especially social cognitive psychology. However, the reader is warned that the disparate, eclectic streams of research into entrepreneurial thinking are not as well connected as one might prefer – nor even as one might reasonably expect. Yet, this eclecticism can be also be viewed as a far-from-complete "mosaic tile" where the quality "tiles" are building toward a more comprehensive picture. Again, the key is research based on theory *a priori*, not simply digging up theory to explain what might be an *ad hoc* finding. The good news is that scholars such as Robert Baron (1998, 2000a), Ron Mitchell et al. (2000) and others (e.g., Gaglio, 1997; Gaglio and Katz, 2001; Shepherd and Douglas, 1997) are showing us that entrepreneurial cognition is incredibly fertile ground for important and interesting research.

Obviously, if the "heart" of entrepreneurship is this orientation toward seeking opportunities, developing a much deeper understanding of this cuts to the very essence of entrepreneurship. If we understand how we learn to see opportunities, we unlock much of the heretofore "black box" of entrepreneurship. Some of the most promising recent models of entrepreneurship focus on cognitive processes, showing the importance of an opportunity-friendly cognitive infrastructure (e.g., Busenitz and Lau, 1996; Alvarez and Busenitz, 2001; Mitchell et al., 2000).

Yet even that may not offer us the most valuable payoff. If we understand the cognitive processes associated with entrepreneurial thinking and action, then we have at least a tentative blueprint for *influencing* those processes. For example, if self-efficacy proves critical, then our knowing how to increase individuals' self-efficacy should allow us to increase the quality and quantity of opportunities that they perceive as personally viable. As with much research in cognitive psychology, there will be as many testable implications for teaching and for practice as there are testable implications for research.

Given the admitted eclecticism of research into entrepreneurial cognition, it behooves us to identify those areas that offer the most promise. Again, we will strive to focus on areas where research has been grounded in sound theory. However, this only increases the risk that the reader will find the subsections to be (of necessity) somewhat disjointed. To compensate for this, each section raises crucial unanswered questions.

Before taking entrepreneurial action, there must be a perceived opportunity (Section 2) and intentions toward pursuing that opportunity (Section 3). Intentions are driven by critical attitudes and beliefs such as self-efficacy (Sections 4 and 5). Underneath those beliefs and attitudes are deeper structures that reflect how we structure knowledge representation (Section 6). These deeper structures help inform us about how to nurture entrepreneurial thinking

(Section 7). Let us preview the chapter by describing these subdomains of greatest interest.

Perception: Probably the most important contribution that cognitive science offers the entrepreneurship researcher is that we apprehend reality not directly, but through multiple perceptual lenses. That is, our brains grasp external phenomena through processes of perception. We are unlikely to pursue an opportunity that we do not perceive. What do we notice? How do we interpret what we do notice? What might bias our perceptions? Section 2 below addresses the perception of opportunities.

Intention: In cognitive psychology, intention is the cognitive state immediately prior to executing a behavior. The dominant class of formal intentions models employs two critical antecedents of intentions that can be classified (despite varying terminology) as (a) perceived feasibility and (b) perceived desirability. That is, intentions require the belief that the behavior is feasible and the belief that the behavior is desirable. One remarkable aspect of this is that perceptions of opportunity have essentially the same antecedents, suggesting somewhat of an isomorphism between intentions and opportunity perceptions, in turn suggesting that something important cognitively is at work. Section 3 moves forward from perceptions to entrepreneurial intentions, perhaps the fastest growing area of cognition research in entrepreneurship.

Belief Structures: If intentions (and opportunity perceptions) depend on personal beliefs and attitudes, then researchers interested in entrepreneurial thinking should also explore the antecedents of intentions. In particular, we are beginning to see a groundswell of interest in one key belief that has long been associated with initiating and persisting at goal-directed behavior, Albert Bandura's notion of *perceived self-efficacy*. The power of self-efficacy as a predictor of human decision making would attract the researcher's attention anyway but it appears quite potent as an antecedent of both opportunity perceptions and intentions. (The domain of entrepreneurship also affords unique insights into our understanding of self-efficacy, an opportunity for entrepreneurship studies to contribute to a broader understanding of decision making.) Section 4 will examine self-efficacy research in entrepreneurship.

In other settings, cognition research has identified other beliefs and attitudes that influence human perceptions and human decision making, though usually the impact is indirect (e.g., as a moderating factor). For example, Shapero (1975) proposed that intentions required both a credible opportunity and some propensity to act. In most cognition research, the researcher assumes that the important phenomena vary across both persons and situations (PxS variables) but one cannot peremptorily dismiss personal influences (or situational, as in Busenitz and Barney). Shaver is right: There is no "entrepreneurial personality." However, numerous trait-like personal beliefs and attitudes do appear to offer additional insight to our theory and additional predictive power to our research. As such, Section 4 will briefly survey some individual difference variables that have been associated with entrepreneurial thinking.

Deeper Structures: Cognitive phenomena such as intentions lie relatively close to the surface in the architecture of our thinking. Underneath surface structures are deeper cognitive structures of how we represent knowledge and how it all fits together. Cognitive science has long used methods such as causal maps, schemas and schemata and scripts to illuminate these deeper structures. While this is perhaps the newest domain of cognition research to be applied to entrepreneurship, the potential is immense. Not only do researchers get a more fundamental view of how we learn to think entrepreneurially, this more fundamental look affords us new ways to influence the processes that lie beneath entrepreneurial thinking. That means we have new, more powerful mechanisms by which we can enhance entrepreneurial thinking. (Ron Mitchell and his team at the University of Victoria predicate their entrepreneurship training on changing students' entrepreneurial scripts from relatively novice to relatively expert.) Section 6 provides an overview of this most exciting and most fertile ground for research in entrepreneurship.

Learning: As the foregoing section suggests, one crucial impact of cognition-focused research into entrepreneurship is that if we understand the "why" of entrepreneurial thinking, we can influence the "how." That is, we can use the fruits of this research fairly directly in our teaching and training. However, despite our strong, ongoing interest in understanding how we learn to see opportunities and despite a very extensive literature of entrepreneurship education, we have been less successful at researching how entrepreneurs learn. The descriptive work done in entrepreneurship education has, of course, proven of great benefit. The next step for researchers is, as with intentions, to be much better grounded in theory. Section 7 lays the groundwork for exploring how entrepreneurs learn. Here is more highly fertile ground for researchers to explore.

Future Directions: This preview has already suggested some critical questions that require answering (or perhaps better answers). As noted above, the cry for more theoretical grounding (rather than *post hoc* explanation) in entrepreneurship research is often deafening. Fortunately, cognition research offers well-grounded, immediately applicable theory (and methodology) for the researcher. Section 8 offers a modest list of what seems to this researcher to be the most promising research questions that are already well within our grasp.

A considerable and growing literature focuses on behaviors associated with seeking opportunities, however, one might be startled at the *ad hoc* nature of the conceptual frameworks (if any) employed. However, one is less startled after considering the variety of conceptual approaches, instead one should be startled by the lack of a closer focus on the role of human cognition in the pursuit of opportunity. Of course, we find this lack of focus itself presents us a golden opportunity to provide an overview of what the study of cognitive phenomena has to offer to the entrepreneurship researcher. This is particularly true in understanding the emergence and evolution of entrepreneurial thinking.

PERCEPTIONS

Definitional Issues

"Optimism" as Perceiving Opportunities?: It seems highly reasonable that we focus our quest for understanding the nature of entrepreneurial thinking by focusing upon a widely-held definition of entrepreneurship: An orientation toward seeking (and acting on) opportunities. Without the quest for opportunities, entrepreneurial activity seems unlikely. Would anyone act upon *unperceived* opportunities? Another question that cognition research raises is that of role identity: Do entrepreneurs perceive opportunities or do they perceive themselves as entrepreneurs – or both? Cognition research offers tools to address that question.

Epistemologically, one might argue that opportunities exist and entrepreneurs discover or recognize them or that research is best served by taking that perspective. A more dominant view is that entrepreneurs enact their opportunities, constructing them mentally from their perceptions of the world around them. Both are useful approaches; both can be explored by examining cognitive phenomena (albeit different phenomena) as potential explanators of opportunity perceptions. As such, cognition-based research offers an opportunity for researchers to explore the limits and delimits of each approach. Either way, entrepreneurship scholars might find the theories and methods of pattern recognition research to be highly useful and interesting.

Defining "Opportunity"?

This, however, begs an important question: What do we mean by "opportunity"? Two issues arise in this. First, if opportunity is perceived, then that perception is likely to vary significantly across individuals. And, as Professor Shaver demonstrates, perception of opportunity should also vary across situations. If the perception of opportunity varies across both persons and situations, that suggests "opportunity" to be an artifact of the processes that generated that perception. Reifying "opportunity" might prove misleading at best. We might also ask ourselves if the entrepreneur's goal is to perceive more opportunities (quantity) or better opportunities (quality).

On the other hand, we run a very real risk of circular reasoning by defining opportunity in terms of its antecedents. If opportunities are discovered and not particularly enacted, then we are guilty of Peter Kilby's "Heffalump" fallacy:

If we are researching opportunity perception, then what we study must be opportunities. Strong theory allows us to do better.

Key Antecedents of Perceived Opportunity

Where we begin to understand the role of perceptions can be found in a not inconsiderable amount of research that suggests two critical antecedents of perceived opportunity, both of which themselves are perceptual.

Dutton and Jackson (1987) first mapped out an elegant model of opportunity perception that utilized the cognitive phenomenon of *categorization*. We have significant biases toward simplifying how we represent knowledge; it is much more efficient and convenient to simplify the range of strategic issues that an individual or organization faces by categorizing as many as possible into "opportunities" and "threats." Dutton and colleagues generated a sizeable number of studies that show how strategic issue categorization plays a central role in strategic decision making (Dutton and Jackson, 1987).

The Dutton and Jackson model argues that perception of opportunity is driven by two other key perceptions. First, a situation where the likely outcomes are perceived as positive and that the situation is deemed as within one's personal control would be categorized as an "opportunity." Contrariwise, a situation where the likely outcomes are negative and the situation is seen as beyond one's control would be categorized as a "threat." This elegant model was then tested successfully (Jackson and Dutton, 1988).

Others (including this author) have adapted this framework with great success. Peter Dickson and I tested the impact of perceived competence (i.e., perceived self-efficacy) on opportunity perception and strategic risk taking in a controlled experiment (Krueger, 1989; Krueger and Dickson, 1994). We argued that a critical element of perceived controllability was the decision maker's sense of personal competence at the specified task. Moreover, Bandura (e.g., 1986) himself hints repeatedly that self-efficacy should influence risk taking. Our findings indicated that while self-efficacy perceptions influenced risk taking, the effect was indirect. That is, self-efficacy was strongly associated with both opportunity perceptions (positively) and threat perceptions (negatively). However, risk taking was associated even more strongly with both opportunity and threat perceptions, with little direct impact of self-efficacy.

This tells us two things, I think. First, Dutton and her colleagues are quite correct, in that opportunity and threat perceptions play a key role in strategic behavior. Even as powerful a factor as self-efficacy seems able to influence risk taking only by influencing the perceptions of opportunity and threat. Second, subjects were tested in two closely-related domains but with independent cues for self-efficacy. The two highly similar decision tasks allowed us to show that the self-efficacy → opportunity/threat perception → risk taking model was situation-specific (again, varies across both persons and situations).

The Key Role of Perceptions

Perhaps it may seem obvious that how we make sense of the world and how we make decisions are based not on brute realities but on our perceptions of those realities. Kirzner (1982) argues that entrepreneurs are "alert" to potential opportunities but we differ both in terms of the number of opportunities and in terms of the specific types of opportunities (perhaps depending on where Shapero's "antennae" are tuned?). We can also use cognition research to explore how we learn to perceive ourselves as entrepreneurs, just as we study how we learn to perceive opportunities.

However, while many researchers still seem to take a "short cut" and ignore the perceptual filters through which we see the world, the very fact that so many more researchers employ constructs and measures that are perceptions or perception-based is encouraging. However, we urge researchers continue to consider the cognitive psychology behind these critical perceptions.

At the heart of many textbooks on cognition is an extended discussion of human perception, partly because perception is central to so many other cognitive phenomena. Perception is sometimes an extremely complicated process: What do we see? What don't we see? What do we see accurately? Is "accuracy" even a relevant question? This is something we need much more research about. A delightful study from Lowell Busenitz and Jay Barney shows how entrepreneurs are subject to the same sorts of cognitive biases that we all are prone to (1997). We ignore these very human cognitions at our peril.

Busenitz and his colleagues have explored how human cognitive biases and decision heuristics characterize entrepreneurs just as they characterize anyone else and how these biases and heuristics help or hinder the entrepreneur. For example, the illusion of control will increase the likelihood of the entrepreneur taking action on an opportunity, but it also may serve to blind the entrepreneur to genuine risks. For another example, consider the various framing effects noted by Kahneman and Tversky (e.g., in Hogarth, 1986) such as prospect theory. Prospect theory argues that we are more apt to take risks in a losing situation (or perhaps simply where we are well below our aspiration level (March and Shapira, 1987)). This might partly explain why someone might start a business under dire personal circumstances such as job loss.

Acting on Opportunities – Optimism as Taking Action

Human action has many roots, yet most researchers – even most philosophers – would argue that decision precedes action (Audi, 1993). While other chapters address decision making in some detail as it applies to entrepreneurial activity, cognitive phenomena dictate much of the inputs of those decision processes. One particularly illuminating approach is attribution theory.

Attributional Models – Optimism as Resilience to Adversity

Humans have an innate proclivity to explain important events in their lives. Even when the cause might be diffuse or simply unknowable, we seek actively to identify a plausible explanation. However, we again tend to categorize our attributions along certain dimensions: Internal/external, stable/unstable, global/specific, etc. It is increasingly evident that no matter how one categorizes causal attributions we find that more optimistic attributions seem highly associated with entrepreneurs and with entrepreneurial activity. For example, my dissertation project with Peter Dickson (Krueger, 1989) included a test of the role of causal attributions on this process and we found tentative evidence that the more internal the attribution of causality (e.g., skill or effort), the stronger the impact of the cuing on judgments of self-efficacy.

However, there is much stronger evidence from Kelly Shaver and his colleagues (especially Elizabeth Gatewood and William Gartner) that demonstrates how causal attributions play a major role in initiating and persisting at goal-directed behavior (Gatewood et al., 1995, 2002). It would be a poor opportunity that did not merit taking action, nor persisting in the face of adversity.

Similarly, the work of Martin Seligman also suggests that causal attributions are critical to initiating and persisting at goal-directed behavior (1990). He argues that persistence in the face of adversity requires the attribution that effort will carry the day. However, this would only be true if the goal were deemed a positive outcome and the situation controllable (sound familiar?). At minimum, Seligman's learned optimism should be strongly associated with a propensity to take action (cf. Krueger et al., 2000).

Most recently, Robert Baron and Gideon Markman (2000) tested a different measure of resilience to adversity, the Adversity Quotient (2000), finding that successful entrepreneurs score significantly higher on that measure. Three different approaches to conceptualizing and measuring attributions show that an optimistic resilience seems inherent to entrepreneurial thinking.

Perceived Tradeoffs in Decision Making

This dovetails elegantly with research on human decision making that finds we often make tradeoffs no so much between alternatives *per se*, but the upside and the downside of the given decision under consideration. For example, Lopes (1987) describes this tradeoff as being between "hope" and "fear": Hope for the upside balanced against the fear of the downside. In a more entrepreneurial context, Peter Dickson and Joseph Giglierano (1986) offer the twin metaphors of the "risk of missing the boat" versus the "risk of sinking the boat." All of this suggests that perception of opportunity may indeed depend upon both a strong sense of desirability ("hope") *and* a strong sense of feasibility (minimizing "fear").

However, given that we process positive information and negative information differently and apparently in different parts of our brains, we know from reward-cost orientation theory that rewards ("hope") and costs ("fear") are processed sequentially. Optimists process the positive information first, then negative information in an anchor-and-adjust process (another common human cognitive heuristic like those noted by Busenitz and Barney (1997). Do entrepreneurs prove to be optimists in this sense?

Role Identity

Finally, there is another perception that we have yet to address in great depth: The entrepreneur's perception that "I *am* an entrepreneur." In many career fields, individuals may have a limited, even distorted mental model of what that career entails in terms of role demands. For example, education students might choose whether or not to be a kindergarten teacher based on their mental model of the prototypical (or the optimal) kindergarten teacher. As that mental prototype is usually based on vague memories of one's own kindergarten teacher, it is at best too narrow and at worst quite distorted. Potential entrepreneurs may be deterred or attracted to entrepreneurship from similar mental prototyping, a cognitive phenomenon related to categorization (Jelinek and Litterer, 1995; Krueger and Hamilton, 1996).

INTENTIONS

Optimism as Intentions? If we care about how entrepreneurs emerge, then it cannot be too surprising to see the extent of interest in critical preconditions that facilitate or inhibit this emergence (e.g., Krueger, 2000). Entrepreneurship scholars once used terms such as "budding entrepreneurs" but use of the more specific term, "intentions", has added focus (and thus more rigor) to this fascinating research area. In return, this is an arena where entrepreneurs can perhaps "give back" fruitfully to other disciplines.

If we are interested in studying new ventures, then we need to understand the processes that lead up to their initiation. From a cognition perspective, that entails a better understanding of the intent to initiate entrepreneurial activity. Psychologists have long found intentions to be highly useful in understanding behavior. Also, an increased focus on intentions pushes researchers away from more retrospective research designs toward more prospective designs. It allows a greater emphasis on predicting versus explaining.

Philosophers (Audi, 1993) argue persuasively that intentions are central to voluntary human behavior. Indeed, psychologists and philosophers alike define "intention" as a cognitive state that is temporally prior and immediately proximate to the target behavior. That is, intent is the cognitive state immediately prior to the decision to act. Empirically, intentions are consistently the single best predictor of subsequent behavior (even if the predictive power is underwhelming.) *Why? Any planned behavior is intentional.* Essentially, if a behavior does not result from stimulus–response, it is intentional.

Fortunately, we are blessed with theoretically-sound, empirically-robust formal models of human intentions toward a target behavior. Even more fortunately, the various models offered by marketing (e.g., Bagozzi and

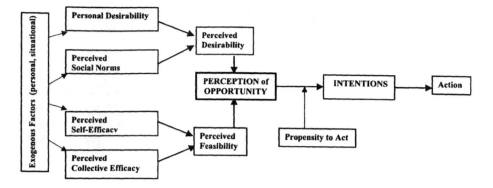

Figure 1. Intentions Model (adapted from Shapero, 1982; Krueger and Brazeal, 1994; Kreuger, 2000)

Warshaw, 1990), political science and other domains converge on highly similar sets of critical antecedents to intentions. The most striking evidence of this consensus about robust predictors of intent lies in the work of Per Davidsson (1991) who independently developed a model of entrepreneurial intentions *de novo* – finding antecedents that map rather nicely onto the known antecedents.

Dutton and Jackson's (1987) antecedents of opportunity perception fits rather nicely within this framework. This suggests that there is a considerable overlap between the two constructs (of opportunity perceptions and intentions).

Theory of Reasoned Action and Theory of Planned Behavior

Ajzen and Fishbein's Theory of Reasoned Action first surfaced in social psychology as a dominant model of intentions. Originally, social psychology tended to look at the inability of attitudes to predict behavior and added intention as a mediating variable. However, a positive attitude toward a behavior did not particularly predict intent, let alone behavior. The theory of reasoned action (TRA) added a theory-based second attitude that reflected the impact of social norms on intentions. The combined impact of personal attitude and social norms proved not only conceptually sound, but also empirically robust. Prediction was improved and the model even proved robust to how the key variables were measured (Sheppard et al., 1988).

However, Ajzen suspected that there was more to the story. Ajzen's Theory of Planned Behavior (TPB) proposed adding a third component, an additional key antecedent, perceived behavioral control. That is, it might be hard to form a strong intent to perform a behavior that is not really within one's control. Certainly one's sense of competence at executing the target behavior should be important (see the discussion elsewhere re Bandura's construct of self-efficacy). Adding this third antecedent typically adds an additional 10% to the variance explained, even predictively (Ajzen, 1991).

Shapero's Model of the Entrepreneurial Event (SEE)

Interestingly, the domain of entrepreneurship had already provided a model quite similar to TPB well before Ajzen formulated it; Shapero's (1975, 1982) proposed the following. The "entrepreneurial event" (defining as initiating entrepreneurial behavior) depends on the presence of a salient, personally-credible opportunity. A credible opportunity depends on two critical antecedents, perceptions of desirability (both personal and social) and perceptions of feasibility (both personal and social), thus presaging Ajzen's TPB by several years. That two different scholars in two different domains converged on highly similar models speaks to the value of intentions models.

[N.B.: Shapero's model also includes a person variable, propensity to act, that he conceived as a separate predictor of action. More important, perhaps, is Shapero's concept (1975, 1982) of the "precipitating event", something that would "displace" the decision maker from the inertia of existing behavior and drive the decision maker to reconsider her/his opportunity set – which might now have entrepreneurship as a salient and most credible personal opportunity. These components are discussed further in Section 5, below.]

For both the Theory of Planned Behavior and for Shapero's model we have a theory-driven and empirically robust model at the surface level (Simon's "semantic" level). However, theory and methods from cognition research offer us the opportunity to dig deeper into the underlying cognitive structures (Simon's "symbolic" level).

Empirical Tests

Shapero's model was first to be tested in the entrepreneurship domain where it found considerable support (Krueger, 1993a). Subsequently, Krueger and Carsrud (1993) proposed consideration of Azjen's TPB. Others, especially Kolveried (1996), have found great success in adapting TPB to entrepreneurial samples. This ultimately spawned a comparative test of TPB and SEE, finding support for *both* models (Krueger, Reilly and Carsrud, 2000). [*Post hoc* analysis suggested that the optimal model would include propensity to act from SEE and social norms from TPB. However, this model has not yet been tested in an independent sample.]

Other Configurations

There are other variations on this theme, each of which offers the researcher some food for thought. One particularly intriguing re-specification comes from Norway. Two different scholars specify the model as multiplicative in nature, rather than additive. This reflects that if a decision maker deems starting a business as completely infeasible (or horribly undesirable), no amount of the other antecedent can possibly compensate. Bjornar Reitan (1997) added a third antecedent, perceived profitability, essentially capturing the overlap between perceived desirability and perceived feasibility. Truls Erickson (2002) offers a simpler multiplicative approach that he dubbed "entrepreneurial capital" that uses only the first two antecedents.

One interesting implication from a multiplicative model consistently yielding a greater percentage of variance explained is that we may have to think in terms of threshold phenomena, something that is rarely examined in management research in general, let alone in entrepreneurship research. No matter how desirable a venture might appear, there is likely a threshold level of perceived feasibility below which decision makers would tend to deter the intent to launch that venture. Similarly, even 100% feasibility would not be enough to compensate for negative levels of desirability.

Another way to look at this is to think not in terms of two additive forces (perceived desirability and perceived feasibility) jointly acting on intentions, but rather that intentions reflect the intersection of two sets (the set of desirable options and the set of feasible options). Intuitively, a set theoretic approach fits the phenomenon, but it begs two questions. First, how do we identify where the threshold might be? Fortunately, Baron notes signal detection theory provides mechanisms for estimating thresholds. Second, in a highly noisy, uncertain context, the vision of the proposed venture has probably not coalesced completely in the decision maker's mind. One might argue that the very definition of "entrepreneurship" is fuzzy – in the mathematical sense. [That is, a given venture need not be perceived as "in" or "out of" the set of "entrepreneurial ventures," it belongs only partially to that set (Smithson, 1982).] Might we find some interesting refinements by employing fuzzy sets (Krueger, 2001a)?

Another highly promising direction to look at intentions is to apply utility theory. As humans tend to make decisions on multiple criteria, we can identify [e.g., via conjoint analysis] subjective utilities associated with not just income, but also independence, work satisfaction, etc. and relate these utilities to individuals' intentions toward starting a business (Douglas and Shepherd, 2000; Shepherd and Douglas, 1997).

What is also intriguing from utility theory is that utility curves are conceptually and empirically related to risk aversion. (Rational risk aversion is a function of the ratio between derivatives of the utility curve.) However, utility curves also reflect the impact of attitude toward uncertainty, i.e., decision makers' optimism or pessimism toward risks that they deem controllable. Hey (1984) elegantly demonstrates the orthogonality of optimism/pessimism (controllable risk) and risk aversion (uncontrollable risk). Similar research that argues we either minimize regret or maximize our subjective utility as theory argues (Loomes and Sugden, 1982). That raises an intriguing question: Is optimism (opportunity-seeking behavior) associated with utility-maximization (while pessimism or threat-avoidance is associated with regret-minimization)? In any event, Brockhaus showed long ago that entrepreneurs need not demonstrate unusual propensities to take risks, but they are nonetheless optimistic. If entrepreneurs are risk-averse but optimistic, that should be reflected quite visibly in entrepreneurs' utility curves.

Advantages of Intentions Models

First, one interesting aspect of this class of models is that it presumes that any other influence operates on intentions (and thus behavior) if and *only* if it influences one or more of the antecedent attitudes. If intentions and its critical antecedents serve as mediating variables, then we can use that knowledge to better assess the impact of other variables (e.g., personality, demographic, situational) on entrepreneurial behavior.

Moreover, it gives us an understanding of *how* that external factor influences intent and behavior. For example, growing up in a family business might enhance one's sense that being entrepreneurial is feasible (Delmar, 2000; Krueger, 1993b, 2000).

Second, we have already noted that the models appear quite robust even to misspecification (e.g., Sheppard et al., 1988). Again, the convergence of models is quite comforting (Krueger et al., 2000). This definitely speaks to the theoretical soundness of this class of models and how it taps into a very important, powerful cognitive mechanism.

Third, intentions models appear to offer predictive power, not just retrospective explanation, partly because intentions (and associated attitudes) are Person X Situation variables (i.e., phenomena vary across both individuals and across situations).

Fourth, intentions remain the single best predictor of subsequent action – not perfect, of course, but still the empirical best. (As intentions have been defined as being the proximal cognitive state prior to deciding to act, this empirical success is comforting.)

Disadvantages of Intentions Models

First, intentions can change, especially for relatively distal or complex behaviors. As such, the intent to start a business is far from persistent. However, this generates a golden opportunity for researchers to study the changes in entrepreneurial intentions. Changing intentions is relatively unexplored in any domain; the entrepreneurship domain should prove especially useful in explicating the underpinnings of changing intentions.

Second, there still is some debate over the direction of causality. In particular, intentions could be seen as simply another attitude, just more visible. Robinson et al. (1991) has argued for the Allportian approach where behavior depends on a troika of critical attitudes: Affective, cognitive and conative [essentially intent], even developing a much-underused measure of entrepreneurial attitudes (Robinson et al., 1991).

However, entrepreneurial intentions are not limited to the decision to launch a new venture. First of all, intentions can be more fine-grained, in that intentionality is focused on more specific elements of a new venture: Intent to grow rapidly or not (Davidsson, 1991)? Intent toward using a specific distribution channel? Second, this also suggests that there are intentional processes that come into play after the venture is launched.

Implementation Intentions

A relatively unresearched area lies in the work of Gollwitzer and Brandstatter (1997) and others that investigates implementation intentions. Strong intentions toward implementing an intended strategy may play a more significant role than we might think. Another decision model of this type is Beach's image theory (1990) where it is argued that decision-makers envision the "image" of the intended behavior or goal, then they envision how to get there. An interesting variation that has already attracted attention is Saras Sarasvarthy's (a protégé of Herbert Simon) notion of "effectuation" as a theory of firm design (1998, 2001). Her effectuation model takes us quite a long way down this intriguing path.

Not only have these two topics not been widely deployed to study entrepreneurial activity, entrepreneurial activity seems an excellent vehicle for testing both of these. For example, we know relatively little about the temporal dimension, thus we can explore intentions toward *when* a prospective entrepreneur might undertake an intended venture (West and Meyer, 1997) and how they enact temporal issues (Fischer et al., 1997).

Nascency

For a simple example, consider nascent entrepreneurs (i.e., those farther along than merely potential but not yet fully launched). Their launch is under way, but not yet completed, so they are still facing numerous complex decisions about future intentional behaviors. Of course, even a long-established entrepreneur faces many complex decisions but entrepreneurial nascency may impose a somewhat more structured set of issues. Research based on the rich data sets compiled by the Entrepreneurial Research Consortium (ERC) has begun, but one must suspect that we will find some intriguing results – and not a few surprises.

"Vision"?

Let us step back from the relatively narrow construct of intentions and consider the concept of "vision". Vision is a broader construct than intent that encompasses a much richer mental model of what the intended vision is – and will be. Bird (unpublished) takes an essentially Aristotelian approach and indeed found a rich web of qualitative influences that underlay the entrepreneurs' vision (see also Ward, 1993). Robert Baum and colleagues have developed a more quantitative view of entrepreneurial vision (Baum et al., 1998, 2001). This approach incorporates the influence of goals, particularly Locke's approach toward goals and goal-setting theory.

Growth Motivation

Above we alluded to the intent to grow a venture (as opposed to launching it). Per Davidsson took the first deep look into this (1991) and found the intent to "continue" venturing was just as amenable to formal intentions models. Subsequently, Davidsson and his colleagues such as Frederic Delmar (1999, 2000) and Johan Wiklund (Wiklund and Shepherd, 2000) have continued to push their research into growth motivation from this social psychological perspective.

Social Influences

Finally, we have already noted many times that social norms and other extra-personal influences play a striking role in human decision making, i.e., modeling effects that help us perceive ourselves as entrepreneurs (or not). Entrepreneurial phenomena are no different with respect to the cognitive forces beyond the individual.

Let us consider the "entrepreneurial organization". Covin and Slevin (1991) argue persuasively that the entrepreneurial firm is proactive, innovative and risk-accepting. We have done relatively little to understand the cognitive aspects behind strategic behaviors such as these (Kuratko et al., 1993; Krueger and Brazeal, 1994; Brazeal and Herbert, 1999).

For example, Kassicieh (1997) found in federal research labs, a supportive organization may be important but not unless lab personnel *perceive* it as truly supportive. Perceived support outweighed individual innovativeness as a predictor of their innovativeness. But, from whence do these perceptions of a supportive environment arise?

Mariann Jelinek (Jelinek and Litterer, 1995) used her extensive research into organizational innovativeness [with Schoonhoven and others] to paint a striking picture of what an entrepreneurial organization really looks like. One particularly powerful discovery was that we need not find many entrepreneurial individuals in a highly entrepreneurial organization. Perhaps paradoxically, there may be corporate mavericks who "go it alone" but for the organization as a whole to be truly entrepreneurial, successful corporate entrepreneurs often operate much less independently. For example, they often seek "buy-in" from other key players such as a source of needed resources. This, of course, also requires a supportive, entrepreneurship-friendly organizational setting that members perceive as truly supportive.

Social Cognition

Even a solo entrepreneur does not operate in a vacuum. As Granovetter pointed out, almost all of economic activity is irretrievably embedded in its social context. Leo-Paul Dana has studied a wide array of economies around the world and finds that "opportunity" is very much culture-dependent (1995).

One obvious impact is through the social norms antecedent of intentions, but social cues can also affect perceptions of self-efficacy. However, there is a deeper issue: In a social setting the attitudes, beliefs and intentions of a team (or larger group) need not reflect simply the 'average' perceptions of the team members. A team's beliefs, attitudes and intentions may differ significantly from those of the team's members (once again, modeling effects need to be better explored). The rich, far-ranging literature on social cognition has not been particularly applied to the entrepreneurship domain despite its promise (Shepherd and Krueger, 2002).

Cognitive Infrastructure

The intentions perspective affords us important insights into how to nurture the entrepreneurial potential of an organization or a community. *Again*: Entrepreneurial potential depends on the quantity and quality of potential entrepreneurs (Krueger and Brazeal, 1994). Increasing the quality and quantity of potential entrepreneurs requires increasing the quality and quantity of entrepreneurial thinking. Thus, the entrepreneurial organization must operate in directions that support its members in perceiving more – and better – opportunities. For example, encouraging corporate entrepreneurship is supported by beliefs and activities that foster internal entrepreneurs to see intrapreneurship as desirable and feasible (Kuratko et al., 1993; Brazeal and Herbert, 1999). For example, it is reasonable to assume that modeling effects are critical – that the impact of mentors and role models serve (in part) to enhance processes of modeling entrepreneurial behavior and attitudes (Carsrud et al., 1987; Krueger, 2000; Shepherd and Krueger, 2002).

The entrepreneurial organization does require a tangible infrastructure of resources and mechanisms that support entrepreneurial activities, yet field research shows that is clearly insufficient to yield significant levels of entrepreneurship (e.g., Kassicieh et al., 1996). Rather, organization members must perceive that tangible infrastructure as supportive (Kuratko et al., 1993; Krueger and Brazeal, 1994; Brazeal and Herbert, 1999). It is not enough to provide the "proper" reward system. What if organization members perceive that reward system as being actually hostile to entrepreneurship?

This implies that organizations (or, for that matter, communities) need to provide and develop a "cognitive infrastructure" that nurtures entrepreneurial thinking. The intentions perspective that implies mechanisms that increase the quantity and quality of perceived opportunities. That requires mechanisms that broaden the set of possibilities that organization members perceive as feasible and as desirable. In turn, that suggests that organizations seek to address each of the key antecedents: Personal attitude, social norms, self-efficacy and collective efficacy (Krueger, 2000).

There is immense potential in digging deeper into this cognitive infrastructure behind entrepreneurship within organizations. Understanding how to stimulate entrepreneurial thinking in teams or in an organization is one key element needed to promote more entrepreneurial organizations (Brazeal, 1993; Kuratko et al., 1993; Krueger and Brazeal, 1994; Brazeal and Herbert, 1999). This seems a most fruitful avenue for further study as researchers can test the impact of various strategic prescriptions on these key antecedents. For example, does the presence of a strong champion enhance perceptions of efficacy (e.g., by modeling successful behavior) or enhance social norms (e.g., by demonstrating that the organization does support entrepreneurial activity)? Similarly, shortfalls in entrepreneurial activity may be diagnosed by testing these same antecedents.

BELIEF STRUCTURES: PERCEPTIONS OF EFFICACY

If underneath the intentionality of opportunity (and thus entrepreneurial) emergence are critical antecedents, it becomes critical to explore the sources of those antecedents. While we have already addressed the role of experience-driven perceptions, let us delve deeper into one specific antecedent, perceived feasibility, and the belief structure that drives it: Bandura's construct of self-efficacy.

One powerful attitude that drives human decision making is our sense of competence, our belief that we can execute a target behavior (Bandura, 1986, 1995). Bandura would argue that sizeable changes in self-efficacy reflect cognitive change at a very deep level. Self-efficacy is best influenced by direct mastery experiences, however, vicarious learning (e.g., behavioral modeling) is also well-documented. Since Bandura proposed self-efficacy theory over 20 years ago, its research literature has become broad and deep. Of late, entrepreneurship research has increasingly taken advantage of self-efficacy theory.

While Bandura's description of the self-efficacious individual (optimistically persistent) sounds as though he is referring to entrepreneurs, the first inkling of self-efficacy's importance came from Robert Scherer and his associates (1989) who found that parents' impact on their children's entrepreneurial attitudes depended on whether they influenced the children's sense of entrepreneurial competence. Alan Carsrud and colleagues (1987) came to similar conclusions about role models and mentors, suggesting that changing critical attitudes such as self-efficacy perceptions is an important element in promoting entrepreneurial thinking.

Key Conceptual Work

Even earlier, Shapero and Sokol (1975, 1982) had discussed the centrality of perceived feasibility in the judgment that a potential opportunity is personally credible, though without using the term self-efficacy. As noted above, Dutton and Jackson's model (1987) of perceived opportunity included perceived controllability as one of two key antecedents. This led to operationalizing Shapero's model of the entrepreneurial event with self-efficacy as the key antecedent of perceived feasibility (Krueger and Brazeal, 1994).

While interest was slow to increase in using self-efficacy in entrepreneurship (Krueger, 1989; Boyd and Vozikis, 1994), Terrence Brown (1996) proposed a look at self-efficacy regarding resource acquisition, marshalling resources being a crucial element in successful entrepreneurship. This narrower domain illustrates the need to focus on the critical dimensions of entrepreneurial competencies. While Brown focused on a specific dimension, Alex DeNoble and associates (1999) developed a measure to tap multiple entrepreneurial competencies while Chen and colleagues' (1998) measure is broader still. Although Bandura considers self-efficacy as being task-specific, measures of general (not task-specific) self-efficacy have been proposed and validated; Robert Baron argues that this broadest conception of entrepreneurial competency should also be useful.

Key Empirical Work

While self-efficacy was originally conceived as a Person X Situation variable, some scholars have explored self-efficacy as a person variable. Although the term self-efficacy was not used, an interesting study by Gaylen Chandler and Erik Jansen (1992) developed and tested a measure of perceived competence to great success: Entrepreneurs *do* perceive themselves as highly competent. More recently, Baron did find that entrepreneurs score higher on a measure of general self-efficacy. Gatewood and colleagues (2002) explored links between perceived ability and expectancies. These latter three studies reinforce the potency of self-efficacy as a useful construct in this domain, but they also suggest that we need to be careful that the theoretical basis for research is aligned with the empirical methods that we employ. An excellent example of this is the recent article by Brown and colleagues where they developed and tested a useful instrument that should prove quite useful (Brown, Davidsson and Wiklund, 2001).

The work of Scherer, of Shapero, and of Dutton and Jackson led to a major experimental study that directly tested the impact of self-efficacy on opportunity and threat perceptions and on risk taking (Krueger, 1989; Krueger and Dickson, 1994). This study found that self-efficacy significantly influenced opportunity and threat perceptions [in opposite directions]; in turn, opportunity and threat perceptions influenced risk taking in two different tasks. More important, the findings show that the impact of self-efficacy was task-specific; that is, despite the two tasks being highly similar, self-efficacy on one task did not influence self-efficacy on the other.

Measurement is important and challenges remain in measuring entrepreneurial self-efficacy. Chen and colleagues (1998) developed a self-efficacy instrument that attempts to capture the key dimensions of entrepreneurial competency. DeNoble and colleagues (1999) developed an instrument that attempts to capture a narrower notion of entrepreneurial competency that focuses less on managerial tasks. Both instruments appear psychometrically sound and demonstrate considerable validity. For example, participants in business plan competitions score significantly higher on entrepreneurial self-efficacy (Neupert, Krueger and Chua, 2000). Similarly, students in entrepreneurship classes demonstrate small, but significant, positive changes in entrepreneurial self-efficacy even over a semester (Krueger, 2001b).

Collective Efficacy

Bandura argues there is another important aspect of efficacy perceptions: Collective efficacy, one's judgment that the group (or team or organization) is capable of executing the target behavior. Brazeal and Herbert (1999) might argue that in an organizational setting (such as corporate entrepreneurship) we should find that perceptions of collective efficacy would become a significant antecedent of perceived feasibility, perhaps an even more important antecedent. As the brief section above on social cognition suggests, measurement of collective efficacy may be fraught with peril (e.g., Shepherd and Krueger, 2002), but should yield important results for understanding (and assisting) entrepreneurial activity at a less individual level. This should prove particularly useful in dealing with domains such as social ventures (e.g., Michael Lounsbury's 1997 article on collective entrepreneurship in a nonprofit setting).

Future Directions

However, there still remains considerable work ahead in developing (and deploying) more refined self-efficacy measures. Terrence Brown's example of developing a reliable, valid measure of a more specific competency fits well with the conception of self-efficacy as task-specific; other competencies are worthy of similar analysis. We should also assess the relative impact of more task-specific measures and of general self-efficacy (the latter offers an opportunity to identify the relative impact of measures that are relatively situation-specific versus relatively cross-situational).

Finally, we should also test the relationship between levels and changes in self-efficacy with deeper cognitive structures. If Bandura is correct, major shifts in self-efficacy should be associated with significant change in scripts and maps [see Section 7]. For example, is a high level of self-efficacy at opportunity recognition associated with evidence of an expert script for opportunity recognition? In many ways, the entrepreneurship domain should prove ideal for testing these as yet untested relationships.

BELIEF STRUCTURES: INDIVIDUAL DIFFERENCES?

If, as Baron suggests, generalized self-efficacy also characterizes the entrepreneur, then that suggests there is indeed a role to play for individual differences. In fact, cognition research brings the entrepreneur back into entrepreneurship in productive new directions. The history of our field is littered with studies that try to identify stable personality traits that characterize entrepreneurs. Even to this day, there is a lingering sense that if entrepreneurs are such special people, we should be able to distinguish between entrepreneurs and non-entrepreneurs. However, as Kelly Shaver has long argued, it is difficult to demonstrate stable personality traits that unambiguously explain entrepreneurial activity (such as entrepreneurial thinking), let alone predict it.

On the other hand, Robert Baron reminds us that individual differences comprise much more than personality traits. As we argued at the outset, cognition theory and research offer a way to return the entrepreneur to entrepreneurship. That is, even if the "entrepreneurial personality" is illusive we can fruitfully seek to identify non-personality individual differences in entrepreneurial thinking.

Part of this derives from key phenomena related to entrepreneurial thinking are not person variables, but person x situation variables (intentions, self-efficacy, etc.) Moreover, characteristics that apparently identify entrepreneurs are also shared by other populations – such as successful managers (Shaver and Scott, 1992). It might also be useful to focus on more specific, more clearly-defined variables (such as opportunity perception, rather than entrepreneurship *per se*) where there is good *theoretical* reason for a personal characteristic to affect entrepreneurial thinking (Gartner, 1989).

There is *also* evidence that personality-type measures can have indirect effects such as moderating the relationship between two other key constructs. For example, upper echelon theory (Hambrick and Mason, 1984; Miller and Toulouse, 1986) argues that the characteristics of top managers may not be directly associated with key organizational outcomes, but there might be indirect (e.g., moderating) effects.

We will thus focus here on a few selected variables that theory would suggest as having at least the potential for significantly influencing entrepreneurial thinking.

A Personal Entrepreneurial Orientation?

Covin and Slevin (1991) contend that an entrepreneurial firm exhibits three key characteristics: Innovativeness, proactiveness and risk taking. Their theory would suggest that high levels of entrepreneurial thinking should be associated with individual measures that correspond to these dimensions. Recent work (Krueger, 1999) found that measures of opportunity perception did correlate with such measures on all three dimensions.

Innovativeness – An attitude favoring new ideas and divergent thinking should be a positive for seeing new opportunities. Buttner and Gryskiewicz (1993) found that entrepreneurs tended to score as more innovative. However, there is much more fertile ground for future research, especially linking this to other aspects of creativity.

Proactiveness – While Jill Kickul and Lisa Gundry (2002) found interesting associations between proactiveness and entrepreneurial activity, we need more theory to guide us regarding entrepreneurial thinking. Seligman's learned optimism (1990) has been consistently associated with proactive goal-directed behavior, but other measures should be worth testing. Action-taking is an important frontier we need to explore.

Risk Taking – Human risk taking is highly situational and driven by risk perceptions, thus a general measure of risk taking is likely to be highly misleading (March and Shapira, 1987; Palich and Bagby, 1995; Saravathy et al., 1998; Simon et al., 2000). Robert Brockhaus's landmark study (1986) found that entrepreneurs tend to have only moderate risk-taking propensity – just like most of us. Entrepreneurs are better described as accepting Knightian uncertainty, a seemingly critical aspect of accepting a new opportunity. As such, Covin and Slevin here refer more to risk acceptance. Finally, we also have considerable evidence that risk taking is strongly associated with opportunity and threat perceptions, especially in less-novel situations where decision makers have signals about their competence and thus the feasibility of that possible opportunity (Krueger and Dickson, 1994).

Propensity to Act

Shapero's model (1975, 1982) argues that entrepreneurial thinking should include some sort of propensity to take action on new opportunities (thus overlapping "proactiveness", above), suggesting that it may be difficult to perceive a potential opportunity as credible and personally-viable if there is no propensity to act. A lower level of propensity to act might result in decision makers perceiving (and acting upon) smaller, less discontinuous opportunities. Shapero proposed locus of control as a proxy for propensity to act, other research has employed desire for control (Krueger, 1993a) and Seligman's learned optimism (Krueger et al., 2000). In both cases, propensity to act was a significant predictor of entrepreneurial intentions.

Dark Side?

Finally, we would be remiss if we did not consider individual characteristics that might constrain the perception of opportunities. The obvious starting point is Kets de Vries's (1985) "dark side of entrepreneurship" which illustrates how entrepreneurs can emerge through psychodynamic processes that need not be fully functional. That is, the forces that helped mold them into entrepreneurs may also bias their perceptions.

On the other hand, there is also growing research that suggests that competent decision making tends to reflect more constructive patterns of thinking (e.g., Epstein's notion of "constructive thinking"). For example, Katz (1992) found that "recognized cognitive heuristic processes" are inherent in career choices. Competent entrepreneurial thinking is already influenced by common decision biases. Busenitz and Barney (1997) show that entrepreneurs are no different than others in being vulnerable to Kahneman/Tversky-type biases such as illusion of control, the availability heuristic, etc. However, Epstein (1998) shows there are other biases that can affect decision making competence, such as categorical ["black and white"] thinking, magical thinking, and the like. Once again, entrepreneurial thinking might prove the ideal domain for testing the impact of constructive thinking and its subscales.

DEEPER STRUCTURES

However, if critical attitudes such as self-efficacy lie beneath the intentions, what lies beneath intentions? In Simon's terms, we move now from the "semantic" level of knowledge representation to the "symbolic" level and exploring how these levels interact.

Cognitive science has long shown how attitudes and beliefs that are expressed on the surface also reflect their genesis in deeper structures of how we represent knowledge and how knowledge is interrelated. That is, knowledge does not exist just as discrete "data", but knowledge is interconnected. Think of it as a relational database where data entries include how each datum is linked to other data. Again, this suggests that skillful application of theory and methods relating to pattern recognition could prove extremely illuminating.

It is critical to understand how these various cognitive phenomena are interconnected. Barbara Bird argued early on (1992 and 1997) that entrepreneurs' intentions are driven by deeper structures such as schema and schemata. More important, though, is that this under-researched arena could prove immensely fruitful, not just for research but also for enhancing our ability to stimulate entrepreneurial thinking at a very deep level.

Again, this is much more than metaphor. These deeper structures are powerful influences on how we think. If we are to enhance entrepreneurial thinking beyond a superficial level, we need to help entrepreneurs change these deeper structures in appropriate directions.

Schemata

Probably the earliest effort to explore a deeper structure underneath entrepreneurial thinking was by Stapleton (Stapleton and Stapleton, 1996) who identified how entrepreneurs differed in terms of schemata (cognitive mechanisms that categorize incoming information). More important, this research appears to show that the type of training influences the development of more entrepreneurial schemata.

Scripts

This area has seen the most development and the most fruitful results. The work of Ron Mitchell and Chesteen (1995) and associates has been highly visible, even outside the field of entrepreneurship (e.g., Mitchell et al., 2000). The key trigger for this whole approach has been the realization that experts think differently than novices. How experts become experts is reflected in the development of an "expert" script. (A script is, as its name suggests, a cognitive mechanism that comprises the key elements in a decision situation and the likely ordering of events.)

The "expert" script can differ from the "novice" script in any number of ways: It can be more complex but is often more parsimonious. In most cases, the knowledge involved will differ (the obvious case being that experts will typically have more accurate information). We cannot readily identify a script directly, but we can recognize the degree to which an expert (or novice) script is present. We do so by identifying critical cues that signal expertise.

Mitchell's original work focused primarily on differences between expert and novice scripts regarding entrepreneurship writ large (1995). However, he and his colleagues have continued by identifying expert scripts for subprocesses (e.g., expert script for marshalling resources or for identifying opportunities, etc.) As we shall see in the next section, this has powerful implications.

Connie Marie Gaglio and Jerome Katz (2001) approach the same topic of entrepreneurial scripts but from the perspective of seeking opportunity, to use Kirzner's (1982) felicitous term, entrepreneurial "alertness." Again, an overall expert script is a valuable tool, but drilling down to more specific cognitive processes (e.g., counterfactual thinking) affords the researcher a look at the most fundamental aspects of entrepreneurial (or non-entrepreneurial) thinking. This too has powerful implications for teaching and training.

Maps

Finally, cognitive maps (or causal maps) have already proven a powerful tool in strategic management (e.g., Huff, 1990) and elsewhere in management (e.g., Bougon et al., 1977). This tool has not been widely deployed in entrepreneurship research (Russell, 1999). One recent study by Jenkins and Johnson (1997) cleverly links the cognitive maps of entrepreneurs to measures of intention. Given the evidence from Mitchell and his colleagues that entrepreneurial training can measurably change an individual's scripts toward those of an expert, so too should we see measurable changes in an entrepreneur's (nascent or otherwise) maps. (We might also find it useful to see how maps and scripts relate to each other. Entrepreneurship could prove an ideal venue for such research that would offer a contribution far beyond entrepreneurship research.)

ENTREPRENEURIAL LEARNING

One reason that we should care about these deeper structures is that we are to truly stimulate entrepreneurial thinking in a fundamental way, then it is likely that there will be important changes in these deeper structures, as they reflect how we represent and process information. As we noted in regard to self-efficacy, mere transfer of information is insufficient to fundamentally alter behavior. This has important implications for *learning* how to think entrepreneurially.

What do entrepreneurs need to learn? How do they best learn that knowledge and skills? For example, it seems reasonable that entrepreneurs need to learn how to identify opportunities. A tremendous amount of descriptive research has delved into entrepreneurship education, though there is an increasing interest in theory-driven research (similar to the state of research into opportunity recognition). This area cries out for extensive theory-driven research. However, we have less theory to guide us in studying entrepreneurial learning – or do we?

"Filling a Pail" or "Lighting a Fire"?

There are two dominant paradigms in education. The traditional approach focuses on fact-based learning (includes rote memorization, repetitive drilling and similar mechanisms). Instructors typically provide the models and framework for knowledge being transferred to students. *Constructivism* argues for situated learning where students acquire knowledge but also have to develop their own ways of organizing the knowledge (building and changing their own mental models to represent knowledge). "Learning the answers" versus "finding the questions" is one way to think about the difference or one might use the words of W.B. Yeats paraphrased in the subhead above. Entrepreneurship educators tend to fall into the second camp.

Traditional methods provide greater control to the instructor and can appear as more efficient for large groups of students. Constructivistic methods tend to be much more student-centered, but this actually reflects how humans actually learn in daily life: By trial and error in a social setting. Moreover, if one wishes to change deeper cognitive structures such as scripts, then more student-centered learning is imperative.

For example, Albert Bandura's Social Learning Theory suggests an iterative process by which deeply held beliefs and attitudes co-evolve as learners actively acquire, process and organize new knowledge. Supporting this is another interesting wrinkle: The strong evidence that entrepreneurs tend to perceive themselves as self-directed learners (Guglielmino and Klatt, 1993).

Thomas Monroy was perhaps first to articulate that traditional classroom methods were not only less frequently used in entrepreneurship classes but they probably are less effective than more experiential approaches (Monroy, 1995). Rather we tend to emphasize "problem-based learning" where learners focus on real-world issues, a focus that is a staple of most entrepreneurship courses. Indeed, the most popular and successful training techniques used in entrepreneurship tend to strongly reflect the constructivistic model: Living cases (e.g., SBI), business plans, shadowing, etc. (Krueger and Hamilton, 1996).

Experiences

Again, if developing entrepreneurial thinking requires changes in deeper cognitive structures, then we have many opportunities to research the specific impacts of different training activities and other experiences. Prior experience certainly influences perception of future opportunities (Shane, 2000). The Center for

Creative Leadership has found that top managers share a surprisingly small set of developmental experiences and an even smaller set of the lessons learned (McCall et al., 1988). We might profitably reprise that research for entrepreneurs. For example, we have some evidence that growing up in a family business influences attitudes and intentions toward entrepreneurship (Krueger, 1993b; Delmar, 2000).

Formal training/teaching does seem to matter. Nicole Peterson's thesis work found that an entrepreneurial training program significantly influenced the various antecedents of entrepreneurial attitudes and intentions (Peterson and Kennedy, 2002). Even formal coursework (Cox, 1996; Krueger, 2001b) appears to have a small but measurable impact on critical beliefs (e.g., self-efficacy) and attitudes (including intent). This could be readily extended to more fine-grained analyses as such acquisition of specific skills.

Skills

All of this begs the question of what specific kinds of skills, what specific kinds of training and what specific kinds of experiences are truly transformative in terms of enhancing entrepreneurial thinking. For example, Robert Baum and colleagues (Baum et al., 2001) found that venture growth depended on both specific motivations and specific skills. Monroy (1995) argued for an Inputs–Throughputs–Outputs model for assessing entrepreneurial education where "throughputs" emphasize the changes between output and input *and* the mechanisms by which change was induced.

Education researchers argue that skills acquisition is a critical phenomenon, whether acquired via hands-on mastery or vicarious learning through behavioral modeling. Self-efficacy theory suggests that just acquiring skills is not enough to fundamentally change how we think, it also requires believing in those skills (perceived efficacy versus actual efficacy). However, Bandura himself would also argue that acquiring the correct skills is also imperative for long-term, sustained change in our thought processes. In the entrepreneurship domain, Lanny Herron (e.g., 1993) and colleagues have identified skills that appear to give the most impact on subsequent entrepreneurial behavior. Fiet and Barney (2002) show that certain key skills related to identifying highly-credible opportunities can be identified and taught. There are also surprises in the skills that are beneficial to entrepreneurs. For example, Baron and Markman found that the ability to apply social skills (essentially EQ) is quite invaluable (2000).

Finally, let us return to the issue of how learning processes can change deep mental models in the direction of better entrepreneurial thinking, whether in terms of learning to see more/better opportunities or to see oneself as an entrepreneur (or, as we have noted, both). Both Baron (2000b) and Gaglio (2002) demonstrate how the cognitive mechanism of counterfactual reasoning is a potent lever for stimulating students to question their existing mental models. Similarly, at the University of Victoria, Ron Mitchell, Eric Morse,

Brock Smith and Brian MacKenzie have developed a pedagogy that heavily emphasizes helping students acquire expert scripts (2000). This clearly suggests that measures of deep structures, whether scripts or maps or other possibilities, can be usefully deployed to research how entrepreneurial thinking changes across a training program (Mitchell et al., 2000; Krueger, 2001b). Similarly, James Fiet and his colleagues have focused their teaching and training on transferring the key opportunity-identification skills he has elucidated.

More Directions for Future Research

Despite the signal honor of being asked to write this chapter, it would be fatuous – if not arrogant – to predict the most fruitful directions for future research. The history of research in both cognitive science and entrepreneurship studies suggests that many surprises lie in store for researchers. I would also argue strenuously that the long-term health of the field of entrepreneurship studies rests in research that contributes to other fields. For example, we know relatively little about how intentions change and even less about intentions about the timing of behavior. Given that entrepreneurial intentions change quite significantly over time, entrepreneurship might well prove an ideal for exploring these questions – to the benefit of intentions researchers across the board.

   Having said that, what we have discovered so far does seem instructive. That is, the answers uncovered to date have, as always happens in science, also uncovered even more intriguing questions – and good places to start. In this chapter, it has seemed useful to point out questions with great potential as we explored the disparate threads of entrepreneurial cognition. However, let us consider some additional questions that seem especially worth pursuing.

Are opportunities "discovered" or "enacted"?

As suggested at the outset, there is at least a middling debate over whether opportunities are discovered or enacted. Given that perceptions play a critical role either way, studying entrepreneurial cognitions is likely to be quite illuminating. That is, cognition research should be able to assess the relative contributions of both perspectives. We should also be able to dig deeper into the question of whether we should distinguish between the quality and the quantity of entrepreneurial thinking – what leads to perceiving more opportunities? What leads to perceiving better opportunities?

Are there personality-like effects? If so, how do they operate (specifically)?

Above we suggested that there should be useful results from research into characteristics that influence entrepreneurial thinking indirectly (e.g., moderator effects). Research that is much more fine-grained (e.g., does an extrovert prefer an outside sales force while introverts prefer selling through catalogs?) Are entrepreneurs more cognitively complex?

Do entrepreneurs adapt cognitively?

Conventional wisdom finally appears to have swung in favor of the conclusion that entrepreneurs are "made" not "born." If that is true, then a focus on entrepreneurial thinking should help us understand at a very deep level how entrepreneurs are "made." (We might also find that it is not just an adaptive process where individuals learn to think more entrepreneurially, but also a selection process wherein those who think less entrepreneurially are weeded out (Krueger, 2001b).)

How do specific learning experiences translate into specific decisions?

Again, more fine-grained analysis could prove quite powerful (see Cox, 1996; Peterson and Kennedy, 2002). For example, high-tech opportunities merit more consideration (Corbett, 2002). Different experiences should yield different results; however, cognition-based studies can provide strong theory to identify useful (and testable) hypotheses. A large enough body of such findings could give us a "celestial mechanics" guidebook for tailoring specific experiences to encourage specific results. For example, what are the critical training processes (and content) to enhance knowledge and skills necessary for a "born global" firm?

How to translate findings into practice/teaching?

Similarly, we can take these findings to design training programs and even coursework. I refer again to the efforts at the University of Victoria which emphasize helping students develop decision scripts closer to those employed by experts. Or, consider how Guth and his colleagues transformed research (Guth et al., 1991) to successful practice (Mezias et al., 2001). How do we best train people to perceive themselves as entrepreneurial? How do we best train people to see personally-credible opportunities?

What other tools might be usefully applied to the entrepreneurship domain?

Not only have we merely begun to scratch the surface of models and theories from cognition, there are more tools that we can deploy toward a better understanding. We have already mentioned Baron's suggestion of signal detection theory (for threshold phenomena). Another example might be the Brunswik lens. The various "flavors" of counterfactual thinking need more analysis (Gaglio, 2002).

However, the key is to skillfully adapt theories and methods and test their value in understanding entrepreneurial thinking; the potential for useful research using cognition models is immense. For example, if entrepreneurs perceive opportunities in patterns of signals and cues from the environment, then we need to use the well-established theory and methods that cognitive science has developed – and use it rigorously.

What about entrepreneurial activity within organizations (e.g., corporate entrepreneurship)?

Deborah Brazeal and Ted Herbert (1999) echo the earlier assertions of Kuratko et al. (1993), Shapero (1982), Hodgkinson (1997), Guth et al. (1991) and Mezias et al. (2001) that corporate entrepreneurs must think entrepreneurially, maybe even more so because of organizational obstacles. Those barriers might even render corporate entrepreneurship as the ideal setting for research into entrepreneurial thinking. Certainly, recent work argues that different facets of the cognitive infrastructure (and tangible infrastructure) have a differential influence upon critical attitudes (Shepherd and Krueger, 2002).

What other domains of entrepreneurial activity should we explore in terms of understanding how entrepreneurial thinking develops?

Along those same lines, we have seen even less research into entrepreneurial thinking in related domains: Franchising, family business, nonprofit or social entrepreneurship, even multilevel marketing. (Successful MLM requires training those in your downline to be more entrepreneurial, hence this might be another ideal domain.)

"Push" or "necessity" entrepreneurs may differ from "opportunity" or "pull" entrepreneurs. For example, one would expect that an entrepreneur pushed into self-employment by necessity would focus first on feasibility perceptions whereas an entrepreneur "pulled" by an opportunity would consider desirability perceptions first. This might manifest itself in differences in information-seeking.

Other dimensions of entrepreneurial thinking need more analysis. For example, Teal and Carroll have opened an interesting door into entrepreneurs' moral reasoning (1999). How do cultural norms influence attitudes and intentions (Dana, 1995)?

What other domains of cognitive science, especially cognitive psychology, might we fruitfully explore?

At a recent conference, Robert Baron suggested that we might consider Tory Higgins's regulatory focus theory, and we might revisit signal detection theory. Shepherd and McMullen found some promising evidence of its value (2002). If we are dealing with threshold phenomena (recall the earlier mention of set theoretic considerations), then we need something akin to SDT to properly assess phenomena such as categorization.

We might continue exploring temporal dimensions of entrepreneurial thinking. Barbara Bird and Page West recently guest edited a special journal issue on this very topic (1997).

I would add that we also need a better empirical understanding of how cognitive phenomena (associated with entrepreneurial cognition) are interrelated across Simon's three levels: Neurological, symbolic and semantic. What "semantic" level cues are associated with "symbolic" level structures underlying opportunity perception? The rich cognitive science literature on pattern recognition could be exploited most fruitfully to address this.

Where might research into entrepreneurial cognition inform other fields?

A field's maturity can often be measured by how much it informs other fields of study, not just borrowing from them. Mitchell's work is beginning to be considered by educational psychologists, but there are many opportunities for entrepreneurial cognition research to contribute elsewhere. For example, work on entrepreneurial intentions should offer new wrinkles to the broader work on intentions.

We certainly should be able to shed considerable light on important, irrevocable ("bet the farm") decisions. Economics has long nibbled at the cognitive aspects of decision making (see Hogarth's (1986) special journal issue and Daniel Kahneman's 2002 Nobel Prize) and "strategic thinking" is now a fast-growing domain of interest in strategic management.

In Conclusion

Several years ago, Ian MacMillan and Jerry Katz suggested that we seek out equally "idiosyncratic milieus" for help in understanding the "idiosyncratic milieu" known as entrepreneurship, a call that this researcher saw as a call to adventure. The suggestions offered above are just the beginning, but I look forward to the ongoing adventure of answering those questions (and the questions those answers will inevitably raise).

If we are ever to truly understand entrepreneurship, it is imperative that we understand the multi-faceted nature of entrepreneurial thinking and of its genesis.

REFERENCES

Ajzen, I. (1987). Attitudes, traits, and actions: Dispositional prediction of behavior in social psychology. *Advances in Experimental Social Psychology*, **20**, 1–63.

Ajzen, I. (1991). The theory of planned behavior. *Organizational Behavior and Human Decision Processes*, **50**, 179–211.

Alvarez, S. and L. Busenitz (2001). The entrepreneurship of resource-based theory. *Journal of Management*, **27**(6), 755–775.

Audi, R. (1993). *Action, Intention, and Reason*. Ithaca, NY: Cornell University Press.

Bagozzi, R. and P. Warshaw (1990). Trying to consume. *Journal of Consumer Research*, **17**(2), 127–140.

Bandura, A. (1986). *The Social Foundations of Thought and Action*. Englewood Cliffs, NJ: Prentice-Hall.

Bandura, A. (1995). Exercise of personal and collective efficacy in changing societies. In A. Bandura (ed.), *Self-efficacy in Changing Societies*. New York: Cambridge University Press.

Baron, R. (1998). Cognitive mechanisms in entrepreneurship: Why and when entrepreneurs think differently than other people. *Journal of Business Venturing*, **13**, 275–294.

Baron, R. (2000a). Psychological perspectives on entrepreneurship: Cognitive and social factors in entrepreneurs' success. *Current Directions in Psychological Science*, **9**(1), 15–18.

Baron, R. (2000b). Counterfactual thinking and venture formation: The potential effects of thinking about "what might have been". *Journal of Business Venturing*, **14**(1), 106–116.

Baron, R. and G. Markman (2000). Beyond social capital: How social skills can enhance entrepreneurs' success. *The Academy of Management Executive*, **14**(1), 106–116.

Baum, J.R., E. Locke and S. Kirkpatrick (1998). A longitudinal study of the relation of vision and vision communication to venture growth in entrepreneurial firms. *Journal of Applied Psychology*, **83**(1), 43–54.

Baum, J.R., E. Locke and K. Smith (2001). A multidimensional model of venture growth. *Academy of Management Journal*, **44**(2), 292–303.

Beach, Lee Roy (1990). *Image Theory*. New York: Wiley.

Bird, B. (1992). The operation of intentions in time: The emergence of the new venture. *Entrepreneurship Theory and Practice*, **17**(1), 11–20.

Bird, B. (2002). What is entrepreneurial vision? Manuscript under review.

Bird, B. and P. West (1997). Time and entrepreneurship. *Entrepreneurship Theory and Practice*, **22**(2), 5–9.

Bougon, M., K. Weick and D. Binkhorst (1977). Cognition in organizations: An analysis of the Utrecht Jazz Orchestra. *Administrative Science Quarterly*, **22**, 606–631.

Boyd, N. and G. Vozikis (1994). The influence of self-efficacy on the development of entrepreneurship. *Entrepreneurship Theory and Practice*, **18**(4), 63–77.

Brazeal, D. (1993). Organizing for internally developed corporate ventures. *Journal of Business Venturing*, **8**, 75–100.

Brazeal, D. and T. Herbert (1999). The genesis of entrepreneurship. *Entrepreneurship Theory and Practice*, **23**(3), 29–46.

Brockhaus, R. and P. Horwitz (1986). The psychology of the entrepreneur. In D. Sexton and R. Smilor (eds.), *The Art and Science of Entrepreneurship*, Cambridge: Ballinger, pp. 25–48.

Brown, T. (1996). Resource orientation, entrepreneurial orientation and growth: How the perception of resource availability affects small firm growth. Unpublished doctoral dissertation, Rutgers University.

Brown, T., P. Davidsson and J. Wiklund (2001). An operationalization of Stevenson's conceptualization of entrepreneurship as opportunity-based firm behavior. *Strategic Management Journal*, **22**(1), 953–968.

Busenitz, L. and J. Barney (1997). Differences between entrepreneurs and managers in large organizations: Biases and heuristics in strategic decision-making. *Journal of Business Venturing*, **12**(1), 9–30.

Busenitz, L. and C.-M. Lau (1996). A cross-cultural cognitive model of new venture creation. *Entrepreneurship Theory and Practice*, **20**(4), 25–39.

Buttner, E.H. and N. Gryskiewicz. Entrepreneurs' problem-solving style: An empirical study using Kirton's adaption/innovation theory. *Journal of Small Business Management*, **32**(1), 22–32.

Carsrud, A., C. Caglio and K. Olm (1987). Entrepreneurs – mentors, networks and successful venture development. *Entrepreneurship Theory and Practice*, **12**(2), 13–18.

Carsrud, A. and N. Krueger (1996). Entrepreneurship and social psychology. In J. Katz (ed), *Advances in Entrepreneurship, Firm Emergence, and Growth*. Greenwich, CT: JAI Press.

Chandler, G. and E. Jansen (1992). The founder's self-assessed competence and venture performance. *Journal of Business Venturing*, **7**(3), 223–236.

Chen, C., P. Greene and A. Crick (1998). Does entrepreneurial self-efficacy distinguish entrepreneurs from managers? *Journal of Business Venturing*, 13(4), 295–316.

Corbett, A. (2002). Recognizing high-tech opportunities: A learning and cognitive approach. Babson-Kauffman Entrepreneurship Research Conference, Boulder, CO, June 2002.

Covin, J. and D. Slevin (1991). A conceptual model of entrepreneurship as firm behavior. *Entrepreneurship Theory and Practice*, 16(1), 7–25.

Cox, L. (1996). The goals and impact of educational interventions in the early stages of entrepreneur career development. Paper presented at the Int-ENT Conference, Nijmegen, Netherlands, July.

Dana, L.-P. (1995). Entrepreneurship in a remote sub-Arctic community. *Entrepreneurship Theory and Practice*, 20(1), 57–72.

Davidsson, P. (1991). Continued entrepreneurship. *Journal of Business Venturing*, 6(6), 405–429.

Delmar, F. (1999). Entrepreneurial growth motivation and actual growth – a longitudinal study. Presented at RENT XIII, London, UK.

Delmar, F. (2000). The psychology of the entrepreneur. In S. Carter and D. Jones Evans (eds.), *Enterprise and Small Business: Principles, Practice and Policy*, pp. 132–154.

DeNoble, A., D. Jung and S. Ehrlich (1999). Entrepreneurial self-efficacy: The development of a measure and its relationship to entrepreneurial action. Paper presented at the Babson Frontiers of Entrepreneurship Research Conference, Columbia, SC, May.

Dickson, P. and J. Giglierano (1986). Missing the boat and sinking the boat: A conceptual model of entrepreneurial risk. *Journal of Marketing*, 50(3), 58–70.

Douglas, E. and D. Shepherd (2000). Entrepreneurship as a utility maximizing response. *Journal of Business Venturing*, 15(3), 231–251.

Dutton, J. and S. Jackson (1987). Categorizing strategic issues: Links to organizational action. *Academy of Management Review*, 12(1), 76–90.

Epstein, S. (1998). *Constructive Thinking: The Key to Emotional Intelligence*. New York: Praeger.

Erickson, T. (2002). Entrepreneurial capital: The emerging venture's most important asset and competitive advantage. *Journal of Business Venturing*, 17(3), 275–290.

Fiet, J. and J. Barney (2002). *The Systematic Search for Entrepreneurial Discoveries*. New York: Quorum.

Fischer, E., A.R. Reuber, M. Hababou, W. Johnson and S. Lee (1997). The role of socially constructed temporal perspectives in the emergence of rapid-growth firms. *Entrepreneurship Theory and Practice*, 22(2), 13–30.

Gaglio, C. (1997). Opportunity identification: Review, critique and suggested research directions. In J. Katz (ed.), *Advances in Entrepreneurship, Firm Emergence and Growth*, 3, 139–202. Greenwich, CT: JAI Press.

Gaglio, C. (2002). The role of mental simulations and counterfactual thinking in the opportunity identification process. *Entrepreneurship Theory and Practice*, 2003.

Gaglio, C. and J. Katz (2001). The psychological basis of opportunity identification: Entrepreneurial alertness. *Small Business Economics*, 16(2), 95–111.

Gartner, W.B. (1989). Some suggestions for research on entrepreneurial traits and characteristics. *Entrepreneurship Theory and Practice*, 14(1), 27–38.

Gatewood, E., K. Shaver and W. Gartner (1995). A longitudinal study of cognitive factors influencing startup behaviors and success at venture creation. *Journal of Business Venturing*, 10(5), 371–391.

Gatewood, E., K. Shaver and W. Gartner (2002). The effects of perceived entrepreneurial ability on task effort, performance and expectancy. *Entrepreneurship Theory and Practice*, forthcoming.

Gollwitzer, P. and V. Brandstatter (1997). Implementation intentions and effective goal pursuit. *Journal of Personality and Social Psychology*, 73(1), 186–199.

Guglielmino, P. and L. Klatt (1993). Entrepreneurs as self-directed learners. *Proceedings*. ICSB World Conference, Las Vegas.

Guth, W., A. Kumaraswamy and M. McErlean (1991). Cognition, enactment and learning in the entrepreneurial process. O. Hagan (ed.), *Frontiers of Entrepreneurship Research*, Pittsburgh: Babson College, pp. 242–253.

Hambrick, D. and P. Mason (1984). Upper echelons: The organization as a reflection of its top managers. *Academy of Management Review*, **9**(2), 193–206.

Herron, L. and R. Robinson (1993). A structural model of the effects of entrepreneurial characteristics on venture performance. *Journal of Business Venturing*, **8**(3), 281–294.

Hey, J. (1984). The economics of optimism and pessimism. *Kyklos*, **37**(2), 181–205.

Hodgkinson, G. (1997). The cognitive analysis of competitive structures: A review and critique. *Human Relations*, **50**(6), 625–654.

Hogarth, R. (1986). Editor's introduction, 'Behavioral foundations of economic theory.' *Journal of Business*, **59**(4, pt 2), S225 *et seq*.

Huff, A.S. (ed.) (1990). *Mapping Strategic Thought*, New York: Wiley.

Jackson, S. and J. Dutton (1988). Discerning threats and opportunities. *Administrative Science Quarterly*, **33**(3), 370–387.

Jelinek, M. and J. Litterer (1995). Toward entrepreneurial organizations: Meeting ambiguity with engagement. *Entrepreneurship Theory and Practice*, **19**(3), 137–168.

Jenkins, M. and G. Johnson (1997). Entrepreneurial intentions and outcomes: A comparative causal mapping study. *Journal of Management Studies*, **34**(6), 895–920.

Kassicieh, S., R. Radosevich and J. Umbarger (1996). A comparative study of entrepreneurship incidence in national laboratories. *Entrepreneurship Theory and Practice*, **20**(3), 33–49.

Katz, J.A. (1992). A psychosocial cognitive model of employment status choice. *Entrepreneurship Theory and Practice*, **17**(1), 29–37.

Katz, J.A. (1993). The dynamics of organizational emergence: A contemporary group formation perspective. *Entrepreneurship Theory and Practice*, **17**(2), 97–101.

Kets de Vries, M.F.R. (1985). The dark side of entrepreneurship. *Harvard Business Review*, **63**(6), 160–167.

Kets de Vries, M.F.R. (1996). The anatomy of the entrepreneur: Clinical observations. *Human Relations*, **49**(7), 853–883.

Kickul, J. and L. Gundry (2002). Prospecting for strategic advantage: The proactive entrepreneurial personality and small firm innovation. *Journal of Small Business Management*, **40**(2), 85–97.

Kirzner, I. (1982). The theory of entrepreneurship in economic growth. In C. Kent et al. (eds.), *The Encyclopedia of Entrepreneurship*, Englewood Cliffs, NJ: Prentice-Hall, pp. 272–276.

Kolvereid, L. (1996). Prediction of employment status choice intentions. *Entrepreneurship Theory and Practice*, **21**(1), 47–57.

Krueger, N. (1989). *The Role of Perceived Self-Efficacy in the Formation of Entrepreneurial Risk Perceptions.* Unpublished dissertation, Ohio State University.

Krueger, N. (1993a). The impact of prior entrepreneurial exposure on perceptions of new venture feasibility and desirability. *Entrepreneurship Theory and Practice*, **18**(1), 5–21.

Krueger, N. (1993b). Growing up entrepreneurial? *Proceedings.* Academy of Management, Atlanta.

Krueger, N. (1999). Identifying growth opportunities. Paper presented at Babson-Kauffman Entrepreneurial Research Conference, Columbia, SC, June.

Krueger, N. (2000). The cognitive infrastructure of opportunity emergence. *Entrepreneurship Theory and Practice*, **24**(3), 5–23.

Krueger, N. (2001a). Opportunity emergence: A fuzzy look at the evolution of strategic vision. Western Academy of Management, Sun Valley.

Krueger, N. (2001b). Adapt or select? Babson-Kauffman Entrepreneurial Research Conference, Jönköping, Sweden.

Krueger, N. and D. Brazeal (1994). Entrepreneurial potential and potential entrepreneurs. *Entrepreneurship Theory and Practice*, **18**(3), 91–104.

Krueger, N. and A. Carsrud (1993). Entrepreneurial intentions: Applying the theory of planned behavior. *Entrepreneurship and Regional Development*, **5**, 315–330.

Krueger, N. and P. Dickson (1994). How believing in ourselves increases risk taking. *Decision Sciences*, **25**(3), 385–400.

Krueger, N. and D. Hamilton (1996). Constructivistic entrepreneurship education. *Proceedings*, Project for Excellence in Entrepreneurship Education, Atlanta.

Krueger, N., M. Reilly and A. Carsrud (2000). Competing models of entrepreneurial intentions. *Journal of Business Venturing*, 15(5/6), 411–532.

Kuratko, D., J. Hornsby, D. Naffziger and R. Montagn (1993). Implement entrepreneurial thinking in established organizations. *SAM Advanced Management Journal*, 58(1), 28–39.

Loomes, G. and R. Sugden (1982). Regret theory: An alternative theory of rational choice under uncertainty. *Economic Journal*, 92, 805–824.

Lopes, L. (1987). Between hope and fear: The psychology of risk. *Advances in Experimental Social Psychology*, 20, 255–295.

Lounsbury, M. (1997). Collective entrepreneurship: The mobilization of college and university recycling coordinators. *Journal of Organizational Change Management*, 11(1): 50–81.

March, J. and Z. Shapira (1987). Managerial perspectives on risk and risk taking. *Management Science*, 33, 1404–1418.

McCall, M., M. Lombardo and A. Morrison (1988). *The Lessons of Experience: How Successful Executives Develop on the Job*. Lexington, MA: Lexington Books.

Mezias, J., P. Grinyer and W. Guth (2001). Changing collective cognition: A process model for strategic change. *Long Range Planning*, 34(1), 71–95.

Miller, D. and J.M. Toulouse (1986). Chief executive personality and corporate strategy and structure in small firms. *Management Science*, 32(11), 1389–1409.

Mitchell, R. and S. Chesteen (1995). Enhancing entrepreneurial expertise: Experiential pedagogy and the new venture expert script. *Simulation and Gaming*, 26(3), 288–306.

Mitchell, R., B. Smith, K. Seawright and E. Morse (2000). Cross-cultural cognitions and the venture creation decision. *Academy of Management Journal*, 43(5), 974–993.

Monroy, T. (1995). Getting closer to a descriptive model of entrepreneurship education. In T. Monroy, J. Reichert and F. Hoy (eds.), *The Art and Science of Entrepreneurship Education*, MES: Berea, Ohio, Vol. III, pp. 205–217.

Neupert, K., N. Krueger and B.L. Chua (2000). Entrepreneurial Self-Efficacy and its Relationship to Business Plan Competitions: An International Examination, 2nd McGill Conference on International Entrepreneurship, Montreal, September 2000.

Palich, L. and D.R. Bagby (1995). Using cognitive theory to explain entrepreneurial risk taking: Challenging conventional wisdom. *Journal of Business Venturing*, 10(6), 425–438.

Peterson, N. and J. Kennedy (2003). The impact of entrepreneurial training on entrepreneurial beliefs. *Entrepreneurship Theory and Practice*, forthcoming.

Reitan, B. (1997). Where do we learn that entrepreneurship is feasible, desirable and profitable? Paper presented at ICSB World Conference, San Francisco, June.

Robinson, P., D. Stimpson, J. Huefner and K. Hunt (1991). An attitude approach to the prediction of entrepreneurship. *Entrepreneurship Theory and Practice*, 15(4), 13–31.

Russell, R. (1999). Developing a process model of intrapreneurial systems: A cognitive mapping approach. *Entrepreneurship Theory and Practice*, 23(3), 65–84.

Sarasvathy, S. (2001). Causation and effectuation: Toward a theoretical shift from economic inevitability to entrepreneurial contingency. *Academy of Management Review*, 26(2), 243–263.

Sarasvathy S., H. Simon and L. Lave (1998). Perceiving and managing business risks: Differences between entrepreneurs and bankers. *Journal of Economic Behavior and Organizations*, 33(2), 207–225.

Scherer, R., J. Adams, S. Carley and F. Wiebe (1989). Role model performance effects on development of entrepreneurship. *Entrepreneurship Theory and Practice*, 13(3), 53–72.

Seligman, M. (1990). *Learned Optimism*. New York: Knopf.

Shane, S. (2000). Prior knowledge and the discovery of entrepreneurial opportunities. *Organization Science*, 11, 448–469.

Shapero, A. (1975). The displaced, uncomfortable entrepreneur. *Psychology Today*, 8, 83–88.

Shapero, A. (1985). Why entrepreneurship? *Journal of Small Business Management*, October, 23(4), 1–5.

Shapero, A. and L. Sokol (1982). Some social dimensions of entrepreneurship. In C. Kent, D. Sexton and K. Vesper (eds.), *The Encyclopedia of Entrepreneurship*. Englewood Cliffs, NJ: Prentice-Hall, pp. 72–90.

Shaver, K. and L. Scott (1992). Person, process and choice: The psychology of new venture creation. *Entrepreneurship Theory and Practice*, 16(2), 23–46.

Shepherd, D. (1999). Venture capitalists' introspection: A comparison of "in use" and "espoused" decision policies. *Journal of Small Business Management*, 37(2), 76–87.

Shepherd, D. and E. Douglas (1997). Entrepreneurial attitudes and intentions in career decision makers. Paper presented at ICSB World Conference, San Francisco, June 1997.

Shepherd, D. and N. Krueger (2002). Cognition, entrepreneurship and teams: An intentions-based model of entrepreneurial teams' social cognition. *Entrepreneurship Theory and Practice*, 27(2), 167–185.

Shepherd, D. and J. McMullen (2002). Action bias and opportunity recognition: An empirical examination of entrepreneurial attitude as regulatory focus. Babson-Kauffman Entrepreneurship Research Conference, Boulder, CO, June.

Shepherd, D. and A. Zacharakis (2002). Venture capitalists' expertise: A call for research into decision aids and cognitive feedback. *Journal of Business Venturing*, 17(1), 1–20.

Sheppard, B., J. Hartwick and P. Warshaw (1988). The theory of reasoned action: A meta-analysis of past research. *Journal of Consumer Research*, 15(3), 325–343.

Simon, M., S. Houghton and K. Aquino (2000). Cognitive biases, risk perception and venture formation: How individuals decide to start businesses. *Journal of Business Venturing*, 15(2), 113–134.

Smithson, M. (1982). Applications of fuzzy set concepts to the social sciences. *Mathematical Social Sciences*, 11(2), 161–182.

Stapleton, R. and D. Stapleton (1996). The significance of schemata and scripts in entrepreneurship education and development. In F. Hoy (ed.), *The Art and Science of Entrepreneurship Education*, MES: Berea, Ohio, Vol. IV.

Stavrou, E. (1999). Succession in family businesses: Exploring effects of demographic factors on offspring intentions to join and take over the business. *Journal of Small Business Management*, 37(3), 43–61.

Stevenson, H. and J.C. Jarillo (1990). A paradigm of entrepreneurship: Entrepreneurial management. *Strategic Management Journal*, 11, 17–27.

Teal, E. and A. Carroll (1999). Moral reasoning skills: Are entrepreneurs different? *Journal of Business Ethics*, 19(3, pt 2), 229–240.

Ward, K. (1993). Vision and entrepreneurship: Usefulness of the concept in classifying venture founders. *Proceedings*, Midwest Academy of Management, Indianapolis.

West, G.P. and G.D. Meyer (1997). Temporal dimensions of opportunistic change in technology-driven ventures. *Entrepreneurship Theory and Practice*, 22(2), 31–52.

Wiklund, J. and D. Shepherd (2000). Intentions and growth: The moderating role of resources and opportunities. Presentation in 2001 Babson conference, Jönköping, Sweden, June.

Zacharakis, A. and G.D. Meyer (1998). A lack of insight: Do venture capitalists really understand their own decision processes? *Journal of Business Venturing*, 13(1), 57–76.

Zacharakis, A., G.D. Meyer and J. DeCastro (1999). Differing perceptions of new venture failure: A matched exploratory study of venture capitalists and entrepreneurs. *Journal of Small Business Management*, 37(1), 1–14.

Zacharakis, A. and D. Shepherd (2001). The nature of information and overconfidence on venture capitalists' decision making. *Journal of Business Venturing*, 16(4), 311–332.

SARAS D. SARASVATHY[1], NICHOLAS DEW[2],
S. RAMAKRISHNA VELAMURI[2] and SANKARAN VENKATARAMAN[2]
[1]University of Maryland, [2]University of Virginia

7.   Three Views of Entrepreneurial Opportunity

INTRODUCTION

*"Although we are not usually explicit about it, we really postulate that when
a market could be created, it would be."*   – Kenneth Arrow (1974a)

For almost fifty years now, following the trail of issues raised by economists
such as Hayek, Schumpeter, Kirzner and Arrow, researchers have studied the
economics of technological change and the problem of allocation of resources
for invention (invention being the production of information). The bulk of this
literature simply assumes that new technical information will either be traded
as a commodity or become embodied in products and services (hereafter called
"economic goods"), without addressing any specific mechanisms or processes
for the transformation of new information into new economic goods or new
economic entities (such as new firms and new markets). It is inside this gap
that we begin our quest for the concept of an "entrepreneurial opportunity."

In a recent interview with CNN, Whitfield Diffy, the inventor of public key
encryption (currently an employee of Sun Microsystems), explained that
although his entire subsequent career had benefited from his invention and he
had done very well financially in the process, it did not occur to him to start
a company to commercialize his invention. In fact he expressed astonishment
at the "hundreds and hundreds of people trying to turn a buck on it." The
designers of the MIR space station would no doubt express similar astonishment at the venture capitalists that recently bid (in vain) several million dollars
to turn it into an advertising/tourist resort – just as the scientists working with
DARPA did not foresee the age of e-commerce. The history of technological
invention is full of unanticipated economic consequences. And, yet, the study
of the economics of technological change is full of "just-so" stories[1] that

---

[1] *Just so stories* (based on Rudyard Kipling's (1909) collection of short stories of the same title)
are stories that explain why things are the way they are. Such stories also tend to celebrate things
the way they are – subscribing to the fallacy that because certain things came to be, there is some
element of "optimality" or "correctness" attached to their origin and structure. This approach leads
us to discount the significance of pre-histories because if existence by itself is the starting point of
theory building, almost *any* story could *ex-post* serve as sufficient explanation for the pre-history.
One delightful example is the story of an arbitrage struggle between an elephant and a crocodile

Z.J. Acs and D.B. Audretsch (eds.), Handbook of Entrepreneurship Research, 141–160.
© 2003 *Kluwer Academic Publishers. Printed in Great Britain.*

seemingly demonstrate the inevitability of commercialization of all new technologies through familiar recurring patterns such as the technology adoption curve. Unfortunately, of course, we do not have any data on all the new products and markets that were *not* created to commercialize new technologies in the past.

This paper challenges the assumption underlying current theories of technological change, laid out so pithily by Arrow in the initial quote, viz., "*when a market could be created, it would be*". Instead, it focuses on Arrow's exhortation to researchers to tackle one of the central problems in economics today: "... *the uncertainties about economics are rooted in our need for a better understanding of the economics of uncertainty; our lack of economic knowledge is, in good part, our difficulty in modeling the ignorance of the economic agent.*" The central premise of this paper is that there exists an important area for research in the conceptual gap between a technological innovation and the markets that come into existence based on that innovation – a gap in our understanding of economics that is filled by the notion of "entrepreneurial opportunity." In this paper, we outline some initial steps in the study of entrepreneurial opportunity by summarizing how existing literature instructs us to proceed and then making a conjectural leap toward grappling with the complexities inherent in this phenomenon.

We begin our exposition with a definition of entrepreneurial opportunity. Then we delineate its elements and examine it within three views of the market process: i.e., the market as an allocative process; as a discovery process; and as a creative process (Buchanan and Vanberg, 1991). Within each stream, we examine the assumptions about the knowledge (ignorance) of the decision maker with regard to the future, and the implications of those assumptions for strategies to recognize, discover, and create entrepreneurial opportunities. We end the essay with a set of conjectures that challenge the inevitability of technology commercialization and argue for a more contingent approach to the study of the central phenomena of entrepreneurship.

Entrepreneurial Opportunity

The Oxford English Dictionary defines opportunity as "A time, juncture, or condition of things favorable to an end or purpose, or admitting of something being done or effected." If we believe that ends are not always specified prior to the pursuit of an entrepreneurial opportunity, but may emerge endogenously over time, we can unpack the constituents of an entrepreneurial opportunity from the second part of the above sentence. An entrepreneurial opportunity, therefore, consists of a set of ideas, beliefs and actions that *enable* the creation of future goods and services in the absence of current markets for them

---

that explains how the elephant came to have a long trunk! Relatedly, almost all the social sciences seem perfectly capable of explaining every creation after the fact, but can predict nothing before the creation.

(Venkataraman, 1997). For example, the entrepreneurial opportunity that led to the creation of Netscape involved (a) the idea of a user-friendly Web browser (Mosaic); (b) the belief that the internet could be commercialized; and (c) the set of decision-actions that brought together Marc Andreesen (the creator of Mosaic) and Jim Clark (the ex-founder of Silicon Graphics) to set up base in the small town of Mountain View.

In sum, our notion of an entrepreneurial opportunity consists of:

1. New idea/s or invention/s that may or may not lead to the achievement of one or more economic ends that become possible through those ideas or inventions;
2. Beliefs about things favorable to the achievement of possible valuable ends; and,
3. Actions that generate and implement those ends through specific (imagined) new economic artifacts (the artifacts may be goods such as products and services, and/or entities such as firms and markets, and/or institutions such as standards and norms).

Our ontological stance in defining an entrepreneurial opportunity in this manner transcends purely subjective and purely objective notions. An opportunity presupposes actors *for whom* it is *perceived* as an opportunity; at the same time, the opportunity has no meaning unless the actor/s actually act upon the real world within which the opportunity eventually has to take shape. As is made clear in the rest of the chapter, this ontological stance enables us to take a pluralistic approach toward the phenomenon without falling into the mire of naïve relativism.

THREE VIEWS OF ENTREPRENEURIAL OPPORTUNITY

Drawing upon three streams of economic literature pertinent to entrepreneurial opportunity – i.e., market as an allocative process, market as a discovery process, and market as a creative process – we could model an entrepreneurial opportunity as a function, or a process or a set of decisions, respectively. The antecedents for the three views presented here specifically draw upon three works, i.e., Hayek (1945), Knight (1921), and Buchanan and Vanberg (1991) – all of which grapple with the central problem demarcated by Arrow (quoted earlier) in terms of understanding uncertainties in the economy and modeling the ignorance of the economic agent.

In an important essay in 1945, Hayek postulated the concept of dispersed knowledge where no two individuals share the same knowledge or information about the economy. Hayek distinguished between two types of knowledge: First, the body of scientific knowledge, which is stable and can be best known by suitably chosen experts in their respective fields; second, the dispersed information of particular time and place, whose importance only the individual possessing it can judge. Hayek pinpointed the harnessing of this latter type of knowledge as a key and underestimated element in the economic development of society. This dispersion has two extremely important implications as far as entrepreneurial opportunities are concerned. First, dispersion of knowledge is a root explanation for the presence of uncertainty, which gives rise to opportunities in the first place. Second, dispersion of knowledge is another root explanation of the nexus of the enterprising individual and the opportunity to discover, create and exploit new markets (Venkataraman, 1997; Shane, 2000). Without this nexus of the individual and the opportunity, most inventions will lie fallow. Frank Knight (1921) clearly realized the implications of uncertainty for economic organization.

In his seminal dissertation, *Risk, Uncertainty, and Profit*, Knight distinguished between three types of uncertainties about the future that an economic agent may face:

- The first consists of a future whose distribution exists and is known, and therefore decisions would only involve calculating the odds of a particular draw and placing one's bets based on the analysis. In this case, risks can be reduced through diversification. This assumes that all possible outcome scenarios are equally likely, *ex ante*.
- The second consists of a future whose distribution exists but is not known in advance. The agent, in this case, has to estimate the distribution through repeated trials and can then treat it the same as the first case. Furthermore, as the environment changes dynamically, successful strategies evolve through adaptive processes including careful experimentation and learning over time. Although we do not know the probabilities attached to each of the outcome scenarios, the probabilities do exist, and their distribution can be uncovered over time.
- The third type of uncertainty, which Knight called true uncertainty, consists of a future that is not only unknown, but also unknowable – with unclassifiable instances and a non-existent distribution. The economic agent, or entrepreneur, who takes on this true uncertainty, gets compensated for it through "profit" – a form of residual return after the normal factors of production are paid for and all market contracts fulfilled.

Knight did not explicate how the entrepreneur deals with this true uncertainty, instead, he argued that:

"The ultimate logic, or psychology, of these deliberations is obscure, a part of the scientifically unfathomable mystery of life and mind. We must simply fall back upon a 'capacity' in the intelligent animal to form more or less correct judgments about things, an intuitive sense of values. We are so built that what seems to us reasonable is likely to be confirmed by experience, or we could not live in the world at all."

In this third case of Knightian uncertainty, there is no meaning to the attachment of probabilities to the opportunity vectors. Instead, we need to understand the process through which the different levels of actors interact. The benefits get created endogenously, in the very unfolding of those interactions.

Later researchers, especially Austrian economists such as Von Mises (1949) and Kirzner (1997), and subjectivists such as Lachmann (1976) and Shackle (1979), have tried to tackle this problem of Knightian uncertainty. Fixing a rather penetrating philosophical gaze on the works of these economic theorists since Hayek and Knight, Buchanan and Vanberg (1991) contrast the three views of economic theory presented here as follows: "*The market as an allocative process, responding to the structure of incentives that confront choice-makers; the market as a discovery process, utilizing localized information; or the market as a creative process that exploits man's imaginative potential ...*" They argue that "the perceptual vision of the market as a *creative process* offers more insight and understanding than the alternative visions that elicit interpretations of the market as a *discovery process*, or, more familiarly, as an *allocative process*. In either of the latter alternatives, there is a telos imposed by the scientist's own perception, a telos that is nonexistent in the first instance. And removal of the teleological inference from the way of looking at economic interaction carries with it significant implications for any diagnosis of the failure or success, diagnosis that is necessarily preliminary to any normative usage of scientific analysis."

But for the purposes of this chapter, the key issue is not which of the three views is "*right*", but rather which view is more useful under what conditions of uncertainty. Such a pragmatic approach allows us to *utilize* the three views explicated so far to construct a rather simple typology of entrepreneurial opportunities based on the pre-conditions for their existence, as follows:

1. *Opportunity Recognition*

If both sources of supply and demand exist rather obviously, the opportunity for bringing them together has to be "recognized" and then the match-up between supply and demand has to be implemented either through an existing firm or a new firm. This notion of opportunity has to do with the exploitation of existing markets. Examples include arbitrage and franchises.

2. *Opportunity Discovery*

If only one side exists – i.e., demand exists, but supply does not, and vice versa – then, the non-existent side has to be "discovered" before the match-up can be implemented. This notion of opportunity has to do with the exploration of existing and latent markets. Examples include: Cures for diseases (Demand exists; supply has to be discovered); and applications for new technologies such as the personal computer (Supply exists, demand has to be discovered).

3. *Opportunity Creation*

If neither supply nor demand exist in an obvious manner, one or both have to be "created", and several *economic* inventions in marketing, financing, etc. have to be made, for the opportunity to come into existence. This notion of opportunity has to do with the creation of new markets. Examples include Wedgwood Pottery, Edison's General Electric, U-Haul, AES Corporation, Netscape, Beanie Babies, and the MIR space resort.

Table 1 presents a summary comparison of the three views along several different dimensions. In the next three sections, we trace the implicit notions

Table 1. Comparing the three views of entrepreneurial opportunity

View	Allocative View	Discovery View	Creative View
What is an opportunity?	Possibility of putting resources to good use to achieve given ends	Possibility of correcting errors in the system and creating new ways of achieving given ends	Possibility of creating new means as well as new ends
Focus	Focus on System	Focus on Process	Focus on Decisions
Method	Opportunities "recognized" through deductive processes	Opportunities "discovered" through inductive processes	Opportunities "created" through *abductive* processes
Domain of application	When both supply and demand are known	Only one or the other (supply or demand) known	When both supply and demand are unknown
Distribution of opportunity vectors	Opportunity vectors are equally likely	Existent, but unknown probability of opportunity vectors	Probabilities for opportunity vectors are non-existent
Assumptions about information	Complete information available at both aggregate and individual levels	Complete information at the aggregate level, but distributed imperfectly among individual agents	Only partial information even at the aggregate level, and ignorance is key to opportunity creation
Assumptions about expectations	Homogeneous expectations both at the micro and macro levels	Homogeneous expectations at the macro level; heterogeneous expectations at the micro level	Heterogeneous expectations at both micro and macro levels
Management of uncertainty	Uncertainty managed through: Diversification	Uncertainty managed through: Experimentation	Uncertainty managed through: Effectuation
Definition of success	Success is a statistical artifact	Success is outliving failures	Success is a mutually negotiated consensus among stakeholders
Unit of competition	Resources compete	Strategies compete	Values compete
Outcomes	Strategies for: Risk management	Strategies for: Failure management	Strategies for: Conflict management

of entrepreneurial opportunity through each of the three literature streams on market process and develop key characteristics of the nature of entrepreneurial opportunities based on each of these perspectives.

THE ALLOCATIVE PROCESS VIEW

Neoclassical economic theory discusses several efficiency properties of markets – allocative, productive, coordinative, and informational. We will focus in this section on the allocative efficiency of markets and its implications for opportunity recognition. Allocative efficiency is achieved when: (a) the income of consumers is optimally allocated to consumption, i.e., they are able to buy the goods and services that they value most; and (b) resources (factors) are optimally allocated to production, i.e., they are used to produce the goods and services that consumers desire.

Allocative efficiency is achieved in a perfectly competitive market, whose characteristics are as follows: There is a very large number of buyers and sellers, all of whom are so small that none of them individually can affect prices; prices of homogeneous goods and factors are uniform throughout the economy; all factors are perfectly mobile; returns to scale are constant; and all economic agents have perfect knowledge about available alternatives. There is an assumption of complete markets, i.e., there are markets for all possible products and services. Furthermore, agents are free to enter and exit the market. Disequilibria are short-term phenomena, and are quickly cleared to bring the situation back to equilibrium through the tatonnement process – prices go up when demand exceeds supply and down when supply exceeds demand – which functions through the mythical figure of the Walrasian auctioneer. There are further requirements for the achievement of an optimal allocation of resources, such as the absence of any divergence between private and social costs and the existence of perfect competition in all sectors of the economy. When a market has achieved allocative efficiency, it complies with two conditions: First, price is equal to marginal cost, which is also equal to minimum average cost ($P = MC = minAC$); and second, Pareto optimality is achieved, which means that resources cannot be redistributed to make anyone better off without making someone else worse off.

The allocative view concerns itself with the optimal utilization of scarce resources. In this view, an opportunity is any possibility of putting resources to better use. At equilibrium, there are no opportunities, because resources have been optimally allocated. However, profits can arise in two ways. First, to the extent that a perfectly competitive market is not in equilibrium, opportunities for short-term profits are available, but they quickly disappear when new firms enter the market attracted by the profits. Second, if we assume that all information is available in the system but is randomly distributed, and therefore acquiring information involves a costly search process, then the opportunity for profit is simply the difference between the benefit of the information and its cost. However, the random distribution of information means that no agent has the possibility of systematically benefiting from superior information. The core idea is that all products and ideas that can potentially exist are all known to be feasible but costly to produce. When the cost problem is solved (for example, due to scientific breakthroughs in laboratories), opportunities arise. However, opportunity is not specific to any one person because there is no informational advantage within this view. Thus there is no heterogeneity between economic agents that enables one agent to be systematically better than another in acquiring information, and consequently in the recognition and pursuit of opportunities. Which agent recognizes the opportunity is therefore a purely random variable. Moreover, since there is no divergence between private cost and social cost (that is, the opportunity cost for an individual agent of a resource in a particular use is the same as the social opportunity cost of the resource in that use), any possibility of a Pareto improvement at the system level is equivalent to an opportunity at the individual agent level.

Arrow (1962) discussed three reasons why a perfectly competitive market could lead to a sub-optimal allocation of resources to invention: *inappropriability*, *indivisibility*, and *uncertainty*. In what follows, we analyze how allocative efficiency is compromised as a result of these three reasons.

Inappropriability

An issue that has been debated for many decades is whether there is any incentive to innovate in a perfectly competitive market, because it does not, by definition, permit the appropriation of rents in a sustained fashion. Kamien and Schwartz (1975) study the relationship between market structure and innovation, and conclude that "few, if any, economists maintain that perfect competition efficiently allocates resources for technical advance" (p. 2). Arrow (1962) argued that the incentive to innovate could exist even in perfectly competitive markets: "It may be useful to remark that an incentive to invent can exist even under perfect competition in the product markets though not, of course, in the 'market' for the information contained in the invention. This is especially clear in the case of a cost reducing invention. Provided only that suitable royalty payments can be demanded, an inventor can profit without disturbing the competitive nature of the industry. The situation for a new product invention is not very different; by charging a suitable royalty to a competitive industry, the inventor can receive a return equal to the monopoly profits" (p. 619).

For Arrow's point to be valid, the assumption of all sectors of the economy being in a perfectly competitive equilibrium must be relaxed. Schumpeter (1976) was of the opinion that the propensity of a firm to innovate was directly proportional to its size and market share. He based his view on the considerable resources required to innovate and the incentive of adequate return. Nutter (1956) disagreed – "Desire and necessity drive competitive and monopolistic producers alike to innovate: Desire for better-than-average profits motivates the venturesome and industrious to introduce new products and techniques; loss of profits forces the cautious and passive to imitate or perish" (p. 523).

Villard (1958) offered a view that ran counter to that of Nutter, concluding that innovation was unlikely at both extremes. "Industries where 'competitive oligopoly' prevails are likely to progress most rapidly and that therefore 'competitive oligopoly' may well be the best way of organizing industry. The basic point is that progress is likely to be rapid (1) when firms are large enough or few enough to afford and benefit from research and (2) when they are under competitive pressure to innovate – utilize the results of research" (p. 491). Scherer (1967) agreed with Villard, arguing that moderate levels of concentration lead to the highest levels of innovation.

Indivisibility

Blaug (1985) defines indivisibility as follows: "If two productive agents are perfect substitutes of each other when used in combination to produce a given output, they are necessarily infinitely divisible: The isoquants in this case are straight lines, meaning that the marginal rate of substitution of the two factors is a constant" (p. 454).

Arrow (1962) argues that "a given piece of information is by definition an indivisible commodity, and the classical problems of allocation in the presence of indivisibilities appear here" (p. 615). He goes on to explain the problems: "In the absence of special legal protection, the owner cannot, however, simply sell information on the open market. Any one purchaser can destroy the monopoly, since he can reproduce the information at little or no cost. Thus the only effective monopoly would be the use of the information by the original possessor. This however, will not only be socially inefficient, but also may not be of much use to the owner of the information either, since he may not be able to exploit it as effectively as others" (p. 615).

Economic theory assumes that in the absence of property rights, the original creator or discoverer of particular information would lose control of it once it was reproduced and accessible to other parties. Thus a large part of the discussion on appropriate institutional structures revolves around establishing the right incentives – copyright laws, patent laws, etc. – for agents to innovate. However, there may be some classes of information that can be used only in combinations with other assets, such as human and physical capital. For this reason the rents from the use of such information may not accrue to parties who do not possess these assets, and this difficulty may provide adequate protection for the innovator, even in the absence of specific legal protection. There are many industries in which firms do not patent inventions in spite of the existence of patent laws. The distinction between information and knowledge becomes relevant here. Brown and Duguid (2000) argue that knowledge differs from information in three ways: First, knowledge is tied to a knower; second, it is harder to detach than information; and third, it is hard to give and receive because it requires more by way of assimilation. They also distinguish between the explicit and tacit dimensions of knowledge: "[S]trategy books don't make you into a good negotiator, any more than dictionaries make you into a speaker or expert systems make you into an expert. To become a negotiator requires not only knowledge of strategy, but skill, experience, judgment, and discretion. These allow you to understand not just how a particular strategy is executed, but when to execute it. The two together make a negotiator, but the second comes only with practice" (Brown and Duguid, 2000, pp. 133–134).

Thus, although information is indivisible and the costs of reproducing it are close to zero, we may relate it to a resource, as defined in the resource based view of the firm. Knowledge, on the other hand, would be a capability, in that it represents a combination of information, physical capital and human capital. Focusing exclusively on raw information makes us view opportunities as arbitrage possibilities, which are not agent specific. On the other hand, focusing on knowledge opens up rich vistas of agent specific opportunities, whose recognition depends upon already owned knowledge and other assets (Shane, 2000).

Uncertainty

Akerlof (1970) argued in his famous "lemons" paper that an extreme case of information asymmetry could lead to a complete market failure. Information asymmetry leads to uncertainty that causes a downward bias in demand and supply. This is because, at very high levels of uncertainty, agents will need concessions so large from the other party to the transaction that neither will recognize any opportunity in the exchange. Institutional support is then often needed to overcome the uncertainty and to restore trade in the market. For example, organizations such as the SEC ensure certain minimum levels of transparency and fair play, which benefit all participants in the form of an increase in the volume of trade. Markets themselves can correct for this asymmetry – firms specializing in information gathering, analysis, and dissemination pervade all markets. These firms lower an individual agent's search costs while increasing the quality of information. Institutions such as guarantees, brand names, and licensing practices are some of the other ways of overcoming the uncertainty caused by information asymmetry.

The other major reason for uncertainty according to Arrow (1974a) is the nonexistence, except in a very limited number of commodities, of futures goods markets:

"Hence, the optimizer must replace the market commitment to buy or sell at given terms by expectations: Expectations of prices and expectations of quantities to be bought or sold. But he cannot know the future. Hence, unless he deludes himself, he must know that both sets of expectations may be wrong. In short, the absence of the market implies that the optimizer faces a world of uncertainty." (p. 6).

According to Arrow, this uncertainty leads to the economic agent taking steps to reduce risks, such as the holding of inventories, preference for flexible capital equipment, etc. It also leads to the creation of new markets for the shifting of risks, such as the equity market. However, while conceding that probabilities are subjective, because different agents have access to different information, he implies that each agent can know his own distribution of probabilities from his own past. He states that uncertainty means:

"[T]hat we do not have a complete description of the world which we fully believe to be true. Instead, we consider the world to be in one or another of a range of states. Each state of the world is a description that is complete for all relevant purposes. Our uncertainty consists in not knowing which state is the true one" (1974b).

The views of Frank Knight (and perhaps more importantly, the different interpretations of what he actually meant) on the distinction between risk and uncertainty become very relevant here.

In summary, there are several implications of viewing the market as an allocative process. First, the focus is on the system and not on individuals or firms, which are all homogeneous in their access to technology and in their cost structures. Second, *ex ante*, all economic agents are equally likely to detect a given opportunity. Opportunity recognition is thus a purely random process. Third, the term competition is as appropriately applied to factor markets as it is to the market for goods and services. In both cases, the markets are assumed to be in competitive equilibrium.

THE DISCOVERY PROCESS VIEW

Two factors influencing the distribution and use of new information have therefore attracted attention from researchers. The first is that access to information sources is extremely important, leading some researchers to suggest that the prime determinant of entrepreneurship is whether the entrepreneur has an advantageous network position from which informational advantages accrue (Burt, 1992). For instance, information is often "sticky" (von Hippel, 1994), in that it is tacitly accumulated by users, which means that access to the relevant information for discovery to occur is only available to a few individuals who have direct and intimate contact with users. Second, new information or knowledge often requires complementary resources in order to be useful, such as a prior knowledge (Venkataraman, 1997; Shane, 2000) that is also often tacit in nature. Such prior knowledge creates the "absorptive capacity" necessary for an individual to make use of new information (Cohen and Levinthal, 1990).

The second reason why people possess different beliefs about the prices at which markets should clear is because, as Kirzner (1997) has observed, the process of discovery in a market setting requires the participants to guess each other's expectations about a wide variety of things. However, the regular supply of new information from endogenous sources creates uncertainty (Knight, 1921) owing to the fact that the discovery of genuinely novel information by other agents can affect the value of resources. Such discoveries cannot be known ahead of time and may add previously unimagined categories of usage for particular resources, thus changing the structure of the decision problem the entrepreneur faces (Langlois, 1984). Since it is impossible to have accurate expectations about inventions that have yet to be made, people form expectations based on hunches, intuition, heuristics, and accurate and inaccurate information, leading their expectations to be incorrect some of the time.

The problem of forming accurate expectations given the genuine uncertainty caused by the endogenous supply of novel information is compounded by some characteristics of human decision-making. All individuals utilize knowledge that is subjectively held, incomplete and tacit. Entrepreneurs therefore form beliefs and expectations about future events that are indeterminate for at least three reasons. First, because much knowledge is tacit (Polanyi, 1966), other individuals – upon whose actions the correctness of the entrepreneur's expectations depend – often base their decision making on invisible elements of experience that are hard to verbalize, but are observed instead only as hunches, intuition and judgement. Second, situations calling for prediction are not given self-evidently because the essence of any situation is how it is enacted by individuals (Weick, 1979). People often produce part of the situation they face (they "enact" it). The dependency of enactment on tacit cues imposed on a situation by individuals means that there is an indeterminacy in how individuals produce situations, just as there is an indeterminacy to how they react to them. This is especially so when multiple actors interact, making the production of a situation dependent on an "inter-enactment" process. The third reason why outcomes are indeterminate is because interaction among individuals gives rise to emergent outcomes. One example of an emergent outcome of the interaction of many individuals in a market is a structure of prices, but many other emergent outcomes are not so predictable, hence their discovery as an aspect of market processes. One of the traits of complex adaptive systems such as market processes is level differences: Observed patterns of behavior differ dramatically between the micro and macro levels. In other words, macro-level phenomena are often indeterminate from micro-level observations. Hence the opportunity to discover is an outcome of the very inability to predict, or form accurate expectations, about such complex dynamic phenomena.

Since entrepreneurial opportunities depend on asymmetries of information and beliefs, entrepreneurs' buying and selling decisions are not always correct and this process leads to "errors" that create shortages, surpluses, and misallocated resources. An individual alert to the presence of an "error" may buy resources where prices are "too low," recombine them and sell the outputs where prices are "too high." The notion that individuals can make these genuine discoveries about misallocated resources has led some researchers to stress the role of "surprise" (Kirzner, 1997) in this process. The nature of overlooked profit opportunities is that they are *completely* overlooked, and therefore individuals are genuinely surprised when they identify a hitherto unexpected profit opportunity. Such surprises are not searched for at the cost of a deliberate search process. Instead, individuals are totally ignorant of these misallocated resources and their total ignorance precludes a deliberate search process. Given that uncertainty and indeterminacy make expectation formation difficult, it is reasonable suggest that regular surprises will be a feature of the discovery process.

One factor that leads to stability in expectations is the role of institutions, which are routinized patterns of action. The presence of routines makes expectation formation a possibility, since certain patterns of human behavior can be reasonably predicted based on the observation of routines. Given the limitations on human cognition (Simon, 1997), routines are an essential aspect of human action for two reasons: First, because they allow each particular individual to preserve scarce decision-making resources for application to non-routine decisions; and second, because they allow all other individuals to economize on scarce decision-making resources because they can make reasonable predictions about the actions of others based on observation of their routines.

Routines are therefore pervasive at the individual level, where we usually describe them as habits, as well as at the organizational level. Every individual has a particular regime of unreflective habits that are accumulated over a lifetime of experience and experimentation (James, 1907). The particular habits of an individual amount to a specialized collection of routines. Organizations such as firms also accumulate specialized collections of routines (Nelson and Winter, 1982). In fact, one example of a predictable routine is the entrepreneurial process described as follows: *People can reasonably forecast that some other people are conjecturing resources are undervalued in their current use and can be purchased and recombined and put to more valuable use. On the other hand, people can also reasonably forecast that many other individuals are simply carrying on with their daily lives, i.e. being a fireman, or minding their children, or relaxing in their old age.* In fact, were it not for the presence of imperfect information and a wide variety of routine modes of behavior (i.e. non-alert, non-entrepreneurs), the entrepreneurial discovery process would not work (Loasby, 1999).

Institutions are important because they impose structure on the world, and as we have already seen, an absence of structure creates the kind of uncertainty that makes forming accurate expectations an impossibility. But to the extent that institutions do exist, expectation formation is a reasonable possibility. Institutional routines therefore are an important part of the discovery process in two ways: First, because routines create a stable interpretative scheme, they enable the entrepreneur to impose order on and make sense out of the "bloomin' buzzin' confusion" of experience (James, 1907); and second, because individuals know what a stable structure is, they are able to notice exceptions. In essence, the notion of surprise only makes sense because an individual knows when he/she is *not* surprised. Since cognitive limits mean individuals cannot be attentive to everything at once, entrepreneurial alertness (Kirzner, 1997) is a function of what is *not* given attention; that is, it is a function of other routinized modes of behavior. In other words, entrepreneurial alertness is a scarce resource that comes with the opportunity cost of that which has been taken for granted. Given that opportunity cost is the essential feature of resource use in choice, this economic calculation ought to come as no surprise to us.

Of course, as the structure of a particular market becomes well established and routinized, eventually entrepreneurial opportunities become cost inefficient to pursue. This occurs for two reasons. First, the opportunity to earn entrepreneurial profit will provide an incentive to many economic actors. As opportunities are exploited, an externality is created. Information diffuses to other members of society at no cost or low cost, and these individuals can imitate the innovator and appropriate some of the innovator's entrepreneurial profit. This diffusion through imitation is one of the most important yet under-researched aspects of the entrepreneurial process (Nelson and Winter, 1982). Although the entry of imitating entrepreneurs may initially validate the opportunity and increase overall demand, eventually competition begins to dominate (Hannan and Freeman, 1984). When the entry of additional entrepreneurs reaches a rate at which the costs from new entrants exceeds the benefits, the incentive for people to pursue the opportunity is reduced because the entrepreneurial profit becomes divided among more and more actors (Schumpeter, 1934).

The second reason entrepreneurial opportunities eventually become cost inefficient to pursue is that the exploitation of opportunity provides information to resource providers about the value of the resources that they possess, leading them to raise resource prices over time to capture some of the entrepreneur's profit for themselves (Kirzner, 1997). In short, the diffusion of information and learning about the accuracy of decisions over time, combined with the lure of profit, will reduce the incentive for people to pursue any given opportunity.

The duration of any given opportunity depends on a variety of factors. The duration is increased by the "inability of others (due to various isolating mechanisms) to imitate, substitute, trade for or acquire the rare resources required to drive down the surplus" (Venkataraman, 1997, p. 133). For instance, the provision of monopoly rights, as occurs with patent protection or an exclusive contract, increases the duration. Similarly, the slowness of information diffusion, or lags in the timeliness with which others recognize information, also increase the duration, particularly if time provides reinforcing advantages, such as occur with the adoption of technical standards (network externalities) or learning curves.

What makes the discovery process metaphor powerful is that the dual premises of a continuous supply of new information and a continuous process of realizing information about the "errors" of prior expectations suggest the market process will be a continuous one. This view of the market as a process distinguishes the discovery view from the allocative view, where the metaphor of equilibrium leads to the perception of markets in static terms. In contrast, the discovery process illustrates how the market is necessarily "alive" and a hive of human activity.

THE CREATIVE PROCESS VIEW

The origins of the creative process view are more recent than the older views based on the market as a discovery process and the even older and established view of the market as an allocative process. Consequently, this view is not yet as well developed as the other two. The key idea in this view, as Buchanan and Vanberg (1991) point out, is that *telos* is neither ignored nor imposed on the phenomena concerned. Instead, ends emerge endogenously within a process of interactive human action (based on heterogeneous preferences and expectations) striving to imagine and create a better world.

The origins of the allocative process view lie in the philosophy of Adam Smith and the equilibrium-based calculus of Marshall (1920), Walras (1954), Arrow (1984) and Debreu (1991) and others; the development of the discovery process view owes its origins to the philosophical roots of evolution going back to Darwin (1859), and is steeped in the calculus of asymmetric information explicated by Hayek (1945), Nelson and Winter (1982) and others; similarly, the creative process view originates in the philosophy of pragmatism professed by James (1907) and Dewey (1917), and takes its cue for shedding a large portion of historical and even evolutionary determinism, instead moving toward a calculus of *contingency* based on the notion of human "free will."

In 1996, founding his arguments on the work of pragmatic philosophers, and drawing from reputed scholars in a variety of social sciences, Hans Joas (1996) sought to establish the creative nature of all human action. Key to his theorizing is a triad of arguments that demonstrate that action (as an empirical fact) is: (a) always situated (i.e., cannot presuppose purposes or be divorced from the sources of the actor's intentions); (b) intrinsically corporeal (i.e., cannot be freed from the constraints and possibilities of the body of the actor); and, (c) essentially social (i.e., cannot originate or occur meaningfully in the absence of others). The three sets of arguments challenge the existing conceptions of human action based on formal or normative models based on "rationality" (for example, models of subjective expected utility). In Joas's own words, "... I have argued that some approaches towards a conceptualization of human creativity have actually drawn an artificial rift between creative action and the totality of human action. My intention is therefore to provide not a mere extension to, but instead a fundamental restructuring of the principles underlying mainstream action theory" (1996, p. 145).

Joas shows that to the extent that an actor is capable of new/plural purposes, lacks control over his own body, and is not autonomous *vis-à-vis* his fellow human beings and environment, his actions are creative. In other words, they end up creating novelties in our world. Hence, in Joas's conception, instead of being anomalies to be explained, surprise and novelty become natural desiderata of a theory of human action that is not confined to so-called "rational" action.

The creative process view urged by Buchanan and Vanberg (1991), although developed independently of Joas's work, asks us essentially to speculate on a creative model of human action, and to develop non-teleological theories of economics. In other words, if human beings are not assumed to be "rational" actors, but instead if human behavior is deemed inherently creative, what kind of an economics (or any other social science, for that matter) would we get?

Joas (1996) and Buchanan and Vanberg (1991) are not isolated in their exhortation to scholars to pursue this line of inquiry. March's garbage-can model of decision making contains one such set of attempts (March, 1994). In his own words, "In a garbage can process, it is assumed that there are exogenous, time-dependent arrivals of choice opportunities, problems, solutions, and decision makers. Problems and solutions are attached to choices, and thus to each other, not because of any means–ends linkage but because of their temporal proximity" (1994, p. 200). Examples of garbage cans include committee and board meetings where a variety of problems, solutions, and decision makers come into temporal proximity with or without particular means–ends chains being involved in the coming into being of particular choices. Building further upon such attempts, March urges us to build a "technology of foolishness" or theories of decision making in the absence of pre-existent goals (March, 1982).

Other attempts in this direction include the empirical work based on Weick's theories of enactment and sensemaking (Weick, 1979). Just as March's *oeuvre* on decision-making highlights the endogeneity of goals, Weick in his theory of enactment focuses on the endogeneity of the environment. He points out how theorizing about "organization" and "environment" as two separate entities prevents organizational scholars from asking important questions. In his own words, "But the firm partitioning of the world into the environment and the organization excludes the possibility that people *invent* rather than discover part of what they think they see" (1979, p. 166).

As early as 1969, Simon (1996) had talked about designing or planning without final goals and the *artificial* nature of the world we live in. His exposition brought out the role of current action in the design of future environments. In his own words, "The real result of our actions is to establish initial conditions for the next succeeding stage of action. What we call 'final' goals are in fact criteria for choosing the initial conditions that we will leave to our successors." Therefore, how we want to leave the world for the next generation becomes an important question in theories based on the creative view.

In sum, the crux of the creative process view is the need to build non-teleological theories of human action, wherein values and meaning emerge endogenously. Recent empirical work in expert entrepreneurial decision-making (Sarasvathy, 2001b) has led to the development of such a non-teleological theory in entrepreneurship. This theory posits an alternative to predictive (causal) rationality, called effectuation, that underlies decisions made by entrepreneurs in bringing new firms and markets into existence (Sarasvathy, 2001a). Starting without given goals, effectuation inverts the key principles and logic of predictive rationality to carve out an alternative paradigm to rational choice. In this view opportunities do not pre-exist – either to be recognized or to be discovered. Instead they get created as the residual of a process that involves intense dynamic interaction and negotiation between stakeholders seeking to operationalize their (often vague and unformed) aspirations and values into concrete products, services and institutions that constitute the economy.

INTEGRATING THE THREE VIEWS

In the foregoing exposition we have outlined and briefly discussed three views of entrepreneurial opportunity under the broader umbrella of the three views of the market process as allocative, discovery, and creative. We now turn to the question of how to integrate the three views into our practice and pedagogy and future scholarship, particularly in the area of entrepreneurship.

One way to look at the three views would be to simply consider them three equally valid and non-overlapping modes of thinking about entrepreneurial opportunities. Such an approach focuses only on the distinctions between the views and overlooks both the possibilities of relationships and interactions between them, and also the fact of empirical confounding in the way they are embodied in economic phenomena. Table 1 sets out all three views along certain key dimensions and allows us to discuss from a bird's eye view, as it were, both distinctions and overlaps.

For example, looking at the operationalization of the three views as the recognition, discovery, and creation of opportunities suggests that the creative view might be more general than and prior to the other two views. This is because creative processes contain recognition and discovery as necessary inputs, while recognition and discovery can do without most key aspects of creativity. A simple example of this point is that before we can "recognize" or "discover" great art, that art has to have been created. Similarly, entrepreneurial opportunities may be posited to have been "created" through the decisions and actions (conscious or unintended) of economic actors before someone can "recognize" or "discover" them. For instance, once specific goals, values and preferences have been formed through the creative process, discovery processes can discover various means to achieve the goals. And when both ends and means become manifest, allocative processes figure out which particular means can best achieve which particular ends.

We could argue the case of Starbucks as an illustration. The original founders (before Howard Schultz came into the picture) acted effectually to create a shop selling fresh roasted beans in Seattle, mostly because one of the founders happened to love coffee from fresh ground beans. It did not even strike them to brew coffee and allow customers to taste it, let alone a vision of the Starbucks coffee bar market as it exists today. After customers actually asked to taste the coffee, the firm turned into a coffee shop that then allowed Schultz to "discover" the potential market for coffee bars and franchise the idea nationally. Today, presumably almost anyone with the basic resource requirements can open up a Starbucks franchise. In this particular case, we can see how each of the three views of entrepreneurial opportunity is empirically valid at different stages of market creation.

Another way to integrate the three views would be to recognize that they are extremely context-dependent. In other words, each view is useful under different circumstances, problem spaces and decision parameters. For example, when resources are clearly specified and goals are given, the allocative view will be the most appropriate. In contrast, when the problem spaces are characterized by enormous uncertainties, and value criteria for making choices are highly ambiguous, a creative approach might be called for.

The essence of our exposition is not to establish the superiority of any one of the three views or even to completely characterize them in all their possible relationships. Rather, our explicit intention here is to demonstrate that the study of entrepreneurial opportunity is a far richer and substantially more textured and interesting area of inquiry than it has hitherto been supposed to be. Furthermore, it derives its interest and promise as much from the practitioner's desire to earn higher profits as from the philosopher's and artist's dreams of creating a better world. But perhaps *most importantly*, an inquiry into entrepreneurial opportunity has the potential to unlock one of the greatest intellectual puzzles of our time, namely the creation of new value in society.

SUMMARY AND CONCLUSIONS

In conclusion, every invention[2] engenders opportunities for the creation of several possible economic (as well as other types of socially significant) effects. In the foregoing sections we have examined three sets of views with regard to how these effects come to be. Approaches based on the view of the market as an allocative process focus entirely on the final effects of opportunity creation, treating the processes leading to these final effects as mere detail; approaches based on the view of the market as a discovery process emphasize only the origins of the opportunity for creation, treating the final effects as inevitable products of competitive markets; and finally, approaches based on the view of the market as a creative process emphasize the decisions and actions of the agents, making both origins and final effects contingent upon those decisions and actions.

In our view, if we are to deepen our understanding of entrepreneurial opportunity, we need to integrate these three approaches, emphasize contingencies rather than inevitabilities in each. As a first step in that direction, we offer the following fundamental argument for the study of the central phenomena of entrepreneurship – namely, entrepreneurial opportunities.

---

[2]The term "invention" need not be limited to technological (i.e., science-based) inventions. Inventions can occur in all spheres of human activity – in the arts (surrealism), in sports (snowboarding) and in philosophy (pragmatism), to name only a few.

Conjecture 1:

The set of all possible economic goods based on any invention is larger than the set of economic goods actually created within a finite period of time after the invention.

Conjecture 2:

Not all actual economic goods created from an invention will be created by existing economic entities. In other words, the creation of new economic goods often entails the creation of new economic entities such as new firms and new markets.

Conjecture 3:

From the point of view of economic welfare, not all actual economic goods and economic entities arising out of any invention are equally "desirable".

Ergo, the lags (temporal and otherwise) between any invention and the creation of new economic welfare enabled by it, require not only the ability and alertness to recognize, and the perception and perseverance to discover opportunities for the achievement of pre-determined goals such as increasing profits and larger market shares, but also necessitate decisions and actions based often only on human imagination and human aspirations, that may or may not in time lead to new products, firms and markets.

REFERENCES

Arrow, K. (1962). Economic welfare and the allocation of resources for inventions. In R. Nelson (ed.), *The Rate and Direction of Inventive Activity*. Princeton, NJ: Princeton University Press.

Arrow, K.J. (1974a). Limited knowledge and economic analysis. *American Economic Review*, 64(1), 1–10.

Arrow, K. (1974b). *The Limits of Organization*. New York: Norton.

Arrow, K.J. (1984). *General Equilibrium*. Cambridge, MA: Belknap.

Blaug, M. (1985). *Economic Theory in Retrospect*, 4th edition. Cambridge: Cambridge University Press.

Brown, J.S. and P. Duguid (2000). *The Social Life of Information*. Boston, MA: Havard Business School Press.

Buchanan, J.M. and V.J. Vanberg (1991). The market as a creative process. *Economics and Philosophy*, 7, 167–186.

Burt, R.S. (1992). *Structural Holes: The Social Structure of Competition*. Cambridge, MA: Harvard University Press.

Cohen, W. and D. Levinthal (1990). Absorptive capacity: A new perspective on learning and innovation. *Administrative Science Quarterly*, 35, 128–152.

Darwin, C. (1859). *On the Origin of Species by Means of Natural Selection*. London: Murray.

Debreu, G. (1991). The mathematization of economic theory. *American Economic Review*, 81, 1–7.

Dewey, J. (1917). The need for a recovery of philosophy. In J. Dewey, A.W. Moore, H.C. Brown, G.H. Mead, B.H. Bode, H.W. Stuart, J.H. Tufts and H.M. Kallen (eds.), *Creative Intelligence. Essays in the Pragmatic Attitude*. New York: Henry Holt, pp. 3–69.

Hannan, M.T. and J. Freeman (1984). Structural inertia and organizational change. *American Sociological Review*, 49(2), 149–164.

Hayek, F.A.v. (1945). The use of knowledge in society. *American Economic Review*, 35(4), 519–530.

James, W. (1907). *Pragmatism: A New Name for Some Old Ways of Thinking*. New York: Longman.

Joas, H. (1996). *The Creativity of Action*. Chicago: University of Chicago Press.

Kamien, M.I. and N.L. Schwartz (1975). Market structures and innovation: A survey. *Journal of Economic Literature*, 13(1), 1–37.

Kipling, R. (1909). *Just So Stories for Little Children*. New York: Doubleday.

Kirzner, I. (1997). Entrepreneurial discovery and the competitive market process: An Austrian approach. *Journal of Economic Literature*, 35, 60–85.

Knight, F. (1921). *Risk, Uncertainty and Profit*, 1933 edition. New York: Houghton Mifflin.

Lachmann, L.M. (1976). From Mises to Shackle: An essay on Austrian economics and the Kaleidic Society. *Journal of Economic Literature*, 14(1).

Langlois, R.N. (1984). Internal organization in a dynamic context: Some theoretical considerations. In M. Jussawalla and H. Ebenfield (eds.), *Communication and Information Economics: New Perspectives*. Amsterdam: North-Holland, pp. 23–49.

Loasby, B.J. (1999). *Knowledge, Institutions, and Evolution in Economics*. London and New York: Routledge.

March, J.G. (1982). The technology of foolishness. In J.G. March and J.P. Olsen (eds.), *Ambiguity and Choice in Organizations*. Bergen: Universitetsforlaget.

March, J.G. (1994). *A Primer on Decision Making*. New York: The Free Press.

Marshall, A. (1920). *Principles of Economics*, 8th edition. London: Macmillan.

Nelson, R. and S. Winter (1982). *An Evolutionary Theory of Economic Change*. Cambridge: Harvard University Press.

Nutter, G.W. (1956). Monopoly, bigness, and progress. *Journal of Political Economy*, 64(6), 520–527.

Polanyi, M. (1966). *The Tacit Dimension*. New York: Doubleday.

Sarasvathy, S.D (2001a). Causation and effectuation: Toward a theoretical shift from economic inevitability to entrepreneurial contingency. *Academy of Management Review*, 26(2), 243–288.

Sarasvathy, S.D. (2001b). Effectual reasoning in entrepreneurial decision making: Existence and bounds. *Best Paper Proceedings, Academy of Management 2001*, Washington DC. Full version available at eff.org.

Scherer, F. (1967). Market structure and the employment of scientists and engineers. *American Economic Review*, 57, 524–531.

Schumpeter, J. (1934). *The Theory of Economic Development*. Oxford: Oxford University Press, pp. 128–156.

Schumpeter, J. (1976). *Capitalism, Socialism, and Democracy*. New York: Norton.

Shackle, G.L.S. (1979). *Imagination and the Nature of Choice*. Edinburgh, UK: Edinburgh University Press.

Shane, S. (2000). Prior knowledge and the discovery of entrepreneurial opportunities. *Organization Science*, 11(4), 448–469.

Simon, H.A. (1996). The architecture of complexity. *Sciences of the Artificial*, 3rd edition. Cambridge, MA: MIT Press.

Simon, H.A. (1997). *Administrative Behavior*. New York: The Free Press.

Venkataraman, S. (1997). The distinctive domain of entrepreneurship research. In *Advances in Entrepreneurship, Firm Emergence and Growth*, Volume 3, pp. 119–138. Greenwich, CT: JAI Press.

Villard, H.H. (1958). Competition, oligopoly, and research. *Journal of Political Economy*, 66(6), 483–497.

Von Hippel, E. (1994). Sticky information and the locus of problem solving: Implications for innovation. *Management Science*, 40(4), 429–439.

Von Mises, L. (1949). *Human Action: A Treatise on Economics*. New Haven, CT: Yale University Press.

Walras, L. (1954). *Elements of Pure Economics; or, The Theory of Social Wealth* (Trans. Jaffe, W.). London: Allen and Unwin.

Weick, K. (1979). *The Social Psychology of Organizing*, 2nd edition. New York: McGraw Hill.

SCOTT SHANE[1] and JONATHAN ECKHARDT[2]

[1]*University of Maryland,* [2]*University of Wisconsin*

8.   The Individual-Opportunity Nexus*

INTRODUCTION

In their efforts to define a distinctive domain for the field of entrepreneurship, researchers have recently shifted attention away from equilibrium approaches, which focus on identifying those people in society who prefer to become entrepreneurs, and towards understanding the nexus of enterprising individuals and valuable opportunities (Venkataraman, 1997). This new focus has been prompted by the need for scholars to explain the existence, identification, and exploitation of opportunities.

Several articles (e.g., Shane and Venkataraman, 2000; Venkataraman, 1997) have previously sought to outline this theoretical perspective. This chapter extends those articles in three ways. First, we broaden the treatment of the topic. Second, we clarify dimensions of the organizing framework that were unclear in these earlier efforts. Third, we update the earlier works by reviewing more recent contributions.

This chapter proceeds as follows: In the next section, we outline the equilibrium perspective on entrepreneurship and explain why we believe that it is inadequate. In the second section, we describe the disequilibrium perspective. In the third section, we discuss the existence of entrepreneurial opportunities. The fourth section offers some typologies of entrepreneurial opportunities. The fifth section discusses the identification of opportunities. The sixth section considers the locus of that identification. The seventh section discusses the exploitation of opportunities. The eighth section considers the locus of exploitation. The final section offers a conclusion.

EQUILIBRIUM THEORIES OF ENTREPRENEURSHIP

For the past thirty years, the dominant theories in entrepreneurship have been equilibrium theories. These theories have overlooked the importance of opportunities, and have sought to explain entrepreneurship as a function of the types

* The authors thank Mike Van Roo for his assistance with preparing this manuscript for publication. Portions of this chapter appeared in the *Journal of Management* under the title, "The Importance of Prices and Opportunities to Entrepreneurship."

Z.J. Acs and D.B. Audretsch (eds.), Handbook of Entrepreneurship Research, 161–191 of people engaged in entrepreneurial activity. From the equilibrium perspective, entrepreneurship depends on differences among people rather than differences in the information they possess. For example, Khilstrom and Laffont (1979) argue that people with a greater preference for uncertainty prefer to be entrepreneurs, while those with a lesser preference for uncertainty prefer to be wage employees. Unfortunately, the equilibrium approach has been largely unsuccessful in explaining entrepreneurship (Gartner, 1990), in part because entrepreneurial activity is episodic, making it unlikely to be explained by factors that influence human action in the same way all of the time (Carroll and Mosakowski, 1987).

To successfully explain entrepreneurship requires researchers to assume *disequilibrium*. To show why disequilibrium is necessary for entrepreneurship, we first summarize the basic assumptions of equilibrium theories and explain why these theories fail to capture entrepreneurship adequately.

Equilibrium theories assume that market economies exist in a state in which participants have no incentive to change their present actions, as they are satisfied with the current combination of prices and quantities that are bought or sold (Pearce, 1992). This assumption imposes very strict constraints, which are inconsistent with the entrepreneurial process.

First, equilibrium theories assume that prices convey all of the relevant information necessary to direct resources. By incorporating the information from all members of society, the price system provides the means to incorporate everyone's information in a way that allows them to coordinate resources accurately (Hayek, 1945). However, for the price system to work as a resource allocator, all relevant information must be reducible to price bids. Unfortunately, prices do not perfectly convey all of the information necessary to make decisions about resource allocation. For example, prices do not convey information regarding how a new technology will change future demand or future production costs for a good. Only after entrepreneurs engage in organizing activities and market transactions designed to utilize the new technology do prices incorporate such information.

Second, equilibrium theories assume that all information and expectations of market participants about the future can be reduced to current price bids for resources (Arrow, 1974). For future information to be reducible to current price information, futures markets must exist for all goods and services. However, futures markets do not exist for creative activities due to two fundamental problems. Primarily, activities that are novel or unique are plagued by information problems because there is no way of separating bad luck from low effort or low quality. As a result, futures markets for creative acts fail from moral hazard and adverse selection problems. Secondarily, market participants are unable to base decisions on information that is fundamentally unknowable in the present period (Simon, 1955).

Third, equilibrium theories assume that all decisions are optimizing decisions. When all of the information necessary to make decisions is incorporated into prices, decision-making becomes a mechanical process of applying mathematical rules of optimization (Casson, 1982). However, many important decisions about how to allocate resources are not made by optimizing within given constraints. Rather, these decisions involve creative processes, such as developing conjectures on the basis of assumption, rather than information, about what a change in technology or a regulation means for an industry.

Fourth, by assuming that prices always accurately direct productive resources, equilibrium theories ignore temporary disruptions in the price system that would allow one to buy or sell resources in response to beliefs about the profit potential of new combinations, or in response to conjectures regarding errors in judgment by other economic actors. In an equilibrium system, no one can possess such information because prices automatically shift in response to changes in supply and demand. As Hayek (1945, p. 527) explains, "the marvel is that in a case like that of a scarcity of one raw material, without an order being issued, without more than perhaps a handful of people knowing the cause, tens of thousands of people ... are made to use the material or its products more sparingly."

But why are people "made to use" resources in this way? In reality, prices do not shift automatically, but respond to the purchasing decisions of the "handful of people knowing the cause." If this is so, then prices change because a handful of entrepreneurs recognized a disequilibrium situation and purchased resources in response to beliefs about the future profit potential of possessing the resource.

MOVING AWAY FROM EQUILIBRIUM THEORIES OF ENTREPRENEURSHIP

Given the problems of taking an equilibrium perspective on entrepreneurship, we assume that equilibrium is either never fully realized in market economies (Kirzner, 1985), or is intermittently disrupted by the profit-seeking actions of individuals (Schumpeter, 1934). Thus, in contrast to equilibrium theories, which assume away the existence of entrepreneurial opportunities, we view entrepreneurship as the interaction between individuals and those opportunities (Shane, 2000).

Following Venkataraman (1997), we define entrepreneurship as the discovery, evaluation, and exploitation of future goods and services. This definition suggests that, as a scholarly field, entrepreneurship incorporates study of the "*sources* of opportunities; the *processes* of discovery, evaluation and exploitation of opportunities; and the set of *individuals* who discover, evaluate and exploit them" (Shane and Venkataraman, 2000, p. 218).

As Figure 1 indicates, our perspective suggests that entrepreneurship involves a sequential process. While this process may have feedback loops and certainly is not linear, we theorize that it is directional. Opportunities exist prior to their discovery and opportunities are discovered before they are exploited. The opposite direction is not possible because opportunities cannot be exploited before they exist.

Figure 1. The direction of the entrepreneurial process.

Our perspective does not require several features common to other theories of entrepreneurship. First, we do not view the creation of new organizations as a defining characteristic of entrepreneurial activity. Although entrepreneurship can include firm formation, it can also occur within previously established firms or through market mechanisms (Amit, Glosten and Mueller, 1993; Casson, 1982; Shane and Venkataraman, 2000). In later sections of the chapter, we explore the implications of this possibility for discovery and exploitation within and outside existing firms, as well as the role of markets as a mode of opportunity exploitation.

Second, our perspective does not assume that the same person or firm engages in all parts of the entrepreneurial process. One person may discover an opportunity and sell it or lose it to others. The discoverer may also enlist the help of others in the exploitation parts of the process, making varied the set of people involved in the different stages of the process.

Third, our perspective does not assume that any consistent relationship exists between effort or skill at discovery or exploitation, and entrepreneurial profits earned. For example, people who engage frequently in entrepreneurial discovery could be more likely to discover opportunities, but less likely to reap entrepreneurial profits from those discoveries than those who engage less frequently in discovery.

To date, we have very little information about the entrepreneurial process. For example, we lack simple demographics about what percentage of discovered opportunities is ever evaluated, or what percentage of evaluated opportunities is exploited. Moreover, as readers will see in later sections, we still lack empirical evidence about the factors that influence the entrepreneurial process. As a result, much work still needs to be conducted before a basic understanding of the entrepreneurial process will be achieved. In the following pages, we argue that the individual-opportunity nexus perspective is a useful theoretical approach from which to guide empirical research about this process.

EXISTENCE OF OPPORTUNITIES

In this section, we discuss the presence of entrepreneurial opportunities. To do this, we first define entrepreneurial opportunities and contrast them with other opportunities for profit. We then explain why prices are incomplete indicators of profitable opportunities. We finish the section with an exploration of the lifecycle of entrepreneurial opportunities.

Entrepreneurial Opportunities Defined

Following Casson (1982) and Shane and Venkataraman (2000), we define entrepreneurial opportunities as situations in which new goods, services, raw materials, markets and organizing methods can be introduced through the formation of new means, ends, or means–ends relationships. These situations do not need to change the terms of economic exchange to be entrepreneurial opportunities, but only need to have the potential to alter the terms of economic exchange.

The creation of new means–ends frameworks in entrepreneurial decision making is a crucial part of the difference between entrepreneurial opportunities and situations in which profit can be generated by optimizing within previously established means-ends frameworks (Kirzner, 1997). Entrepreneurial opportunities cannot be exploited by optimizing because the set of alternatives in introducing new things is unknown, precluding mechanical calculations between all possible alternatives (Baumol, 1993). Thus, while non-entrepreneurial decisions maximize scarce resources across previously developed means and ends, entrepreneurial decisions involve the identification of ends and means (Gaglio and Katz, 2001) previously undetected by market participants.

Why Prices are Incomplete Indicators of Opportunity

The market system is a powerful means of coordinating economic activity because prices simultaneously coordinate the production plans, resource availability, and resource requirements of market participants in a way that limits the cognitive demands on any one individual. By efficiently transmitting information, the invisible hand of the market coordinates the actions of millions of people who never have to interact, or even know why or how others produce goods and services (Smith, 1776).

As valuable as the price system is to the coordination of economic activity, it has one major weakness. Prices do not accurately convey all information necessary to coordinate economic decisions. As a result, prices do not accurately guide the discovery and exploitation of entrepreneurial opportunities.

For entrepreneurial opportunities to exist, people must not all agree on the value of resources at a given point in time. For an entrepreneur to exploit an opportunity, he or she must believe that the value of resources, recombined according to a new means–ends framework, would be higher than if exploited in their current form. In addition, the belief cannot be universally shared (Casson, 1982). If all of the current resource owners and other potential entrepreneurs shared the entrepreneur's belief in the correctness of the proposed new means- ends framework, then they would hold the same beliefs about the value of resources as the focal entrepreneur. If they based their decisions on these beliefs, this situation would preclude the focal entrepreneur from obtaining the resources at a price that would allow profitable recombination (Shane and Venkataraman, 2000).

But why, in a market economy, should people fail to agree on the value of resources if the price system provides an efficient means of transmitting information about changes in beliefs between disconnected individuals? The answer is that prices fail to provide all of the necessary information to make all decisions about resources.

First, prices convey only part of the information necessary to direct opportunities to serve markets. Producers are unable to make production decisions and allocate resources simply by producing quantities that set prices to marginal cost, as costs are unknowable before goods and services are created. Prices also fail to provide information on how new markets could be served, how a new technology could be used to improve a production process, or how a new way of organizing will generate value. In addition, prices do not contain information about prior failures at that effort, or articulate how one's approach to recombining resources would stand *vis-à-vis* the approaches of potential competitors.

Second, prices convey even less information to direct opportunities to serve markets that do not yet exist. While market participants might be satisfied today, a future condition might emerge that would lead them to desire a new good or service. However, as Arrow (1974) explained, there are no contingent prices for future goods and services. In the absence of futures markets for goods and services, there is no way to use current prices to determine if there would be an opportunity to serve a market that is not yet in existence. Similarly, there is no way for current prices to guide the allocation of resources in the current period in anticipation of resource needs of markets that will exist in the future, but that do not currently exist.

Evidence of the latter problem is most prevalent during periods of technological change, which do not appear to be anticipated by markets. For example, in the nineteenth century, just before the invention of steam ships, prices sent incorrect signals to sailboat producers and customers about the production of sail-powered cargo vessels designed to last for several decades (Slaven, 1993).

Given that prices cannot tell people what future demand will be, they provide limited information about forward marginal costs or revenues. Similarly, because markets set prices on known technology, not new methods that may be discovered in the future, prices do not reflect the relative benefits of different innovations if they would be introduced in the future. However, the appropriateness of resource allocation decisions in the current period, such as investments in durable plant and equipment, are contingent on the characteristics of future markets for goods and services.

Thus, even Hayek's (1945, p. 526) example of the value of the price system in the tin market shows the limitations of the price system for allocating resources for entrepreneurial opportunities. He wrote, "assume that somewhere in the world a new opportunity for the use of some raw materials, say tin, has arisen, or that one of the sources of supply of tin has been eliminated. It does not matter ... which of these two causes has made tin more scarce. All that the users of tin need to know is that some of the tin they used to consume is now more profitably employed elsewhere, and that in consequence they must economize tin." To Hayek, producers need only to look at the prevailing price of tin when making production decisions.

However, Hayek's account only describes how prices guide the decision process of tin producers who are selecting what quantity of a standardized good currently under production to produce. Prices provide little information to guide producers who have developed a novel use for tin or even if they should invest resources in developing such novel uses.

To the entrepreneur seeking to profit from this change, which of the two causes makes tin scarce is of fundamental importance. If an entrepreneur believes that the shortage of tin has resulted from the new use of tin, she may conjecture that using tin in the new way would be profitable. Therefore, purchasing the tin and recombining into the new use and then selling it would result in a profit. However, if the true cause of the tin shortage were a temporary elimination of a source of supply, then the purchase and recombining of tin into a new form would result in an entrepreneurial loss. The difference between entrepreneurial profit and loss in this case lies not in the information about the shortage of tin indicated by the price change, but in the entrepreneurial conjecture as to the *cause* of that shortage.

Discovery Defined

Although price coordination has its shortcomings, the market system remains an extremely efficient means of simultaneously coordinating the unique production plans and preferences of millions of individuals. Because the efficiency of coordination of resources through a price-based market system is achieved only if individuals base decisions on prevailing prices, most market-based decision making resembles a process of optimizing the allocation of resources within known means–ends frameworks that are already reflected in prevailing prices.

However, situations arise in which prices provide insufficient information to allocate resources. In these situations, individuals must make decisions based on information not incorporated in prices, and do so through mechanisms other than optimization. Entrepreneurial discovery is the perception of a new means–ends framework to incorporate information, incompletely or partially neglected by prices, that has the potential to be incorporated in prices and thereby efficiently guide the resource allocation decisions of others.

Entrepreneurs bring new means–ends decision-making frameworks into the price system by forming perceptions and beliefs about how to allocate resources better than they are currently allocated or would be allocated in the future on the basis of information not incorporated in prices. By leading entrepreneurs to buy resources, recombine them, and sell the outputs, these perceptions create new markets or update old ones. The prices that are updated or created through this process of recombination increase the accuracy of decisions of others who coordinate resources by optimizing within the price-based market system.

Formulating a profitable conjecture about an opportunity is far from the trivial exercise of optimizing within existing means–ends frameworks because it requires forming expectations about the prices at which goods and services that do not yet exist will sell (Arrow, 1974; Venkataraman, 1997). When these conjectures prove correct, entrepreneurs earn entrepreneurial profit, but when they prove incorrect, entrepreneurs incur entrepreneurial loss (Casson, 1982; Shane and Venkataraman, 2000).

The process of discovery describes how individuals acting alone, or within firms, perceive of a previously unseen or unknown way to create a new means-ends framework. Although we have used the term "discovery" to maintain consistency with prior literature, individual discovery is a misleading concept, as it implies that sufficient information exists at the moment of initial perception to assess whether a non-zero probability exists that an opportunity does in fact exist. Instead, individuals *perceive* that they have become aware of a profitable opportunity. Whether in fact they have discovered such an opportunity is unknowable at the time of initial perception, as it involves the ability to predict unknowable factors such as the characteristics of future market demand, or the extent to which individuals can be convinced to commit resources sufficient to sustain the effort to pursue the opportunity.

Suppose an individual has perceived, or discovered, that she can produce a new item by a previously unknown means. To establish if the opportunity has value in the first case, the individual must conjecture that a positive probability exists that the future price of the item will exceed its costs, that future demand will exist, and that others will not produce a superior substitute. In the middle case, the individual will need to conjecture that once others are presented with the actual product, they will respond positively to it. In all cases, the individual must attempt to foresee the characteristics of future markets to determine *ex ante* if the opportunity has potential value.

Predicting such things with certainty is not possible, as it requires individuals to possess information that does not yet exist at the time of individual discovery. For example, current customers are unlikely to provide accurate forecasts of their own future demand for new products even when working prototypes exist (Christensen and Bower, 1996). In addition, individuals may be mistaken in their analysis of the characteristics of the usefulness of new items. Therefore, individuals, operating alone or within firms, lack sufficient information to establish if a discovery has been made.

In the process of the exploitation of opportunities, individuals acquire resources and engage in market making activities that change prices and provide information to others. The process of exchange and interaction provides information that increases the mutual awareness among market participants about the characteristics of the opportunity (Arrow, 1974; Jovanovic, 1982;

Venkataraman, 1997). This information may either encourage, or discourage the individual pursuing the opportunity from continuing.

However, the only reliable confirmation that a previously unseen or unknown valuable opportunity has in fact been discovered occurs when a market has been created for the new item. In the absence of market confirmation, the validity of the entrepreneur's perception is unknown; no knowledge is recorded in prices, and therefore the production plans and preferences of individuals are not updated.

The Lifecycle of Opportunities

If an entrepreneur does discover a valuable opportunity and that opportunity generates entrepreneurial profit, that profit is transient due to external and internal factors. First, the disequilibrating shocks that initially generated the opportunity are often replaced by other shocks that open up new opportunities and close up the existing ones (Schumpeter, 1934). Second, even when new shocks are not triggered, the opportunities become exhausted by entrepreneurial competition. The information asymmetry that creates the opportunities in the first place is subsequently reduced by the diffusion of information about the opportunity. When entrepreneurs exploit opportunities, they transfer information to others about what the opportunity is and how to pursue it. Although this imitation might initially legitimate an opportunity, it also generates competition that exhausts the discrepancy to the point where the incentive to act no longer exists (Schumpeter, 1934; Shane and Venkataraman, 2000). Third, information about the opportunity diffuses to resource owners, who seek to capture profits by raising the price of their resources in response to information generated by the actions of the entrepreneurs about the new value of their resources (Kirzner, 1997).

However, the opportunity half-life can last longer or shorter depending on a variety of factors. First, mechanisms that limit imitation by other entrepreneurs, such as trade secrecy, patent protection, or monopoly contracts prolong the life of the opportunity (Shane and Venkataraman, 2000). Second, mechanisms that slow the transmission or recognition of information about the opportunity hinder imitation, thereby extending the life of the opportunity. The latter include the concepts of causal ambiguity commonly discussed in the resource-based view of strategy (Barney, 1991). They also include situations in which few parties have the requisite knowledge to copy a way of exploiting an opportunity, despite its demonstration, as Zucker et al. (1998) have described.

TYPES OF OPPORTUNITIES

Entrepreneurial opportunities manifest themselves in a variety of different ways. We believe that the prior literature has offered three valuable ways of categorizing opportunities: By the locus of the changes that generate the opportunity;

by the source of the opportunities themselves; and by the initiator of the change. In the sections below, we consider these different dimensions.

Locus of Changes

Although most entrepreneurship research implicitly assumes that entrepreneurship involves changes in products or services, entrepreneurial opportunities can, in fact, occur as a result of changes in a variety of parts of the value chain. Schumpeter (1934) suggested five different loci of these changes: Those that stem from the creation of new products or services, those that stem from the discovery of new geographical markets, those that emerge from the creation or discovery of new raw materials, those that emerge from new methods of production, and those that are generated from new ways of organizing.

Certainly, the creation of a new good or service can create an opportunity for entrepreneurial profit, as is the case when the development of accounting software or a surgical device makes possible a recombination of resources that can be sold for greater than its cost of production. However, as we have seen from the development of the Internet, new modes of organizing that do not require bricks and mortar locations also generate opportunities for entrepreneurial profit. Similarly, the discovery that seaweed could be sold as a food in the United States as well as Japan generates the opportunity for entrepreneurial activity, as did the discovery that oil provided a better fuel than many other raw materials previously discovered. Finally, new methods of production, such as the assembly line or computer-aided drug discovery, have provided opportunities for entrepreneurial profit.

In Figure 2, we show that Schumpeter's loci of changes can be arrayed along the value chain. We suggest that considering the relationship between these types of changes and the parts of the value chain would provide an interesting domain for entrepreneurship researchers to explore. For example, are the relationships one-to-one, as our figure suggests, or are they overlapping? If they are overlapping, are some Schumpeterian changes more powerful instigators of changes on certain parts of the value chain than on others?

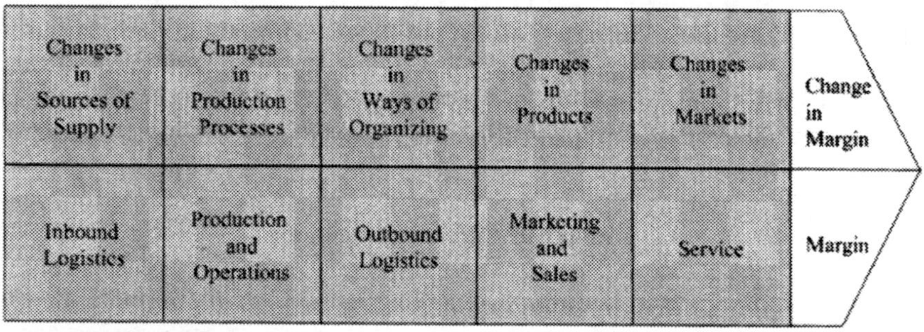

Changes in Sources of Supply	Changes in Production Processes	Changes in Ways of Organizing	Changes in Products	Changes in Markets	Change in Margin
Inbound Logistics	Production and Operations	Outbound Logistics	Marketing and Sales	Service	Margin

Figure 2. The relationship between types of Schumpeterian opportunities and the value chain.

In addition, we think that documenting the frequencies of different types of opportunity-creating changes and their relative causes and effects would be useful. For example, researchers should examine whether the opportunities generated by some types of changes are more long lasting or valuable than others and whether the factors that lead to them are different.

Furthermore, researchers may find that the processes by which opportunities are discovered, evaluated, and exploited differ across loci. Exploration of the potential contingencies between these loci of changes and the three parts of the entrepreneurial process would be a valuable addition to the field of entrepreneurship.

Sources of Opportunities

Opportunities also vary as to their source. We believe that prior research suggests four important ways of categorizing opportunities by sources: First considering differences between opportunities that result from asymmetries in existing information between market participants and opportunities that result from exogenous shocks of new information; second, comparing supply and demand side opportunities; third, comparing productivity-enhancing and rent-seeking opportunities; and fourth, identifying the agents that initiate the change which generates the opportunity.

Information Asymmetry vs. Exogenous Shocks

Kirzner (1973) and Schumpeter (1934) disagreed over whether exogenous shocks of information are the primary catalyst of entrepreneurship. In what Venkataraman (1997) termed the strong form of entrepreneurship, Schumpeter (1934) held that periods of market efficiency are punctuated by periods of upheaval. Changes in technology, regulation, and other factors generate new information about how resources might be recombined into more valuable forms. This information changes the equilibrium price for resources, thereby allowing economic actors who have early access to the new information to purchase resources at below-equilibrium prices, use the information to recombine them into a more valuable form, and sell them at an entrepreneurial profit (Schumpeter, 1934; Shane and Venkataraman, 2000).

In contrast, Kirzner (1973, 1985, 1997) holds that opportunities exist even in the absence of this new information. In the absence of prices, he argues, people form beliefs in response to information they possess. Because those beliefs are influenced by a wide variety of ceaselessly changing factors, they are never one hundred percent accurate. As a result, market actors make mistakes in their decisions, creating shortages and surpluses of resources (Gaglio and Katz, 2001). People alert to these mistakes can buy, recombine, and resell resources for a profit (Shane and Venkataraman, 2000).

Supply vs. Demand Side Changes

Opportunities can also be classified on whether the changes that generate them exist on the demand or the supply side. In general, the entrepreneurship literature implicitly focuses on supply side changes. For example, most discussions of opportunity concern changes in inputs, ways of organizing, production processes, or products (Schumpeter, 1934). But changes in demand alone can generate opportunities. Customer preferences influence the allocation of resources because producers need to respond to the preferences and purchasing habits of consumers. Thus, demand changes from exogenous shifts in culture, perception, tastes, or mood can open up opportunities (Schumpeter, 1934; Kirzner, 1997), as in the case of demand for American flags in response to a terrorist attack. The opportunity is created if the increase in demand outpaces investments in production capacity, generating opportunities to add more capacity, perhaps on better economic terms (Drucker, 1985). In addition, growing markets might create new niches (Christensen and Bower, 1996), as well as the opportunity to specialize (Geroski, 2001).

To the extent that observed entry corresponds with the existence of opportunities, some empirical support exists for the existence of opportunities in growing markets. For example, Romanelli (1989), Shankar et al. (1999), Highfield and Smiley (1987), Audretsch (1995) and Acs and Audretsch (1989) all find a positive correlation between market growth and firm entry. However, the research to date addresses this topic only indirectly and more studies should explore demand-driven entrepreneurial opportunities.

Productivity Enhancing vs. Rent Seeking Opportunities

Much of what researchers imply when they discuss entrepreneurship is productive entrepreneurship. In the standard view, the pursuit of entrepreneurial opportunity has productivity enhancing outcomes, as economies are made more efficient. However, it is also possible to think of entrepreneurial actions as rent seeking, which Baumol (1990) has defined as opportunities that generate personal value, but no social value. He points out several types of entrepreneurial opportunities that are not productivity enhancing, including crime, piracy, and corruption.

Merger activity provides a good example of the potential for both productive and unproductive entrepreneurship. The recombination of resources through the merger or break-up of firms can create productive opportunities as new customer relationships or economies of scale are generated. However, mergers may also generate unproductive opportunities, as would be the case if a merger merely shifts wealth from consumers to producers by reducing competition.

Researchers would provide a valuable contribution to understanding entrepreneurship by examining several facets of this categorization of opportunities. Venkataraman (1997) suggests that researchers investigate the social, legal, and political factors that influence the relative distribution of productive and unproductive opportunities across locations. Baumol (1990) suggests that researchers also examine relative distribution over time, arguing that, in the same location at different points in time, the potential to add value from new combinations of resources might be higher or lower than the potential to shift value from others via new combinations of resources.

Initiator of the Change

A final dimension on which opportunities have been classified is by the actor that initiates the change. Different types of entities initiate the changes that result in entrepreneurial opportunities, and the type of initiator is likely to influence the process of discovery and evaluation, as well as the value and duration of the opportunities. Among the different types of actors that researchers have identified are non-commercial entities, such as governments or universities; existing commercial entities in an industry, such as incumbents and their suppliers and customers; and new commercial entities in an industry such as independent entrepreneurs and diversifying entrants (Klevorick et al., 1995).

Although researchers have not often examined the actors that generate opportunities outside the area of technological opportunities, work in that area is instructive. Researchers have shown that two sets of actors are very important to the creation of technologies opportunities: Specialized knowledge creating agencies, such as universities or research laboratories, that lie outside the industrial chain, and firms within the industrial chain, including suppliers and customers (Klevorick et al., 1995). The two sets of actors have a different likelihood of generating opportunity-creating changes under different industry knowledge conditions. Researchers have also examined the conditions under which the actors within the industrial chain that generate opportunity-inducing changes are most likely to be users (Von Hippel, 1988), upstream suppliers, or the incumbent firms themselves (Klevorick et al., 1995). Additional research in this area would increase our understanding of the factors that influence the prevalence of economic opportunities in market economies.

IDENTIFICATION OF OPPORTUNITIES

To profit from the existence of an entrepreneurial opportunity, a person must first perceive that such an opportunity exists (Shane and Venkataraman, 2000). The information asymmetry that under-girds entrepreneurship assumes that only a portion of the population will identify a particular opportunity at a specific moment (Hayek, 1945; Kirzner, 1973). This observation begs the question: Why do some people and not others identify particular entrepreneurial opportunities at a particular point in time? Separate streams of research about access to information and alertness to opportunity offer insight into this question.

Access to Information

Information is unevenly distributed across economic actors (Hayek, 1945) because of limits in the ability of prices to transmit information (Akerlof, 1970), because people specialize in information (Becker and Murphy, 1992), and because people have varied information stocks that result from heterogeneous life experiences (Venkataraman, 1997). As a result, only some portion of the population will possess information about errors in market processes or exogenous shocks to equilibrium conditions at any moment in time. For example, only scientists at MIT might know about the creation of new technology in biologically based computing, while only residents in Topeka, Kansas might know about unmet demand for bakery goods on the north side of the city.

Three mechanisms appear to underlie the variation across people in access to information: Knowledge corridors, search processes, and social networks. We review the implications of these three mechanisms for entrepreneurial discovery in the subsections below.

Knowledge Corridors

Much of the ability to gather information about opportunities "is acquired through each individual's own circumstances including occupation, on-the-job routines, social relationships and daily life" (Venkataraman, 1997, p. 122), or occurrences termed knowledge corridors. These experiences allow people to know about resources that are unused, new technological developments, regulatory changes, or other information before others know about them. Hayek (1945) explained that everyone has superior information over others about some dimension of time and place that provides an advantage in discovering entrepreneurial opportunities. For example, the shipper knows which vessels are half empty before the real estate agent, whereas the real estate agent knows which houses are for sale before the shipper. Because this information advantage allows certain people to learn about the disequilibrium that makes an entrepreneurial opportunity possible before other people can see it, the advantage facilitates the discovery of that opportunity.

Search

People might also possess information before others because they search for it. Search theories argue that an individual searches for information as long as the marginal benefit of searching is anticipated to exceed the marginal cost of search (Stigler, 1961). Because individuals possess different information as a result of experiences transacting in diverse markets, some people can search for specific information more inexpensively than others. Moreover, searching for information closer to what one already knows increases the likelihood of gathering that information. Because information influences the probability of entrepreneurial discovery, and because local search is cheaper than distant search, individuals are likely to discover opportunities within a close proximity to their knowledge base.

Social Ties

Social network theorists postulate that individuals uncover information through the structure and content of the relationships with other members of society (Granovetter, 1973; Burt, 1992). The structure of social relationships determines the quantity of information, the quality of information, and how rapidly people can acquire information necessary to discover opportunities for profit. Further, social capital theorists believe that people are able to purposefully design the structure of their social relationships to enhance their chances of discovering opportunities.

Social relations are depicted as clusters of frequently interacting groups of individuals linked by weaker ties to other clusters of individuals. The interconnectedness of relationships within clusters of individuals leads to redundant ties where information from a single source can be received from a variety of individuals. As a result, information flows rapidly among members of these groups, thereby providing all members with access to the same information.

However, non-redundant social ties with members of other social clusters provide people with information not available to others lacking these ties. These non-redundant ties allow people access to information not broadly shared with others in their group, thereby facilitating the discovery of opportunities.[1]

Although the use of social networks to discover information that facilitates the identification of opportunities is detailed in the theoretical research on social capital, research attempting to measure the connection between the structure of social networks and the discovery of entrepreneurial opportunities is limited. However, in an analysis of 308 responses of a survey of 1,402 founders of information technology consulting firms, Singh et al. (2000) find that the structure of social networks influences the number of new ideas identified by entrepreneurs.

Cognitive Abilities

Access to information is likely to be an incomplete explanation of the identification of opportunities, because opportunities are identified only when people formulate a new means–ends framework in response to that information. As a result, recognizing opportunities from information about changes also involves determining the meaning of that information (Baron, forthcoming).

The need to understand information about changes or prior errors suggests that an important cognitive dimension of the identification of entrepreneurial opportunity is the construct of "alertness." Alertness has been described as individual receptiveness and ability to use information to create new means–ends frameworks from pieces of information (Kirzner, 1997).

---

[1] Social network theories differ from search theories about access to information. In the latter, individuals who gather information search locally for it; whereas, in the former, individuals who build connections to information possessed by individuals with market experience much different than their own are more likely to gather useful information. Therefore, social capital theory implies that local search is of little value for entrepreneurs seeking to discover opportunities for profit that are not yet reflected in market prices.

But why are some people better able than others to create new means–ends frameworks from information about changes? One answer might lie in relative superiority across individuals in this cognitive process. Gaglio and Katz (2001) suggest that alertness to opportunity is a function of variation across people in their ability to deconstruct causal relationships, to see cross-linkages between pieces of information, to understand the workings of economic, social, and physical processes, to critically evaluate information, to challenge assumptions, to re-label categories, to use analogies, to identify counterintuitive patterns, or to engage in counterfactual thinking. Sarasvathy, Simon and Lave (1998) suggest that it is a function of variation in people's cognitive schema, so that some people view new information in terms of opportunities rather than risks. Shackle (1982) suggests that it is a function of variation in people's creativity or imagination.

However, very little empirical research has supported these arguments. In a pilot study of twenty mangers and small business owners, Gaglio and Taub (1992) found evidence that managers approached the evaluation of a series of business case studies differently from owners. Although they interpreted the results as an indication that the cognitive process of trained business managers differs from that of small business owners, the authors did not detect a difference in their construct of alertness between the two sets of individuals.

One reason for this null finding may be that alertness is not an attribute of specific people. Rather, everyone may be alert to certain kinds of information, but not other kinds of information, according to the circumstances. Prior knowledge about a topic might generate an absorptive capacity that allows people to recognize the value of information on that topic (Cohen and Levinthal, 1990). Specifically, prior knowledge about such things as markets, technologies, production processes, industries, and customers influences the ability of people to comprehend or interpret new information as it relates to other information.

Shane (2000) provides empirical evidence in support of this argument. He shows that, in response to a single MIT invention, eight individuals discovered different opportunities that were related to their prior knowledge and experiences, but each did not recognize the opportunities identified by the others.

Another reason for this null finding is that there might be a contingency between types of opportunities and the cognitive schema that generate alertness. For example, Gaglio and Katz (2001, p. 100) suggest that "mental models for detecting the 'herd mentality' of other market actors and for developing contrarian positions as the initial reference point" will be likely to identify opportunities that result from information asymmetry between market actors. But, would such dimensions of alertness help to identify opportunities based on new knowledge? A valuable area for future research would be to map the relationship between cognitive schema and types of opportunities.

LOCUS OF OPPORTUNITY DISCOVERY

Our earlier discussion suggested that new firm creation is not a necessary characteristic of entrepreneurial activity. Individuals within existing firms could also discover opportunities. In fact, we expect that individuals within existing firms frequently discover opportunities.

To date, no research explores whether people within organizations are more or less likely than people outside those organizations to identify particular opportunities. Moreover, we know nothing about the types of opportunities that might be more or less likely to be discovered by people within organizations. However, information flows are likely to influence the probability of entrepreneurial discovery, and people within existing organizations receive different information than those outside of organizations. Therefore, the opportunities that people within organizations will discover likely will differ from the opportunities that people outside organizations discover. Similarly, if filters in the hiring process lead people within organizations to have a different distribution of cognitive properties than people outside organizations, then people within organizations are likely to discover different opportunities than those outside organizations.

Another important issue about the locus of opportunity discovery concerns its effect on other stages of the entrepreneurial process. If people within existing organizations are more likely to identify certain opportunities, and mechanisms exist to deter those individuals from exploiting those opportunities on behalf of a new entity (e.g., intellectual property or labor constraints), then the exploitation process becomes path dependent. Exploitation processes that are more common within established organizations will become associated with certain opportunities, and the range of observed approaches to exploitation outside of existing firms will become truncated.

EXPLOITATION

After an entrepreneur has discovered an opportunity, he or she may decide to exploit it, which we define as taking action to gather and recombine the resources necessary to pursue an opportunity, as opposed to the mental activities of recognition and evaluation. This exploitation process depends on several factors, including the attributes of both entrepreneurs and the opportunities that they pursue.

The attributes of opportunities are themselves important to the exploitation process because the asymmetric information that makes entrepreneurial opportunities possible influences the process of exploitation (Venkataraman, 1997). To exploit an opportunity, an entrepreneur must gather and recombine resources to pursue a perception of an opportunity that may or may not prove valuable. As a result, resource owners must provide resources to the entrepreneur despite significant uncertainty about the accuracy of the entrepreneur's conjecture. Moreover, because the identification of opportunities is influenced by the possession of information that others do not possess, significant asymmetries of information exist between entrepreneurs and resource providers (Venkataraman, 1997).

These information asymmetries raise the threat of moral hazard and adverse selection problems that could undermine markets for resources (Amit et al., 1990). Moreover, these problems are exacerbated by the behavior of entrepreneurs. To reduce the likelihood that others will imitate their approach to pursuing opportunities, entrepreneurs seek not to disclose the information that allowed them to identify their opportunities or their strategies for pursuing them. This reluctance to disclose requires resource providers to make decisions about supporting the opportunity with less information than the entrepreneur possesses (Shane and Cable, 2001), making it difficult for resource providers to avoid problems of adverse selection.

The entrepreneurs' reluctance to disclose information about their opportunities or exploitation strategies also makes it difficult to monitor them against opportunistic behavior (Cable and Shane, 1997). As a result, the information asymmetry between entrepreneurs and resource providers raise the potential for moral hazard on the part of entrepreneurs. These conditions suggest three very important factors in the exploitation of opportunities: Access to financial capital, contracting solutions, and social capital. We discuss these factors below.

Financial Capital

One solution to the problem of information asymmetry between entrepreneurs and resource providers is for entrepreneurs to invest their own capital in their ventures. By self-financing, entrepreneurs can overcome the information asymmetry problem by placing the financing decision in the hands of those people who have all the information about the opportunity. Thus, people with greater financial capital are more likely to exploit opportunities than people with lesser financial capital (Evans and Leighton, 1989).

The question of whether or not entrepreneurs need to self-finance provides an important distinction between the entrepreneurship theories of Schumpeter (1934) and Knight (1921). Schumpeter (1934) did not consider the importance of information asymmetry to resource acquisition, and thus argued that entrepreneurship involved only the identification and exploitation of opportunity. To Schumpeter (1934), entrepreneurs do not have to provide capital, and thus, do not bear uncertainty. Knight (1921), however, presaged modern finance theory when he recognized the information problems that would occur if entrepreneurs formulated their opportunities on the basis of information that resource providers did not have. Given these problems, Knight (1921) explained that entrepreneurs must provide capital to exploit their own opportunities, thereby making them bearers of uncertainty.

Contracting Solutions

Another way to mitigate the problems of information asymmetry and uncertainty lies in the allocation of ownership rights between entrepreneurs and resource providers (Gompers and Lerner, 1999; Kaplan and Stromberg, 1999).

Because entrepreneurial opportunities are uncertain, much of the information necessary to separate successful from unsuccessful ones is not available at the time that the entrepreneur identifies the opportunity. Under these circumstances, resource providers want to make only those investments that are necessary to gather needed information and postpone other investments until later (Dixit and Pindyk, 1994). Thus, resource providers supply resources in stages. These investment options give them the right, but not the obligation, to continue their financial support (Sahlman, 1990).

Resource providers also protect themselves against problems of information asymmetry and uncertainty by limiting entrepreneurs' control rights. Gompers (1997) explains that venture capitalists often write covenants that preclude the entrepreneur from receiving compensation until the investors have earned their return. Hoffman and Blakely (1987) point out that many resource providers force entrepreneurs to lose part of their ownership if the venture does not meet investor return targets. Resource providers also contractually require entrepreneurs to bear a significant portion of the risk in their ventures (Gompers and Lerner, 1999; Kaplan and Stromberg, 1999).

Social Capital

Unfortunately, explicit contracts can rarely completely eliminate the problems engendered by information asymmetry and uncertainty (Arrow, 1974). Therefore, investors also use social capital to manage these problems (Venkataraman, 1997; Aldrich and Zimmer, 1986). Social ties provide two benefits that mitigate adverse selection and moral hazard. First, social ties link the provision of resources to social obligation and social norms of fairness and trustworthiness (Gulati, 1995). This leads parties to avoid exploiting information asymmetries that might exist in their favor. Social ties also provide a way to gather information quickly and cheaply, thereby reducing the information asymmetry itself (Aldrich and Zimmer, 1986; Gulati and Gargiulo, 1999; Uzzi, 1996).

Some empirical support currently exists for the importance of social capital in the resource acquisition process. Shane and Cable (2001) show that investors are more likely to make seed stage investments if they have direct or indirect social ties to the entrepreneurs who bring them the investment. Shane and Stuart (2002) show that spin-offs from MIT are significantly more likely to have raised venture capital if they had pre-existing social ties to investors at the time of firm formation. Larson (1992) shows that other resource providers, such as strategic alliance partners, are also more likely to provide those resources if social ties exist between the entrepreneur and the resource provider.

The Characteristics of the Opportunity

Another factor that influences opportunity exploitation is the characteristics of the opportunity itself. The exploitation of opportunities is endogenous to their identification because people discover opportunities of varying value in response to a given change. For example, in response to a single MIT invention, entrepreneurs identified opportunities with markets as small as a few million dollars and as large as several billion (Shane, 2000). The perceived value of the opportunity will influence the exploitation decision because entrepreneurs have other options for their time, such as wage employment. As a result, empirical research has shown that opportunities will be more likely to be exploited when markets are larger (Schmookler, 1965; Schumpeter, 1934), profit margins are higher (Dunne, Roberts and Samuelson, 1988), levels of competition are lower (Hannan and Freeman, 1984), and capital is cheaper (Shane, 1996).

Another factor that influences the perceived value of opportunities is the appropriability regime related to a given opportunity. Appropriability is the condition under which one party can prevent others from capturing the returns from the exploitation of an opportunity (Levin et al., 1987). If the entrepreneur cannot appropriate the returns from exploiting an opportunity, the entrepreneur will likely abandon that opportunity or fail to initiate exploitation.

The Fit with the Person

Several characteristics of the entrepreneur will also influence the exploitation process. Venkataraman (1997) points out that entrepreneurs do not evaluate opportunities on the basis of relative performance. Rather, they evaluate opportunities relative to their personal alternatives. In particular, entrepreneurs look at their opportunity cost, and their premia for uncertainty and illiquidity, and compare those factors to their conjecture of the expected value of their opportunity.

This process of opportunity evaluation has important implications for opportunity exploitation. Given variation in the characteristics of the discoverer of opportunity, not everyone will be willing to exploit a given discovery. For example, the discovery of a need for a hot dog stand on a particular corner in Manhattan might lead an unemployed and illiterate individual to exploit it, but is unlikely to lead an investment banker on Wall Street to act. The magnitude of the opportunity cost will likely be a major deterrent to entrepreneurial exploitation by the investment banker (Venkataraman, 1997).

In addition, the fit with the person extends to skills necessary to exploit an opportunity that has been discovered. An individual may have the ability to recognize that a given opportunity exists, but may lack the managerial ability or social connections necessary to implement a business based on the concept. As a result, a particular opportunity that has been discovered may not be exploited, or a different person may exploit it.

Psychological Differences

Psychological differences between people also influence their decisions to exploit opportunities. For example, McClelland (1961) argued that individuals high in need for achievement will be more likely to exploit entrepreneurial opportunities because they prefer to take responsibility for finding solutions to problems, master complex tasks, take risks based on goals and skills, and seek financial rewards for success. In fact, Collins et al. (2000) conducted a meta analysis of 63 need for achievement studies in entrepreneurship and found that individuals high in need for achievement appear to be more likely to be entrepreneurs than the general population.

People higher in internal locus of control are more likely to exploit entrepreneurial opportunities. Individuals with a strong internal locus of control believe that they can understand and control the outcome of events, while individuals with a strong external locus of control perceive the outcomes of events as beyond their personal control (Rotter, 1966; Spector, 1992). Individuals with a greater internal locus of control are more likely to exploit entrepreneurial opportunities because it leads them to believe that their actions to recombine resources will have positive outcomes.

People higher in risk taking propensity are more likely to exploit entrepreneurial opportunities (Khilstrom and Laffont, 1979; Knight, 1921). Entrepreneurs must make decisions that involve bearing true uncertainty (Knight, 1921) because they must invest resources before they know the outcome of those investments (Venkataraman, 1997), in the absence of insurance, futures markets, or strategies for diversification (Arrow, 1974). Begley (1995) as well as Sexton and Bowman (1996) found differences in risk preferences between entrepreneurs and managers, and Brockhaus (1980) reported differences in risk preferences between entrepreneurs and the overall population. Stewart and Roth (2001) conducted a meta-analysis of risk taking propensity and found that entrepreneurs have a higher risk taking propensity than managers.

People higher in tolerance for ambiguity are more likely to exploit entrepreneurial opportunities. Tolerance for ambiguity is the tendency for individuals to accept ambiguous circumstances as attractive in contrast to intimidating (Budner, 1982). As the process of entrepreneurship is uncertain and fraught with alternatives without clear solutions, individuals with higher tolerance for ambiguity will be more likely to become entrepreneurs. In a review of four studies, Sexton and Bowman (1996) report that entrepreneurs have a higher tolerance for ambiguity than managers. Further, Begley and Boyd (1987) and Miller and Drodge (1986) similarly find evidence that entrepreneurs have higher tolerance for ambiguity than managers.

People higher in self-efficacy are more likely to exploit entrepreneurial opportunities. Self-efficacy is a measure of individual task-specific confidence, formally defined as the degree to which an individual believes he or she has the ability to achieve a certain level of achievement for a given task (Bandura, 1997). Those high in self-efficacy will have a greater probability of exploiting opportunities because that activity demands such confidence in one's ability to execute the exploitation successfully (Chen, Greene, and Crick, 1998).

LOCUS OF OPPORTUNITY EXPLOITATION

What modes of exploitation will be used to exploit entrepreneurial opportunities? Because only individuals are capable of discovering opportunities, the locus of decision-making about exploitation of discovered opportunities lies with people. As Audretsch (1997) has argued, this means that decisions about the locus of opportunity exploitation can be attributed to decisions that entrepreneurs make about how best to appropriate the returns from their discovery. Two dimensions of this choice appear to be important. First, can the opportunity be effectively pursued through markets? Second, are new or established firms better entities for undertaking the opportunity exploitation process? In the sections below, we review factors that might influence these decisions.

Markets or Firms?

Sometimes entrepreneurial opportunities are pursued through market mechanisms, as in the case of franchising and licensing. However, much of the time, entrepreneurial opportunities are pursued through firms. The exploitation of entrepreneurial opportunities through market mechanisms is influenced by three sets of factors: Cost, timing, and information (Venkataraman, 1997).

Entrepreneurial opportunities are often pursued through market mechanisms because such mechanisms prove less expensive than hierarchical arrangements. New organizations lack existing cash flow, which requires them to raise capital from external entities to pursue opportunities. Not only capital that must be raised through market mechanisms more costly than internal capital, but the rationing of financing for new entities makes it difficult for entrepreneurs to raise the total amount of capital they need (Evans and Leighton, 1989). As a result, capital strapped entrepreneurs often seek to use market mechanisms to pursue opportunities. Not only does the use of franchising and licensing allow them to use others' capital (Shane, 1998), but also exploitation through markets requires the ownership of fewer assets, reducing capital intensity (Martin, 1988). This argument suggests that the use of market-based mechanisms to pursue opportunities increases with the capital constraints of entrepreneurs, as well as with the capital intensity of the opportunities themselves.

Entrepreneurial opportunities are often pursued through market mechanisms because such mechanisms prove faster to implement than hierarchical arrangements. Because entrepreneurial opportunities are often short-lived, the rapid establishment of the infrastructure necessary to pursue those opportunities depends on the quick implementation of the value-chain necessary to pursue the opportunity (Venkataraman, 1997). This argument suggests that the use of market-based mechanisms to pursue opportunities increases with the shortness of the life span of the opportunity. In addition, it suggests that market-based mechanisms will be more common when the entity pursuing the opportunity needs to create the value-chain from scratch, as is the case with independent entrepreneurs.

Entrepreneurial opportunities are also more likely to be pursued through market-based mechanisms when information conditions suggest that such approaches are effective. As the literature on franchising suggests, when shirking problems are more severe than free riding problems in the exploitation of opportunities, market-based mechanisms will be preferred (Shane, 1998). In contrast, when hold-up problems plague market-based transactions, entrepreneurs will be more likely to use hierarchical arrangements (Azoulay and Shane, 2001).

Several characteristics of the opportunities themselves also influence the use of markets. First, markets are more likely to be employed when the opportunity can be well codified, as is the case for the economic sectors in which franchising typically occurs (Michael, 1996). An inability to describe the characteristics of an opportunity in written form will make the opportunity much harder to sell through markets because of the difficulty of executing contracts.

Second, markets for opportunities are facilitated when patents are effective means of protecting intellectual property. Patent protection mitigates the disclosure problem for opportunities by ensuring that the buyer will have to pay for the opportunity once its value is demonstrated (Arrow, 1962). Moreover, patent protection mitigates moral hazard problems, in which the buyer shirks in their commitment to pay the seller, by making the opportunity and its exploitation process more easily verified by third parties (Anand and Khanna, 2000). Finally, patents mitigate hold-up problems by codifying information about opportunities, thereby facilitating the writing of explicit contracts about them (Teece, 1981).

Third, market-mechanisms are more likely to be used to exploit routine opportunities. When different parties are more likely to agree on the value of opportunities, transactions are less likely to break down due to disagreements over price (Audretsch, 1997). However, when knowledge conditions increase the variance in people's perception of the value of an opportunity, as is the case when the opportunity is technically radical, market-based mechanisms may fail because transactors cannot agree on value.

New or Established Firms

Another question about the locus of opportunity concerns whether new or established firms are the entities that exploit those opportunities. To date we have several types of evidence about factors that influence whether opportunities are better exploited by new or established firms. We categorize this evidence in three sets: Those that are a function of industry characteristics, those that are a function of opportunity characteristics, and those that are a function of firm characteristics.

Industry-Level Factors

Several industry conditions increase the likelihood that new firms will be a mode of opportunity exploitation. First, new firms are more common models of exploitation when industries have more capital available for start-up activity, as is the case when they have easier access to venture capital or angel financing (Cohen and Levin, 1989). Second, new firms are more common models of exploitation when industries do not have high economies of scale or powerful first mover advantages, because these factors favor established producers (Shane and Venkataraman, 2000). Third, new firms are more common modes of exploitation when the opportunities are less reliant on complementary assets in manufacturing, marketing, or distribution, because established firms can compete with innovators more easily when the basis of competitive advantage lies in assets other than the innovation itself (Teece, 1986). Fourth, new firms are more common modes of exploitation when industries are new, because new markets are generally initially too small to interest established firms with a higher opportunity cost (Shane, 2001a) and a focus on serving their major customers (Christensen and Bower, 1996), and because learning curve advantages do not yet exist (Nelson, 1995). Fifth, new firms are more likely to be a mode of opportunity exploitation when patents are effective means of preventing competition, because patents allow entrepreneurs to establish an organization and value-chain before the means of opportunity exploitation is imitated (Teece, 1987); because effective patents will give the entrepreneur time to adjust the product or service to market needs (Shane, 2001b); and because strong patents will allow competition on the basis of factors other than cost, in which established firms will be advantaged due to the benefits of size and experience.

Opportunity-Level Factors

Several dimensions of an opportunity itself may make opportunities more likely to be exploited by new firms. First, radical opportunities will be more likely to be exploited by new firms because such opportunities undermine the competence advantages of existing firms (Tushman and Anderson, 1986), because established firms do not like to invest in opportunities that cannibalize their existing operations (Arrow, 1962), and because the routines of established firms focus their attention away from new information and new activities (Henderson, 1993). Second, low capital demands to exploit an opportunity will increase the likelihood that a new firm will be used to exploit the opportunity as new firms lack existing cash flow necessary to finance capital intensive projects. Third, stronger intellectual property protection for an opportunity, as is the case with broad scope patents, will facilitate exploitation by a new firm because that protection allows the entrepreneur to get the value-chain in place before the means of exploiting the opportunity are imitated by others (Shane, 2001b).

Firm Level Factors

Several firm-level factors also influence the locus of opportunity exploitation. The first is structure of the organization. The exploitation of entrepreneurial opportunities often requires organizational flexibility to manage their uncertainty. However, established organizations often seek to minimize flexibility in order to enhance their monitoring of existing operations, thereby undermining the willingness to engage in entrepreneurial exploitation within the firm (Holmstrom, 1989). Thus, organization design will influence the willingness of people to exploit opportunities within the confines of an existing organization, especially when managers are monitored closely and held strictly accountable for variance from their targets.

Second, organization scholars assert that institutional arrangements and organizational structures within mature firms spawn inertial forces that inhibit the ability for these firms to rapidly respond to changes (Hannan and Freeman, 1977, p. 1984). Because the exploitation of entrepreneurial opportunities often demands speed, organizations that have high levels of inertia will be less likely to be exploiters of such opportunities.

Third, the stronger the reputation of an existing firm, the less likely it will be to exploit entrepreneurial opportunities. Because the established firm has a reputation that it might not want to risk losing, it will be unwilling to make necessary decisions about entrepreneurial opportunities for fear that those decisions would prove incorrect and hinder the firm's reputation (Holmstrom, 1989).

Fourth, the greater the importance of existing customers to the organization, the less likely it will be to exploit entrepreneurial opportunities. Christensen and Bower (1996) argue that industry incumbents respond to contemporary expectations of established customers. They provide evidence that established customers do not seek new products or services, because those products or services are initially inferior to prevailing alternatives. As a result, established firms cede new market niches to new firms.

Fifth, the organizational reward structure might influence the locus of exploitation. An entrepreneur might perceive a greater expected value from exploiting the opportunity independently, rather than through a firm, if the incentive structure in the firm would not let the entrepreneur share as fully in the potential returns. This would be the case if the organization did not allow the individual sufficient stock ownership to replicate that of independent firm ownership (Audretsch, 1997).

The Relationship between the Locus of Discovery and Exploitation

In Figure 3, we consider a matrix that compares the discovery and exploitation of opportunities by new and established firms. This figure identifies four different types of efforts to pursue opportunity that depend on whether the discoverer was within or outside an existing firm and whether the exploiter is within or outside an existing firm.

This matrix provides several issues for researchers to consider. First, it raises the question of whether entrepreneurship researchers should focus their attention on the independent start-up cell, as they tend to do. The absence of research on the demographics of this matrix means that we do not know how

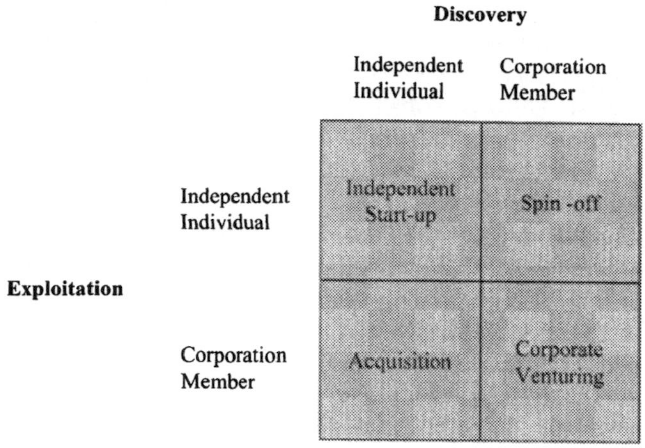

Discovery

	Independent Individual	Corporation Member
Independent Individual	Independent Start-up	Spin-off
Corporation Member	Acquisition	Corporate Venturing

Exploitation

Figure 3. Types of entrepreneurial efforts as a function of the locus of discovery and exploitation.

common the different cells are. Without information on what proportion of efforts to pursue opportunities fall in each of the four cells, we do not know whether concentrating research efforts on explaining independent start-ups makes sense.

Second, we do not know how the processes of pursuing these opportunities differ across each of the four cells. Casual empiricism alone indicates that pursuing opportunities through independent start-ups must differ in fundamental ways from pursuing them through corporate venturing. But we lack systematic empirical evidence that explains how these processes differ. For example, are resources acquired in the same way? Are the tools to evaluate the opportunities different? Future research is necessary to explain the ways in which independent start-ups, corporate venturing, acquisitions, and spin-offs are similar and different.

Third, we lack information on what factors lead opportunities to be pursued in each of the four ways described in the cells. Most of the problem lies in our lack of information about the locus of discovery. So far, we have information only about new firm versus existing firm exploitation, regardless of the source of opportunity discovery. To compare opportunities across the four cells, we need the additional information about discovery.

Nevertheless, some researchers have considered the relationship between the corporate venturing cell and the spin-off cell, both theoretically and empirically. When the opportunity depends more on human capital than on physical assets, spin-offs are more common, because entrepreneurs cannot move physical assets with them when they exit a firm.

In addition, several authors have attributed an increase in spin-offs to characteristics possessed by the firms in which the discovery was made. When innovations are architectural and therefore reconfigure the way in which products are developed, spin-offs will be more common because established firms have a hard time exploiting such innovations (Henderson and Clark, 1990). Similarly, when a new product or service is appropriate primarily to a small market niche, spin-offs are more common because an existing customer base will restrict an incumbent firm from focusing attention on the new niche (Christensen and Bower, 1996).

A third line of reasoning attributes the frequency of spin-offs to characteristics of the discoverer. For example, Bankman and Gilson (1999) attribute the variance in the locus of exploitation between corporate venturing and spin-offs to the nature of the person discovering the opportunity. More risk averse people will not launch spin-offs to pursue the opportunity.

CONCLUSION

The purpose of this chapter was to extend and elaborate on the individual-opportunity nexus framework on entrepreneurship presented in Shane and Venkataraman (2000) and Venkataraman (1997). We explained the weaknesses of the dominant equilibrium approaches to entrepreneurship and showed why entrepreneurship needs to be examined through a disequilibrium framework. We discussed the existence of entrepreneurial opportunities, particularly as they relate to the limits of the price system. The chapter also reviewed several typologies of opportunities. We discussed the process of opportunity discovery and explained why some actors are more likely to discover a given opportunity than others. We considered the opportunity exploitation process from the perspective of the individual-opportunity nexus. Finally, we considered the locus of opportunity discovery and exploitation. For all of these topics, we presented the logical arguments for the individual-opportunity approach to entrepreneurship and the empirical evidence gathered to date in support of the dimensions of this approach. Given the limited empirical evidence to date, we suggested many areas for future research. We hope that this chapter stimulates other scholars to join the effort to refine this framework and gather robust empirical evidence to examine the validity of it.

REFERENCES

Acs, Z. and Audretsch, D. (1989). Births and firm size. *Southern Economic Journal*, 56(2), 467–476.

Akerlof, G. (1970). The market for "lemons": Quality uncertainty and the market mechanism. *Quarterly Journal of Economics*, 84(3), 488–500.

Aldrich, H. and C. Zimmer (1986). Entrepreneurship through social networks. In Donald Sexton and Raymond Smilor (eds.), *The Art and Science of Entrepreneurship*. New York: Ballinger.

Amit, R., L. Glosten and E. Mueller (1990). Entrepreneurial ability, venture investments, and risk sharing. *Management Science*, 38(10), 1232–1245.

Amit, R., L. Glosten and E. Mueller (1993). Challenges to theory development in entrepreneurship research. *Journal of Management Studies*, 30(5), 815–834.

Anand, B. and T. Khanna (2000). The structure of licensing contracts. *Journal of Industrial Economics*, 48(1), 103–135.

Arrow, K. (1962). Economic welfare and the allocation of resources for inventions. In R. Nelson (ed.), *The Rate and Direction of Inventive Activity*. Princeton, NJ: Princeton University Press.

Arrow, K. (1974). Limited knowledge and economic analysis. *American Economic Review*, **64**(1), 1–10.

Audretsch, D. (1995). *Innovation and Industry Evaluation*. Cambridge: MIT Press.

Audretsch, D. (1997). Technological regimes, industrial demography and the evolution of industrial structures. *Industrial and Corporate Change*, **6**(1), 49–82.

Azoulay, P. and S. Shane (2001). Entrepreneurs, contracts and the failure of young firms. *Management Science*, **47**(3), 337–358.

Bandura, A. (1997). *Self-efficacy: The Exercise of Self Control*. New York: W.H. Freeman and Company.

Bankman, J. and R. Gilson (1999). Why start-ups? *Stanford Law Review*, **51**, 289.

Barney, J. (1991). Firm resources and sustained competitive advantage. *Journal of Management*, **17**(1), 99–120.

Baron, R. (forthcoming). OB and entrepreneurship: Why both may benefit from closer links. In B. Staw and R. Kramer (eds.), *Research in Organizational Behavior*. Greenwich, CT: JAI Press.

Baumol, W. (1990). Entrepreneurship: Productive, unproductive, and destructive. *Journal of Political Economy*, **98**(5), 893–921.

Baumol, W. (1993). Formal entrepreneurship theory in economics: Existence and bounds. *Journal of Business Venturing*, **8**, 197–210.

Becker, G. and K. Murphy (1992). The division of labor, coordination costs and knowledge. *Quarterly Journal of Economics*, **107**, 1137–1160.

Begley, T. (1995). Using founder status, age of firm, and company growth rate as the basis of distinguishing entrepreneurs from managers of smaller businesses. *Journal of Business Venturing*, **10**, 249–263.

Begley, T. and D. Boyd (1987). A comparison of entrepreneurs and managers of small business firms. *Journal of Management*, **13**, 99–108.

Brockhaus, R. (1980). Risk taking propensity of entrepreneurs. *Academy of Management Journal*, **23**, 509–520.

Budner, S. (1982). Intolerance of ambiguity as a personality variable. *Journal of Personality*, **30**, 29–50.

Burt, R.S. (1992). The social structure of competition. *Networks and Organizations: Structure, Form and Action*. 57–91. N. Nohria and R. Eccles (eds.). Harvard Business School Press, Cambridge, MA.

Cable, D. and S. Shane (1997). A prisoner's dilemma approach to entrepreneur-venture capitalist relationships. *Academy of Management Review*, **22**(1), 142–176.

Carroll, G. and E. Mosakowski (1987). The career dynamics of self-employment. *Administrative Science Quarterly*, **32**, 570–589.

Casson, M. (1982). *The Entrepreneur*. Totowa, NJ: Barnes & Noble Books.

Chen, C., P. Greene and A. Crick (1998). Does entrepreneurial self-efficacy distinguish entrepreneurs from managers? *Journal of Business Venturing*, **13**(4), 295–316.

Christensen, C. and J. Bower (1996). Customer power, strategic investment, and the failure of leading firms. *Strategic Management Journal*, **17**, 197–218.

Cohen, C. and Levin (1989). Firm size and R&D intensity: A re-examination. *Journal of Industrial Economics*, **35**(4), 543–566.

Cohen, W. and D. Levinthal (1990). Absorptive capacity: A new perspective on learning and innovation. *Administrative Science Quarterly*, **35**(1), 128–153.

Collins, C., E. Locke and P. Hanges (2000). The relationship of need for achievement to entrepreneurial behavior: A meta-analysis. *Working Paper*, University of Maryland at College Park.

Dixit, A. and R. Pindyk (1994). *Investment Under Uncertainty*. Princeton, NJ: Princeton University Press.

Drucker, P. (1985). *Innovation and Entrepreneurship*. New York: Harper and Row.

Dunne, T., M. Roberts and L. Samuelson (1988). Patterns of firm entry and exit in U.S. manufacturing industries. *Rand Journal of Economics*, **19**(4), 495–515.

Evans, D. and L. Leighton (1989). Some empirical aspects of entrepreneurship. *American Economic Review*, 79(3), 519–535.

Gaglio, C. and J. Katz (2001). The psychological basis of opportunity identification: Entrepreneurial alertness. *Small Business Economics*, 16, 95–111.

Gaglio, C. and R. Taub (1992). Entrepreneurs and opportunity recognition. *Frontiers of Entrepreneurship Research: Proceedings of the Second Annual Babson College Entrepreneurship Research Conference*. Wellesley, MA, June 1992.

Gartner, W. (1990). What are we talking about when we talk about entrepreneurship? *Journal of Business Venturing*, 5(1), 15–29.

Geroski, P. (2001). Exploring the niche overlaps between organizational ecology and industrial economics. *Industrial and Corporate Change*, 10(2), 507–540.

Gompers, P. (1997). An examination of convertible securities in venture capital investments. Harvard University Working Paper.

Gompers, P. and J. Lerner (1999). *The Venture Capital Cycle*. Cambridge, MA: MIT Press.

Granovetter, M. (1973). The strength of weak ties. *American Journal of Sociology*, 78, 1360–1380.

Gulati, R. (1995). Does familiarity breed trust? The implications of repeated ties for contractual choice in alliances. *Academy of Management Journal*, 38(1), 85–112.

Gulati, R. and M. Gargiulo (1999). Where do interorganizational networks come from? *American Journal of Sociology*, 105(5), 1439–1494.

Hannan, M. and Freeman, J. (1977). The population ecology of organizations. *American Journal of Sociology*, 82, 929–964.

Hannan, M. and J. Freeman (1984). Structural inertia and organizational change. *American Sociological Review*, 49(2), 149–164.

Hayek, F. (1945). The use of knowledge in society. *The American Economic Review*, 35(4), 519–530.

Henderson, R. (1993). Underinvestment and incompetence as responses to radical innovation: Evidence from the photolithographic alignment equipment industry. *Rand Journal of Economics*, 24(2), 243–266.

Henderson, R. and K. Clark (1990). Architectural innovation: The reconfiguration of existing product technologies and the failure of established firms. *Administrative Science Quarterly*, 35(1), 9–30.

Highfield, R. and R. Smiley (1987). New business starts and economic activity. *International Journal of Industrial Organization*, 5, 51–66.

Hoffman, H. and J. Blakely (1987). You can negotiate with venture capitalists. *Harvard Business Review*, 65(2), March–April, 6–24.

Holmstrom, B. (1989). Agency costs and innovation. *Journal of Economic Behavior and Organization*, 12(3), 305–327.

Jovanovic, B. (1982). Selection and the evolution of industry. *Econometrica*, 50(3), 649–670.

Kaplan, S. and P. Stromberg (1999). Financial contracting meets the real work: An empirical analysis of venture capital contracts. *Working Paper*, University of Chicago.

Khilstrom, R. and J. Laffont (1979). A general equilibrium entrepreneurial theory of firm formation based on risk aversion. *Journal of Political Economy*, 87(4), 719–748.

Kirzner, I. (1973). *Competition and Entrepreneurship*. Chicago: University of Chicago Press.

Kirzner, I. (1985). *Discovery and the Capitalist Process*. Chicago, IL: University of Chicago Press.

Kirzner, I. (1997). Entrepreneurial discovery and the competitive market process: An Austrian approach. *The Journal of Economic Literature*, 35, 60–85.

Klevorick, A., R. Levin, R. Nelson and S. Winter (1995). On the sources of significance of interindustry differences in technological opportunities. *Research Policy*, 24, 185–205.

Knight, F. (1921). *Risk, Uncertainty, and Profit*. New York, NY: Augustus Kelly.

Larson, A. (1992). Network dyads in entrepreneurial settings: A study of the governance of exchange relationships. *Administrative Science Quarterly*, 37(1), 76–105.

Levin, R., A. Klevorick, R. Nelson and S. Winter (1987). Appropriating the returns from industrial research and development. *Brookings Papers on Economic Activity*, 3, 783–832.

McClelland, D. (1961). *The Achieving Society*. New York: Free Press.

Martin, R. (1988). Franchising and risk management. *American Economic Review*, 78(5), 954–969.

Michael, S. (1996). To franchise or not to franchise: An analysis of decision rights and organizational form shares. *Journal of Business Venturing*, 11, 57–71.

Miller, D. and C. Drodge (1986). Psychological and traditional determinants of structure. *Administrative Science Quarterly*, 31, 539–560.

Nelson, R. (1995). Recent evolutionary theorizing about economic change. *Journal of Economic Literature*, 33(1), 48–90.

Pearce, W. (1992). *The MIT Dictionary of Modern Economics*. Cambridge MA: MIT Press.

Romanelli, E. (1989) Environments and strategies of organization start-up: Effects on early survival. *Administrative Science Quarterly*, 34, 369–387.

Rotter, J. (1966). Generalized expectancies for internal versus external control of reinforcement. *Psychological Monographs: General and Applied*, 80, 609.

Sahlman, W. (1990). The structure and governance of venture capital organizations. *Journal of Financial Economics*, 27, 473–521.

Sarasvathy, D., H. Simon and L. Lave (1998). Perceiving and managing business risks: Differences between entrepreneurs and bankers. *Journal of Economic Behavior and Organization*, 33, 207–225.

Schmookler, J. (1965). Technological change and economic theory. *American Economic Review*, 55(1–2), 333–341.

Schumpeter, J.A. (1934). *The Theory of Economic Development: An Inquiry into Profits, Capital Credit, Interest, and the Business Cycle*. Cambridge, MA: Harvard University Press.

Sexton, D. and Bowman, N. (1996). Validation of a personality index: Comparative psychological characteristics analysis of female entrepreneurs, managers, entrepreneurship students and business students. *Frontiers of Entrepreneurship Research: Proceedings of the Sixth Annual Babson College Entrepreneurship Research Conference*. Wellesley, MA, June 1996.

Shackle, G. (1982). *Imagination and the Nature of Choice*. Edinburgh, Scotland: Edinburgh University Press.

Shane, S. (1996). Explaining variation in rates of entrepreneurship in the United States: 1899–1988. *Journal of Management*, 22(5), 747–781.

Shane, S. (1998). Making new franchise systems work. *Strategic Management Journal*, 19(7), 697–707.

Shane, S. (2000). Prior knowledge and the discovery of entrepreneurial opportunities, *Organization Science*, 11(4), 448–469.

Shane, S. (2001a). Technology opportunities and new firm creation. *Management Science*, 47(2), 205–220.

Shane, S. (2001b). Technology regimes and new firm formation. *Management Science*, 47(9), 1173–1181.

Shane, S. and D. Cable (2001). Social relationships and the financing of new ventures. *Working Paper*, University of Maryland.

Shane, S. and T. Stuart (2002). Organizational endowments and the performance of university start-ups. *Management Science*, 48(1), 154–170.

Shane, S. and S. Venkataraman (2000). The promise of entrepreneurship as a field of research. *Academy of Management Review*, 26(1), 217–226.

Shankar, V., G. Carpenter and L. Krishnamurthi (1999). The advantages of entry in the growth stage of the product life cycle: An empirical analysis. *Journal of Marketing Research*, 36, 269–276.

Simon, H. (1955). A behavioral model of rational choice. *Quarterly Journal of Economics*, 69, 99–118.

Singh, R., G. Hills, G. Lumpkin and R. Hybels (2000). The entrepreneurial opportunity recognition process: Examining the role of self-perceived alertness and social networks. *Working Paper*, University of Illinois at Chicago.

Slaven, A. (1993). Shipbuilding in nineteenth-century Scotland. In: S. Ville (ed.), *Shipbuilding in the United Kingdom and the Nineteenth Century: A Regional Approach*, St. John's, Newfoundland: International Maritime Economic History Association.

Smith, A. (1776). *An Inquiry Into the Nature and Causes of the Wealth of Nations*. Edinburgh, Scotland: University of Edinburgh Press.

Spector, P. (1992). Behavior in organizations as a function of locus of control. *Psychological Bulletin*, 91, 482–497.

Stewart, W. and P. Roth (2001). Risk taking propensity differences between entrepreneurs and managers: A meta-analytic review. *Journal of Applied Psychology*, **86**(1), 145–153.

Stigler, G. (1961). The economics of information. *Journal of Political Economy*, **69**(3), 213–225.

Teece, D. (1981). The market for know-how and the efficient international transfer of technology. *Annals of the American Academy*, **458**, 81–96.

Teece. D. (1986). Transactions cost economics and the multi-national enterprise: An assessment. *Journal of Economic Behavior and Organization*, **7**(1), 21–46.

Teece, D. (1987). Technology transfer by multinational firms: The resource cost of transferring technological know-how. *Economic Journal*, **87**, 242–261.

Tushman, M. and Anderson, P. (1986). Technological discontinuities and organizational environments. *Administrative Science Quarterly*, **31**, 439–465.

Venkataraman, S. (1997). The distinctive domain of entrepreneurship research. *Advances in Entrepreneurship, Firm Emergence and Growth*, **3**, 119–138.

Von Hippel, E. (1988). *The Sources of Innovation*. New York: Oxford University Press.

Weick, K. (1995). *Sensemaking in Organizations*. London, England: Sage Publications.

Uzzi, B. (1996). The sources and consequences of embeddedness for the economic performance of organizations: The network effect. *American Sociological Review*, **61**, 674–698.

Zucker, L., M. Darby and M. Brewer (1998). Intellectual human capital and the birth of U.S. biotechnology enterprises. *American Economic Review*, **88**(1), 290–305.

PART FOUR

The Emergence of New Ventures

If new firms are important in the mix of market exploitation, how firms emerge is an important question. The three chapters in this section examine this question from different aspects. In Chapter 9, "Entrepreneurial Behavior and Firm Organizing Processes," William B. Gartner and Nancy M. Carter offer insights and evidence about the process of organization formation. They examine the founding of independent for profit business for insights into the nature of organization formation. They view entrepreneurship as an organizational phenomenon and as an organizing process and posit that the roots of entrepreneurship are embedded in social processes and consider the process or organizational formation to be the core characteristic of entrepreneurship.

In Chapter 10 Mark Casson examines the relationship between entrepreneurship and the theory of the firm. According to Casson, there is a gulf between economic theories of entrepreneurship, which tend to be abstract, and studies of entrepreneurial behavior, which tend to be more about individual behavior. The purpose of the chapter is to bridge this gap by developing a naturally consistent set of hypotheses about entrepreneurial behavior from a parsimonious set of assumptions. The key to bridging the gap according to Casson is to relax some of the very restrictive assumptions about human motivation and decision making that underpin conventional economic theory. The main assumptions that need to be relaxed concern the objectivity of information, autonomy of preferences and cost-less optimization. Relaxing these assumptions makes it possible to accommodate theoretical insights derived from other social sciences. Once these assumptions are relaxed, it becomes evident that theories of entrepreneurship are closely related to modern theories of the firm, such as transaction cost theories and resource-based theories.

The relationship between entrepreneurship and strategy is examined by Sharon A. Alvarez in Chapter 11, "Resources and Hierarchies: Intersections between Entrepreneurship and Business Strategy." For many years, there has been a cozy relationship between strategy and entrepreneurship. In fact many have viewed entrepreneurship as simply an extension of strategy, and have called for close work between them. Strategy and entrepreneurship come into close contact when we are dealing with an innovation that the firm is trying to develop internally, or corporate venturing.

WILLIAM B. GARTNER[1] and NANCY M. CARTER[2]

[1] University of Southern California, [2] University of St. Thomas

9. Entrepreneurial Behavior and Firm Organizing Processes

INTRODUCTION

The purpose of this chapter is to offer some ideas and evidence about the processes of organization formation. We look at the founding of independent for-profit businesses for insights into the nature of organization formation, in general, realizing that other kinds of organizations, such as voluntary organizations, non-profit organizations, and governmental organizations, may be founded in different ways (Aldrich, 1999; Gartner, 1993a; Gartner and Gatewood, 1993; Scott, 1997). The focus of research on entrepreneurial behavior is about exploring "how" various activities undertaken by individuals emerge into organizations. Entrepreneurial behavior is a type of organizational behavior (Bird, 1989). Entrepreneurial behavior involves the activities of individuals who are associated with creating new organizations rather than the activities of individuals who are involved with maintaining or changing the operations of on-going established organizations (Gartner, Bird and Starr, 1992; Gartner and Starr, 1993). This chapter does not attempt to investigate the factors and causes that might lead to the initiation of organization formation activities. Discussions of theory and evidence about "why" organizations are likely to be formed have been addressed by a number of scholars (Aldrich, 1999; Kirchhoff, 1994; Reynolds, 1992; Reynolds, Hay, Bygrave, Camp and Autio, 2000; Reynolds and White, 1997; Schoonhover and Romanelli, 2001; Storey, 1994), and were also the subject of two special issues of *Entrepreneurship Theory and Practice* (1992, 1993).

We view entrepreneurship as an organizational phenomenon, and more specifically, as an organizing process. Without belaboring the etymology of the word "entrepreneurship" [see for example, Baumol (1993), Bull and Willard (1993), and Herbert and Link (1988), for discussions of a history of entrepreneurship definitions; and Amit, Glosten and Muller (1993) and Gartner (1990, 1993, 2001) for recent interpretations], its root, *entreprendre* [i.e. go ahead, take in hand, undertake, take a hold of (Crookall, 1994, p. 333)] is fundamentally about organizing [as in a "generic category of assembly rules," (Weick, 1979, p. 235)]. *Organizing* involves the coordination and establishment of routines, structures and systems (Becker and Gordon, 1966; Leibenstein, 1968;

Z.J. Acs and D.B. Audretsch (eds.), Handbook of Entrepreneurship Research, 195 221
© 2003 *Kluwer Academic Publishers. Printed in Great Britain.*

Nelson and Winter, 1982; Ronen, 1982). Organizing processes are accomplished through interactions among people, continually re-accomplished and renewed over time (Pfeffer, 1982). We posit that the roots of entrepreneurship are, therefore, embedded in social processes (Katz, 1993; Katz and Gartner, 1988) and we consider the processes of organization formation to be the core characteristic of entrepreneurship (Carter, Gartner and Reynolds, 1996; Gartner, 1985, 1988, 2001).

Parts of this chapter are devoted to defining the scope and boundaries of entrepreneurial behavior, as a topic area in the field of entrepreneurship. In the next section of this we attempt to alert the reader to what we consider to be some of the primary characteristics of the phenomenon of entrepreneurial behavior. We believe that entrepreneurial behavior is an individual level phenomenon, which occurs over time (is a process), and results in an organization as the primary outcome of these activities. We then identify an issue that we believe has caused considerable confusion in the entrepreneurship field: Namely the assumption that the study of new organizations is comparable to the study of emerging organizations. We argue that the information gained from the retrospections, insights, or the current behaviors and thought processes of individuals who are operating established new businesses are not comparable to the experiences of individuals actually in the process of organization creation. Research on individuals already in business tells only one side of the story about the process of organization creation – about outcomes of emergence. We will argue that research based on samples of individuals in new firms are biased in a way that renders them unusable for answering fundamental questions about how entrepreneurs create organizations. If the reader accepts our point of view about the need to use samples of individuals in the process of starting businesses for research on organization formation, then, prior empirical research that is germane to this literature review dramatically decreases.

The third part of this chapter specifies the outcomes of entrepreneurial behavior: The characteristics of new organizations. We believe the reader gains some important insights into the process of entrepreneurial behavior through this exploration of the kinds of organizational characteristics that can be used to manifest a "new organization." It is not apparently easy to specify the characteristics of a new organization, and since (as will be shown) new organizations manifest themselves, over time, in various ways, appreciating the variety of characteristics that constitute the existence of a new organization suggests the variety of behaviors that might lead to generating these characteristics.

The fourth and fifth sections of this chapter offer ideas and empirical evidence about the overall "gestalt" of entrepreneurial activities and possible ways these sequences of activities might be combined in order for an organization to emerge. The gist of the fourth section is to show that the formation of an organization requires a broad range of different activities that occur over time. We point out the limited number of empirical studies that focus on the activities of individuals involved in founding organizations that have been conducted. In the fifth section, we suggest a few possible ways that research on entrepreneurial behavior might be approached. Finally, the chapter ends with a few recommendations for future research in this area.

CHARACTERISTICS OF ENTREPRENEURIAL BEHAVIOR

There are a number of assumptions that influence this overview of research on entrepreneurial behavior that differs dramatically with assumptions that guide the work of other scholars who focus on other aspects of organization creation. First, the process of creating a new organization is, inherently, an individual level phenomenon. Individual behaviors are the principal necessary ingredients for organization formation to occur. Without the organization creation activities of individuals, there are no organizations. So, while organization formation occurs within a particular context (Gartner, 1985; Schoonhoven and Romanelli, 2001) – environmental, economic, social, community, political – organizations are not created by their context. Entrepreneurs are necessary for entrepreneurial behavior, and it is through the actions of entrepreneurs that organizations come into existence. We see entrepreneurial behavior as something that individuals engage in, rather than firms (Lumpkin and Dess, 1996). We are not suggesting that entrepreneurs, as firm organizers, are inherently unique, *per se*, compared to individuals undertaking other kinds of activities. Rather, we stipulate that organization formation requires activity, and that activity occurs through the actions of individuals. From the entrepreneurial behavior perspective, it is the behaviors that matter (as the primary way in which variation among individuals would be ascertained), not the characteristics of these individuals, themselves (Gartner, 1988). This perspective assumes that there are individual differences both between new firm founders (nascent entrepreneurs) compared to non-founders and among firm founders, themselves. The study of individual differences are of interest in ascertaining those factors that might prompt some individuals to engage in firm formation activities (compared to others), as well as specifying why nascent entrepreneurs engage in different entrepreneurial activities. Individual characteristics matter, therefore, in that they are likely to be associated with differences in individual behaviors. But, it is the behaviors, themselves, that produce organizations. It should also be pointed out that the behaviors involved in organization formation are likely to be imbedded in the actions of many individuals, rather than through a single individual. A significant percentage of firm formation activities involve teams of individuals (Ruef, Aldrich and Carter, 2002). Therefore, it would be the behaviors of all individuals involved in the formation of a firm that would comprise the process of organization creation.

Second, entrepreneurial behavior is a process. When we discuss the activities of individuals engaged in entrepreneurial activities, we hope the reader realizes that these activities occur over a period of time. While the ways in which we observe and report on entrepreneurial activities might lead one to think that these activities are concrete and limited events, we recognize that most entrepreneurial activity requires a set of actions or series of actions, over time.

Third, the creation of an organization is the principal outcome of entrepreneurial behavior, that is, our primary dependent variable for research on entrepreneurial behavior is determining whether an organization comes into existence, or not. While a number of other outcomes of entrepreneurial activity might occur in the organization formation process (e.g., the creation of new products, the identification of new markets, new customers and groups of customers, the acquisition of new skills and knowledge), the fundamental outcome of entrepreneurial behavior is the organization, itself. We are cognizant that there are numerous quantitative and qualitative differences in the kinds of organizations that are created. Such organizational characteristics as size (in sales and employees), rate of growth, profitability, and innovativeness are certainly important to recognize when making judgments about the subsequent value of the outcomes of entrepreneurial behavior.

Finally, we note that the process of entrepreneurial behavior is a multi-level phenomenon and that it is often difficult to separate what constitutes an independent variable (an entrepreneurial activity) from a dependent variable (a characteristic of a new organization). For example, the activity of "making sales" is both an important individual-level entrepreneurial behavior and an important characteristic that indicates that an organization exists. An individual is actually involved in creating a sales transaction, that is, an organization can't actually sell: An individual must undertake those activities. Yet, "making sales" is a critical signifier of an important organizational characteristic (Katz and Gartner, 1988; Reynolds and Miller, 1992). Is "making sales" an individual-level or an organization-level phenomenon? It is difficult to keep separate what appear to be individual-level activities and events from what essentially is something that is, or becomes, the organization, itself. This problem is omnipresent in research on entrepreneurial behavior: At some point individual entrepreneurial activity emerges into organizational behavior. Demarcating when this transition actually occurs is surprisingly difficult to do (Reynolds and Miller, 1992).

Much of our discussion about the current state of knowledge on the topic of entrepreneurial behavior and possible directions for future research on entrepreneurial behavior is informed by our insights and experiences with developing the Panel Study of Entrepreneurial Dynamics – PSED (Reynolds, 2000; Shaver, Carter, Gartner and Reynolds, 2001). The PSED has detailed longitudinal survey information on 830 individuals that were identified while they were in the process of starting new businesses. This sample of nascent entrepreneurs was generated from a random sample of 64,622 working age adults in the United States. The PSED is a representative, generalizable sample of all entrepreneurial activity in the United States. The nascent entrepreneurs in the PSED dataset have been interviewed three times over the following three years (from 1998 to 2002 depending on when they were originally contacted) about their startup activities and the subsequent outcomes of their endeavors.

Over 120 scholars were involved in the development of the PSED. Since this project was initially conceived in 1996, thirty-three universities and private foundations, the National Science Foundation, and the Kauffman Center for Entrepreneurial Leadership have provided over two million dollars in financial support to this effort.

The PSED is the first national database to offer systematic, reliable and generalizable data on the process of business formation. The PSED includes information on: The proportion and characteristics of the adult population involved in attempts to start new businesses, the kinds of activities these nascent entrepreneurs undertake during the business start-up process, and the proportion and characteristics of the start-up efforts that become new firms. As we are writing this overview on research on entrepreneurial behavior, findings from the PSED are just beginning to surface as conference presentations (Allen and Stearns, 2002; Carter, 2002; Carter, Gartner and Greene, 2002; Crosa, Aldrich and Keister, 2002; Gartner and Shaver, 2002; Matthews and Human, 2000; Ruef, Aldrich and Carter, 2002; Stearns and Allen, 2001), journal articles (Carter, Gartner, Shaver and Gatewood, in press), book chapters (Gartner, Carter and Hills, in press; Greene, Carter and Reynolds, in press), and books (Gartner, Shaver, Carter and Reynolds, in press). We believe that research results from analyses of the PSED will have a significant impact on our understanding of how firms emerge, as well as on all future theoretical and empirical research on entrepreneurial behavior and entrepreneurship, overall. Our overview will, therefore, offer some of the ways in which entrepreneurial behavior was conceptualized and operationalized in the PSED survey. Some preliminary results from the PSED on the activities of these nascent entrepreneurs will also be presented.

"NEW" ORGANIZATIONS ARE NOT "EMERGING" ORGANIZATIONS

One of our frustrations with attempting to provide an overview of prior empirical research on entrepreneurial behavior is in discovering only a very small number of empirical studies that have explored the activities of individuals while they are in the process of starting a new business. There are very few "facts" about the process of organization formation as it actually occurs, and a great deal of speculation. Most studies of firm organizing activities have been retrospective explorations of the startup behaviors of individuals who are, already, in business. This is a significant problem. As has been pointed out by other scholars, surveys of entrepreneurs who have successfully started firms introduce a significant selection bias into any research program that attempts to explore issues involved with the creation of organizations (Aldrich, 1999; Aldrich et al., 1989; Delmar and Shane, 2002; Katz and Gartner, 1988). Obviously, when only those individuals who have successfully started businesses are surveyed, no information on startup activities is provided on those individuals who failed in their startup attempts. Indeed, it is the knowledge gained from studying the "failures" that provides reasonable contrasts for making sense of the "successes." Information gleaned from the individuals who successfully started new businesses cannot be used to infer whether the unsuccessful nascent entrepreneurs behaved differently. For example, if a survey of individuals who successfully started a new business indicates that 75% of these individuals initiated a particular organization creation activity, this finding cannot be used to imply that individuals who did not successfully start a new business did not undertake this activity. It could be plausible that the same percentage of the unsuccessful nascent entrepreneurs also initiated this same activity. It is very difficult to ascertain whether a behavior undertaken by a successful entrepreneur, is indeed, important, without information from the unsuccessful nascent entrepreneurs on whether they undertook such behaviors, or not. If the outcome of entrepreneurial behavior is an organization, then, exploring the behaviors of entrepreneurs who all had successful outcomes (new organizations) doesn't really seem to address the variation between those that were successful and those that didn't start organizations.

Some scholars have assumed that the identification of all new organizations in a particular population of organizations are likely to represent all of the variation that occurred during prior attempts at founding, and that studies of new organizations would likely be an adequate surrogate for speculations about the creation of variation in organization populations (Carroll and Hannan, 2000). We suggest that the activities involved with attempts at creating organizations are likely to be where the majority of possible variations, and sources of variations in possible new organizations are likely to occur (Aldrich, 1999; Katz and Gartner, 1988). The process of attempting to start businesses are experiments that are conducted by millions of nascent entrepreneurs to test their hypotheses about whether their ideas, skills, capabilities and actions might result in successful outcomes (e.g., establishing an ongoing organization). It is in the process of organization formation that there are likely to be more degrees of freedom to generate a variety of organizations and new types of organizations. To assume that samples of individuals who had successful solutions to the problem of organization creation represent all of the possible ways that nascent entrepreneurs might have engaged in organization creation is a substantial leap of faith. We believe that scholarship on entrepreneurial behavior should be based, primarily, on studies that observe individuals in the process of organization creation.

Our inclination is to focus only on studies that have used samples of nascent entrepreneurs, that is, to look at individuals in the process of starting businesses, and to ignore evidence from studies that survey founders of new on-going organizations. We try to point out, in our overview of research on entrepreneurial behaviors, the composition and characteristics of the individuals in the samples analyzed. We believe that the evidence provided in the following sections of this chapter support the view that research on organization formation processes needs to study these activities while they occur. Samples used in research on organization creation need to reflect all possible attempts at organization creation, not just those attempts that resulted in new firms.

THE CHARACTERISTICS OF EMERGING ORGANIZATIONS

If entrepreneurial behavior involves creating organizations, then, an important aspect of scholarly study of the organization creation process involves specifying, what, exactly, is being created. Identifying when a new organization occurs, as well as what constitutes a new organization, is a challenge. For example, one way to measure the successful creation of a new business is whether a business license exists. It is entirely possible for an individual to acquire a business license without an idea about what the business is going to do, without any sales, without any specific resources, and without a physical location. In fact, the first activity an entrepreneur could engage in could be the acquisition of a business license. Is the possession of a business license an organization? Should a business license, then, be the primary measure of whether an organization has been created? Every measure that can be used to indicate whether an organization exists has both benefits and problems.

There are numerous ways in which organizations can demonstrate their existence. In a review of theory and empirical research on the characteristics of organizations in the process of creation, Katz and Gartner (1988) suggested that there are four "properties" that could be used to identify their emergence: *intention* (characteristics that demonstrate purpose and goals), *resources* (physical components, such as human and financial capital), *boundary* (barrier conditions that distinguish the organization, as such – incorporation, phone listing, a tax identification number), and *exchange* (transactions between the emerging organization and others, such as sales, loans or investment). They indicated that an emerging organization would "reveal" itself in different ways, and that a focus on any one of these four properties would result in an observer noticing, at different times, the newly created organization. As a way to explore these four properties, we will look at the problems involved in finding organizations *that are already in existence* as a way to see whether these properties might be useful to identifying organizations in the process of emergence.

Scholars who have attempted to find organizations (new and "old") have found that different data sources of organizations and different methods for finding organizations result in substantially different numbers and types of organizations identified (Aldrich, Kalleberg, Marsden and Cassell, 1989; Birley, 1984, 1986; Kalleberg, Marsden, Aldrich and Cassell, 1990; Busenitz and Murphy, 1996; Murphy, 2002). For example, Kalleberg et al. (1990), demonstrated that in a comparison of five methods for identifying organizations in a specific geographical area (enumeration – physically canvassing an area, telephone white pages, ES202 state unemployment insurance files, DMI – Dun and Bradstreet Market Identifier Files, and Chamber of Commerce listings), using telephone white pages revealed the largest number of businesses (6,220) and using Chamber of Commerce listings revealed the least (1,131). Only 52.6% of the businesses identified by these methods were listed in more than one data source, and only 5% of the businesses identified were found in all five data sources. Other studies have found little overlap among the businesses identified using different data sources, as well as indications that each data source of organizations has certain inherent biases towards certain kinds of organizations by type of industry, size, and ownership (Aldrich et al., 1989; Birley, 1986; Busenitz and Murphy, 1996, Murphy, 2002). These studies implicitly assume that organizations "exist" and that the only difficulty for scholars is in finding them. But, in fact, the measures used for identifying organizations "defines" whether they actually "exist." Recognizing that these studies were intended to find organizations in existence, rather than organizations in the process of coming into existence, suggests that the problem of identifying when an organization has been created is likely to be even more difficult. We believe that there are a number of different "birthdays" for an emerging organization. These "birthdays" depend on the measures used to indicate "birth."

Some studies have attempted to trace the various properties of firm emergence over time. Reynolds and Miller (1992) used samples derived from DMI files in Minnesota and Pennsylvania to identify firm founders who were interviewed about the occurrence (month and year) of four "gestation markers" in the creation of their businesses: *personal commitment* (when members of the startup team first made an investment of personal time and resources), *financial support* (when first outside financial support was obtained), *sales* (when first sales income received), and *hiring* (when firm first hired anyone, full or part time). They found that:

> "... *none* of these features of gestation in living systems are shared by new firms. Not all events occur. Every possible sequence of events was present. There is substantial variation in length of the gestation period." (Reynolds and Miller, 1992, p. 408)

Firms do not "signal" their emergence in the same way. About one half of all of the firms in their sample did not report all four events. When computing the time between the first events reported and the last event reported (irregardless of how many events were reported) they found that about 80% of all of the firms underwent the gestation process within two years. The first event for over 80% of new firms is personal commitment. In addition, the first event for 40% of new firms is sales. About half of all firms reported simultaneous first events of two or more activities. Last events reported ranged from 50% of firms indicating hiring employees or receiving sales income, 40% of firms indicating receiving financial support, and 25% indicating personal commitment. After a number of analyses to explore various sequences of startup events, Reynolds and Miller (1992) summarize their findings by suggesting that:

> "The most important implication is the importance of separating the founding process into two parts. The gestation period, from conception to birth, should be treated separately from the post-birth period." (p. 416)

Upon reflection however, it is quite difficult, in practice, to actually specify the point at which the gestation period ends, and the post-birth period begins. When the PSED survey was constructed there was considerable discussion about the kinds of "firm birth markers" that might be used to indicate the emergence of a new business. We decided to used markers similar to those used in the firm identification studies: (a) listing in the telephone book, (b) ES202 – state unemployment insurance tax payments, (c) payment of FICA (Federal Social Security taxes), (d) filing of a federal tax return, and (e) the nascent entrepreneur's knowledge of whether the firm was listed in the Dun and Bradstreet DMI files. In addition, we asked nascent entrepreneurs for a self-report measure, both at one and two years after the initial interview, of whether they thought their gestation efforts were in one of four categories: (1) a new ongoing firm, (2) still actively engaged in the startup process, (3) "on hold" with expectations of continuing startup efforts later, (4) or an abandoned effort (gave up).

In Table 1 we present a preliminary analysis of the "first behaviors" of the PSED nascent entrepreneurs at the time of the initial interview. This list of first behaviors also includes the firm birth markers. What is interesting to notice is that, at the outset of the firm formation process, some entrepreneurs specify new firm birth markers as their first activities. Of the 715 startup activity reports analyzed for this table, 17 nascent entrepreneurs first filed a federal tax report, 3 first paid FICA taxes, 1 first indicated having a business phone listing, and 1 nascent entrepreneur first paid state unemployment tax. (No nascent entrepreneurs initially began their business formation activities by receiving a Dun and Bradstreet identifier.) It is surprising that events that one would assume would mark the culmination of the firm formation process appears in some emerging organizations as indicators of a nascent entrepreneur's first efforts.

The gist of this section on the kinds of characteristics that might be used to identify organizations would imply that researchers interested in the process of *how* organizations come into existence should also pay attention to *what* kinds of properties will be used to demonstrate that these organizations are, indeed, "on-going" organizations, or in some state of emergence.

The issue of determining whether individual activity represents the activity of a nascent entrepreneur, or that of a owner of a new business, was a much discussed conundrum in determining who would be included as a nascent entrepreneur in the PSED. We determined an individual was a nascent entrepreneur if an affirmative answer was provided to either of these two questions:

- Are you, alone or with others, now trying to start a new business?
- Are you, alone or with others, now starting a new business or new venture for your employer? An effort that is part of your job assignment?

In addition, in order to be considered as a nascent entrepreneur, individuals were to meet three additional criteria:

- They expect to be owners or part owners of the new firm.

Table 1. Distribution of most frequent business startup behaviors that occurred first

	N^1	$\%^2$
Spent a lot of time thinking about starting business	404	57
Took classes or workshops on starting business	115	16
Saving money to invest in business	109	15
Invested own money in business	98	14
Developed model or procedures for product/service	82	12
Defined market opportunities	58	8
Raw materials, inventory, supplies purchased	52	7
Business Plan prepared	50	7
Startup team organized	40	6
Major items like equipment, facilities or property purchased, leased	24	3
Files federal tax income tax return	17	2
Marketing or promotional activities started	17	2
Arranged childcare or household help to allow time for business	16	2
Devoted full time to business	13	2
Credit from supplier established	14	2
Projected financial statements developed	9	1
Bank account opened exclusively for this business	9	1
Received money, income or fees from sale of goods or services	8	1
Applied for patent, copyright or trademark	8	1
Asked financial institutions or people for funds	5	>1
Hired employees or managers	2	>1
Paid federal social security taxes (FICA)	3	>1
Monthly revenues exceeded monthly expenses	2	>1
Business has own phone listing	1	>1
Business has own phone line	2	>1
Paid state unemployment insurance	1	
Paid managers who are owners a salary	0	
Business listed with D&B	0	

[1] Total doesn't sum to number of eligible nascent entrepreneurs (715) since some respondents indicated simultaneous first behaviors.
[2] % of 715 eligible nascent entrepreneurs who reported item as one of first behaviors.

- They have been active in trying to start the new firm in the past 12 months.
- The effort is still in the startup or gestation phase and is not an infant firm.

The third criteria was measured by asking these individuals whether the startup effort has a positive monthly cash flow that covers expenses and the owner-manager salaries for more than three months (Reynolds, 2000, pp. 170–171). Surprisingly, 27% of the individuals who responded "yes" to one of the first two questions (Are you trying to start a business?) also responded "yes" to the third criteria. That is, individuals that, by our criteria, we considered to be owner-managers of new firms thought of themselves as nascent entrepreneurs – still in the process of starting a business. This finding does point out the difficulty, for both the individuals involved in starting new organizations, as well as for scholars studying the process of organization formation, of trying to make sense of whether the properties of the situation demonstrate that an organization "exists" or whether these situations represent the process of organization formation.

ENTREPRENEURIAL BEHAVIORS: FIRM FORMATION ACTIVITIES

A number of scholars have suggested a variety of activities that are necessary for organization creation, as well as an explicit, or sometimes implied, sequence of how these activities will occur. For example, Gartner and Starr (1993) identified 24 different lists of entrepreneurial activities taken from various scholarly books and articles when they attempted to generate a comprehensive list of entrepreneurial behaviors and sequences of entrepreneurial behaviors. It should be noted that most of these lists of activities were based on anecdotal evidence, rather than on systematic research studies. Gartner and Starr (1993) indicated that the predominant way in which entrepreneurial activity was construed involved viewing the process of organization creation in a mechanistic way (Morgan, 1996), that is, seeing entrepreneurial activity as a set of behaviors involved with assembling various resources that can ultimately be combined into an organization. Van de Ven et al. (1989) describes this process of assembly as an accumulation or epigenetic model of change: "Over time, these entrepreneurs accumulate the external resources and technology necessary to transform their ideas into a concrete reality by constructing a new business unit" (p. 225). For example, Vesper (1990, p. 109) specifies that the process of organization creation involves the acquisition of five key ingredients: (1) *technical know-how* to generate the company's product or service, (2) the *product or service idea* which provides direction for the organization's efforts, (3) *personal contacts*, "because ventures are not started in isolation," (4) *physical resources*, and (5) *customer orders*. He then presents anecdotal evidence to indicate that these five key ingredients can be combined in a variety of differences sequences (e.g., 1–2–3–4–5, 4–1–5–2–3, 5–3–1–4–2, etc.). As was shown earlier in the Reynolds and Miller (1992) study, Vesper's suggestion that the sequence of startup activities may not follow what appears to be a logical progression (e.g., 1–2–3–4–5), seems to have systematic empirical support. Yet, most lists of entrepreneurial activities do suggest a particular sequence of activities, such as Birley (1984) who assumes that the venture creation process will occur in the following order: (1) decision to start a business, (2) quit job, (3) incorporate, (4) establish bank account, (5) acquire premises and equipment, (6) receive first order, (7) pay first tax, (9) hire full-time employees.

Since the Gartner and Starr (1993) overview of entrepreneurial behavior research, there have been few systematic empirical studies of how entrepreneurial activities might lead to the formation of an organization. The empirical studies that have explored a comprehensive view of the constellation of activities that might result in organization formation can be identified as those involved with in-depth event histories of a few organizations created while studying the innovation process (Garud and Van de Ven, 1992; Van de Ven and Polley,

1992; Van de Ven, Venkataraman, Polley and Garud, 1989; Venkataraman and Van de Ven, 1989) and studies that have explored whether a specified list of entrepreneurial activities are involved in creating a broad range of different types of firms (Carter et al., 1996; Gatewood, Gartner and Shaver, 1995). Since Van de Ven and his colleagues have primarily focused on the nature of innovation within established organizations as a way to understand entrepreneurial behavior, and since their line of research has been discussed, in detail, elsewhere (Poole, Van de Ven, Dooley and Holmes, 2000), we will summarize their efforts by suggesting that their findings indicate a multitude of different entrepreneurial activities and a variety of sequences of these activities can result in the formation of a new business. Indeed, in a very thoughtful reanalysis of data from two of their previous innovation studies (Cheng and Van de Ven, 1996), what appear to be random events and activities in the initial stages of a venture's development can be understood as following a chaotic pattern. Overall, the findings from these innovation studies indicate that the pattern of activities that might lead to organization formation does not appear to follow the same sequential process.

Gatewood et al. (1995) studied 147 nascent entrepreneurs who had contact with a Small Business Development Center between October 1990 and February 1991, and explored whether certain cognitive factors as well as certain entrepreneurial activities led to the formation of a business (measured by whether sales had occurred) one year later (by February 1992). After a review of previous literature to identify specific entrepreneurial activities, and the use of a focus group of SBDC counselors to enlarge and revise this list, 29 separate entrepreneurial activities were generated that were grouped into five categories of behavior: Gathering market information, estimating potential profits, finishing the groundwork for the business, developing the structure of the company, and setting up business operations. This list of 29 entrepreneurial activities was mailed to the nascent entrepreneurs in the follow-up survey. Nascent entrepreneurs were asked to indicate whether any of the 29 activities were undertaken, and, for those activities, to estimate the number of hours they had devoted to them. When an analysis of these responses were undertaken, Gatewood et al. (1995) found that activities involved with setting up business operations (e.g., purchasing raw materials and supplies; hiring and training employees; producing, distributing and marketing a product or service) were significantly correlated to the creation of a new firm (as measured by sales). The other categories of activities were not significantly correlated to the subsequent establishment of a firm. It should be noted that this study did not attempt to explore whether any particular sequence of these activities might result in a new firm since specific dates for each activity were not ascertained on the survey.

Carter et al. (1996) using data from a random sample of 683 adult residents in Wisconsin, and 1,016 adults across the United States, identified 71 nascent entrepreneurs who had provided information on their startup activities. These nascent entrepreneurs were initially surveyed about their startup activities between 1992 and 1993 and were re-interviewed six to 18 months later. This study explored three broad questions: What activities do nascent entrepreneurs initiate when attempting to start a business? How many activities do they initiate? When are particular activities initiated? Approximately one half of the respondents had initiated a business by the time of the follow-up interview, over 30% were still engaged in activities to start a business, and 20% had given up on their efforts at business formation. In general, those nascent entrepreneurs who were able to establish a business were more likely to engage in more business formation activities, and engage in these business formation activities earlier, than the other two groups. For the first year of the startup process, the activity levels of those nascent entrepreneurs who "gave up" were very similar to the activity levels of those nascent entrepreneurs who established businesses. In subsequent periods the nascent entrepreneurs who gave up engaged in fewer activities than those that successfully established firms. Those nascent entrepreneurs who were in the "still trying" stage were likely to engage in fewer activities compared to the other two groups. Similar to the findings of Gatewood et al. (1995), it appeared that the nascent entrepreneurs who were able to successfully start a new business engaged in activities that made their businesses more tangible to others: They looked for facilities and equipment, they sought and got financial support, formed a legal entity, bought facilities and equipment, and were more likely to devote full time to the business. For those nascent entrepreneurs who indicated that they had started a business: 94% had sales, 71% had filed a Federal income tax statement for their business, 50% had positive cash flow, and 47% were paying FICA taxes. Surprisingly, nascent entrepreneurs in the other two groups (still trying and gave up) had also achieved some of these new firm startup markers: 50% of those that gave up and 48% of those who indicated they were still trying had achieved sales, 19% of both those who gave up and those who were still trying reported positive cash flow, and 19% of those still trying and 6% of those who had given up had filed a federal income tax form for their business.

In undertaking the Carter et al. (1996) study, it became apparent that only a limited amount of knowledge could be gleaned from a sample of 71 nascent entrepreneurs. It was at this point, that Nancy M. Carter, William B. Gartner, and Paul D. Reynolds conceived of a plan to involve other scholars in an effort to raise funds for the development of much larger sample of nascent entrepreneurs. Except for the pilot studies that served as the samples for Carter et al. (1996) previous efforts by Paul Reynolds to raise funds from government agencies for a national panel study of nascent entrepreneurs had been unsuccessful (Reynolds, 2000). It was believed that if a sufficient number of scholars could convince their institutions to provide $20,000 each, these funds might be sufficient for a sample of hundreds of nascent entrepreneurs. And, not only could more insights be gained into the activities of nascent entrepreneurs, other questions about their startup efforts (e.g., their backgrounds, attitudes, network, net worth, and skills) could also be explored. The genesis of the PSED was born; therefore, out of the frustrations of having information on the behaviors of such a small sample of 71 nascent entrepreneurs.

The organization formation activities that were asked of the nascent entrepreneurs in the PSED are listed in Table 2. This list of behaviors was generated, primarily, from combining lists of behaviors from Carter et al. (1996) and Gatewood et al. (1995). Additional activities were also added. The behavior, "arranged child care ..." was added because there was prior theory and evidence to suggest that this activity might predict the likelihood that female nascent entrepreneurs would have the time to successfully start new businesses (Carter, 1997; Gilbert, 1997). As we noted earlier, activities that might be considered as markers of the existence of an organization are also listed as startup behaviors. We added four other startup marker activities: Bank account opened; business has own phone listing; business has own phone line; and paid managers who are owners a salary. These particular activities were added after reviewing the literature on identifying organizations (Aldrich, Kalleberg, Marsden and

Table 2. Sources of entrepreneurial behaviors in the PSED

PSED behavior	Carter et al., 1996	Gatewood et al., 1995
Spent a lot of time thinking about starting business		X
Took classes or workshops on starting business		X
Saving money to invest in business	X	X
Invested own money in business	X	
Developed model or procedures for product/service	X	X
Defined market opportunities		X
Raw materials, inventory, supplies purchased	X	X
Business Plan prepared	X	X
Startup team organized	X	X
Major items like equipment, facilities or property purchased, leased	X	X
Files federal tax income tax return	X	
Marketing or promotional activities started		X
Arranged childcare or household help to allow time for business		
Devoted full time to business	X	
Credit from supplier established	X	X
Projected financial statements developed		X
Bank account opened exclusively for this business		
Received money, income or fees from sale of goods or services	X	X
Applied for patent, copyright or trademark	X	X
Asked financial institutions or people for funds	X	X
Hired employees or managers	X	X
Paid federal social security taxes (FICA)	X	
Monthly revenues exceeded monthly expenses	X	
Business has own phone listing		
Business has own phone line		
Paid state unemployment insurance	X	
Paid managers who are owners a salary		
Business listed with D&B	X	

Cassell, 1989; Birley, 1984, 1986; Kalleberg, Marsden, Aldrich and Cassell, 1990; Busenitz and Murphy, 1996; Murphy, 2002). It is our contention that these markers might also be important behaviors in the organization formation process, as well. Such activities as "business has own phone listing," is not only a signifier for determining that an organization might exist, it is a way for a nascent entrepreneur to demonstrate to others (potential customers, investors, employees, suppliers) that the emerging organization should merit their involvement (Gartner et al. 1992). Indeed, in a recent study by Delmar and Shane (2002) which used data on nascent entrepreneurs from a research effort in Sweden that was run parallel to the PSED in the United States, arguments and empirical evidence are offered to support the idea that certain startup markers (such as acquiring a business license) can be seen as legitimizing activities (Aldrich and Fiol, 1994; Hannan and Freeman, 1984) and that such activities significantly improves the chances that an ongoing organization will come into existence.

Specific information on this list of activities of these nascent entrepreneurs can be ascertained in a number of ways. In the Gatewood et al. (1995) study, nascent entrepreneurs were asked to indicate whether an activity was initiated and to estimate the number of hours spent on that particular activity. In Carter et al. (1996) nascent entrepreneurs were also asked to indicate whether a startup activity had been initiated and, if so, to provide a year and month when this activity was undertaken. In the PSED, questions and responses for each startup activity were similar to Carter et al. (1996) since we thought that the designation of a time when certain startup activities occurred would be very useful for conducting event history analyses. We did not request an estimation of the number of hours devoted to each startup activity because we were concerned about the ability of nascent entrepreneurs to: (1) accurately recall the number of hours devoted to a particular startup activity and (2) accurately recall the amount of time for a particular effort *vis-à-vis* their other efforts. In addition, we were concerned about the relevance of comparisons between the amount of time devoted to particular startup efforts for various nascent entrepreneurs *vis-à-vis* other nascent entrepreneurs given that there is significant variation in when certain startup activities occur, the duration between startup events, and the sequence of each startup activity in relationship to other startup activities. Even if computational techniques can solve, in some form, some of our concerns about whether hourly estimations could reasonably reflect the effort of nascent entrepreneurs on particular startup behaviors, for the reasons mentioned above, and, because of the time limitations for the number of questions we desired to ask on the phone survey, estimations of the hours devoted to each startup behavior, were not asked. It should also be noted that many efforts at starting new businesses involve team efforts (Ruef, Aldrich and Carter, 2002). Attempting to ascertain the effort undertaken (estimating the number of hours worked) on various startup activities of the various team members of the startup would have been difficult, if not impossible, to achieve in the phone and mail survey. By asking whether an activity had been attempted (and accomplished) in the firm formation process by any member of the venture team seemed to be a response that any member of a venture team could reasonably offer. What should be emphasized in looking at the data on entrepreneurial behaviors in the PSED is that this sample is over 10 times larger (830 nascent entrepreneurs) than the sample of 71 nascent entrepreneurs used in Carter et al. (1996).

WAYS TO EXPLORE ENTREPRENEURIAL BEHAVIORS IN THE PSED

While a substantial amount of descriptive information on the activities of individuals in the process of starting businesses is likely to be generated from the PSED, scholars are likely to want to understand *why* certain entrepreneurial behaviors and sequences of behaviors might affect the likelihood of successful organization creation. A variety of theories and explanations may be appropriate. As we mentioned earlier, Delmar and Shane (2002) offer theory and evidence indicating that activities involved with legitimating the organization reduces the likelihood that the organizing effort will have disbanded in its first 30 months. Their ideas on legitimating are thoughtfully pulled together from various threads of ideas from institutional theory (Meyer and Rowan, 1977), the social relationship school of evolutionary theory (Stinchombe, 1965) and the Schumpeterian strand of evolutionary theory (Schumpeter, 1934). We propose a number of other theories that might offer insights into why certain behaviors or sequences of behaviors might lead to organization formation.

Daft and Weick (1984) suggest that organizations are systems of interpretations, and offer a three stage model of the interpretation process that involves scanning, interpretation, and learning. Two key dimensions are offered as a way to explain differences in how organizations behave in different interpretive modes: Beliefs about the analyzability of the external environment (unanalyzable or analyzable), and the extent to which the organization intrudes into the environment to understand it (passive or active). They advocate four organizational interpretive modes based on these two dimensions: Unidirected viewing (unanalyzable and passive), conditioned viewing (analyzable and passive), enacting (unanalyzable and active), and discovering (analyzable and active). We believe that this approach can be used to identify different ways that nascent entrepreneurs focus their activities during the organization creation process, that is, these four interpretive modes might also be useful as four categories of ways that nascent entrepreneurs behave. For example, we might expect that nascent entrepreneurs who undertook greater numbers of external actions (i.e., asked for funds, defined market opportunity, began marketing and promotion) would be more likely to pursue enacting and discovering interpretation modes. Nascent entrepreneurs who pursued a discovering mode would likely be more systematic in their activities (e.g., took classes on starting a business, formally prepared as business plan, spent a lot of time thinking about the business) than nascent entrepreneurs who used an enacting approach (opportunity suddenly occurred, the business plan is unwritten but "in head," received revenue from sales early on). In Table 3 we show how activities in the PSED might be used to distinguish between nascent entrepreneurs using two of the interpretive approaches: Enacting and discovering.

Another approach that has significant merit for understanding the processes of organization creation is being championed by Lichtenstein (1999; 2000). He uses ideas from complexity theory (Dooley, 1997; Leifer, 1989; McKelvey, 1999; West, 1985) to suggest that organization creation activities: (1) will not occur at a constant rate over time, (2) will not obviously aggregate from specific activities, (3) will be mutually interdependent, and (4) that the outcomes of these activities will be non-proportional. While not wanting to simplify his

Table 3. Discovering and enacting modes of organization formation

	Discovering	Enacting
A. Assumption about the Environment		
Extent to which environment is analyzable	Yes	No
Opportunity changes over time	No	Yes
The best ideas just come (reverse scale)	No	Yes
B. Scanning (*Data Collection*)		
Effort to define market opportunities	Yes	No
Engaged in deliberate systematic search for business idea	Yes	No
Contacted helpful programs	Yes	No
Opportunity identification involved learning over time	Yes	No
C. Interpreting (*Data Given Meaning*)		
Spent a lot of time thinking about business	No	Yes
Pro forma developed	Yes	No
Developed models, prototypes	Yes	No
Have plan or feasibility study	Yes	No
Formality of business plan	Formally written	Unwritten in Head
D. Learning (*Action Taken*)		
Saving money to invest	Yes	No
Taking classes on starting a business	No	Yes
Invested own money	Yes	No
Asked for funds	No	Yes
Arranged childcare	No	Yes
Received revenues from sales	No	Yes
Devoted full time	Yes	No
Establish business bank account	Yes	No
Purchased raw materials, inventory, supplies, etc.	Yes	No
Began marketing efforts	No	Yes
New business telephone line and listing	Yes	No
Hired employees	No	Yes
Purchased equipment, facilities, property	Yes	No
Filed federal income tax return	Yes	No
Established credit with supplier	No	Yes
D&B Listing	No	Yes

logic and ideas, we view the promise of using non-linear approaches for exploring entrepreneurial behavior for their ability to show "order" in what appear to be random patterns of activity. Lichtenstein (1999, 2000) has also been able to demonstrate how complexity theory has practical implications for how individuals might behave in emergent situations. We think there will be considerable value in applying these ideas to the PSED, particularly for exploring issues of how momentum occurs (Gersick, 1988, 1994) in these entrepreneurial activities, overall.

The list of entrepreneurial behaviors in the PSED can also be used to explore a broad range of issues involved in the formation of organizations. We will explore one particular issue here. Because of Shane and Venkataraman's (2000) recent article on the importance of opportunity to the study of entrepreneurship, there has been a great deal of thoughtful discussion about definitions of the attributes of opportunity and explorations of the processes by which opportunity occurs, as well as the beginnings of specifying the value of the concept of opportunity to entrepreneurial studies (Erikson, 2001; Schoonhoven and Romanelli, 2001; Shane and Venkataraman, 2001; Singh, 2001; Zahra and Dess, 2001). While there is some systematic evidence about the nature of opportunity by which these current ideas can be tested (Busenitz, 1996; Hills and Schrader, 1998; Kaish and Gilad, 1991; Shane, 2000; Singh, Hills and Lumpkin, 1999), the interpretations of these results are, at best, equivocal (Gaglio and Katz, 2001). The evidence from individuals involved in opportunity discovery and recognition is meager. We believe that data from the PSED can provide many insights into how the process of opportunity discovery and recognition actually occurs.

Discussions about the nature of opportunity are discussions about how circumstances external to the entrepreneur are construed. Most scholars currently pursue a line of reasoning about the nature of opportunity that suggests that opportunities are, sort-of-speak, concrete realities waiting to be noticed, discovered, or observed by entrepreneurs (Kirzner, 1979; Shane, 2000; Shane and Venkataraman, 2000). We label this viewpoint the "opportunity discovery" perspective. Such a perspective uses the economics literature to emphasize the importance of alertness, observation and the informational asymmetries among all individuals who are pursing their best interests (Hayek, 1945). We propose another alternative. We argue that in many circumstances, opportunities are enacted, that is, the salient features of an opportunity only become apparent through the ways that entrepreneurs make sense of their experiences (Gartner, Bird and Starr, 1992; Sarasvathy, 2001; Weick, 1979). Indeed, we suggest that merely by talking about opportunities as a part of the circumstances of entrepreneurship, scholars invoke a way of making sense of the phenomenon of entrepreneurship that provokes entrepreneurs to see their experiences in a certain way. Entrepreneurs may talk about "discovering opportunities" because that is the way we (academic scholars) ask them to talk about opportunity.

In the opportunity enactment perspective, opportunities are seen to emerge out of the imagination of individuals by their actions and their interactions with others (Daft and Weick, 1984; Dutton, 1993a, 1993b; Dutton and Jackson, 1987; Gioia, Schultz and Corley, 2000; Hill and Levenhagen, 1995; Jackson and Dutton, 1988; Scott and Lane, 2000; Thomas, Clark and Gioia, 1993). Conceptualizing entrepreneurship and opportunity as an emergent cognitive and social process is not new to the field of entrepreneurship (Gartner, 1993a, b; Gartner, Bird and Starr, 1992; Shaver and Scott, 1991), yet social psychological approaches to the study of this phenomenon seem to have been lost in the current fashion for an economic rationality to this process.

Since the theory and logic of these two perspectives are covered in more detail elsewhere (Gartner, Carter, Hills, in press), we will hint, here, that preliminary results from the PSED indicates there is no preponderance of evidence for either view. Table 4 indicates that a little more than a third of the respondents indicated that the idea came first; while 44% indicated the desire to start came first, and 21.5% indicated that both the desire and idea came at the same time. In Table 5, we cross tabulate the responses in Table 4 with data in Table 1 to see whether we can ferret out any differences among those nascent entrepreneurs who "have an idea first" compared to those nascent entrepreneurs who indicated a "desire to start first." As was shown in Table 1, a large proportion of nascent entrepreneurs first spent time thinking about starting a business, so it would not be a surprise that 50% of these individuals desired to start a business first. If we attempt to generate a profile of differences between those who have the idea/opportunity first, compared to those who had a desire to start first, we offer the following insights. In proportion to the other two groups (idea and both), for those who had a desire to start a business first, it appears that these nascent entrepreneurs first undertook actions to "prepare" themselves for aspects of the startup process: Some spent time thinking about the business, some took classes, some saved money, and some devoted full time effort to the startup. In proportion to the other two groups (desire and both) for those who had the idea/opportunity first, it appears that these nascent entrepreneurs were more likely to first undertake actions that involved the startup process, itself: Some defined a market opportunity, some purchased materials and supplies, some filed federal tax returns and some arranged for childcare.

Table 4. Which came first? Idea or desire

Question (A2): Which came first for you, the business idea or your decision to start some kind of business?

Frequency	Percent	Response
164	34.5%	Business idea or opportunity came first
209	44.0	Desire to start a business came first
102	21.5	Idea or opportunity and desire to have a business came at the same time
475	100.0%	

We believe that the primary insights to be gained from studying the results in Tables 1, 4 and 5 would be an appreciation that the phenomenon of entrepreneurial activity is very diverse, and that for many nascent entrepreneurs, a broad range of startup activities are occurring before they appear to "discover" their opportunity. Indeed, we wonder whether many of these nascent entrepreneurs ever "discover" an opportunity, at all. Overall, we do not believe there is a preponderance of support for a belief that most entrepreneurs see opportunities in an objective way, that is, there is not very much evidence that opportunities are discovered in the manner assumed by some academic scholars (Gaglio

Table 5. Distribution of most frequent first behavior by A2 (desire/idea)

	Which came first			
	Idea/ oppor- tunity	Desire to start	Both same time	Total N
Spent a lot of time thinking about starting business	32%	50%	18%	266
Took classes or workshops on starting business	28%	49%	23%	83
Saving money to invest in business	37%	49%	15%	74
Invested own money in business	39%	51%	11%	57
Developed model or procedures for product/service	38%	48%	14%	50
Defined market opportunities	46%	32%	22%	41
Raw materials, inventory, supplies purchased	47%	30%	23%	30
Business Plan prepared	34%	44%	22%	32
Startup team organized	24%	44%	32%	25
Major items like equipment, facilities or property purchased, leased	46%	46%	9%	11
Files federal tax income tax return	40%	20%	40%	15
Marketing or promotional activities started	30%	50%	20%	10
Arranged childcare or household help to allow time for business	46%	27%	27%	11
Devoted full time to business	30%	60%	10%	10
Credit from supplier established				
Projected financial statements developed				
Bank account opened exclusively for this business				
Received money, income or fees from sale or goods or services				
Applied for patent, copyright or trademark				
Asked financial institutions or people for funds				
Hired employees or managers				
Paid federal social security taxes (FICA)				
Monthly revenues exceeded monthly expenses				
Business has own phone listing				
Business has own phone line				
Paid managers who are owners a salary				
Paid state unemployment insurance				
Business listed with D&B				

Sample size reduction comes from moving to mail survey data for A2 on opportunities.
Percentages reported only when "first" behavior was reported by 10, or more, respondents.

and Katz, 2001; Kirzner, 1997; Shane and Venkataraman, 2000). Others may interpret the evidence we have presented in a different manner.

Finally, there are likely to be a number of other theories and ideas that might be amenable for exploring entrepreneurial behaviors, in total, and the relationship of these entrepreneurial behaviors to other issues involved in the formation of organizations. We suggest that Van de Ven and Poole's (1995) framework for explaining development and change in organizations might be an important point of departure for this effort.

RECOMMENDATIONS FOR FUTURE RESEARCH

It is our belief that the Panel Study of Entrepreneurial Dynamics is a decisive moment in the study of entrepreneurship. The PSED is the first large-scale national database to offer systematic, reliable and generalizable data on the process of business formation. While no data set can provide all of the answers about firm formation processes, it is our expectation that the PSED can offer a foundation of generalizable findings about entrepreneurial behavior. What should not be underestimated is the value of having the depth and breadth of information on this sample of nascent entrepreneurs. A major complaint about many entrepreneurship studies has been the idiosyncratic nature of the samples used (Gartner, 1989). It has been difficult to judge whether a sample of entrepreneurs is similar or different to other kinds of samples of entrepreneurs, to entrepreneurs overall, or to non-entrepreneurs. Since the PSED is a generalizable sample of all nascent entrepreneurs in the population (as well as a generalizable sample of non-nascent entrepreneurs), the PSED provides a way to compare any sample of entrepreneurs to the population of nascent entrepreneurs, and to the population of non-nascent entrepreneurs. In addition, given the longitudinal nature of the PSED, the dataset also will be valuable for studying differences between the population of nascent entrepreneurs to those individuals who become the founders of established businesses. Studies of nascent entrepreneurs in the PSED should therefore provide important signposts for guiding all knowledge development in the entrepreneurship field. We hope that more scholars will devote the time and effort needed to explore this rich source of information on entrepreneurs.

Besides studies that utilize the PSED, there are a number of other ways that research on firm formation processes can and should be conducted. We suggest certain methodologies, rather than specific studies of entrepreneurial situations, best apply those approaches.

There is a great need for scholars to undertake in-depth case studies (Stake, 2000) of the activities of individuals involved in the process of starting business. Firm formation involves a multitude of interdependent activities among a variety of individuals (e.g., founders; investors; prospective employees, buyers and suppliers; and paid and unpaid mentors and advisors). Systematic evidence needs to be generated to better understand how all of these different actors interrelate during the founding process. In addition, there is very little evidence about the "micro-behaviors" of organization founders. For example, there is not much beyond anecdotal evidence about the specific behaviors and the sequences of these behaviors when nascent entrepreneurs actually negotiate with others for critical resources to start a new business. What, specifically, occurs when nascent entrepreneurs attempt to convince other individuals to become investors? Do nascent entrepreneurs follow similar negotiating strategies and tactics (compared to managers or individuals in other negotiation situations), or are there unique characteristics of organization formation that require different behaviors? We would assume that the indeterminate and future oriented characteristics of firm founding would influence how the process of negotiation occurred among nascent entrepreneurs and others, and that these characteristics of the situation (indeterminacy and future orientation) would be different than other kinds of negotiations.

We would also hope that some scholars would devote their efforts to documenting and discussing their own involvement in entrepreneurial activities through participant observation (Tedlock, 2000), action research (Kemmis and McTaggart, 2000), and the exposition of their own narratives and stories of organization formation through reflexivity, personal narrative, and autoethnography (Ellis and Bochner, 2000). In addition, many highly successful entrepreneurs have written autobiographies of their experiences that could be explored for insights (Silverman, 2000).

Finally, while there can, and should, be scholarly efforts to explore entrepreneurial behavior using more controlled methodologies (e.g., lab studies and simulations), it is our belief that major gains in scholarship on organization formation activities will primarily occur through field research. The phenomenon of organization formation, itself, is larger than a particular theoretical perspective or methodology. So, we celebrate using multiple theories and multiple methods to understand organization formation that can look at this phenomenon comprehensively. We take seriously Weick's admonition to "Complicate Yourselves" (Weick, 1979), that is, scholars need to recognize that no one particular theory or method can adequately explain the phenomenon under observation, and that a variety of approaches are required.

If our experiences studying the process of organization formation have shown us anything, it is that there is: Substantial variation in the kinds of organizations that are started by nascent entrepreneurs; substantial variation in the characteristics that would signal to researchers that these organizations, do, indeed exist; and substantial variation in when these characteristics that signal the existence of these new organizations occur. There is no escaping this fact – entrepreneurial behavior is fundamentally an activity involved with generating "variation" as an organizational phenomenon (Aldrich, 1999; Katz and Gartner, 1988; Weick, 1979). There is no one particular way in how organizations emerge because there is no one particular kind of organization that results as an outcome of the startup process (Gartner, Mitchell and Vesper, 1989). Research that can both recognize variation in the phenomenon of organization creation, while also offering insights into how these diverse activities might lead to patterns of successful formation of organizations is needed and required.

REFERENCES

Aldrich, H.E. (1999). *Organizations Evolving*. London: Sage Publications.
Aldrich, H.E. and M. Fiol (1994). Fools rush in? The institutional context of industry creation. *Academy of Management Review*, **19**(4), 645–670.
Aldrich, H., A. Kalleberg, P. Marsden and J. Cassell (1989). In pursuit of evidence: Sampling procedures for locating new businesses. *Journal of Business Venturing*, **4**(6), 367–386.
Allen, K.R. and T.M. Stearns (2002). Nascent high tech entrepreneurs: Who are they and how they compare with no-technology entrepreneurs. Paper presented at the Babson College Kauffman Foundation Entrepreneurship Research Conference, Boulder, CO, June.
Amit, R., L. Glosten and E. Muller (1993). Challenges to theory development in entrepreneurship research. *Journal of Management Studies*, **30**(5), 815–834.
Baumol, W.J. (1993). Formal entrepreneurship theory in economics: Existence and bounds. *Journal of Business Venturing*, **8**, 197–210.
Becker, S.W. and G. Gordon (1966). An entrepreneurial theory of formal organizations. Part I: Patterns of formal organizations. *Administrative Science Quarterly*, **XX**, Vol. 11, 315–344.
Bird, B.A. (1989). *Entrepreneurial Behavior*. Glenview, IL: Scott, Foresman and Company.
Birley, S. (1984). Finding the new firm. *Academy of Management Proceedings*, **47**, 64–68.
Birley, S. (1986). The role of new firms: Births, deaths, and job generation. *Strategic Management Journal*, **7**(4), 361–376.
Bull, I. and G.E. Willard (1993). Towards a theory of entrepreneurship. *Journal of Business Venturing*, **8**, 183–195.
Busenitz, L.W. (1996). Research on entrepreneurial alertness. *Journal of Small Business Management*, **34**(4), 35–44.
Busenitz, L.W. and G.B. Murphy (1996). New evidence in the pursuit of locating new businesses. *Journal of Business Venturing*, **11**(3), 221–231.
Carroll, G.R. and M.T. Hannan (2000). *The Demography of Corporations and Industries*. Princeton, NJ: Princeton University Press.
Carter, N.M. (1997). Entrepreneurial processes and outcomes: The influence of gender. In P.D. Reynolds and S.B. White (eds.), *The Entrepreneurial Process*. Westport, CT: Quorum Books, pp. 163–178.
Carter, N.M. (2002). The role of risk orientation on financing expectations in new venture creation: Does sex matter? Paper presented at the Babson College Kauffman Foundation Entrepreneurship Research Conference, Boulder, CO, June.
Carter, N.M., W.B. Gartner and P.D. Reynolds (1996). Exploring start-up event sequences. *Journal of Business Venturing*, **11**(3), 151–166.
Carter, N.M., W.B. Gartner and P.G. Greene (2002). Already there? The career reasons of minority nascent entrepreneurs. Paper presented at the National Academy of Management Meetings. Denver, CO, August.
Carter, N.M., W.B. Gartner, K.G. Shaver and E.J. Gatewood (in press). The career reasons of nascent entrepreneurs. *Journal of Business Venturing*.
Cheng, Y. and A.H. van de Ven (1996). Learning the innovation journey: Order out of chaos? *Organization Science*, **7**(6), 593–614.
Crookall, D. (1994). Editorial: Entrepreneurship education. *Simulation and Gaming*, **25**(3), 333–334.
Crosa, B., H.E. Aldrich and L. Keister (2002). Is there a wealth affect? Financial and human capital as determinants of business startups. Paper presented at the Babson College Kauffman Foundation Entrepreneurship Research Conference, Boulder, CO, June.

Daft, R.L. and K.L. Weick (1984). Toward a model of organizations as interpretation systems. *Academy of Management Review*, 9(2) 284–295.

Delmar, F. and S. Shane (2002). Legitimating first: Organizing activities and the survival of new ventures. *Working Paper*. College Park, MD: R.H. Smith School of Business, University of Maryland.

Dennis, W.J. (1997). More than you think: An inclusive estimate of business entries. *Journal of Business Venturing*, 12, 175–196.

Dooley, K. (1997). A complex adaptive systems model of organization change. *Nonlinear Dynamics, Psychology and Life Sciences*, 1, 69–97.

Dutton, J.E. (1993a). Interpretations on automatic: A different view of strategic issue diagnosis. *Journal of Management Studies*, 30(3), 339–357.

Dutton, J.E. (1993b). The making of organizational opportunities: An interpretive pathway to organizational change. *Research in Organizational Behavior*, 15, 195–226.

Dutton, J.E. and S.E. Jackson (1988). Categorizing strategic issues: Links to organizational action. *Academy of Management Review*, 12(1), 76–90.

Ellis C. and A.P. Bochner (2000). Autoethnography, personal narrative, reflexivity: Researcher as subject. In N.K. Denzin and Y.S. Lincoln (eds.), *Handbook of Qualitative Research*, 2nd edition. Thousand Oaks, CA: Sage Publications, pp. 733–768.

Entrepreneurship: Theory and Practice (1992) 17(1).

Entrepreneurship: Theory and Practice (1993) 17(2).

Erikson, T. (2001). The promise of entrepreneurship as a field of research: A few comments and some suggested extensions. *Academy of Management Review*, 26(1), 12–13.

Gaglio, C.M. and J.A. Katz (2001). The psychological basis of opportunity identification: Entrepreneurial alertness. *Small Business Economics*, 16(2), 95–111.

Gartner, W.B. (1985). A conceptual framework for describing the phenomenon of new venture creation. *Academy of Management Review*, 10, 696–706.

Gartner, W.B. (1988). Who is an entrepreneur? Is the wrong question. *American Journal of Small Business*, 12(4), 11–32.

Gartner, W.B. (1989). Some suggestions for research on entrepreneurial traits and characteristics. *Entrepreneurship Theory and Practice*, 14(1), 27–38.

Gartner, W.B. (1990). What are we talking about when we talk about entrepreneurship? *Journal of Business Venturing*, 5, 15–28.

Gartner, W.B. (1993a). Organizing the voluntary association. *Entrepreneurship: Theory and Practice*, 17(2), 103–106.

Gartner, W.B. (1993b). Words lead to deeds: Towards an organizational emergence vocabulary. *Journal of Business Venturing*, 8, 231–240.

Gartner, W.B. (2001). Is there an elephant in entrepreneurship? *Entrepreneurship Theory and Practice*, 25(4), 27–39.

Gartner, W.B., B.J. Bird, and J. Starr (1992). Acting as if: Differentiating entrepreneurial from organizational behavior. *Entrepreneurship: Theory and Practice*, 16(3), 13–32.

Gartner, W.B., N.M. Carter and G.E. Hills (in press). The language of opportunity. In C. Steyaert and D. Hjorth (eds.), *New Movements in Entrepreneurship*. London: Edward Elgar.

Gartner, W.B. and E.J. Gatewood (1993). And now for something completely different. *Entrepreneurship: Theory and Practice*, 17(2), 87–90.

Gartner, W.B., T.R. Mitchell and K.H. Vesper (1989). A taxonomy of new business ventures. *Journal of Business Venturing*, 4(3), 169–186.

Gartner, W.B. and S.A. Shane (1995). Measuring entrepreneurship over time. *Journal of Business Venturing*, 10, 283–301.

Gartner, W.B. and K.G. Shaver (2002). The attributional characteristics of opportunities and problems described by nascent entrepreneurs in the PSED. Paper presented at the Babson College Kauffman Foundation Entrepreneurship Research Conference, Boulder, CO, June.

Gartner, W.B., K.G. Shaver, N.M. Carter and P.D. Reynolds (in press). *The Handbook of Entrepreneurial Dynamics: The Process of Organization Creation*. Thousand Oaks, CA: Sage.

Gartner, W.B. and J. Starr (1993). The nature of entrepreneurial work. In S. Birley and I.C. MacMillan (eds.), *Entrepreneurship Research: Global Perspectives*. Amsterdam: North-Holland, pp. 35–67.

Garud, R. and A.H. vn de Ven (1992). An empirical evaluation of the internal corporate venturing process. *Strategic Management Journal*, 13, 93–109.

Gatewood, E.J., K.G. Shaver and W.B. Gartner (1995). A longitudinal study of cognitive factors influencing start-up behaviors and success at venture creation. *Journal of Business Venturing*, 10(5), 371–391.

Gersick, C. (1988). Time and transition in work teams. *Academy of Management Journal*, 29, 9–41.

Gersick, C. (1994). Pacing strategic change: The case of a new venture. *Academy of Management Journal*, 4, 9–45.

Gilbert, M.R. (1997). Identity, space and politics: A critique of the poverty debates. In J.P. Jones III, H.J. Nast, and S.M. Roberts (eds.), *Thresholds in Feminist Geography: Difference, Methodology, Representation*. Oxford, U.K.: Rowman & Littlefield, pp. 29–45.

Gioia, D.A., M. Schultz and K.G. Corley (2000). Organizational identity, image, and adaptive instability. *Academy of Management Review*, 25(1), 63–81.

Greene, P.G., N.M. Carter and P.D. Reynolds (in press). Minority entrepreneurship: Trends and explanations. In C. Steyaert and D. Hjorth (eds.), *New Movements in Entrepreneurship*. Cheltenham, UK: Edward Elgar.

Hannan, M. and J. Freeman (1984). Structural inertia and organizational change. *American Sociological Review*, 45, 149–164.

Hayek, F. (1945). The use of knowledge in society. *American Economic Review*, 35, 519–530.

Herbert, R.F. and A.N. Link (1988). *The Entrepreneur*. New York: Praeger.

Hill, R.C. and M. Levenhagen (1995). Metaphors and mental models: Sensemaking and sensegiving in innovative and entrepreneurial activities. *Journal of Management*, 21(6), 1057–1074.

Hills, G. and R. Shrader (1998). *Successful entrepreneur's insights into opportunity recognition. Frontiers of Entrepreneurship Research*. Wellesley, MA: Babson College, pp. 30–43.

Jackson, S.E. and J.E. Dutton (1988). Discerning threats and opportunities. *Administrative Science Quarterly*, 33, 370–387.

Kaish, S. and B. Gilad (1991). Characteristics of opportunity searches of entrepreneurs versus executives: Sources, interests, general alertness. *Journal of Business Venturing*, 6(1), 45–61.

Kalleberg, A.L., P.V. Marsden, H.E. Aldrich and J.W. Cassell (1990). Comparing organizational sampling frames. *Administrative Science Quarterly*, 35(4), 658–688.

Katz, J.A. (1993). The dynamics of organizational emergence: A contemporary group formation perspective. *Entrepreneurship Theory and Practice*, 17(2), 97–102.

Katz, J.A. and W.B. Gartner (1988). Properties of emerging organizations. *Academy of Management Review*, 13(3), 429–441.

Kemmis, S. and R. McTaggart (2000). Participatory action research. In N.K. Denzin and Y.S. Lincoln (eds.), *Handbook of Qualitative Research*, 2nd edition. Thousand Oaks, CA: Sage Publications, pp. 567–606.

Kirchhoff, B.A. (1994). *Entrepreneurship and Dynamic Capitalism*. Westport, CT: Praeger.

Kirzner, I. (1997). Entrepreneurial discovery and the competitive market process. An Austrian approach. *Journal of Economic Literature*, 35, 60–85.

Leibenstein, H. (1968). Entrepreneurship and development. *American Economic Review*, 58(2): 72–83.

Leifer, R. (1989). Understanding organization transformation using a dissipative structure mode. *Human Relations*, 42, 899–916.

Lichtenstein, B. (1999). A dynamic model of non-linearity in entrepreneurship. *Journal of Business and Entrepreneurship*, 6(1), 24–55.

Lichtenstein, B. (2000). Emergence as a process of self-organizing: New assumptions and insights from the study of nonlinear dynamic systems. *Journal of Organizational Change Management*, 13, 526–544.

Lumpkin, G.T. and G.G. Dess (1996). Clarifying the entrepreneurial orientation construct and linking it to performance. *Academy of Management Review*, 21, 135–172.

McKelvey, B. (1999). Complexity theory in organization science: Seizing the promise or becoming a fad? *Emergence*, 1(1), 5–31.

Matthews, C.H. and S.E. Human (2000). *The Little Engine that Could: Uncertainty and growth expectation of nascent entrepreneurs.* Frontiers of Entrepreneurship Research 2000. Wellesley, MA: Babson College.

Meyer, J. and B. Rowan (1977). Institutional organizations: Formal structure as myth and ceremony. *American Journal of Sociology*, 83, 340–363.

Morgan, G. (1996). *Images of Organization*, 2nd edition. Thousand Oaks, CA: Sage.

Murphy, G.B. (2002). The effects of organizational sampling frame selection. *Journal of Business Venturing*, 17(3), 237–252.

Nelson, R. and S. Winter (1982). *An Evolutionary Theory of Economic Change.* New York: Belknap Press.

Pfeffer, J.E. (1982). *Organizations and Organization Theory.* Cambridge, MA: Ballinger.

Poole, M.S., A.H. van de Ven, K. Dooley and M.E. Homes (2000). *Organizational Change and Innovation Processes: Theory and Methods for Research.* Oxford: Oxford University Press.

Reynolds, P.D. (1992). Predicting new firm births: Interactions of organizational and human populations. In D.L. Sexton and J.D. Kasarda (eds.), *The State of the Art of Entrepreneurship.* Boston, MA: PWS-Kent, pp. 268–297.

Reynolds, P.D. (2000). National panel study of U.S. business startups: Background and methodology. In J.A. Katz (ed.), *Advances in Entrepreneurship, Firm Emergence, and Growth* (Vol. 4). Stamford, CT: JAI Press, pp. 153–227.

Reynolds, P.D., M. Hay, W.D. Bygrave, S.M. Camp and E. Autio (2000). *Global Entrepreneurship Monitor: 2000 Executive Report.* Kansas City: Kauffman Center for Entrepreneurial Leadership.

Reynolds, P.D. and B. Miller (1992). New firm gestation: Conception, birth, and implications for research. *Journal of Business Venturing*, 7(5), 405–418.

Reynolds, P.D. and S.B. White (1997). *The Entrepreneurial Process.* Westport, CT: Quorum Books.

Ronen, J. (1982). *Entrepreneurship.* Lexington, MA: Lexington Books.

Ruef, M., H.E. Aldrich and N.M. Carter (2002). *Don't go to strangers: Homophily, strong ties and isolation in the formation of organizational founding teams.* Chicago: American Sociological Association.

Sarasvathy, S.D. (2001). Causation and effectuation: Towards a theoretical shift from economic inevitability to entrepreneurial contingency. *Academy of Management Review*, 26(2), 243–263.

Schoonoven, C.B. and E. Romanelli (2001). *The Entrepreneurship Dynamic.* Stanford, CA: Stanford University Press.

Schumpeter, J. (1934). *The Theory of Economic Development.* New York: Harper and Row.

Scott, R.W. (1997). *Organizations: Rational, Natural and Open Systems*, 4th edition. Englewood Cliffs, NJ: Prentice-Hall.

Scott, S.G. and V.R. Lane (2000). A stakeholder approach to organizational identity. *Academy of Management Review*, 25(1), 43–62.

Shane, S. (2000). Prior knowledge and the discovery of entrepreneurial opportunities. *Organization Science*, 11(4), 448–469.

Shane, S. and S. Venkataraman (2000). The promise of entrepreneurship as a field of research. *Academy of Management Review*, 25(1), 217–226.

Shaver, K.G., N.M. Carter, W.B. Gartner and P.D. Reynolds (2001). Who is a nascent entrepreneur? Decision rules for identifying and selecting entrepreneurs in the Panel Study of Entrepreneurial Dynamics. Paper presented at the Babson College Kauffman Foundation Entrepreneurship Research Conference, Jönköping, Sweden, June.

Shaver, K.G. and L.R. Scott (1991). Person, process, choice: The psychology of new venture creation. *Entrepreneurship Theory and Practice*, 16(2), 23–45.

Silverman, D. (2000). Analyzing talk and text. In N.K. Denzin and Y.S. Lincoln (eds.), *Handbook of Qualitative Research*, 2nd edition. Thousand Oaks, CA: Sage Publications, pp. 821–834.

Singh, R.P. (2001). A comment on developing the field of entrepreneurship through the study of opportunity recognition and exploitation. *Academy of Management Review*, 26(1), 11–12.

Singh, R.P., G.E. Hills and G.T. Lumpkin (1999). New venture ideas and entrepreneurial opportunities: Understanding the process of opportunity recognition. Proceedings, United States Association for Small Business and Entrepreneurship National Meeting, San Diego, pp. 657–671.

Stake, R.E. (2000). Case studies. In N.K. Denzin and Y.S. Lincoln (eds.), *Handbook of Qualitative Research*, 2nd edition. Thousand Oaks, CA: Sage Publications, pp. 435–454.

Stearns, T.M. and K.R. Allen (2001). *The Foundations of High Technology Start-ups: The who, where, when and why*. Frontiers of Entrepreneurship Research, 2000. Wellesley, MA: Babson College.

Storey, D.J. (1994). *Understanding the Small Business Sector*. London: Routledge.

Stinchcombe, A. (1965). Social structure and organizations. In J. March. (ed.), *Handbook of Organizations*. Chicago: Rand McNally.

Tedlock, B. (2000). Ethnography and ethnographic representation. In N.K. Denzin and Y.S. Lincoln (eds.), *Handbook of Qualitative Research*, 2nd edition. Thousand Oaks, CA: Sage Publications, pp. 455–486.

Thomas, J.B., S.M. Clark and D.A. Gioia (1993). Strategic sensemaking and organizational performance: Linkages among scanning, interpretation, action, and outcomes. *Academy of Management Journal*, 36(2), 239–270.

Van de Ven, A.H., H.L. Angle and M.S. Poole (1989). *Research on the Management of Innovation*. New York: Harper and Row.

Van de Ven, A.H. and D. Polley (1992). Learning while innovating. *Organization Science*, 3(1), 92–116.

Van de Ven, A.H. and N.S. Poole (1995). Explaining development and change in organizations. *Academy of Management Review*, 20, 510–540.

Van de Ven, A.H., S. Venkataraman, D. Pooley and R. Garud (1989). Processes of new business creation in different organizational settings. In A.H. van de Ven, H. Angel and M.S. Poole (eds.), *Research on the Management of Innovation: The Minnesota Studies*. New York: Harper & Row, pp. 221–298.

Venkataraman, S. and A.H. van de Ven (1989). Qnetics new business creation case. In A.H. van de Ven, H. Angel and M.S. Poole (eds.), *Research on the Management of Innovation: The Minnesota Studies*. New York: Harper & Row, pp. 228–243.

Vesper, K.H. (1990). *New Venture Strategies*, 2nd edition. Englewood Cliffs, NJ: Prentice-Hall.

Weick, K.E. (1979). *The Social Psychology of Organizing*, 2nd edition. New York: Random House.

West, B. (1985). *On the Importance of Being Nonlinear*. Berlin: Spinger-Verlag.

Zahra, S. and G.G. Dess (2001). Entrepreneurship as a field of research: Encouraging dialogue and debate. *Academy of Management Review*, 26(1), 8–10.

MARK CASSON

The University of Reading

10. Entrepreneurship, Business Culture and the Theory of the Firm

INTRODUCTION

This chapter is concerned with the relationship between the entrepreneur and the firm. It is written from the perspective of the modern economic theory of the entrepreneur, which is explained in the first part of the chapter. This perspective is rather different from that which dominates the small business literature, as reflected in some of the other chapters in this Handbook.

In the small business literature the entrepreneur is often identified with the founder of a firm, or with the owner-manager of it. The entrepreneur is self-employed, and may employ others, but is never an employee. This creates the paradox that the Chief Executive Officers of large firms are not entrepreneurs because they are salaried employees. However 'entrepreneurial' their firm may be, they are not entrepreneurs because they are employees. This paradox is caused entirely by reliance on an unsuitable definition of the entrepreneur.

The definition of entrepreneurship in term of running a small business has wide appeal because it invokes a popular cultural stereotype of the individualistic and competitive founder of a successful firm. Despite all the evidence that many small firms fail, the stereotype perpetuates the mistaken idea that people who found firms are successful people who deserve admiration. This appeal to misleading stereotypes is a weakness rather than a strength of popular theories of the entrepreneur.

The economic theory of entrepreneurship presented in this chapter helps to place the analysis of entrepreneurship on a more rigorous basis. Critics have alleged that the resulting theory is too abstract, or too philosophical, to be of much practical use. In fact, however, the theory has proved extremely useful in the field of business history, and is widely used by business historians to explain differences in performance between firms. The theory is also increasingly used by economic historians to address long-term 'big issues' such as the causes and consequences of the rise and decline of nations, and the influence of politics and religion on national economic life (see for example Godley, 1996). It is, indeed, somewhat ironic that the field of small business research, which professes to specialise in the study of entrepreneurship, has been particularly

Z.J. Acs and D.B. Audretsch (eds.), Handbook of Entrepreneurship Research, 223–246
© 2003 *Kluwer Academic Publishers. Printed in Great Britain.*

notable for neglecting the practical application of the economic theory of the entrepreneur.

A possible reason why small business researchers have neglected economic theories of entrepreneurship is that they may believe that the theory is still rooted in the 'neoclassical' thinking which dominated the economic theory of the firm in the 1960s. As other chapters in this Handbook show, however, this view of modern economic theory is misleading. Economics is a dynamic and evolving discipline, and many of the restrictive assumptions of neoclassical economics, which limited its usefulness in small business research, have now been relaxed.

The main assumptions that have been relaxed concern the objectivity of information, autonomy of preferences and costless optimisation. Relaxing these assumptions makes it possible to accommodate theoretical insights derived from other social sciences. To retain predictive power, however, it is necessary to replace the assumptions that have been relaxed with specific postulates about how people handle information within a social environment. These postulates generate hypotheses about entrepreneurial behaviour which can be tested at the individual, corporate, industry and national level.

Once these assumptions are relaxed, it become evident that theories of entrepreneurship are closely related to modern theories of the firm, such as transactions cost theories (Williamson, 1985) and resource-based theories (Penrose, 1959). The theory of entrepreneurship emerges as a powerful mechanism for synthesising the insights of these modern theories of the firm.

It also turns out that, once these assumptions are relaxed, the theory of entrepreneurship can address issues concerning the role of the entrepreneur in cultural change. The 'change management' literature (Peters and Waterman, 1982) has placed considerable emphasis on the role of the entrepreneur in providing employees with a vision of the future, and in inculcating values in the workplace which will serve to realise this vision. Conventional economic theories encounter difficulties in analysing this role because of the assumption of autonomous preferences on which they are based. Relaxing this assumption allows the theory of entrepreneurship to examine the costs and benefits of cultural change, and the role of the entrepreneur in effecting such change.

Finally, it should be pointed out that before the hey-day of the neoclassical theory of the firm, economic theorists did not normally make the very strong assumptions on which the neoclassical theory of the firm was based. Relaxing these assumptions gives intellectual access to the classic writings on entrepreneurship of previous generations. The insights of the great writers of the past can therefore be synthesised with modern thinking in a systematic way. One result of this process is that the reader will notice that many of the references and citations in this chapter are to relatively early literature. The profusion of references to recent papers, which is a hallmark of modern professional literature in business studies, is missing from this chapter. Because of the wide span of publication dates, and the breadth of the issues addressed, only a representative set of references to recent literature on each individual topic is given.

I

ENTREPRENEURIAL JUDGEMENT

The modern economic theory of the entrepreneur has evolved from a series of fundamental contributions going back to Cantillon (1755). Leading twentieth-century writers include Knight (1921), Schumpeter (1934), Hayek (1937), Kirzner (1973) and Baumol (1991). A modern synthesis defines the entrepreneur as *someone who specialises in taking judgemental decisions about the coordination of scarce resources* (Casson, 1982).

In this definition, the term *someone* emphasises that the entrepreneur is an individual. It is the individual and not the firm that is the basic unit of analysis. A full analysis of entrepreneurship must explain the internal structure of the firm as well as its external competitive strategies; in other words, it must explain the place of the entrepreneur within the firm. It cannot be assumed that membership of the firm is so cohesive that the firm has a 'will of its own', and that this 'will' of the firm, as exemplified by its strategies, is simply the will of the entrepreneur. This starting point of the theory reflects the methodological individualism which the economic theory of entrepreneurship shares with other branches of economics.

Judgemental decisions are decisions for which no obviously correct procedure exists – a judgemental decision cannot be made simply by plugging available numbers into a scientific formula and acting on the basis of the number that comes out. The need for judgement reflects both the costliness of factual information, and the partial and limited nature of the conceptual frameworks used interpret this information when arriving at a decision. The entrepreneur does not normally possess a correct model of the environment, and even if they did possess one, much of the information they would need to apply the model would only be available at prohibitive cost.

Judgement is defined here in terms of what it is *not* – namely the routine application of a standard rule. What it is can best be explained by describing when it is most likely to be required. Judgement is most important in taking decisions where relevant information is very scarce. Key facts may be missing, or the facts may be known but, in the absence of a suitable model, their meaning may be unclear. It is where information is scarce that good judgement is of the greatest value. Judgement draws upon intuition, and the capacity to reflect on relevant experience, to supplement meagre resources of objective information. Judgement is particularly important in improving the quality of decisions that must be taken *urgently* in *novel* and *complex* situations where objectives are *ambiguous*. The urgency of decisions is often stimulated by *competitive forces*; in particular, by the need to recognise and exploit profit opportunities before others do so. The novelty of decisions, as reflected in the absence of suitable precedents, tends to be greatest when the business environment is rapidly *changing*, and is *evolving* in such a way that the same situation never occurs twice. Complexity is often associated with *long-term* decisions taken in situations where the potentially *adversarial reactions* of other people must be taken into account (Casson, 1990a, chapter 3). Ambiguity is exemplified by a situation where a number of stakeholders have clubbed together to undertake a project (for example, the entrepreneur may have borrowed funds from business partners). Although the stakeholders share a commitment to the success of the project, their interests may differ in other respects, and these conflicting interests can lead to tensions. Under these conditions the entrepreneur may have to negotiate key decisions with the individual stakeholders rather than simply impose the decision that he would favour himself. This not only complicates the decision-making process, but also slows it down.

Information is always scarce (Simon, 1983), and so judgement is required for many different types of decision, as diverse as selecting a marriage partner or choosing a career. The emphasis in the definition on *scarce resources* confines attention to decisions of an economic kind – such as business decisions. Reference to the *coordination* rather than the allocation of resources emphasises the dynamic aspect – coordination *changes* the allocation in order to improve the situation. It should be emphasised, though, that entrepreneurial activity does not necessarily improve the situation from everyone's point of view. An entrepreneur's decisions may have adverse effects on third parties who have no right of redress because they possess no property rights through which they can articulate their opposition.

In principle, judgemental decision-making could be a once-for-all rather than a continuing process. In an economic system, where everything depends on everything else, each individual faces a single integrated life-time problem – namely how best to allocate their time, their wealth and their effort over the rest of their life. To cope with uncertainty, each individual could develop a contingent inter-temporal plan which would specify how every moment of the remainder of his (or her) life would be spent. Reactions to new events would be pre-planned, by calculating in advance the best response to every situation that could possibly occur. Provided all possibilities were considered at the outset, all decision-making could be telescoped into the present.

In practice, of course, such planning is prohibitively costly, and so many decisions are deferred on the basis that the situations to which they relate may never materialise. While entrepreneurs may well find it useful to pre-plan their responses to the most commonly occurring types of situation, because the costs of identifying the situations and calculating the appropriate responses are fixed costs which can be spread over repeated occurrences, pre-planning is uneconomic for situations which are unlikely to occur, and whose recurrence is even more improbable. Plans are therefore left open-ended, covering only the major contingencies, and consequently they need to be refined as and when improbable or unexpected situations occur. In the volatile environment in which entrepreneurs operate, change is endemic and so improbable and unexpected situations of this kind arise on a regular basis. Thus entrepreneurial decision-making becomes a continuing process.

THE MENTAL DIVISION OF LABOUR AND INTELLECTUAL COMPARATIVE ADVANTAGE

An integrated decision problem may be decomposed into constituent parts. For example, an entrepreneur may decide to separate the question of whether to invest in some asset from the decision of how best to utilise that asset on a daily basis later on. In certain cases the logic of a problem may permit exact decomposition, but this is fairly unusual. Decomposition normally involves ignoring some of the interdependencies in a situation. This introduces errors which would be unacceptable to an individual who faced costless information. But when information is very costly the overall quality of decision-making may actually improve. This is because the cost of the information required to take a sequence of simple decisions is often much less than the cost of the information required to take a single complex one. This is mainly because information on current situations is usually far easier to collect than information which will predict future situations. Because of this, short-term decision-making is often artificially separated from the long-term decision-making by replacing a long-term strategic objective with a sequence of short-term tactical ones. Tactics can then be altered without changing the entire strategy.

A strategy that has been immunised against tactical change need not be continuously reconsidered. A sensible response is only to reconsider strategies when it seems likely that a significant change may be required. This involves establishing some norm for an acceptable risk of error, and passively following a no change policy in strategy until the norm has been breached. Individuals working with norms tend to re-examine their strategies only when they have been surprised (Shackle, 1979). Problem-solving thus becomes an intermittent process driven by what appears to the problem-solver to be stochastic events.

The sub-problems generated by decomposition can usually be specified more precisely than the integrated problem from which they have been derived. Moreover they tend to be of a standard type. Thus whilst an overall strategic problem may be idiosyncratic, it may simply be an unusual permutation of tactical problems, each of a common type.

When a problem has been decomposed in this way, different sub-problems can be allocated to different people. Because different types of integrated problem can generate the same kind of sub-problem, several different people may call upon the same person to solve a given sub-problem. By concentrating his effort on a particular sub-problem, the person concerned may acquire considerable expertise. Efficiency therefore dictates that problem-solving should be concentrated on specialists.

This is a particular manifestation of the *division of labour* – albeit applied to the intellectual task of problem-solving rather than the physical tasks of production. The related principle of *comparative advantage* implies that people with particular aptitudes should concentrate on particular types of problem. Specifically, some problems call for greater judgement than others – and it is people who specialise in judgemental decision-making that become entrepreneurs. Thus while everyone takes judgemental decisions from time to time, it is only entrepreneurs that *specialise* in doing so.

DELEGATION

The division of labour in problem-solving can be effected either by *referring* problems or *transferring* them. *Referral* involves *delegation* – someone is instructed to solve the problem on someone else's behalf. Shareholders, for example, delegate corporate managers to solve the problem of how the wealth they have invested in the firm is to be used. The senior managers may in turn delegate some responsibility to junior managers. For example, the problem of factory management may be decomposed functionally into a production planning problem, a personnel problem and a financial problem, each of which is delegated to a different manager. Since the solutions to these sub-problems must complement each other, those involved must work as a team.

In a managerial division of labour the chief executive is responsible for synthesising the overall solution. The chief executive's role normally requires the greatest judgement and so carries the main entrepreneurial responsibility. Whether other managers share this responsibility depends on whether they are given discretion to exercise their judgement. If so, the team is a coalition of entrepreneurs; if not, it is a hierarchy in which the members obey instructions on information-processing dictated by a solitary entrepreneur.

A problem is *transferred* when the resources to which the problem pertains are allocated to someone else. Problems can be transferred either *between principals* or *between delegates*. The first involves an *arm's length transaction* between two ownership units. Consumers, for example, pay producers for solutions to problems. These solutions are embodied in consumer goods and services. Problems relating to the production of those services are entirely the responsibility of firms. Producers may also pay other producers for solutions – a firm may sell off a component factory, for example, and buy back components at arm's length from the subcontractor. In this case the assembly firm has transferred problems of component manufacture to another firm.

The transfer of a problem between delegates is effected by an *internal transaction*. Assuming both delegates work for the same principal, the transfer occurs within the ownership unit. In a vertically integrated production sequence, for example, responsibility for the quality of intermediate products may be transferred from an upstream division to a downstream division as the products flow down the chain. Under long-term corporate restructuring, an entire facility may be transferred from one division to another – as when a central research laboratory is 'captured' by one of the application-centred divisions.

II

SUBJECTIVITY

In an evolving economy, the division of labour will adapt as new problems arise and existing ones are solved. Environmental change is endemic because of population ageing, resource depletion, wars, etc. But it is the *perception* as well as the reality of problems that is important. Information lags mean that real problems may not be immediately perceived, whilst cultural changes mean that new problems may be perceived even if the underlying reality is unchanged.

At the root of this is the *subjectivity* of problems. This pertains both to their identification and solution.

Identification is subjective because people have different objectives and different norms. Conventional economics stresses that objectives differ because of differences in tastes. But the problem goes deeper than this. People also need to morally legitimate their wants, so objectives are affected by personal morality too (Casson, 1991). Differences in taste and morality mean that in the same situation one person may perceive one problem and another person another.

Differences in norms are important too. In economic problems efficiency considerations are paramount and so the emphasis is on performance norms. A person with high norms may perceive a problem where a person with low norms does not.

Solutions are subjective because of both the information available and the model (or 'mental map') used. Because information sources are localised, different people have access to different information, but even where access is similar, opinions may differ as to reliability. No item of information can authenticate itself, and so one person may dismiss as false and misleading information which someone else regards as true. People capable of synthesising information from diverse sources are the best judges of veracity because they can use different items to corroborate each other.

The interpretation of information requires a model. Models are typically very simple in relation to the environment they claim to represent, and so in many situations – particularly complex ones – there may be several models representing different aspects of the situation. At the other extreme, in an unprecedented situation there may be no adequate model at all. The decision-maker may have to rely on very crude analogies instead. People who have been educated in a different way may be biased towards particular types of model or analogy and so interpret information very differently.

Thus a consumer products industry, which involves the continuous innovation of novel designs, may require entrepreneurs who are good at taking decisions without a carefully-specified model and with only limited information. A mature process industry, by contrast, may require entrepreneurs who are good at reconciling different models which deal with complementary aspects of a very complex production system. The principle of comparative advantage applied to subjective decision-making therefore implies that people with different personal qualities will gravitate to different industries. Individuals who are good at coping with ignorance due to shortage of data will incline to innovative industries, whilst those who are good at synthesising different models will opt for mature industries with complex technologies.

INNOVATION AND ARBITRAGE

In a free enterprise economy anyone can devote their time to identifying and solving any kind of problem they wish – provided they are willing to pay the opportunity cost involved. Profit opportunities provide the material incentive to use their time in this way.

Profit opportunities are exemplified by *innovation* (Schumpeter, 1934) and *arbitrage* (Kirzner, 1973, 1979). The most dramatic forms of innovation are those concerned with *infrastructure* – notably transport, communication, and the distribution systems associated with utilities (electricity grids, gas mains, etc). These innovations solve crucial problems relating to the movement of people and freight, the exploitation of scale economies in energy-generation, etc. Also significant, but less dramatic, are ordinary *product and process* innovations. A consumer product innovation, for example, may be based on the solution of a common household problem. The solution is embodied in the design of an ingenious durable good. The production and marketing of this good may form the basis of profitable corporate activity.

Innovation usually involves the entrepreneur in the active *management* of resources under his control (though see section 9). Arbitrage, on the other hand, does not. Arbitrage deals with problems which lie purely in the domain of *ownership*. For example, one party may require resources urgently to resolve a pressing problem, but the relevant resources may initially belong to someone else. Alternatively, someone may be mismanaging resources which would be better placed under someone else's control. A single transaction can solve problems of this kind, and recognition of this solution provides an opportunity for arbitrage. When the problem lies in the future rather than the present, the opportunity becomes a speculative one instead.

The successful appropriation of profit depends upon maintaining a monopoly of the solution until the appropriate contractual arrangements have been made. Competition from other entrepreneurs exploiting a similar solution will drive up the prices of resources it is planned to acquire, and depress the prices of resources which are to be sold.

Even with a monopoly, however, the appropriation of profit may be impeded if a key resource required to implement the solution is monopolised by someone else. To avoid being held to ransom, the entrepreneur must understate his valuation of the resource – withholding relevant information as a secret – so that the other monopolist underestimates his own market power. *Negotiation skills* of this kind are very important to the entrepreneur.

Because the economy is in a continual state of flux there is always uncertainty about whether any particular solution is really the best. The prudent entrepreneur will ask himself whether the problem is really as easy to tackle as he believes, and whether his solution is really the best available. Has he really discovered something that other people do not know, or has he merely overlooked some aspect of the problem that they have recognised? This issue can never really be resolved until the outcome is known. Indeed, even then it can never be fully resolved – for what seems in immediate retrospect to have been a failure may turn out even later to look like a success. Nevertheless the entrepreneur must be prepared for the fact that the consensus of opinion, acting on hindsight, may condemn the judgement that underpinned his solution.

The entrepreneur therefore needs to be not only *optimistic* that the problem can indeed be solved, but also *confident* that his optimism, even though it is not shared by others, is still justified. He must also be able to *tolerate the stress* of waiting for the outcome to materialise, and wondering if he can find a suitable excuse if it is a disaster. Indeed, it is because of his optimism and confidence that the entrepreneur is likely to have a monopoly of the opportunity – there is a subjective 'barrier to entry' into the exploitation of the solution created by the relative scepticism of the other people involved.

CAPITAL REQUIREMENTS AS AN ENTRY BARRIER

When the resources required to exploit a solution are large, however, the entrepreneur may himself become the victim of an entry barrier – namely lack of funds. To capitalise an enterprise properly, the funds must be sufficient to meet contractual obligations in the event of failure as well as in the event of success (Casson, 1990b). These funds may be quite large in relation to the entrepreneur's personal wealth. Because of subjective differences in the perception of risk, potential financiers will be less optimistic than the entrepreneur. There is, moreover, a "catch-22" problem, because if the entrepreneur presents potential backers with convincing evidence for his optimism then they may decide to invest directly themselves. Since they have the funds and he does not, they can cut him out altogether. The evidence must therefore be presented with some crucial information withheld.

The success of the solution may also depend on the effort supplied by the entrepreneur after the funds have been made available. To provide a suitable material incentive, the backers may insist that the entrepreneur place some of his own personal wealth 'on the line'. It is in this way that the entrepreneur becomes an uncertainty-bearer (Knight, 1921).

If the entrepreneur does not have funds of his own then the backers may insist on powers of supervision. In effect, the entrepreneur becomes an employee. He receives a basic salary, and will normally be 'incentivised' by bonuses, share-options, or other forms of performance-related pay. His job security may be limited too – if he performs badly then he can be fired from his job.

The fact that an entrepreneur becomes an employee does not imply that his role becomes a purely passive one. In many large companies the directors on the board may each represent a particular 'constituency' – such as a particular group of shareholders – and the chairman may be quite independent, leaving the chief executive, who makes the key decisions, as the entrepreneur, even though he is an employee. The board is there to exercise oversight, appoint auditors, and to fix the chief executive's remuneration. Thus the employee, rather than the owner-employers, takes the key strategic decisions that govern the performance of the firm. The main responsibility of the owners is to decide which chief executive to hire.

Some writers dub the employed entrepreneur an 'intrepreneur'. This is quite helpful if it is understood that the intrapreneur is a special type of entrepreneur – namely an employee – but it can be confusing if it is taken to mean that the intrapraneur is not a proper fully-fledged entrepreneur.

The entrepreneur may, however, be reluctant to submit to supervision, or to share authority with outside shareholders. An entrepreneur who values autonomy may confine his backing to family sources. Relatives may interfere less because they trust the entrepreneur more than do other people. In cases where the older generation of the family are lending to a descendent, the entrepreneur is effectively taking a loan against his own inheritance. In the absence of family sources, the entrepreneur may be able to realise other assets – taking a second mortgage on his house (particularly useful if he has obtained capital gains), selling his second car, and so on. Apart from this he will have to rely on savings out of income from work.

III

INTERMEDIATION

The flexibility of a private enterprise economy owes much to the individual initiative of the entrepreneur. The decentralisation of initiative is, in turn, promoted by specific institutional arrangements – in particular, *money* and *markets*. *Money* is important because it allows complex multilateral networks of trade to be resolved into separate bilateral arrangements. These are sufficiently loosely coupled that anyone of them can normally be renegotiated without simultaneously changing all the others. *Markets* are important because they facilitate switching between trading partners – switching which can be informed by price comparisons obtained at convenient central places.

In a market economy a good deal of entrepreneurial effort is normally devoted to the problem of improving trading arrangements – i.e. to *reducing transaction costs*. Transaction costs are incurred in seeking out a partner (including advertising), specifying requirements, negotiating terms, transferring title (and exchanging physical custody of goods where appropriate), checking compliance and sanctioning defaulters.

Two transaction cost-reducing strategies are particularly important for the entrepreneurial firm – namely *intermediation* and *internalisation*. Both involve a significant measure of *building trust*.

Intermediation is exemplified by entrepreneurial activity in retailing and commodity broking, which is finely tuned to reducing customer's transaction costs. Reputation is very important to an intermediator. An intermediator with a reputation for integrity can establish a chain of trust between a buyer and seller who do not directly trust each other. The gains from reputation are such that even if the intermediator is not particularly moral, it is in his own interests to maintain any reputation that he has incidentally acquired because of the profit it will yield in the long run. Thus the customers' collective trust in the intermediator has a self-validating property.

An intermediator with a widespread customer base will also wish to establish a reputation for taking a hard line in negotiations – *i.e.* quoting a firm price and sticking to it – particularly where low-value items are involved. Otherwise the time costs of negotiation will become prohibitive. Intermediation is particularly entrepreneurial when it involves buying and re-selling goods on own account, rather than simply charging customers a fee, because it affords opportunities for speculation as well.

Some of the inputs into intermediation are of a very specialised nature. Since transactions normally involve the transfer of legal title, lawyers have an important role. Monitoring the timeliness of payment and managing the associated cash-flow problems is the prerogative of accountants. The demand for transaction cost savings therefore creates a derived demand for specialist employees.

The hiring of specialists in turn creates its own transaction cost problems – in particular assessing individual competence, which is very difficult for the layman to do. Professional accreditation, backed by examination and peer group review, has emerged as an important mechanism for guaranteeing quality. It is financed by professional membership fees paid by licensed practitioners out of the economic rents that flow from their accredited status. The employment of qualified professionals is an important feature of large-scale entrepreneurial activity, and the integration of different professions into a harmonious management team is a potential source of problems which require considerable judgement to resolve.

INTERNALISATION

Internalisation is another important strategy for reducing transaction costs. Internalisation is effected by bringing both the buying activity and the selling activity under common ownership and control (Coase, 1937). It is most appropriate when there are regular flows of intermediate products between two or more activities in the business sector. Internalisation is particularly useful in a low-trust environment as it eliminates the incentives to haggle and default.

Internalisation of the market in innovative solutions (see section 6) is particularly important for the entrepreneur. An entrepreneur can assure the technical quality of the solution most easily if it is generated by employed inventors working under his supervision. He therefore integrates backwards into R&D. Given the limitations of the patent system, it is often difficult to appropriate rents effectively by delegating exploitation to a licensee. He therefore integrates forward into production too. Economies of scale in transport and in wholesale and retail facilities normally discourage full forward integration into distribution, but nevertheless most entrepreneurs employ their own sales force to monitor the distribution channel and ensure adequate point-of-sale promotion (Casson, 1990c). Thus transaction costs are minimised by establishing a firm which embraces several functional areas, rather than by simply arbitraging in an intellectual property market for innovations.

Some ideas have very wide applicability. For example, a knowledge of how low-income households can improve their status by conspicuous consumption of certain types of product may have implications for the marketing of an entire range of mass-produced goods. Such general concepts, exploited through internalisation, can lead the firm to develop a diversified product range. Similarly, concepts which are general in a geographical sense – for example, pharmaceutical treatments – can lead to exporting and multinational production.

THE GROWTH OF THE FIRM

Entrepreneurs are often identified as the founders of new firms or as the owner-managers of small and medium-size enterprises (SMEs). Economic principles indicate, however, that entrepreneurship is much broader than this, and encompasses a senior management role in long-established large firms. Indeed, a marketing manager in a large firm may take judgemental decisions much more regularly than the founder of an SME, whose exercise of judgement may be confined largely to a one-off decision to work for themselves instead of for someone else.

The frequency with which judgement has to be exercised within a firm is partly a consequence of its size, but is also dependent on the volatility of the environment in which the firm operates. Volatility creates a stream of new problems, and of new opportunities, for the firm. Volatility creates opportunities for the firm when it creates problems for other people that the firm can help them to solve – in other words, when it creates new customers for its products. Problems and opportunities may well occur together. For example, an increase in local raw material prices may create problems for the firm on account of higher costs. On the other hand, higher raw material prices faced by its customers may encourage the customers to invest in new technology to cut down waste, and this may generate new orders for equipment. An entrepreneurial firm is constantly on the look out for opportunities of this kind.

In terms of 'resource-based' theories of the firm (Teece and Pisano, 1994), this argument suggests that entrepreneurship is the key resource possessed by the firm. Indeed, much of the literature on resource-based theory can be interpreted as a restatement of propositions in the theory of entrepreneurship with the word 'resource' substituted for 'entrepreneur'. The greater is the firm's endowment of entrepreneurship, the higher is the rate of profit it will earn for a given degree of risk, and the faster the firm will grow relative to the average for its industry. Indeed, the theory goes beyond resource-based theories, by highlighting the role of factors such as volatility in driving a wedge between the performance of average firms and the performance of highly entrepreneurial ones. In an industry with high volatility, differences in performance between firms will tend to be wider because differences in entrepreneurial endowments will have a greater impact on profitability and growth.

IV

CULTURE

Subjectivity has hitherto been discussed as an individualistic phenomenon – as in the Austrian literature (Hayek, 1937; Mises, 1949). But subjectivity can also be collective. Culture may, indeed, be usefully defined (from an economic standpoint) as a collective subjectivity – a shared set of values, norms and beliefs.

Because culture deals with values and beliefs to which everyone in a group conforms, individual members are often not aware of its influence. This in turn means that they are not naturally critical of these beliefs. Some of these beliefs may be quite naive because they are imparted in childhood when people are uncritical anyway. Culture is important both for geographical units, such as the nation or the region, and for organisational units, such as the firm. The discussion below focuses on geographical units first.

Values are reflected in the legitimation of objectives – for example, one culture may see scientific progress as an important collective endeavour, while another may see it as a purely utilitarian exercise. Since different values legitimate different objectives, and different objectives generate different kinds of problem, societies with different cultures will tend to focus on distinctive types of problem-solving. 'Learning by doing' is an important aspect of problem-solving, and so learning effects will give each culture a distinctive kind of problem-solving expertise. This may show up in the industrial pattern of comparative advantage between different cultural groups.

Absolute advantage as well as comparative advantage is important to a group. Absolute advantage confers high productivity on the comparatively advantaged sectors, thereby raising the standard of living. A culture that establishes *high norms* will keep group members 'on their toes', and so develop the high-level expertise that underpins absolute advantage of this kind.

Values and norms are also reflected in the relative status accorded to different roles. A culture that promotes *industrial progress effected through structural change* will confer high social status on entrepreneurs. Conversely, a culture that promotes *stability maintained by formal authority* will accord high status to politicians and bureaucrats instead.

It is beliefs about the *social environment*, rather than the *natural environment*, that are of greatest moment for the entrepreneur. Such beliefs can affect the political choice of the economic system within which the entrepreneur has to work. A belief that *only a few people of a certain type are well-informed* tends to support centralised decision-making by the state, as in socialist planned economies, whereas a belief that potentially anyone may be well-informed tends to support decentralisation through private enterprise based on individual property rights. In the centralised state entrepreneurial activity is concentrated on the planners, whereas under private enterprise it is much more widely diffused. In the intermediate case of a 'mixed economy', culture can affect the amount of bureaucratic intervention and market regulation to which private enterprise is subject.

Beliefs about *genetics* can be important too. Non-scientific beliefs may lend support to traditional systems of authority – kingship at the state level, paternalism in the family, etc. Tradition often favours hereditary systems such as primogeniture – which is important to entrepreneurship because it maintains the personal concentration of wealth within family dynasties (see section 7). Tradition can also reduce social mobility by discouraging trade or intermarriage between different classes or castes.

Perhaps the single most important set of beliefs, however, relate to the question of *who can be trusted* (see section 8). When few people can be trusted transaction costs become very high. This affects relations both between firms and within them. Inter-firm relations are undermined because licensors cannot rely on licensees, assemblers cannot rely on subcontractors, and *vice versa*. In response to this, internalisation becomes a widespread strategy. Industrial activities become divided up between a small number of large integrated firms.

Unfortunately, however, internalisation encounters its own problems of distrust within the firm. To discourage slacking, complex and intrusive monitoring systems have to be established using a formal hierarchy supported by accountants, work-study specialists, and the like.

In a high-trust culture, by contrast, complex interdependencies between firms can be sustained by arm's length contracts, and within each firm the owner can rely on the loyalty and integrity of employees. One important implication of this is that it is a high-trust culture rather than a low-trust culture that sustains an industrial structure based on a large number of small highly productive firms.

The high-trust culture and the low-trust culture are, of course, the two extremes of a continuous spectrum. In the middle of this spectrum culture influences perception of where exactly trust should be placed. Some authoritarian cultures suggest that subordinates must trust their superiors irrespective of their personal qualities, thereby allowing superiors to exercise moral suasion purely by virtue of their role. Other cultures require superiors to win the respect of their subordinates by 'getting along side them' – reducing 'power distance' in Hofstede's (1980) terms. Management is clearly much easier in the first situation than in the second, though arguably good management, when available, can achieve much more in the second situation than in the first.

THE ENTREPRENEUR AS LEADER: CORPORATE CULTURE AS AN INSTRUMENT OF STRATEGY

The basic cultural unit is the social group. Each group typically has a leader whose role is to engineer the values and beliefs to which members conform. The firm is the basic social unit in which people work. Although a firm does not necessarily consist of a single entrepreneur, one of the entrepreneurs in any given firm may well be the dominant personality, and this dominant entrepreneur is likely to act as the leader, and to fashion the corporate culture of the firm. In other words, even if entrepreneurship is not unitary, leadership is.

Where the members of a firm are recruited from similar backgrounds, corporate culture may well 'free ride' on national culture, or on values and beliefs inspired by religion or social class. Religions that stress freedom of conscience and the subduing of nature are most likely to sustain entrepreneurship. It is on this basis that Protestantism and Quakerism have been said to promote entrepreneurial behaviour (Kirby, 1984). Furthermore, 'middle class' attitudes that endorse social competitiveness, wealth accumulation and upward mobility are more likely to encourage entrepreneurship than 'working class' values of conformity and solidarity with fellow employees.

The 1980s has witnessed a surge of interest in corporate culture (Schein, 1985) which has been sustained ever since. The engineering of corporate culture is claimed to hold the key to long-run corporate performance. Much of the analysis has centred on the large enterprise. Since managerial effort, being mental rather than physical, is difficult to monitor, managerial motivation cannot easily be achieved by supervision alone. Moral manipulation may be more effective. By creating a corporate ethic of integrity and dedication, the owner of the firm may encourage employees to punish themselves emotionally for lack of effort. External supervision is replaced by internal monitoring by the individual himself, and from an information-handling point of view this is much more effective (Casson, 1990a).

Moral manipulation thus provides a useful complement to supervision. While supervision is helpful in discouraging gross misconduct, because such misconduct is easily observed, manipulation is valuable in eliciting that extra degree of effort of which only the employee himself is immediately aware. It may be suggested that it is a capacity for moral manipulation that distinguishes the true 'business leader' from a mere 'entrepreneur'.

V

DEMAND AND SUPPLY OF ENTREPRENEURS

The market for entrepreneurship equates demand and supply. The demand for entrepreneurship determines the number and nature of the entrepreneurial roles that need to be filled. Supply factors govern the availability of suitable candidates to fill these roles.

It has been stressed throughout this chapter that the demand for entrepreneurship is highly subjective. This means, firstly, that the roles created reflect a perceived need for solutions to problems rather than any underlying reality. Secondly, and more importantly, it means that some roles may be specifically created by individuals who believe that it is their mission to occupy them. This is typically the situation of the self-employed entrepreneur, who has created his own demand for the role he plays.

The overall intensity of entrepreneurial demand will reflect the level of norms in the population for, as noted in section 5, high norms generate problems that low norms do not. Coordination problems are particularly intense when there is a perceived need for structural change. Structural change requires a pervasive reallocation of resources from declining industries into growth industries, and generates substantial profit opportunities for the entrepreneur. It is, therefore, amongst a population with high norms that perceives a far-reaching need for structural change that there is likely to be the most intense demand for entrepreneurs.

The supply of entrepreneurs is governed by occupational choice. The options include manual work as well as intellectual work and, within intellectual work, the rule-governed as well as judgemental. Other options include unpaid work – housework, charitable work – and no work at all – unemployment, leisure. It follows that, for a given distribution of entrepreneurial aptitudes, recruitment to entrepreneurship depends upon the entire spectrum of rewards to alternative uses of time.

These rewards may contain a significant non-pecuniary element. These may be a moral element (as in the case of charitable work). Negative moral attitudes to profit-seeking – especially low-level activities such as arbitrage – may inhibit entry into entrepreneurship. The social dimension can be important too. Some roles carry a much higher status than others. Status may be particularly important in choosing between a professional career as a lawyer or accountant or a more broadly-based entrepreneurial career.

It has been emphasised that entrepreneurs must continually put their personal judgement to the test, and that in doing so they must also place some of their own resources, and their personal reputation at risk. They must also be able to work in partnership with other risk-bearers too. The supply of entrepreneurs is therefore influenced by the level of confidence, tolerance of stress, moderation of risk-aversion and willingness to share responsibility – all factors which have been mentioned earlier.

Occupational choice will also reflect educational background. Basic education increases the supply of entrepreneurs by inculcating basic literacy and numeracy. Further education has a more ambiguous effect. On the one hand it can help to refine entrepreneurial judgement – for example, by providing historical awareness of the endemic nature of change – and so increase the rewards to entrepreneurship. On the other hand, it can open up artistic and scientific careers that can entice people away from business.

Early specialisation in education can also reduce entrepreneurship by encouraging other people to enter narrowly-defined professions instead. Although these professions support entrepreneurial activity indirectly, the support they give is often limited by the inability of complementary specialisms to coordinate with each other under the direction of the entrepreneur (see section 8).

The market for entrepreneurship will tend to adjust to equilibrium through changes in the pecuniary rewards offered to entrepreneurs. These rewards may be in the form of profits for owner-entrepreneurs or salaries for employee-entrepreneurs. It is, of course, anticipated rather than actual rewards that are important – expected profits may not materialise and even expected salaries may not get paid if the employer goes bankrupt. Because anticipations are liable to change even when there is no change in the underlying situation, the market for entrepreneurs is potentially volatile. The tendency to equilibrium is, therefore, only a fairly weak one in the short run. In the long run the underlying situation too is liable to change, and so the equilibrium to which the market tends is itself a moving target.

Subject to these reservations, though, certain predictions about market behaviour can be deduced using the method of comparative statics. A real resource shock, for example, such as a substantial oil price increase, will create a perceived need for structural change which stimulates the demand for entrepreneurs. Although the initial impact of this may be modified through macroeconomic effects caused by wage and price rigidities, the profit opportunities created by potential substitution possibilities will stimulate entrepreneurial demand in new and growing industries. The anticipated reward to entrepreneurship will rise, and new recruits will be attracted to these industries. While there may be some transfer of entrepreneurs from obsolescing industries, this will be limited by the industry-specificity of many people's skills. Many of the new recruits will therefore be people drawn away from non-entrepreneurial occupations.

The increased pressure on a limited supply of competent entrepreneurs will reduce the average quality of judgement amongst practising entrepreneurs. Thus while there will be more entrepreneurs earning a higher reward for a given quality of judgement, many new recruits, though earning more than they would in some other occupation, may not earn anywhere near as much as the more able and experienced entrepreneurs.

Entry into entrepreneurship will be effected most smoothly when new recruits have an accurate perception of their own quality of judgement. If they overestimate this quality, however, then too many people of poor quality will enter. Mistakes will be made because of poor judgement – and as expectations fail to be realised, confidence will be undermined, and entrepreneurs will withdraw from the industry in an atmosphere of crisis. In certain cases the effect may be severe enough to precipitate a macroeconomic recession (Schumpeter, 1939).

A similar analysis can be provided for shifts in supply. This shows, for example, that a shift to greater breadth in further education, by stimulating entrepreneurial supply, will lead to a greater number of people entering business because their potential productivity in more specialised work has been reduced. This will lead to greater entrepreneurial activity, but lower anticipated rewards for each entrepreneur because of greater competition between them.

Because state education is subject to government policy shifts, a public perception of rising demand for entrepreneurs may indirectly induce an increase in supply. Because the supply response refers to a flow of newly trained entrants, however, it will take a long time to impact significantly on the total stock of entrepreneurs. By the time the supply effect works through, demand may have changed, and so this lagged response may generate a 'cobweb' cycle in the market for entrepreneurs.

THE ROLE OF FINANCIAL INSTITUTIONS

The preceding analysis was silent on the crucial question of how exactly the market for entrepreneurs adjusts towards an equilibrium. It followed a long tradition amongst economists of fudging this issue. According to Adam Smith (1776), the market works through an 'invisible hand' – a concept which later economists attempted to formalise in terms of the hypothetical Walrasian auctioneer. Austrian economists have rightly criticised the Walrasian notion and stressed that the market is a process. They emphasise the decentralised nature of the process, and tend to suggest that the market generally 'gets it right'.

The view that the market gets it right is dubious, however. Few markets get it right in the short run, and there are special reasons for believing that the market for entrepreneurs is one of the least efficient in the economy. While entrepreneurial activity may well improve the functioning of other markets, it has only a limited impact on the market for entrepreneurs itself.

One reason is that – like other labour markets – the market for entrepreneurs is a market in people and, in the absence of slavery – or transferable long-term employment contracts generally – opportunities for intermediators to arbitrage are limited. The main potential for arbitrage lies in identifying able entrepreneurs who are in the wrong job and offering them the right job for only a little additional pay. If the entrepreneur is loyal to his new employer he may refrain from demanding increased pay and so allow the employer to retain the arbitrage profit generated by his 'headhunting' activity. There is only limited scope for exploiting this approach, however, because of the problem of adverse selection

– those who are most easily enticed to quit their present job are likely to turn out to be disloyal in the future.

Another problem with the market is that it is difficult to screen accurately for entrepreneurial qualities. Indeed, until recently, the backward state of entrepreneurial theory has meant that it was not even clear what the desirable qualities were.

Because of these difficulties, intermediation in the market is confined mainly to the activities of financial institutions. There are grounds for believing that these institutions may systematically select inappropriate people for entrepreneurial roles. Key decisions are concentrated in the hands of a few institutions operating behind substantial barriers to entry, and the decisions of these institutions may well reflect shared – and possibly inaccurate – culturally-specific values.

Pension funds are major shareholders in large corporations and can influence the selection of chief executives, while clearing banks and venture capitalists can regulate start-ups by potential self-employed entrepreneurs through their procedures for approving loan applications. The agglomeration of financial decision-makers in major financial centres (see section 15) facilitates the formation of a distinctive culture based on frequent social interaction between them. This culture may evolve stereotypes of other social groups, which influences financiers' decisions whether to place financial resources under the control of members of particular groups. An inappropriate financial culture can therefore undermine performance at the micro-level even though at the macro-level the underlying demand and supply conditions are favourable.

If true, this proposition has important implications for economic performance. It suggests that good economic performance is not just the consequence of an intense demand for entrepreneurship driven by high norms, sourced by an abundant supply of able entrepreneurs, but also depends on the micro-level efficiency with which individual entrepreneurs are matched to particular roles. Are potentially good entrepreneurs overlooked and incompetents appointed in their place? Are entrepreneurs who would be good at managing innovation in high-growth consumer product industries mismatched to jobs managing complexity in mature process industries, and vice versa? Are young entrepreneurs who lack experience promoted too soon to positions of responsibility, and are old entrepreneurs allowed to stay on when they should be retired?

An economy that has a good supply of entrepreneurs, but serious inefficiencies in the domestic market for entrepreneurs, may find that entrepreneurs emigrate to exploit opportunities overseas. In addition, foreign capital may enter the country to employ the able entrepreneurs that domestic institutions are unwilling to support. Thus international migration and capital flows may emerge to compensate (partially) for the inefficiencies of the domestic market.

THE SPATIAL DIMENSION

The division of labour has an important spatial dimension. This applies both to the physical division of labour in production and to the mental division of labour in problem-solving. It is the spatial division of labour in problem-solving that holds the greatest significance for the location of entrepreneurial activity.

Economies of internalisation mean that in a global economy many production plants are branch plants owned by multinational firms. The headquarters of these firms are drawn to large financial centres because of the importance to managers of face-to-face contact with financiers and professional specialists such as international lawyers, tax advisers, and so on. Access to government for lobbying, and to major corporate clients for marketing intermediate goods, may also be important. The agglomeration of headquarters activities around major financial centres means that most high-level judgemental decisions will be taken by people living within commuting distance of such centres. Only lower-level decisions will be taken elsewhere.

The most important centres may become international service centres, and play an important role in cross-cultural communication. Merchants, bankers and businessmen from different cultures meet there to make contracts. For a city to achieve the status of an international service centre the local culture must support religious and ethnic toleration. Respect for business confidentiality, and impartiality in the legal enforcement of contracts, are important too.

Such centres are attractive to frustrated foreign entrepreneurs who cannot get backing from their own domestic financiers. They are also attractive to exiles. At any one time, civil wars and persecutions create refugees who need to re-establish their culture overseas. Exiled people, though dispersed, often maintain contact amongst themselves, creating channels of international communication along which commercial as well as personal and domestic information can flow. These channels are particularly well adapted to developing the international trade of the entrepôt, and to speculation and arbitrage in international financial markets.

Certain exile groups – 'wandering Jews', 'sojourning Chinese', and so on – have very strong business-oriented cultures which can survive persecution and take root in new locations. The creative intellectual tension generated by the arrival of these groups can transmit – through parental influence and schooling – a strongly entrepreneurial culture to the next generation of both indigenous and immigrant people. In this way the international service centre may be able to maintain its economic base even though the original rationale – such as port activity – goes into decline as a result of the geographical restructuring of trade.

THE LIFE CYCLE OF THE ENTREPRENEUR

The co-existence, within the division of labour, of high-level and low-level problems is important for the career structure of the entrepreneur. High-level problem-solving typically requires a broader range of relevant experience and hence calls for older people to take it on. These people should have 'spiralled upwards' in their careers through a variety of more functionally-specialised roles. Senior professionals who have remained within the same functional area all their life are not well-suited to these roles. They may be important as advisors to the high-level entrepreneurs (as noted above) but are not capable of filling the roles themselves.

Those who occupy high-level roles also require personal skills to elicit relevant information from delegates. They need team-building skills to handle their subordinates, and an extensive network of contacts to allow them to access a wide variety of consultants. This suggests that the successful high-level entrepreneur will typically have followed a career path which begins with a fairly routine functionally-specialised role ('learning the business' in his twenties) and switches to a more responsible innovative role (in his thirties). This role, as it expands, gives him team-building experience and brings him into contact with a wider group of people. He can then move, in his forties, to a leadership role – acting as an exemplar to an increasing number of subordinates and representing his organisation to other institutions. He can retain this role until it becomes increasingly symbolic rather than executive (in his sixties). Finally he retires and functions purely as an 'elder statesman' of business in a consultative and counselling capacity.

In exceptional circumstances the entrepreneur's responsibilities may grow along with the firm he has founded, so that his career development is also the biography of the firm. More usually, though, where high-level entrepreneurs are concerned, he will have acquired his initial experience of the industry as an employee of a large firm. In some cases he may remain with this firm throughout his career. In other cases he may quit to found his own business at the innovative stage of his career. When the innovation becomes successful, and the scale of operations grows, the entrepreneur may then sell out to a larger firm in return for a seat on the board, and pursue his rise to the top by internal promotion at board level. On this analysis, those most likely to reach the top are people who are willing, when necessary, not merely to share responsibility with, but even to subordinate themselves to others, and are willing to move geographically around production locations to learn the business and then transfer to the metropolis to take up a high-level post. The most successful entrepreneur, therefore, is unlikely to be the ruggedly independent self-employed individual of popular myth.

SUMMARY

The preceding analysis has used a fairly conventional economic methodology to generate an unconventional synthesis of insights derived from various social sciences. The entrepreneur has been defined as someone who specialises in judgemental decision-making. Judgement is required in finding urgent solutions to novel, complex and ambiguous problems. Within a private enterprise economy, specialisation is normally effected in two distinct stages. Firstly, problems are decomposed and allocated to separate ownership-units. The coordination of problem-solving between ownership units is then effected by the market mechanism. Further decomposition of problems can then be effected within the ownership unit if desired.

The firm itself is an institutional product of the first stage of the specialisation process. It takes over from consumers the problem of finding solutions to common household problems. It takes over from wealth-holders the problem of how to manage the resources they own. It takes over from workers the problem of how to organise themselves as a team. The second stage of specialisation is exemplified by the delegation of decisions to functional roles within the firm. Because delegates can enjoy considerable discretion, entrepreneurship is not necessarily confined to the owner or chief executive of the firm. The entrepreneurial firm is an opportunity-seeking information system, geared to identifying profit opportunities, based on solving other people's problems, and to setting up administrative systems to exploit these opportunities in an efficient way. It is also a problem-solving system, employing professional specialists to tackle its own internal coordination problems as and when they occur. New problems and opportunities continually arise with a frequency that reflects the underlying volatility of the firm's environment.

Innovation is a very judgement-intensive activity – particularly where infrastructure investments are concerned. Arbitrage and speculation require a rather different kind of judgement, since they are concerned, not with the management of resources, but merely with the transfer of resources between one ownership unit and another. Internalisation economies explain why innovation leads to managerial involvement – problems of insecure intellectual property rights and difficulties in quality control encourage backward integration into technical research and forward integration into production.

The demand for entrepreneurship is partly created by entrepreneurs themselves who perceive opportunities that they believe they are personally well-equipped to exploit. A culture that emphasises high norms will stimulate this perceptual process. Another source of demand arises from people who perceive a need for economic restructuring but who wish to hire entrepreneurs to take decisions on their behalf. While the first source of demand leads to self-employment, the second source leads to the recruitment of entrepreneurial employees.

The supply of entrepreneurs depends upon natural abilities, the nature of the educational system (in particular the degree of specialisation) and the relative status of entrepreneurial careers. Demographic factors are important because few entrepreneurs acquire the breadth of experience needed for high-level entrepreneurship until early middle age.

Entrepreneurial rewards, in the form of profits for the self-employed or salaries for employees, tend to adjust to balance overall supply and demand. Adjustment is subject to substantial disequilibrium fluctuation, however, because it is anticipated rewards rather than real rewards to which supply and demand respond. Inefficiencies are even more serious where the matching of people to specific roles is concerned. Thus consumer product industries may require individuals who can take urgent and novel decisions of a fairly simple kind, while mature process industries may require people who can cope with complexity instead. Because it is difficult to screen for the necessary qualities, suitable placements can often be found only by trial and error.

The matching process is typically intermediated by financial institutions. Cultural stereotyping may result in group affiliation being used as a surrogate for personal qualities in deciding whether entrepreneurs are to receive financial backing. If the financial community has its own culture, then the stereotyping may merely reflect one culture's views of other cultures, and the outcome of the process may be quite poor.

Financial institutions tend to agglomerate around international financial centres which then compete to attract business from entrepreneurs. Any centre needs a culture of tolerance and impartiality. It also needs a culture that employs stereotypes which are realistic – or ideally uses personal information that is so good that stereotyping is not required.

The international competitiveness of an economy will depend crucially on entrepreneurial factors. The norms and values of the domestic culture will determine the types of problems that are researched, and hence the industrial structure of the expertise that is developed. This expertise can be exploited internationally through either exporting, licensing or foreign direct investment. Education policy and the social ranking of occupations will govern the supply of indigenous intrepreneurs, whilst toleration and impartiality will govern the supply of immigrant entrepreneurs. A combination of buoyant demand, abundant supply and efficient matching will sustain international competitive advantage through entrepreneurship.

REFERENCES

Alchian, A.A. and H. Demsetz (1972). Production, information costs and eonomic organisation. *American Economic Review*, **62**, 777–795.

Baumol, W.J. (1993). *Entrepreneurship, Management and the Structure of Pay-offs*. Cambridge, Mass.: MIT Press.

Cantillon, R. (1755). *Essai sur la Nature du Commerce en Generale* (H. Higgs, ed.), London: Macmillan, 1931.

Casson, M.C. (1982). *The Entrepreneur: An Economic Theory*. Oxford: Martin Robertson.

Casson, M.C. (1990a). *Enterprise and Competitiveness: A Systems View of International Business*. Oxford: Clarendon Press.

Casson, M.C. (1990b). Entrepreneurship: A model of risky innovation under capital constraints. *University of Reading Discussion Chapters in Economics*.

Casson, M.C. (1990c). Internalization theory and beyond. *University of Reading Discussion Chapters in International Investment and Business Studies*.

Casson, M.C. (1991). *Economics of Business Culture: Game Theory, Transaction Costs and Economic Performance*. Oxford: Clarendon Press.

Coase, R.H. (1937). The Nature of the firm. *Economica (New Series)*, **4**, 386–405.

Godley, A.C. (1996). Cultural determinants of Jewish immigrant entrepreneurship in the UK and USA, 1880–1914. In A.C. Godley and O.M. Westall (eds.), *Business History and Business Culture*. Manchester: Manchester University Press, pp. 222–240.

Hayek, F.A. von (1937). Economics and knowledge. *Economica (New Series)*, **4**, 33–54.

Hofstede, G. (1980). *Culture's Consequences*. Beverly Hills, Calif.: Sage.

Kirby, M.W. (1984). *Men of Business and Politics*. London: Allen & Unwin.

Kirzner, I.M. (1973). *Competition and Entrepreneurship*. Chicago: University of Chicago Press.

Kirzner, I.M. (1979). *Perception, Opportunity and Profit*. Chicago: University of Chicago Press.

Knight, F.H. (1921). *Risk, Uncertainty and Profit* (G.J. Stigler, ed.). Chicago: University of Chicago Press.

Mises, L. von (1949). *Human Action: A Treatise on Economics*, London: William Hodge.

Penrose, E.T. (1959). *The Theory of the Growth of the Firm*. Oxford: Blackwell.

Peters, T.J. and R.H. Waterman, Jr. (1982). *In Search of Excellence*. New York: Harper & Row.

Schein, E.H. (1985). *Organisational Culture and Leadership*. San Francisco, Calif.: Jossey-Bass.

Schumpeter, J.A. (1934). *The Theory of Economic Development*. Cambridge, Mass.: Harvard University Press.

Schumpeter, J.A. (1939). *Business Cycles: A Theoretical, Historical and Statistical Analysis of the Capitalist Process*. New York: McGraw-Hill.

Shackle, G.L.S. (1979). *Imagination and the Nature of Choice*. Edinburgh: Edinburgh University Press.

Simon, H.A. (1983). *Reason in Human Affairs*. Oxford: Blackwell.

Smith, A. (1776). *An Inquiry into the Nature and Causes of the Wealth of Nations* (R.H. Campbell, A.S. Skinner and W.B. Todd, eds.). Oxford: Clarendon Press, 1976.

Teece, D.J. and G. Pisano (1994). The dynamic capabilities of firms: An introduction. *Industrial and Corporate Change*, **3**, 537–556.

SHARON A. ALVAREZ*

Ohio State University

11. Resources and Hierarchies: Intersections between Entrepreneurship and Strategy

INTRODUCTION

While the two fields of entrepreneurship and strategic management have developed largely independent of each other, scholars in both fields have long been interested in understanding sources of organizational renewal, growth, firm competitive advantage, and the generation of entrepreneurial rents. However, typically, strategic management research has overlooked entrepreneurial insight and entrepreneurial capabilities, and entrepreneurship research has remained elusive as to the potential advantages that could result from the protection of more valuable resources such as entrepreneurial insights and capabilities. Recently several scholars have called for the integration of entrepreneurial and strategic thinking (Hitt, Ireland, Camp, Sexton, 2002; McGrath and MacMillan, 2000; Meyer and Heppard, 2000; Alvarez and Busenitz, 2001).

While there have been calls for research at the intersection of entrepreneurship and strategy (Hitt, Ireland, Camp, Sexton, 2002; Meyer and Heppard, 2000), most of this research is phenomena based and typically does not address the intersection at a theoretical level. In an earlier chapter of this book, Casson suggests that the theory of the entrepreneurial firm is embedded within the resource-based theory and the transactions cost theory of the firm. While there has been some work done in this area (Alvarez and Busenitz, 2001; Alvarez and Barney, 2002), there is still more work to be done in understanding how these theories inform both entrepreneurship and strategy.

For the purposes of this chapter, entrepreneurship is defined following Schumpeter (1934). Entrepreneurship is the creation and commercialization of new resources or the recombination of existing resources in novel ways that result in the formation of a firm (Schumpeter, 1934; Alvarez and Busenitz, 2001).[1] Entrepreneurs engage in these activities through the development and commercialization of new products and services, moving into new markets, or

---

* I would like to thank Mike Hitt and Jay Barney for their thoughtful comments on this paper.

[1] The author acknowledges other definitions of entrepreneurship such as those of Kirzner, and Shane and Venkataraman. However, because this chapter is concerned with resources the most applicable definition is in Alvarez and Busenitz, 2001.

Z.J. Acs and D.B. Audretsch (eds.), Handbook of Entrepreneurship Research, 247–263
© 2003 *Kluwer Academic Publishers. Printed in Great Britain.*

servicing new customers (Ireland, Hitt, Camp and Sexton, 2001). We define strategy as a firm's theory of how to gain competitive advantage (Barney, 2002). In this chapter strategic management is defined as the process the firm goes through to conceive of and implement its strategies. This process is a function of a firm's competitive position as defined by a bundle of unique resources and relationships that are adjusted and renewed as time, competition, and change erode their value. This adjustment and renewal of resources effects the survival and success of the firm. If we focus on resources within a firm as the unit of analysis and how those resources are created and renewed and protected by the firm over time to give the firm a sustainable competitive advantage, it becomes clear that entrepreneurial and strategic perspectives can be integrated. Moreover, this chapter takes the view that many entrepreneurs are rent seeking in their behavior and are thus focused on competitive advantages that sustain their firms and produce entrepreneurial rents. There are entrepreneurs that are not rent seeking, and this chapter acknowledges that fact, however we do not focus on these entrepreneurs.

This chapter examines the intersection of entrepreneurship and strategic management as rent seeking behavior through entrepreneurship in either established firms or in newly forming firms with the recognition that entrepreneurship is intimately connected with the appearance and adjustment of unique and idiosyncratic resources. This chapter extends both resource-based theory and transactions cost economics by introducing the entrepreneurial firm that allows us to view firm formation and renewal from these theoretical perspectives.

THE INTERSECTION OF ENTREPRENEURSHIP AND STRATEGY

As early as the Pittsburgh conference in 1978 when the field of strategic management began to emerge as a distinct field of research, the intersection between entrepreneurship and strategic management has interested academic researchers (Schendel and Hofer, 1978). As the intersection between entrepreneurship and strategic management evolved two streams of research emerged, one from an economics perspective (Rumelt, 1987), and one from a management perspective (Meyer and Heppard, 2000).

The majority of the work done in the entrepreneurship-strategy intersection from an economics perspective is concerned with understanding how entrepreneurial activity can result in economic rents. Rumelt (1987) asked the question, "where do new businesses come from?" In his work he took a strong Schumpeterian view of entrepreneurship and built his definition on Schumpeter's work defining entrepreneurship as the creation of new businesses that have some element of novelty. Rumelt suggested that entrepreneurial activity was motivated by the chance for gain and that entrepreneurial insight, and the entrepreneur's ability to acquire resources, determined the potential returns to entrepreneurial activity. The potential returns to entrepreneurial activity he later defines as entrepreneurial rents.

Teece (1986) was also concerned with the intersection of entrepreneurship and strategy, although he did not use the word entrepreneurship. Teece (1987) extended transaction cost economics beyond Williamson's work on efficient contracting. Teece included production and organizational economies and was interested in the distinctive ways that enterprises accomplished heterogeneous performance leading to competitive advantage among certain firms. While Teece did not use the entrepreneurship word, his work and that of Rumelt's certainly began the early conversations on the intersection of economic strategy and entrepreneurship.

While many organizational economists have found the entrepreneurship question and phenomena of importance, they typically considered entrepreneurship to be very difficult to examine (Rumelt, 1987). Entrepreneurship is not particularly amenable to economic analysis or mathematical modeling, both of which have become exceedingly popular in traditional economics. Moreover, economics typically deals with industry-level analysis and the firm's production function is assumed to be homogeneous, often the theory of the firm in traditional economics leaves the firm out of the theory (Williamson, 1975). It has been through the development of transaction cost theory and resource-based theory that a more micro unit of economic analysis is addressed opening the possibility to examine an individual economic actor and thus the economic consequences of individual behavior, the entrepreneurial firm. Traditional neoclassic economic theory does not address the individual and thus does not address the entrepreneurial firm, leading to a paucity of work in this area.

The latest work on the intersection between entrepreneurship and strategy from an economics perspective comes from Casson (see the earlier chapter in this book) and Alvarez and Barney (2002). Both of these bodies of work begin to address the entrepreneurial theory of the firm from a transactions cost and resource-based theory lens. Alvarez and Barney explicitly tie the outcome of rent generation to entrepreneurial knowledge and the effective coordination of that knowledge in the entrepreneurial firm leading not just to the generation of rents, but also to the appropriation of these rents. They particularly address the importance of rent appropriation to the entrepreneurial firm's survival and the continued ability to generate new knowledge leading to innovation through the investment of appropriated entrepreneurial rents.

General management researchers in the strategy field also recognized the importance of entrepreneurship to strategy and it is through the general management literature that interest in this area began to really develop and a name became attached to this stream of research. About 1997, Meyer was one of the first management scholars to directly address the intersection of entrepreneurship and strategy. The first serious attempt to deal with the intersection between the two fields was an edited volume by Meyer and Heppard (2000) which addressed the subject through a collection of papers written by what was at the time doctoral students, paired with senior scholars in the field of strategy.

The theme of the book was to uncover for firms, regardless of size, the components of an entrepreneurial dominant logic. What surfaced was the connection between innovation of new products and entrepreneurship.

In *Entrepreneurship as Strategy*, it is predicted that the entrepreneurial function can make firms both large and small resemble each other in terms of organizational culture and structure (Brown, Eisenhardt, and Neck). Hitt and Reed, suggest that firms need to develop dynamic core competencies to creat and re-create products in the new competitive landscape. Miles, Heppard, Miles and Snow address the management function and the recruitment and hiring of employees for entrepreneurial firms and Amit, Brigham and Markman suggest empowering these employees. The final chapter by Cooper, Markman, and Niss is a historical review of the field of entrepreneurship. With few exceptions (i.e., The chapter by Alvarez and Barney), the book typically focused on entrepreneurial phenomena and not on theoretical development (Michael, 2001). Alvarez and Barney provided a review of entrepreneurship and economic theory and began the conversation about knowledge as the core strategy for firms.

More recently we have several works by Hitt, Ireland, Camp, and Sexton (2001, 2002) that address the intersection between entrepreneurship and strategic management. Hitt, Ireland, Camp, and Sexton edited special issues of *The Academy of Management Executive* (2001), *The Strategic Management Journal* (2001), and the book *Strategic Entrepreneurship* (2002). This group coined the term strategic entrepreneurship, which they define as the integration of entrepreneurial (i.e., opportunity seeking actions) and strategic (i.e., advantage-seeking actions) perspectives to design and implement entrepreneurial strategies that create wealth. All three of these edited works address the intersection of the phenomena between entrepreneurship and strategy. The collection of papers include areas of entrepreneurship that intersect with innovation, alliances and networks, international entrepreneurship, growth, leadership.

In the final work by these authors the book *Strategic Entrepreneurship (2002)*, there is concern in the first three chapters with trying to define the differences and similarities between entrepreneurship and strategy. For example, Meyer, Neck and Meeks suggest that entrepreneurship is about creation and strategic management is about competitive advantage. Michael, Storey, and Thomas's chapter suggests that entrepreneurship is about creation of new business and strategic management is about coordination and loss prevention. Johnson and Van de Ven provide a framework for entrepreneurial strategies. They incorporate four models and suggest that the models each call for a different entrepreneurial mindset. However, as the book evolves there is more concern with theoretical development and some important issues in entrepreneurship theory begin to surface. There is a chapter by Alvarez and Barney that suggests that entrepreneurial knowledge and the coordination of that knowledge lead entrepreneurs to identify opportunities and exploit those opportunities through the creation of a firm. Smith and Di Gregorio argue that it is the firm's dis-equilibrating actions that can produce long-term competitive advantages. Hoskisson and Busenitz suggest that entrepreneurial firms account for most technological advances.

While the work in management began to illuminate the many possibilities for intersecting entrepreneurship and strategy, and began some of the theoretical conversations, the potential for new theoretical groundwork still exists and has yet to be completed. What the rest of this chapter does is to address the intersection of entrepreneurship and strategy from a pure theoretical basis using resource-based theory and transactions cost theory.

RESOURCES AND ENTREPRENEURSHIP

If we begin with the primary assumption that a firm's competitive position is defined by a bundle of unique resources and relationships that need to be adjusted and renewed over time in response to competitive pressures and value erosion, then the concepts of entrepreneurship and resource heterogeneity are complimentary. Entrepreneurship can help develop and maintain resource heterogeneity. In emerging entrepreneurial firms it is often not recognized soon enough that the unique bundle of resources an emerging firm starts with may determine its future growth.

Regardless of calls for more dynamic theories of the firm, there is still a typical assumption in strategic management that a firm will select its production function from a known bundle of technological possibilities. Moreover, another underlying assumption in strategic management is that there exists a finite set of known factors of production and that their marginal productiveness can be discerned. Even in the case of resource-based theory where resource heterogeneity and product market imperfections exist, much of strategic management research has taken the view that new production functions are a given and not an outcome. The view has been that opportunities exist because of factor or product market failures, thus the firm is a result of market failure.

However, suppose that there exists an irreducible uncertainty connected with the creation of a new production function? In this case we will have heterogeneous firm resources with heterogeneous firm outcomes (Barney, 1986; Rumelt, 1987), or entrepreneurship (Alvarez and Busenitz, 2001). Resource heterogeneity is the most basic condition of resource-based theory and it assumes that resource bundles and capabilities underlying production can be heterogeneous across firms (Barney, 1991).

Similar to RBT, heterogeneous resources are also a basic condition of entrepreneurship (Kirzner, 1997). Some scholars (Kirzner, 1979; Casson, 1982) suggest that entrepreneurial opportunities exist when different agents have insight into the value of resources that other agents do not, and the agents with the insight act upon these un-exploited opportunities. If these agents are correct, an entrepreneurial rent will be earned; if not, an opportunity loss will occur (Rumelt, 1987; Alvarez and Barney, 2000).

The uncertainty in the production function occurs for two reasons; first, from the production function itself whereby there is ambiguity as to what the factors of production really are and how they interact, and second, the uncertainty that is is created by the entrepreneurial coordination of these production factors. The production function and the entrepreneurial coordination can interact causing further ambiguity. We now have causal ambiguity since we cannot exactly determine the reasons for success or failure, even *ex post*. If there is causal ambiguity surrounding this entrepreneurial activity of coordinating the production function in new and creative ways, this ambiguity will act to block firm homogenization relative to other firms entering an industry through imitation and we will have a sustained competitive advantage. However more importantly, this manner of looking at a firm's superior performance as the entrepreneurial coordination of resources into a production function, views the firm as a success and not a market failure.

A less frequently addressed question by entrepreneurship scholars that directly impacts the field is; under what conditions can opportunities be most efficiently realized through market exchanges (Kirzner, 1997), and when can they be most efficiently realized through the firm (Schumpeter, 1934; Coase, 1937)? The market versus firm debate remains currently blurred and ambiguous in the study of entrepreneurship and is an extension of transactions cost theory. In the field of entrepreneurship the distinction between the discovery of market opportunities (Kirzner, 1979) and the exploitation of these opportunities (Schumpeter, 1934) is a crucial element in entrepreneurship theory that has only recently begun to be addressed (Alvarez and Barney, 2002). The important question to ask is not whether price theory models or the perfect competition model addresses the role of entrepreneurship, because several scholars have already answered this question (Knight, 1921; Schumpeter, 1934; Coase, 1937; Kirzner, 1979). Instead we argue that the important question is, "when is it less costly for the entrepreneur via the firm to coordinate resources and disparate knowledge and when is it less costly for the market to coordinate resources?" This is an old question first asked by Coase (1937) and later expanded upon by Williamson (1975, 1985) in what has now become transactions cost theory. However, as suggested in the next section, traditional transaction costs arguments have focused on the firm as a market failure, but when transaction costs incorporates an entrepreneurial view the firm now becomes more efficient to the market when certain resources need to be coordinated.

COASE, TRANSACTION COSTS, RESOURCE-BASED THEORY, AND ENTREPRENEURSHIP

In his seminal work, Coase (1937) began to address the scale and scope of the firm through what has become transaction costs economics, a theory of why firms exist, and resource-based theory, a theory of firm performance differences that lead to a competitive advantage. However, both of these theories while

being important and popular approaches in the field of strategy have largely ignored the role of entrepreneurship. The field of entrepreneurship has been equally neglectful, in that it has largely ignored Coase's work on the firm and the implications of transaction costs theory and resource-based theory.

Coase (1937) suggested that outside of the firm, price movements direct production that is coordinated through a series of exchange transactions or contracts. Within the firm these market transactions are eliminated and are substituted by the entrepreneur who is the coordinator of production. In this view the entrepreneur recognizes opportunities in factor and production markets and understands how to coordinate processes in a firm that are too costly to coordinate through the market. Coase further goes on to put limits on the firm size and the entrepreneurial function.

Coase suggests that as firms get larger the costs of organizing additional transactions within the firm may rise and the returns to the entrepreneurial function decrease. Once a firm reaches the point where the cost of organizing an extra transaction becomes greater than the market costs either the transaction will be organized through the market or a new entrepreneur will enter and organize the new knowledge. The entrepreneurial knowledge of resource reorganization that is critical to the transformation of inputs into heterogeneous outputs becomes lost as the firm grows and the now large firm begins to resemble the market.

This Coaseian view of the firm resulting from the entrepreneurial function of resource coordination has largely been ignored in the literature. The next sections will address transaction costs economics and resource-based theory from an entrepreneurial perspective.

TRANSACTION COSTS ECONOMICS AND ENTREPRENEURSHIP

One of the most prevalent theories in the field of strategy is transaction costs economics (TCE) (Williamson, 1975; Coase, 1937). However, one of the weaknesses of transaction costs economics is that its emphasis is on a static comparative analysis and on identifying generalized boundary conditions that exist between firms and markets (Liebeskind, 1996). In fact, transactions costs theories of the firm have traditionally been more effective at explaining the scope of manufacturing firms than service or knowledge firms such as R&D or consulting firms (Liebeskind, 1996), and thus TCE has evolved to more of a theory of contracts than a theory of the firm (Joskow, 1987; Parkhe, 1993; Reuer and Ariño, 2002). However, Williamson (1985) argued that innovation is more likely to occur in smaller firms and larger firms are more effective at manufacturing and distributing those innovations. Acs and Audretsch (1987) found that in industries that are innovative small firms appear to have an advantage, and in capital intensive industries large firms have an advantage. The implication to this argument that has not been addressed is that not only do firms result when it is less expensive to organize transactions, but firms result when the opportunities recognized by an entrepreneur are better coordinated within a firm.

In the case of entrepreneurship, a TCE argument with regard to the firm has implications for the protection of entrepreneurial heterogeneous resources that we will refer to as entrepreneurial knowledge.[2] Indeed, TCE suggests that when property rights to knowledge are weak, as is often the case with entrepreneurial knowledge that often tends to be tacit in nature, the firm through the use of organizational arrangements is able to protect entrepreneurial knowledge. Through the use of the firm the rents generated by entrepreneurial knowledge can be appropriated by the creator of the knowledge (Alvarez and Barney, 2002). A theory of the entrepreneurial firm should consider knowledge and knowledge protection since the generation of new knowledge is dependent upon the degree to which the creator of this knowledge can appropriate the rent stream for future investment.

If it is assumed that new knowledge is produced by investment in innovation (Liebeskind, 1996) then it follows that innovators are entrepreneurs (Schumpeter, 1934) and thus the knowledge that we are addressing is entrepreneurial knowledge. This entrepreneurial knowledge is not distributed evenly among entrepreneurs and thus not distributed evenly among entrepreneurial firms, firms are heterogeneous and earn heterogeneous rents. If some firms are better able to protect the value of their knowledge, these firms will be better able to appropriate the rents that the knowledge has generated and have more incentives to innovate.

In many ways this seems rather intuitive if we consider factors of production in a traditional manner. However, if we begin to consider entrepreneurial knowledge as a factor of production, the protection of knowledge becomes less clear. It is not difficult to understand that machines and factories must be protected from thievery (or appropriation), nor is it difficult to understand that the knowledge that helped build those machines and factories should be protected. What is difficult to grasp is that it is the innovative process that keeps the firm inventing one new machine after another that must be protected.

A better example is technology and the exploitation of technology through the firm. For several decades researchers have looked to market structure to answer the question of when firms form to exploit a technology and appropriate the rents generated from the technology. Yet, the results of years of research has suggested that firm formation as a result of the market structure or market failure is at best inconclusive (Cohen and Levinthal, 1989; Kamien and Schwartz, 1982; Shane, 2001). This is not surprising since one of the early criticisms of transaction costs theory is that it is a non-trivial task to distinguish purchase prices across a market from in-house production prices because

---

[2]For the purposes of this paper we adopt the definition of entrepreneurial knowledge used by Alvarez and Busenitz (2001). Entrepreneurial knowledge is the ability to take conceptual, abstract information of where and how to obtain undervalued resources, explicit and tacit, and how to deploy and exploit these resources.

in-house production involves the use of inputs that are purchased. If to this complexity we add entrepreneurial knowledge and coordination costs, the correct equation would be whether the sum of entrepreneurial knowledge, coordination, and production costs are less in the firm relative to the market?

Newly created knowledge is often not widely diffused (Schumpeter, 1934; Knight, 1921). For example, an economic actor in an existing firm may have different insights about the value of newly created knowledge versus the value placed on that knowledge by other economic actors in that organization. The greater the knowledge asymmetries between the first economic actor and the rest of the actors in the firm, the more likely the first economic actor will be to leave the present firm and start a new firm (Audretsch, 1995).

In this section we suggest that the generalized institutional capabilities of the firm allow protection of entrepreneurial knowledge from expropriation and imitation more effectively than the protections available through markets. However, a question that should be further explored is given that the protection of entrepreneurial knowledge through firms is expensive, it is important to resolve what knowledge should be protected and what knowledge should not be protected.

This stream of research is important to entrepreneurship scholars because it is the protection of entrepreneurial knowledge through the firm that helps the entrepreneur move beyond the exploitation and generation of rents to the appropriation of rents that enable entrepreneurs to continue to invest in future entrepreneurial endeavors.

Traditional transactions cost theory suggests that when the knowledge exchanged in a transaction is explicit, the most efficient way to manage this transaction will generally be non-hierarchical governance (Williamson, 1975, 1985). Non-hierarchical governance includes both intermediate governance (e.g., strategic alliances) and market governance (e.g., market contracts).[3] Non-hierarchical governance is preferred in this setting because explicit knowledge is codifiable, and thus usually can be converted, at low cost, into contracts of various kinds. These contracts can then be used to monitor the actions of exchange partners and reduce the threat of opportunism in coordinating the resources needed to take advantage of a market opportunity at low cost.

However, in this context, traditional transactions cost logic has some important limitations. In particular, decisions about organizing the generation of economic rents cannot be separated from decisions about organizing the appro-

---

[3] The analysis in this chapter is based on a hierarchy called the firm. The author acknowledges that there are other forms of hierarchy such as alliances. Alliances and networks have emerged as a major form of organizing to acquire the resources and capabilities necessary to compete effectively in markets (Hitt, Ahlstrom, Dacin, and Levitas, 2001). Alliances and networks can be of particular importance to entrepreneurial firms since these often resource-constrained firms can acquire resources such as managerial talent, firm legitimacy, information, channels of distribution and many other resources (Alvarez and Barney, 2000). See Cooper (2002) in *Strategic Entrepreneurship*, Hitt, Ireland, Camp, and Sexton (eds) for a review of the alliance literature at the intersection of entrepreneurship and strategic management.

priation of these rents. In particular, when the knowledge about a market opportunity is explicit, and absent barriers to knowledge diffusion, the decision to coordinate the resources needed to generate an economic rent through non-hierarchical means is likely to have the effect of increasing the competitiveness of the market for taking advantage of a market opportunity. This increased competition reduces the ability of the economic actors attempting to generate a rent to appropriate it.

For example, suppose an economic actor – based on explicit knowledge – recognizes an opportunity to generate economic rents but concludes that others will have to become involved to fully realize this opportunity. Because explicit knowledge is easy to understand, once discussions with others to coordinate these multiple resources begin, these other parties will be able to recognize the value of this opportunity. Once these other parties understand the value of this opportunity, they will seek ways to appropriate any rents it might generate, for example, by trying to capitalize on this opportunity through contacting other parties that possess the requisite resources. They will be at no competitive disadvantage compared to the individual who first spots this opportunity in organizing to take advantage of it. In this case, the act of using non-hierarchical governance to coordinate the resources needed to capitalize on an opportunity has the effect of increasing competition around that opportunity. This increased competition reduces the amount of the rent that any one of these individuals can appropriate.

Of course, those using explicit knowledge to generate the rents associated with a market opportunity will typically anticipate the increased competition associated with contacting others to work together to take advantage of that opportunity. For this reason, these actors will often attempt to place one or more "isolating mechanisms" in place in the contracts they sign with other economic actors. These isolating mechanisms are the externally imposed constraints on information diffusion mentioned earlier and can take many different forms, including patents on key technologies, the use of trademarks and copyrights, non-complete clauses, and so forth (Rumelt, 1984).

If these isolating mechanisms are effective in preventing competition around a market opportunity from developing, i.e., if they can be written and enforced at low cost, non-hierarchical governance will be preferred over hierarchical governance for organizing the resources needed to capitalize on explicit knowledge about market opportunities.

However, in many circumstances, isolating mechanisms have been shown to be ineffective in preventing the dissemination of explicit knowledge. For example, Mansfield, Schwartz, and Wagner (1981) have shown that 60% of all patents are imitated within four years of being granted, without legally violating patent rights obtained by innovators. More generally, Lieberman and Montgomery (1988) show that first mover advantages based on explicit knowledge are, in most industries, difficult to sustain. In general, when the property rights associated with proprietary but explicit knowledge are insecure, isolating mechanisms are not effective in preventing the diffusion of explicit information

(Milgrom and Roberts, 1992).[4] And when these mechanisms are ineffective, economic actors looking to generate and appropriate economic rents by using explicit knowledge about market opportunities must look for other sources of protection.

In the case of strategic management this article suggests that firms protect knowledge and view the firm as an isolating mechanism and not that isolating mechanisms protect the firm and its knowledge. The implication becomes if there is knowledge that is a potential source of rent generation, then in order to protect the knowledge and appropriate the rents, the most cost-efficient manner to do this is through the firm.

RESOURCE-BASED THEORY AND ENTREPRENEURSHIP

Strategy researchers have become increasingly aware of the importance of heterogeneous firm assets (relative to competitor firms) in achieving a firm's sustainable competitive advantage. Barney (1986) and Dierickx and Cool (1989) were the first to draw attention to the importance of tacit socially complex assets. Paradoxically, while the importance of resource heterogeneity among firms has been acknowledged, strategists have given scant attention to the process by which these resources are discovered, turned from inputs into heterogeneous outputs, and exploited to extract greater profits. Thus, we argue that entrepreneurship informs strategic management about the process of how resources are discovered and recombined to provide more complex unique resources that lead to sustained competitive advantage.

Resource heterogeneity is the most basic condition of resource-based theory and it assumes at least some resource bundles and capabilities underlying production are heterogeneous across firms (Barney, 1991). Resource-based theory suggests that heterogeneity is necessary but not sufficient for a sustainable advantage. For example, a firm can have heterogeneous assets, but not the other conditions suggested by resource-based theory, and those assets will only generate a short-term advantage until they are imitated.

Similar to RBT, heterogeneous resources are also a basic condition of entrepreneurship (Kirzner, 1997). Entrepreneurial opportunities are thought to exist when different agents have insight into the value of resources that other agents do not, and the agents with the insight act upon these un-exploited opportunities (Kirzner, 1979; Casson, 1982). If these agents are correct, an entrepreneurial rent will be earned; if not, an opportunity loss will occur (Rumelt, 1987; Alvarez and Barney, 2000).

Kirzner (1979) developed the term "entrepreneurial alertness" as the ability to see where products (or services) do not exist or have unsuspectedly emerged as valuable. Alertness exists when one individual has an insight into the value

---

[4] In this sense, both transactions cost and resource-based theories of the entrepreneurial firm are related to the asset ownership approach discussed by Grossman and Hart (1986).

of a given resource when others do not. From this perspective, entrepreneurial alertness refers to "flashes of superior insight" that enable one to recognize an opportunity when it presents itself (Kirzner, 1997). In distinguishing between entrepreneurial alertness and the knowledge expert, Kirzner (1979) argues that the knowledge expert does not fully recognize the value of their knowledge or how to turn that knowledge into a profit or else the expert would be an entrepreneur. The entrepreneur may not have the specific knowledge of the expert (such as technological expertise), but it is the entrepreneur who recognizes the value and the opportunity of the expert's knowledge. While the entrepreneur may have specialized knowledge, it is the tacit generalized knowledge of how to organize specialized knowledge that is the entrepreneur's critical intangible resource.

In the case of entrepreneurship, the specialized knowledge is often knowledge about opportunities created by the environment or a new product or even the opportunities of a potential new product. As we uncover the phenomenon surrounding entrepreneurial cognition, it is becoming clearer why entrepreneurs see new discoveries more readily than their counterparts (Busenitz and Barney, 1997). Their heuristic-based logic appears to give them a competitive advantage in quickly learning about new changes and what the implication of those changes are for the development of specific discoveries.

Resource-based logic identifies the kinds of resources and capabilities that require specific investment in order for their full economic value to be realized – resources and capabilities that are socially complex, path dependent, tacit, and so forth (Barney, 1995). Thus, when the realization of the economic value associated with an entrepreneurial opportunity depends on the use of socially complex, path dependent, or tacit resources and capabilities, it is more likely that hierarchical governance – a firm – will be used to realize this value than non-hierarchical governance.

These ideas suggest that conditions which require the efficient coordination of and integration of knowledge are those in which entrepreneurial firms[5] are likely to arise in an economy (Coase, 1937; Hayek, 1945; Kirzner, 1997). Schumpeter (1934) distinguished between invention and innovation, with invention being the discovery of an opportunity and innovation the exploitation of a profitable opportunity. The importance of the distinction between invention and innovation is that it focuses on the firm as a problem-solving institution (Demsetz, 1991). Instead of concentrating on the market, the focus is on the role of entrepreneurship as the integration of disparate specialized knowledge (as suggested by both Schumpeter and Coase). Firm formation is essentially an entrepreneurial act because in order to coordinate and transmit tacit knowledge the firm is often required. Firms are a bundle of commitments to technology, human resources, and processes all blanketed by knowledge that is specific

---

[5]While there are many theories of the firm and thus many definitions of a firm, many of which are valid, this chapter defines the entrepreneurial firm as a firm that is formed as a repository, isolating mechanism and coordinating vehicle for new knowledge.

to the firm. It is this bundle, and how the entrepreneur coordinates this bundle, that allow firms to be heterogeneous and thus these firms cannot be easily altered or imitated. We conclude, similarly to the previous section, that the firm itself can be an isolating mechanism and thus a source of sustained competitive advantage for entrepreneurial knowledge.

CONCLUSION

While this chapter has used received theories of the firm as a foundation, the ideas presented in this chapter go beyond traditional applications of resource-based theory and transactions cost logic found in strategic management, and extend these theories to the problem of entrepreneurship.

In the case of resource-based theory the chapter illustrates how entrepreneurial knowledge is an idiosyncratic resource that is capable of generating and sustaining a competitive advantage. Entrepreneurial knowledge is the ability to take conceptual, abstract information of where and how to obtain undervalued resources, explicit and tacit, and how to deploy and exploit these resources. Both Kirzner (1979) and Schumpeter (1934) describe the entrepreneurial role as the decision to direct inputs into certain processes rather than into other processes. In fact, entrepreneurship involves what Schumpeter termed "new combinations" of resources. Early work on resource-based theory did not address the choice of how to deploy and obtain unique resources, instead it viewed idiosyncratic heterogeneous resources already in place within the firm. It isn't until resource-based theory is addressed through an entrepreneurial lens that the entrepreneurial ability to deploy resources and recombine them is viewed as a unique resource in its own right.

The process of strategic management is the redeployment of a firm's unique resources potentially leading to a sustained competitive advantage and superior firm performance. A firm's stability and profitability fundamentally depend upon entrepreneurial coordination and knowledge that drives the recombination of resources in a firm resulting in heterogeneous firms. Resource-heterogeneity resulting in firm heterogeneity are corner stones of both entrepreneurship and strategic management. It is through the integration of views from both fields that we get a better understanding of firm renewal and competition.

While firm performance is an accepted paradigm in strategic management, performance is also a non-trivial part of entrepreneurship research. Wealth creation, which in the case of the firm is driven by firm performance, appears to be central to both entrepreneurship and strategic management. In his 1937 work Coase's main purpose was to explain why economic activity was organized within the firm. In later work by Williamson (1975) firms became alternatives to markets when the market failed. However, in this chapter it is suggested that the firm is a success, in that through the coordination of the entrepreneur the firm is able to organize knowledge and resources in a way that markets cannot. Thus by using an entrepreneurial lens, transactions cost theory becomes more informative, in that it now addresses the production and organizational activities of a firm as unique coordination activities by the entrepreneur that result in superior firm performance and a potential source of competitive advantage.

As mentioned earlier in this chapter Casson (2002) suggests that resource-based and transactions cost theories are closely related to the theory of entrepreneurship and that a theory of entrepreneurship is a powerful mechanism for synthesizing the insights of these theories. What this chapter begins to suggest is that previous theories of the firm such as resource-based theory and transactions cost theory are the foundation for an entrepreneurial theory of the firm. Moreover that when the entrepreneurial theory of the firm is written it will in return provide insights into current theories of the firm that have hereto not been understood.

In the search for why firms exist several theories of the firm have been put forth. Indeed what has become known as the theory of the firm is one of the major topics in many disciplines. However, the present state of theories of the firm are diverse theories that each field has developed to address a particular set of characteristics and behaviors of interest to that field. For example, specific investments (Coase, 1937; Williamson, 1975, 1985), measurement problems (Alchian and Demsetz, 1972), and asset ownership (Grossman and Hart, 1986) have all been cited as explanations of the existence and the scope of the firm in industrial organization economics. In finance, agency costs (Jensen and Meckling, 1976) have been cited as a primary determinant of the existence and scope of the firm. More recently, several strategic management scholars have begun focusing on costly to imitate resources and capabilities as an important explanation of the existence and scope of the firm (Conner and Prahalad, 1996; Grant, 1996; Liebeskind, 1996; Barney, 2002).

While all of the current theories of the firm have proved to be informative and have provided an intellectual backbone for many principles in many different fields, the type of firm that these theories seek to understand is the traditional business corporation. This firm is asset-intensive, vertically integrated, with tight control over its employees, with clear, definable, stable firm boundaries, all the parameters found in transactions cost theory and agency theory. The firms of today in many ways no longer resemble more traditional organizations that these theories were developed to address. Firm assets now tend to be knowledge-based, with innovative firms having looser forms of collaboration rather than vertical integration, and boundaries that are sometimes fluid and sometimes not very well defined at all.

The foundation for previous theories of the firm are a set of initial premises which help to predict and define the object of analysis – the established firm. In fields such as organization behavior, economics, and strategy, once a theory of the firm is defined most questions can be developed without constantly referencing the underlying theory of the firm. However, what all of these theories presuppose is that the firm is a given and not the process of why new firms are created; this would constitute an entrepreneurial theory of the firm.

Questions about the existence and scope of entrepreneurial firms have also been an important area of research. Some of this work dates back centuries (e.g., Cantillon). Last century, entrepreneurship played a significant role in several explorations of the existence and scope of the firm, especially in the work of Knight (1921), Coase, (1937), Schumpeter (1934), and Kirzner (1979). More recently, the determinants of the existence and scope of the entrepreneurial firm have been discussed by Casson (2002), Sautet (2000), and Shane and Venkataraman (2000).

While the field of entrepreneurship has often been the bearer of criticism, that entrepreneurship is a collection of war stories reflecting practitioners' common sense, today entrepreneurship is quickly becoming a bona fide discipline, taught to both future practitioners and doctoral students. The quality and the impact of current research in entrepreneurship are heralding a "golden age" for entrepreneurship.

Given the amount of research in the field of entrepreneurship, it is not surprising that the attention of entrepreneurship scholars has been drawn to questions about the existence and scope of the entrepreneurial firm. These questions are central to the development of entrepreneurship as a field of study, and are relevant to many of the core issues in the field of entrepreneurship, including: What is an entrepreneur?, what is an entrepreneurial firm?, how can market opportunities be created and exploited? (Shane and Venkataraman, 2000), and how can any economic rents generated by creating or exploiting a market opportunity be appropriated? (Alvarez and Barney, 2001). More broadly, while the field of entrepreneurship is to a large extent formed we still continue to lack specific theories or theoretical frameworks (Bruyat and Julien, 2001). In many ways the field struggles to define itself, entrepreneurship, and the fundamental questions of the field. The next important paper to be written in this field will help define but a small slice within the domain of entrepreneurship, the entrepreneurial theory of the firm. In the field of entrepreneurship, fundamental questions regarding the theory of the firm are now a precondition for any further developments in entrepreneurship.

REFERENCES

Acs, Z.J. and D.B. Audretsch (1987). Innovation, market structure, and firm size. *Review of Economics and Statistics*, **LXIX**, 567–574.

Alvarez, S.A. and J.B. Barney (2000). Entrepreneurial capabilities: A resource-based view. In Meyer and Heppard (eds.), *Entrepreneurship as Strategy: Competing on the Entrepreneurial Edge*. Thousand Oaks, CA: Sage Publications.

Alvarez, S.A. and J.B. Barney (2002). Organizing rent generation and appropriation: Toward a theory of the entrepreneurial firm. *Journal of Business Venturing*. (In press.)

Alvarez, S.A. and L.W. Busenitz (2001). The entrepreneurship of resource-based theory. *Journal of Management*, **27**, 755–775.

Audretsh, David B. (1995). *Innovation and Industry Evolution*. Cambridge, MA: MIT Press.

Barney, J.B. (1986). Strategic factor markets: Expectations, luck and business strategy. *Management Science*, 42, 1231–1241.

Barney, J.B. (1991). Firm resources and sustained competitive advantage. *Journal of Management*, 17, 99–120.

Barney, J.B (1995). Looking inside for competitive advantage. *Academy of Management Executive*, 9, 49–61.

Barney, J.B. (2002). *Gaining and Sustaining Competitive Advantage*, 2nd edition. Upper Saddle River, NJ: Pearson Education, Inc.

Barney, J.B. and S. Alvarez (2002). Social network structure and information about market opportunities: The role of strong and weak ties. Unpublished. Center for Entrepreneurship, Fisher College of Business, The Ohio State University.

Busenitz, L. and J.B. Barney (1997). Differences between entrepreneurs and managers in large organizations: Biases and heuristics in strategic decision making. *Journal of Business Venturing*, 12(1), 9–30.

Casson, M. (1982). *The Entrepreneur: An Economic Theory*, 2nd edition. Oxford: Martin Robertson.

Casson, M. (2002). Entrepreneurship, business culture, and the theory of the firm. In Z.J. Acs and D.B. Audretsch (eds.), *The Handbook of Entrepreneurship Research*. Kluwer: Boston.

Coase, R.H. (1937). The nature of the firm. *Economica*, 4, 386–405.

Cohen, W.M. and D.A. Levinthal (1989). Innovation and learning: The two faces of R&D. *Economic Journal*, 99, 397, 569–610.

Cohen, W.M. and D.A. Levinthal (1990). Absorptive capacity: A new perspective on learning and innovation. *Administrative Science Quarterly*, 35, 128–152.

Conner, K.R. and C.K. Prahalad (1996). A resource-based theory of the firm: Knowledge versus opportunism. *Organization Science*, 7(5), 477–501.

Cooper, A.C. (2002). Networks, alliances and entrepreneurship. In M.A. Hitt, R.D. Ireland, S.M. Camp and D.L. Sexton (eds.), *Strategic Entrepreneurship*, Cornwall: Blackwell Publishers Ltd., pp. 203–222.

Demsetz, H. (1991). The theory of the firm revisited. In O.E. Williamson and S.G. Winter (eds.), *The Nature of the Firm*. New York: Oxford University Press, pp.159–178.

Dierickx, I. and Cool, K. (1989). Asset stock accumulation and sustainability of competitive advantage. *Management Science*, 35, 1504–1511.

Grossman, S. and O. Hart (1986). The cost and benefits of ownership: A theory of vertical and lateral integration. *Journal of Political Economy*, 94, 691–719.

Hayek, F.V. (1945). The use of knowledge in society. *American Economic Review*, 35, 519–530.

Hitt, M.A., D. Ahlstrom, M.T. Dacin and E. Levitas (2001). The economic and institutional context of international strategic alliance partner selection: China vs. Russia. Paper presented at the *Academy of Management* meetings, August, Washington, D.C.

Hitt, M.A., R.D. Ireland, S.M. Camp and D.L. Sexton (2002). *Strategic Entrepreneurship. Creating a New Mindset*. Oxford, UK: Blackwell Publishers Ltd.

Ireland, R.D., M.A. Hitt, S.M. Camp and D.L. Sexton (2001). Integrating entrepreneurship and strategic management actions to create firm wealth. *Academy of Management Executive*, 15(1), 49–63.

Jensen, M. and W.H. Meckling (1976). Theory of the firm: Managerial behavior, agency costs and ownership structure. *Journal of Financial Economics*, 3, 305–360.

Joskow, P.L. (1987). Contract duration and transaction specific investment: Empirical evidence from coal markets. *American Economic Review*, 77, 168–185.

Kamien, M.I. and N.L. Schwartz (1982). In Kamien and Schwartz (eds.), *Strategic Entrepreneurship: Market Structure and Innovation*, Boston: Cambridge University Press, pp. 223–245.

Kirzner, I. (1979). *Perception, Opportunity, and Profit*. Chicago: University of Chicago Press.

Kirzner, I (1997). Entrepreneurial discovery and the competitive market process: An Austrian approach. *Journal of Economic Literature*, 35, 60–85.

Knight, R.H. (1921). Cost of production and price over long and short periods. *Journal of Political Economy*, 29, 332.

Lieberman, M.B. and D.B. Montgomery (1988). First-mover advantages. *Strategic Management Journal*, **9**, 41–58.

Liebeskind, J.P. (1996). Knowledge, strategy, and the theory of the firm. *Strategic Management Journal*, **17** (Winter Special Issue), 93–107.

McGrath, R.G. and I. MacMillan (2000). *The Entrepreneurship Mindset*. Boston, MA: Harvard Business School Press.

Mansfield, E., M. Schwartz and S. Wagner (1981). Imitation costs and patents: An empirical study. *Economic Journal*, **91**, 907–918.

Meyer, G.D. and K.A. Heppard (2000). *Entrepreneurship as Strategy: Competing on the Entrepreneurial Edge*. Thousand Oaks, CA: Sage Publications.

Michael, S.C. (2001). *Academy of Management Review*, **26**(1), 133.

Milgrom, P. and J. Roberts (1992). *Economics, Organization, and Management*. Englewood Cliffs, NJ: Prentice-Hall. ·

Parkhe, A. (1993). Strategic alliance structuring: A game theoretic and transaction costs examination of interfirm cooperation. *Academy of Management Journal*, **36**, 794–829.

Reuer, J.J. and A. Ariño (2002). Contractual renegotiations in strategic alliances. *Journal of Management*, **28**, 51–74.

Rumelt, R.P. (1984). Toward a strategic theory of the firm. In. R. Lamb (ed.), *Competitive Strategic Management*. Upper Saddle River, NJ: Prentice Hall.

Rumelt, R.P. (1987). Theory, strategy, and entrepreneurship. In D.J. Teece (ed.). *The Competitive Challenge: Strategies for Industrial Innovation and Renewal*. Cambridge, MA: Ballinger, pp. 137–158.

Sautet, F.E. (2000). *An entrepreneurial theory of the firm*. London: Routledge.

Schendel, D. and C.W. Hofer (1978). Introduction to the Pittsburgh Conference. In D.E. Schendel and C.W. Hofer (eds.), *Strategic Management: A New View of Business Policy and Planning*. Boston: Little, Brown.

Schumpeter, J. (1934). *The Theory of Economic Development*. Cambridge, MA: Harvard University Press.

Shane, S. (2001). Technology regimes and new firm formation. *Management Science*, **47**(9), 1173–1190.

Shane, S. and S. Venkataraman (2000). The promise of entrepreneurship as a field of research. *Academy of Management Review*, **25**(1), 217–226.

Teece, D.J. (1987). *The Competitive Challenge: Strategies for Industrial Innovation and Renewal*. Cambridge, MA: Ballinger Publishing Company.

Venkataraman, S. and S.D. Sarasvathy (2001). Strategy and entrepreneurship: Outlines of an untold story. In M.A. Hitt, E. Freeman and J.S. Harrison (eds.), *Handbook of Strategic Management*. Oxford, UK: Blackwell, pp. 650–68.

Williamson, O.E. (1975). *Markets and Hierarchies: Analysis and Antitrust Implications*. New York: Free Press.

Williamson, O.E. (1985). *The Economic Institutions of Capitalism*. New York: Free Press.

PART FIVE

Financing the New Venture

Finance plays a central role in entrepreneurship and is the topic of Part V of this Handbook. The two chapters comprising this section provide an overview about what has been learned about the role that finance plays in entrepreneurship. In Chapter 12, "Equity Financing," Paul Gompers and Joshua Lerner focus on equity financing for entrepreneurial firms. This is a topic that has attracted increasing considerable attention in both the popular press and academic literature. The dramatic growth in the venture capital industry, as well as angel financing, in the past two decades has been accompanied by new academic research that explores its form and function. In particular, Gompers and Lerner provide two contributions with their chapter: (1) They summarize and synthesize what scholarly research has established about equity finance, and (2) identify the important questions that future research needs to address.

In Chapter 13, Allen Berger and Gregory Udell examine "Small Business and Debt Finance." Berger and Udell analyze how small-firm debt finance differs from that by large corporations. In particular, they identify the idiosyncratic nature of small firm debt financing. This includes a discussion of the motivation for debt finance in small firms, and the different sources of small firm debt. Berger and Udell examine the nature of debt contracting in small firm finance, focusing on contracting tools – such as collateral, guarantees, covenants, maturity, and menu pricing – that can be used to solve the problems associated with informational opacity that plague many small businesses. They show how lenders use these contracting tools in very different ways to address the information problems associated with small firm finance. Berger and Udell also examine some of the key factors that affect the supply of small business credit, including the global consolidation of the banking industry, credit crunches, discrimination in lending, and the impact of technological innovation.

PAUL GOMPERS and JOSHUA LERNER*

Harvard University, Harvard University

12. Equity Financing

INTRODUCTION

Equity financing for entrepreneurial firms has attracted increasing attention in both the popular press and academic literature. The dramatic growth in the venture capital industry in the past two decades has been accompanied by new academic research that explores its form and function. Angel financing, while less well understood, is also attracting attention. At the same time, many of the questions that are most critical to policy-makers remain unanswered. Thus, this chapter has a two-fold role: To summarize and synthesize what we do know about equity finance or entrepreneurial firms from recent research, and to indicate the important questions that we cannot yet answer.

A natural first question is what constitutes venture capital and angel financing. Many start-up firms require substantial capital. A firm's founder may not have sufficient funds to finance these projects alone, and therefore must seek outside financing. Entrepreneurial firms that are characterized by significant intangible assets, expect years of negative earnings, and have uncertain prospects are unlikely to receive bank loans or other debt financing. Venture capital organizations finance these high-risk, potentially high-reward projects, purchasing equity stakes while the firms are still privately held. At the same time, not everyone who finances these firms is a venture capitalist. We define venture capital as independently managed, dedicated pools of capital that focus on equity or equity-linked investments in privately held, high growth companies. Individual investors (or "angels") also finance these firms, putting their own capital to work in these concerns.

Three limitations should be acknowledged at the outset. The primary focus of this chapter is on drawing together the empirical academic research on venture capital and angel investing. The many theoretical papers that examine various aspects of the equity financing of entrepreneurial firms are beyond the scope of this chapter. Much of the theoretical literature examines the role that these investors play in mitigating agency conflicts surrounding entrepreneurial firms. The improvement in efficiency might be due to the active monitoring

* Harvard University and National Bureau of Economic Research. This chapter is based in part on the works of Gompers and Lerner (1999b, 2001). All errors are our own.

Z.J. Acs and D.B. Audretsch (eds.), Handbook of Entrepreneurship Research, 267–298
© 2003 *Kluwer Academic Publishers. Printed in Great Britain.*

and advice that is provided (Cornelli and Yosha, 2002; Hellmann, 1998; Marx, 1994), the screening mechanisms employed (Chan, 1983), the incentives to exit (Berglöf, 1994), the proper syndication of the investment (Admati and Pfleiderer, 1994), or the staging of the investment (Bergemann and Hege, 1998). This work has improved our understanding of the factors that affect the relationship between equity investors and entrepreneurs.

Nor do we seek to duplicate the guides that explain the intricacies of the equity financing process to practitioners. Numerous excellent volumes exist (especially Bartlett, 1995; Halloran et al., 1995 and Levin, 1995), which document the legal and institutional considerations associated with raising such financing at much greater depth than could be done in this chapter.

Third, we will not consider the upstream relationships between equity financiers of entrepreneurial firms and the institutions that provide them with capital at much length. Over the past several years, a series of research papers have given us a better understanding of how venture capital funds are structured, and how incentive issues that arise are (or are not addressed). This topic, however, would take us too far from our central mission. The interested reader is referred to Gompers and Lerner (1999b).

The rest of the chapter is organized as follows: Section 2 presents a brief history of financing of entrepreneurial firms. The selecting of investments, structuring of deals, monitoring of firms, and exiting of investments by venture capitalists and angels are taken up in Section 3. Section 4 discusses two public policy issues. The final section highlights an area that urgently needs future research: The internationalization of the U.S. venture capital industry and its implications.

THE DEVELOPMENT OF THE EQUITY FINANCING

Angel financing is probably as old as civilization. Certainly, examples can be found of entrepreneurs raising capital from financiers (e.g., for trading expeditions) from Babylonian times and early medieval European and Arabic nations. The venture capital industry – using the definition above – was, on the other hand, a much more recent and a predominantly American phenomenon. Only gradually has it spread to elsewhere around the globe.

It is important to note that, in many ways, venture capital is an outgrowth of angel investing. The industry had its origins in the family offices that managed the wealth of high net worth individuals in the first decades of last century. Wealthy families invested in and advised a variety of business enterprises, including the Rockefeller family (Douglas Aircraft and Eastern Airlines) and the Phipps (Ingersoll Rand and International Paper). Gradually, these families began involving outsiders to select and oversee these investments. In many cases, these entities formed the nuclei for what would ultimately become independent groups. These included J.H. Whitney & Co. (Whitney family) and Venrock Associates (Rockefeller family).[1]

The first venture capital firm satisfying the criteria delineated above, however, was not established until after World War II. American Research and Development (ARD) was formed in 1946 by MIT President Karl Compton, Harvard Business School Professor Georges F. Doriot, and local business leaders. A small group of venture capitalists made high-risk investments into emerging companies that were based on technology developed for World War II. The success of the investments ranged widely: Almost half of ARD's profits during its 26-year existence as an independent entity came from its $70,000 investment in Digital Equipment Company (DEC) in 1957, which grew in value to $355 million. Because institutional investors were reluctant to invest, ARD was structured as a publicly traded closed-end fund and marketed mostly to individuals (Liles, 1977). Many of the other venture organizations begun in the decade after ARD's formation were also structured as closed-end funds.

The first venture capital limited partnership, Draper, Gaither, and Anderson, was formed in 1958. Imitators soon followed, but limited partnerships accounted for a minority of the venture pool during the 1960s and 1970s. Most venture organizations raised money either through closed-end funds or small business investment companies (SBICs), federally guaranteed risk-capital pools that proliferated during the 1960s. While the market for SBICs in the late 1960s and early 1970s was strong, incentive problems ultimately led to the collapse of the sector. The annual flow of money into venture capital during its first three decades never exceeded a few hundred million dollars and usually was substantially less.

The activity in the venture industry increased dramatically in late 1970s and early 1980s. Table 1 and Figure 1 provide an overview of fundraising by venture partnerships, highlighting the changing volume of investments over the years, as well as the shifting mixture of investors. Industry observers attributed much of the shift to the U.S. Department of Labor's clarification of ERISA's "prudent man" rule in 1979. Prior to this year, the Employee Retirement Income Security Act (ERISA) limited pension funds from investing substantial amounts of money into venture capital or other high-risk asset classes. The Department of Labor's clarification of the rule explicitly allowed pension managers to invest in high-risk assets, including venture capital. In 1978, when $424 million was invested in new venture capital funds, individuals accounted for the largest share (32 percent). Pension funds supplied just 15 percent. Eight years later, when more than $4 billion was invested, pension funds accounted for more than half of all contributions.[2]

---

[1] These family offices are not the only antecedents to modern venture capital firms. For instance, patent agents in the United Kingdom and United States also played an intermediary role during the late nineteenth and early twentieth centuries, introducing individual inventors to wealthy potential investors. They typically did not, however, raise funds or invest their own capital into these firms. For a discussion, see Lamoreaux and Sokoloff (2000) and MacLeod (1992).

[2] The annual commitments represent pledges of capital to venture funds raised in a given year. This money is typically invested over three to five years starting in the year the fund is formed.

Table 1. Summary statistics for venture capital fund-raising by independent venture partnerships. All dollar figures are in millions of 1992 dollars

	1978	1979	1980	1981	1982	1983	1984	1985	1986	1987	1988	1989	1990	1991	1992	1993	1994	1995	1996	1997	1998	1999	2000
First closing of funds																							
Number of funds	23	27	57	81	98	147	150	99	86	112	78	88	50	34	31	46	80	84	80	103	161	209	228
Size (millions of 1992 $)	414	469	1,208	1,661	2,026	5,289	4,694	4,065	4,295	5,217	3,606	3,354	2,431	1,483	1,950	2,480	3,582	4,045	6,805	8,060	16,933	33,633	60,339
Sources of funds																							
Private pension funds	15%	31%	30%	23%	33%	26%	25%	23%	39%	27%	27%	22%	31%	25%	22%	59%	47%	38%	43%	40%	37%	43%	40%
Public pension funds	a	a	a	a	a	5%	9%	10%	12%	12%	20%	14%	22%	17%	20%	a	a	a	a	a	10%	a	a
Corporations	10%	17%	19%	17%	12%	12%	14%	12%	11%	10%	12%	20%	7%	4%	3%	8%	9%	2%	13%	30%	18%	14%	4%
Individuals	32%	23%	16%	23%	21%	21%	15%	13%	12%	12%	8%	6%	11%	12%	11%	7%	12%	17%	9%	13%	11%	10%	12%
Endowments	9%	10%	14%	12%	7%	8%	6%	8%	6%	10%	11%	12%	13%	24%	18%	11%	21%	22%	21%	9%	8%	17%	21%
Insurance/banks companies/banks	16%	4%	13%	15%	14%	12%	13%	11%	10%	15%	9%	13%	9%	6%	14%	11%	9%	18%	5%	1%	3%	16%	23%
Foreign investors/other	18%	15%	8%	10%	13%	16%	18%	23%	11%	14%	13%	13%	7%	12%	11%	4%	2%	3%	8%	7%	13%	b	b
Independent venture partnerships as																							
a share of the total venture pool[c]	40%	44%	58%	68%	72%	73%	75%	78%	80%	79%	80%	80%	81%	78%	78%								

[a] Public pension funds are included with private pension funds in these years.

[b] Foreign investors are included with other investors in 1999 and 2000.

[c] This series is defined differently in different years. In some years, the *Venture Capital Journal* states that non-bank SBICs and publicly traded venture funds are included with independent venture partnerships. In other years, these funds are counted in other categories. It is not available after 1994.

Source: Compiled from the unpublished Venture Economics funds database and various issues of the *Venture Capital Journal*. The numbers differ slightly from Lerner and Gompers (1996) due to continuing emendations to the funds database.

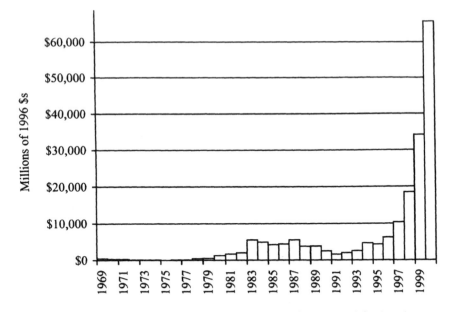

Figure 1. Commitments to the venture capital industry. Commitments are defined as the amount of money that is pledged to venture capital funds in that year. Amounts are in millions of 1996 dollars.
Source: Venture Economics and Asset Alternatives.

One important change in the venture capital industry around this time was the rise of the limited partnership as the dominant organizational form. Limited partnerships have an important advantage that makes them attractive to tax-exempt institutional investors: Capital gains taxes are not paid by the limited partnership. Instead, the (taxable) investors only pay taxes. Venture partnerships have pre-determined, finite lifetimes (usually ten years though extensions are often allowed). Investors in the fund are limited partners. In order to maintain limited liability, investors must not become involved in the day-to-day management of the fund.

The subsequent years saw both very good and trying times for venture capitalists. On the one hand, venture capitalists backed during the 1980s and 1990s many of the most successful high-technology companies, including Apple Computer, Cisco Systems, Genentech, Netscape, and Sun Microsystems. A substantial number of service firms (including Staples, Starbucks, and TCBY) also received venture financing. At the same time, commitments to the venture capital industry were very uneven. As Figure 1 and Table 1 depict, the annual flow of money into venture funds increased by a factor of ten during the early 1980s, peaking at just under six billion 1996 dollars. From 1987 through 1991, however, fundraising steadily declined. Over the past decade years, the pattern has been reversed. 2000 represented a record fundraising year, in which over

$68 billion was raised by venture capitalists. This process of rapid growth and decline has created a great deal of instability in the industry.

As Figure 2 depicts, returns on venture capital funds had declined in the mid-1980s, apparently because of overinvestment in various industries and the entry of inexperienced venture capitalists. As investors became disappointed with returns, they committed less capital to the industry. The recent activity in the IPO market and the exit of many inexperienced venture capitalists led to an increase in returns. New capital commitments rose again in response, increasing by more than twenty times between 1991 and 2000. While systematic data are not available, most indications are that angel investing underwent a dramatic increase during this period as well.

The question of how equity financing for entrepreneurial firms will evolve over the next decade is a particularly critical one because the recent growth and subsequent decline has been so spectacular. As will be highlighted below, short-run shifts in the supply of or demand for such equity investments can have dramatic effects. For instance, periods with a rapid increase in capital commitments have historically led to less restrictions on venture capital funds, larger investments in portfolio firms, higher valuations for those investments, and lower returns for investors. These patterns have led many practitioners to conclude that this activity is inherently cyclical. In short, this view implies that periods of rapid growth generate sufficient problems that periods of retrenchment are sure to follow. These cycles may lead us to be pessimistic about the prospects in the years to come.

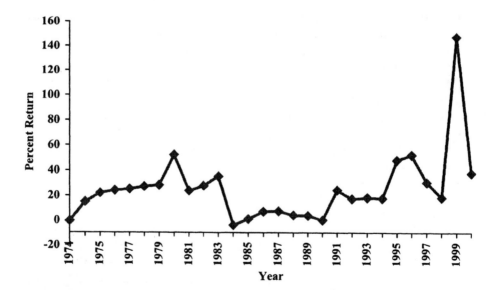

Figure 2. Return on venture capital. The average annual internal rate of return on venture capital funds, net of fees and profit-sharing, is plotted by year.
Source: Compiled from Venture Economics (2000b) and their unpublished data.

It is important, however, to consider the *long-run* determinants of the level of equity investors, not just the short-run effects. In the short run, intense competition between investors may lead to a willingness to pay a premium for certain types of firms (e.g., firms specializing in tools and content for the Internet). This is unlikely to be a sustainable strategy in the long run: Investors that persist in such a strategy will earn low returns and eventually either run out of funds or be unable to raise follow-on funds.

The types of factors that determine the long-run steady-state supply of equity for entrepreneurial firms in the economy are more fundamental. These are likely to include the pace of technological innovation in the economy, the degree of dynamism in the economy, the presence of liquid and competitive markets for investors to sell their investments (whether markets for stock offerings or acquisitions), and the willingness of highly skilled managers and engineers to work in entrepreneurial environments. However painful the short-run adjustments, these more fundamental factors are likely to be critical in establishing the long-run level.

When one examines these more fundamental factors, there appears to have been quite substantial changes for the better over the past several decades.[3] Consider two of the determinants of the long-run supply of equity investments for entrepreneurial firms in the United States: The acceleration of the rate of technological innovation and the decreasing "transaction costs" associated with such investments.

While the increase in innovation can be seen though several measures, probably the clearest indication is in the extent of patenting. Patent applications by U.S. inventors, after hovering between forty and eighty thousand annually over the first 85 years of last century, have surged over the past decade to over 120 thousand per year. This does not appear to reflect the impact of changes in domestic patent policy, shifts in the success rate of applications, or a variety of alternative explanations. Rather, it appears to reflect a fundamental shift in the rate of innovation.[4] The breadth of technology appears wider today than it has been ever before. The greater rate of intellectual innovation provides fertile ground for future investments, especially by venture capitalists.

A second change has been decreasing cost of making new equity investments in entrepreneurial firms. The efficiency of the equity investment process has been greatly augmented by the emergence of other intermediaries familiar with its workings. The presence of such expertise on the part of lawyers, accountants, managers and others – even real estate brokers – has substantially lowered the transaction costs associated with forming and financing new firms or restructuring existing ones. The increasing number of professionals and managers familiar with and accustomed to the employment arrangements offered by these firms

---

[3] It is also worth emphasizing that despite its growth, the pool of equity for entrepreneurial firms today remains very small relative to the overall pool of public equities, which has also grown rapidly during these years.

[4] These changes are discussed in Kortum and Lerner (1998).

Table 4. Number and dollar amount of venture capital disbursements for all industries in the ten states with the most venture capital activity, by state and five-year period. The count of venture capital investments in each five-year period is the sum of the number of firms receiving investments in each year. All dollar figures are in millions of 1992 dollars

Panel A: Venture Capital Investments (#s)

State	1965–69	1970–74	1975–79	1980–84	1985–89	1990–96
California	65	179	310	1,863	2,645	3,380
Massachusetts	45	93	155	708	1,014	1,028
Texas	18	71	84	373	584	489
New York	28	90	73	311	324	276
New Jersey	15	35	47	171	291	336
Colorado	5	22	31	194	258	298
Pennsylvania	8	21	32	120	290	311
Illinois	16	29	31	133	214	312
Minnesota	12	34	42	170	186	194
Connecticut	3	20	37	136	217	210
Total, all states	302	847	1,253	5,365	8,154	9,406

Panel B: Venture Capital Disbursements (millions of 1992 $s)

State	1965–69	1970–74	1975–79	1980–84	1985–89	1990–96
California	218	546	691	6,711	9,670	13,603
Massachusetts	61	155	197	1,943	2,829	3,386
Texas	37	140	148	1,161	2,171	2,010
New York	32	154	162	688	1,404	1,394
New Jersey	33	82	77	370	1,214	1,711
Colorado	12	50	46	493	805	951
Pennsylvania	18	41	116	370	1,530	1,109
Illinois	59	134	117	287	1,208	1,413
Minnesota	6	90	44	270	406	522
Connecticut	1	32	85	319	1,463	724
Total, all states	$687	$1,935	$2,259	$15,261	$30,742	$37,162

Source: Based on tabulations of unpublished Venture Economics databases.

only) over the past three decades; and Table 4 provides a summary of investments in the ten states with the most venture capital activity over the past three decades.

The industry results in Tables 2 and 3 highlight the continuing focus by venture capitalists on high technology firms (e.g., communication, computers, electronics, biotechnology, and medical/health). The percentage of venture capital invested in high technology firms never falls below 70% of annual investments. Industry investment composition suggests that venture capitalists specialize in industries in which monitoring and information evaluation are important.

Why This Concentration?

Uncertainty and informational asymmetries often characterize young firms, particularly in high-technology industries. These information problems make it difficult to assess these firms, and permit opportunistic behavior by entrepreneurs after financing is received. This literature has highlighted the role of informed investors such as angels and venture capitalists in alleviating these information problems.

To briefly review the types of conflicts that can emerge in these settings, Jensen and Meckling (1976) demonstrate that conflicts between managers and investors ("agency problems") can affect the willingness of both debt and equity holders to provide capital. If the firm raises equity from outside investors, the manager has an incentive to engage in wasteful expenditures (e.g., lavish offices) because he may benefit disproportionately from these but does not bear their entire cost. Similarly, if the firm raises debt, the manager may increase risk to undesirable levels. Because providers of capital recognize these problems, outside investors demand a higher rate of return than would be the case if the funds were internally generated.

Even if the manager is motivated to maximize shareholder value, informational asymmetries may make raising external capital more expensive or even preclude it entirely. Myers and Majluf (1984) and Greenwald, Stiglitz, and Weiss (1984) demonstrate that equity offerings of firms may be associated with a "lemons" problem (first identified by Akerlof, 1970). If the manager is better informed about the investment opportunities of the firm and acts in the interest of current shareholders, then managers only issue new shares when the company's stock is overvalued. Indeed, numerous studies have documented that stock prices decline upon the announcement of equity issues, largely because of the negative signal sent to the market. These information problems have also been shown to exist in debt markets by Stiglitz and Weiss (1981) and others.

More generally, the inability to verify outcomes makes it difficult to write contracts that are contingent upon particular events. This inability makes external financing costly. Many of the models of ownership (e.g., Grossman and Hart, 1986), and Hart and Moore, 1990) and financing choice (e.g., Hart and Moore, 1998) depend on the inability of investors to verify that certain actions have been taken or certain outcomes have occurred. While actions or outcomes might be observable, meaning that investors know what the entrepreneur did, they are assumed not to be verifiable: i.e., investors could not convince a court of the action or outcome. Start-up firms are likely to face exactly these types of problems, making external financing costly or difficult to obtain.

If the information asymmetries could be eliminated, financing constraints would disappear. Financial economists argue that specialized financial intermediaries, such as venture capital organizations, can address these problems. By intensively scrutinizing firms before providing capital and then monitoring them afterwards, they can alleviate some of the information gaps and reduce capital constraints. Thus, it is important to understand the tools employed by venture investors discussed below as responses to this difficult environment, which enable firms to ultimately receive the financing that they cannot raise from other sources. It is the nonmonetary aspects of venture capital that are critical to its success.

The Specific Tools

One of the most common features of equity investors in entrepreneurial firms is the meting out of financing in discrete stages over time. Sahlman (1990) notes that staged capital infusion is the most potent control mechanism such an investor can employ. Prospects for the firm are periodically reevaluated. The shorter the duration of an individual round of financing, the more frequently the investors monitors the entrepreneur's progress and the greater the need to gather information. Staged capital infusion keeps the owner/manager on a "tight leash" and reduces potential losses from bad decisions.[5]

The research on conflicts between investors and managers discussed above suggests several factors that should affect the duration and size of these investments. Investors should weigh potential agency and monitoring costs when determining how frequently they should reevaluate projects and supply capital. The duration of funding should decline and the frequency of reevaluation should increase when the venture capitalist expects conflicts with the entrepreneur are more likely.

If monitoring and information gathering are important – as models by Admati and Pfleiderer (1994), Amit, Glosten, and Muller (1990a, 1990b), and Chan (1983) suggest – the most specialized investors in entrepreneurial firms, venture capitalists, should invest in firms in which asymmetric information is likely to be a problem. The value of oversight will be greater for these firms. The capital constraints faced by these companies will be very large and the information gathered will help alleviate the constraint. Early-stage companies have short or no histories to examine and are difficult to evaluate. Similarly, high-technology companies are likely to require close monitoring. A significant fraction of venture capital investment should therefore be directed towards early-stage and high technology companies.

In practice, equity investors in entrepreneurial firms incur costs when they monitor and infuse capital. Monitoring costs include the opportunity cost of generating reports for both the venture capitalist and entrepreneur. If investors need to "kick the tires" of the plant, read reports, and take time away from other activities, these costs can be substantial. Contracting costs (e.g., legal fees) and the lost time and resources of the entrepreneur must be imputed as well. These costs lead to funding being provided in discrete stages.

[5]Two related types of agency costs exist in entrepreneurial firms. Both agency costs result from the large information asymmetries that affect young, growth companies in need of financing. First, entrepreneurs might invest in strategies, research, or projects that have high personal returns but low expected monetary payoffs to shareholders. For example, a biotechnology company founder may choose to invest in a certain type of research that brings him/her great recognition in the scientific community but provides little return for the venture capitalist. Similarly, entrepreneurs may receive initial results from market trials indicating little demand for a new product, but may want to keep the company going because they receive significant private benefits from managing their own firm. Second, because entrepreneurs' equity stakes are essentially call options, they have incentives to pursue highly volatile strategies, such as rushing a product to market when further testing may be warranted.

Even though equity investors periodically "check-up" on entrepreneurs between capital infusions, entrepreneurs still have private information about the projects that they manage. Gorman and Sahlman (1989) show that between financing rounds, the lead venture capitalist visits the entrepreneur once a month on average and spends four to five hours at the facility during each visit. Venture capitalists also receive monthly financial reports. Gorman and Sahlman show, however, that venture capitalists do not usually become involved in the day-to-day management of the firm. Major reviews of progress and extensive due diligence are confined to the time of refinancing. The checks between financings are designed to limit opportunistic behavior by entrepreneurs between evaluations.

The nature of the firm's assets also has important implications for expected agency costs and the structure of staged equity investments. Intangible assets should be associated with greater agency problems. As assets become more tangible, equity investors can recover more of their investment in liquidation. This reduces the need to monitor tightly and should increase the time between refinancings. Industries with high levels of R&D should also have more frequent agency problems, and investors should shorten funding duration. Finally, a substantial finance literature (e.g., Myers, 1977) argues that firms with high market-to-book ratios are more susceptible to these agency costs, thus investors should increase the intensity of monitoring of these firms.

Gompers (1995) tests these predictions using a random sample of 794 venture capital-financed companies. The results confirm the predictions of agency theory. Venture capitalists concentrate investments in early stage companies and high technology industries where informational asymmetries are significant and monitoring is valuable. Venture capitalists monitor the firm's progress. If they learn negative information about future returns, the project is cut off from new financing. Firms that go public (these firms yield the highest return for venture capitalists on average) receive more total financing and a greater number of rounds than other firms (which may go bankrupt, be acquired, or remain private). Gompers also finds that early stage firms receive significantly less money per round. Increases in asset tangibility increase financing duration and reduce monitoring intensity. As the role of future investment opportunities in firm value increases (higher market-to-book ratios or R&D intensities), firms are refinanced more frequently. These results suggest the important monitoring and information generating roles played by equity investors in entrepreneurial firms. Consistent evidence regarding the actual contractual terms in these agreements is found in Kaplan and Stromberg's (2002) analysis of 130 venture partnership agreements.

Why cannot other financial intermediaries that focus on debt financing (e.g., banks) undertake the same sort of monitoring? First, because regulations limit banks' ability to hold shares, they cannot freely use equity to fund projects. Though several papers focus on monitoring by banks (James, 1987; Petersen and Rajan, 1994, 1995; Hoshi, Kashyap, and Scharfstein, 1991), banks may not have the necessary skills to evaluate projects with few collateralizable assets and significant uncertainty. In addition, Petersen and Rajan (1995) argue that banks in competitive markets will be unable to finance high-risk projects because they are unable to charge borrowers rates high enough to compensate for the firm's riskiness. Taking an equity position in the firm allows the venture capitalist or angel to proportionately share in the upside, guaranteeing that the venture capitalist benefits if the firm does well. Finally, angels' personal investments and venture capital funds' high-powered compensation schemes give these investors incentives to monitor firms more closely, because their individual compensation is closely linked to the funds' returns. Corporations, investment banks, and other institutions that have sponsored venture funds without such high-powered incentives have found it difficult to retain personnel, once the fund managers have developed a performance record that enables them to raise a fund of their own.

In addition to the staged capital infusions, venture capitalists and angels will usually make investments with other investors. One investor will originate the deal and look to bring in others. This syndication serves multiple purposes. First, it allows the investors to diversify. If the investor had to invest alone into all the companies in his portfolio, then he could make many fewer investments. By syndicating investments, the venture capitalist or angel can invest in more projects and largely diversify away firm-specific risk.

For example, a typical venture capital firm may raise a fund of between two hundred million dollars. In any one particular round in recent years, a portfolio company receives between five and twenty million dollars. If the typical venture-backed company receives four rounds of venture financing, any one firm might require about forty or fifty million dollars of financing. If the venture capital firm originating the deal were to make the entire investment, the fund could only make four or five investments. Hence, the value of bringing in syndication partners for diversification is large.

A second potential explanation for syndication patterns is that involving other investors provides as a second opinion on the investment opportunity. There is usually no clear-cut answer as to whether any of the investments that an equity investor undertakes will yield attractive returns. Having other investors approve the deal limits the danger that bad deals will get funded. This is particularly true when the company is early-stage or technology-based.

Lerner (1994a) tests this "second opinion" hypothesis in a sample of biotechnology venture capital investments. In a sample of 271 firms, Lerner finds that in the early rounds of investing, experienced venture capitalists tend to syndicate only with venture capital firms that have similar experience. Lerner argues that if a venture capitalist were looking for a second opinion, then he would want to get a second opinion from someone of similar or better ability, certainly not from someone of lesser ability.

The advice and support provided by equity investors is often embodied by their role on the firm's board of directors. Lerner (1995) examines the decision of venture capitalists to provide this oversight. He examines whether venture capitalists' representation on the boards of the private firms in their portfolios is greater when the need for oversight is larger. This approach is suggested by Fama and Jensen (1983) and Williamson (1983), who hypothesize that the composition of the board should be shaped by the need for oversight. These authors argue that the board will bear greater responsibility for oversight – and consequently that outsiders should have greater representation – when the danger of managerial deviations from value maximization is high. If venture capitalists are especially important providers of managerial oversight, their representation on boards should be more extensive at times when the need for oversight is greater.

Lerner examines changes in board membership around the time that a firm's chief executive officer (CEO) is replaced, an approach suggested by Hermalin and Weisbach's (1988) study of outside directors of public firms. The replacement of the top manager at an entrepreneurial firm is likely to coincide with an organizational crisis and to heighten the need for monitoring. He finds that an average of 1.75 venture capitalists are added to the board between financing rounds when the firm's CEO is replaced in the interval; between other rounds, 0.24 venture directors are added. No differences are found in the addition of other outside directors. This oversight of new firms involves substantial costs. The transaction costs associated with frequent visits and intensive involvement are likely to be reduced if the venture capitalist is proximate to the firms in his portfolio. Consistent with these suggestions, he find that geographic proximity is an important determinant of venture board membership: Organizations with offices within five miles of the firm's headquarters are twice as likely to be board members as those more than 500 miles distant. Over half the firms in the sample have a venture director with an office within sixty miles of their headquarters.

Another mechanism utilized by equity investors in entrepreneurial firms to avoid conflicts is the widespread use of stock grants and stock options. Managers and critical employees within a firm receive a substantial fraction of their compensation in the form of equity or options. This tends to align the incentives of managers and investors, unlike large public companies, where the CEO's personal wealth typically increases by only a dollar or two for each $1000 increase in firm value.

Equity investors also employ additional controls on compensation to reduce potential gaming by the entrepreneur. First, venture capitalists usually require vesting of the stock or options over a multi-year period. In this way, the entrepreneur cannot leave the firm and take his shares. Similarly, the venture capitalist can significantly dilute the entrepreneur's stake in subsequent financings if the firm fails to realize its targets. This provides additional incentives for the entrepreneur. In order to maintain his stake, the entrepreneur will need to meet his stated targets.

Distortions to the Equity Investment Process

Until this point, this section has highlighted the ways in which equity investors can successfully address agency problems in portfolio firms. Practitioners, however, often make the argument that equity financing has gone through periods of disequilibrium. During periods when the amount of money flowing into the industry has dramatically grown, they argue, the valuations at which investments are made or the likelihood that certain transactions get funded can shift dramatically. If there are only a certain number of worthy projects to finance, then a substantial increase in the amount of venture fundraising may increase the prices that are paid to invest in these companies. These higher prices may ultimately affect the returns on investment in the industry.

Sahlman and Stevenson (1987) chronicle the exploits of angel investors and venture capitalists in the Winchester disk drive industry during the early 1980s. Sahlman and Stevenson believe that a type of "market myopia" affected equity investing in the industry. During the late 1970s and early 1980s, nineteen disk drive companies received venture capital financing. Two-thirds of these investments came between 1982 and 1984, the period of rapid expansion of the venture industry. Many disk drive companies also went public during this period. While industry growth was rapid during this period of time (sales increased from $27 million in 1978 to $1.3 billion in 1983), Sahlman and Stevenson question whether the scale of investment was rational given any reasonable expectations of industry growth and future economic trends.[6] Similar stories are often told concerning investments in software, biotechnology, and the Internet. The phrase "too much money chasing too few deals" is a common refrain in the equity financing market during periods of rapid growth.

Gompers and Lerner (2000) examine these claims through a dataset of over 4000 venture investments between 1987 and 1995 developed by the consulting firm VentureOne. They construct a hedonic price index that controls for various firm attributes that might affect firm valuation, including firm age, stage of development, and industry, as well as macroeconomic variables such as inflow of funds into the venture capital industry. In addition, they control for public market valuations through indexes of public market values for firms in the same industries and average book-to-market and earnings-to-price ratios.

The results support contentions that a strong relation exists between the valuation of venture capital investments and capital inflows. While other variables also have significant explanatory power – for instance, the marginal impact of a doubling in public market values was between a 15% and 35% increase in the valuation of private equity transactions – the inflows variable is significantly positive. A doubling of inflows into venture funds leads to between a 7% and 21% increase in valuation levels.

The overall price index is depicted in Figure 3. The index is constructed such that the price level in the first quarter of 1987 is set equal to 100. The index controls for differences in the underlying deals in the venture industry.

---

[6]Lerner (1997) suggests, however, that these firms may have displayed behavior consistent with strategic models of "technology races" in the economics literature. Because firms had the option to exit the competition to develop a new disk drive, it may have indeed been rational for venture capitalists to fund a substantial number of disk drive manufacturers.

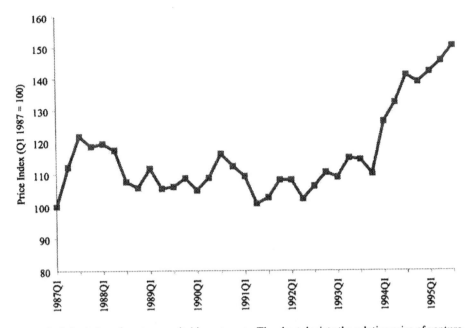

Figure 3. Price index of venture capital investments. The chart depicts the relative price of venture capital investments, controlling for changes in the companies funded.
Source: Gompers and Lerner (2000).

While prices rose somewhat in 1987, they declined and remained quite flat through the 1990s. Starting in 1994, however, prices steadily increased. This increase coincided with the recent rise in venture fundraising. The regression results show that this rise in fundraising is an important source of the increase in prices.

The results are particularly strong for specific types of funds and funds in particular regions. Because funds have become larger in real dollar terms, with more capital per partner, many venture capital organizations have invested larger amounts of money in each portfolio company. Firms have attempted to do this in two ways. First, there has been a movement to finance later-stage companies that can accept larger blocks of financing. Second, venture firms are syndicating less. This leads to greater competition for making later-stage investments. Similarly, because the majority of money is raised in California and Massachusetts, competition for deals in these regions should be particularly intense and venture capital inflows may have a more dramatic effect on prices in those regions. The results support these contentions. The effect of venture capital inflows is significantly more dramatic on later-stage investments and investments in California and Massachusetts.

Gompers and Lerner also examine whether increases in venture capital inflows and valuations simultaneously reflect improvements in the environment for young firms. If shifts in the supply of venture capital are contemporaneous with changes in the demand for capital, their inferences may be biased. They show that success rates – whether measured through the completion of an initial public offering or an acquisition at an attractive price – did not differ significantly between investments made during the early 1990s, a period of relatively low inflows and valuations, and those of the boom years of the late 1980s. The results seem to indicate that the price increases reflect increasing competition for investment.

Exiting Equity Investments in Entrepreneurial Firms

The final stage in the investment process is exiting. In order to make money on their investments, equity investors need to turn illiquid stakes in private companies into realized return. Typically, as was discussed above, the most profitable exit opportunity is an initial public offering (IPO). In an IPO, the investor assists the company in issuing shares to the public for the first time. Table 5 summarizes the exiting of investments in entrepreneurial firms through initial public offerings.

Initial empirical research into the role of equity investors in exiting investments focused on the structure of IPOs. Barry, Muscarella, Peavy and Vetsuypens (1990) focus on establishing a broad array of facts about the role of venture capitalists in IPOs, using a sample of 433 venture-backed and 1123 non-venture IPOs between 1978 and 1987.

Barry et al., document that venture capitalists hold significant equity stakes in the firms they take public (on average, the lead venture capitalist holds a 19% stake immediately prior to the IPO, and all venture investors hold 34%), and hold about one-third of the board seats. They continue to hold their equity positions in the year after the IPO. Finally, venture-backed IPOs have less of a positive return on their first trading day. The authors suggest that this implies that investors need less of a discount in order to purchase these shares (i.e., the offerings are less "underpriced"), because the venture capitalist has monitored the quality of the offering.

Megginson and Weiss (1991) argue that because venture capitalists repeatedly bring firms to the public market, they can credibly stake their reputation. Put another way, they can certify to investors that the firms they bring to market are not overvalued. Certification requires that venture capitalists possess reputational capital, that the acquisition of such a reputation is costly, and that the present value of lost reputational capital by cheating is greater than the one-time gain from behaving in a duplicitous manner.

The certification model yields several empirical implications. First, because venture capitalists repeatedly take firms public, they build relationships with underwriters and auditors. These relationships may lead to the average venture-backed IPO having higher-quality underwriters and auditors than non-venture IPOs. Megginson and Weiss also argue that these relationships and the existence of reputation should lead to greater institutional holdings of the venture-backed firm after IPO. Megginson and Weiss also argue that the retention of

Table 5. The distribution of venture-backed and non-venture IPOs for the period 1978–1999. This table compares the distribution of IPOs in this sample versus all IPOs recorded over this period of time. All dollar figures are in millions of 1992 dollars:

Year	Number of venture-backed IPOs	Amount raised in venture-backed IPOs	Total number of IPOs	Total amount raised in all IPOs	Venture-backed IPOs as percent of all IPOs (number)	Venture-backed IPOs as percent of all IPOs (amount)
1978	6	$134	42	$485	12.50%	21.59%
1979	4	$62	103	$777	3.74%	7.34%
1980	24	$670	259	$2,327	8.48%	22.35%
1981	50	$783	438	$4,848	10.25%	13.91%
1982	21	$738	198	$1,901	9.59%	27.97%
1983	101	$3,451	848	$17,999	10.64%	16.09%
1984	44	$731	516	$5,179	7.86%	12.37%
1985	35	$819	507	$13,307	6.46%	5.80%
1986	79	$2,003	953	$23,902	7.66%	7.73%
1987	69	$1,602	630	$19,721	9.87%	7.52%
1988	36	$915	435	$6,679	8.28%	13.70%
1989	39	$1,110	371	$6,763	10.51%	16.41%
1990	43	$1,269	276	$4,828	15.58%	16.29%
1991	119	$3,835	367	$16,872	32.43%	22.73%
1992	157	$4,317	509	$23,990	30.84%	17.99%
1993	193	$4,905	707	$40,456	27.30%	12.12%
1994	159	$3,408	564	$27,786	28.19%	12.26%
1995	205	$6,251	566	$36,219	36.22%	17.26%
1996	284	$10,976	845	$38,245	33.61%	28.70%
1997	138	$4,419	628	$40,278	21.34%	10.60%
1998	78	$3,388	319	$31,075	24.45%	10.90%
1999	271	$20,757	485	$56,952	55.87%	36.45%

Sources: Barry et al. (1992), Ritter (1998), and various issues of the *Going Public: The IPO Reporter* and the *Venture Capital Journal.*

large stakes of equity both before and after the IPO is a "bonding mechanism" that increases the effectiveness of the venture capitalist's certification. Any benefit to issuing overpriced shares would be minimized because the venture capitalist sells few or no shares at IPO. Megginson and Weiss test these ideas using a matched set of 640 venture-backed and non-venture IPOs between 1983 and 1987, and find results generally consistent with their hypotheses.

More recent research has examined the timing of the decision to take firms public and to liquidate the equity investors' holdings (which frequently occurs well after the IPO). Several potential factors affect when firms go public. One of these is the relative valuation level of publicly traded securities. Lerner (1994b) examines when venture capitalists choose to finance a sample of biotechnology companies in another private round versus taking the firm public in. Using a sample of 350 privately held venture-backed firms, he shows take firms public at market peaks, relying on private financings when valuations are lower. Seasoned venture capitalists appear more proficient at timing IPOs.

The results are robust to the use of alternative criteria to separate firms and controls for firms' quality. The results are not caused by differences in the speed of executing the IPOs, or in the willingness to withdraw the proposed IPOs.

Another consideration may be the reputation of the investor, at least in the case of venture capitalists that need to raise money from outside investors. Gompers (1996) argues that young venture capital firms have incentives to "grandstand": i.e., they take actions that signal their ability to potential investors. Specifically, young venture capital firms bring companies public earlier than older venture capital firms in an effort to establish a reputation and successfully raise capital for new funds. He examines a sample of 433 venture-backed initial public offerings (IPOs) between 1978 and 1987, as well as a second sample consisting of the first IPOs brought to market by 62 venture capital funds. The results support predictions of the grandstanding hypothesis.

The typical equity investor, however, does not sell their equity at the time of the IPO. The negative signal that would be sent to the market by an insider "cashing out" would prevent a successful offering. In addition, most investment banks require that all insiders, including the venture capitalists, do not sell any of their equity after the offering for a pre-specified period (usually six months). Once that lock-up period is over, however, venture capitalists can return money to investors in one of two ways. They can liquidate their position in a portfolio company by selling shares on the open market after it has gone public and then paying those proceeds to investors in cash. More frequently, however, venture capitalists make distributions of shares to investors in the venture capital fund. Many institutional investors have received a flood of these distributions during the past several years and have grown increasingly concerned about the incentives of the venture capitalists when they declare these transfers.

Gompers and Lerner (1998) examine how investors might be affected by distributions. These distributions have several features that make them an interesting testing ground for an examination of the impact of transactions by informed insiders on securities prices. Because they are not considered to be "sales," the distributions are exempt from the anti-fraud and anti-manipulation provisions of the securities laws. The legality of distributions provides an important advantage. The institutional investors compile comprehensive records of these transactions and the intermediaries who invest in venture funds, addressing concerns about sample selection bias. Like trades by corporate insiders, transactions are not revealed at the time of the transaction. Venture capitalists can immediately declare a distribution, send investors their shares, and need not register with the SEC or file a report under Rule 16(a). Rather, the occurrence of such distributions can only be discovered from corporate filings with a lag, and even then the distribution date cannot be precisely identified. To identify the time of these transactions, one needs to rely on the records of the partners in the fund. They characterize the features of the venture funds making the distributions, the firms whose shares are being distributed, and the changes associated with the transactions in a way that can discriminate between the various alternative explanations for these patterns.

From the records of four institutions, Gompers and Lerner construct a representative set of over 700 transactions by 135 funds over a decade-long period. The results are consistent with venture capitalists possessing inside information and of the (partial) adjustment of the market to that information. As depicted in Figure 4, after significant increases in stock prices prior to distribution, abnormal returns around the distribution are a negative and significant −2.0 percent, comparable to the market reaction to publicly announced secondary stock sales. The sign and significance of the cumulative excess returns for the twelve months following the distribution appear to be negative in most specifications, but are sensitive to the benchmark used.

CURRENT PUBLIC POLICY ISSUES

In this section, we consider two of the debates swirling about public policies to encourage equity investments in entrepreneurial firms. First, we consider the evidence about the relationship between venture capital and innovation. We then explore the advisability of steps to encourage angel investing.

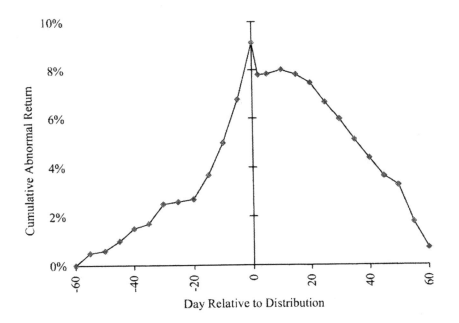

Figure 4. Stock price around distribution of equity by venture capitalists. The graph plots the cumulative abnormal return from 60 days prior to distribution to 60 days after distribution. *Source*: Gompers and Lerner (1998).

obtain external financing limits many forms of business investment. Particularly relevant are works by Hall (1992), Hao and Jaffe (1993), and Himmelberg and Petersen (1994). These show that capital constraints appear to limit research-and-development expenditures, especially in smaller firms.

However compelling the evidence for capital constraints limiting investments by small, technology-intensive firms,[8] these studies' relevance for policy-makers today is unclear. Many of these works examine firms during the 1970s and early 1980s, when the venture capital pool was relatively modest in size. As noted above, the pool of venture capital funds has grown dramatically in recent years. Thus, even if small high-technology firms had numerous value-creating projects that they could not finance in the past, it is not clear that this problem remains today.

A second set of arguments is based on the perceived limitations of the venture capital industry. Venture capitalists fund a modest number of firms each year, and these investments are highly concentrated. Furthermore, venture investors tend to only consider investing in firms that have a substantial need for capital. We next review and assess these arguments.

Venture capitalists back only a tiny fraction of the technology-oriented businesses begun each year. In 2000, a record year for venture disbursements, just under 3000 companies received venture financing for the first time (National, 2001). (By way of comparison, the Small Business Administration estimates that in recent years close to one million businesses have been started annually.) Furthermore, these funds – as in previous years – have been very concentrated. 92% went to firms specializing in information technology and the life sciences, and 46% went to Internet-related companies (National, 2001).

It is not clear, however, what lessons to draw from these funding patterns. Concentrating investments in such a manner may well be an appropriate response to the nature of opportunities. Consider, for instance, the geographic concentration of awards. Recent models of economic growth – building on earlier works by economic geographers – have emphasized powerful reasons why successful high-technology firms may be very concentrated. The literature highlights several factors that lead similar firms to cluster in particular regions, including knowledge spillovers, specialized labor markets, and the presence of critical intermediate good producers. (The theoretical rationales for such effects are summarized in Krugman, 1991.) Case studies of the development of high-technology regions (e.g., Saxenian, 1994) have emphasized the importance of intermediaries such as venture capitalists, lawyers, and accountants in facilitating such clustering.

A related argument for encouraging angel investors is that structure of venture investments may be inappropriate for many young firms. Venture funds tend to make quite substantial investments, even in young firms. The mean

---

[8] A related body of literature documents that investments in R&D yield high private and social rates of return (e.g., Griliches, 1986; Mansfield et al., 1977). These findings similarly suggest that a higher level of R&D spending would be desirable.

venture investment in a start-up or early-stage business even before the current growth was quite substantial: Between 1961 and 1992 (expressed in 2000 dollars), the mean investment was $2.2 million (Gompers, 1995).

The substantial size of these investments may be partially a consequence of the demands of institutional investors. The typical venture organization raises a fund (structured as a limited partnership) every few years. Because investments in partnerships are often time-consuming to negotiate and monitor, institutions prefer making relatively large investments in venture funds (typically $10 million or more). Furthermore, governance and regulatory considerations lead institutions to limit the share of the fund that any one limited partner holds. (The structure of venture partnerships is discussed at length in Gompers and Lerner, 1996.) These pressures lead venture organizations to raise substantial funds. Because each firm in his portfolio must be closely scrutinized, the typical venture capitalist is typically responsible for no more than a dozen investments. Venture organizations are consequently unwilling to invest in very young firms that only require small capital infusions.[9] This problem may be increasing in severity with the growth of the venture industry. As the number of dollars per venture fund and dollars per venture partner have grown, so too has the size of venture investments: For instance, the mean financing round for a start-up firm has climbed (in 2000 dollars) from $1.8 million in 1991 to $11.5 million in 2000 (National, 2001).

Again, it is not clear what lessons to draw from these financing patterns. Venture capitalists may have eschewed small investments because they were simply not profitable, because of either the high costs associated with these transactions or the poor prospects of the thinly capitalized firms. (For a theoretical discussion of why poorly capitalized firms are less likely to be successful, see Bolton and Scharfstein, 1990.) Encouraging individuals to make such small investments may be counter-productive and socially wasteful if the financial returns are unsatisfactory and the companies financed are not viable.

Support for these claims is found in recent work on the long-run performance of initial public offerings (IPOs). Brav and Gompers (1997) show that IPOs that had previously received equity financing from venture capitalists outperform other offerings, such as those firms who were backed by individual investors. Field (1996) shows that the long-run returns of IPOs are positively correlated with the willingness of institutional (as opposed to individual) investors to purchases shares in the offering. Taken together, these findings underscore concerns about policies that seek to encourage individuals to invest in companies that are rejected by professional investors.

---

[9]There are two primary reasons why venture funds do not simply hire more partners if they raise additional capital. First, the supply of venture capitalists is quite inelastic. The effective oversight of young companies requires highly specialized skills that can only be developed with years of experience. A second important factor is the economics of venture partnerships. The typical venture fund receives a substantial share of its compensation from the annual fee, which is typically between 2% and 3% of the capital under management. This motivates venture organizations to increase the capital that each partner manages.

Beyond this question, there are many challenges associated with the design of programs to encourage individual investors. Because of the relatively little research done on the topic of "angel" investors, this discussion is necessarily speculative in nature. Thus, we only seek to raise questions about how these efforts should be designed and implemented:

- *How to insure the involvement of value-added individual investors?* Field studies – see, for instance, Wetzel and Seymour (1981) and Freear, Sohl, and Wetzel, 1994) – have highlighted the heterogeneity of angel investors. Some are very sophisticated former entrepreneurs who may be of a great deal of assistance to the new businesses that they finance; but other individual investors may be quite naïve about the risks and delays associated with building an entrepreneurial firm. In fact, in some cases the involvement of unsophisticated individual investors can make it more difficult for an entrepreneurial firm to raise outside capital (e.g., Das and Lerner, 1995). One challenge facing public efforts is how to insure the involvement of angels who can add the most value.
- *How to address concerns about disclosure and securities laws?* In order to participate in ACE-Net, entrepreneurs need to file offering documents under such securities provisions as Regulation A, Regulation D, or Rule 504, as well as appropriate state filings. When private companies raise money informally through angel investors, they very rarely are required to undertake such filings. Small privately held companies frequently resist disclosing financial or business data, lest they provide their larger rivals with competitively useful information about their strategy and/or technology. It may be important to consider whether public initiatives can be developed which do not require such disclosures.
- *How should public initiatives interact with similar private-sector efforts?* An Internet search reveals that a variety of for-profit entities have introduced services which seek to match entrepreneurs with angel investors. Examples include American Venture Capital Exchange, Capital Matchmaker, FinanceHub, MoneyHunter, and Venture Capital Report. Determining how public and private efforts should interact will be an important policy priority.

Thus, important unanswered questions remain, both about the overall need for and the desirable structure of public efforts to encourage angel investments in entrepreneurial firms. One conclusion is certain: Angel finance is a ripe area for more intensive research, on both an empirical and theoretical level, by financial economists. While data limitations have been a substantial barrier to researchers in the past, through careful and creative exploration of new data sets, we may gain a better understanding of these issues.

FUTURE RESEARCH

While financial economists know much more about equity financing of entrepreneurial firms than they did a decade ago, there are many unresolved issues that would reward future research. While we have indicated a number of these in the course of the discussion, this section highlights the area where research is most needed: The internationalization of venture capital.

The rapid growth in the U.S. venture capital market has led institutional investors to look increasingly at private equity alternatives abroad. Until very recently, outside of the United Kingdom (where performance of funds has been quite poor) and Israel there has been little venture capital activity abroad.[10] (Table 6 provides an international comparison of venture capital activity.) Black and Gilson (1998) argue that the key source of the U.S. competitive advantage in venture capital is the existence of a robust IPO market. Venture capitalists can commit to transfer control back to the entrepreneur when a public equity

Table 6. The size of the venture capital pool in 21 nations in 1995. We use Jeng and Wells's figures for early-stage funds in each country outside the U.S. because we believe it to be most comparable to venture capital funds as defined in the U.S. Figures for Australia and New Zealand are 1994 estimated levels; figures for Israel are a 1995 estimate; and figures for Portugal are the actual level in 1994. All dollar figures are in millions of current U.S. dollars.

Country	Total Venture Capital Under Management
Australia	54
Austria	0.4
Belgium	8
Canada	182
Denmark	4
Finland	1
France	35
Germany	116
Ireland	1
Israel	550
Italy	60
Japan	11
Netherlands	100
New Zealand	1
Norway	7
Portugal	9
Spain	24
Sweden	9
Switzerland	1
United Kingdom	36
United States	3,651

Source: Compiled from Jeng and Wells (1999), as slightly amended by the authors.

[10]One potential source of confusion is that the term venture capital is used differently in Europe and Asia. Abroad, venture capital often refers to all private equity, including buyout, late stage, and mezzanine financing (which represent the vast majority of the private equity pool in most overseas markets). In the U.S., these are separate classes. We confine our discussion of international trends – as the rest of the paper – to venture capital using the restrictive, U.S. definition.

market for new issues exists. This commitment device is unavailable in economies dominated by banks, such as Germany and Japan.

These arguments, however, have less credibility in light of the events of the past two years. There has been a surge in venture capital investment, particularly relating to the Internet, in a wide variety of nations across Asia, Europe, and Latin America. While some of these investments have been made by local groups (many recently established), much of the activities have been driven by U.S.-based organizations.

The changes in Europe are illustrative. On the venture capital side, the same changes have happened on a much more accelerated time frame. As the European private equity industry emerged in the early 1980s, there was a significant representation of venture capital investments. Over time, however, the venture capital portion dwindled dramatically. The shrinking representation of venture capital investments reflected their poor performance. Between 1980 and 1994, for instance, while the average mature large buyout fund in Great Britain boasted a net return of 23.1% and the average mid-sized buyout fund had a return of 14.7%. Meanwhile, the typical venture fund had a net return of 4.0% over the same period ("European Performance," 1996). As a result, most venture capital specialists were unable to new funds, and generalist investors (such as Apax and 3i) shifted to an emphasis on buyouts.

This situation began reversing itself around 1997. The shifting attitudes were in part triggered by American venture groups, particularly East Coast-based organizations such as General Atlantic and Warburg Pincus. Attracted by the modest valuations of European technology and biotechnology start-ups relative to their European counterparts, general partners began increasingly traveling to Europe to invest in portfolio companies. This trend accelerated at the end of the decade, as American groups such as Benchmark and Draper Fisher Jurvetson began targeting large amounts of capital (sometimes in dedicated funds) for European venture investments. The trend was also helped by the superior performance of venture investments in the last years of the decade. In fact, by the end of 1999, the ten year performance of venture capital funds (17.2%) was almost indistinguishable from that of buyout ones (17.5%) (Venture Economics (2000a)) (Generalist funds performed significantly more poorly, with 9.5% rate of return over this period.)

Meanwhile, European-based funds also became more active. The increase in activity was manifested in three ways. First, groups that had been active for a number of years, such as Atlas Ventures, were able to raise significantly larger amounts of funds. Second, new entrants – in many cases modeled after American groups – became increasingly active. (Examples include Amadeus in the United Kingdom and Early Bird in Germany). Finally, generalist funds increased their allocation to venture capital again: For instance, over the late 1990s, 3i moved from a 15% allocation to technology funds to a 40% share.

In a pioneering study, Jeng and Wells (1999) examine the factors that influence venture capital fundraising in 21 countries. They find that the strength of the IPO market is an important factor in the determinant of venture capital commitments, echoing the conclusions of Black and Gilson. Jeng and Wells find, however, that the IPO market does not seem to influence commitments to early-stage funds as much as later-stage ones. While this work represents an important initial step, much more remains to be explored regarding the internationalization of venture capital.

One provocative finding from the Jeng and Wells analysis is that government policy can have a dramatic impact on the current and long-term viability of the venture capital sector. In many countries, especially those in Continental Europe, policymakers face a dilemma. The relatively few entrepreneurs active in these markets face numerous daunting regulatory restrictions, a paucity of venture funds focusing on investing in high-growth firms, and illiquid markets where investors do not welcome IPOs by young firms without long histories of positive earnings. It is often unclear where to being the process of duplicating the success of the United States. Only very recently have researchers begun to examine the ways in which policymakers can catalyze the growth of venture capital and the companies in which they invest. (Three recent exceptions are Irwin and Klenow, 1996; Lerner, 1999; and Wallsten, 1996.) Given the size of recent initiatives undertaken both in the United States and abroad (summarized in Lerner, 1999) and Gompers and Lerner (1999a), much more needs to be done in this arena.

Finally, the interaction between angel and venture capital investors needs to be explored. To what extent did the venture groups "crowd out" the angel investors that have hitherto been the dominant providers of equity capital in these markets? Or instead, were the two types of investments complements: Did the entry of venture investors lead to more wealthy entrepreneurs, who in turn became angel investors? These topics will reward research in the years to come.

REFERENCES

Admati, A. and P. Pfleiderer (1994). Robust financial contracting and the role for venture capitalists. *Journal of Finance*, **49**, 371–402.

Akerlof, G. (1970). The market for "lemons": Qualitative uncertainty and the market mechanism. *Quarterly Journal of Economics*, **84**, 488–500.

Amit, R., L. Glosten and E. Muller (1990a). Does venture capital foster the most promising entrepreneurial firms? *California Management Review*, **32**, 102–111.

Amit, R., L. Glosten and E. Muller (1990b). Entrepreneurial ability, venture investments, and risk sharing. *Management Science*, **36**, 1232–1245.

Barry, C.B., C.J. Muscarella, J.W. Peavy III and M.R. Vetsuypens (1990). The role of venture capital in the creation of public companies: Evidence from the ongoing public process. *Journal of Financial Economics*, **27**, 447–471.

Bartlett, J.W. (1995). *Equity Finance: Venture Capital, Buyouts, Restructurings, and Reorganizations*. New York: John Wiley.

Bergemann, D. and U. Hege (1998). Dynamic venture capital financing, learning, and moral hazard. *Journal of Banking and Finance*, **22**, 703–735.

Berglöf, E. (1994). A control theory of venture capital finance. *Journal of Law, Economics, and Organization*, **10**, 247–267.

Black, B. and R. Gilson (1998). Venture capital and the structure of capital markets: Banks versus stock markets. *Journal of Financial Economics*, **47**, 243–277.

Bolton, P. and D. Scharfstein (1990). A theory of predation based on agency problems in financial contracting. *American Economic Review*, **80**, 93–106.

Brav, A. and P.A. Gompers (1997). Myth or reality?: Long-run underperformance of initial public offerings: Evidence from venture capital and nonventure capital-backed IPOs. *Journal of Finance*, **52**, 1791–1821.

Chan, Y. (1983). On the positive role of financial intermediation in allocation of venture capital in a market with imperfect information. *Journal of Finance*, **38**, 1543–1568.

Cornelli, F. and O. Yosha (2002). Stage financing and the role of convertible debt. *Review of Economic Studies*, forthcoming.

Das, S.R. and J. Lerner (1995). Apex Investment Partners (A) and (B). Cases No. 9-296-028 and 9-296-029, Harvard Business School.

European Performance Surveyed – A Tentative First Step, 1996. *European Venture Capital Journal*, 3–6.

Fama, E.F. and M.C. Jensen (1983). Separation of ownership and control. *Journal of Law and Economics*, **26**, 301–325.

Field, L.C. (1996). Is the institutional ownership of initial public offerings related to the long-run performance of these firms? Working paper, Pennsylvania State University.

Freear, J., J.E. Sohl and W.E. Wetzel, Jr. (1994). Angels and non-angels: Are there differences? *Journal of Business Venturing*, **9**, 109–123.

Gompers, P. (1995). Optimal investment, monitoring, and the staging of venture capital. *Journal of Finance*, **50**, 1461–1489.

Gompers, P. (1996). Grandstanding in the venture capital industry. *Journal of Financial Economics*, **42**, 133–156.

Gompers, P.A. and J. Lerner (1996). The use of covenants: An empirical analysis of venture partnership agreements. *Journal of Law and Economics*, **39**, 463–449.

Gompers, P. and J. Lerner (1998). Venture capital distributions: Short- and long-run reactions. *Journal of Finance*, **53**, 2161–2183.

Gompers, P. and J. Lerner (1999a). *Capital Market Imperfections in Venture Markets: A Report to the Advanced Technology Program*. Washington, DC, Advanced Technology Program, U.S. Department of Commerce.

Gompers, P. and J. Lerner (1999b). *The Venture Capital Cycle*. Cambridge, MA: MIT Press.

Gompers, P. and J. Lerner (2000). Money chasing deals? The impact of fund inflows on private equity valuations. *Journal of Financial Economics*, **55**, 239–279.

Gompers, P. and J. Lerner (2001). *The Money of Invention*. Boston, MA: Harvard Business School Press.

Gorman, M. and W.A. Sahlman (1989). What do venture capitalists do? *Journal of Business Venturing*, **4**, 231–248.

Greenwald, B.C., J.E. Stiglitz and A. Weiss (1984). Information imperfections in the capital market and macroeconomic fluctuations. *American Economic Review Papers and Proceedings*, **74**, 194–199.

Griliches, Z. (1986). Productivity, R&D, and basic research at the firm level in the 1970s. *American Economic Review*, **76**, 141–154.

Grossman, S. and O. Hart (1986). The costs and benefits of ownership: A theory of vertical and lateral integration. *Journal of Political Economy*, **94**, 691–719.

Hall, B.H. (1992). Investment and research and development: Does the source of financing matter? Working Paper No. 92-94, Department of Economics, University of California at Berkeley.

Halloran, M.J., L.F. Benton, R.V. Gunderson, Jr., K.L. Kearney and J. del Calvo (1995). *Venture Capital and Public Offering Negotiation*. Englewood Cliffs, NJ: Aspen Law and Business.

Hao, K.Y. and A.B. Jaffe (1993). Effect of liquidity on firms' R&D spending. *Economics of Innovation and New Technology*, **2**, 275–282.

Hart, O. and J. Moore (1990). Property rights and the nature of the firm. *Journal of Political Economy*, **98**, 1119–1158.

Hart, O. and J. Moore (1998). Default and renegotiation: A dynamic model of debt. *Quarterly Journal of Economics*, **113**, 1–41.

Hellmann, T. (1998). The allocation of control rights in venture capital contracts. *Rand Journal of Economics*, **29**, 57–76.

Hellmann, T. and M. Puri (2000). The interaction between product market and financing strategy: The role of venture capital. *Review of Financial Studies*, **13**, 959–984.

Hermalin, B.E. and M.S. Weisbach (1988). The determinants of board composition. *Rand Journal of Economics*, **19**, 589–606.

Himmelberg, C.P. and B.C. Petersen (1994). R&D and internal finance: A panel study of small firms in high-tech industries. *Review of Economics and Statistics*, **76**, 38–51.

Hoshi, T., A. Kashyap and D. Scharfstein (1990). The role of banks in reducing the costs of financial distress in Japan. *Journal of Financial Economics*, **45**, 33–60.

Hubbard, R.G. (1998). Capital-market imperfections and investment. *Journal of Economic Literature*, **36**, 193–225.

Irwin, D.A. and P.J. Klenow (1996). High tech R&D subsidies: Estimating the effects of Sematech. *Journal of International Economics*, **40**, 323–344.

James, C. (1987). Some evidence on the uniqueness of bank loans. *Journal of Financial Economics*, **19**, 217–235.

Jeng, L. and P. Wells (1999). The determinants of venture capital funding: Evidence across countries. *Journal of Corporate Finance*, **6**, 241–289.

Jensen, M.C. and W.H. Meckling (1976). Theory of the firm: Managerial behavior, agency costs and ownership structure. *Journal of Financial Economics*, **3**, 305–360.

Kaplan, S. and P. Stromberg (2002). Financial contracting theory meets the real world: Evidence from venture capital contracts, *Review of Economic Studies*, forthcoming.

Kortum, S. and J. Lerner (1998). Stronger protection or technological revolution: What is behind the recent surge in patenting? *Carnegie-Rochester Conference Series on Public Policy*, **48**, 247–304.

Kortum, S. and J. Lerner (2000). Assessing the contribution of venture capital to innovation. *Rand Journal of Economics*, **31**, 674–692.

Krugman, P.R. (1991). *Geography and Trade*. Cambridge, MA: MIT Press.

Lamoreaux, N.R. and K.L. Sokoloff (2000). Intermediaries in the U.S. market for technology, 1870–2000, Working paper, University of California at Los Angeles.

Lerner, J. (1994a). The syndication of venture capital investments. *Financial Management*, **23**, 16–27.

Lerner, J. (1994b). Venture capitalists and the decision to go public. *Journal of Financial Economics*, **35**, 293–316.

Lerner, J. (1995). Venture capitalists and the oversight of private firms. *Journal of Finance*, **50**, 301–318.

Lerner, J. (1997). An empirical exploration of a technology race. *Rand Journal of Economics*, **28**, 228–247.

Lerner, J. (1998). Angel financing and public policy: An overview. *Journal of Banking and Finance*, **22**, 773–783.

Lerner, J. (1999). The government as venture capitalist: The long-run effects of the SBIR program. *Journal of Business*, **72**, 285–318.

Levin, J.S. (1995). *Structuring Venture Capital, Private Equity, and Entrepreneurial Transactions*. Boston, MA: Little, Brown.

Liles, P. (1977). *Sustaining the Venture Capital Firm*. Cambridge, MA: Management Analysis Center.

MacLeod, C. (1992). Strategies for innovation: The diffusion of new technology in nineteenth-century British industry. *Economic History Review*, **45**, 285–307.

Mansfield, E., J. Rapoport, A. Romeo, S. Wagner and G. Beardsley (1977). Social and private rates of return from industrial innovations. *Quarterly Journal of Economics*, **91**, 221–240.

Marx, L. (1994). Negotiation and renegotiation of venture capital contracts, Working paper, University of Rochester.

Megginson, W.C. and K.A. Weiss (1991). Venture capital certification in initial public offerings. *Journal of Finance*, **46**, 879–893.

Myers, S. (1977). Determinants of corporate borrowing. *Journal of Financial Economics*, **5**, 147–175.

Myers, S. and N.M. Majluf (1984). Corporate financing and investment decisions when firms have information that investors do not have. *Journal of Financial Economics*, **13**, 187–221.

National Venture Capital Association (2001). *NVCA Yearbook*, Washington, DC, National Venture Capital Association.

Petersen, M.A. and R.G. Rajan (1994). The benefits of lending relationships: Evidence from small business data. *Journal of Finance*, **49**, 3–37.

Petersen, M.A. and R.G. Rajan (1995). The effect of credit market competition on lending relationships. *Quarterly Journal of Economics*, **110**, 407–443.

Ritter, J.R. (1998). Initial public offerings. In D. Logue and J. Seward (eds.), *Warren, Gorham, and Lamont Handbook of Modern Finance*. New York: WGL/RIA.

Sahlman, W.A. (1990). The structure and governance of venture capital organizations. *Journal of Financial Economics*, **27**, 473–524.

Sahlman, W.A. and H. Stevenson (1987). Capital market myopia. *Journal of Business Venturing*, **1**, 7–30.

Saxenian, A. (1994). *Regional Advantage: Culture and Competition in Silicon Valley and Route 128*. Cambridge, MA: Harvard University Press.

Stiglitz, J and A. Weiss (1981). Credit rationing in markets with incomplete information. *American Economic Review*, **71**, 393–409.

U.S. Small Business Administration, Office of Advocacy (1996a). *Creating New Capital Markets for Emerging Ventures*. U.S. Small Business Administration, Washington, DC.

U.S. Small Business Administration, Office of Advocacy (1996b). *The Process and Analysis behind ACE-Net*. U.S. Small Business Administration, Washington, DC.

Venture Economics (2000a). *Investment Benchmark Reports: International Private Equity*. Newark, NJ: Venture Economics.

Venture Economics (2000b). *Investment Benchmark Reports: Venture Capital*. Newark, NJ: Venture Economics.

Wallsten, S.J. (2000). The effects of government-industry R&D programs on private R&D: The case of the Small Business Innovation Research program. *Rand Journal of Economics*, **31**, 82–100.

Wetzel, W.E. and C.R. Seymour (1981). *Informal Risk Capital in New England*. Center for Industrial and Institutional Development, University of New Hampshire, Durham, New Hampshire.

Williamson, O.E. (1983). Organization form, residual claimants, and corporate control. *Journal of Law and Economics*, **26**, 351–366.

ALLEN N. BERGER[1] and GREGORY F. UDELL[2]

[1] *Board of Governors of the Federal Reserve System and Wharton Financial Institutions Center,*
[2] *Indiana University*

13. Small Business and Debt Finance

INTRODUCTION

It is tempting to view debt as the less glamorous side of entrepreneurial finance. In the context of an entrepreneurial firm's financial growth cycle, it is generally believed that infusions of external debt typically follow infusions of external equity (e.g., see Pratt and Morris, 1987). Moreover, the organized venture capital market – a relative newcomer on the financial stage that primarily provides external equity – has garnered much of the publicity associated with financing technology-oriented start-ups.

This characterization in which equity is of overwhelming importance, however, masks the vital role played by debt in entrepreneurial finance. The proportion of debt in the capital structure of small businesses in the U.S. is similar to the 50% overall proportion of debt in the capital structure of all U.S. businesses. Perhaps surprisingly, this also holds true for the youngest firms in the U.S. (firms less than two years old) where debt represents about 52% of the capital structure.[1] Even for high-growth start-ups in which private equity financing dominates in the earliest growth stages, debt financing assumes a major role in the capital structure by the time these firms go public. For the 3,676 firms that went public between 1985 and 1999, the average debt/asset ratio just before the initial public offering (IPO) was about 33%.[2]

While the proportion of debt in the capital structure of small firms is similar to that of large firms, the debt financing itself is quite different in terms of the type of debt issued, the contracting tools used, the lending technologies employed, and the roles of intermediaries in the process. For large firms, the majority of debt is in the form of traded instruments, such as commercial paper, syndicated bank loans, and public bond issues. For small firms, in

The opinions expressed do not necessarily reflect those of the Board of Governors or its staff. The authors thank Raphael Bostic and David Smith for helpful comments.

[1] Sources: Federal Reserve National Survey of Small Business Finance and the Federal Reserve Flow of Funds Accounts for the United States.

[2] This excludes 20 firms that went public during this period with a significant negative book net worth and total debt/total asset ratios greater than 10 (source: Securities Data Corp. Global New Issues Data Base).

Z.J. Acs and D.B. Audretsch (eds.), Handbook of Entrepreneurship Research, 299–328
© 2003 *Kluwer Academic Publishers. Printed in Great Britain.*

contrast, virtually all of the debt is nontraded – the biggest portion of which is in non-syndicated commercial loans. Moreover, the typical terms of small firm debt contracts are significantly different than those in large firm debt contracts because of the informational opacity often associated with small businesses. As shown below, small business debt differs specifically with respect to the use of contracting tools such as maturity, covenants, collateral, and guarantees. Also discussed below, different lending technologies – such as relationship lending, asset-based lending, credit scoring, and trade credit – are often employed in lending to small firms to make up for the dearth of informative financial information, problems of low firm quality, and lack of well-developed external reputations. Finally, small firm debt is often issued with the help of financial intermediaries like commercial banks and finance companies that specialize in using the contracting tools and lending technologies noted above to originate and monitor loans to informationally opaque small businesses.

Another striking difference between small and large firms is their governance. With the exception of venture capital-backed start-ups, most small firms are owner-managed. One advantage of this is that the wedge between ownership and management is removed, eliminating the agency costs associated with outside equity holders trying to control professional managers. However, other contracting problems may be exacerbated. For example, the incentive to shift risk on creditors (the agency cost of debt of Jensen and Meckling, 1976) may be greater in owner-managed firms. In a professionally-managed firm, risk averse managers may choose safer strategies than stockholders would prefer in order to preserve their human capital, and this may inadvertently help debtholders (e.g., Amihud and Lev, 1981). Unburdened by the risk aversion of a professional manager, small firm owners may be less constrained in shifting risk onto creditors.[3] The opportunity to exploit the wedge between the interest of the owner-manager and creditors may also be exacerbated in small firms because they are often very informationally opaque. Consequently, it is not surprising that debt contracts associated with small firm finance are much richer in the type of contracting features that address these problems than the debt contracts of large firms.

In this chapter, we explore the idiosyncratic nature of small firm debt financing. Section 2 discusses the motivation for debt finance in small firms, and breaks down the sources of small firm debt. Section 3 examines the nature of debt contracting in small firm finance, focusing on contracting tools – such as collateral, guarantees, covenants, maturity, and menu pricing – that can be used to solve the problems associated with informational opacity that plague many small businesses. In section 4, we argue that lenders use these contracting tools in very different ways to address the information problems associated with small firm finance. Specifically, lenders use these tools in the context of a

---

[3] However, it is also possible that entrepreneurs may behave in a *more* risk averse fashion than professional managers because of their idiosyncratic risk aversion.

variety of distinct technologies which involve very different uses of labor, physical capital, software, and data. Five lending technologies used in small business finance are identified: Financial statement lending, relationship lending, asset-based lending, credit scoring and similar quantitative techniques, and trade finance. We also note which types of financial intermediaries tend to specialize in each of these different lending technologies. In section 5, we examine some of the key factors that affect the supply of small business credit, including the global consolidation of the banking industry, credit crunches, discrimination in lending, and the impact of technological innovation. Section 6 concludes.

MOTIVATION FOR AND SOURCES OF DEBT FOR SMALL BUSINESSES

In this section we briefly present some of the theoretical motivations for debt and give a rough empirical overview of the sources of debt for small businesses in the U.S.

It is often argued that firms establish a "pecking order" in developing their financing strategies, drawing first on the funds that are the cheapest and proceeding to more and more expensive funds (e.g., Myers, 1984; Myers and Majluf, 1984). At the top of the pecking order is internally generated cash flows provided by the entrepreneur, and perhaps "nearly internal" funds provided by other members of the start-up team, family, and friends. These internal and nearly internal funds are relatively low cost because of minimal issue costs and information problems. If external funds are needed, debt may be preferred to equity for several reasons. First, external debt has a distinct advantage to the entrepreneur over external equity, in that it does not dilute ownership. Moreover, it likely conveys less control to outsiders, although covenants and other contracting features may still cede considerable control to external creditors. If the firm has collateral available, or if the entrepreneur has personal collateral or wealth that can be pledged or used to support a personal guarantee, this allows external debt to essentially extend the benefits of internal finance and maintain full ownership and control so long as the firm remains solvent.

External debt may also be preferred over external equity because it reduces verification costs (e.g., Townsend, 1979; Diamond, 1984). That is, an outside debtholder only has to go to the cost of verifying the firm's cash flows if the debt repayment is not made in full, whereas an outside equityholder may have to bear the costs of verifying cash flows under a much greater set of circumstances. Similarly, some have found that adverse selection favors external debt over external equity (e.g., Myers, 1984; Myers and Majluf, 1984; Nachman and Noe, 1994). Outside investors may offer debt contracts instead of equity contracts to separate out firms that (privately) know they have good prospects from those that (privately) know they have poor prospects. This is because firms with poor prospects are more likely to agree to share the poor expected profits, whereas firms with good prospects are more likely to agree to pay off a fixed loan and keep the residual high expected profits.

In contrast, external equity may be preferred over external debt in cases of significant moral hazard, i.e., when the firm cannot be stopped from shifting into a riskier strategy after the funds are injected. Risk can be shifted onto outside debtholders, but not onto outside equity holders, so the moral hazard incentive to risk-shift is blunted by using outside equity in place of outside debt. Moral hazard problems are most likely to occur when the amount of external finance needed is large relative to the amount of internal and nearly internal funds (inclusive of any personal wealth at risk via pledges of personal collateral or guarantees). This suggests that external equity finance may be particularly important when relatively large amounts of external funds are needed. The fact that high-growth, high-risk new ventures often obtain external equity (e.g., via angel finance or venture capital) before obtaining significant external debt suggests that the moral hazard problem may be particularly acute for these firms. Finally, we simply note that external equity and debt decisions may also be driven by tax considerations and issuing costs, which may be substantial.

Table 1 breaks down small business finance in the U.S. in 1993 (the most recent data available) into a number of different equity and debt financing sources.[4] As noted above, equity and debt have about equal shares in small firm capital structure on average. Most of the equity financing for small businesses is internal capital supplied by the principal owners. Most of the remainder is "other equity," which is likely partially composed of the "nearly internal" funds described above, provided by other members of the start-up team, family, and friends. In contrast, debt financing for most firms comes mostly from external sources. For the most part, the data are consistent with the main implications of the theory described above: 1) much of the funding is from internal and nearly internal sources, and 2) most of the external finance is from debt, which may reduce problems of external ownership and control, costly state verification, and adverse selection. However, for the subset of high potential start-ups, a considerable portion may be provided by external equity from angel investors and venture capitalists, which may reduce moral hazard problems.

Table 1 reflects the fact that the two biggest sources of small business debt finance are commercial banks and trade creditors who supply about 19% and 16%, respectively, of total financing. The next largest – commercial finance companies – supplies about 5%.[5] A substantial proportion of bank and com-

---

[4]This table is from Berger and Udell (1998, table 1), which is based on data from the Federal Reserve's National Survey of Small Business Finance for 1993. The survey uses the Small Business Administration's definition of a "small business" as one with less than 500 full-time equivalent employees.

[5]Commercial finance companies are institutionally distinct from commercial banks. Like commercial banks they invest in business loans. However, unlike commercial banks they do not fund these loans with deposits.

Table 1. U.S. small business finance – estimated distributions of equity and debt – percent of total equity plus debt (top numbers), and billions of dollars (bottom numbers)

| | Sources of equity | | | | | Sources of debt | | | | | | | | | | | |
| | | | | | | Financial institutions[a] | | | Nonfinancial business and government | | | Individuals | | | | |
	Prin. owner[b]	Angel fin.	Venture capital	Other equity	Total equity	Comm. banks	Fin. comps.	Other fin. insts.	Trade credit[c]	Other bus.	Govt.	Prin. owner[d]	Credit card[e]	Other indls.	Total debt	Total equity plus debt
All small businesses[f]	31.33% $524.3	3.59% $60.0	1.85% $31.0	12.86% $215.2	49.63% $830.6	18.75% $313.8	4.91% $82.1	3.00% $50.1	15.78% $264.1	1.74% $29.2	0.49% $8.1	4.10% $68.5	0.14% $2.4	1.47% $24.5	50.37% $842.9	100.00% $1,673.4

[a] Financial institutions include commercial banks, finance companies, thrift institutions, leasing companies, brokerage firms, mortgage companies, and insurance companies.
[b] For proprietorships, principal owner's share of equity is by definition 100 percent.
[c] Trade credit is defined as accounts payable for year-end 1992.
[d] Only partnerships and corporations have principal owner loans. By definition, proprietorships do not have loans from owners.
[e] Credit card debt is estimated using the typical monthly balances of business charges to both personal and business credit cards after monthly payments were made on these accounts. Personal and business totals could not be accurately separated using the NSSBF data.
[f] Represents enterprises in 1993 with fewer than 500 full-time equivalent employees, excluding real estate operators and lessors, real estate subdividers and developers, real estate investment trusts, agricultural enterprises, financial institutions, not-for-profit institutions, government entities, and subsidiaries controlled by other corporations.

Sources: From Berger and Udell (1998). All data except for angel finance and venture capital are from the 1993 National Survey of Small Business Finance (NSSBF). These data are weighted to replicate to nation's small business population as a whole. The NSSBF data are from year-end 1993, except that the principal owner's equity, total equity, and trade credit are from balance sheets at year-end 1992, and credit card debt is from typical monthly balances during 1993. The angel figure is based on survey data summarized in Freear, Sohl and Wetzel (1994) and should be considered to be just one point in a large range. The venture figure is estimated from data in Venture Economics using methods employed in Fenn, Liang and Prowse (1997).

mercial finance company loans are not entirely external because many of them are personally guaranteed or backed by personal collateral owned by the firms' principal owner (Berger and Udell, 1995, 1998; Avery, Bostic, and Samolyk, 1998). These guarantees permit recourse to the owner and thus represent a contingent claim against the owner's wealth.

Small businesses generally tap external debt financing to address specific funding needs. Trade credit and short-term commercial loans, often in the form of lines of credit, are typically used for working capital purposes (i.e., to finance accounts receivable and inventory); long-term debt is typically used to finance fixed assets such as plant and equipment. As the firm grows, the need for these types of financing grows with it. Bank and finance company commercial loans are also used in small firm acquisitions, leveraged buyouts, and management buyouts. Other lenders may participate in these types of transactions along with commercial banks and finance companies. These include life insurance companies and mezzanine debt funds who typically provide long-term subordinated debt with an equity "kicker," such as a convertible provision or stock options (Carey et al., 1993). Commercial banks and particularly commercial finance companies also provide financing for companies in distress, including DIP (debtor in possession) and pre-DIP financing.

THE TOOLS OF SMALL BUSINESS PRIVATE DEBT CONTRACTING

The informational opacity of many small firms makes financial contracting quite problematic. Adverse selection problems at origination are reflected in the incentive for borrowers to understate their risk, and moral hazard problems after funding are reflected in the incentive to shift to higher risk. These problems may be exacerbated in younger firms that have not had the opportunity to establish a reputation for nonexploitive behavior. In the absence of any mechanisms to address these problems, lenders may be forced to charge very high interest rates or to ration credit (Stiglitz and Weiss, 1981, 1987).

Fortunately, the participants in this market possess a tool box of contracting devices that can help mitigate these problems. We next examine the most important of these tools and how they are deployed in the small business debt market. These include collateral, guarantees, covenants, maturity, and menu pricing.

Collateral

Collateral is widely used in small business lending. For example, the majority of small business lines of credit are secured (Berger and Udell, 1995). Moreover, many other types of loans, such as motor vehicle, equipment, and commercial real estate loans are virtually always secured by the asset underlying the loan. It is important to draw a distinction between "outside" and "inside" collateral. Outside collateral involves pledging assets owned outside of the firm as security for a loan to the business. This typically occurs in small business lending when the owner pledges a personal asset, such as a home, as collateral for a business loan. In contrast, inside collateral involves pledging specific business assets such as accounts receivable, inventory, or equipment to a specific lender as security for a business loan.

The theoretical literature on outside collateral demonstrates that it can be used to reduce adverse selection problems (Stiglitz and Weiss, 1981, 1986; Bester, 1985; Chan and Kanatas, 1985; Besanko and Thakor, 1987a, b) and mitigate moral hazard problems (Boot, Thakor, and Udell, 1991). Outside collateral has an incentive effect similar to an infusion of equity by the entrepreneur, because it effectively exposes the entrepreneur's wealth to the losses of the firm.

The power of inside collateral derives from an entirely different source. Unlike outside collateral, inside collateral does not involve a contingent claim on the entrepreneur's wealth. Instead it rearranges the capital structure of the firm by reordering creditor priority in bankruptcy. Secured lenders have a claim on specific firm assets which means that all proceeds from the liquidation of those assets will generally be applied first to repayment of the secured lender's debt, and unsecured creditors will be paid only if there are remaining funds. This reordering of claims can be a powerful contracting tool. It can mitigate the Myers (1977) underinvestment problem by giving the incremental lender a senior position, so the proceeds of its loan do not principally accrue to the benefit of other lenders (Stulz and Johnson, 1985). Inside collateral can also reduce risk shifting because collateralized assets that may be associated with low-risk business strategies cannot be sold without the lienholder's permission (Smith and Warner, 1979). It may also help enforce covenants during financial distress (Gorton and Kahn, 1997), facilitate optimal firm closure (Swary and Udell, 1988), and reduce the costs of allocating assets in bankruptcy (Welch, 1997).[6]

Personal Guarantees. Personal guarantees are another important contracting tool in small business lending. When entrepreneurs personally guarantee loans to their businesses, they convey contingent claims on their personal assets to the lender. This claim gives the lender legal recourse against the entrepreneur (or other guarantor) for any deficiency in the loan's repayment. In other words, if the business cannot fully repay its loan, the bank has recourse for any shortfall against the entrepreneur.

Personal guarantees operate in a similar manner to outside collateral with three important distinctions. First, recourse under outside collateral is limited to the specific personal assets pledged as collateral, while a personal guarantee generally conveys a claim against the entire wealth of the guarantor.[7] Second,

---

[6] However, inside collateral might also exacerbate the agency cost of debt by discouraging maintenance of secured assets (John, Lynch, and Puri 1999).

[7] In small business lending entrepreneurs typically guarantee the entire business loan. However, guarantees can be structured with a ceiling that caps the guarantor's dollar exposure.

outside collateral conveys a significant measure of control over the specific assets pledged to the lender. In particular, the collateral cannot be sold without the permission of the lender (the lienholder). However, in the case of a personal guarantee, no control over any personal assets is conveyed to the lender. Thus, the lender has no assurance that the entrepreneur (i.e., the guarantor) will have any remaining assets if the firm fails to repay a loan in the future. Third, legislation may limit a general claim operating through a guarantee against the entrepreneur's personal assets. For example, some states have "homestead acts" that may protect personal residences against general creditors in bankruptcy (Berkowitz and White, 1998).

The use of personal guarantees and outside collateral as contracting mechanisms is widespread in small business lending, accounting for about 40% of all loans and 60% of loan dollars (Ang, Lin, and Tyler, 1995; Avery, Bostic, and Samolyk, 1998). In addition to the direct effect from having recourse against assets outside the firm, the incentive affects can be powerful in aligning the interests of business lenders and entrepreneurs. Arguably, these incentive effects may be quite powerful even if the entrepreneur has little wealth relative to the size of the business loan. As long as the personal assets that are exposed represent a substantial portion of the wealth of the entrepreneur, the entrepreneur may have a strong incentive to repay the loan.

Debt Covenants and Maturity

Because small firms are often more informationally opaque and have more difficulty developing widely known reputations than larger firms, it is not surprising that we observe that they have less access to long-term debt. Lenders must have confidence that their borrowers will not shift their risk profile significantly during the life span of their loans. To avoid exposure from risk shifting, lenders structure debt contracts with shorter maturities and/or stricter covenants to small businesses, depending on the degree of informational opacity (Carey et al., 1993).[8] For example, access to working capital financing to the smallest and most informationally opaque borrowers that receive external debt may be entirely limited to spot loans with maturities considerably less than one year. As the business grows and becomes more transparent, it is more likely to have access to lines of credit (usually under one-year commitments), which provide more flexible financing arrangements.[9] However, the stringency of the terms of its line of credit will likely still depend on the lender's confidence

---

[8] Empirical evidence on differences on maturity structure across firm sizes is limited. For a comprehensive survey on debt maturity, see Ravid (1996).

[9] One study that analyzed small business access to lines of credit found that while firm size was positively related to the probability of having a line of credit, the age of the firm was not related (Jayaratne and Wolken 1999). Moreover, this study found that the firm's repayment performance and its profitability were negatively related to the probability of having a line of credit, which runs contrary to our arguments in the text.

in the borrower and the strength of its relationship (Berger and Udell, 1995; Harhoff and Körting, 1998a).

Covenants can be viewed as a partial substitute for maturity. Debt covenants are promises by borrowers to lenders regarding firm characteristics, actions, or events. These often include promises to meet certain financial goals (e.g., financial ratios) or to engage in or refrain from certain types of behavior (e.g., to continue in a particular line of business or to refrain from acquisitions). A covenant violation typically gives the lender the right to demand immediate repayment of the loan – i.e., to completely accelerate the loan's maturity.

Covenants can be used to require the borrower to obtain permission from its lender when it seeks to pursue strategic opportunities that will change the financial profile of the company (Smith and Warner, 1979; Berlin and Loeys, 1988). This gives the lender the opportunity to prevent exploitive behavior, and to adjust the other terms of these loans as the situation dictates. This arrangement also allows the borrower to pursue new value-enhancing projects, provided that the borrower compensates the lender for any increase in risk borne by the lender. Theory suggests that the firms with more credit risk and more moral hazard incentives will likely borrow under stricter covenants (Berlin and Mester, 1993). This is consistent with the observation that covenants on public debt issued by large corporations are much less stringent than those associated with debt issued by small and mid-size business borrowers (Carey et al., 1993). Not surprisingly, the more stringent are the covenants, the higher is the frequency of renegotiation (Carey et al., 1993; Kwan and Carleton, 1993).

While covenants and maturity are closely related, they are not perfect substitutes for at least two reasons. First, the conditions under which a lender can refuse to renew a loan at maturity differ from the conditions under which a covenant can be triggered. A lender is relatively unconstrained in its ability to refuse to renew a loan at maturity – at least from a legal and contractual perspective. That is, loan renewal can be based on mutually observable, but not necessarily verifiable characteristics, actions, or events (Hart and Moore, 1989; Sharpe, 1990). However, a covenant can only be based on something that is mutually observable *and* verifiable.[10] Thus, a sufficiently short maturity can be viewed as stronger than any covenant because the decision to not renew can be based on unverifiable events, such as a decrease in the lender's confidence in the entrepreneur. This likely explains why small businesses which are extremely informationally opaque are significantly limited in their access to long-term debt even though covenants could be written on this debt to address moral hazard problems.

A second reason why covenants and maturity are imperfect substitutes relates to the feasibility of covenants in small business lending. As noted above, covenants must be contingent on verifiable characteristics, actions, or events. Often this verifiability requires the costly production of information by third parties. For example, covenants based on financial ratios require audited, or

---

[10] Practically speaking, verifiable means supportable in a court of law.

at least CPA-prepared, financial statements. Because audited financial statements are likely prohibitively expensive for some firms, particularly the smallest, maturity may dominate covenants as a contracting device for these firms.

Menu Pricing

Many of the products that businesses purchase from financial institutions are priced in a number of dimensions. For example, in addition to the loan rate, commercial loans may have collateral requirements, guarantee requirements, covenants, and fees (if extended under a loan commitment). The combination of all of these determines the overall price. However, beyond just determining the level of pricing, lenders may be able to manipulate the menu of prices associated with certain products to encourage informationally opaque borrowers to reveal their true quality or to choose safer or higher net present value strategies. Any and all of these dimensions of price can be traded off against one another to improve incentives and to encourage borrowers to sort themselves by quality. For example, lenders can utilize the pricing menu on loan commitments in this manner by offering alternative contracts that differ in terms of the up-front fees, the usage fees, compensating balances, and the interest rate (Boot, Thakor and Udell, 1987; Kanatas, 1987; Thakor and Udell, 1987; Berkovitch and Greenbaum, 1991).

Menu pricing has also been investigated in conjunction with consumer checking accounts. Banks might sort borrowers by manipulating the fee structure of checking accounts by varying such elements as the maintenance fee and the not sufficient funds (NSF) fee. For example, one bank might charge a very high NSF fee combined with a low maintenance fee in order to attract high-quality customers, while another bank might charge a low NSF fee and a high maintenance fee to attract (and to compensate for) low-quality customers (Udell, 1986). This type of menu pricing can be used to improve pricing efficiency across products. For example, the bank that offers the high NSF fee checking account might also offer lower loan rates to its checking account customers because it knows it is attracting a higher quality customer (Allen, Saunders and Udell, 1991). While the NSF case has not been investigated in small business banking, it would not be surprising if these results obtain given that the products and pricing elements are similar.

LENDING TECHNOLOGIES

We argue here that small business lenders use a variety of different lending technologies to address the information opacity problems often associated with small businesses. We discuss several of these technologies here – financial statement lending, relationship lending, asset-based lending, credit scoring and similar quantitative techniques, and trade finance. In part, these technologies reflect different combinations of the contracting tools for dealing with the information problems discussed above, but the differences go beyond just the tools themselves. We also argue that these methods may be rightfully considered as different lending technologies because they represent different approaches to gathering information and addressing information-related problems that require very different uses of labor, physical capital, software, and data inputs. Some of these differences are evident, for example, in how these technologies use financial data: 1) financial statement lending puts most of its effort into evaluating firm financial statements; 2) relationship lending focuses primarily on proprietary information gained though continuous contact over time with the small business, its owner, and its local community; 3) asset-based lending pays primary attention to the valuation of certain types of collateral; 4) small business credit scoring applies statistical techniques to quantitative data on both the small business and the entrepreneur; and 5) trade credit is based in part on knowledge of the industry and information culled from trade payment patterns. We emphasize that our characterization of these different lending approaches as different technologies represents our unique view that is not necessarily shared by other financial researchers.

These lending technologies tend to be associated with different types of financial intermediaries that have comparative advantages in different technologies. For example, some commercial banks may have a comparative advantage in relationship lending by using information gathered over time through checking accounts and other types of contact with the small business, whereas some commercial finance companies may specialize in and develop comparative advantages in asset-based lending, and goods and services suppliers have obvious advantages in supplying trade credit along with selling products to the firm. Despite all the differences, however, these lending technologies are not entirely mutually exclusive. In fact, the same lender may use more than one technology in evaluating a single loan to a single small business. For example, a bank may spend considerable effort in doing conventional analysis of financial statements, evaluate proprietary data from its historical relationship with the firm, evaluate the accounts receivable and inventory pledged as collateral, and generate or purchase a credit score for the same small business. The findings from the different technologies may be given various weights in choosing whether to extend additional credit and in the choice of the contract terms of that credit.

Financial Statement Lending

This represents the most traditional approach to lending. It emphasizes standard financial statement analysis with a focus on traditional financial ratios including liquidity ratios, asset management ratios, debt and solvency ratios, and profitability ratios.[11] Due diligence includes not only an assessment of the

---

[11] For a more detailed discussion of these ratios and what we refer to as the traditional lending approach see Cornett and Saunders (1999), chapter 10.

small business and its prospects, but also the managerial expertise of the entrepreneur and the management team. Any or all of the contracting tools discussed above may be incorporated into the loan contract. Empirical evidence suggests that riskier borrowers are more likely to pledge inside or outside collateral (Orgler, 1970; Hester, 1979; Scott and Smith, 1986; Berger and Udell, 1990, 1992, 1995; Booth, 1992; Booth and Chua, 1996) and that many of these loans will be personally guaranteed (Berger and Udell, 1995, 1998; Avery, Bostic and Samolyk, 1998).[12] An important characteristic of this type of lending, however, is that the loan itself will not be principally based on the collateral or guarantee. Recourse against collateral or against the entrepreneur's personal assets is viewed only as a secondary source of repayment if the loan becomes distressed. Instead the loan is principally based on the financial strength of the business as reflected in the traditional ratios mentioned above. This type of lending may be most associated with larger banks, with better credits, and with larger businesses.

Financial statement lending, however, may be problematic if a borrower's risk is too high or if the borrower does not have highly informative financial statements. This latter condition may occur because the business is too young, because audited or CPA-prepared financial statements are prohibitively expensive, or because the main value of the firm lies in an idea or technology that has not yet generated accounting profits. In substantial part, the remaining lending technologies discussed are designed to compensate for excessive borrower risk or to make up for the lack of highly informative financial statements by uncovering information in different ways or from different sources.

Relationship Lending

Under this technology, the relationship between the lender and the entrepreneur and the small business become more important than the pure financial condition of the company. This contrasts with financial statement lending which is much more transactions-based as opposed to relationship-based. Specifically, under relationship lending, the lender acquires proprietary information about the entrepreneur and the business over time with respect to the provision of loans (Petersen and Rajan, 1994; Berger and Udell, 1995) and the provision of other products (Nakamura, 1993; Cole, 1998; Mester, Nakamura, and Renault, 1998; Degryse and van Cayseele, 2000) beyond information that is readily available to the public and information available in the firm's financial statements. The lender also gathers information about the local community/business

---

[12]This empirical evidence from these papers does not explicitly focus on traditional financial statement lending. However, it is likely that most of these results are driven by this technology, given that these studies focus primarily on traditional bank loans, which are generally dominated in numbers and size by financial statement loans. The loans studied were generally issued prior to the advent of credit scoring, and do not include asset-based loans by commercial finance companies or trade credit extended by suppliers.

environment and the entrepreneur's and the business's interaction with that environment.

Information culled from the relationship appears to benefit borrowers and helps determine the price of credit and whether credit is extended. Empirically, this may be reflected in an association between the strength or existence of the relationship and lower loan interest rates (Berger and Udell, 1995; Harhoff and Körting, 1998a; Scott and Dunkelberg, 1999; Degryse and van Cayseele, 2000), reduced collateral requirements (Berger and Udell, 1995; Harhoff and Körting, 1998a; Scott and Dunkelberg, 1999), greater debt seniority for relationship lenders (Longhofer and Santos, 2000), lower dependence on trade debt (Petersen and Rajan, 1994, 1995), greater protection against the interest rate cycle (Berlin and Mester, 1999; Conigliani, Ferri and Generale, 1997; Ferri and Messori, 2000) and increased credit availability (Cole, 1998; Elsas and Krahnen, 1997; Scott and Dunkelberg, 1999; Machauer and Weber, 2000).[13] Just as with traditional financial statement lending, relationship-based loan contracts may incorporate any or all of the contracting tools mentioned in the previous section, but their use may be adjusted as the relationship matures.

The dark side of relationship lending is that it may be associated with two types of costs – the hold-up problem and the soft-budget constraint problem. The hold-up problem arises because the acquisition of proprietary information about the borrower through relationship lending necessarily conveys some market power to the lender that may result in higher loan costs (Rajan, 1992). This may lead to the use of longer-term implicit contracts in which borrowers receive a subsidized rate in the short term and then compensate lenders in later periods (Sharpe, 1990). The use of multiple lenders would also likely solve this problem but would necessarily dilute the value of the relationship. The soft-budget constraint problem refers to the problem of banks being locked in as their borrower's primary source of external funding. This may convey to borrowers the ability to coerce their banks into providing additional funds to avoid losses on previously issued credit (Dewatripont and Maskin, 1995; Bolton and Scharfstein, 1996). Collateral or the seniority of bank debt may be used to ameliorate this problem (Boot, 2000).

An important issue in the empirical literature on relationship lending is how to measure the strength of a relationship. Alternative measures include the existence of a relationship (Cole 1998), length of the relationship (Berger and Udell, 1995; Petersen and Rajan, 1994, 1995; Scott and Dunkelberg, 1999;

---

[13] These results are consistent with the theoretical models in Boot and Thakor (1994) and Petersen and Rajan (1995), but inconsistent with those of Greenbaum, Kanatas, and Venezia (1989), and Sharpe (1990). However, not all of the empirical literature finds this result that credit terms improve with the strength of the relationship. Angelini, Salvo and Ferri (1998) found a negative relationship between the length of the relationship and loan rates offered by Italian credit cooperatives. Blackwell and Winters (1997) found no clear relationship between the duration of the relationship and loan rates, and Petersen and Rajan (1994) found the same result for a sample that included all types of business loans (as opposed to Berger and Udell, 1995, and Harhoff and Körting, 1998a, who focused only on lines of credit).

Ongena and Smith, 2000), the breadth of a relationship (Cole, 1998; Scott and Dunkelberg, 1999; Degryse and van Cayseele, 2000), the degree of mutual trust (Harhoff and Körting, 1998a), the number of different account managers (Scott and Dunkelberg, 1999), the presence of a hausbank (Elsas and Krahnen, 1997), and multiple banking sources (Harhoff and Körting, 1998a; Berger, Klapper, and Udell, 2000; Ferri and Messori, 2000; Machauer and Weber, 2000; Ongena and Smith, 2001).

Another important, but as yet unaddressed, issue in relationship lending is the extent to which the relationship with the bank resides with the loan officer or with the banking organization. It seems plausible to argue that the loan officer may be an especially important repository of the proprietary information associated with relationship lending – particularly the qualitative component that determines the level of mutual trust (Harhoff and Körting, 1998a). If this is the case, then we would expect that banks who specialize in relationship lending would delegate significant lending authority to their loan officers. Such delegation, however, may create a significant agency problem if the objectives of the loan officer do not correspond well with the objectives of the institution as a whole. While there is no direct evidence associating relationship lending with delegation of loan authority *per se*, one study has found that some banks delegate significantly more lending responsibility to their loan officers than others and as a result invest significantly more in monitoring their loan officers (Udell, 1989). This is also an important public policy issue because if relationship lending is principally extruded through loan officers, then bank failures and bank mergers and acquisitions may be less likely to destroy small business banking relationships. That is, loan officers could move from extinguished banks to surviving banks or start new banks and take their relationship borrowers with them.

Relationship lending is typically better suited to small business lending than large business lending because small businesses are generally more informationally opaque. Empirical evidence provides support for this argument. In particular, several studies have found evidence indicating that larger firms are more likely to have multiple banking relationships which necessarily implies less relationship intensity (Harhoff and Körting, 1998b; Ongena and Smith, 2000; Machauer and Weber, 2000).

With respect to the delivery of relationship lending, banks may have a comparative advantage over other financial institutions because they jointly deliver both deposits and loans (Diamond and Rajan, 1999; Berlin and Mester, 1999). The vast majority of small businesses identify commercial banks as their primary financial institutions, and these businesses typically stay with the same bank for many years (Berger and Udell, 1998). Moreover, because banks offer such a wide variety of services and because small businesses tend to cluster their purchases of financial services in a single, primary bank with a nearby office (Cole and Wolken, 1995; Kwast, Starr-McCluer, and Wolken, 1997), banks may be ideally suited for culling information about their borrowers.

Empirical evidence suggests that large banks may be less likely to deliver relationship lending to small businesses than small banks. Specifically, large banks are more likely to extend generic low risk loans (Berger and Udell, 1996) and less likely to make loans based on the strength of the relationship instead of financial ratios (Cole, Goldberg, and White, 1999). This may be the result of organizational diseconomies that occur when large banks attempt to deliver relationship lending along with transactions-based financial statement lending.

Asset-Based Lending

Collateral in the form of accounts receivable and inventory can be used in the context of either traditional financial statement lending or relationship lending so long as it is viewed as a secondary source of repayment. However, when the liquidation of accounts receivable and inventory is viewed as the primary source of repayment and traditional financial statement ratios and lender-borrower relationships are viewed as secondary or irrelevant considerations in making a working capital loan, then the loan falls under the category of asset-based lending. Specifically, under asset-based lending, lenders principally base their credit decision on the collectability and liquidation value of the accounts receivable and inventory, respectively.

Financial statement analysis is still important under asset-based lending. However, the focus is much different. Instead of emphasizing ratios on liquidity, debt, solvency, and profitability, lenders emphasize ratios on accounts receivable and inventory turnover, sales returns and other stress tests on the conditions of these specific assets. Profitability and leverage ratios are subordinate to an assessment of the likelihood that the proceeds from the liquidation of accounts receivable and inventory equal or exceed the loan balance.

Interestingly, the genesis of asset-based lending is factoring, a by-product of the fourteenth century wool industry in England (Lazere, 1968). While factoring still exists today, it is not really lending in a technical sense. Instead it is the outright purchase of receivables by the "factor." The largest part of the asset-based lending industry in the U.S., however, involves collateralized lending against accounts receivable and inventory, which began as a distinct business around 1900 (Lazere, 1968). These assets are intensively monitored. In the case of accounts receivable, the monitoring is typically so intense that the lender generates information every day on the status of every receivable. Moreover, in some cases, the lender has the invoice payments sent to a post office box over which the lender has sole dominion in order to preclude a diversion of funds.

One study modeled asset-based lending as a technology whose monitoring conveys real-time information to the lender about firm solvency, and dominion over the collateral provides a mechanism to insure optimal firm closure (Swary and Udell, 1988). An implication of this model is that asset-based lending is particularly valuable as a lending technology for high-risk, informationally opaque firms where the probability of suboptimal late closure is higher. This accords with industry practice where asset-based lending is often used to finance extremely risky transactions, including small firm LBOs and MBOs (management buyouts), and DIP and pre-DIP financing. It also accords with empirical evidence that asset-based lending is associated with higher-risk borrowers (Klapper, 1998; Carey, Post, and Sharpe, 1998). However, conventional empirical proxies for informational opacity fail to confirm that it is associated with asset-based lending (Carey, Post, and Sharpe, 1998).

Credit Scoring and Similar Quantitative Techniques

Over the past 25 years, a variety of statistical techniques to evaluate credit risk have been developed. The most common of these are statistical models falling under the general label of credit scoring that are used to quantify default probability or default risk classification. These include the linear probability model, logit models, and linear discriminant analysis (Saunders, 2000).[14] Credit scoring has been widely used in consumer lending for some time. However, as recently as 1995, only one large bank, Wells Fargo, had been able to generate a sufficiently large loan database to develop a reliable proprietary model (Acs, 1999). Since 1995, however, small business credit scoring models have been available from outside venders. A recent study found that by 1998 over 60% of the largest banks in the U.S. had adopted credit scoring for small business loans and only 12% of these used proprietary models. Notably, only 42% of those adopting credit scoring used it to make automatic approval/rejection decisions (Frame, Srinivasan, and Woosley, 2001). Smaller banks, however, do not have sufficient loan volume to develop their own proprietary models (Acs, 1999), and likely have not as widely adopted credit scoring for their small business lending.

Credit scoring seems particularly appropriate in bank micro-business lending, which could be defined as business loans under $250,000. While the credit scoring models used in this manner are more complex than those used in consumer lending they still place considerable weight on factors associated with the financial history of the entrepreneur (Feldman, 1997). This is not surprising given that for small businesses, the creditworthiness of the owner is closely intertwined with the creditworthiness of the business (Ang, 1992; Mester, 1997). Thus, adapting the type of credit scoring-based underwriting used in consumer lending to commercial lending would appear to be much easier than adapting it to middle market commercial lending where evaluating creditworthiness is arguably more complex, and much more dependent on the business than the entrepreneur.

It has been argued that the increasing use of credit scoring will affect small business lending in terms of the interaction between borrowers and lenders, loan pricing, and the availability of credit (Feldman, 1997). Like traditional balance

---

[14]See Saunders (2000) for a more detailed discussion of credit scoring models and other newer quantitative techniques that can be used for credit risk measurement and pricing.

sheet lending, credit scoring emphasizes quantitative analysis and de-emphasizes the value of the lender-borrower relationships. To the extent that credit scoring reduces underwriting costs, it could lead to a lower cost of credit for some borrowers in the micro-business loan market.[15] Recent empirical evidence suggests that credit scoring is associated with a larger allocation of large bank assets to small business lending, particularly to relatively risky "marginal applicants" (Frame, Srinivasan, and Woosley, 2001; Berger, Frame, and Miller, 2002).

Trade Credit

Trade credit is financing extended by suppliers who sell to businesses on account. As reflected in Table 1, trade credit to small business provides nearly 16% of small business finance. Empirical evidence suggests that stronger firms are able to get more trade credit, although suppliers appear willing to extend credit to cash-constrained growing firms (Petersen and Rajan, 1997). Some theories of trade credit emphasize factors such as comparative advantages in funding (Schwartz, 1974), production/inventory management (Emery, 1987), price discrimination (Meltzer, 1960; Schwartz and Whitcomb, 1979; Brennan, Maksimovic and Zechner, 1988; Mian and Smith, 1992; Petersen and Rajan, 1997) or product quality guarantees (Long, Malitz, and Ravid, 1994).

Some theories of trade credit, however, emphasize the underwriting and lending process itself. For example, some models emphasize that trade creditors may have an informational advantage over financial intermediaries such as banks and finance companies in evaluating their customers' ability to pay (Emery, 1984), solving incentive problems more effectively (Biais and Gollier, 1997), or in repossessing and reselling goods in the event of default (Mian and Smith, 1992; Petersen and Rajan, 1997). Trade creditors may also have an advantage over banks and other financial intermediaries in controlling borrower behavior by threatening to withdraw future supplies. This could be a stronger threat than a bank's threat to withhold future credit (Petersen and Rajan, 1997). Because trade credit employs a short-term maturity, it can be withdrawn based on observable but not verifiable information. Some evidence suggests that access to trade credit may be viewed by bankers as a necessary condition for access to the bank loan market in some developing nations, suggesting that trade credit technology may be particularly useful when other methods of addressing informational opacity are not as well developed (Cook, 1999).[16]

FACTORS AFFECTING THE SUPPLY OF CREDIT TO SMALL BUSINESSES

There has been considerable research on factors that affect the supply of credit to small businesses. While we cannot discuss all of these, we can examine a few of the most important and visible factors.

---

[15] See Mester (1997) for a discussion of the limitations of credit scoring.
[16] See Petersen and Rajan (1997) for a more complete summary of theories of trade credit.

Macroeconomic Factors

There has been interest recently in the possibility that the transmission mechanism of monetary policy may operate at least partially through bank credit, particularly bank credit to small businesses that do not have access to the public debt markets. There are two distinct hypothesized "credit channels" that may operate alongside the traditional interest rate and money channels. The "bank lending view" suggests that a contraction of bank reserves forces banks to contract their supplies of credit to their borrowers. In turn, this reduction in credit supply may have a real effect on business spending and the performance of the macroeconomy (e.g., Bernanke and Blinder, 1988). Empirical evidence suggests that tight monetary policy reduces bank lending and reduces economic growth (see Kashyap and Stein, 1997 for a survey) and the growth and investment of small businesses (Gertler and Gilchrist, 1994; Bernanke, Gertler and Gilchrist, 1996).

The second hypothesized credit channel, the "balance sheet" or "financial accelerator," operates through the impact of higher interest rates on the creditworthiness of potential borrowers. Rising interest rates depresses collateral value and the balance sheet value of potential borrowers, particularly small firms who are more likely to depend on collateral values. Empirical evidence provides support for this view and the impact of monetary policy on small business balance sheets (e.g. Bernanke and Gertler, 1995; Bernanke, Gertler, and Gilchrist, 1996).

Another macroeconomic factor is the impact of credit crunches on the availability of credit to small business. The early 1990s has been identified as credit crunch in the U.S. principally because of the decline in business lending by U.S. banks, and that this may have disproportionately affected small businesses (Dunkelberg and Dennis, 1992; Avery, Bostic and Samolyk, 1998). Considerable research effort has focused on the causes of this credit crunch, focusing on hypotheses that range from implementation of the Basle-Accord risk-based capital standards, capital shocks and excessive regulatory scrutiny (Bernanke and Lown, 1991; Bizer, 1993; Hancock and Wilcox, 1993, 1994a,b, 1997; Haubrich and Wachtel, 1993; Berger and Udell, 1994; Peek and Rosengren, 1994, 1995a,b; Hancock, Laing, and Wilcox, 1995; Shrieves and Dahl, 1995; Wagster, 1999; Berger, Kyle, and Scalise, 2001).

Consolidation of the Banking Industry

The global consolidation of the financial services industry has raised a policy issue over whether small business credit availability will be adversely affected. The concern stems in great part from the empirically negative association between bank size and the allocation of assets to small business lending (Berger, Kashyap, and Scalise, 1995; Keeton, 1995; Levonian and Soller, 1995; Berger and Udell, 1996; Peek and Rosengren, 1996; Strahan and Weston, 1996). It may be the case that there are organizational diseconomies associated with jointly delivering capital market products to large businesses and private banking services to small businesses particularly those that require relationship lending.

This issue has been addressed in a variety of different ways empirically. Arguably, the most compelling empirical evidence comes from studies that have investigated the dynamics of bank mergers and acquisitions by evaluating small business lending behavior after consolidation (Keeton, 1996, 1997; Peek and Rosengren, 1996, 1998; Strahan and Weston, 1996, 1998; Craig and Santos, 1997; Kolari and Zardkoohi, 1997a,b; Zardkoohi and Kolari, 1997; Walraven, 1997; Berger, Saunders, Scalise, and Udell, 1998; Avery and Samolyk, 2000; Bonaccorsi di Patti and Gobbi, 2000). While the specific results differ by type of merger or acquisition, size of participating banking organizations and the comparison period, the most common finding is that large banking organization consolidation tends to reduce small business lending. However, this reduction appears to be offset at least in part by an external effect where other banking organizations in the same market increase their lending in response (Berger, Saunders, Scalise, and Udell, 1998; Avery and Samolyk, 2000; Berger, Goldberg, and White, 2001). There may also be an external effect in the form of an increase in de novo entry – new banks that form in markets where M&As occur. The evidence is mixed on this issue (Seelig and Critchfield, 1999; Berger, Bonime, Goldberg, and White, forthcoming). However, it should be noted that even if the external effect completely offsets the reduction in credit by the participating banks, some of the affected small businesses may suffer search costs and a higher cost of credit because they are forced to seek out and begin a new banking relationship.

Discrimination in Lending

Small businesses are important for building local communities, and so the availability of credit to small businesses in low-income and minority communities has been the subject of considerable concern and a number of public policy initiatives. Studies of the consumer lending market have found evidence of racial discrimination after controlling for borrower characteristics and selection bias (e.g., Duca and Rosenthal, 1993). Concern over discrimination in lending to small business is likewise intense. In part, the concern is fueled by the consolidation in the bank industry, which often brings in distantly-based institutions. Studies have shown that small businesses typically purchase their services from providers in the local market (e.g., Elliehausen and Wolken, 1990, 1993; Kwast, Starr-McCluer, and Wolken, 1997).

There has been a considerable amount of new research in this area spurred by new data sets that permit analysis of small business lending behavior, including the National Survey of Small Business Finance (NSSBF) and a new Community Reinvestment Act (CRA) database. Overall, the evidence suggests that the relationship between small business lending and race/ethnicity may be quite complex. Some evidence suggests that the distribution of small business loans closely reflects the distribution of businesses across neighborhoods and that the number of loans varies with racial composition, although evidence on the dollar amount of lending is mixed (Canner, 1999; Immergluck, 1999; Squires and O'Conner, 1999). Other evidence suggests that small business loan approval rates are statistically significantly less for black-owned businesses than white-owned businesses, although evidence on differences in approval rates between white-owned and Hispanic-owned businesses are mixed and appear to depend on model specification (Cavalluzzo and Cavalluzzo, 1998; Bostic and Lampani, 1999; Cavalluzzo, Cavalluzzo, and Wolken, 2000). The data also suggests the concentration in the bank loan market may affect denial rates for black-owned small businesses (Cavalluzzo, Cavalluzzo, and Wolken, 2000). Other research suggests that minorities may gain access to credit markets differently. One study found that black owners start their businesses with less capital and less access to trade credit less than Hispanic owners. This could be associated with significantly different business survival rates (Huck, Rhine, Townsend, and Bond, 1999).

It should be noted that drawing strong conclusions about whether these results on differential access to credit imply the existence of discrimination is difficult because of data and statistical issues associated with disentangling demand and supply effects. An important research problem is that there are legitimate borrower, loan, and market characteristics that are used by lenders, but are not measured or are imprecisely measured in the survey data sets available to researchers. To the extent that these unmeasured or poorly measured variables are associated with ethnicity, the data cannot reveal whether differences in loan denial or credit access result from legitimate differences across groups versus illegal discrimination (Avery, 1999a, b).[17] These problems may be even more acute in analyzing discrimination in business lending than consumer lending because of the difficulties in evaluating collateral value, the complexity of business loan pricing, the intertwining of entrepreneurial credit-worthiness with business creditworthiness, and issues of measuring the strength of the bank-borrower relationship (Yezer, 1999). These confounding issues may be somewhat mitigated in the micro-business loan market, in which banks are much more likely to employ credit scoring as a tool in evaluating loan applications. Credit scoring may improve the objectivity of their loan underwriting (Padhi, Woosley, and Srinivasan, 1999) and make it easier for banks to document the link between lending decisions and the underwriting criteria (Mester, 1997).

Technological Innovation

Technology has obviously had an enormous impact on the financial services industry. For example, technological innovation was clearly associated with the transformation of much of the industry from a local to a national market.

---

[17] Two types of discrimination are illegal in the U.S. "Statistical discrimination" occurs when lenders use race or ethnicity as proxies for variables the lender does not measure that are thought to be related to likely future performance of the loan. "Non-economic discrimination" occurs when lenders apply a penalty for race or ethnicity that is not related to expected future performance. See Avery (1999).

For instance, the creation of money market mutual funds and cash management accounts would not have been possible without significant advances in information technology. The impact of technology on the lending segment of the industry, however, is much more difficult to assess. As noted earlier, credit scoring techniques have certainly had an impact on consumer and micro-business lending. Innovations in database management and computing technology, as well as improvements in the analytical technology itself, were necessary conditions for the adoption of credit scoring. Similarly, modern software programs and internet networking have reduced the costs of analyzing, spreading, and transmitting financial statements and other financial information, and made more efficient the monitoring of specific kinds of collateral, such as accounts receivable.

Technology has also had a large impact on third-party information exchanges. Specifically, hardware and software innovations have likely significantly reduced the cost of information acquisition for public credit registries and private mercantile rating agencies such as Dun and Bradstreet (Kallberg and Udell, 2000; Miller, 2000). This has likely benefited small, informationally opaque firms more than large, informationally transparent firms, because trade credit payment history may play a larger role in analyzing the former type of firm. Some empirical evidence suggests that the power of mercantile payment information exceeds the power of financial statement information in predicting firm failure (Kallberg and Udell, 2000).

Some recent data show evidence on the economic impact of technological innovation on credit availability to small business. The studies mentioned above on credit scoring that found that credit scoring is associated with a larger allocation of large bank assets to small business lending provides some direct evidence (Frame, Srinivasan, and Woosley, 2001; Berger, Frame, and Miller, 2002). Indirect evidence also suggests the possibility that the impact of technology is nontrivial. One study found that the average distance between small businesses and their banks has increased and that communications between banks and small business borrowers occurs less often on a face-to-face basis. Moreover, these changes appear to be associated with changes in bank productivity suggesting that to some degree on-line banking, software technology, and hardware technology have helped displace human input in the lending function (Petersen and Rajan, 2002).

One of the most important financial innovations of the past two decades, securitization, appears to have had little impact on small business lending. Securitization has transformed other markets – most dramatically the market for residential mortgages where the reduction of the liquidity premium in mortgage rates directly benefits home buyers. Increased use of credit scoring over time could lead to an expansion of securitization in this market by increasing the commoditization of small business loans (Acs, 1999). However, more research may be needed to determine how well credit scoring works, the extent to which a secondary market is necessary and the extent to which relationship lending imposes an economic barrier (Mester, 1999).

CONCLUSION

Debt financing is as important for small firms as it is for large firms, although the form and process are strikingly different. While large firms issue debt instruments that are traded on secondary markets, small firms issue nontraded instruments that are generally held by their lenders until maturity. We argue here that informational opacity drives many of the differences between small firm debt and large firm debt. Unlike large firm debt, small firm debt is substantially delivered by financial intermediaries. These intermediaries use a variety of financial contracting tools and employ an array of lending technologies to help mitigate the problems associated with relatively poor information about the projects that will be funded and their prospective payoffs.

In this paper, we examine the capital structure of small firms, why they issue debt, and the sources of that debt. The theory suggests that internal and "nearly internal" funds in the form of equity financing from the entrepreneur, other members of the start-up team, friends, and family is likely first in the "pecking order" of least costly sources of finance. After internal and nearly internal funds are exhausted, additional funding from external debt financing may be preferred over external equity for several reasons. Outside debt avoids diluting the entrepreneur's ownership and may cede less control to outsiders. Relative to outside equity, outside debt also helps reduce verification costs and adverse selection problems faced by the outside investors. Outside equity may be preferred when moral hazard is a significant problem, such as occurs when relatively large sums are needed for high risk ventures. Small firms obtain their debt from a number of different sources, but most of it comes from commercial banks, trade creditors, and finance companies.

We also explore how small firms obtain credit from these sources, emphasizing that entrepreneurs often know much more about future cash flows and payoff probabilities than potential lenders, and this informational opacity puts lenders at a severe disadvantage. We identify and discuss two distinct dimensions on which lenders address this informational wedge. This first dimension is the type of contracting tools that lenders can use in constructing debt contracts including collateral, personal guarantees, covenants, maturity, and menu pricing. These tools may be used to solve adverse selection problems by encouraging borrowers to reveal their types, or to mitigate moral hazard problems by discouraging entrepreneurs from shifting into riskier projects.

The second dimension that we identify is the lending technologies available to underwrite and monitor small business loans. These include financial statement lending, relationship lending, asset-based lending, credit scoring and similar quantitative techniques, and trade finance. These technologies differ not only in how they utilize contracting tools, but also in how they deploy labor, physical capital, software, and data to address information problems. These technologies tend to be associated with particular categories of lenders. Financial statement lending tends to be associated with larger banks, relationship lending with smaller community banks, asset-based lending with commercial finance companies or asset-based lending divisions or subsidiaries of large banking organizations, credit scoring with larger banks, and trade credit with product vendors.

Finally, we explore a number of important factors that affect the overall supply of credit to small business. These include monetary policy, credit crunches, the consolidation of the banking industry, discrimination in lending, and technological innovation.

Research in entrepreneurial finance is growing rapidly, in part because a number of new data sources have recently become available (e.g., see Dunkelberg, 1998; Wolken, 1998). In this paper, we highlight many of the key issues in small firm debt finance and the extant academic literature on these topics. We offer an overall framework for thinking about small business lending which we hope will be useful in focusing future research in this area.

REFERENCES

Acs, Z.A. (1999). The development and expansion of secondary markets for small business loans. In J.L. Blanton, A. Williams and S.L.W. Rhine (eds.), *Business Access to Capital and Credit*. A Federal Reserve System Research Conference, pp. 625–643.

Allen, L., A. Saunders and G.F. Udell (1991). The pricing of retail deposits: Concentration and information. *Journal of Financial Intermediation*, 1, 335–361.

Amihud, Y. and B. Lev (1981). Risk reduction as a managerial motive for conglomerate mergers. *Journal of Economics*, 12(2), 605–617.

Ang, J.S. (1992). On the theory of finance for privately held firms. *Journal of Small Business Finance*, 1, 185–203.

Ang, J.S., J.W. Lin and F. Tyler (1995). Evidence on the lack of separation between business and personal risks among small businesses. *Journal of Small Business Finance*, 4, 197–210.

Angelini, P., Salvo, R.D., Ferri, G. (1998). Availability and cost for small businesses: Customer relationships and credit cooperatives. *Journal of Banking and Finance*, 22, 929–954.

Avery, R.B. (1999a). Access to credit for minority-owned businesses. In J.L. Blanton, A. Williams and S.L.W. Rhine (eds.), *Business Access to Capital and Credit*. A Federal Reserve System Research Conference, pp. 277–286.

Avery, R.B. (1999b). Access to credit for minority-owned businesses. In J.L. Blanton, A. Williams and S.L.W. Rhine (eds.), *Business Access to Capital and Credit*. A Federal Reserve System Research Conference, pp. 362–389.

Avery, R., R.W. Bostic and K.A. Samolyk (1998). The evolution of small business finance: The role of personal wealth. *Journal of Banking and Finance*, 22.

Avery, R.B. and K.A. Samolyk (2000). Bank consolidation and the provision of banking services: The case of small commercial loans, Federal Deposit Insurance Corporation Working Paper.

Berger, A.N., S.D. Bonime, L.G. Goldberg and L.T. White, forthcoming. The dynamics of market entry: The effects of mergers and acquisitions on entry in the banking industry. *Journal of Business*.

Berger, A.N., W.S. Frame and N.H. Miller (2002). Credit scoring and the availability, price, and risk of small business credit, Federal Reserve Board working paper.

Berger, A.N., L.G. Goldberg and L.J. White (2001). The Effects of Dynamic Changes in Bank Competition on the Supply of Small Business Credit. *European Finance Review*, 5, 115–139.

Berger, A.N., A.K. Kashyap and J.M. Scalise (1995). The transformation of the U.S. banking industry: What a long, strange trip it's been. Brookings Papers on Economic Activity, Vol. 2, pp. 55–218.

Berger, A.N., L.F. Klapper and G.F. Udell (2000). The ability of banks to lend to informationally opaque small businesses. *Journal of Banking and Finance*, **25**, 2127–2167.

Berger, A.N., M.K. Kyle and J.M. Scalise (2001). Did U.S. bank supervisors get tougher during the credit crunch? Did they get easier during the banking boom? Did it matter to bank lending? In F.S. Mishkin (ed.), *Prudential Supervision: What Works and What Doesn't, National Bureau of Economic Research* (Chicago, IL: University of Chicago Press), 301–349.

Berger, A.N., A. Saunders, J.M. Scalise and G.F. Udell (1998). The effects of bank mergers and acquisitions on small business lending. *Journal of Financial Economics*, **50**, 187–229.

Berger, A.N. and G.F. Udell (1990). Collateral, loan quality, and bank risk. *Journal of Monetary Economics*, **25**, 21–42.

Berger, A.N. and G.F. Udell (1992). Some evidence on the empirical significance of credit rationing. *Journal of Political Economy*, **100**, 1047–1077.

Berger, A.N. and G.F. Udell (1993). Securitization, risk, and the liquidity problem in banking. In M. Klausner and L.J. White (eds.), *Structural Change in Banking*. Homewood, IL: Irwin Publishing, pp. 227–291.

Berger, A.N. and G.F. Udell (1994). Did risk-based capital allocate bank credit and cause a "credit crunch" in the U.S.? *Journal of Money, Credit and Banking*, **26**, 585–628.

Berger, A.N. and G.F. Udell (1995). Relationship lending and lines of credit in small firm finance. *Journal of Business*, **68**, 351–382.

Berger, A.N. and G.F. Udell (1996). Universal banking and the future of small business lending. In A. Saunders and I. Walter (eds.), *Financial System Design: The Case for Universal Banking*. Burr Ridge, IL: Irwin Publishing, pp. 559–627.

Berger, A.N. and G.F. Udell (1998). The economics of small business finance: The roles of private equity and debt markets in the financial growth cycle. *Journal of Banking and Finance*, **22**, 613–673.

Berkovitch, E. and S.I. Greenbaum (1991). The loan commitment as an optimal financing contract. *Journal of Financial and Quantitative Analysis*, **26**, 83–95.

Berkowitz, J. and M.J. White (1999). The effect of personal bankruptcy law on small firms' access to credit. In *Business Access to Capital and Credit*. In J.L. Blanton, A. Williams and S.L.W. Rhine (eds.), *A Federal Reserve System Research Conference*, pp. 445–466.

Berlin, M. and J. Loeys (1988). Bond covenants and delegated monitoring. *Journal of Finance*, **43**, 397–412.

Berlin, M. and L.J. Mester (1993). Debt covenants and renegotiation. *Journal of Financial Intermediation*, **2**, 95–133.

Berlin, M. and L.J. Mester (1997). Why is the banking sector shrinking? Core deposits and relationship lending. Working Paper No. 96-18R. Federal Reserve Bank of Philadelphia.

Berlin, M. and L.J. Mester (1998). On the profitability and cost of relationship lending. *Journal of Banking and Finance*, **22**, 873–897.

Berlin, M. and L.J. Mester (1999). Deposits and relationship lending. *Review of Financial Studies*, **12**, 579–607.

Bernanke, B. (1983). Non-monetary effects of the financial crisis in the propagation of the great depression. *American Economic Review*, **73**, 257–276.

Bernanke, B.S. and A. Blinder (1988). Credit, money, and aggregate demand. *American Economic Review*, **78**, 435–439.

Bernanke, B.S. and M. Gertler (1995). Inside the black box: The credit channel of monetary policy transmission. *Journal of Economic Perspectives*, **9**, 27–48.

Bernanke, B., M. Gertler and S. Gilchrist (1996). The financial accelerator, and the flight to quality. *Review of Economics and Statistics*, **78**, 1–15.

Bernanke, B.S. and C. Lown (1991). The credit crunch. *Brookings Papers on Economic Activity*, 205–248.

Besanko, D. and A.V. Thakor (1987a). Collateral and rationing: Sorting equilibria in monopolistic and competitive markets. *International Economic Review*, **28**, 671–689.

Besanko, D. and A.V. Thakor (1987b). Competitive equilibrium in the credit market under asymmetric information. *Journal of Economic Theory*, **42**, 167–182.

Bester, H. (1985). Screening vs. rationing in credit markets with imperfect information. *American Economic Review*, 75, 850–855.

Biais, B. and C. Gollier (1997). Trade credit and credit rationing. *Review of Financial Studies*, 10, 903–937.

Billett, M.T., M.J. Flannery and J.A. Garfinkel (1995). The effect of lender identity on a borrowing firm's equity return. *Journal of Finance*, 50, 699–718.

Bizer, D.S. (1993). Regulatory discretion and the credit crunch. Working paper, U.S. Securities and Exchange Commission, Washington DC (April).

Blackwell, D. and D.B. Winters (1997). Banking relationships and the effect of monitoring on loan pricing. *Journal of Financial Research*, 20, 275–89.

Bolton, P. and D.S. Scharfstein (1996). Optimal debt structure and the number of creditors. *Journal of Political Economy*, 104, 1–25.

Bonaccorsi di Patti, E. and G. Gobbi (2000). The effects of bank consolidation on small business lending: Evidence from market and firm data, Bank of Italy working paper.

Boot, A.W.A. (2000). Relationship banking: What do we know? *Journal of Financial Intermediation*, 9, 7–25.

Boot, A.W.A. and A.V. Thakor (1994). Moral hazard and secured lending in an infinitely repeated credit market game. *International Economic Review*, 35, 899–920.

Boot, A.W.A., A.V. Thakor and G. Udell (1987). Competition, risk neutrality and loan commitments. *Journal of Banking and Finance*, 11, 449–471.

Boot, A.W.A., A.V. Thakor and G.F. Udell (1991). Secured lending and default risk: Equilibrium analysis and policy implications and empirical results. *Economic Journal*, 101, 458–472.

Booth, J.R. (1992). Contract costs, bank loans, and the cross-monitoring hypothesis. *Journal of Financial Economics*, 31, 2–41.

Booth, J.R. and L. Chua (1996). Loan collateral decisions and corporate borrowing costs. Arizona State University working paper.

Bostic, R.W. and K.P. Lampani (1999). Racial differences in patterns of small business finance: The importance of local geography. In J.L. Blanton, A. Williams and S.L.W. Rhine (eds.), *Business Access to Capital and Credit*. A Federal Reserve System Research Conference, pp. 149–179.

Brennan, M., V. Maksimovic and J. Zechner (1988). Vendor financing. *Journal of Finance*, 43, 1127–1141.

Canner, G.B. (1999). Evaluation of CRA data on small business lending. In J.L. Blanton, A. Williams and S.L.W. Rhine (eds.), *Business Access to Capital and Credit*. A Federal Reserve System Research Conference, pp. 53–84.

Carey, M. (1996). Financial covenants, private debt, and financial intermediation. Board of Governors of the Federal Reserve working paper.

Carey, M., M. Post and S.A. Sharpe (1998). Does corporate lending by banks and finance companies differ? Evidence on specialization in private debt contracting. *Journal of Finance*, 53, 845–878.

Carey, M., S. Prowse, J. Rea and G.F. Udell (1993). The economics of private placements: A new look. *Financial Markets, Institutions and Instruments*, 2.

Cavalluzzo, K. and L. Cavalluzzo (1998). Market structure and discrimination: The case of small business. *Journal of Money, Credit and Banking*.

Cavalluzzo, K., L. Cavalluzzo and J. Wolken (2000). Competition, small business financing, and discrimination: Evidence from a new survey. Federal Reserve Board working paper.

Chan, Y.-S. and G. Kanatas (1985). Asymmetric valuation and the role of collateral in loan agreements. *Journal of Money, Credit and Banking*, 17, 85–95.

Cole, R.A. (1998). The importance of relationships to the availability of credit. *Journal of Banking and Finance*, 22.

Cole, R.A., L.G. Goldberg and L.J. White (1999). Cookie-cutter versus character: The microstructure of small business lending by large and small banks. In J.L. Blanton, A. Williams and S.L.W. Rhine (eds.), *Business Access to Capital and Credit*. A Federal Reserve System Research Conference, pp. 362–389.

Cole, R.A. and J.D. Wolken (1995). Sources and uses of financial services by small businesses: Evidence from the 1993 National Survey of Small Business Finances. *Federal Reserve Bulletin*, 81, 629–670.

Conigliani, C., G. Ferri and G. Generale (1997). The impact of bank-firm relations on the propagation of monetary policy squeezes: An empirical assessment for Italy. *Banca Nazionale del Lavoro Quarterly Review*, **50**, 271–299.

Cook, L. (1999). Trade credit and bank finance: Financing small firms in Russia. *Journal of Business Venturing*, **14**, 493–518.

Cornet, M.M. and A. Saunders (1991). *Fundamentals of Financial Institutions Management*. Boston, MA: Irwin McGraw-Hill.

Craig, B.R. and J.C.D. Santos (1997). Banking consolidation. Impact on small business lending. Working Paper, Federal Reserve Bank of Cleveland.

Degryse, H. and P.V. Cayseele (2000). Relationship lending within a bank-based system: Evidence from European small business data. *Journal of Financial Intermediation*, **9**, 90–109.

Dewatripont, M. and E. Maskin (1995). Credit and efficiency in centralized and decentralized economies. *Review of Economic Studies*, **62**, 541–555.

Diamond, D.W. (1984). Financial intermediation and delegated monitoring. *Review of Economic Studies*, **51**, 393–414.

Diamond, D.W. and R. Rajan (1999). Liquidity risk, liquidity creation and financial fragility: A theory of banking working paper, University of Chicago.

Duca, J.V. and S.S. Rosenthal (1993). Borrowing constraints, household debt, and racial discrimination in loan markets. *Journal of Financial Intermediation*, **3**, 77–103.

Dunkelberg, W. (1998). Credit, banks and small business in America. *Journal of Banking and Finance*, **22**, 1085–1088.

Dunkelberg, W.C. and W.J. Dennis, Jr. (1992). The small business "credit crunch". The NFIB Foundation, Washington DC.

Elliehausen, G.E. and J.D. Wolken (1990). Banking markets and the use of financial services by small and medium-sized businesses. *Federal Reserve Bulletin*, **76**, 801–817.

Elliehausen, G.E. and J.D. Wolken (1993). The demand for trade credit: An investigation of motives for trade credit by small businesses. Staff study 165, Board of Governors of the Federal Reserve System, Washington DC.

Elsas, R. and J.P. Krahnen (1997). Is relationship lending special? Evidence from credit-file data in Germany. *Journal of Banking and Finance*, **22**, 1283–1316.

Emery, G.W. (1984). A pure financial explanation for trade credit. *Journal of Financial and Quantitative Analysis*, **19**.

Emery, G.W. (1987). An optimal financial response to variable demand. *Journal of Financial and Quantitative Analysis*, **22**, 209–225.

Feldman, R. (1997). Banks and a big change in technology called credit scoring. The Region, Federal Reserve Bank of Minneapolis, September, pp. 19–25.

Fenn, G.W., N. Liang and S. Prowse (1997). The private equity market: An overview. *Financial Markets, Institutions and Instruments*, **6**, 1–106.

Ferri, G. and M. Messori (2000). Bank-firm relationships and allocative efficiency in northeastern and central Italy and in the south. *Journal of Banking and Finance*, **24**, 1067–1095.

Ferris, J.S. (1981). A transactions theory of trade credit use. *Quarterly Journal of Economics*, **96**, 243–270.

Frame, W.S., A. Srinivasan and L. Woosley (2001). The effect of credit scoring on small business lending. *Journal of Money, Credit and Banking*, **33**, 813–825.

Freear, J., J.E. Sohl, W.E. Wetzel, Jr. (1994). The private investor market for venture capital. *Financier*, **1**, 7–19.

Gertler, M. and S. Gilchrist (1994). Monetary policy, business cycles, and the behavior of small manufacturing firms. *Quarterly Journal of Economics* **109**, 309–340.

Goldberg, L.G. and L.J. White (1998). De novo banks and lending to small businesses. *Journal of Banking and Finance*, **22**, 851–867.

Gorton, G. and J. Kahn (1997). The design of bank loan contracts, collateral, and renegotiation. University of Pennsylvania Working Paper.

Greenbaum, S.I., G. Kanatas and I. Venezia (1989). Equilibrium loan pricing under the bank-client relationship. *Journal of Banking and Finance*, **13**, 221–235.

Hancock, D., A. Laing and J.A. Wilcox (1995). Bank balance sheet shocks and aggregate shocks: Their dynamic effects on bank capital and lending. *Journal of Banking and Finance*, 19, 661–677.

Hancock, D. and J.A. Wilcox (1993). Has there been a "capital crunch" in banking? The effects on bank lending of real estate market conditions and bank capital shortfalls. *Journal of Housing Economics*, 3, 31–50.

Hancock, D. and J.A. Wilcox (1994a). Bank capital and the credit crunch: The roles of risk-weighted and unweighted capital regulations, *AREUEA*, 22, 59–94.

Hancock, D. and J.A. Wilcox (1994b). Bank capital, loan delinquencies, and real estate lending. *Journal of Housing Economics*, 4, 121–146.

Hancock, D. and J.A. Wilcox (1997). Bank capital, nonbank finance, and real estate activity. *Journal of Housing Research*, 8, 75–105.

Hancock, D. and J.A. Wilcox (1998). The "Credit crunch" and the availability of credit to small business. *Journal of Banking and Finance*, 22, 983–1014.

Harhoff, D. and T. Körting (1998a). Lending relationships in Germany: Empirical results from survey data. *Journal of Banking and Finance*, 22, 1317–1354.

Harhoff, D. and T. Körting (1998b). How many creditors does it take to tango? Discussion paper. Conference on Industrial Structure and Input Markets, Center for Economic Policy Research, Deutsche Forschungsgemeinschaft, Zentrum für Europaische Wirtschaftsforschung, Mannheim, Germany.

Hart, O. and J. Moore (1989). Default and renegotiation: A dynamic model of debt. London School of Economics Discussion Paper, 57.

Haubrich, J. and P. Wachtel (1993). Capital requirements and shifts in commercial bank portfolios. *Federal Reserve Bank of Cleveland Economic Review*, 29 (Quarter 3), 2–15.

Hester, D. (1979). Customer relationships and terms of loans: Evidence from a pilot survey. *Journal of Money, Credit and Banking*, 11, 349–357.

Huck, P., S.L.W. Rhine, R. Townsend and P. Bond (1999). A comparison of small business finance in two Chicago minority neighborhoods. In J.L. Blanton, A. Williams and S.L.W. Rhine (eds.), *Business Access to Capital and Credit*. A Federal Reserve System Research Conference, pp. 467–502.

Immergluck, D. (1999). Intraurban patterns of small business lending: Findings from the new community reinvestment act. In J.L. Blanton, A. Williams and S.L.W. Rhine (eds.), *Business Access to Capital and Credit*. A Federal Reserve System Research Conference, pp. 123–138.

Jayaratne, J. and Wolken, J.D. (1999). How important are small banks to small business lending? New evidence from a survey to small businesses. *Journal of Banking and Finance*, 23, 427–458.

Jensen, M.C. and W.H. Meckling (1976). Theory of the firm: Managerial behavior, agency costs, and ownership structure. *Journal of Financial Economics*, 3, October, 305–360.

John, K., A.W. Lynch and M. Puri (1997). Collateral and perquisite consumption: Theory and evidence. New York University working paper.

Kallberg, J. and G.F. Udell (2000). The value of private sector credit information: The U.S. case, Indiana University working paper.

Kanatas, G. (1987). Commercial paper, bank reserve requirements, and the informational role of loan commitments. *Journal of Banking and Finance*, 11, 425–448.

Kashyap, A.K. and J.C. Stein (1997). The role of banks in monetary policy: A survey with implications for the European Monetary Union. Economic Perspectives, Federal Reserve Bank of Chicago, September/October, pp. 3–18.

Keeton, W.R. (1995). Multi-office bank lending to small businesses: Some new evidence. *Federal Reserve Bank of Kansas City Economic Review*, 80(2), 45–57.

Keeton, W.R. (1996). Do bank mergers reduce lending to businesses and farmers? New evidence from tenth district states. *Federal Reserve Bank of Kansas City Economic Review*, 81(3), 63–75.

Keeton, W.R. (1997). The effects of mergers on farm and business lending at small banks: New evidence from tenth district states. Working Paper, Federal Reserve Bank of Kansas City.

Klapper, L. (1998). Short-term collateralization: Theory and evidence. New York University working paper.

Kolari, J. and A. Zardkoohi (1997a). The impact of structural change in the banking industry on small business lending. Report to the Small Business Administration.

Kolari, J. and A. Zardkoohi (1997b). Bank acquisitions and small business lending. Working paper, Texas A&M University.

Kwan, S.H. and W.T. Carleton (1993). The structure and pricing of private placement corporate loans. University of Arizona working paper.

Kwast, M., M. Starr-McCluer and J.D. Wolken (1997). Market definition and antitrust in banking. *Antitrust Bulletin*, **42**, Winter, 973–995.

Lazere, M.R. (1968). Commercial financing. National Commercial Finance Conference.

Levonian, M. and J. Soller (1995). Small banks, small loans, small business. Federal Reserve Bank of San Francisco working paper.

Long, M.S., I.B. Malitz and S.A. Ravid (1994). Trade credit, quality guarantees, and product marketability. *Financial Management*, **22**, 117–127.

Longhofer, S.D. and J.A.C. Santos (2000). The importance of bank seniority for relationship lending. *Journal of Financial Intermediation*, **9**, 57–89.

Machauer, A. and M. Weber (2000). Number of bank relationships: An indicator of competition, borrower quality, or just size? University of Mannheim working paper.

Meltzer, A.H. (1960). Mercantile credit, monetary policy, and size of firms. *Review of Economics and Statistics*, **42**, 429–437.

Mester, L.J. (1997). What's the point of credit scoring? *Business Review*, Federal Reserve Bank of Philadelphia, September/October, pp. 3–16.

Mester, L.J. (1999). Credit scoring and securitization of small business loans. In J.L. Blanton, A. Williams and S.L.W. Rhine (eds.), *Business Access to Capital and Credit*. A Federal Reserve System Research Conference, pp. 650–664.

Mester, L.J., L.I. Nakamura and M. Renault (1998). Checking accounts and bank monitoring. Federal Reserve Bank of Philadelphia working paper.

Mian, S. and C. Smith (1992). Accounts receivable management policy: Theory and evidence. *Journal of Finance*, **47**, 169–200.

Miller, M. (2000). Credit reporting systems around the globe: The state of the art in public and private credit registries. World Bank working paper.

Myers, S. (1977). Determinants of corporate borrowing. *Journal of Financial Economics*, **5**, 147–175.

Myers, S. (1984). Presidential address: The capital structure puzzle. *Journal of Finance*, **39**, 575–592.

Myers, S.C. and N.C. Majluf (1984). Corporate financing and investment decisions when firms have information that investors do not have. *Journal of Financial Economics*, **13**, 187–221.

Nachman, D.C. and T.H. Noe (1994). Optimal design of securities under asymmetric information. *Review of Financial Studies*, **7**, 1–44.

Nakamura, L.I. (1993). Commercial bank information: Implications for the structure of banking. In M. Klausner and L.J. White (eds.), *Structural Change in Banking*. Homewood, IL: Irwin, pp. 131–160.

Nilsen, J.H. (1994). Trade credit and the bank lending channel of monetary policy. Working paper, Princeton University.

Ongena, S. and D.C. Smith (2000). What determines the number of bank relationships? *Journal of Financial Intermediation*, **9**, 26–56.

Ongena, S. and D. Smith (forthcoming). The duration of banking relationships. *Journal of Financial Economics*, **61**, 449–475.

Orgler, Y. (1970). A credit scoring model for commercial loans. *Journal of Money, Credit and Banking*, **2**, 435–445.

Padhi, M.S., L.W. Woosley and A. Srinivasan (1999). Credit scoring and securitization of small business loans. In J.L. Blanton, A. Williams and S.L.W. Rhine (eds.), *Business Access to Capital and Credit*. A Federal Reserve System Research Conference, pp. 587–624.

Peek, J. and E.S. Rosengren (1994). Bank real estate lending and the New England capital crunch. *AREUEA*, **22**, 33–58.

Peek, J. and E.S. Rosengren (1995a). The capital crunch: Neither a borrower nor a lender be. *Journal of Money, Credit and Banking*, **27**, 625–638.

Peek, J. and E.S. Rosengren (1995b). Bank regulation and the credit crunch. *Journal of Banking and Finance,* 19, 679–692.

Peek, J. and E.S. Rosengren (1996). Small business credit availability: How important is size of lender? In A. Saunders and I. Walter (eds.), *Financial System Design: The Case for Universal Banking.* Burr Ridge, IL: Irwin Publishing.

Peek, J. and E.S. Rosengren (1998). Bank consolidation and small business lending: It's not just bank size that matters. *Journal of Banking and Finance,* 22, 799–819.

Petersen, M.A. and R.G. Rajan (1994). The benefits of firm-creditor relationships: Evidence from small business data. *Journal of Finance,* 49, 3–37.

Petersen, M.A. and R.G. Rajan (1995). The effect of credit market competition on lending relationships. *Quarterly Journal of Economics,* 110, 407–443.

Petersen, M.A. and R.G. Rajan (1997). Trade credit: Theories and evidence. *The Review of Financial Studies,* 10, 661–669.

Petersen, M.A. and R.G. Rajan (2002). Does distance still matter? The information revolution in small business lending. *Journal of Finance.*

Pratt, E.S. and J.K. Morris (1987). Pratt's guide to venture capital sources. Venture Economics, Inc., Wellesley.

Rajan, R.G. (1992). Insiders and outsiders: The choice between informed and arm's-length debt. *Journal of Finance,* 47, 1367–1399.

Rajan, R.G. and A. Winton (1995). Covenants and collateral as incentives to monitor. *Journal of Finance,* 50, 1113–1146.

Ravid, S.A. (1996). Debt maturity – a survey. *Financial Markets, Institutions and Instruments,* 5(3), 1–68.

Saunders, A. (2000). *Financial Institutions Management.* Boston, MA: Irwin McGraw-Hill.

Schwartz, R.A. (1974). An economic model of trade credit. *Journal of Financial and Quantitative Analysis,* 9, 643–657.

Schwartz, R.A. and D. Whitcomb (1979). The trade credit decision. In J. Bicksler (ed.), *Handbook of Financial Economics.* Amsterdam: North Holland.

Scott, J.A. and Dunkelberg, W.C. (1999). Bank consolidation and small business lending: A small firm perspective. In J.L. Blanton, A. Williams and S.L.W. Rhine (eds.), *Business Access to Capital and Credit.* A Federal Reserve System Research Conference, pp. 328–361.

Scott, J.A. and T.C. Smith (1986). The effect of the Bankruptcy Reform Act of 1978 on small business loan pricing. *Journal of Financial Economics,* 16, 119–140.

Seelig, S.A. and T. Critchfield (1999). Determinants of de novo entry in banking. Federal Deposit Insurance Corporation Working Paper, 99–101.

Sharpe, S.A. (1990). Asymmetric information, bank lending, and implicit contracts: A stylized model of customer relationships. *Journal of Finance,* 45, 1069–1087.

Shrieves, R.E. and D. Drew (1995). Regulation, recession, and bank lending behavior: The 1990 Credit Crunch. *Journal of Financial Services Research,* 9, 5–30.

Smith, C. and J. Warner (1979). Bankruptcy, secured debt, and optimal capital structure: Comment. *Journal of Finance,* 34, 247–251.

Smith, J.K. (1987). Trade credit and information asymmetries. *Journal of Finance,* 42, 863–872.

Squires, G.D. and S. O'Connor (1999). Access to capital: Milwaukee's small business lending gaps. In J.L. Blanton, A. Williams and S.L.W. Rhine (eds.), *Business Access to Capital and Credit.* A Federal Reserve System Research Conference, pp. 85–122.

Stiglitz, J. and A. Weiss (1981). Credit rationing in markets with imperfect information. *American Economic Review,* 71, June, 393–410.

Stiglitz, J. and A. Weiss (1987). Credit rationing: Reply. *American Economic Review,* 77, March, 228–231.

Strahan, P.E. and J. Weston (1996). Small business lending and bank consolidation: Is there cause for concern? *Current Issues in Economics and Finance.* Federal Reserve Bank of New York, 2, 1–6.

Strahan, P.E. and J. Weston (1998). Small business lending and the changing structure of the banking industry. *Journal of Banking and Finance,* 22, 821–845.

Stulz, R. and H. Johnson (1985). An analysis of secured debt. *Journal of Financial Economics*, **14**, 501–522.

Swary, I. and G.F. Udell (1988). Information production and the secured line of credit. New York University working paper.

Thakor, A.V. and G.F. Udell (1987). An economic rationale for the pricing structure of bank loan commitments. *Journal of Banking and Finance*, **11**, 271–289.

Townsend, R. (1979). Optimal contracts and competitive markets with costly state verification. *Journal of Economic Theory*, **21**, 265–93.

Udell, G.F. (1986). Pricing returned check charges under asymmetric information. *Journal of Money, Credit, and Banking*, **18**, 495–505.

Wagster, J.D. (1999). The Basle Accord of 1988 and the International Credit Crunch of 1989–1992. *Journal of Financial Services Research*, **15**, 123–143.

Wagster, J.D. (1997). The Basle Accord of 1988 and the International Credit Crunch of 1989–1992. Working paper, Wayne State University.

Walraven, N. (1997). Small business lending by banks involved in mergers. Finance and Economics Discussion Series 97-25, Board of Governors of the Federal Reserve.

Welch, I. (1997). Why is bank debt senior? A theory of asymmetry and claim priority based on influence costs. *Review of Financial Studies*, **10**, 1203–1236.

Wilson, P.F. (1993). The pricing of loans in a bank-borrower relationship. Indiana University working paper.

Wolken, J.D. (1998). "New" data sources for research on small business finance. *Journal of Banking and Finance*, **22**, 1067–1076.

Yezer, A.M.J. (1999). Studies of CRA data on small business lending. In J.L. Blanton, A. Williams and S.L.W. Rhine (eds.), *Business Access to Capital and Credit*. A Federal Reserve System Research Conference, pp. 139–148.

Zardkoohi, A. and J. Kolari (1997). The effect of structural changes in the U.S. banking industry on small business lending. Working paper, Texas A&M University.

PART SIX

The Social Context

The social context looks at social outcomes that are larger than individuals. If entrepreneurship is important, and one of the outcomes of entrepreneurial behavior is new organization, then how the organizations relate to each other is the formation of larger social groups is important to study. In Part VI the outcome of social performance is examined. In Chapter 14, "The Social Psychology of Entrepreneurial Behavior," Kelly G. Shaver suggests that the social psychology is important for the study of entrepreneurship because the creation of a new venture is a truly social enterprise. The chapter examines four major areas of theory and research in social psychology and indicates how each has found its place in the study of entrepreneurial activity.

In Chapter 15, "Entrepreneurship as Social Construction: An Evolutionary Approach," Howard Aldrich and Martha Martinez analyze the multi-level selection processes that apply across three different levels of entrepreneurial social construction: organizations, populations and communities. The chapter emphasizes the inexorable tension between selection forces at the three levels that affect variations generated by entrepreneurs. Sometimes these forces work in concert and sometimes they do not. Their main goal is to describe the entrepreneurial process as a form of social construction that goes beyond the firm itself to the creation of populations and communities. Following an evolutionary argument, the survival of a firm, population or community depends as much on the existence of favorable environmental forces as on the effectiveness of individual entrepreneurs. This is especially important for entrepreneurs that are innovators creating new organizations, populations and communities. They emphasize the importance of collective action, which depends on social psychology, in providing entrepreneurs with the capacity to shape their environments.

Patricia Thornton and Katherine Flynn in Chapter 16, "Entrepreneurship, Networks and Geographies," provide an example of the role of organizations and regions in the firm formation process. Organizations are increasingly important in forming new organizations. How these environments spawn new entrepreneurs and create new business remains relatively understudied. Although these organization and regional environments have been described as network structures and geographic clusters, research that links the spatial and relational aspects of these larger contexts to the micro process of entrepreneurship is relatively underdeveloped.

KELLY G. SHAVER

College of William and Mary

14.   The Social Psychology of Entrepreneurial Behaviour

INTRODUCTION

The purpose of this chapter is to describe four major areas of theory and research in social psychology, and to indicate how each has found its place in the study of entrepreneurial activity. Economic conditions in an industry may favor the emergence of new entrants, venture capital may be readily available, technological advances may create market opportunities, but as Shaver and Scott (1991) have noted, there will be no new companies created without focused and sustained entrepreneurial *behaviour*. Such entrepreneurial action may be the work of an individual, or it may be the work of a team. In either case, the behavioural processes involved are ones normally considered within the domain of social psychology. As team-based entrepreneurship is often treated separately from individual entrepreneurship (see, for example, Cooper and Daily, 1997; Stewart, 1989), this chapter will concentrate on what social psychology refers to as the "intrapersonal" processes of an individual entrepreneur. These include social cognition, attribution, attitudes, and the self. The specific topics to be discussed were selected because (a) they are traditional concerns of social psychology, and (b) they have been the subject of numerous papers in entrepreneurship. Our review is necessarily selective, but will still advance a strong case for further consideration of the social psychological processes that guide the entrepreneur's venture-organizing activities.

Some Initial Distinctions

Social psychology is "the scientific study of the personal and situational factors that affect individual social behaviour" (Shaver, 1987, p. 18). The field is traditionally distinguished from psychology on the one hand and from sociology on the other, by the level of analysis inherent in most work in each field. Social psychology concentrates on the *socially meaningful actions* of an individual person (actions, for example, like those associated with starting a new venture). In contrast, the "dependent variable" for much of psychology is at a more molecular level. How much change must there be in the wavelength of a projected colored light for a person to shift from calling the light "blue" to

Z.J. Acs and D.B. Audretsch (eds.), Handbook of Entrepreneurship Research, 331–357
© 2003 *Kluwer Academic Publishers. Printed in Great Britain.*

calling it "green?" Is there a "critical period" among humans during which the person must hear other human speech in order to develop a full and sophisticated vocabulary? What does reaction time tell us about the internal structure of the cognitive apparatus? These questions, and others at a comparable level of analysis have engaged psychological researchers for years, and have contributed to our overall understanding of human beings. But in virtually all of such studies, the dependent variables are not socially meaningful chunks of behaviour.

As psychology concentrates on dependent variables "smaller" than the individual person, sociology concentrates on structures and processes that are larger than any *particular* individual. A business school consists of a Dean, area or department heads, faculty members, support staff, and students at various levels. Each participant in this system behaves in large part according to role expectations and social status. Of course there are individual variations, but replacing one, or several, particular faculty members with other people whose training is comparable does not convert the business school to an art school. Demographics matter, culture matters, the structure matters; particular individuals typically do not matter.

Through the years of entrepreneurship as a separate field of inquiry, more than a few definitions have been offered for entrepreneurial action. Indeed, the diversity of chapters in this volume provides eloquent testimony to the intellectual eclecticism of the field. Yet there are important common threads – opportunity seeking and recognition, innovation, creation of value, assumption of risk, disregard for resources controlled (see, for example, Hisrich and Peters, 1998; Stevenson and Gumpert, 1985; Timmons, 1994). In a refreshingly open approach to the problem of definition, Mitton (1989) noted that "Entrepreneurship and pornography have a lot in common: They are both hard to define" (p. 9). He continued the analogy, building on Justice Potter Stewart's comment, by saying "I can't define it – at least not to everyone else's satisfaction – but I know it when I see it" (p. 9). The reason that Mitton, and many of the rest of us, can "know it when we see it," is that entrepreneurial behaviour involves precisely the *socially meaningful actions of individuals* that are the province of social psychology.

Methodological Approach

Although one of the early extensive studies of entrepreneurial behaviour was conducted by the psychologist David McClelland (1961), it is fair to say that, on balance, most research in entrepreneurship has not been informed by the extensive methodological contributions of experimental social psychology. Management scholars are well aware of classics like the "Hawthorne" experiments (Roethlisberger and Dickson, 1939), but have rarely conducted the sort of laboratory research that is the stock in trade of social psychologists. As a consequence, entrepreneurship researchers trained in the management tradition are less likely to be skeptical about some of the traditional means of examining entrepreneurial behaviour.

Because their research involves the meaningful actions of individuals capable of problem-solving and intentional action, social psychologists often talk about the "experimenter-subject interaction" as a particular sort of scripted interchange. This is especially true in a traditional laboratory setting, but applies with nearly equal force to other research venues as well. Regardless of where the work is conducted, the researcher begins a project with what Rosenthal (1966, 1994) called *experimenter expectancies* – a sort of personal prediction about what the data will likely show. Given that most experimental work involves hypothesis testing, rather than hypothesis generation, it is not at all surprising that the person conducting the research should have expectations about the outcome. The difficulty comes in the ease by which these experimenter expectancies can be communicated to the research participants, often in ways so subtle that they are well outside the conscious awareness of either party. Patterns of speech by the experimenter, degree and timing of eye contact, changes in body position, can all convey the "right answer" to a research participant. Expectancies have been implicated in everything from behavioural medicine studies of stress (Krantz and Ratliff-Crain, 1989) to police line-ups (Wells, 1993). The production of expected responses is not limited to interactions between researchers and participants, nor is it limited to face-to-face interactions. For example, in one early study of a domain that has become known as *behavioural confirmation* (Snyder, 1984) researchers produced important behavioural differences during telephone interviews (Snyder, Tanke and Berscheid, 1977). In this study, male undergraduates were asked to conduct a 10-minute telephone conversation with female undergraduates, ostensibly for the purpose of getting acquainted. Before the conversation began, each male was given a folder containing biographical information about the female he was to call, and a Polaroid picture purported to be her photograph. In fact, the photographs had been preselected to be either highly attractive or unattractive (but in neither case were they the actual picture of the target female). The telephone conversations were unstructured, and done through headphones and microphones, so that each party's side of the conversation could be recorded on a separate channel. The conversations of the female targets were later rated by judges who had no idea about the nature of the experiment (and who did not hear the males' sides of the conversations). These ratings showed that females who had been talking to males who *thought* they were highly attractive were rated to be more attractive and socially skilled than females who had been talking to males who thought they were less attractive. The expectations of the male callers had somehow produced the very behaviour they expected. In social interaction, what you get may be what you expect to see.

Not all of the potential biases in a research interchange are introduced by the experimenter; some are situationally induced and others are inherent in the participants. Whether they are undergraduates in a social psychological laboratory, or presidents of start-up companies being interviewed in their offices, people who know that their behaviour is being scrutinized are susceptible to several important biases. One of the situational biases is the presence of *demand characteristics*, the sum total of cues that a participant uses to discover the "true purpose" of the research (Orne, 1959). The magical phrase "this is an experiment," legitimizes almost any request, from the mindless turning of pegs in a board (Festinger and Carlsmith, 1959), through providing what were believed to be painful electric shocks to a hapless victim (Milgram, 1963) to being asked how much one likes the feel of a sex partner's "sweat on my body" after having previously responded to a series of true-false questions about death (Goldenberg, Pyszczynski, McCoy, Greenberg and Solomon, 1999). In "research" apparently, anything goes, regardless of how dull, frightening, or intensely personal it might be in normal everyday life. And for their part, the problem-solving research subjects use whatever information is available to try to "understand" the interviewer's objectives and help achieve them.

Unless, of course, helping the researcher conflicts with maintaining or enhancing one's own self-esteem. This particular problem begins with what Rosenberg (1965) called *evaluation apprehension:* concern about the impression one is making with a researcher. This concern is so pervasive that it has almost attained the status of a ritual. When introduced as "a psychologist," one can see the micromomentary expression – "Oh, my God! He's *analyzing* me!" – on the other person's face. One almost feels the need to put the person at ease either by pointing out that "No, I'm not *that* kind of psychologist," or by making the standard joke, "Yes, I *can* read your mind and you should be ashamed!" Having in one way or another acknowledged the person's unease, you can then continue the conversation on a much more routine basis. When the interchange occurs in the structured setting that typifies most studies of human behaviour, the research participant's concern is likely to be greater than it would be in the context of everyday social exchange. And the researcher does not need to be a psychologist for evaluation apprehension to occur: A business professor (or even graduate student) with any extensive functional expertise will likely know more about his or her specialty than does the entrepreneur being interviewed. More importantly, the researcher has made the contact, structured the setting, constructed questions in advance, and (presumably) considered what the "right" answers might be. To borrow a term from the venture capital literature, there is "information asymmetry" between scholar and research participant.

How does a research participant behave when placed at this sort of disadvantage? He or she emphasizes the positive, minimizes the negative, and omits any details that would complicate the picture, thus falling into a *social desirability* response set (Crowne and Marlowe, 1964). The interviewee takes credit for success and deflects responsibility for failure, a frequent form of self-serving attributional bias (Bradley, 1978). Or falls prey to the "hindsight bias" (Fischhoff, 1975), evaluating the likelihood of choices on the basis of their known effects, regardless of whether those effects could have been anticipated at the time the original choice was made. If the research subject is led to feel inadequate in some area, he or she may attempt what Wicklund and Gollwitzer (1982) have called "symbolic self-completion," the tendency to increase one's self-esteem through associations with valued entities and people. It is important to note that none of these biases is the result of *deliberation* on the part of the research participant. On the contrary, most are so non-conscious that the participant would be legitimately offended if the response sets, errors and biases were pointed out.

Nearly all of these complicating factors were originally identified by social psychologists (demand characteristics being the notable exception). For this reason, social psychologists have developed strong disciplinary preferences about which sorts of research techniques are least susceptible to the many potential complications. We prefer experiments to non-experimental methods, because the former permit random assignment of participants to conditions, thereby virtually eliminating subject-based response biases. Whether the method is experimental or non-experimental, we prefer to have the data collected by assistants who are unaware of the specific hypotheses of the research. We prefer closed-ended questions, designed using scales and adverbs with known psychometric properties, to open-ended questions that by their very nature are more likely to facilitate the appearance of unwanted biases. If we must resort to open-ended questions, we prefer to have them coded according to clear theoretical principles specified in advance, and to have the coding done by people who do not know the predictions to which those theoretical principles would lead. Taken together, these methodological preferences lead social psychologists to be highly skeptical of the results, for example, of a series of "in-depth interviews" conducted over time with a few haphazardly selected successful entrepreneurs by a researcher who has some preconceived opinion about what the data might, or might not, show. To no small degree, social psychology's methodological preferences also influence my choice of what content to include in the remainder of the present chapter.

SOCIAL COGNITION

Social cognition has been defined as "thinking about people" (Fiske, 1995, p. 151). This definition suggests that *social* cognition can be distinguished from abstract conceptual reasoning, problem solving, or thinking about inanimate objects, all of which are surely cognitive processes, but none of which necessarily involves people as a critical part of the content. Thus, for example, an entrepreneur's memory of an encounter with a venture capitalist would be a topic for social cognition, whereas the entrepreneur's memory for the factors that affect first-year cash flow would not be. Social *cognition* is also described as a "cold" process, distinguished from internal processes that are "hot" – such as emotion and motivation – regardless of whether the content relates to people. So an entrepreneur's beliefs about the industry preferences of a venture capital firm would be a topic for social cognition, but the entrepreneur's disappointment at learning of this preference during a meeting in which a plan was rejected would not be.

In many respects, processes of social cognition are similar to those of *non*social cognition. Both involve cognitive categorization (Bruner, 1957), internal representations of the external world (see Carlston and Smith, 1996) such as prototypes and schemata, and what Fiske (1995) calls "unabashed mentalism" (p. 154). This latter focus on psychological processes that are not directly observable is a return to some of psychology's early roots in the study of sensation and mental states (see, for example, the "structuralism" of Edward Titchener, or the extensive theorizing of William James, both admirably described by Hilgard, 1987). Now, in the midst of "the cognitive revolution," it is difficult to believe that the prevailing ideology in psychological science was, for years, guided by Skinner's version of behaviourism (e.g., 1938) that denied the importance, if not the existence, of the mental.

Biases in Social Cognition

The processes of social cognition that have received the most attention within entrepreneurship are the cognitive biases and heuristics, and the principles of attribution. Cognitive heuristics were first identified by Kahneman and Tversky (1973) in a more general discussion of why people are poor intuitive statisticians. People, as opposed to statisticians (who happen to be thinking like statisticians rather than like people), have a proclivity to make judgments on the basis of particular individual cases rather than on the basis of base rate probabilities, even though those probabilities might be stated explicitly. For example, in one of Kahneman and Tversky's best-known examples, people were asked to judge the likelihood that a particular individual was either a lawyer or an engineer. Half of the research participants received a description of a gathering said to contain 30% lawyers, and 70% engineers, the other half received a description that claimed there were 70% lawyers and only 30% engineers. Then both sets of participants were given a series of brief descriptions, such as "Dick is a 30-year-old man. He is married with children. A man of high ability and high motivation, he promises to be quite successful in his field" (p. 242). After each description, the participants were asked to estimate the likelihood that the target person was either a lawyer or an engineer. Obviously, the "correct" guess, regardless of the description, is either 30% or 70%, depending on the condition or the question. The results showed why "cognitive heuristics" are often considered in the domain of *social* cognition: With no individuating information, the answers followed the base rates; when there was individuating information, however, the judgments differed significantly from the appropriate base rate.

In some ways, it is easy to suggest a very social explanation for studies involving failures of base rates. Assume for the moment that one asks, as social psychologists do, "What does the research participant think his or her task really is?". A research participant, concerned about what the researcher might think of his or her performance, would scour the demand characteristics of the study for the answer, assuming all the while that the answer sought could not *possibly* be mere repetition of the percentage value just mentioned. "This is really a test of my interpersonal perception ability ..." Participants who had this view would attend to every detail of the description, and would respond on the basis of whatever personal cognitive structures were activated. So, for example, a person who believes (outside the laboratory) in a stereotyped view of engineers as computer-geeks who have no social life would use that stereotype as justification for the assumption that, because Dick is married, he *must* be a lawyer. In this way, what began as an exercise in applied cognition concludes as a judgment adversely affected by a social stereotype.

Two other failures of the intuitive statistician may have played a part in the findings of a number of recent studies in entrepreneurship. These particular cognitive biases are the *availability heuristic* (Kahneman and Tversky, 1973) and the idea of *illusory correlation* (Chapman, 1967). As we have seen, people make mistakes in estimating relative frequency even when they have all of the information needed for the judgment. When there is uncertainty about the "truth," estimates of relative frequency are likely to be based on the particular cases that can easily be recalled, ones that are "available" without a lot of detailed searching. Though availability affects thought in a wide variety of domains, its reliability in the entrepreneurship domain has turned it into a classroom exercise. Ask students in any undergraduate or MBA entrepreneurship course to write down the name of "the first entrepreneur who comes to your mind." There will be lots of "Bill Gates," some "Richard Branson," some "Steve Jobs," and perhaps some "Ted Turner." What there will *not* be, is a different person for every student in the class. This kind of demonstration of availability assumes greater importance when one realizes the number of people who – in order to decide whether they personally have "what it takes" – adopt one of these highly available targets as their standard of comparison.

Just as surely as availability compromises the selection of cases for review, illusory correlation can compromise the inferences made from those cases. Especially when (a) a data pattern is incomplete, and (b) a perceiver brings his or her prior theories to the examination of that data pattern, the perceiver is likely to "find" an association that does not actually exist. Theory-confirming examples are noted, theory-disconfirming features of the situation are ignored.

For example, a venture capitalist might say "we've always had excellent success when we've gone with the management and the idea, instead of relying exclusively on the numbers." Such an assertion could, in fact, be true. On the other hand, the statement ignores two blunt facts of the venture capital business. The first of these is that entrepreneurs whose business plans do not contain the right numbers will rarely, if ever, get to the point of an interview with a venture capital partner, so the sample of firms the partner sees is necessarily limited. The second fact, to put it mildly, is that some VC-backed firms fail to become roaring successes. It is within the realm of possibility that the particular venture capitalist may be associated with a firm that has never lost money on one of those good business ideas proposed by an excellent management team. On the other hand, to learn from the prior discussion of base rates, it is more likely that the venture investor is just not remembering the failures, or the good ideas and management teams that were rejected. From the combination of availability and illusory correlation, the venture capitalist has become *overconfident*.

Support for this speculation comes from recent research by Zacharakis and Shepherd (2001). These investigators asked venture capitalists to make two judgments – estimated likelihood of venture success, and personal confidence in this likelihood estimate – for each of 50 brief investment cases. The cases had been created with the assistance of venture capitalists not involved in the study, and all identifying information (entrepreneur identity, industry, even financial cues) had been purged from the cases. What remained as cues in the case differed across three experimental conditions. In the "base cognitive cues" condition, cases contained information about market familiarity, leadership experience, level of proprietary protection, market size, and market growth. In the "additional cognitive cues" condition the base cues were supplemented by information concerning start-up team track record, and the number and strength of direct competitors. Finally, in a "task cues" condition, the material from the other two conditions was replaced by four statistically-derived index variables previously discovered (by Roure and Keeley, 1990).

Differences among the three conditions were used to test several of Zacharakis and Shepherd's hypotheses, but for our purposes, it is more important to describe the overall outcome. Of the 50 cases presented to each venture capitalist, 25 had been based on actual funded ventures that, at the time of the research, had a known outcome. The "successful" venture with the smallest return on investment (ROI) had achieved a 31% ROI, the "failed" venture with the highest ROI had achieved a 6% ROI. The existence of these very clear cases allowed the investigators to compare the VC predictions to the actual outcomes, thus establishing the accuracy of the predictions (percentage of correct predictions out of 25). Now, in a perfect world, a venture capitalist's confidence in his or her predictions ought to correlate perfectly with accuracy. After all, if your predictions are consistently faulty, you ought not be very confident in your ability. Not surprisingly, however, across the three treatment conditions, some 96% of the VCs were *over*confident (percentage confidence exceeding percentage accuracy), with 29 VCs having at least 60% confidence in their judgments, regardless of their level of accuracy. Moreover, there were no differences in overconfidence based on years of experience in the business – VCs with years of experience were just as overconfident as VCs new to the business. The availability heuristic, and perhaps also illusory correlation, appear to be alive and well in the venture investor community.

It is important to note that similar findings of overconfidence have also been obtained in studies of entrepreneurs by Busenitz and Barney (1997), and Simon, Houghton, and Aquino (1999). The first of these is especially interesting from our perspective, primarily because of a metatheoretical assumption to which we shall return in a moment. Busenitz and Barney selected their entrepreneur sample from the records of a state comptroller's office, limiting the search to seven SIC codes that included the manufacturing of plastics, electronics, and instruments, on the premise that these industries would represent a higher percentage of new firms. The managers were selected, with participation by their publicly-traded parent companies, from five SIC codes, three of which were the same as those in the entrepreneur sample (62% of entrepreneurs, and 86% of managers came from these three industries). Once the data had been collected, the entrepreneur sample was further restricted to those who had (a) founded the firm, and (b) done so within the past two years (or were planning another start-up). Managers had to have responsibility for at least two functional areas.

To assess overconfidence, all respondents were asked to answer a series of five questions used by Fischhoff and his associates (Fischhoff, Slovic and Lichtenstein, 1977; Lichtenstein and Fischhoff, 1977). Each item is a two-choice question about what sorts of diseases and accidents produce the most fatalities. In addition to making the choice, respondents use a separate scale to indicate their confidence in the judgment. This scale ran from 50% (in a two-choice setting, this is clearly the value for "just guessing"), to 100%. Scores were transformed so that confidence could be compared to a "perfect calibration" line like that used by Zacharakis and Shepherd (2001). The results were as expected: Not only were entrepreneurs more highly overconfident than managers, the level of overconfidence was able to separate the two groups quite reliably (when some standard control variables were not). Comparable results were also obtained for the representativeness heuristic, with entrepreneurs falling into its trap more frequently than did managers.

Taking Busenitz and Barney's (1997) results a step further, and combining overconfidence with two other biases – the illusion of control and the belief in the law of small numbers – Simon, Houghton and Aquino (1999) tested the influences of cognitive biases on risk perception. These researchers asked MBA students to evaluate the well-known "contact lenses for chickens" case (Clarke, 1988). The "revolutionary" contact lenses are said to reduce the tendency to fight, and the reduction in injuries among confined chickens has substantial economic implications. To increase the risk involved, Simon, Houghton and Aquino doubled the original product costs and made the claimed market demand less predictable. Respondents completed measures of three cognitive biases, estimated the risk of the venture, stated their willingness to start, and answered a number of control variables.

The results showed that as the perception of risk associated with beginning the venture decreased, likelihood of proceeding increased. This perception of venture risk, in turn, was decreased (a) as the illusion of control (being able to control events that others might not be able to control) increased, and (b) by a belief in small numbers (e.g., the market can be assessed adequately by asking one or two people). Interestingly, the overconfidence bias did not affect perceived risk, nor did it affect willingness to begin the venture. The Simon,

Houghton and Aquino (1999) study, like many of its predecessors, measured overconfidence *outside* the domain of entrepreneurship. The authors argued that this should not have been a problem,

"because people are overconfident across domains, ... suggesting the items do not need to reflect the case. Furthermore, entrepreneurs' decisions stem from a wide range of non-business and untraditional information, indicating that it is appropriate to use diverse items ..." (p. 126).

Emotion and Cognition

As it happens, however, there may be a much more *social* and much less purely cognitive explanation. A recent review by Lowenstein, Weber, Hsee and Welch (2001) argues that risk, and the perception of risk, involve hefty doses of *emotional* content. Lowenstein et al. point out that the study of judgments under risk grew out of economics and cognitive psychology, two disciplines that share an assumption that human decision-making is essentially rational. Rational decision-making may sometimes be in error, but it is not presumed to be affected adversely by feelings, emotions, or motivation. (This, of course, is not a widespread assumption in social psychology, despite the popularity of research in social cognition.) Drawing on literature from social psychology (e.g., Clore, Schwarz and Conway, 1994; Zajonc, 1980, 1998) and neuroscience (LeDoux, 1996) the authors present a "risk as feelings" model of decision-making. In this model, the emotions generated either by the fact of having to make the decision or by the nature of the consequences, are given the same weight as the more cognitive features of the judgment task.

One statement from Lowenstein et al. (2001) that is especially relevant in the present context is the fact that the factors influencing people's emotional reactions to risks "include the vividness with which consequences can be imagined, *personal exposure* to or experience with outcomes, and *past history* of conditioning. Cognitive assessments of risk, on the other hand, tend to depend more on objective features of the risky situation, such as probabilities of outcomes and assessments of outcome severity" (p. 271, emphasis added). This view has two implications for entrepreneurship research. First, on the methodological side, it might not be possible to obtain accurate estimates of overconfidence among entrepreneurs by asking the traditional questions that have nothing whatsoever to do with starting a new venture. Second, a related point is that because of entrepreneurs' prior experience, the possibility of failure might simply carry less emotional content than it would for managers. Especially in the case of "serial entrepreneurs" (Westhead and Wright, 1998), there might be very little real fear associated with the possibility of failure. One is reminded here of the often heard entrepreneurial claim "I've been poor, I've been rich, I'm poor again, but I'll be rich again." Such a claim might be nothing more than an elaborate form of self-deception, but it might also be an accurate expression of the very "routine-ness" of entrepreneurial behaviour. In the language of another recent study, an entrepreneur's beliefs concerning future success may be "comparative optimism," rather than "unrealistic optimism" (Radcliffe and Klein, 2002).

Person and Situation

As noted above, an interesting feature of Busenitz and Barney's (1997) study is one of its implicit metatheoretical assumptions. The authors begin their paper by describing the decision environments facing entrepreneurs, and managers in large corporations (the two groups of people subsequently compared). Managers exist in a corporate environment where historical data provide a backdrop for decisions, the cost of gathering additional information is relatively low, and the time frame for most decisions is relatively forgiving. By contrast, entrepreneurs have limited "people resources," essentially no hard historical data, cannot obtain (or afford) additional information, and must decide quickly. Appropriate research is cited to support both of these quite reasonable characterizations. Then they go on to say "Thus, we argue that those who are more susceptible to the use of biases and heuristics in decision-making are the very ones who are most likely to become entrepreneurs. The more cautious decision-makers will tend to be attracted to larger organizations where more methodical information tends to be more readily available. Entrepreneurial activities simply become too overwhelming to those who are less willing to generalize through the use of heuristics and biases" (p. 14).

Without knowing that they have done so, Busenitz and Barney (1997) have just taken a position on one of the long-standing debates within social and personality psychology (Bowers, 1973; Funder and Colvin, 1991; Mischel, 1968; Pervin, 1989). In the early years of research on individual differences in behaviour, personality theorists asserted that people could be characterized by their location on a variety of relatively enduring "traits" (see, for example, Allport, 1937). Identify the primary traits that describe a person, and you have gone a long way toward being able to predict what the individual will do in a novel setting.

Unfortunately, research examining the correlation between assessed personality traits and behaviour in different settings began to find that traits were not very helpful in predicting "cross-situational consistency" in behaviour (see reviews by Bem and Allen, 1974; Bem and Funder, 1978; Mischel and Peake, 1982). The failure of the "pure personality" approach led one highly influential writer to suggest that the study of personality be supplanted by the study of variations in situations (Mischel, 1968). The response was immediate, and highly critical (see Bowers, 1973). Indeed, in the late 1970s the Society for Personality and Social Psychology (Division 8 of the American Psychological Association) nearly split into two armed camps – the "personological" personality researchers versus the "situational" social psychologists. The Society managed to avoid splintering apart, and its journal is still called the *Personality and Social Psychology Bulletin*. As for the conceptual controversy, most social and personality psychologists subscribe to some version of *interactionism*, a view that behaviour in a given setting is a function of *both* the more personological individual differences and the more social features of the situation.

Returning to entrepreneurship, the interactionist position has been the basis for an argument against the existence of an "entrepreneurial personality" whose behaviour is presumed to be constant regardless of the situation (Shaver, 1995). What is a bit surprising is that the myth of the entrepreneurial personality survived as long as it did. After all, the leadership literature – the topical focus of which is at least a first cousin to entrepreneurship – has subscribed to an interactionist view for over 30 years (at least since Fiedler, 1964).

ATTRIBUTION PROCESSES

The person and the situation can both be seen in the social psychological literature on *attribution*, the cognitive processes by which people explain their own behaviour, the actions of others, and events in the world. Indeed, in the work that provided the foundation for attribution theory, Heider (1958) explicitly argued that behaviour was a function of both person and external environment:

$$B = f(P, E).$$

For any particular behaviour or event the perceiver's task is to determine the relative contributions of person and environment to the production of the effects observed. People bother to explain causes because doing so presumably helps them predict behaviour and events in the future. If we can identify particular "dispositional properties" – enduring characteristics – of either persons or the environment, we are better able to predict what might happen in a novel setting. The possibility of distinguishing situational effects from personal effects has recently increased with the use in social psychology of statistical techniques for multi-level modeling (see, for example, Nezlek, 2001).

In Heider's view the "naïve" (really meaning "non-scientific") perceiver begins with an observed action or event, and then reasons backward to decide why the action or event occurred. For a person to have accomplished an action, the person's internal ability must typically have had to exceed the difficulty of the task (in Heider's terms, the person "can" perform the action). The qualifier, "typically," is there because opportunity or luck might have made the success possible this time, though it would not be possible in the future. Working still farther backward in the explanatory chain, being able to complete a task does not mean that the task will necessarily be accomplished. In addition to "can," there must be an intention to complete the task, and effort must be expended in order to reach the goal contained within the intention. Thus we believe that a successful performance will most often have involved some intention on the part of the actor, effort expended in the service of that intention, and a level of ability sufficient to overcome the natural difficulty of the task. When an action has moral overtones, we will hold the person "responsible" for the outcome only to the extent of the person's contribution to the occurrence.

Attributions of Causality

Because Heider's (1958) theory included both the determination of causality and the moral judgment of responsibility, its conceptual and empirical descendants have diverged into two separate literatures. Research on the attribution of causality is normally traced to Kelley's formalization of some of Heider's observations (Kelley, 1967, 1973), whereas research on the attribution of responsibility is usually traced to Jones's specification of how perceivers might determine *why* an action was undertaken (Jones and Davis, 1965; Jones and McGillis, 1976). Relationships among the three theories have been outlined in detail by Shaver (1975), who has also developed a comprehensive theory of the attribution of blame (Shaver, 1985).

Because entrepreneurship deals with positive outcomes (or, even in the case of venture failure, *unintended* negative ones), questions of responsibility are less frequent than questions of causality. So I shall concentrate on Kelley's (1967, 1973) theory and research that follows in its tradition. Fundamentally, the theory argues that people have two different ways of coming to understand the causes of events. In one of these, multiple observations of the behaviour or event are possible – starting a second or third company, conducting successive waves of market research, the daily (or more frequent) fluctuations in the financial markets. When multiple observations are possible, people rely on a principle of *covariation*. If there are no repeated occurrences, then people rely on the second way of deriving attributions, *schemata*.

First, consider covariation. Specifically, an event or behaviour is attributed to presumed causes that vary with the occurrence of the presumed effect, rather than to presumed causes that remain constant over the multiple observations. Kelley's theory lists three attributional dimensions: Entities (targets for the attribution), time/modality (the circumstances under which the multiple observations take place), and persons (the number of observers who share the perceiver's view of the situation. Whether the behaviour or event will be attributed to the target individual with it depends on the status of three attributional criteria, one associated with each dimension. If the behaviour is "distinctive" (not all entities perform it), if it is "consistent" over circumstances, and if there is consensus among the persons who view the behaviour, then the action will most likely be attributed to the person. Alternatively, if the behaviour is not at all distinctive (everyone does it), and there is consistency and consensus, then the action will be attributed to forces within the situation.

Turning to schemata (or "schemas" in some places), Kelley's use of the term is essentially the same as the original (Bartlett, 1932): A schema is a cognitive structure that serves as a template for organizing incoming information. How the cause is identified for a one-time occurrence depends on the features of the information. If there is only one cause of an event, the attribution problem is trivial. When there are multiple sufficient causes, the problem is much more difficult. Any one of the multiple sufficient causes might have produced the effect, or collections of them might have combined to do so (how this happens has been a matter of some debate). Because of these multiple possibilities, the *discounting* principle comes into play: The more plausible potential causes there are, the less certain the perceiver can be that any selected one of them is *the* cause. Did the new venture fail because there was insufficient cash? Because the development time was much longer than expected? Because the market evaporated? Because general economic conditions became unfavorable? Because the venture investor wielded too much (or not enough) weight in his or her position on the Board? Because the firm's management just was not up to the task? And the list goes on.

Causal Dimensions

Rather than attempt to identify specific causal patterns for every sort of event or action, attribution researchers have concentrated on dimensions, derived from Heider (1958), that simplify the judgment required. Specifically, potential causes of events and behaviours can be separated on a dimension known as "locus of causality" into those that are *internal* to the person, and those that are *external*. Within these categories, potential causes can be separated along a dimension known as "stability" into those that are *stable* and those that are *variable*. The result is a four-fold table whose cells are the familiar ability (internal, stable), effort (internal, variable), task difficulty (external, stable), and luck (external, variable). It is important here to note that locus of causality, as used in the attribution literature, is *not* the same as "locus of control" (Rotter, 1966). The former characterizes events and behaviours, whether or not any individual person might be able to exert effective control over them. In contrast, the latter is regarded as an individual-differences variable that represents the extent to which people believe that they are able to produce outcomes – in social, political, and personal domains among others – that they seek. Although locus of control has been popular in the entrepreneurship literature, very few studies (such as Mueller and Thomas, 2001) have made certain that their versions of the scale were *uni*dimensional (see Shaver and Scott, 1991, for a detailed critique). Because the social psychological approach concentrates more on situational variables than on individual difference variables, we shall not discuss locus of control further.

Returning to locus of causality, other attributional dimensions have been suggested, such as "globality" – the number of different domains across which a judgment is made (Abramson, Seligman, and Teasdale, 1978) – and "controllability" (Anderson, 1991). But these two are not likely to contribute added value to our understanding of entrepreneurship. In theoretical terms, new venture creation is an intentional act that involves repeated attempts to exercise control over the process in a specific domain, in order to achieve the desired outcome. This is exactly the sort of activity that Malle (1999) has argued ought to be described as "reason-based," not "cause-based." Whether true control *can* be exerted is not the issue. Indeed, it is entirely possible that for some activities, the environment's contribution to success may exceed that of the person. But this particular empirical fact would not change the conceptual point: In principle, the act of business creation is *a* domain-specific intentional action (see Bird, 1988; Krueger, Reilly and Carsrud, 2000) that requires control.

Just as the locus of causality and stability dimensions can be used to characterize an event that has already happened, they can also be used to help understand the reasons an entrepreneur might offer for going into business in the first place. The first entrepreneurship study to do an attributional classification of reasons to go into business was a study conducted among clients of a small business development center (SBDC) by Gatewood, Shaver and Gartner (1995). At their first meeting with the SBDC staff, clients were asked why they wanted to go into business. Although this question was open-ended, and could have produced any number of responses, the modal number was only two. The four most frequently cited answers were (a) identified market need, (b) desire for autonomy and independence, (c) desire to make more money, and (d) desire to use existing knowledge and experience. All answers were first parsed into separate elements, then categorized as either external or internal, then as either stable or variable (details of attributional coding are described for another data set by Shaver, Gartner, Crosby, Bakalarova and Gatewood (2001).

A year after the initial testing, 85 of the original 142 clients estimated the amount of time they had put into each of 29 organizing activities during the intervening year. These activities included gathering market information, estimating potential profits, completing the groundwork, developing the structure of the company, and actually getting into business. Results showed that entrepreneurs whose reasons were internal and stable had spent more time on structuring their companies than had people with other attribution patterns. When only those respondents who had made a sale were considered, there was a sex difference in the attributional patterns. Women who had made sales had, a year earlier, provided primarily internal reasons for wanting to start. By contrast, men who had made sales had, a year earlier, provided primarily external reasons for wanting to start. So the "why" of entering seems to make a difference in the "what" is later accomplished, though the particular reasons differ across sex.

Within social (and indeed, clinical) psychology, the locus of causality dimension has known implications for self-esteem. The well-known "self-serving bias" (Bradley, 1978) in attribution is the tendency to attribute one's successes internally, and one's failures externally. By contrast, the alternative, attributing one's successes to luck, and one's failures internally (if this is across many domains) is a recipe for depression (Abramson, Seligman and Teasdale, 1978). Consequently, people engage in "self-handicapping," by attempting to create conditions for behaviour that will favor externalization of failure and internalization of success (Berglas and Jones, 1978). After a failure, people offer excuses designed to absolve them of responsibility, if not of causal participation (Snyder and Higgins, 1988). Even the possibility of being held accountable is threatening, leading to *defensive* attributions of responsibility (Shaver, 1970). Given all of this evidence, we should not be surprised when an entrepreneur chooses to explain venture failure by pointing to uncontrollable external conditions, whereas the venture capitalist who has lost a great deal of money places the cause of failure squarely on the shoulders of the entrepreneur. Self-serving biases have been noted in both the management literature (Clapham and Schwenk, 1991) and in the entrpreneurship literature (Baron, 1998).

If the locus of causality dimension is implicated in feelings of self-worth, the stability dimension is implicated in the expectations for future success (Anderson, Krull and Weiner, 1996). Specifically, one can hope to change the course of the future only if it can be considered malleable. In entrepreneurship the importance of the stability dimension has recently been shown by Gartner, Shaver and Aggarwal (2001). As part of a large-scale survey of small business firms conducted by the Los Angeles *Times*, these investigators asked business owner/managers to identify what they considered to be the opportunities and problems facing their enterprises. In the overall sample of 1,686, 1,300 people answered the question about problems and 1,024 answered the question about opportunities (a total of 806 provided answers to both questions). The first opportunity mentioned, and the first problem mentioned, were each coded according to the two dimensions – locus of causality and stability. Thus for anyone who answered both questions, there are 16 possible attribution patterns (the combination of four codes for opportunities with four codes for problems). More than half of the people who answered both items gave descriptions of opportunities that were external and *stable*. Similarly, more than half who answered both items gave descriptions of problems that were external, but *variable*. There were, however, only 261 people whose answers fit the modal response to both questions (external stable opportunities plus external variable problems). This *enterprise-serving* pattern makes it possible for the owner/manger to believe that (a) opportunities exist for the taking, now and in the future, and (b) problems are external, but solvable. The past growth obtained, and the future growth expected, were higher for the 261 people with the enterprise-serving pattern than they were for people with any of the 15 other patterns, or for people who had not mentioned both an opportunity and a problem. This is a good demonstration, in the entrepreneurship domain, of the traditional attribution theory view that changes in stability are implicated in expectancies for future success.

ATTITUDES

The concept of an attitude has been a central element of social psychology throughout most of the discipline's history. The first volume with the title, *Handbook of Social Psychology*, was published in 1935 (Murchison, 1935), but few of its topics have been retained in subsequent versions. The exception is a chapter on attitudes. The next *Handbook of Social Psychology*, published in 1954, did not call itself the second edition (Lindzey, 1954), and was to contain two chapters on attitudes (one omitted at the last minute). Subsequent editions have been numbered from the Lindzey version: The 2nd edition (Lindzey and Aronson, 1968–69), the 3rd edition (Lindzey and Aronson, 1985), and most recently the 4th edition (Gilbert, Fiske and Lindzey, 1998). The concept of an attitude assumes a prominent place in every edition. Beyond its content, attitude research has also contributed to the development of methodology in social psychology. Thurstone scaling (Thurstone and Chave, 1929), Likert scaling (Likert, 1932), and semantic differential scaling (Osgood, Suci and Tannenbaum, 1957) were all developed as attitude measurement techniques. In the 1960s the controversy between cognitive dissonance (Festinger, 1957) and incentive theory views of attitude change gave us the notion of evaluation apprehension (Rosenberg, 1965), the technique of "balanced replication" (Linder, Cooper and Jones, 1967), and one of the very first physiological measures of a social psychological process (Brehm, Back and Bogdanoff, 1964).

Components of Attitudes

It is easy to see why attitude research and theory have been at the core of social psychology. Traditional definitions of the concept divide an attitude into three components – a cognitive component, an affective component, and a behavioural component. The first represents one's beliefs about the attitude object, and many of these are organized according to processes of social cognition. The second component is evaluative, involving both judgments of the attitude target and one's own reasons for holding the attitude (what Katz and Stotland, 1959, described as the "functions" of an attitude). The third component is often regarded as a general tendency to respond in a favorable or unfavorable manner toward the attitude object, represented more precisely by the notion of "behavioural intentions" (Fishbein and Ajzen, 1975). Including cognition, emotion, and behaviour within a single concept makes that concept sound very much like the stated domain of the field: The socially meaningful actions of particular individuals. In entrepreneurship, this tripartite representation of attitudes is the basis for the *Entrepreneurial Attitude Orientation* (EAO) scale developed by Robinson, Stimpson, Huefner and Hunt (1991). These investigators included dimensions such as innovation and achievement, but were particularly careful to tap behaviours as well as beliefs and values, thus covering all three of the elements of an attitude.

Cognitive Consistency

Recent treatments of attitudes have tended to concentrate on the evaluative or emotional elements (Tesser and Martin, 1996), particularly when the topic is limited to attitude change (Petty, 1995). This, too, is not surprising. After all, people rarely change their beliefs and attitudes unless there is some reason to do so. A long-standing tradition in attitude theory is that a primary motivation for change comes from an inconsistency between one's expressed attitudes and one's actual behaviour. "If I believe that, why am I doing *this*?" The search for consistency between thought and action is best represented by *cognitive dissonance theory* (Cooper and Fazio, 1984; Festinger, 1957).

Typical of the cognitive consistency theories of attitude change, dissonance theory partitions the mental landscape into cognitive elements and the relations among them. Three such relationships are possible: Consonance (agreement in content), dissonance (one implies the opposite of another), and irrelevance. The elements can represent emotions, beliefs, or behaviours, though the latter two are by far the most frequently studied. According to the more recent version of the theory (Cooper and Fazio, 1984), dissonance will occur if (a) one's actions produce consequences one considers negative, (b) one cannot avoid personal responsibility for the consequences, and (c) the resulting general motivational arousal cannot be attributed to some external source. Because it is easier to change an attitude than to change a behaviour (indeed, a person's past public actions cannot be changed), the usual result of dissonance is attitude change.

Cognitive dissonance, and its first cousin, *escalation of commitment* (Brockner, 1992; Staw, 1981) would appear to have widespread applications in entrepreneurship. What is "single-mindedness of purpose" in the organizing phase of a new venture may become "unwillingness to listen to constructive advice" should trouble develop. Venture investors may continue to put cash into an enterprise that is well on its way to becoming one of the "living dead." Members of advisory boards sometimes take strong public positions that effectively prevent them from modifying their views in response to changing circumstances. Indeed, a recent study by Blanton, Pelham, DeHart and Carvallo (2001) suggests a dissonance-based explanation of the overconfidence bias.

But those who would look for dissonance as an explanation for venture continuance need to be careful in their search. A first caution concerns the target chosen for study. Dissonance exists within the mind (based on the behaviour) of one person. So, for example, to study dissonance as an explanation for continuation despite clear indications that the venture should be scrapped, all the data must be collected from the original *founder*. A manager will not do as a substitute, because dissonance is person-based, not firm-based. A second caution is based on the Cooper and Fazio (1984) revision of the theory. Merely having a bad outcome is not enough. Only if the bad outcome should have been anticipated, and there are few alternatives to accepting personal responsibility will dissonance be the result.

Planned Behaviour

Although the components of attitudes and the motivation involved in attitude change have parallels in the entrepreneurship literature, by far the most influential attitude theory has been the theory of reasoned action (Fishbein and Ajzen, 1975) and its successor, the *theory of planned behaviour* (Ajzen, 1991, 1996).

The theory of planned behaviour (TPB) begins with an assumption quite congenial to entrepreneurship, namely that most important behaviour is volitional. Such volitional behaviour is presumed to be the product of intentions, which are themselves a function of the person's overall attitude and the "subjective norms" that represent social pressure either to perform or not perform the action. Regardless of attitude and subjective norms, intentions will be exercised only if the individual believes that he or she has perceived behavioural control.

In formal terms, the TPB holds that

$$B \cong I\alpha[\omega_1 A_b + \omega_2 SN + \omega_3 PBC]$$

where B is the behaviour, I is the behavioural intention, A_b is the attitude toward the action, SN is the set of social norms, and PBC is the perceived behavioural control. The three weights are empirically determined.

Although the model is simple in principle, testing its implications requires substantial detail. The attitude toward the behaviour or object (A_b) is often considered the sum of beliefs about the object, with each belief multiplied by its perceived goodness. So the question, "what is your attitude toward (some new product)?" really reduces to a series of smaller questions about its design, the likelihood that it will meet its market need, whether it can be produced with sufficient margins to make a profit, and so forth. Similarly, the social norms component (SN) is also a sum, this time of the judgments of any person whose opinion matters, with each judgment multiplied by the motivation to comply with the opinion. Finally, even the perceived control component (PBC) is subdivided into the constraints as they exist, and as they are perceived.

As Ajzen (1996) notes, there is a sizable volume of research in social psychology that supports the overall predictions of the TPB. But perhaps for understandable reasons, the theory's influence in entrepreneurship has been more apparent in theorizing than in research. Social psychologists who are interested in testing the TPB often do not have a content objective beyond understanding the nature of attitude structure. So it is in their interest to identify all of the relevant beliefs about an attitude object and obtain evaluative ratings of each; to identify all the people who might contribute normative pressure and estimate the likelihood of compliance; to create relatively precise measures of perceived control in experimental settings where the range of possible values for actual control is either limited or nonexistent. For entrepreneurship scholars, however, the situation is quite different. If the attitude to be measured is one concerning a new process or product – or worse, a new industry – some of the "beliefs" are not likely to be known. The subjective norms involved are seldom those imposed by individual people, rather they are estimated by proxy from categories of targets (e.g., customers, suppliers, or the financial community). And the number of factors that can (and often do) limit the entrepreneur's freedom of action is quite large. Nevertheless, the TPB has made its way into entrepreneurship, primarily in the work of Krueger and his associates (Krueger, 2000, Krueger and Brazeal, 1994; Krueger, Reilly and Carsrud, 2000). Much of this work has taken the position that perceived behavioural control is best estimated with measures of self-efficacy (Bandura, 1986), so its discussion will occur later in the chapter.

THE SELF

Who are you, and how did you get that way? This question covers more than your beliefs, biases, attributions, and attitudes. Indeed, searching a psychological data base for all "self-" compounds is a guarantee of eye strain. Part of the reason that the topic covers so much ground is that the self both "is" and "does" (a distinction originally made by William James, 1892). James considered the self-as-object (the "Me") to include the material self (physical being and possessions), the spiritual self (personality traits, verbal skills, attitudes, inner experience), and the social *selves* (the plural indicates that we have, at minimum, a slightly different social self for every category of people with whom we come in contact). In contrast, James argued that there is only one self who "does." This self-as-subject (the "I"), does the knowing, does the thinking, is the sum of our conscious processes. If all of this sounds like a version of the mind/body problem, that is because psychology's origins derive from a philosophy contrasting Hobbesian materialist identity theory with Cartesian dualism (see, for example, Churchland, 1988; Robinson, 1979). Not surprisingly, devising ways to study ongoing conscious processes has been a technical problem for scientific psychology ever since Wilhelm Wundt established what many consider the first psychological laboratory in 1879. But with modern advances in neuroscience, this problem may be getting more tractable (see, for example, Zillmann and Zillmann, 1996). Despite the increasing contact between social psychology and neuroscience, most researchers have not yet had broad access to procedures (such as magnetic resonance tomography) now used to study the conscious mind as it thinks. As a consequence, a majority of the social psychological inquiry into the self has emphasized either the contents or processes of the "self-as-does." And in entrepreneurship, there has been the most interest in what social psychology would describe as issues of self-evaluation.

Self-Evaluation

In the development of our social selves, we must often choose between accuracy and distortion. We need to know our capabilities, but we would like them to be more extensive than they are. We need to know what our core as a person might be, but we would also like people to think well of us. This conflict between accuracy and distortion can be seen in a great deal of theorizing about the self (Shaver, 1987).

One place where the tension is clear is in the case of *social comparison theory* (Festinger, 1954; Kruglanski and Mayseless, 1990, Suls and Wills, 1991). This theory has three fundamental elements. First, it holds that people have a drive to evaluate their opinions and abilities. Second, it claims that people will prefer objective standards for evaluation, when those standards are available. And finally, when there are no objective standards, people will use social comparison with others who are similar to them in ways relevant to the comparison. The original statement of the theory was not clear on the precise meaning of "evaluate." Specifically, does it mean "locate relative to others," or does it mean "place a value upon." Later work shows clearly that when people are faced with learning their "location" in a manner that might reduce their self-esteem, they will engage in "downward" social comparison, finding their location relative to people who are expected to be worse off (Wills, 1991).

At this point, social comparison theory has not made its way into entrepreneurship research. But a real opportunity exists. Consider the various organizations to which many entrepreneurs belong – local technology councils, breakfast roundtables sponsored by entrepreneurship centers, even more formal and expensive options like the Entrepreneur's Edge or The Executive Committee. Why would an entrepreneur take time away from his or her business to "attend a bunch of meetings?" Certainly part of the answer is that business networks provide sources of competitive intelligence, access to capital and suppliers, and the opportunity to get one's business known in the local community. But there may be more. If it is lonely at the top of a large organization, it is every bit as lonely at the top of a small one. Worse, if you have started at the top of the small one, you lack the years of relevant company experience that can provide some comfort to the CEO of a large corporation. Not only can entrepreneurs learn "facts" from one another about how to solve problems facing their firms, they can also get a sense of how well they are performing in their role as CEO.

There is a practical research implication of considering "networking" from the standpoint of social comparison. To return to the issue of the "overconfidence bias," suppose that a researcher attempts to collect performance expectations from all businesses within a narrow industry sector. Further suppose that the number of such businesses can be identified with confidence from local tax or unemployment records, but that for convenience the research is conducted at meetings of a local network organization for the industry sector. Finally, suppose that only 30% of the local companies belong to the organization. Then if the respondents say that their firms are in some way "better" than 70% of firms in the sector, this response could be "overconfidence bias," or it could only be an accurate reflection of their belief that the organization members perform at a higher level than the remainder of the local firms in the sector. In short, social comparison theory would urge us to be careful in the specification of potential reference groups.

Consequences of Self-Concept

Social comparison processes describe the ways in which we come to understand just how well we do. Certainly there are some objective benchmarks as well: Firm size, revenue growth, market penetration. But what exactly does it *mean* to say that one's firm has 15% of the market? Is that a lot? Is it a little? Is it enough to justify a large venture investment? The answer, of course, depends on the size of the market segment, the number of other firms in the segment, and on what their level of market share might be. In other words, there must be a kind of social comparison of the objective information. The question now is what we do with the performance information we glean. How does it enter into our self-concepts, and more particularly, how does it affect our behaviour?

Although there are several theories in social psychology about the relationship between self-maintaining processes and social behaviour, the one that has received most attention in entrepreneurship is *self-efficacy* (Bandura, 1986, 1997). Fundamentally, Bandura's theory is one of personal causation, involving "the origins of efficacy beliefs, their structure and function, the processes through which they produce diverse effects, and their modifiability" (1997, p. 10), and is presumed to operate at both the individual level and the collective level. In a nutshell, perceived self-efficacy is a set of domain-specific beliefs about whether one can produce a certain action. In that sense it can be distinguished from locus of control beliefs and expectancies that presume to summarize the relationship between action, once performed, and outcomes or consequences of that action. A person's self-efficacy increases as a result of his or her mastery experiences, modeling or "vicarious experience" (often obtained through a form of social comparison), verbal persuasion from others, and even from close monitoring of internal affective states during a performance or activity (how much does it really hurt to be a "weekend quarterback?"). The self-efficacy cues derived from all of these sources guide behaviour in the future.

In one sense, the notion of self-efficacy has an interesting status as a concept. It is at once an individual difference variable and a capability susceptible to outside influence or training. This joint status makes it quite different from more than a few related ideas. For example, the usual connotation of "individual difference variable" is something equivalent to a personality trait – a relatively enduring, cross-situationally consistent, feature of the person. True, personality traits are clearly shaped during socialization, but over a long period of years. They are not regarded (at least by the therapeutic community) as changeable in the short term without truly dramatic interventions. On the other hand, a person's beliefs can be shifted by persuasive communication, often with only minimal effort. So the idea of a set of beliefs – open to change through verbal persuasion – that nevertheless constitute an individual difference variable – on which people will be relatively normally distributed – is not always easy to translate into research practice.

Despite this obstacle, self-efficacy has found a home in entrepreneurship, largely through the work of Krueger and his associates (Krueger, 2000; Krueger and Brazeal, 1994; Krueger, Reilly and Carsrud, 2000). Specifically, Krueger has used self-efficacy in the entrepreneurial domain as a replacement for the "perceived behavioural control" that is part of the theory of planned behaviour (TPB). For example, Krueger (2000) describes self-efficacy as a personal estimate of venture feasibility, and extends the analysis to include the "collective efficacy" in an organization that might act to support or inhibit the perceived control of individual members of the team. Experiences that provide the opportunity for mastery will, of course, enhance perceived venture feasibility. In Krueger's work self-efficacy is then combined with perceived desirability of entrepreneurial action (the social norms component of TPB) and with a version of the "entrepreneurial event" outlined by Shapero (1982) to create intentions for entrepreneurial action.

CONCLUSION

The creation of a new venture is a truly social enterprise. It begins with the recognition of an opportunity (an act of social perception), continues through an organizing process that necessarily involves interaction with others, and culminates in a business that will reflect a "corporate culture" derived (intentionally or not) from its founders. For this reason, the theories and methods of social psychology would seem to be especially appropriate as ways to help understand the process. When the discipline of social psychology requires nearly 2,000 pages to capture (the size of the 4th edition of the Handbook), it is clearly impossible to bring all of social psychology to bear on the phenomenon of entrepreneurial behaviour. To do justice to the concepts involved, and to describe at least some of the resulting entrepreneurship research, this chapter has concentrated on the intrapersonal processes involved prior to the existence of an organization. To our consideration of social cognition, attribution, attitudes, and self-beliefs, many social psychologists might hope to add topics like equity, bargaining and negotiation, investments in close relationships, to name a few. At this point in the development of the discipline of entrepreneurship, social psychological theory and methods have already had a significant impact. The sheer amount of what is *not* covered here suggests that social psychology's value to entrepreneurship can only increase in the future.

REFERENCES

Abramson, L.Y., M.E.P. Seligman and J. Teasdale (1978). Learned helplessness in humans: Critique and reformulation. *Journal of Abnormal Psychology*, **87**, 49–74.

Ajzen, I. (1991). The theory of planned behaviour. *Organizational Behaviour and Human Decision Processes*, **50**, 179–211.

Ajzen, I. (1996). The social psychology of decision making. In E.T. Higgins and A.W. Kruglanski (eds.), *Social Psychology: Handbook of Basic Principles*, pp. 297–325. New York: Guilford.

Allport, G.W. (1937). *Personality: A Psychological Interpretation*. New York: Holt, Rinehart and Winston.

Anderson, C.A. (1991). How people think about causes: Examination of the typical phenomenal organization of attributions for success and failure. *Social Cognition*, **9**, 295–329.

Anderson, C.A., D.S. Krull and B. Weiner (1996). Explanations: Processes and consequences. In E.T. Higgins and A.W. Kruglanski (eds.), *Social Psychology: Handbook of Basic Principles*, pp. 271–296. New York: Guilford.

Bandura, A. (1986). *The Social Foundations of Thought and Action.* Englewood Cliffs, NJ: Prentice-Hall.

Bandura, A. (1997). *Self-efficacy.* New York: Freeman.

Baron, R.A. (1998). Cognitive factors in entrepreneurship: Why and when entrepreneurs think differently than other people. *Journal of Business Venturing,* 13, 275–294.

Bartlett, F.C. (1932). *Remembering: A Study in Experimental and Social Psychology.* Cambridge: Cambridge University Press.

Bem, D.J. and A. Allen (1974). On predicting some of the people some of the time: The search for cross-situational consistencies in behaviour. *Psychological Review,* 81, 506–520.

Bem, D.J. and D.C. Funder (1978). Predicting more of the people more of the time: Assessing the personality of situations. *Psychological Review,* 85, 485–501.

Bird, B. (1988). Implementing entrepreneurial ideas: The case for intention. *Academy of Management Review,* 13, 442–453.

Berglas, S. and E.E. Jones (1978). Drug choice as a self-handicapping strategy in response to non-contingent success. *Journal of Personality and Social Psychology,* 36, 405–417.

Blanton, H., B.W. Pelham, T. DeHart and M. Carvallo (2001). *Journal of Experimental Social Psychology,* 37, 373–385.

Bowers, K.S. (1973). Situationism in psychology: An analysis and a critique. *Psychological Review,* 80, 307–336.

Bradley, G.W. (1978). Self-serving biases in the attribution process: A reexamination of the fact or fiction question. *Journal of Personality and Social Psychology,* 36, 56–71.

Brehm, M.L., K. Back and M.D. Bogdanoff (1964). A physiological effect of cognitive dissonance under stress and deprivation. *Journal of Abnormal and Social Psychology,* 69, 303–310.

Brockner, J. (1992). The escalation of commitment to a course of action: Toward theoretical progress. *Academy of Management Review,* 17, 39–61.

Bruner, J.S. (1957). On perceptual readiness. *Psychological Review,* 64, 123–152.

Busenitz, L.W. and J.B. Barney (1997). Differences between entrepreneurs and managers in large organizations: Biases and heuristics in strategic decision making. *Journal of Business Venturing,* 12, 9–30.

Carlston, D.E. and E.R. Smith (1996). Principles of mental representation. In E.T. Higgins and A.W. Kruglanski (eds.), *Social Psychology: Handbook of Basic Principles,* pp. 184–210. New York: Guilford.

Chapman, L.J. (1967). Illusory correlation in observational report. *Journal of Verbal Learning and Verbal Behaviour,* 6, 151–155.

Churchland, P.M. (1988). *Matter and Consciousness* (rev. ed.). Cambridge, MA: MIT Press.

Clapham, S.E. and C.R. Schwenk (1991). Self-serving attributions, managerial cognition and company performance. *Strategic Management Journal,* 12, 219–229.

Clarke, C.R. (1988). *Optical Distortion.* Boston, MA: Harvard Business School Press.

Clore, G.L., N. Schwarz and M. Conway (1994). Affective causes and consequences of social information processing. In R.S. Wyer and T.K. Srull (eds.), *Handbook of Social Cognition,* Vol. 1, pp. 323–417. Hillsdale, NJ: Lawrence Erlbaum Associates.

Cooper, A.C. and C.M. Daily (1997). Entrepreneurial teams. In D.L. Sexton and R.W. Smilor (eds.), *Entrepreneurship 2000.* Chicago: Upstart.

Cooper, J. and R.H. Fazio (1984). A new look at dissonance theory. In L. Berkowitz (ed.), *Advances in Experimental Social Psychology,* Vol. 17, pp. 229–266. New York: Academic Press.

Crowne, D.P. and Marlowe, D. (1964). *The Approval Motive.* New York: Wiley.

Festinger, L. (1954). A theory of social comparison. *Human Relations,* 7, 117–140.

Festinger, L. (1957). *A Theory of Cognitive Dissonance.* Stanford, CA: Stanford University Press.

Festinger, L. and J.M. Carlsmith (1959). Cognitive consequences of forced compliance. *Journal of Abnormal and Social Psychology,* 58, 203–210.

Fiedler, F.E. (1964). A contingency model of leadership effectiveness. In L. Berkowitz (ed.). *Advances in Experimental Social Psychology,* Vol. 1, pp. 149–190. New York: Academic Press.

Fischhoff, B. (1975). Hindsight-foresight: The effect of outcome knowledge on judgment under uncertainty. *Journal of Experimental Psychology: Human Perception and Performance,* 1, 288–299.

Fischhoff, B., P. Slovic and S. Lichtenstein (1977). Knowing with certainty: The appropriateness of extreme confidence. *Journal of Experimental Psychology: Human Perception and Performance*, **3**, 552–564.

Fishbein, M. and I. Ajzen (1975). *Belief, Attitude, Intention, and Behaviour: An Introduction to Theory and Research*. Reading, MA: Addison-Wesley.

Fiske, S.T. (1995). Social cognition. In A. Tesser (ed.), *Advanced Social Psychology*, pp. 149–193. New York: McGraw-Hill.

Funder, D.C. and C.R. Colvin (1991). Explorations in behavioural consistency: Properties of persons, situations, and behaviours. *Journal of Personality and Social Psychology*, **60**, 773–794.

Gartner, W.B., K.G. Shaver and N. Aggarwal (2001). Opportunity or problem? The enterprise-serving attributional bias. Unpublished manuscript, University of Southern California.

Gatewood, E.J., K.G. Shaver and W.B. Gartner (1995). A longitudinal study of cognitive factors influencing start-up behaviours and success at venture creation. *Journal of Business Venturing*, **10**, 371–391.

Gilbert, D.T., S.T. Fiske and G. Lindzey (1998). *The Handbook of Social Psychology*, 4th edition. New York: Oxford University Press.

Goldenberg, J.L., T. Pyszczynski, S.K. McCoy, J. Greenberg and S. Solomon (1999). Death, sex, and neuroticism: Why is sex such a problem? *Journal of Personality and Social Psychology*, **77**, 1173–1187.

Heider, F. (1958). *The Psychology of Interpersonal Relations*. New York: Wiley.

Hilgard, E.R. (1987). *Psychology in America: A Historical Survey*. San Diego, CA: Harcourt Brace Jovanovich.

Hisrich, R.D. and M.P. Peters (1998). *Entrepreneurship*, 4th edition. Boston, MA: Irwin/McGraw-Hill.

Jones, E.E. and K.E. Davis (1965). From acts to dispositions: The attribution process in person perception. In L. Berkowitz (ed.), *Advances in Experimental Social Psychology*, Vol. 2, pp. 219–266. New York: Academic Press.

Jones, E.E. and D. McGillis (1976). Correspondent inferences and the attribution cube: A comparative reappraisal. In J.H. Harvey, W.J. Ickes and R.F. Kidd (eds.), *New Directions in Attribution Research*, Vol. 1, pp. 389–420. Hillsdale, NJ: Lawrence Erlbaum Associates.

Kahneman, D. and A. Tversky (1973). On the psychology of prediction. *Psychological Review*, **80**, 237–251.

Katz, D. and E. Stotland (1959). A preliminary statement to a theory of attitude structure and change. In S. Koch (ed.), *Psychology: Study of a Science*, Vol. 3, pp. 423–475. New York: McGraw-Hill.

Kelley, H.H. (1967). Attribution processes in social psychology. In D. Levine (ed.), *Nebraska Symposium on Motivation*, pp. 192–238. Lincoln, NE: University of Nebraska Press.

Kelley, H.H. (1973). The processes of causal attribution. *American Psychologist*, **28**, 107–128.

Krantz, D.S. and J. Ratliff-Crain (1989). The social context of stress and behavioural medicine research: Instructions, experimenter effects, and social interactions. In N. Schneiderman, S.M. Weiss and P.G. Kaufmann (eds.), *Handbook of Research Methods in Cardiovascular Behavioural Medicine*, pp. 383–392. New York: Plenum.

Krueger, N.F. Jr. (2000). The cognitive infrastructure of opportunity emergence. *Entrepreneurship Theory and Practice*, **24**, 5–23.

Krueger, N.F. Jr. and D.V. Brazeal (1994). Entrepreneurial potential and potential entrepreneurs. *Entrepreneurship Theory and Practice*, **18**, 91–104.

Krueger, N.F. Jr., M.D. Reilly and A.L. Carsrud (2000). Competing models of entrepreneurial intentions. *Journal of Business Venturing*, **15**, 411–432.

Kruglanski, A.W. and O. Mayseless (1990). Classic and current social comparison research: Expanding the perspective. *Psychological Bulletin*, **108**, 195–208.

LeDoux, J. (1996). *The Emotional Brain*. New York: Simon and Schuster.

Lichtenstein, S. and B. Fischhoff (1977). Do those who know more also know more about what they know? *Organizational Behaviour and Human Performance*, **20**, 159–183.

Likert, R. (1932). A technique for the measurement of attitudes. *Archives of Psychology*, **140**, 5–53.

Linder, D.E., J. Cooper and E.E. Jones (1967). Decision freedom as a determinant of the role of incentive magnitude in attitude change. *Journal of Personality and Social Psychology,* **6**, 245–254.

Lindzey, G. and E. Aronson (eds.) (1968–1969). *Handbook of Social Psychology,* 2nd edition, Vols. 1–5. Reading, MA: Addison-Wesley.

Lindzey, G. and E. Aronson (eds.) (1985). *Handbook of Social Psychology,* 3rd edition, Vols 1–2. New York: Random House.

Lowenstein, G.F., E.U. Weber, C.K. Hsee and N. Welch (2001). Risk as feelings. *Psychological Bulletin,* **127**, 267–286.

McClelland, D.C. (1961). *The Achieving Society.* Princeton, NJ: VanNostrand.

Malle, B.F. (1999). How people explain behaviour: A new theoretical framework. *Personality and Social Psychology Review,* **3**(1), 23–48.

Milgram, S. (1963). Behavioral study of obedience. *Journal of Abnormal and Social Psychology,* **67**, 371–378.

Mischel, W. (1968). *Personality and Assessment.* New York: Wiley.

Mischel, W. and P.K. Peake (1982). Beyond déjà vu in the search for cross-situational consistency. *Psychological Review,* **89**, 730–755.

Mitton, D.G. (1989). The complete entrepreneur. *Entrepreneurship Theory and Practice,* **13**(3), 9–19.

Mueller, S.I. and A.S. Thomas (2001). Culture and entrepreneurial potential: A nine country study of locus of control and innovativeness. *Journal of Business Venturing,* **16**, 51–75.

Murchison, C. (ed.) (1935). *Handbook of Social Psychology.* Worcester, MA: Clark University Press.

Nezlek, J.B. (2001). Multilevel random coefficient analyses of event- and interval-contingent data in social and personality psychology research. *Personality and Social Psychology Bulletin,* **27**, 771–785.

Orne, M.T. (1959) (September). *The Demand Characteristics of an Experimental Design and Their Implications.* Paper presented at the meeting of the American Psychological Association, Cincinnati.

Osgood, C.E., G.J. Suci and P.H. Tannenbaum (1957). *The Measurement of Meaning.* Urbana, IL: University of Illinois Press.

Pervin, L.A. (1989). Persons, situations, interactions: The history of a controversy and a discussion of theoretical models. *Academy of Management Review,* **14**, 350–360.

Petty, R.E. (1995). Attitude change. In A. Tesser (ed.), *Advanced Social Psychology,* pp. 195–255. New York: McGraw-Hill.

Radcliffe, N.M. and W.M.P. Klein (2002). Dispositional, unrealistic, and comparative optimism: Differential relations with the knowledge and processing of risk information and beliefs about personal risk. *Personality and Social Psychology Bulletin,* **28**, 836–846.

Robinson, D.N. (1979). *Systems of Modern Psychology.* New York: Columbia University Press.

Robinson, P.B., D.V. Stimpson, J.C. Huefner and H.K. Hunt (1991). An attitude approach to the prediction of entrepreneurship. *Entrepreneurship Theory and Practice,* **15**, 13–31.

Roethlisberger, F.J. and W.J. Dickson (1939). *Management and the Worker: An Account of a Research Program Conducted by the Western Electric Company, Hawthorne Works, Chicago.* Cambridge, MA: Harvard University Press.

Rosenberg, M.J. (1965). When dissonance fails: On eliminating evaluation apprehension from attitude measurement. *Journal of Personality and Social Psychology,* **1**, 28–42.

Rosenthal, R. (1966). *Experimenter Effects in Behavioural Research.* New York: Appleton-Century-Crofts.

Rosenthal, R. (1994). On being one's own case study: Experimenter effects in behavioural research – 30 years later. In W.R. Shadish and S. Fuller (eds.), *The Social Psychology of Science,* pp. 214–229. New York: Guilford.

Rotter, J.B. (1966). Generalized expectancies for internal versus external locus of control of reinforcement. *Psychological Monographs,* **80**, 1–28.

Roure, J.B. and R.H. Keeley (1990). Predictors of success in new technology based ventures. *Journal of Business Venturing,* **5**, 201–220.

Shapero, A. (1982). Some social dimensions of entrepreneurship. In C. Kent, D. Sexton and K. Vesper (eds.), *The Encyclopedia of Entrepreneurship.* Englewood Cliffs, NJ: Prentice-Hall.

Shaver, K.G. (1970). Defensive attribution: Effects of severity and relevance on the responsibility assigned for an accident. *Journal of Personality and Social Psychology*, **14**, 101–113.

Shaver, K.G. (1975). *An Introduction to Attribution Processes*. Cambridge, MA: Winthrop.

Shaver, K.G. (1985). *The Attribution of Blame: Causality, Responsibility, and Blameworthiness*. New York: Springer-Verlag.

Shaver, K.G. (1987). *Principles of Social Psychology*, 3rd edition. Hillsdale, NJ: Lawrence Erlbaum Associates.

Shaver, K.G. (1995). The entrepreneurial personality myth. *Business and Economic Review*, **41**(3), 20–23.

Shaver, K.G., W.B. Gartner, E. Crosby, K. Bakalarova and E.J. Gatewood (2001). Attributions about entrepreneurship: A framework and process for analyzing reasons for starting a business. *Entrepreneurship Theory and Practice*, **26**(2), 5–32.

Shaver, K.G. and L.R. Scott (1991). Person, process, choice: The psychology of new venture creation. *Entrepreneurship: Theory and Practice*, **16**(2), 23–45.

Simon, M., S.M. Houghton and K. Aquino (1999). Cognitive biases, risk perception, and venture formation: How individuals decide to start companies. *Journal of Business Venturing*, **15**, 113–134.

Skinner, B.F. (1938). *The Behaviour of Organisms: An Experimental Analysis*. New York: Appleton-Century.

Snyder, C.R. and R.L. Higgins (1988). Excuses: Their effective role in the negotiation of reality. *Psychological Bulletin*, **104**, 23–35.

Snyder, M. (1984). When belief creates reality. In L. Berkowitz (ed.), *Advances in Experimental Social Psychology*, Vol. 18, pp. 247–305. New York: Academic Press.

Snyder, M., E.D. Tanke and E. Berscheid (1977). Social perception and interpersonal behaviour: On the self-fulfilling nature of social stereotypes. *Journal of Personality and Social Psychology*, **35**, 656–666.

Staw, B.M. (1981). The escalation of commitment to a course of action. *Academy of Management Review*, **6**, 577–587.

Stevenson, H.H. and D.E. Gumpert (1985). The heart of entrepreneurship. *Harvard Business Review*, **63**(2), March/April 1985, pp. 85–94.

Stewart, A. (1989). *Team Entrepreneurship*. Newbury Park, CA: Sage.

Suls, J. and T.A. Wills (eds.) (1991). *Social Comparison: Contemporary Theory and Research*. Hillsdale, NJ: Lawrence Erlbaum Associates.

Tesser, A. and L. Martin (1996). The psychology of evaluation. In E.T. Higgins and A.W. Kruglanski (eds.), *Social Psychology: Handbook of Basic Principles*, pp. 400–432. New York: Guilford.

Thurstone, L.L. and E.J. Chave (1929). *The Measurement of Attitude*. Chicago: University of Chicago Press.

Timmons, J.A. (1994). *New Venture Creation*, 4th edition. Burr Ridge, IL: Irwin.

Wells, G.L. (1993). What do we know about eyewitness identification? *American Psychologist*, **48**, 553–571.

Westhead, P. and M. Wright (1998). Novice, portfolio, and serial founders: Are they different? *Journal of Business Venturing*, **13**, 173–204.

Wicklund, R.A. and P.M. Gollwitzer (1982). *Symbolic Self-completion*. Hillsdale, NJ: Lawrence Erlbaum Associates.

Wills, T.A. (1991). Similarity and self-esteem in downward comparison. In J. Suls and T.A. Wills (eds.), *Social Comparison: Contemporary Theory and Research*, pp. 51–78. Hillsdale, NJ: Lawrence Erlbaum Associates.

Zacharakis, A.L. and D.A. Shepherd (2001). The nature of information and overconfidence on venture capitalists' decision making. *Journal of Business Venturing*, **16**, 311–332.

Zajonc, R.B. (1980). Feeling and thinking: Preferences need no inference. *American Psychologist*, **35**, 151–175.

Zajonc, R.B. (1998). Emotions. In D. Gilbert, S. Fiske and G. Lindzey (eds.), *The Handbook of Social Psychology*, 4th edition, Vol. 1, pp. 591–632. New York: Oxford University Press.

Zillmann, D. and M. Zillmann (1996). Psychoneuroendocrinology of social behaviour. In E.T. Higgins and A.W. Kruglanski (eds.), *Social Psychology: Handbook of Basic Principles*, pp. 39–71. New York: Guilford.

HOWARD E. ALDRICH and MARTHA MARTINEZ
The University of North Carolina at Chapel Hill

15. Entrepreneurship as Social Construction: A Multi-level Evolutionary Approach[1]

INTRODUCTION

Organizations are social structures – patterned and relatively stable arrangements of roles and statuses – that constitute the building blocks of modern capitalist societies. Efforts to understand their emergence typically focus on the role of entrepreneurs and concentrate on the firm level. Such firm-level analyses make sense in already existing populations and communities, because most new firms follow the paths of their predecessors and survive by filling an existing niche. However, in the case of new ventures that are the first of their kind, the formation of a firm cannot be the final step. Entrepreneurs creating organizations that depart from the established order must not only create a coherent and self-sustaining entity, but must also organize with other entrepreneurs to build a new, more favorable context.

In a fundamental sense, then, entrepreneurship involves the social construction of new social entities. Whereas entrepreneurs in established populations benefit from the work already completed by antecedent firms, entrepreneurs in new populations must create and give form to their own social environments. Entrepreneurs building new populations must engage in activities that range from making people and organizations aware of their existence and value to creating a system of cooperation and competition that facilitates their long-term survival. In these cases, entrepreneurial work does not stop at the organizational level, but goes on to involve the construction of populations and communities. Environmental change and entrepreneurs' capacities for adaptation to change, as well as the interaction of these two factors, influence the success or failure of such efforts.

The other chapters of this book provide an in-depth look at entrepreneurial processes at the firm and individual levels. In contrast, the purpose of our chapter is to review and analyze the multi-level selection processes that apply across three different levels of entrepreneurial social constructions: Organizations, populations, and communities. We emphasize the inexorable

---

[1] We thank Linda Renzulli, Scott Shane, and an anonymous reviewer for their helpful comments on an earlier draft.

Z.J. Acs and D.B. Audretsch (eds.), Handbook of Entrepreneurship Research, 359–399
© 2003 *Kluwer Academic Publishers. Printed in Great Britain.*

tension between selection forces at the three levels that affect variations generated by entrepreneurs. Sometimes selection forces work in concert, but often they do not.

The Social Construction of Entrepreneurship at the Organizational Level

The concept of "nascent entrepreneur" captures the flavor of the chaotic and disorderly process driving the creation of new firms. A nascent entrepreneur is defined as someone who initiates serious activities that are intended to culminate in a viable business startup (Reynolds and White, 1997). In evolutionary terms, nascent entrepreneurs comprise a major source of organizational variations, beginning with their diverse intentions and continuing through a wide range of heterogeneous activities oriented toward a realized founding.

Recent data on startup rates shows the widespread prevalence of entrepreneurial activities not only in American society, but in other nations, as well. If we define nascent entrepreneurs as those individuals engaged in two or more activities directed toward the founding of a firm within the past 6 months, then 4.3 percent of the population could be classified as nascent entrepreneurs in a representative sample of 683 Wisconsin residents in the United States in 1993. In a nationally representative sample of all adult residents of the United States in 1997, 3.9 percent were classified as nascent entrepreneurs (Reynolds, 1999). Another nationally representative study in the United States, conducted in 1997, arrived at comparable estimates, after allowing for slight differences in definitions (Dennis, 1997).

Extrapolating from these results, millions of adults participate each year in some form of entrepreneurial activity in the United States, even though most activities do not lead to firm formation or positive financial results in the short run. Perhaps as many as 7 million people become involved in such activities each year, launching as many as 3.3 million firms that reach a point where they are potentially viable businesses. Viewed from the perspective of their working careers, about 40 percent of American adults experience spells of self employment in their lifetime (Reynolds and White, 1997).

International information on startup rates is becoming available through various collaborative efforts, such as the GEM Project (Reynolds et al., 1999, 2000). The GEM project found that the rate of nascent entrepreneurship varies widely across nations, with the United States at the high end, with more than one in 12 people in 1999, versus about one in every 67 people in Finland. Rates in Australia are about 1 in 12, in Germany about 1 in 25, about 1 in 33 in the United Kingdom, about 1 in 50 in Sweden, and about 1 in 100 in Ireland. "In the highly active countries (i.e. U.S., Canada and Israel), it is rare to find a person who doesn't personally know someone who is trying to start a business. In the less active countries (i.e. Finland and Japan), it may be rare to find a person who knows of anyone trying to start a new firm" (Reynolds et al.,

1999). Countries also differ in the extent to which startups are sponsored by existing businesses and in the level of personal financial support invested in a new business.

Although this inclination toward entrepreneurship in some nations implies the potential for a torrent of organizational innovation, the actual pool of startups contains mostly mundane replications of the familiar. Based on survey and ethnographic accounts, the founding process appears complex, chaotic, and compressed in time, and highly vulnerable to intense selection pressures. Most entrepreneurs thus fail in their attempts to create new entities, and less than one in ten new ventures grows (Duncan and Handler, 1994; Reynolds and White, 1997). Even when they succeed, the products of entrepreneurial efforts (stable, self-sustainable organizations) are typically simple replications of existing organizational forms (Gartner, 1985; Aldrich and Fiol, 1994; Low and Abrahamson, 1997; Aldrich and Martinez, 2001). Imitation and the reproduction of organizational forms constitute the norm, rather than the exception.

Of course, some mundane replications of the familiar carry the potential of becoming very large. For example, some people start new firms in the belief that they can create a new franchise chain. A franchise is a classic replication because, from the very beginning, new establishments are intended to be identical to the original template. However, even following the route of replication, rather than innovation, does not guarantee success, as most new franchise systems fail within ten years (Shane, 1996).

For modern societies, apparently so oriented toward radical change, the small proportion of innovative entrepreneurs seems shocking. To explain this apparent anomaly, we consider three questions in this section on firm-level entrepreneurship: Why are entrepreneurs so inclined to imitate existing forms? In the face of powerful pressures, why does innovation nonetheless often occur? Finally, what selection forces face innovating entrepreneurs?

Imitation Reproduces Existing Forms

On a continuum between the two poles of reproducers and innovators, *reproducer organizations* are defined as those organizations started in established populations whose routines and competencies vary minimally, if at all, from those of existing organizations. They bring little or no incremental knowledge to the populations they enter, organizing their activities in much the same way as their predecessors. At the other end of the continuum, *innovative organizations* are those organizations started by entrepreneurs, intentionally or not, whose routines and competencies vary significantly from those of existing organizations (Picot et al., 1989).

The forces that favor imitation and the reproduction of existing structures, rather than innovation and replacement, lie at the core of sociological theory and have been given special emphasis by neo-institutional theorists. As with other wide-ranging perspectives, institutional theories have many faces (DiMaggio and Powell, 1991; Suchman and Edelman, 1996). At the most general level, institutional theories argue that reproduction takes place because of the existence of socially created "truths" about such questions as: What is possible and impossible, how do markets and industries work, what goals should organizations pursue, and what are the appropriate means to accomplish organizational goals? (Meyer and Rowan, 1977).

Many definitions of organizational form have been proposed, as noted by Carroll and Hannan (2000). All definitions share a concern with characterizing a bounded population of organizations, but they differ in the principles used to achieve that goal. Many definitions treat an organizational form as a "cluster of features," such as Weber's definition of the bureaucratic form of organization (Carroll and Hannan, 2000), or McKelvey's (1982) concept of organizational species as polythetic groupings. Although they began in the 1970s with conceptions emphasizing organizational architecture, population ecologists eventually adopted ideas from institutional theory and developed a conception of organizational forms as social constructions (Hannan and Henry, 1986).

Carroll and Hannan (2000) proposed a new definition of form as "a recognizable pattern that takes on rule-like standing." Deeply grounded in a sociological view of organizations, this definition emphasizes cognitive recognition and external enforcement of the features an organization can legitimately display. Organizational forms thus depend for their existence on insiders and outsiders expecting particular features and negatively sanctioning organizations that fail to live up to their expectations. Defining organizations as social constructions, of course, immediately raises the issue of when and why a new kind of organizational form emerges. In this chapter, we focus on the role entrepreneurs play in constructing new forms.

Organizations are the dominant, taken for granted tools of collective action in our world. Indeed, knowledge of "organizations" as a social form is deeply embedded in the cultures of all industrial societies. At the individual level, the received idea of "organization" creates a strongly held set of expectations and behaviors, including the need to modify our ideas according to the opinions of other people (Zucker, 1977; Blackmore, 1999). Not surprisingly, as cultural products, particular strategies of action differ across societies. Resources for constructing strategies of action are generated by "the symbolic experiences, mythic lore, and ritual practices of a group or society [that] create moods and motivations, ways of organizing experience and evaluating reality, modes of regulating conduct, and ways of forming social bonds" (Swidler, 1986).

In most Western industrial societies, these rules constitute part of the behavioral repertoire of socialized adults who understand and use the rules as guides through most social situations. Used appropriately, such rules help individuals "economize on their interactions with others" (Drazin and Sandelands, 1992). Indeed, in all societies, fundamental rules of organizing are available to people from a very early age. "Models of organization are part of the cultural tool kit of any society and serve expressive or communicative as well as instrumental functions" (Clemens, 1993). Potential entrepreneurs usually take for granted such culturally defined building blocks of rules, thus channeling most new ventures in the direction of reproducing existing organizational forms (Carroll, 1993).

Beyond the general and very abstract effect of taken for granted "truths," practical reasons may direct entrepreneurs to imitation. By definition, all first-time entrepreneurs are learning how to construct an organization, even while in the process of creating one. They learn by doing, as they engage in trial and error learning. *Learning by doing* puts powerful pressures on newcomers to adopt the role of student *vis-à-vis* established entrepreneurs who already run successful organizations. In fact, managerial education, including programs designed for entrepreneurs and courses taught to MBAs, reinforces imitation by focusing on successful cases. Because failed organizing attempts are usually not available for study, whereas apparently successful ones are, nascent entrepreneurs will engage in quite a bit of superstitious learning.

People often pick models to imitate that contain subtle selection biases that are easy to overlook, as Denrell (2000) noted. For example, the business press frequently celebrates entrepreneurs as aggressive risk takers, noting that the most successful firms in an industry have pursued higher risk strategies than others. What such comparisons fail to note, however, is that many firms pursuing a high-risk strategy simply failed. Such firms are thus missing from the comparative assessments made by current commentators. A more balanced assessment would conclude that high-risk strategies are actually quite dangerous and unpredictable, as likely to lead to a firm's demise as its success. In truly uncertain environments, nascent entrepreneurs are, by definition, flying blind (Knight, 1921).

Under conditions of uncertainty, entrepreneurs' absorptive capacities influence their ability to see opportunities, as Shane (2000) pointed out, building on an argument by Dosi (1982) on technological paradigms. Human cognitive processes drive people to see things related to their existing knowledge. As a result, "creativity" is actually more about assembling prior knowledge in new ways than about dreaming up something totally new. Prior paradigms and problem-solving approaches thus constrain most innovative thinking, restricting potential variation in ideas.

Even if nascent entrepreneurs could resist isomorphic pressures (DiMaggio and Powell, 1983), they still face deep-seated temptations to imitate. With all the complexity, risks, and uncertainty related to the founding of a firm, the safest choice lies in imitating practices, products, and processes that have already proven successful. Obviously, imitation does not eliminate risks, because entrepreneurs do not have access to unbiased information about entrepreneurial failures that used the imitated practices, products, and processes. Nonetheless, imitation is a relatively inexpensive mode of social construction. By contrast, innovation is expensive and risky because it requires not only the acquisition of resources but also the creation of new knowledge.

Why Innovations Still Occur

Given powerful pressures to imitate, why and how do entrepreneurs ever innovate? First, individuals do not always act like simple machines, slavishly conforming to the world as they find it (Shane, 2000). As Harper (1996) argued, entrepreneurs make reasoned conjectures about the world and then act on them. Sometimes their conjectures are about worlds that do not exist yet. Second, innovations, as well as the behaviors that lead to them (experimentation, play, and make believe), have proved historically useful for human adaptation and survival (Campbell, 1969). Creativity, experimentation and accidents, play, and make-believe, in contrast to the cultural conformity induced by social processes, are naturally occurring behaviors through which individuals "disobey" ingrained cultural routines, norms, and habits.

The continuum from reproducer to innovator is defined by outcomes, not intentions (Aldrich and Kenworthy, 1999). Some entrepreneurs deliberately intend to depart from existing knowledge, whereas others give it no thought. Irrespective of intentions, individuals face a tension between deviating from existing routines and competencies and conforming to them, as Campbell (1994, p. 35) noted: "There is, perhaps, always a potential conflict between the freedom to vary, which makes advance possible, (versus) the value of retaining the cultural accumulation." Playfulness and experimentation are natural impulses that have been wired into humans because of their utility. However, the full expression of these tendencies is opposed by another set of wired-in impulses: Humans' tendencies to defer to the beliefs of others. Indeed, pressures for obedience to cultural routines can be powerful enough to intimidate individuals with unorthodox beliefs (Aldrich and Kenworthy, 1999).

Given that the odds of survival are low, under what conditions might people nonetheless become involved in innovative entrepreneurship? Campbell (1994) identified several dimensions that distinguish innovators from reproducers. First, individuals may just be plain egotistic or narcissistic, putting competitive behaviors and a sense of their "uniqueness" above group interests. Some people may thus believe that they can avoid group-level selection pressures, and set out to single-mindedly pursue their own idiosyncratic course of action. Discerning readers will recognize this description as the classic portrait of an entrepreneur, a depiction that has been substantially but not totally discredited by researchers (Aldrich and Wiedenmayer, 1993). It serves as a siren song, tempting new generations of researchers to employ it, regardless of the serious methodological problems frequently encountered but rarely solved (Baum, 2001).

Second, individuals may "doubt" the appropriateness, practicality, or simple functionality of current cultural templates. Innovation, whether intended or not, requires an ability to challenge, and often disregard, dominant cultural routines. Challenging the dominant paradigm constitutes an overwhelming obstacle for many entrepreneurs. For example, resource requirements for founding, via loans or venture capital funding, may result in coercive isomorphism (DiMaggio and Powell, 1983) with a new firm forced to adopt a taken-for-granted form. Strong selection pressures may thus quash individual variation in solutions chosen to startup problems.

Nonetheless, some entrepreneurs may succeed in maintaining their skepticism because they have confidence in alternative decision algorithms learned through experience, or because they are embedded in highly diverse social networks. Even if nascent entrepreneurs discover a very promising idea for a start-up, they still require help from others to actually build an organization. About half of all nascent organizing attempts in the United States involve more than one founder who will also own equity in the new venture (Ruef et al., 2002). Given the lure of further experimentation and the diversity of their contacts, innovative founders and founding teams may dissipate their energies before an organization can take form.

Third, an alternative path to the non-conformist, innovative creation of new organizational knowledge may occur via ignorance of existing cultural norms. Circumstances may occur where individuals simply do not know what prevailing forces dictate. For example, truly innovative start-ups are often the result of creative experimentation with new ideas by outsiders to an industry. Indifference to industry routines and norms gives outsiders the freedom to break free of the cognitive constraints on incumbents. Innovative entrepreneurs often have human capital that has been developed outside of the industry they wish to enter. For these individuals, and the organizations they found, ignorance or blindness to the norms of the population encourages creative, innovative organizational emergence (Cliff, 1997).

Some theorists have argued that recognizably valuable opportunities are essential for the success of nascent ventures. Investors often talk of the importance of things like potential market size in funding ventures, for example. In a very well-articulated statement of this position, Shane and Venkataraman (2000) argued that "Although recognition of entrepreneurial opportunities is a subjective process, the opportunities themselves are objective phenomena that are not known to all parties at all times." We acknowledge that, after the fact, objective observers may agree that an entrepreneur took advantage of an opportunity, but from an evolutionary perspective, we question whether *a priori* identification of objective opportunities should be built into a model of nascent entrepreneurship.

Entrepreneurs creating organizations in new populations face uncertainty, not simply "risk," in making their decisions. Knight (1921), in his classic analysis of risk and uncertainty, "restricted the concept of risk to situations in which both the set of possibilities and the probability distribution over this set are known, either by argument *a priori*, as in calculating the expected results of throwing dice, or by statistical analysis of appropriate evidence" (Loasby, 2001). Under conditions of uncertainty, decisions are usually made on grounds other than logical calculation (Thaler, 1994). Evolutionary thinking posits an open future that is enacted by myopic agents who are hampered by ignorance and environmental complexity as they grapple with uncertainty. Entrepreneurs can assemble what they think they need, but whether their choices match up successfully with selection forces is an open question.

Selection Forces Affecting Innovative Entrepreneurs

Given their difficulties in acquiring resources, are innovating entrepreneurs subject to stronger selection forces than their imitating counterparts? Some innovative entrepreneurs create routines and competencies that vary in ways *favored* by selection criteria. The new organizational knowledge they generate may thus transform an existing population or create a new one, although the innovating firm itself may not survive. From a population point of view, they have created *competence-enhancing, competence-destroying* (Anderson and Tushman, 1990), or *competence-extending innovations* (Hunt and Aldrich, 1998).

Competence-enhancing innovations involve substantial improvements that build on existing routines and competencies within a product/service class and can be adopted by existing organizations (Abernathy and Clark, 1985; Utterback and Abernathy, 1975). For example, most typewriter manufacturers switched relatively smoothly from producing mechanical typewriters to producing electric ones. Competence-extending innovations permit existing firms to pursue new opportunities that allow them to stretch their existing competencies into complementary ventures. Unlike competence-enhancing opportunities, these new ventures are not straightforward extensions of current routines and competencies and therefore cannot be pursued with minimal effort. At the same time, however, these opportunities are not direct threats to existing firms' competencies. Instead, they are potential opportunities for expanding their domains. The World Wide Web (henceforth, just "the Web") and the biotechnology communities offer examples of this process. Most competence-enhancing and extending innovations can be adopted by existing organizations.

Competence-enhancing and -extending innovating startups find themselves in a very weak position, because they encounter an environment already occupied with organizations that can easily absorb their very temporary competitive advantage. Existing organizations also have more experience with successful practices in their industry. Selection forces might thus give only a marginal advantage to start-ups based on such incremental innovations. Nonetheless, their efforts give birth to the population-level benefits of increasing the fitness and survival capabilities of all organizations in the population (even if they are part of it for only a short time).

In contrast to the incremental effects of competence-enhancing and extending innovations, competence-destroying innovations require new knowledge, routines, and competencies in the development and production of a product/service. They fundamentally alter the set of relevant competencies required of an organization. Accordingly, they put existing organizations at a disadvantage. The development of computers as word processors was a competence-destroying innovation that has driven the typewriter industry to near extinction. Typewriter manufacturers' attempts to offer some of the same features as word processors, such as being able to edit and save electronic documents, have been insufficient to maintain their position in the market.

Entrepreneurs who try to create organizations based on competence-destroying technologies thus plant the seeds that might germinate a new population, or at least lead to a mass extinction of existing organizations and their replacement by a new cohort of organizations. New industries, as opposed to new markets within existing industries, are typically opened by independent new ventures. New independent ventures often cannot rely on existing institutions to provide external legitimacy.

Because the new ventures constitute an entirely new population, much of the knowledge they need will not be available via experience and imitation (Van de Ven et al., 1988). Founders of the first innovative ventures in a new population operate in a situation with few, if any, precedents for the core new activity in which they are engaged. They must learn about new markets and develop the organizational knowledge to exploit them. They also often face situations in which potential members and resource providers question their legitimacy. Learning and legitimacy are thus two of the most important factors for the survival of a firm, but individual firms only partially control their own fate. Much of the critical learning and legitimacy creation takes place at the population level, which we discuss in the next section.

Summary: Organizational Level Entrepreneurship

Nascent entrepreneurs face four powerful forces inhibiting innovation. First, given the chaotic and unpredictable process of creating new firms, reproduction is typically more cost-effective than innovation. Second, overarching institutional frameworks constrain imitators' thinking regarding what is possible or impossible, acceptable or unacceptable. Third, innovators have a hard time convincing key constituencies to provide them the scarce resources required to build new firms. Finally, existing firms often assimilate competence-enhancing and competence-extending innovations, leaving innovators without a sustainable competitive advantage and lots of organizational problems.

Given these four problems, it is remarkable that entrepreneurial innovation takes place at all in modern societies. Nonetheless, several factors do contribute to the persistence of innovative efforts, even in the face of serious constraints. First, curiosity and the need for exploration are as highly engrained in human nature as is the need for stability. Second, the quite sensible act of doubting the system, a common phenomenon in many societies, gives people reasons to look for new ways to perform tasks. Some people are quite willing to face societal wrath in pursuit of their vision, regardless of the costs. Third, ignorance of existing forms can lead to accidental innovation.

However, simply creating an innovative venture is insufficient. In a world ruled by inertia, entrepreneurs must still discover how to make it last. Powerful selection forces conspire against most innovative foundings. Ultimately, successful collective action at the population and community levels allows entrepreneurs to create environments favorable to their existence.

POPULATION FORMATION AND GROWTH

Populations appear and disappear with great regularity in modern economies. Given a long-enough period of observation, almost all populations show an inverted-U shaped growth pattern, with numbers of organizations rising and falling as a population ages. In this section, we focus on two problems facing entrepreneurs in new populations: They must develop effective new routines and competencies, and they must carve out a legitimate niche for the population. When we assert that innovating entrepreneurs must create their own niches, we are referring to their need to obtain resources and legitimacy by acting on their environments. First, we describe the context in which these two problems arise. Second, we review the cognitive requirements confronting startups and then examine common strategies enacted to meet them. Third, we conduct a similar analysis of sociopolitical requirements and strategies.

Problems Confronting Entrepreneurs in New Populations

Two specific problems confront nascent entrepreneurs in new populations. First, they must discover or create effective routines and competencies under conditions of ignorance and uncertainty. When the number of organizations in a new industry is small, organizational members must learn new roles without the luxury of established role models. Of course, not all information is population-specific, and thus occasionally new firms have an opportunity to learn from other populations. Second, new organizations must establish ties with an environment that might not understand or acknowledge their existence (Stinchcombe, 1965; Hannan and Carroll, 1992). In particular, they must search for strategies that give them legitimacy.

In Aldrich and Fiol (1994), two forms of legitimacy were identified: Cognitive and sociopolitical. *Cognitive legitimacy* refers to the acceptance of a new kind of venture as *a taken for granted* feature of the environment. The highest form of cognitive legitimacy exists when a new product, process, or service is accepted as part of the sociocultural and organizational landscape. When an activity becomes so familiar and well known that people take it for granted, founders can conserve time and other organizing resources, and their likelihood of success increases. From a producer's point of view, cognitive legitimacy means that new entrants to an industry are likely to copy an existing organizational form, rather than experiment with a new one. From a consumer's point of view, cognitive legitimacy means that people are committed users of the product or service. Cognitive legitimacy thus depends upon knowledge – in the form of routines, structures, products, and strategies – being acquired and then diffused.

Sociopolitical legitimacy refers to the acceptance by key stakeholders, the general public, key opinion leaders, and government officials of a new venture as appropriate and right. It contains two components: *moral acceptance*, referring to conformity with cultural norms and values, and *regulatory acceptance*, referring to conformity with governmental rules and regulations. Clemens (1993, p. 771) noted that "the adoption of a particular organizational form influences the ties that an organized group forms with other organizations." Signs of conformity to moral norms and values include (a) the absence of attacks by religious and civic leaders on the new form, and (b) heightened public prestige of its leaders. For example, in the 19th century, clergy and church leaders initially vilified the life insurance industry for profaning the sacredness of life (Zelizer, 1978). Signs of conformity to governmental rules and regulations include (a) laws passed to protect or monitor the industry, and (b) government subsidies to the industry. For example, the passage of the Wagner Act in 1935 in the United States gave special status under federal law to unions that conformed to federal guidelines.

The process of learning and building legitimacy begins at the organizational level and continues up through the various levels: Within populations, between populations, and the entire community of populations. Table 1 (Aldrich, 1999) summarizes the different strategies that organizations follow to gain knowledge

Table 1. Strategies facilitating the growth of populations

Level of analysis		Cognitive strategies		Sociopolitical strategies
	Learning	Cognitive legitimacy	Moral legitimacy	Regulatory legitimacy
Organizational	Create knowledge base through experimentation	Link new ventures to the past via symbolic language and behaviors	Build on local networks of trust	Avoid entanglement with government agencies as long as possible
Within-population	Deepen a knowledge base by encouraging convergence around a dominant design	Collaborate to create standard-setting bodies	Foster perceptions of reliability by mobilizing to take collective action	Present a united front to political and government officials
Between-population	Spread knowledge base by promoting alliance and third party activities	Create cross-population groups and associations	Develop a reputation of a new activity as a reality by negotiation and compromise with other industries	Co-opt government agencies as allies against competing populations
Community	Solidify a knowledge base by creating linkages with established educational curricula	Cooperate with independent certifying institutions	Embed legitimacy by organizing collective marketing and lobbying efforts	Embed the population within the political system via PACs and hiring of former government officials

Source: Aldrich (1999).

and legitimacy at these different levels of selection. We use the term "strategy" in a generic sense to refer not necessarily to consciously articulated plans of action, but rather to a consistent stream of actions intended to further an entrepreneur's objectives (Mintzberg, 1978). When achieved, legitimacy and population level knowledge become resources that cloak the foundings of all organizations in a population, regardless of their individual characteristics (Rao, 1994).

Cooperation versus Competition in New Populations

Building a new population involves the creation of a market, a very important collective task for entrepreneurs. In the process of constructing a market, tensions arise among new firms between pressures toward cooperation as opposed to competition. On the one hand, given the complexity of product and consumer needs (status, preferences, and roles), most markets cannot be dominated by a single firm (Podolny, 1993). Few markets resemble the "winner take all" conditions described by Shapiro and Varian (1999) in which a single firm's technology or marketing power allows it to crush its competitors. New ventures must thus compete, as individuals, to gain the most profitable segment(s) of their emerging market. On the other hand, new ventures must pursue collective efforts to efficiently accumulate knowledge and acquire legitimacy among the segments of society constituting their intended market or resource providers.

The balance a new population achieves between competition and cooperation internally and *vis-à-vis* other groups of organizations ultimately determines its boundaries. Members struggle with recognizing and responding to constraints and opportunities as they strive to construct a population's boundaries. Their struggle is very much a collective effort, although not necessarily a collaborative one. Indeed, in the early days, founders might compete with each other to set a direction for the new population, pushing for a direction that will benefit their own firms.

Cognitive Requirements Confronting New Populations

The most pressing issues facing founders of entirely new activities involve cognitive rather than sociopolitical problems. In capitalist nations, firms benefit from a "diffuse belief that profit-seeking activities are valid, unless otherwise specified" (Delacroix et al., 1989). Though it may be legally validated in the form of a legal charter, an entirely new activity often begins with low levels of knowledge, depressed cognitive legitimacy, or both. Given the absence of codified knowledge, pioneering founders begin at the organizational level by creating a knowledge base in their own organization. Early on, they might also struggle with the founders of other organizations in their emerging population. If the transfer of knowledge and evidence from other populations is acceptable in a particular situation, then entrepreneurs can base their initial trust building strategies on objective external evidence from them. However, if such transfers are not possible, then they must concentrate on framing the unknown in such a way that it becomes believable (Aldrich and Fiol, 1994).

Learning and cognitive legitimacy must be developed not only at the firm level but also at higher levels of social structures. *Within-population processes* constrain the emergence of new populations by the way in which the environment for new ventures unfolds. Entrepreneurs, in their collective quest for knowledge and cognitive legitimacy, face two main problems. First, they need to develop effective routines and competencies. Second, they need collective agreement on standards and designs, so that the population or its products and/or services can become a taken for granted reality for all relevant agents.

During the period following a radical innovation that potentially sparks a new population, an *era of ferment* may arise in which struggles occur between contending designs. Beneficial templates are scarce within an emerging population, thus hampering learning. Instead, pioneering entrepreneurs must learn new schemata or extensively modify old ones. In the early days of a new population, disagreement among firms on dominant design increases entry rates and holds down exit rates as contending firms struggle to have their design accepted. In their review of the literature on technology cycles, Tushman and Murmann (1998) noted that the emergence of dominant designs substantially affects population dynamics. By contrast, when a dominant design emerges, disbandings increase and entry slows because the incumbent firms are advantaged and new entrants have a much lower likelihood of changing the population's standards.

The era of ferment ends when participants settle on a dominant design, and it is followed by an era of incremental change (Anderson and Tushman, 1990). Convergence toward an accepted design occurs rapidly if new ventures find it easy to imitate pioneers, rather than seek further innovation. Early on, founders within a population implicitly compete to have their approach taken for granted, appealing to potential customers, investors, and others to accept their version (Aldrich, 1999). Although this competition may elevate their status in an incipient market, they face countervailing obligations to cooperate in the creation of a population standard. Otherwise, the competition between companies creates confusion, thereby undermining the cognitive legitimacy of the industry as a whole. If achieved, consensual standards and subsequent cognitive legitimacy will increase the number of imitators that will try to enter the new market. As Rosenkopf and Tushman (1994) noted, the process of achieving standards is a socio-cultural one, rather than being purely technologically driven.

Populations with imitable innovations generate more collective action than populations with innovations that are difficult to imitate. If innovations, even when competence-destroying, are easy to imitate, founders will have to deal with new competitors. Thus, they gain a strong incentive to cooperate on stabilizing conditions in the industry by creating standards that favor them. By contrast, when products or technologies are not easily imitated, founders can protect their core competencies from being widely diffused (Shapiro and Varian, 1999). Such fiercely competitive individual strategies hinder, or simply make unnecessary, a united collective front by a population. For example, since it's founding, the so-called "e-book" producers have struggled over a common standard for the format of e-books' content presentations, despite the clear benefits of an industry wide resolution on a shared format. As of 2002, the struggle showed no signs of abating. Several different, incompatible, formats were contending for dominance, and consumers seemed to be holding back, waiting until a clear winner emerged.

Imitability's effects appear paradoxical unless we pay careful attention to different levels of selection. For a population, easier imitability means growth. New firms enter more easily and an expanding market means that proportionately more entrants might survive. For individual ventures, however, easier imitability makes organizational survival more problematic, as their market becomes crowded with equally competent rivals and survival becomes contingent on fairly small differences between ventures. One common pattern involves the survival of new entrants at the expense of earlier entrants who have not learned fast enough to keep up.

However, for individual firms, extreme uniqueness may also be a disadvantage. The monopoly of a technological innovation by a single organization does not preclude success by others. Independent firms may choose to exchange and even diffuse their technologies (in contrast to protecting them under patent enforcement) to create a group of products that can be offered as a package to the market. The existence of imitators and complementary products increases the likelihood of a particular innovation being adopted and diffusing, creating economies of scale that can increase company profitability (Funk and Methe, 2001, p. 591).

The experience of Apple Computer provides a well-known example of the consequences of a firm not supporting open technological standards that would allow a limited degree of imitation. Although the Macintosh OS was considered a superior product to Microsoft's Windows, Apple's decision to not license the hardware, therefore closing the door to cheaper copies of their models, severely hampered their business. With only a limited number of computers able to run Macintosh software, the company never reached the economies of scale that allowed it to become a standard and promote the creation of suitable applications. Thus, neither extreme imitability nor extreme uniqueness apparently favors a firm's survival within new populations. The net effect of imitability is contingent on whether a population has converged on a dominant design and on the relative balance between underlying growth in a market, new entries, and exits from the population.

The nature of relations *between industries*, whether competing or cooperating, affects the distribution of resources in the environment and the terms on which they are available to entrepreneurs. Lack of cognitive legitimacy may be both an advantage and a disadvantage for new ventures when dealing with already established populations. Sometimes a low level of cognitive legitimacy is an advantage, such as when established organizations do not treat the activity as a serious threat. For example, early ecommerce firms were simply ignored by established firms, which were very slow to move into on-line commerce. Neglect of the ecommerce space by established firms gave Web-based startups a few months' or even a few years' head start, although the gap was eventually closed.

Organizations that feel threatened by a newcomer can undermine a new venture's cognitive legitimacy through rumors and information suppression or inaccurate dissemination. For example, early mail- and phone-order computer supply stores in the United States were highly specialized, selling mainly to people very knowledgeable about electronics who were building or modifying their own equipment. When the industry began to grow rapidly in the 1980s, selling to "amateurs," traditional walk-in stores argued that mail- and phone-order firms did not provide after-sales service and thus were an inferior form (Aldrich, 1999).

Similarly, health maintenance organizations (HMOs) confronted bitter opposition from traditional physician practices, which argued that HMOs violated customary expectations about effective physician–patient relationships, and thus delivered inferior services to patients (Scott et al., 2000). Physicians fought HMOs through a national organization, the American Medical Association (AMA), as well as state associations. They found a powerful ally in the American Association of Retired Persons (AARP), which argued that HMOs shortchanged senior citizens. HMOs grew slowly until other organizations intervened on their behalf, such as large insurance companies.

Community-level conditions affect the rate at which an industry grows by affecting the diffusion of knowledge about a new activity and the extent to which it is publicly or officially accepted. If founders have pursued effective trust-building and reliability-enhancing strategies within their emerging industry, and have established a reputation *vis-à-vis* other industries, they have laid the groundwork for attaining cognitive legitimacy at the community level. If not, then population survival becomes problematic. We will examine community level entrepreneurship more fully later in this chapter.

Cognitive Strategies in Populations

We turn now to the specific strategies that organizations follow to achieve shared learning and cognitive legitimacy: Interorganizational relations, collective interest associations, and access to colleges and universities. Entrepreneurs who pursue strategies of total autonomy face formidable obstacles. By contrast, collective action, if successful, can spell the difference between success and failure for new populations. Collective action can be as simple as dyadic cooperation (Larson, 1992) or as complex as multi-organizational small firm networks (Human and Provan, 2000).

Inter-organizational Relations

At the within-population level, *interorganizational relations* can be a route through which successful routines are transferred from one organization to another, as shown in research on organizational and industry-wide learning curves (Zimmerman, 1982; Auster, 1994). In their study of Liberty Ship construction yards during World War II, Argote et al. (1990) found that shipyards beginning production later in the war benefited from knowledge acquired from shipyards that had begun production earlier. In a study of 36 pizza stores operated by 10 different franchisees, Argote and her colleagues found evidence that knowledge acquired through learning by doing transferred across stores owned by the *same* franchisee (Darr et al., 1995). For example, one store discovered a better way of arranging pizza boxes next to the ovens, so that fewer steps were required and fewer pizzas dropped. This boxing innovation quickly spread to the other stores owned by the same franchisee, with the knowledge spread via phone calls, personal acquaintances, and meetings.

Interorganizational relations depend heavily upon trust, and trust arises from patterns of collective interaction over the long term. In such cases, the number of trust-based ties does not depend on strictly dyadic interaction, but instead develops from a collective understanding. Uzzi (1997), building upon earlier studies, conducted a field and ethnographic analysis of 23 women's dress firms in the New York City apparel industry. Although the firms often engaged in straightforward economic exchange relationships, they also depended very heavily on embedded relationships. Trust, rather than calculated risk, smoothed transactions between firms. Fine-grained information transfer allowed the spread of tacit knowledge across firms. Building on their underlying social relationships, they also were able to use joint problem-solving arrangements. However, Uzzi's (1996) study also showed that when firms increased their dependence on particular actors, instead of creating more within-population ties, their likelihood of survival decreased sharply. Thus, the totality of relationships between firms within a population, rather than relationships between just two or three firms, ultimately determines a population's fate.

Collective Interest Associations

Initial collaborations between organizations begin informally, in networks of inter-firm relations, but some later develop into more formalized strategic alliances, consortia, and trade associations (Powell, 1990). In some kinds of technology regimes, new-to-the-world innovations tend to be pursued by a handful of parallel, independent actors, as Van de Ven and Garud (1991) found in their study of the cochlear implant industry. People come to know one another through personal interaction and through traveling in similar social/technical circles, such as attending the same industry conferences and technical committee meetings. This small handful of actors can generate social networks that, in the aggregate, result in population-level collective action (Van de Ven, 1991). Some standard-setting bodies evolve into trade associations, but most do not.

The Bluetooth Special Interest Group is an example of inter-firm collaboration that may catalyze a new population. In February of 1998, Ericsson, Nokia, IBM, Toshiba, and Intel formed an alliance to promote a low power, low cost radio interface between mobile phones and their accessories. Their announced ultimate goal was to eliminate cables between mobile phones, PC cards, headsets, printers, and other desktop devices (Bluetooth, 2000). The Bluetooth standard system was designed to minimize interference with other wireless protocols and provide increased security by offering a range of up to 33 feet for data transmission. As a special interest group, Bluetooth's main goal was to promote their wireless solution as *the* standard for person-to-person technologies and connectivity between closely located computer devices.

However, companies such as Apple and Lucent Technologies, who supported the HomeRF and 8002.11b standards, questioned Bluetooth's claims of not interfering with other kinds of short-range wireless transmission. The Bluetooth chip can be used for wireless communication outside as well as inside the home but it has an extremely short range (10 meters at most). In contrast, the HomeRF was designed for wireless communication inside a house or a particular business, and the 802.11b technology works as a wireless Ethernet. The Bluetooth Special Interest Group has made a point of showing that their transmission technology is compatible with both HomeRF and 802.11b and that their system serves consumer needs in ways that offset compatibility issues. HomeRF and 802.11b are competing to become the predominant technology to serve the same basic need: Wireless access to the Internet within particular buildings (Batista, 2000).

The creation of industry standards may increase the potential for synergy among participants in an informal network of organizations and increase the survival capabilities of the population in an aggregate, but standards also play a role in discouraging entry and eliminating some organizations within the industry. The application service provider (ASP) industry that began emerging in early 1999 provides an example of how standards might be beneficial for a population as a whole but disadvantageous for single firms in the population. The industry leases software over the Internet to small and medium sized firms, and potential customers have been very concerned about issues of data security, privacy, and the reliability of the service. Spurred by the Application Service Provider Industry Consortium, formed in mid-1999, firms began offering service level agreements (SLAs) that spelled out strict security and reliability terms. As many segments of the industry appear to be moving toward "winner take all" markets, firms rapidly escalated their promises, with some promising 99.999 percent up time (the so-called "five nines" standard). Such SLAs substantially enhanced the cognitive legitimacy of the industry, but many small and undercapitalized new firms found the emerging standards inordinately expensive to meet.

Trade associations are an example of collective interest associations that work together to advance the interests of an organizational population. For example, trade associations pursue interests common to most firms in an industry by formulating product/process standards via trade committees and publishing trade journals. They also conduct marketing campaigns to enhance an industry's standing in the eyes of the public and promote trade fairs at which customers and suppliers can gain a sense of the industry's stability. Trade associations are *minimalist organizations* – able to operate on low overhead and quickly adapt to changing conditions – and thus are easier to found than, for example, production organizations (Halliday et al., 1987). An *industry champion* often steps forward as a catalyst to an association's founding by volunteering to cover the costs of running the association until it recruits enough members to gain a stable dues base. Typically, the largest firms in an industry do this, and they dominate an association's board of directors. Many trade associations, following the example of state bar and other voluntary associations, operate out of the offices of member firms in their early years. Law firms representing the largest firms in the industry administer many smaller trade associations.

Trade associations can facilitate within-population learning, disseminating knowledge of effective routines and competencies. For example, state bar associations learned from early mistakes, as associations founded later in the population's growth apparently benefited from the knowledge gained from earlier foundings (Halliday et al., 1987). Similarly, Aldrich et al. (1990) found that trade association disbandings were reduced in specific industry niches that already had large numbers of existing associations. Previous associations had developed organizing templates that subsequent associations adopted.

At the between-population level, business interest associations and political action groups that organize across industry boundaries facilitate population-level learning and cognitive legitimacy. For example, in 1943, a diverse group of 25 California electronics manufacturers formed the West Coast Electronics Manufacturers Association (WCEMA) in response to the War Production Board's (WPA) announcement of a cutback in defense contracts awarded to west coast firms. The WCEMA – later renamed the Western Electronics Manufacturers Association (WEMA) – lobbied the WPA for a larger share of defense contracts. They argued that a disproportionate share was going to eastern firms, such as Raytheon and General Electric. In the 1960s, WEMA concentrated its efforts on the smaller entrepreneurial firms in Silicon Valley, and "sponsored seminars and educational activities that encouraged the exchange of ideas and information, including management training sessions on subjects ranging from finance and technology marketing to production and export assistance" (Saxenian, 1994). WEMA eventually expanded outside of California and was renamed the American Electronics Association (AEA) in 1978. The WCEMA's transformations into the WEMA and the AEA illustrate the advantages of cross-industry organizing efforts, as well as the flexibility of minimalist organizations.

Not all efforts at cross-population organizing succeed in promoting joint standards or a common public policy position. When the largest firms in cross-industry alliances disagree, they may impede convergence on a common standard. For example, throughout the 1980s, computer and software manufacturers, software users, and other interested parties struggled over Unix standards for technical workstations, an industry with over $10 billion in sales by 1990 (Axelrod et al., 1995). The original Unix operating system was developed at Bell Laboratories during the 1960s, and subsequently software developers wrote more than 250 versions. An early attempt to develop a common standard, the X/Open group, failed when two large firms – AT&T and Sun Microsystems – pulled out and announced their own effort to develop a system that would be available under proprietary license to others. Seven major firms, including IBM and DEC, formed an alternative coalition – the Open Software Foundation – and eventually recruited nine full sponsors. AT&T and Sun responded by forming Unix International, an alliance of ten firms. Both alliances eventually released their own commercial versions of Unix. As this example illustrates, large firms play a crucial role in mobilizing other firms to join a standard-setting coalition, and conflicts between them can fragment alliances.

Educational Institutions

Finally, at the community level, *educational institutions* create and spread knowledge about dominant competencies (Romanelli, 1989), thus putting resources in the hands of potential founders. New populations must either build on the competencies already supported by educational institutions or find ways to encourage the provision of new ones. To the extent that specific competencies underlie particular populations, the activities of educational institutions may increase the diversity of organizational communities. Universities, research institutes, and associated programs not only conduct research, but also train persons who become competent enough to exploit the latest research products. Educational institutions also "formalize and centralize information by establishing courses and degree programs that train students in basic competencies. Once technologies are understood, and stabilized and identifiable jobs (e.g., computer engineer) emerge in industry, colleges and universities take over much of the training of skilled personnel" (Romanelli, 1989). Historically, the growth of national educational systems has spurred founding rates by spreading generalized competencies that give nascent entrepreneurs the necessary skills to succeed (Nelson, 1994).

The wireless telecommunications industry has worked extremely hard to establish connections with academic research and educational programs. Academic wireless programs can be found at UC Berkley, Columbia, Purdue, the University of Washington, the University of Pennsylvania and Georgia Tech, among others. Most of these programs were funded by, and have direct links to, the main wireless telecommunications companies. For example, the MPRG program at the Virginia Polytechnic Institute and State University has formed an Industrial Affiliates Program with major firms as charter members: AT&T, FBU, GTE, Motorola, Apple Computer, Nortel, Bellsouth, Rockwell and Southwestern Bell. Through their experience in the MPRG program, over 100 undergraduate and graduate students have taken state-of-the art knowledge to the rapidly expanding wireless industry (MPRG, 2000).

Sociopolitical Requirements and Strategies

The acquisition of sociopolitical legitimacy for a new population depends on its capacity to create collective action and, therefore, on the willingness of individual entrepreneurs to compromise their independent, possibly rebellious, dispositions. In a fashion similar to cognitive strategies, the key events affecting the emergence of new populations as stable entities involve the formation of other types of organizations (Delacroix and Rao, 1994). Gaining moral legitimacy for a new population involves altering or fitting into existing norms and values, something individual organizations sometimes lack the resources to accomplish. Similarly, winning legal and regulatory acceptance generally requires campaign contributions, political action committees, lobbying, and other costly activities that are often beyond the reach of individual organizations. Thus, early in a new population's growth, interorganizational collective action will have to address sociopolitical issues or the population will remain vulnerable to attacks on its legitimacy.

In the interior construction of a population, sociopolitical approval – especially regulatory approval from governmental agencies – may be jeopardized if collective action fails. Failure to agree upon common standards leaves a new population vulnerable to illegal and unethical acts by feckless members. Such actions may bring the entire population into moral disrepute and jeopardize its legitimacy. In contrast, mobilization around a shared goal may enable new populations to shape the course of government regulation and win favorable treatment. As Edelman and Suchman (1997) noted, organizations and associations not only submit to laws but also shape them. If early founders succeed in creating an interpretive frame that links a new population to established norms and values, subsequent founders will mobilize support much more easily.

Two examples show how associations may attempt to solicit their own regulation to ward off more drastic action by government. In the United States, both the Information Industry Association, representing the pay per call industry, and the American Gaming Association, representing gambling casinos, became involved in issues that initially raised questions concerning their populations' moral legitimacy. Ultimately, the issues they confronted were dealt with as regulatory matters. The Information Industry Association was formed only after the industry was stigmatized by the reckless actions of some firms, whereas the American Gaming Association was formed in response to the potential for greater federal regulation of an industry that has always had a rather shady reputation (Aldrich, 1999).

Populations that succeed in creating a strong organization to represent their interests may use their position to block the way for alternative organizational forms. Populations that not only solicit favorable treatment from the state, but also cloak themselves in moral legitimacy, are especially blessed. For example, funeral home owners in the United States enjoyed great success for many years in thwarting state regulation of the industry (Torres, 1988). Locally owned homes controlled most state boards regulating the industry by playing on the twin themes of local control of business and respect for the sacredness of their practices. For almost a century, state boards blocked alternatives to traditional means of disposal of the dead, opposing crematoriums, burial societies, and chain-owned funeral homes. Their actions kept the founding rates of technically superior alternatives very low, almost totally suppressing the emergence of competing industries. Only when changing political currents in the 1980s began to favor deregulation did regional and national chains gain the upper hand.

Many inter-industry relations involving moral and regulatory acceptance are more matters of education and negotiation than of zero-sum conflict. For example, *moral* legitimacy arguments for technology-intensive patient care emphasize the health care system's obligation to do all it can for the quality of human life, and *regulatory* legitimacy arguments stress equitable treatment of citizens covered by government and private insurers. To benefit from complying with these legitimacy requirements, new biomedical and health-care industries must convince third parties – insurance companies and the government – to pay the costs that patients cannot bear, such as for CAT scans or cochlear implants. Thus, firms in the industry must cooperate to educate and influence these third parties to include the product or service in their payment reimbursement systems (Van de Ven and Garud, 1991).

Finally, lack of community-level support for new populations may undercut their efforts to secure sociopolitical approval. Most new forms of business enterprise have enjoyed at least moral and regulatory tolerance of their existence (Delacroix et al., 1989; Zucker, 1989). Nonetheless, this apparent easy success should not blind us to the many occasions on which support has been withheld. The first newspaper editor in the United States was jailed (Delacroix and Carroll, 1983), and many forms of inter-business alliances were ruled illegal in the 19th century (Staber and Aldrich, 1983).

The human genome project exemplifies the moral limitations of basic "business" concepts and institutions. Two different types of organizations have pursued this project: a) publicly funded non-profit institutes and agencies, and b) private biotechnology firms. In the 1990s and into the early years of the 21st century, private bio-technology companies have been trying to obtain patents over particular sequences of genes, while the publicly funded project has been committed to the open publication and use of findings (Outlook, 2000). These two strategies follow from the moral legitimacy framework of Western political culture, which posits that government sponsored research should be public, whereas private companies should pursue the exclusive exploitation of their findings. Nonetheless, controversy over the property rights status of genes has exploded, particularly in the United States and Great Britain.

Although the U.S. Patent and Trademark Office has given some patents for gene sequences, it has not yet processed a large backlog of claims. For example, over the past five years, a single company, ZymoGenetics, has applied for over 500 novel gene sequences (ZymoGenetics, 2000). In March of the year 2000, President Bill Clinton and Prime Minister Tony Blair publicly affirmed the need to maintain open access to the human genome raw genetics sequences. Immediately after their statement, the stock value of the biotech firms involved in the genome field decreased dramatically. Although the controversy has not been resolved, it appears that human genetic information has reached the limit of what our conventional concept of intellectual property rights can handle, thereby jeopardizing the continued acquisition of resources by biotechnology firms. The industry's future remains uncertain.

Some members of the public sector and the scientific community believe that patents on genes should just be prohibited, whereas others believe that simply modifying the patenting system to include the possibility of obligatory licensing systems would be adequate. The latter system would give firms the right to receive compensation, but they could not restrict public access to information. Another suggested modification to the existing system would be to raise patent standards by asking for substantial, specific and credible evidence of the use of a particular gene (Shulman, 2000).

Summary: Population Formation and Growth

In this section, we described the context in which learning and legitimacy problems arise for entrepreneurs in new populations. We also reviewed the cognitive and sociopolitical requirements confronting startups and examined common strategies enacted to meet them. We argued that organizations with competence-destroying innovations have two main tasks that are mainly accomplished through collective action: The creation of routines and working standards and the creation of ties with important societal actors. To survive, new organizations must create a balance between competition and cooperation. Successful efforts can enhance their positions in favorable segments of emerging markets, if they manage to collectively construct a clear image of themselves, their products or services, and their proposed advantages.

Although the process of learning and creating legitimacy starts at the organizational level, ultimately it requires actions at higher levels of the social structures. Collective efforts to create a knowledge base and gain legitimacy must take place within populations, between populations, and within communities. The process of collective action starts with the creation of interorganizational ties to companies within the industry, as well as with educational institutions. Some of these ties evolve into special interest groups, industry trade associations, and inter-industry interest associations.

Building Organizational Communities

An *organizational community* is *a set of coevolving organizational populations joined by ties of commensalism and symbiosis through their orientation to a common technology, normative order, or legal-regulatory regime.* Symbiosis denotes a mutual dependence between dissimilar units, whereas *commensalism* means that units make similar demands on the environment. Populations in different niches that are pursuing different resources and benefit from each other's existence are in a symbiotic relation. For example, information technology firms often provide the knowledge accumulation and retrieval systems for biotechnology firms. Commensalism, "literally interpreted, means eating from the same table" (Hawley, 1950), and this condition puts organizations from such populations in situations of potential competition from each other. We present many examples of commensalism in this section.

Investigators define a community for a particular historical period, and its geographic scope is an empirical matter. A community may well encompass an entire regional, national, or global economic system, depending on the core chosen. In this chapter, we focus on national communities. The extent to which social actors are interdependent is also ultimately an empirical question.

In this section, we first map out the 8 possible relations between populations, showing that relations are more complex than a simple competition/cooperation dimension. We argue that three forces are primarily responsible for generating new organizational communities, although we focus mainly on one of them – technological innovation – in this section. Finally, we consider the selection processes affecting acceptance of a new community as legitimate, concentrating on collective action, government actions, and the role of community institutions.

Types of Relations between Populations

Populations are not equal within a community, but have different status and relationships, depending on their overall pattern of inter-population relations. The most common expression of commensalism is *competition*, in which populations, old and new, seek the same resources. For example, the telephone and cable industries have invested heavily in developing wired means for multimedia data transmission, forcing the telecommunications industry to improve its wireless data transmission technology to remain competitive in the e-commerce sector. Whereas telephone companies can now offer internet services with Digital Subscriber Lines (DSL) that provide speeds between 384 kilobytes and 1.5 megabytes per second (OIT, 2000), the wireless industry can currently only handle data transmissions of 144 to 300 kilobytes per second. Such slow speeds are far from the 2.4 megabytes per second required to provide services like e-mail, web browsing, and mobile e-commerce (Buckley, 2000). Thus, competitive pressures have compelled wireless firms to innovate or fall behind.

The extent of competition between populations depends on the relative size of each and the degree of similarity or niche overlap between them. Populations based on competence-destroying capabilities essentially aim to seize the resources of the old population they hope to replace. Commensalism can also lead to mutualism, if populations making similar demands on the environment combine their efforts, intentionally or otherwise. Cross-population mutualism, in the form of business associations or inter-industry councils, can improve the joint standing of those involved by increasing their capacity for sociopolitical legitimacy and their access to resources.

Relations between populations in an evolving community revolve simultaneously around symbiotic and commensalistic axes. Innovative entrepreneurs must be willing to compromise some of their autonomy to enter a complex set of cooperative relationships, while simultaneously competing in an even broader environment and with a greater variety of actors. Based on the distinction between symbiotic and commensalistic relations, we can distinguish eight types of relations between populations, as shown in Table 2 (Brittain and Wholey,

Table 2. Eight possible relations between organizational populations

I.   *Commensalism*

   (−, −) Full Competition: growth in each population detracts from growth in the other. E.g. competition between voluntary associations for members from the same socio-demographic groups (McPherson, 1983).

   (−, 0) Partial competition: relations are asymmetric, with only one having a negative effect on the other. E.g. industrial unions suppressed the founding of craft unions in the 1930s (Hannan and Freeman, 1987).

   (+, −) Predatory competition: one population expands at the expense of the other. E.g. television stations' revenue grew at the expense of radio stations (Dimmick and Rothenbuhler, 1984).

   (0, 0) Neutrality: populations have no effect on each other. E.g. founding rates of commercial and savings banks in Manhattan had no effect on each other between 1792 and 1980 (Ranger-Moore et. al., 1991).

   (+, 0) Partial mutualism: relations are asymmetric, with only one population benefiting from the presence of the other. E.g. the growth of brewpubs between 1975 and 1990 stimulated foundings of microbreweries, but not vice-versa (Carroll and Swaminathan, 1992).

   (+, +) Full mutualism: two populations in overlapping niches benefit from the presence of the other. E.g. small and large railroads and telephone companies benefited from the other's presence (Dobbin, 1994; Barnett, 1995).

II. *Symbiosis*

   (+, +) Symbiosis: two populations are in different niches and benefit from the presence of the other. E.g. venture capitalists make profits by investing in high technology firms, thereby enabling both populations to grow (Brittain, 1994).

III. *Dominance*

   A dominant population controls the flow of resources to other populations. Effects depend on the outcome of commensalistic and symbiotic relations.

Legend: Signs in parentheses refer to the effect of one population, A, on a second population, B: + Positive effect, 0 No effect, − Negative effect.
Source: Aldrich (1999).

1988). In this table, symbols in parentheses precede each form of interaction, denoting the impact each population has on the other. Six constitute various forms of commensalism (competition and cooperation), and a seventh is symbiosis. Aldrich (1999) included dominance as an eighth type of relation between populations. Dominance emerges as a hierarchical relation between populations, based on the outcome of symbiotic and commensalistic interactions.

Forces Generating New Organizational Communities

Communities emerge not only from forces that generate new organizations and populations, but also from new commensalistic and symbiotic relations between populations. In previous sections, we have explored the foundings of new organizations and the social construction of new populations. To those accounts we now add the activities that cut across populations and contribute to the social construction of communities. Discontinuities in existing populations and communities caused by technical, normative, and regulatory innovations that are exploited by entrepreneurs provoke transformations in existing populations or the emergence of new ones. Processes of competition, mutualism, and symbiosis sort the affected populations into differentiated niches, characterized by hierarchy and dominance. Depending upon their strength, these processes may bind populations into a community sharing a common fate.

Three kinds of discontinuities seem to play particularly important roles as catalysts for changes that generate new communities: (1) shifts in societal norms and values, (2) changes in laws and regulations, and (3) technological innovations. Shifts in societal norms and values may create conditions facilitating the development of new populations. If such populations develop mutualistic or symbiotic relations, they might become the nucleus of a new organizational community. Changes in laws and regulations might also lead to new organizational communities because of the resulting symbiotic networks of government agencies, non-profit organizations, law firms, consultants, research institutes, and academic programs (Galaskiewicz, 1979). However, technological innovations have probably played the most important role in the creation of new communities in recent decades.

Rarely do single key events generate new organizational populations, based on a technological breakthrough (Ziman, 2000). Instead, from an evolutionary view, technological innovation typically involves a cumulative series of interrelated acts of variation, selection, and retention that might culminate in commercial applications (Garud, 1994). Long-term changes in scientific discovery in the 20th century continually generated technological innovations with commercial potential (Dosi, 1988). Some of the innovations have been seized upon by entrepreneurs and pursued with such vigor that new populations were formed, such as the radio broadcasting industry in the 1920s (Leblebici et al., 1991). Although many of the new populations failed, some of those that prospered became segments of existing communities, whereas others became the nucleus of new organizational communities.

For the Web, the introduction of Mosaic software in 1993 was the major technological innovation that facilitated its emergence as a commercial community, but there were many previous events that set the stage for Mosaic to become a catalytic event (Hafner and Lyon, 1996). Many firms (e.g., Digital Equipment Corporation, MCI Telecommunications) were seeking ways in the 1980s and early 1990s to exploit the technology of the Internet for commercial gain. In addition, Mosaic technology was itself an innovation that improved upon the earliest Web browser created by CERN scientists in Switzerland as a more sophisticated means for getting information from the Internet. Because these early efforts occurred in a mutualistic environment of open sharing and standard setting, many individuals contributed to the early enhancements of the Mosaic technology, enabling it to become the dominant standard very rapidly.

Technological innovations have been playing a similar role in the telecommunications industry, with the impending arrival of a third generation (3G) of wireless technologies. The jump to 3G technology has increased the chaotic nature of this emerging industry and created a perceived need for collective action among participants. The new technology will ultimately allow the transmission of multimedia information in a fashion similar to the way customers now receive wired Internet services provided by telephone companies and TV cable providers. The ultimate goal would be to offer web or internet-based commercial services through cellular phones and other similarly wireless devices.

However, achieving the final goal of radically increasing the data transmission capacity of 3 Megabytes per second (to support e-mail, Web browsing, mobile e-commerce and multimedia) implies a migration to different technologies that build upon each other. Depending on their starting technology, companies might have to update their software, make relatively minor investments in infrastructure, or transform their entire set of connectivity networks. Some starting technologies offer cheaper and better migration paths than others. For example, companies whose core technology is based on the CDMA (Code Division Multiple Access) and TDMA (Time Division Multiple Access) systems will have to spend 30 percent less in their upgrading to 3G capacity than those based on GSM (Global System for Mobile Communications) technology (Buckley, 2000).

From an evolutionary perspective, selection forces need not favor the cheapest transition, as regulatory and political considerations may favor more expensive solutions. The migration pattern from CDMA is based only on software enhancement and is cheaper than any other alternative. However, because the GSM migration path (the most predominant system in Europe) tends to converge with TDMA migration (which is the most popular current standard for the Americas), both paths enjoy a competitive advantage over GSM. Global standardization and earlier global connectivity, combined with the support of the 3GPP organization (Third-Generation Partnership Program) have created incentives for firms to follow either the GSM or TDMA technological paths (Buckley, 2000).

Because a population's product or service – hardware and software – is often part of a larger symbiotic system of components, its evolutionary path thus depends on changes in other systems. Some innovations are relatively discrete entities, but many innovations are related to some aspect of a techno-logical system, which can be thought of as composed of core and peripheral subsystems (Tushman and Murmann, 1998). For example, most micro-electronic devices are sold as components of more complex systems (Barley et al., 1992), unlike biotechnology products. A period of incremental change may be relatively stable with respect to the core subsystem, but it may be quite dynamic with respect to innovations in peripheral subsystems. Individuals and organizations can cause temporary uncertainty by creating peripheral subsys-tems that complement the core technology. These new innovations become the basis for populations symbiotically linked to the population producing the core subsystem.

Innovations that occurred in the early days of the Web's evolution into a commercial community fit the concept of core and peripheral subsystems. The introduction of a standardized browser technology was the key innovation that created the core subsystem of the Web's commercial community. Because the community converged around this technology relatively swiftly and Netscape Corporation asserted its dominance within a year after the technology was introduced in 1994, the Netscape browser quickly became the standard within the community. However, using its dominance in personal computer operating systems, Microsoft created an Internet Explorer browser that caught up and surpassed Netscape in subsequent years (Cusumano and Yoffie, 1998). With the core in place, efforts at enhancing the technology of the Web focused on subsystems, such as browser add-ons and other user interfaces. For example, one subsystem innovation involved the transformation of web sites and applica-tions to simplify their use in wireless browsers that the telecommunications industry will provide in 3G technology.

Innovative entrepreneurs play a vital role in capitalizing technological advances in a more rapid fashion than already established bureaucratic organizations and populations. In the Web Internet Service Provider (ISP) population, for example, the thousands of local ISPs that were founded in the mid-1990s overshadowed established firms. New firms took advantage of the slowness with which large firms, such as regional telephone companies, responded to the new technology. Between 1996 and 1997, in fact, more than 1000 new ISPs were founded and the ISP population at the end of 1997 numbered over 5000 (Yoshitake, 1997). Similarly, young entrepreneurs, fresh out of college, founded most of the Web consulting and design firms; some were fleeing established advertising and marketing firms.

In biotechnology, by the mid-1980s, "over 500 freestanding dedicated bio-technology firms had been established worldwide to pursue some form of genetic engineering" (Barley et al., 1992). The early biotechnology firms were mostly independent dedicated biotechnology firms, rather than divisions or spin-offs from existing companies (Hybels et al., 1994). Scientists striving to commercialize discoveries from their university laboratories founded many of these small, science-based companies. By the mid-1990s, independent startups appeared to have achieved more success than those initially sponsored by older and larger firms. Nonetheless, most biotech firms in the late 1990s were still fairly small, measured by their market value. In 1994, only 8 biotechnology firms in the United States had a market value in excess of $500 million. In mid-1998, of the 120 largest firms followed by BioVenture Consultants, only 19 exceeded $500 million in market value (Robbins-Roth, 1998).

Is this social construction of communities by entrepreneurs an intentional process or one just driven by responses to environmental pressures? The search for dominance in a particular community may indicate that community formation, at least for entrepreneurs trying to dominate their environments, is at least partially propelled by strategic intent. Theories of capitalist class integration, upper class cohesion, and bank centrality in capitalist economies go beyond simple ecological analyses of dominance (Mizruchi, 1996). In these theories, dominance results from strategic acts by self-aware or at least self-interested actors. In most of these accounts, powerful actors use director interlocks to shape the flow of resources between organizations and owners or top executives. They need not be aware of a larger collective interest for their actions to have systemic effects. Even if the individual firms act primarily out of self-interest, the aggregate effect of their actions can be substantial, if a group of them behave similarly (Mizruchi, 1992). However, as Mizruchi (1996, p. 273) noted, "there are virtually no systematic data on firms' motives for interlocking." Researchers have inferred motives by examining patterns of interlocking, observing that interlocks seem to follow from the flow of resource dependence. Because researchers have not had direct access to directors, with a few exceptions (Hirsch, 1982), they have been unable to discern the motives underlying the interlocks.

Selection Forces Affecting New Communities

A developing community's viability depends on the extent to which its core populations gain cognitive and sociopolitical legitimacy, as well as on the perceived value of the core populations' products or services (Miner and Haunschild, 1995). Government and regulatory bodies, for example, face decisions regarding the extent to which they need to become involved in the burgeoning community, as overseers and as supporters. Innovating organizations must also consider how to modify or interpret the innovation so that it is readily understandable to their customers or constituency. In making modifications, organizations and regulatory agencies engage in collective action to establish standards, both within and across populations.

The more an emerging community depends on new organizational forms and new populations, the more serious its legitimacy problems (Baum and

Oliver, 1992; Dacin, 1997). How does a developing organizational community achieve legitimacy? In most cases, no "guiding hand" governs from the community center, directing strategic moves toward legitimacy. Instead, community legitimacy depends on three processes. First, new organizations and populations must struggle to achieve legitimacy in their own right. Legitimacy problems are most acute for the first populations in the community. Later, follower populations will have an easier time. Second, organizations and populations achieve legitimacy more easily within the community if they work together to gain government support for industry standards. Third, across the entire community, institutional actors, such as educational organizations and the media, create the laws, regulations, and symbolic resources sustaining organizational communities. Organizational actions to achieve legitimacy have already been discussed in the first part of this chapter, and so in this section we will concentrate on the population and community levels for the acquisition of legitimacy.

Within- and Cross-population Actions

Collective action organizations make population and community level learning much easier, as firms share information and work on solutions to common problems affecting many populations (Miner and Haunschild, 1995). Although individual firms might be able to achieve their own legitimacy, population and community level legitimacy becomes problematic if these firms engage in unbridled full competition to advance their own interests and fail to promote their mutual interests (Aldrich and Fiol, 1994; Garud, 1994). A lack of standard designs, for example, may block the diffusion of knowledge and understanding, thus constraining the new activities. Therefore, founders of new firms are compelled by selection pressures to find strategies for establishing stable sequences of mutualistic relations within their emerging population. They also benefit if they find ways to create symbiotic relations with organizations in other populations. Such actions include developing dominant designs and community-wide standards through the creation of industry councils, cooperative alliances, trade associations, and other vehicles for collective action (Haunschild, 1993).

Across the entire evolving community, partial or full mutualism heightens legitimacy and organizational learning. Such developments mean that new populations generated at later stages in the community's growth will experience more favorable founding conditions than earlier populations. For example, in biotechnology, American firms founded in the 1980s became embedded in mutualistic *networks of learning* that gave them access to knowledge gained through research and development by previous firms (Powell et al., 1996). Once established, these new collective units can concentrate on symbiotic relations with government, educational institutions, and the media. Following the logic of collective action, the combined activities of groups across populations have a more powerful influence on standards and regulations than the actions of isolated organizations or action sets (Olson, 1965; Aldrich and Whetten, 1981).

For example, in the cochlear implant industry, the American Association of Otolaryngology "initiated a committee of representatives from industry, clinics, audiology, psychoacoustics, and other disciplines to study and recommend technical standards" (Garud, 1994). In biotechnology, several practices promoted a relatively unified technological community: Professors took sabbaticals at biotechnology firms, postdoctoral students circulated between universities and firms, and firms made laboratory conditions so attractive that they created a labor market for scientists that cut across universities and industry (Powell et al., 1996).

The Web is an interesting case precisely because collective action organizations – alliances, coalitions, and consortia – formed so quickly and managed to recruit the largest firms in the affected industries to join. As a community of symbiotically linked populations, many of the Web's interest groups were multi-industry, rather than limited to membership from only one population. For example, the World Wide Web Consortium, which set standards for the Web, included more than 100 members. All major software firms joined, as did the major hardware firms, such as IBM, Sun Microsystems, and Silicon Graphics (Lohr, 1995). Other groups that were formed to promote Internet standards included the Internet Engineering Task Force (IETF), the Internet Assigned Number Authority, the Federal Networking Council and the Internet Society. Between 1993 and 1997, four International World Wide Web Conferences were held in Europe and the United States, where Web service providers and businesses discussed ways to resolve some of the common issues they faced. The American Institute of Certified Public Accountants developed a certification program, called the CPA Web Trust, which gave a seal of approval to vendors doing business on the Web who followed secure practices.

Government Support and Regulation

Organizational communities benefit from a strong supporting state infrastructure, in addition to individual and collective efforts. Governmental support and assistance can create a stable nucleus for an evolving organizational community and thus accelerate the speed with which new populations linked to the community achieve legitimacy. State sponsored associations, alliances, and other activities can also create strong incentives for organizations and populations to engage in mutualistic activities, as well as a compliance structure for reducing the likelihood of competitive activities. In her study of the diffusion of charter schools in the United States in the 1990s, Renzulli (2001) found that state laws treating charter schools favorably were a crucial factor affecting the number of submissions from school districts. Regardless of whether a community is generated by technological innovations, shifts in norms and values, or changes in laws and regulations, state actions play a key role in its evolution.

Two domains are particularly significant: Government support for research, and enactment and enforcement of new laws, regulations, and standards.

In communities with deep roots in technological innovation, the essential infrastructure was often built from research and development sponsored by the government, as documented in several studies. In the cochlear implant industry, for example, the first commercial activity was preceded by 22 years of non-commercial research (Van de Ven and Garud, 1993). Research on electronically enhancing human hearing was conducted by academics and sponsored by grants from government, public research foundations, and philanthropists. The commercial radio community grew not only from entrepreneurial activity and collective action by commercial firms, but also from "the emergence and active participation of military, legislative, and regulatory bodies" (Rosenkopf and Tushman, 1994, pp. 413–414). The US Navy was involved because it made heavy use of radio technology in its operations, and it lobbied for federal legislation giving priority to its needs. In the machine tool industry, the US Air Force played a major role in establishing numerically controlled machine tools as a standard, versus the record-playback standard that some firms wanted (Noble, 1984).

Concerning government regulation, major differences exist between nations with decentralized versus centralized political systems. The United States has a political system of divided executive and legislative branches, containing independent regulatory agencies. Thus, newly organized industries ultimately must co-opt, neutralize, form alliances with, and otherwise come to terms with government agencies. Trade associations and other collective action entities focus much of their efforts on direct access to agencies themselves. By contrast, in political systems that have unified executive and legislative branches, as in most European and Asian nations, support from political parties and career civil servants is essential. For example, in Japan, Ministry of Finance career officials wield substantial influence over the banking system, and many retire from the Ministry to take high-level positions in financial institutions. Regardless of a political system's structure, without governmental approval, individual efforts to form organizations and create new populations will be severely hampered.

For example, the early biotechnology industry developed in an environment of great uncertainty, because firms did not have a clear idea of what products would be regulated and what safety tests would be required by the Environmental Protection Agency, the Food and Drug Administration, and the Department of Agriculture. Accordingly, the Industrial Biotechnology Association lobbied the FDA, the EPA and other agencies in an attempt to create a more certain regulatory environment. An FDA ruling in 1981, approving the first diagnostic kit based on a monoclonal antibody, significantly raised the founding rate of biotech firms in the years that followed (Shan et al., 1991). However, for years the industry has been unable to resolve a controversy over their most promising research project – the human genome – and thus they were unable to gain the support of the U.S. Trade Patent and Trademark office.

Unlike the experience of biotechnology, early associations in the Web community succeeded in promoting their collective interests, especially with respect to regulatory control over the community's activities. During the 1996–97 session of Congress, for example, several efforts were made to enact legislation that would have forced independent service providers, such as America Online, to monitor messages sent through their servers. As a result of collective lobbying efforts by community members, however, none of these efforts were successful. By contrast, the biotechnology community fought a long-running battle with government regulators. Only in 1995 did the industry begin receiving the same treatment from the FDA as traditional pharmaceutical firms. The biotechnology community struggled for almost 20 years to achieve the kind of sociopolitical legitimacy that the Web community had apparently already won after only three years, even though investors poured billions of dollars into the biotech industry in the intervening years.

Government agencies can play a role in structuring the inter-organizational environment of new industries in ways that encourage mutualism between firms and populations. Rappa's (1989) study of the development of the gallium arsenide integrated circuit in the United States, Japan, and Western Europe found that the United States had more firms and scientists involved, but that Japan had greater coordination of its firms' and scientists' efforts. In Japan, the Ministry of International Trade and Industry (MITI), a government agency, encouraged inter-firm cooperation in the integrated circuit industry via trade committees, just as it facilitated the formation of research and development consortia in other industries (Aldrich and Sasaki, 1995). The cooperating firms jointly formulated industrial governance policies, developed a competence pool of scientists and managers through training programs and informal information sharing, and also worked on commercial applications of the technology (Fransman, 1990). By contrast, competition between firms in the United States inhibited the development of collective action within the affected industries.

In telecommunications, government plays an important role in two areas: Technology regulations and spectrum allocations. Creating and diffusing a standard is almost impossible for a single a firm and even very difficult for a population. Governments can either provide incentives for cooperation or define the standards to follow (Funke and Methe, 2001, p. 590). However, despite their oft-stated goals of acting as coordinators and organizers, governments may not adequately deal with global issues. Around the world, governments have favored different technologies, creating high uncertainty for the industry. Whereas European governments have forced telecommunication companies to adopt the GSM system, the American government has been reluctant to impose any particular standard, under the argument that they do not want to overly interfere with business and technological developments. The Chinese government apparently has favored the development of CDMA technologies through its alliance with Qualcomm (Buxbaum, 2000). These radically different approaches and selection criteria have delayed the establishment of a unique global standard.

Educational Institutions and the Media

Educational institutions also play a role in how rapidly emerging communities achieve legitimacy. Budding populations can establish symbiotic links with educational institutions by incorporating the skills and knowledge needed for success in the populations into school curricula. In the United States, biotechnology firms attempted to enhance their legitimacy by identifying themselves with elite research universities, such as Harvard, Stanford, and the University of California-San Francisco (Deeds et al., 1997). In many cases, faculty inventors of key technologies actually started new firms. The perceived value of the new firms arose from inventive technological advances, such as the use of restriction enzymes and recombinant DNA. In turn, the legitimacy of the firms and their technologies was heightened by links to the universities.

With respect to the Web, the commercial-university link exemplifies the significance of symbiotic relations in growing communities. In the beginning, the Internet was the sole province of academic and research institutions, and later commercial sites benefited from their early experimental efforts. After commercial enterprises began using the Web, however, private firms initiated most of the developments and changes. Many of the Web entrepreneurs founding organizations in the new Web-based populations were young people who had learned about computers in college classes and part-time jobs.

Mass and specialized media – television, magazines, journals, newsletters, and newspapers – also play a symbiotic role in communities, disseminating information within and between populations. Information diffusion increases the likelihood that potential entrepreneurs will perceive opportunities for combining old resources in new ways, or at least recognize opportunities in already existing populations. The media – especially journalists in print media – played a very key role in establishing the legitimacy of the Web. In 1993, for example, there were only 34 magazine articles and 13 articles in major newspapers that mentioned the Web. During 1994, however, those figures had jumped to 686 and 743 respectively; and during 1995, they reached totals of 6,365 and 10,054. In those early days, many of the articles were published in technical journals and focused on describing what the Web was and how browser technology worked. Eventually, articles appeared in mainstream outlets, focusing on how the Web could affect commercial activity. As the legitimacy of the Web became even more established, references to the Web (usually through provision of a home page address) became integrated into stories of all kinds, such as announcements of upcoming rock concerts and descriptions of new movie releases (Hunt and Aldrich, 1998).

Summary: Building Organizational Communities

Communities are defined as a set of co-evolving populations joined by ties of commensalisms (populations make similar demands on the environment) and symbiosis (mutual dependence between dissimilar units). Communities arise from the creation of new populations, as well as from new symbiotic and commensalistic relations between already existing populations. In this section, we focused on technological change as one of the most important factors for the transformation of new communities. Some entrepreneurs will be successful in implementing new and revolutionary commercial applications of scientific discoveries and be the seed for the creation of successful populations. Some of these populations will join already existing communities (altering the balances of competition–cooperation and symbiosis–commensalism), or will become the central node of new communities.

The survival of a community with new innovative organizations and populations is strongly related to the ability of these two kinds of social actors to achieve legitimacy. Populations that start a new community have to devote more resources and efforts to the construction of legitimacy. At the same time, populations within a community have a better chance of achieving legitimacy by using cross-population collective action. Finally, collective action from the whole community instead of isolated populations and/or organizations is more effective in gaining the support of institutional actors like the government, educational institutions, and the media.

Conclusions and Future Directions

Our main goal has been to describe the entrepreneurial process as a form of social construction that goes beyond the firm itself to the creation of populations and communities. In contrast to the view that the "best" companies will prevail in the modern economy, we have ample evidence that collective action early in the life of a population affects which firms prosper and which do not (Aldrich, 1999). Following an evolutionary argument, the survival of a firm, population, or community depends as much on the existence of favorable environmental forces as on the effectiveness of individual entrepreneurs. We have emphasized the importance of collective actions in providing entrepreneurs with the capacity to shape their environments.

We view this statement as the starting point for a myriad of interesting and unanswered questions at all levels of analysis. At the firm level, we may ask how innovative entrepreneurs become able to collect scarce resources. Are certain markets, organizational fields, or societies more open to providing resources for innovative entrepreneurs than others? What are the specific selection criteria within particular environments? We do not even have an estimate of the prevalence of innovative products, technologies or organizational forms in the total universe of entrepreneurs. How much greater is their likelihood of failure than their non-innovative counterparts?

Even at the firm level, methodological and practical problems make it difficult to study "innovative entrepreneurship," for two reasons. First, although as many as one in ten adults in the United States are engaged in firm formation activities, locating them and soliciting their cooperation has proven difficult.

Even when large-scale national surveys are used to locate nascent entrepreneurs, the yield rate is between four and six percent of the total sample called (Reynolds et al., 2000). Given strong pressures toward imitation, most of these entrepreneurs will not fall into the category of innovators, even in the competence enhancing sense. Therefore, getting a representative and large enough sample of innovative entrepreneurs is both complicated and expensive.

Second, innovation is defined by outcomes, not by intentions. Therefore, the label of reproducer or innovator can only be attached after entrepreneurs have had at least some success in the construction of their firms. Investigators need to follow firms through the early phase of their life course to see which succeed and which succumb. Building fully specified historical models of the process requires a study design that can take account of age, period, and cohort effects (Aldrich, 1999).

Populations and communities, as subjects of research, have been approached in the past through the analysis of specific empirical cases, such as those we have used as examples in this chapter. As in other studies related to entrepreneurship and management in general, investigators tend to choose populations and communities for study that have been successful or that attract more media attention, such as high technology industries. Investigators have not randomly sampled populations or communities, and thus we have very little idea of the distribution of strategies that deal with the balance between competition and cooperation.

We also know very little about how new or changing populations may affect the symbiotic and mutualistic balance within a community. Short-run demands direct entrepreneurs' attentions to organizational issues, where selection pressures are most keenly felt. However, additional selection pressures arise because new organizations are embedded in the larger, more encompassing social structures of populations and communities (Dacin et al., 1999). Founders can pursue strategies individually, but at the more encompassing levels, very little will be accomplished without collaboration with other founders.

Collective action, if successful, leads to the reshaping of population- and community-level environments and benefits the entire population. However, we lack knowledge of what population or community configurations increase the likelihood for their survival. Is there such a thing as too much cooperation and collective action among the members of a population? Are communities where negative mutualism abounds more likely to disappear?

Two tasks appear necessary to advance our knowledge of entrepreneurship as an evolutionary process of social construction. First, we need more fully developed evolutionary models that specify the conditions under which successful innovators, new populations, and new communities emerge. Second, we need methods for understanding how successful innovators at the firm level affect the specific configuration of cooperation and competition within populations. We also need to understand how the interplay of these two elements affects the balance of new and already existing communities. Both tasks require the use of longitudinal and historical data that is unbiased by success, as well as the creation of explanatory models of populations and community structures (Aldrich, 2001). Ideally, our research designs should encompass the systematic comparison of different industry and community arrangements over broad sweeps of historical time.

In the end, we propose a multilevel model that encompasses how interaction between entrepreneurs affects the configuration of populations, and how the configurations of inter-related populations shape community structure. Finally, a comprehensive model should explain how the structures of different communities and their inter-relationships shape societal institutions and the path of social change.

Obviously, data requirements for these kinds of multilevel studies are extremely difficult to overcome. However, they are not so different from some of the goals that general non-evolutionary approaches to entrepreneurship are trying to accomplish. As Katz (2000) argued, entrepreneurship research in general needs to use large representative samples, improve its measures, replicate studies, and use a longitudinal approach. Such methods allow researchers to study the effects of dynamic processes that have strong selection effects. In this sense, we agree with Katz's argument that the only way to study entrepreneurship in general, and through an evolutionary lens in particular, is through collective action by researchers to jointly build high quality datasets. Not surprisingly, as we emphasize the collective nature of entrepreneurial efforts to create and alter their own environments, we also stress the need for collaborative and cumulative work for studying entrepreneurship, such as in national panel studies of startups (Reynolds et al., 2000).

REFERENCES

Abernathy, W. and K.B. Clark. (1985). Innovation: Mapping the winds of creative destruction. *Research Policy*, **14**, 3–22.

Aldrich, H. (1999). *Organizations Evolving*. London: Sage.

Aldrich, H.E. (2001). Who wants to be an evolutionary theorist? *Journal of Management Inquiry* **10**, 115–127.

Aldrich, H.E. and M.C. Fiol (1994). Fools rush in? The institutional context of industry creation. *Academy of Management Review*, **19**(4), 645–670.

Aldrich, H.E. and A. Kenworthy (1999). The accidental entrepreneur: Campbellian antinomies and organizational foundings. In J.A.C. Baum and B. McKelvey (eds.), *Variations in Organization Science: In Honor of Donald T. Campbell*. Newbury Park, CA: Sage.

Aldrich, H.E. and M.A. Martinez. (2001). Many are called, few are chosen: An evolutionary approach to entrepreneurship. *Entrepreneurship: Theory and Practice*, **25**, 41–56.

Aldrich, H.E. and T. Sasaki (1995). R&D consortia in the United States and Japan. *Research Policy*, **24**(2), 301–316.

Aldrich, H.E., U.H. Staber, C. Zimmer and J.J. Beggs (1990). Minimalism and organizational mortality: Patterns of disbanding among U.S. trade associations, 1900–1983. In J.V. Singh (ed.), *Organizational Evolution*. Newbury Park, CA: Sage.

Aldrich, H.E. and D. Whetten (1981). Making the most of simplicity: Organization sets, action sets, and networks. In P. Nystrom and W.H. Starbuck (eds.), *Handbook of Organizational Design*. New York, Oxford University Press, pp. 385–408.

Aldrich, H.E. and G. Wiedenmayer (1993). From traits to rates: An ecological perspective on organizational foundings. In J. Katz and R.H. Brockhaus (eds.), *Advances in Entrepreneurship, Firm Emergence, and Growth.* Greenwich, CT: JAI Press, Vol. 1, pp. 145–195.

Anderson, P. and M. Tushman (1990). Technological discontinuities and dominant designs: A cyclical model of technological change. *Administrative Science Quarterly,* 35(4), 604–633.

Argote, L., S.L. Beckman and D. Epple (1990). The persistence and transfer of learning in industrial settings. *Management Science,* 36(2), 140–154.

Auster, E.R. (1994). Macro and strategic perspectives on interorganizational linkages: A comparative analysis and review with suggestions for reorientation. *Advances in Strategic Management,* 10B, 3–40.

Axelrod, R., W. Mitchell, R.E. Thomas, D.S. Bennett and E. Bruderer (1995). Coalition formation in standard-setting alliances. *Management Science,* 41(9), 1493–1508.

Barley, S.R., J.H. Freeman and R.C. Hybels (1992). Strategic alliances in commercial biotechnology. In N. Nohria and R.G. Eccles (eds.), *Networks and Organizations: Structure, Form, and Action.* Boston, MA: Harvard University Business School, pp. 311–347.

Barnett, W.P. (1995). Telephone companies. In G.R. Carroll and M.T. Hannan (eds.), *Organizations in Industry: Strategy, Structure, and Selection.* New York: Oxford University Press, pp. 337–354.

Batista, E. (2000). Intel: Bluetooth is viable. *Wired News* [online]. Accessed on: November 20, 2000. http://www.wired.com/news/

Baum, J.R.L., E.A. Locke and K.G. Smith (2001). A multidimensional model of venture growth. *Academy of Management Journal,* 44(2), 292–303.

Baum, J.A.C. and C. Oliver (1992). Institutional embeddedness and the dynamics of organizational populations. *American Sociological Review,* 57(4), 540–559.

Blackmore, S. (1999). *The Meme Machine.* Oxford, England: Oxford University Press.

Bluetooth (2000). The Official Bluetooth Website. Accessed on: November 6, 2000. http://www.bluetooth.com/sig/sig/sig.asp.

Brittain, J. (1994). Density-independent selection and community evolution. In J.A.C. Baum and J.V. Singh (eds.), *Evolutionary Dynamics of Organizations.* New York: Oxford University Press, pp. 355–378.

Brittain, J. and D.R. Wholey (1988). Competition and coexistence in organizational communities: Population dynamics in electronic components manufacturing. In G.R. Carroll (ed.), *Ecological Models of Organization.* Cambridge, MA: Ballinger.

Buckley, S. (2000). 3G wireless: Mobility scales new height. *Telecommunications* [online]. Accessed on: November 6, 2000. http://www.telecommagazine.com/issues/200010/tcs/index.html

Buxbaum, P. (2000). A brave new wireless world [online]. Accessed on: November 6, 2000. http://www.chiefexecutive.net/mag/158tech/1people_brave.htm

Campbell, D.T. (1969). Variation and selective retention in socio-cultural evolution. *General Systems,* 14, 69–85.

Campbell, D.T. (1994). How individual and face-to-face-group selection undermine firm selection in organizational evolution. In J.A.C. Baum and J.V. Singh (eds.), *Evolutionary Dynamics of Organizations.* New York: Oxford University Press, pp. 23–38.

Carroll, G.R. (1993). Sociological view on why firms differ. *Strategic Management Journal,* 14(4), 237–249.

Carroll, G.R. and M.T. Hannan (2000). *The Demography of Corporations and Industries.* Princeton, NJ: Princeton University Press.

Carroll, G.R. and A. Swaminathan (1992). The organizational ecology of strategic groups in the American brewing industry from 1975 to 1990. *Industrial and Corporate Change,* 1(1), 65–97.

Clemens, E.S. (1993). Organizational repertoires and institutional change: Women's groups and the transformation of U.S. politics, 1890–1920. *American Journal of Sociology,* 98(4), 755–798.

Cliff, J. (1997). Building on experience: A cross-level, learning-based approach to the design of new firms. Vancouver, Canada.

Cusumano, M.A. and D.B. Yoffie (1998). Competing on Internet time: Lessons from Netscape and its battle with Microsoft. New York: Free Press.

Dacin, M.T. (1997). Isomorphism in context: The power and prescription of institutional norms. *Academy of Management Journal*, 40(1), 46–81.

Dacin, M.T., M. Ventresca and B.D. Beal (1999). The embeddedness of organizations: Dialogue and directions. *Journal of Management*, 25(3), 317–356.

Darr, E.L., L. Argote and D. Epple (1995). The acquisition, transfer, and depreciation of knowledge in service organizations: Productivity in franchises. *Management Science*, 41(11), 1750–1762.

Deeds, D.L., Y. Paul, P.Y. Mang and M. Frandsen (1997). The quest for legitimacy: A study of biotechnology IPO's. Paper presented at the 1997 Academy of Management meetings Boston, MA, August.

Delacroix, J. and G.R. Carroll (1983). Organizational foundings: An ecological study of the newspaper industries of Argentina and Ireland. *Administrative Science Quarterly*, 28(2), 274–291.

Delacroix, J. and M.V.H. Rao (1994). Externalities and ecological theory: Unbundling density dependence. In J.A.C. Baum and J.V. Singh (eds.), *Evolutionary Dynamics of Organizations*. Oxford: Oxford University Press, pp. 255–268.

Delacroix, J., A. Swaminathan and M.E. Solt (1989). Density dependence versus population dynamics: An ecological study of failings in the California wine industry. *American Sociological Review*, 54(2), 245–262.

Dennis, W.J. Jr. (1997). More than you think: An inclusive estimate of business entries. *Journal of Business Venturing*, 12(3), 175–196.

Denrell, J. (2000). Learning, under-sampling of failure, and the myths of management. Unpublished paper, Institute of International Business, Stockholm School of Economics, Stockholm, Sweden.

DiMaggio, P.J. and W.W. Powell (1983). The iron cage revisited: Institutional isomorphism and collective rationality in organizational fields. *American Sociological Review*, 48(2), 147–160.

DiMaggio, P.J. and W.W. Powell (1991). Introduction. In W.W. Powell and P.J. DiMaggio (eds.), *The New Institutionalism in Organizational Analysis*. Chicago, IL: University of Chicago Press, pp. 1–40.

Dimmick, J. and E. Rothenbuhler (1984). Competitive displacement in the communication industries: New media in old environments. In R.E. Rice (ed.), *The New Media: Communication, Research, and Technology*. Beverly Hills, CA: Sage.

Dobbin, F. (1994). *Forging Industrial Policy: The United States, Britain, and France in the Railway Age*. New York: Cambridge University Press.

Dosi, G. (1982). Technological paradigms and technological trajectories: A suggested interpretation of the determinants and directions of technological change. *Research Policy*, 11(3), 147–162.

Dosi, G. (1988). Sources, procedures, and microeconomic effects of innovation. *Journal of Economic Literature*, 26(4), 1120–1171.

Drazin, R. and L. Sandelands (1992). Autogenesis: A perspective on the process of organizing. *Organization Science*, 3(2), 230–249.

Duncan, J.W. and D.P. Handler (1994). The misunderstood role of small business. *Business Economics*, 29(3), 1–6.

Edelman, L.B. and M.C. Suchman (1997). The legal environment of organizations. *Annual Review of Sociology*, 23, 479–515.

Fransman, M. (1990). *The Market and Beyond: Cooperation and Competition in Information Technology Development in the Japanese System*. Cambridge, MA: Cambridge University Press.

Funk, J.L. and D.T. Methe (2001). Market- and committee-based mechanisms in the creation and diffusion of global industry standards: the case of mobile communication. *Research Policy*, 30, 589–610.

Galaskiewicz, J. (1979). The structure of community organizational networks. *Social Forces*, 57(4), 1346–1364.

Gartner, W.B. (1985). A conceptual framework for describing the phenomenon of new venture creation. *Academy of Management Review*, 10(4), 696–706.

Garud, R. (1994). Cooperation and competitive behaviors during the process of creative destruction. *Research Policy*, 23, 385–394.

Hafner, K. and M. Lyon (1996). *Where Wizards Stay Up Late: The Origins of the Internet*. New York: Simon & Schuster.

Halliday, T., M.J. Powell and M.W. Granfors (1987). Minimalist organizations: Vital events in state bar associations, 1870–1930. *American Sociological Review*, 52(4), 456–471.

Hannan, M.T. and G.R. Carroll (1992). *Dynamics of Organizational Populations: Density, Legitimation, and Competition.* New York: Oxford University Press.

Hannan, M.T. and J.H. Freeman (1987). The ecology of organizational founding: American labor unions, 1836–1975. *American Journal of Sociology*, 92(4), 910–943.

Hannan, M.T.F. and J.H. Freeman (1986). Where do organizational forms come from? *Sociological Forum*, 1(1), 50–72.

Harper, D.A. (1996). *Entrepreneurship and the Market Process: An Enquiry into the Growth of Knowledge.* London: Routledge.

Haunschild, P.R. (1993). Interorganizational imitation: The impact of interlocks on corporate acquisition activity. *Administrative Science Quarterly*, 38(4), 564–592.

Hawley, A. (1950). *Human Ecology.* New York: Ronald.

Hirsch, P.M. (1982). Network data versus personal accounts: The normative culture of interlocking directorates. Paper presented at the Annual Meeting of the American Sociology Association, San Francisco, CA, August 1982.

Human, S.E. and K.G. Provan (2000). Legitimacy building in the evolution of small-firm multilateral networks: A comparative study of success and demise. *Administrative Science Quarterly*, 45(2), 327–365.

Hunt, C.S. and H.E. Aldrich (1998). The second ecology: The creation and evolution of organizational communities as exemplified by the commercialization of the World Wide Web. In B. Staw and L.L. Cummings (eds.), *Research in Organizational Behavior.* Greenwich, CT: JAI Press, p. 20.

Hybels, R.C., A.R. Ryan and S.R.A. Barley (1994). Alliances, legitimation, and founding rates in the U.S. biotechnology field, 1971–1989. Unpublished paper presented at the Academy of Management meetings, Dallas, Texas, August 1994.

Katz, J. (2000). Databases for the study of entrepreneurship. *Advances in Entrepreneurship, Firm Emergence and Growth*, edited by Jerome A. Katz. New York, Jai. 4.

Knight, F.H. (1921). *Risk, Uncertainty, and Profit.* Boston, MA: Houghton Mifflin.

Larson, A. (1992). Network dyads in entrepreneurial settings: A study of the governance of exchange processes. *Administrative Science Quarterly*, 37(1), 76–104.

Leblebici, H., G. Salancik, A. Copay and T. King (1991). Institutional change and the transformation of interorganizational fields: An organizational history of the U.S. radio broadcasting industry. *Administrative Science Quarterly*, 36(3), 333–363.

Loasby, B.J. (2001). Making sense of making artefacts: Reflections on John Ziman (ed.), Technological innovation as an evolutionary process. *Evolutionary Theories in the Social Sciences* [online]. Accessed on: May 2. http://www.etss.net/:http://www.etss.net/

Lohr, S. (1995). Telecommunications giants' joint Internet security quest. *New York Times.* New York.

Low, M.B. and E. Abrahamson (1997). Movements, bandwagons, and clones: Industry evolution and the entrepreneurial process. *Journal of Business Venturing*, 12(6), 435–457.

McKelvey, B. (1982). *Organizational Systematics.* Berkeley, CA: University of California Press.

McPherson, J.M. (1983). The ecology of affiliation. *American Sociological Review*, 48(4), 519–532.

Meyer, J.W. and B. Rowan (1977). Institutionalized organizations: Formal structure as myth and ceremony. *American Journal of Sociology*, 82(3), 340–363.

Miner, A.S. and P.R. Haunschild (1995). Population level learning. In B.M. Staw and L.L. Cummings (eds.), *Research in Organizational Behavior.* Greenwich, CT: JAI Press.

Mintzberg, H. (1978). Patterns in strategy Formation. *Management Science*, 24, 934–948.

Mizruchi, M.S. (1992). *The Structure of Corporate Political Action: Interfirm Relations and Their Consequences.* Cambridge, MA: Harvard University Press.

Mizruchi, M.S. (1996). What do interlocks do? An analysis, critique, and assessment of research on interlocking directorates. In J. Hagan and K. Cook (eds.), *Annual Review of Sociology.* Palo Alto, CA: Annual Reviews, Inc., Vol. 22, pp. 271–298.

MPRG (2000). *Virginia Polytechnic Institute and State University* [online]. Accessed on: November 6, 2000. http://www.mprg.ee.vt.edu

Nelson, R.R. (1994). Evolutionary theorizing about economic change. In N. Smelser and R. Swedberg (eds.), *Handbook of Economic Sociology*. Princeton, NJ: Princeton University Press, pp. 108–136.

Noble, D.F. (1984). *A Social History of Industrial Automation*. New York: Knopf.

OIT (2000). ADSL Website. *Office of Information Technology* [online]. Accessed on: November 6, 2000. http://www.oit.duke.edu/helpdesk/adsl/5_steps.html.

Olson, M. Jr. (1965). *The Logic of Collective Action*. Cambridge, MA: Harvard University Press.

Outlook (2000). Genome patents. *The Independent* [online]. Accessed on: November 6, 2000. http://web.lexis-nexis.com

Picot, A., U.D. Laub and D. Schneider (1989). *Innovative Unternehmensgründungen: Eine Ökonomisch-Empirische Analyse*. Berlin: Springer Verlag.

Podolny, J. (1993). A status based model of market competition. *American Journal of Sociology*, 98(4), 829–872.

Powell, W.W. (1990). Neither market nor hierarchy: Network forms of organization. In B.M. Staw and L.L. Cummings (eds.), *Research in Organizational Behavior*. Greenwich, CT: JAI Press, Vol. 12, pp. 295–336.

Powell, W.W., K.W. Koput and L. Smith-Doerr (1996). Interorganizational collaboration and the locus of innovation: Networks of learning in biotechnology. *Administrative Science Quarterly*, 41(1), 116–145.

Rao, H. (1994). The social construction of reputation: Certification contests, legitimation, and the survival of organizations in the American automobile industry: 1895–1912. *Strategic Management Journal*, 15, 29–44.

Rappa, M. (1989). Assessing the emergence of new technologies: The case of compound semiconductors. In A.H. Van de Ven, H.L. Angle and M.S. Poole (eds.), *Research on the Management of Innovation: The Minnesota Studies*. New York: Ballinger/Harper & Row, pp. 439–464.

Renzulli, L.A. (2001). Initiating new organizational forms: The case of charter schools in the United States. Unpublished Ph.D. Dissertation, Department of Sociology, Unversity of North Carolina Chapel Hill, NC.

Reynolds, P.D. (1999). National Panel Study of U.S. Business Start-Ups: First Annual Overview. Entrepreneurial Research Consortium. *Babson College, Wellesely, MA* [online]. Accessed on: 15 August 1999. http://projects.isr.umich.edu/psed/History.htm

Reynolds, P.D., M. Hay, W. Bygrave, M. Camp and E. Autio (2000). *Global Entrepreneurship Monitor: Global Executive Report*. Kauffman Center for Entrepreneurial Leadership [online]. Accessed on: November 20, 2000. http://www.ncoe.org/research/RE-026.pdf

Reynolds, P.D., M. Hay and M. Camp (1999). *Global Entrepreneurship Monitor: Executive Report*. Kansas City, MO: Kauffman Center for Entrepreneurial Leadership.

Reynolds, P.D. and S.B. White (1997). *The Entrepreneurial Process: Economic Growth, Men, Women, and Minorities*. Westport, CN: Quorum Books.

Robbins-Roth, C. (1998). Will Biotech come back? Forbes (September 7), 214.

Romanelli, E. (1989). Organization birth and population variety: A community perspective on origins. In B.M. Staw and L.L. Cummings (eds.), *Research in Organizational Behavior*. Greenwich, CT: JAI Press, Vol. 11, pp. 211–246.

Rosenkopf, L. and M.L. Tushman (1994). The coevolution of technology and organization. In J.A.C. Baum and J.V. Singh (eds.), *Evolutionary Dynamics of Organizations*. New York: Oxford University Press, pp. 403–424.

Ruef, M., H.E. Aldrich and N.M. Carter (2002). Don't go to strangers: Homophily, strong ties, and isolation in the formation of organizational founding teams. Paper presented at the American Sociological Association meeting, Chicago, Illinois, August 2002.

Saxenian, A. (1994). *Regional Advantage: Culture and Competition in Silicon Valley and Route 128*. Cambridge, MA: Harvard.

Scott, W.R., M. Ruef, P.J. Mendel and C.A. Caronna (2000). *Institutional Change and Healthcare Organizations*. Chicago: University of Chicago Press.

Shan, W., J.V. Singh and T.L. Amburgey (1991). Modeling the creation of new biotechnology firms, 1973–1987. In J.L. Wall and L.R. Jauch (eds.), *Academy of Management Best Papers Proceedings 1991*. Miami Beach, FL.

Shane, S.A. (1996). Hybrid organizational arrangements and their implications for firm growth and survival: A study of new franchisors. *Academy of Management Journal*, **39**(1), 216–234.

Shane, S. (2000). Prior knowledge and the discovery of entrepreneurial opportunities. *Organization Science*, **11**(4), 448–469.

Shane, S. and S. Venkataraman (2000). The promise of entrepreneurship as a field of research. *Academy of Management Review*, **25**(1), 217–226.

Shapiro, C. and H.R. Varian (1999). *Information Rules: A Strategic Guide to the Network Economy*. Boston, MA: Harvard Business School Press.

Shulman, S. (2000). Toward sharing the genome. *Technology Review* (Sep–Oct), 61–67.

Staber, U.H. and H.E. Aldrich (1983). Trade association stability and public policy. In R. Hall and R. Quinn, *Organization Theory and Public Policy*. Beverly Hills, CA: Sage, pp. 163–178.

Stinchcombe, A.L. (1965). Social structure and organizations. In J.G. March (ed.), *Handbook of Organizations*. Chicago, IL: Rand McNally, pp. 142–193.

Suchman, M.C. and L.B. Edelman (1996). Legal rational myths: The new institutionalism and the law and society tradition. *Law and Social Inquiry*, **21**(4), 903–941.

Swidler, A. (1986). Culture in action: Symbols and strategies. *American Sociological Review*, **51**(2), 273–286.

Thaler, R.H. (1994). *The Winner's Curse: Paradoxes and Anomalies of Economic Life*. Princeton, NJ: Princeton University Press.

Torres, D.L. (1988). Professionalism, Variation, and Organizational Survival. *American Sociological Review*, **53**(3), 380–394.

Tushman, M.L. and J.P. Murmann (1998). Dominant designs, technology cycles, and organizational outcomes. In B.M. Staw and L.L. Cummings (eds.), *Research in Organizational Behavior*. Greenwich, CT: JAI Press, Vol. 20, pp. 231–266.

Utterback, J.M. and W.J. Abernathy (1975). A dynamic model of product and process innovation. *Omega*, **3**(6), 639–656.

Uzzi, B. (1996). The sources and consequences of embeddedness for the economic performance of organizations: The network effect. *American Sociological Review*, **61**(4), 674–698.

Uzzi, B. (1997). Social structure and competition in interfirm networks: The paradox of embeddedness. *Administrative Science Quarterly*, **42**(1), 35–67.

Van de Ven, A.H. (1991). A systems framework for studying the process of entrepreneurship. Paper presented at a conference on Theories of Entrepreneurship, University of Illinois, Champaign-Urbana, Champaign-Urbana, IL, April 1991.

Van de Ven, A.H. and R. Garud (1993). Innovation and industry development: The case of cochlear implants. In R. Burgelman and R. Rosenbloom (eds.), *Research on Technological Innovation, Management, and Policy*. Greenwich, CT: JAI Press, Vol. 5, pp. 1–46.

Van de Ven, A.H., S. Venkataraman, D. Polley and R. Garud (1988). Processes of new business creation in different organizational settings. In A.H. Van de Ven, H.L. Angle and M.S. Poole (eds.), *Research on the Management of Innovation*. Cambridge, MA: Ballinger, pp. 222–297.

Yoshitake, D. (1997). ISPs hold on to their market [online]. Accessed on: February 13, 1997. http://www.news.com.

Zelizer, V.A. (1978). Human values and the market: The case of life insurance and death in 19th-century America. *American Journal of Sociology*, **84**(3), 591–610.

Ziman, J. (ed.) (2000). *Technological Innovation as an Evolutionary Process*. Cambridge, England: Cambridge University Press.

Zimmerman, M.B. (1982). Learning effects and the commercialization of new energy technologies: The case of nuclear power. *Bell Journal of Economics*, **13**(2), 297–310.

Zucker, L. (1977). The role of institutionalization in cultural persistence. *American Sociological Review*, **42**(5), 726–743.

Zucker, L.G. (1989). Combining institutional theory and population ecology: No legitimacy, no history. *American Sociological Review*, **54**(4), 542–545.

Zymogenetics (2000). Novo nordisk completes private placement of shares in ZymoGenetics. *Lexis-Nexis Academic Universe* [online]. Accessed on: November 6, 2000. http://web.lexis-nexis.com

PATRICIA H. THORNTON and KATHERINE H. FLYNN
Duke University

16. Entrepreneurship, Networks, and Geographies

Introduction

Entrepreneurship is increasingly the domain of organizations and regions, not individuals. These organizations and regions are environments rich in entrepreneurial opportunities and resources and they have been increasing in numbers and in varieties – be they technology licensing offices, bands of angels, venture capital firms, corporate venturing programs, or incubator firms and regions. These environments explicitly influence individuals by teaching them how to discover and exploit entrepreneurial opportunities. These environments also specifically influence new ventures, providing the resources to increase their rate of founding and survival. However, how these environments spawn new entrepreneurs and create new businesses remains relatively understudied.

Although these organizational and regional environments have been described as network structures (Florida and Kenney, 1988) and geographic clusters (Cooper and Folta, 2000), research that links the spatial and relational aspects of these larger contexts to the micro processes of entrepreneurship is relatively underdeveloped. In this review we take inventory of literatures on networks and geographies to examine how these environments affect the ability of entrepreneurs to garner scarce resources. We seek to address questions of how individuals are likely to become entrepreneurs within the context of why and where entrepreneurship is likely to occur. We define entrepreneurship as both the discovery and exploitation of entrepreneurial opportunities (Shane, 2000) and the creation of new organizations, which occur as a context-dependent social and economic process (Low and Abrahamson, 1997).

The study of entrepreneurship has a bifurcated history – typically focusing on either individuals or environments but not linking the two (Thornton, 1999). Supply-side theorists argued that individuals who possess particular psychological traits are more likely to become entrepreneurs and thereby account for the rate of entrepreneurship (Shaver and Scott, 1991). In contrast, demand-side theorists argued that individuals who are structurally situated in entrepreneurial environments are more likely to be entrepreneurs because the availability of opportunities encourages founders to emerge (Aldrich and Wiedenmayer, 1993). While the individual entrepreneur cannot mobilize without an infrastructure, it is also the case that social and economic structures are not actors (Sewell,

Z.J. Acs and D.B. Audretsch (eds.), Handbook of Entrepreneurship Research, 401–433
© 2003 *Kluwer Academic Publishers. Printed in Great Britain.*

1992). Clearly, the discovery and exploitation of entrepreneurship is related to linking both person and place, with the founding of a firm dependent on both the actions of individuals and the structures of environments (Schoonhoven and Romanelli, 2001).

Earlier research in economics and sociology focused on the spatial and relational contexts of entrepreneurship – the demand-side. For example, Weber (1929) was concerned about the influences of hierarchies on innovation. Stinchcombe (1965) argued that it is easier to found organizations in a context that has more organizational experience. Turk (1970) found that organizations are more easily introduced and are more achievement oriented in an environment that is richly connected inter-organizationally. Frankel (1955) argued that the slow rate of diffusion of innovations around the turn of the century in the British textile, iron, and steel industries was due to the absence of vertically integrated firms. Marshall (1916) wrote about the influences of geographies on innovation and trade. However, as the fields of sociology and economics evolved, researchers increasingly shifted their attention to examining the characteristics of the entrepreneur as an abstract and universal actor, independent of the particular time and place.

Recently there has been a resurgence of research on the spatial and relational determinants of entrepreneurship. Two examples are how an entrepreneur's social capital – the quality of their referral network – determines their chances of receiving venture capital (Stuart et al., 1999), and how a region's cultural capital determines its ability to recruit human capital (Florida, 2002). While we can argue that spatial location in a network affects an individual's and an organization's chances for discovering and exploiting entrepreneurial opportunities (Burt, 1992; Warren, 1967), we know little about how this principle of networks applies to higher levels of analysis, such as geographic regions. At the same time, we know that geographic regions have been shown to exhibit entrepreneurial advantages based on differences in their network structures and cultures (Saxenian, 1994); however, the micro processes of these mass effects are relatively understudied in large sample research.

Relational networks exist at multiple levels of analysis because they can tie together individuals, groups, firms, industries, geographic regions, and nation-states. They can tie members of any one of these categories to members of another category. For example, venture capital firms in their efforts to syndicate financing tie together incubator regions (Florida and Kenney, 1988). The location of the research university is pivotal to regional infrastructure because of its networking role in recruiting talent and transferring technology through multiple networks, such as placing students in industry, licensing intellectual property, and spinning-off companies (Powell, Koput and Smith-Doerr, 1996; Florida and Cohen, 1999). It is also the case that the individual characteristics of scientists determine the geographical location of entrepreneurship. The proximity of biotechnology companies and universities is shaped by the roles played by scientists, whether they be that of a star Nobel laureate or other grades of scientific talent that is "bait to the investment community" (Audretsch and

Stephan, 1996). It is through such multilevel ties that networks and geography are inexorably linked in the pursuit of entrepreneurship.

We organize our review first by levels of analysis, focusing on networks and then on geographies. We draw on theoretical perspectives to frame our review, for example, institutional, resource dependence, learning, and status. First, we define the concepts of networks and geographies; then we conclude each section by identifying questions for future research. We close our review by discussing the integration of the work on networks and geographies for the study of entrepreneurship.

DEFINING NETWORKS AND GEOGRAPHIES

Networks

Relational networks can be defined from a number of perspectives. Podolny and Page (1998, p. 3) define relational network forms of organization as any collection of actors (N [greater than equal to] 2) that pursues repeated enduring exchange relations with one another and, at the same time, lacks a legitimate organizational authority to arbitrate and resolve disputes that may arise during the exchange. Laumann (1991) argues that markets and hierarchies are two pure types of organization that can be represented with the basic analytic constructs of nodes and ties – that is, networks are the more general form of organization.

Relational networks are characterized as embedded, for example, in social structures (Granovetter, 1985), and more specifically within and between hierarchies (Dacin, Ventresca, and Beal, 1999; Burt, 2000) such as in the cases of matrix structures (Greiner, 1972), strategic alliances, commodity chains (Gereffi, 1994), and transnational hierarchies (Scott, 1999). Relational networks are also embedded in culture, as in the cases of the relative immunity of relational network forms of organization to acquisition under personal capitalism, but not under market capitalism (Thornton, 2001).

Relational networks are also characterized as governance structures, and in this respect economists and sociologists disagree. From a sociological perspective, Powell (1990, p. 307) argues that relational networks are distinct governance structures, in that they embody in their organizational form unique "logics." The logics associated with network forms of organization serve as governance mechanisms for economic, social, and political exchanges, acting as an alternative to the control mechanisms of markets and formal hierarchies. Relational networks control and dampen the negative effects of market competition because they embody the logics of trust, reciprocity, and cooperation. Williamson (1991) argues the economic view – networks are motivated by lower transaction costs, not by a distinct culture of cooperation. They are "hybrid" forms located on a continuum between markets and hierarchies.

Dore (1983) found that a "spirit of goodwill" explained the network relationships between Japanese buyers and suppliers. Uzzi (1996) demonstrated how the "logics" of networks moderate opportunism in U.S. garment manufacturing. Thornton (2002) showed that the "institutional logics" of personal capitalism explained and fostered the prevalence of relational network structures and suppressed the development of formal hierarchy. Gulati and Gargiulo (1999) found that relational networks arise from prior embeddedness and repeat ties, motivated by lowering search costs and the risk of opportunism.

Relational networks are also a method of analysis that is compatible with economic and organization theories useful to explaining entrepreneurship. From an economic transaction cost perspective, networks are thought to be less costly and a more efficient alternative to formal hierarchy when innovation is autonomous and there is not a "small numbers" problem in the supplier markets (Chesbrough and Teece, 1996). From an institutional perspective, networks are carriers of institutions that shape the identities and behaviors of entrepreneurs and organizations (Scott, 1995, pp. 52–54; Thornton, 2002). From a social capital perspective, networks, that is their level of status and legitimacy, affect a number of entrepreneurial processes, such as the market valuations of privately held biotechnology firms (Stuart, Hoang, and Hybels, 1999), higher-status venture capital firms signaling lower risk to investors (Podolny, 2001), and wealth creation in postsocialist Hungary (Stark, 1996). Networks can be analyzed from an organizational learning perspective in which they are conduits for collaborators to internalize one another's skills, thereby creating new opportunities (Hamel, 1991; Kogut, 1988) and novel syntheses of information (Powell and Brantley, 1992). Networks can also be analyzed from a resource-dependence perspective – as in the case of incubator firms assisting nascent entrepreneurs in networking with other organizations to collect valuable resources (Hansen et al., 2000).

Networks also can be bounded by different political and geographical jurisdictions that may have implications for an increase or decrease in entrepreneurial activity. An example is differences in property rights laws among states that produce regional and national competitive advantages resulting in incubator regions and enterprise zones (Campbell and Lindberg, 1990). Alternatively, differences in legal institutions between nation-states, for example, the European Union with its many divisions, may inhibit a culture and science of innovation. As Guillen (2001) found in his literature review, most empirical studies do not find convergence in political, social or organizational patterns as a result of globalization.

Geographies

Geographic variation in the rates of entrepreneurship has been a recurring finding in research on new firm formation (see Malecki, 1997, for a review of U.S. and international studies). Networks of actors, whether consisting of individuals, organizations, or industries, play a critical role in the formation of these regional patterns. Networks are bounded by a material resource space that varies in geographic location, density, and physical proximity. Geographies can be theorized from each of these perspectives, raising interesting questions about how each affects the diffusion of innovation and the development of entrepreneurship. It is a given that with respect to geographical location (classical theory of regional economic development), natural resources differ from place to place, and, therefore, interregional trade encourages producers to concentrate on these given and comparative advantages.

With respect to density, agglomeration theory argues that density increases entrepreneurship because of the social construction of localized political and cultural assets such as mutual trust, tacit understandings, learning effects, specialized vocabularies, transaction-specific forms of knowledge, and performance-boosting governance structures facilitating entrepreneurship (Scott, 1999, p. 388). Although not working in the tradition of agglomeration theorists, Schoonhoven and Eisenhardt (1993) showed similar effects, in that competition is less important than the effects of cooperation and spatial proximity, features that facilitate organizational learning. Similarly, in the industrial economic tradition, Porter (1980) argues that increases in competition at the local level increase entrepreneurship, which leads to competitive advantage among regions and nation-states at the global level. In contrast, the concept of density, the central force in population ecology theory, increases competition, which in turn suppresses the founding rate of new enterprise. In applying ecology theory in the multicountry context and to the emergence of the automobile, competition was shown to have local effects and culture (cognitive legitimacy) was shown to have global effects (Hannan, Carroll, Dundon, and Torres, 1995).

Even in the age of electronic communication, entrepreneurship is a local phenomenon in which geographic proximity and face-to-face contact in the exchange of information and technological knowledge are critically important in a number of respects. Tacit knowledge is best communicated informally and is vital to found new firms. Such knowledge rarely resides in formulae or blue prints – if it did, it wouldn't be entrepreneurship (see Brown and Eisenhardt, 1995, for a summary). Moreover, the socialization effects of learning to be an entrepreneur must to some extent involve face-to-face contact with entrepreneurs, angel investors, and venture capitalist role models in the immediate environment (Malecki, 1997). Similarly, face-to-face contact is required to obtain funding; it is necessary to present business plans and to develop and demonstrate reputational capital and the management team experience and expertise that is the basis for investment decisions when there are no physical assets to serve as collateral. Likewise, investors also seek to lower risk by hands-on relationships with entrepreneurs and their fledgling companies, and this is not possible without geographic proximity and face-to-face relationships.

Geographies also can be bounded in terms of neighborhoods and cyberspace. Because these entities are likely to be communities, their boundaries may not be material- and resource-based, but instead cognitive- and culture-based. For example, Redding's (1990) Neo-Weberian analysis of the success of Chinese businessmen abroad is based on the Confucian ethic and aspects of the Chinese family – showing that entrepreneurial minority groups in one country are entrepreneurial in others, and evidencing how culture is not just place oriented, but can be transnational and render geographical distance and boundaries irrelevant. Even more impervious to the limits of material boundaries are cyberspace communities based around Internet etiquette, such as in the case of the development of the software product Linux, distance education programs, and less formally organized chat rooms and bulletin boards.

REVIEW OF NETWORKS AND ENTREPRENEURSHIP

The study of networks and their impact on economic transactions stems back to classic literatures in economics and sociology in which social and relational structure influence market processes (Veblen, 1972: Granovetter, 1985). Malecki (1997) argues that entrepreneurial environments exhibit thriving and supportive networks that provide the institutional fabric linking individual entrepreneurs to organized sources of learning and resources. The quantitative research on networks and entrepreneurship has largely concentrated on three different levels of analysis – network ties between individuals, those connecting teams and groups, and those connecting firms and industries.

Individuals

Research indicates that there is a relationship between the structure of a network and the processes inherent in the discovery and exploitation of entrepreneurial opportunities. According to Burt (1992), individual entrepreneurs with deep "structural holes" in their networks – that is, an absence of contact redundancy and substitution – increase their chances of successfully identifying and exploiting entrepreneurial opportunities because they are central to and well-positioned to manipulate a structure that is more likely to produce higher levels of information. Burt (1992) argues further that network structure can help the information process by allowing individuals to evaluate those they do not know through the opinions of those they do know. Burt (2000) provides a comprehensive review of this rapidly growing research literature on networks and social capital.

Shane and Cable (2002) show contrary to structural hole theory, entrepreneurs with networks high in cohesion drive financial investment decisions. Using survey and interview methods, they examined the impact of social networks, referrals, reputation, and direct ties on the likelihood of investment in early stage new ventures. Though companies looking for financing have an upper hand in making deals because they possess more information than do potential investors, investors do not remedy this informational imbalance by entering into stringent contracts. Rather, they invest in companies with whom they have social relations. Additionally, Shane and Cable found that an investor will not invest in an entrepreneur who is unknown in the investor's network, not referred by someone the investor respects, not highly regarded among investors, or not directly connected to the investor, unless the technology of the new company is outstanding. The interconnections between investors and the connections between investors and target firms are highly influential in helping investors select target companies.

Abell (1996) also examines the impact of structural-level determinants on individuals' opportunities for entrepreneurship. At a more macro level of analysis, using the Labor Force Survey in Great Britain, he examines those entering self-employed entrepreneurship. The Gross Domestic Product, unemployment rates, and previous rates of entry to and exit from entrepreneurship have consistently positive effects upon current rates. Abell argues that past rates affect current rates because if rates of entrepreneurship have been high in the past, current potential entrepreneurs are likely to know someone who is, or has been, an entrepreneur, and who can recommend entrepreneurship as a legitimate career option.

Other relational network structures provide socialization experiences which affect individuals' ability to discover entrepreneurial opportunities and to collect the resources to found new firms, such as "mentor-capitalists," angels, and headhunters. Leonard and Swap (2000), using interviews and field methods to develop a case study, explored a phenomenon that arose in Silicon Valley – mentor capitalists. They describe how entrepreneurs receive entrepreneurial training from mentor capitalists who also use their social capital networks to attract human and (follow-on finance) capital for the entrepreneurs of new ventures.

"Bands of angels" are another important source of social capital that provides informal seed capital to entrepreneurs.[1] Angels are wealthy individuals who informally come together in groups to provide early or mid-stage financing to new ventures. Each angel financially contributes to a pool of funds and the angels then meet as a group to decide which ventures to fund. Angels also advise the companies they fund and create connections between them and experts in the field or other, more experienced, companies which also may be able to help the nascent companies with management advice or later-stage funding. Bands of angels are important members of the ecosystem of resources available to nascent entrepreneurs. Angels have symbiotic relationships that form networks in the financial community, serving as referral agents and co-investors with both venture and corporate capitalists.

Finlay and Coverdill (2000) describe headhunters as individuals who are "network builders" – they have a significant impact on helping entrepreneurs develop new ventures. Using interviews, fieldwork, and surveys, they show how headhunters and their ties can help companies find the managers needed to run new ventures. The management team is one of the key assets in a new venture, and if the individual members of the team are well-qualified and have a track record they signal a higher potential for value creation and less risk to

[1] We acknowledge the helpful comments of Mitch Mumma and John Glushik at Intersouth Partners who provided information on angel investors in a personal communication.

potential investors. The search to increase value and lower risk has given increasing importance to the formal organization of headhunters.

Teams and Groups

Founders can pursue strategies individually, however collaboration with other founders and members of the management team is essential (Aldrich and Martinez in this volume; Cooper and Daily 1997). Different types of team experience have been found to predict entrepreneurial success. Roure and Maidique (1986) found that in team-based new companies the breadth of experience that a team had in different functional areas was a major predictor of success in the venture. Higgins and Gulati (2001) theorize that the network ties of the management team to previous employers are determinants of success because they help potential evaluators judge the quality of a nascent firm. In analyzing the 5-year employment experience of more than 3000 executives who were among the top managers of biotechnology firms founded between 1961 and 1994 in the United States, they found that having a management team with experience in companies located downstream, some kinds of upstream companies, and having a management team with a range of experiences predicts success in obtaining financing and public offerings. Higgins and Gulati (2001) also found that the previous employment experience of the entire management team, and not just the CEO or top managers, matters, and that a company's financial success is not mediated by the prestige of its lead bank. In sum, a variety of different types of team experiences were found to predict entrepreneurial success. Birley and Stockley (2000) provide a literature review on entrepreneurial teams and entrepreneurial success.

Firms

Firms as a focal source of entrepreneurship is understudied (Acs and Audresch, 1988) – whether it is in the context of a formal hierarchy, an incubator or venture capital-backed firm, or the result of developing new capabilities by acquisition and joint venture activities (Karim and Mitchell, 2000). While the number of start-ups by means of bootstrapping and family capital may be greater, it is arguable that the more formally organized contexts for founding new ventures are more likely to produce larger firms and higher returns.

In an early case study of the semiconductor industry, Freeman (1986) argues that entrepreneurship depends upon firms – venture capital and others – and upon the relations between them. High-technology firms tend to be started by employees from larger organizations who leave these organizations to found new firms when the environmental conditions are favorable. In a network sense, the number of venture capital sources and the relations among them create an environment in which people in large organizations wish to leave their firms, connect themselves to the venture capitalists, and found new high-technology firms. Freeman (1986, p. 49) argues that the process culminates in the creation of new high-technology firms; his argument works equally well in explaining the founding of venture capital firms.

Phillips (2001) quantitatively tests Freeman's (1986) proposition that firms create entrepreneurship by spinning-off new firms. In a population-level study, Phillips shows with Silicon Valley law firms that new organizations are often founded by members of older organizations within the same population – what he terms the "parent–progeny transfer." He argues that the transfer of routines and resources between a parent organization and its progeny is a function of the employment relationship and career history between the parent firm and the potential founder. Phillips further shows that the higher the previous status of the new founder in his or her former firm, the higher the failure rate of the parent firm and the lower the failure rate of the progeny.

Suchman, Steward, and Westfall (2001) describe how professional services are codified to help entrepreneurs structure their firms according to legal conventions within the venture community. In a case study they show the role of Silicon Valley law firms in standardizing practices in the entrepreneurial community and how entrepreneurship depends as much on convention as on innovation. Local law firms act as dealmakers, counselors, and proselytizers in the routinization of "cookie cutter" organizational forms from which the entrepreneur can select. In their portrayal, the entrepreneur learns the most efficient way to start a firm, thus economizing on entrepreneurial attention (Gifford, 1998) that can in turn be used for the many critical nonroutine decisions that innovating entrepreneurs must make in order to obtain resources and legitimacy (Aldrich and Martinez in this volume).

Although intrapreneurial corporations have a long history of founding new ventures (Block and Macmillan, 1995), most of what we know about the effects of intrapreneurial contexts for founding is based on descriptive case studies that are often flawed by sampling on the dependent variable. Overall, the case study evidence indicates no differences in new ventures funded with corporate as compared to venture capital. The one large sample study by Gompers and Lerner (2000) discovered that firms founded with corporate capital that have a focused "strategic fit" show outcomes comparable to or better than those firms funded with independent venture capital. In particular, they found that firms ventured by corporate capital have the same likelihood of going public as those ventured by independent funds. They further found that, though corporate capitalists make investments at a premium, this premium is not inflated in investments where there is a close fit between corporate strategy and the funded company. Finally, firms capitalized by corporate sources overall were found to be less stable and have shorter life spans than those funded by venture capital. However, corporately funded ventures with a specific focus are as or more stable than firms funded by independent venture capital (Gompers and Lerner, 2000, pp. 119–120).

These results suggest that what really matters in the outcomes of ventured companies is not whether the venture capital is corporate or independent, but how the venture capital source is tied to the firm it is funding. Corporate venture capital funds that have a strong fit with the companies they venture, and are thus able to engage in productive networks and relationships with them, produce outcomes superior to those produced by independent venture capital funds. However, aside from the "complementarities hypothesis," this study points to the lack of a theory explaining why corporate hierarchies may or may not be a superior founding context to that of the markets.

Venture capital firms often decide to review plans and make funding decisions on the basis of well-established referral networks – their social capital (Florida and Kenney, 1988). The recent dot.com market cycle has drawn attention to the potential biases of their decision making processes. For example, as Shaver (in this volume) points out, with the combination of the effects of the availability heuristic and illusory correlation, venture capitalists became overconfident. This created for some a legitimacy crisis in raising future funds in a down-market environment. Some venture capitalists have responded to this problem by developing practices to keep track of deals screened out by their traditional network referral system, although the VCs may not be consciously aware of their cognitive biases of overconfidence. The network-elite context of decision making by venture capitalists motivates the need to study their decision environments, and as Shaver points out, the social science to do so is well-developed.

Incubator firms typically provide a new venture with office space, expertise, network connections, and seed funding in return for equity stakes in the new ventures. The management teams of incubated companies can help one another through the similar problems they all experience; they also can receive training and connections to outside funding from incubator employees. Moreover, incubator firms help to recruit the most talented employees for their new ventures because in theory location in an incubator enhances reputation and reduces the risks and liabilities of new ventures. The overall argument for incubators is that new ventures that enter incubators are paying an equity share to gain access to networks that will enhance their chances at successful entrepreneurship. Although many incubators have gone out of business in the recent down market cycle, there were an estimated 700 incubator firms in North America in the year 2000 (d'Arbeloff, 2000, p. 9; Hanson, Nohria, and Berger, 2000). Eshun (2002) describes the historical origins of incubators in the U.S. and how they lower market entry barriers for entrepreneurs. Jang and Rhee (2002) documented the existence of 259 incubators in Korea alone. Sampling 123 of the relatively mature incubators that had experienced one cycle of hatching, Jang and Rhee found the diversity and quality of support services, the employment of full time staff, and the efficacy of networking distinguished those incubators with better performance.

Podolny (1993) questions whether firms should structure their networks to be rich in structural holes or to have cohesion around high-status players. The idea is that network expansion and exclusion are countervailing principles in determining whether firms have an advantage in discovering and exploiting entrepreneurial opportunities. According to Podolny (2001, pp. 58–59), a focus on structural holes or on status provides a firm two different ways in which it may represent its assets and thereby address different types of market uncertainty.

In a population of firms that made venture capital investments, Podolny showed that a network rich in structural holes is more helpful in resolving egocentric (producer) uncertainty, whereas a network rich in status is more helpful in overcoming altercentic (consumer) uncertainty. Podolny's research identifies some of the contingent effects of social capital from the perspective of whether networks should be conduits for information, that is act as "pipes," or whether networks should serve to "split out" information for evaluation, that is, act as "prisms." The implications of Podolny's theory and research are that there is a tradeoff between the formation of network ties that add structural holes to the network and ties that will augment the actor's status and ability to evaluate actors in the market. Status-based views of social capital have been applied in other research on the exploitation of entrepreneurial opportunities at the stage of exiting investment from venture capital portfolios (Stuart et al., 1999).

Industries

The characteristics of networks have implications for innovation at the industry level of analysis. Powell, Koput, and Smith-Doer (1996) claim that when the knowledge of an industry is broadly distributed and rapidly changing, the locus of innovation will be found in interorganizational networks rather than in individual firms. They find a liability of unconnectedness in which strong-performing biotechnology firms have larger, more diverse alliance networks than do weak-performing firms. Smith and Powell (2002) examine the consequences of geographically bounded social networks on innovation as measured by patenting by biotechnology firms. They find that a diverse portfolio of partners aids firm patenting in physically dispersed networks, but hinders it in a regionally bounded innovation network. Acs et al. (2001) found that the use of patent data is a reliable proxy measure of innovative activity at the regional level. Audretsch and Feldman (1996) show that spillovers are more pervasive in knowledge industries than in non-knowledge industries. Similarly, Anselin et al. (2000) found that university spillovers are specific to certain industries such as electronics and instruments. Moving up another level of analysis, Acs and Armington (2002) examine the impact of interindustry networks as a source of knowledge spillovers and entrepreneurial activity, proposing a model in which local economic growth is dependent on the various information networks present in the regional knowledge base. Combined, these findings have implications for making regional geographies and the network relationships among them the central units of interaction in economies. In the subsequent sections, we highlight literatures that focus on such implications.

QUESTIONS FOR FURTHER RESEARCH

One question relevant to supply- and demand-side perspectives and issues in institutional theory is the degree to which individuals actively versus passively build the networks they access in entrepreneurial undertakings. Staber and Aldrich (1995) found that entrepreneurs maintained old network ties with individuals they knew before they began their businesses rather than strategically constructing new networks, as implied by Burt (1992). At the firm level of analysis, Gulati and Gargiulo (1999) found that networks originate from previous alliances between firms, since one of the central questions with networks is finding a trusted contact. Could the tendency to use existing networks be a case in which norms and understandings of entrepreneurship as possible and desirable simply drift across pre-existing networks? Or, is it a case, as other researchers (Lin et al., 2001) might suggest, that individuals can be much more directed in constructing social networks? Research is needed on how different kinds of networks lead to success with respect to various elements of the entrepreneurial process (Staber and Aldrich, 1995).

While Burt (1992) was the first to link the concepts of network structure and entrepreneurship in his prominent theory of structural holes, scholars have been unable to agree on theories of how network structures affect innovation and entrepreneurship. Should networks be densely interconnected (Coleman, 1988) or rich in structural holes (Burt, 1992)? Do networks rich in structural holes better lead to the discovery of opportunities and networks rich in cohesion better lead to the exploitation of opportunities (Shane and Cable, 2002)? How do networks of personal relations get converted into social capital (Saks, 2002)? Moreover, how does the availability and restricted access to networks in the entrepreneurial process compromise the decision making of entrepreneurs and investors?

Ahuja (2000) finds that a network rich in structural holes is not as effective a network for producing innovations, as is the case when a firm has a large network of indirect ties. On the surface, this seems to contradict the general findings of Shane and Cable (2002). The array of findings is difficult to make sense of as the research contexts and levels of analysis vary significantly. Hence, meta-analytic and large sample research is needed that lends clarity to what we know at this point about the contingent value of social capital for entrepreneurship.

One question that is of particular importance with respect to economic policy issues is whether social capital, or the gains received from social networks, are the same for all groups, and whether or not individuals and groups use networks for entrepreneurial gains in the same or in different ways. Preliminary work along these lines has found that social capital does not operate in the same ways for women and minorities as it does for white men (Burt, 1998; Burt, 2000). Extending this line of work on the inequality among groups of potential entrepreneurs is warranted, since women start more businesses than men but have less access to venture capital and other resources.

These questions need to be investigated within and across the various contexts that are rich in entrepreneurial opportunities and that present competing alternatives from which entrepreneurs collect resources. What are the specific social psychological factors that determine why women, for example might have less social capital with venture capitalists than they might with administrators of publicly-funded incubators (Shaver in this volume)?

In addition to socio-demographic differences, another way to understand differences in how individuals access networks and engage in entrepreneurship is to examine differences in systems of belief – culture. The paper by Aldrich and Martinez (in this volume) provides recent evidence that the rates of entrepreneurship continue to vary widely across nations. While McGrath et al. (1992) show that entrepreneurs have a persistent and characteristic value orientation irrespective of their base culture (nation state), their methods may not have provided adequate variation in the countries that were sampled to show an effect. For example, according to theory (Jepperson, 2001), if France were included in the sample, cultural differences may have been derived. It should not be overlooked that classic studies, considered politically incorrect today, did find cultural differences in levels of individualism and economic development when categorizing culture by religious differences at the family and country levels of analyses, respectively (Winterbottom, 1958; McClelland, 1961). At the same time, the McGrath finding is supportive of recent work in sociology on the profusion of individual roles and identities in the postwar period (Frank and Meyer, 2001, p. 87). This research argues that increasingly society is culturally rooted in the natural, historical, and spiritual worlds through the individual, not corporate entities or groups. The findings on culture are contradictory, suggesting the need for a meta-analytic and multidisciplinary review of this research, as well as the development of fresh approaches.

There is much to be done to theorize and operationalize the "carriers of culture." As Davis and Greve (1997) have elegantly shown, networks themselves don't spread entrepreneurial practices unless they are supported by a legitimate cultural account. Network embeddedness and power approaches by themselves don't lend much of an explanation of why – what are the cultural mechanisms that produce learning, adoption, and diffusion (DiMaggio, 1992; Fligstein, 2001; Stinchcombe, 2002)? However, relational networks as governance structures with their distinct cultural logics may be one way to examine carriers of entrepreneurial culture (Powell, 1990; Thornton, 2002; White, 2002). How else might the effects of culture on entrepreneurship be examined?

We discuss three approaches that might be fruitfully applied to the study of entrepreneurship, institutional logics (Friedland and Alford, 1991; Scott and Meyer, 1994), institutional differentiation (Jepperson, 2001), and organizational culture (Martin, 1992). Scott and Meyer's (1994) research on structural influences on the identities of individuals and organizations argues that those institutional sectors that are most influential are those that have formal organizations with high status and legitimacy. They provide the salient sources of values, norms, language, advice, and occupational identities likely to influence actors to learn to be entrepreneurial. This idea stems back to Weber's (1904) classic statement on the origin of the "entrepreneurial spirit," however it substitutes the influences of the religious sector for those of the modern corporate and market sectors (Friedland and Alford, 1991). Applying this view generates the proposition that the individuals and organizations more likely to adopt entrepreneurial identities and to discover and exploit entrepreneurial opportunities are those that are structurally situated in environments that are higher in status and richer than others in entrepreneurial ideas and resources.

This neoinstitutional perspective holds promise for explaining the origin of entrepreneurial culture in determining regional advantage. Note, it is a cognitive argument and may provide analytic leverage in discussing geographies because it is not place dependent (DiMaggio, 1994, 1997); hence it may be a useful avenue to explore questions on the transgeographical diffusion of entrepreneurship (Redding, 1990; Strang and Meyer, 1994). In a related vein, Jepperson's (2002) typology on institutional differentiation captures the institutional logics and political cultures of the Anglo, Nordic, Germanic, and French "orbits." Such a typology could be used as a conceptual framework to examine potential contrasts in country cultural differences in rates of entrepreneurship. Researchers interested in cultural effects are also usually attuned to the role of symbols. We are not aware of work on the symbolic aspects of entrepreneurship. A potential new application of symbolic management (Zajac and Westphal, 2001) to entrepreneurship may become available for study with the recent emergence of social entrepreneurship programs in corporate settings.

Further research is needed to examine how professional groups that have different normative beliefs influence the rates of entrepreneurship (Audretsch and Stephan, 1996). One such setting is U.S. universities that aspire to be players in the commercialization of technologies by creating incentives and socialization experiences to turn their scientists into entrepreneurs and to create a culture of entrepeneurship. In some sectors of the university, such as professional schools, peer group norms may support entrepreneurial activities; in other sectors of the university for-profit science is held in disdain. Universities are organizations located at the center of entrepreneurial networks and geographies, and as such produce spillovers of innovations from ongoing research (Acs et al., 1994). A better understanding is needed of the interplay between faculty peer group norms and university incentives for scientists to learn to be entrepreneurs. The "contested terrain" of university entrepreneurship is an apt setting to apply classic concepts such as organizational culture (Martin, 1992), goal displacement, and loose coupling (Meyer and Rowan, 1977) in examining how scientists may be converted to alternative contested pathways to university eminence – either scholarship or entrepreneurship.

Our review and discussion assumes that networks lead to learning and to novel syntheses of information and innovation. However, as Podolny and Page (1998) point out, this assumption has not been empirically tested. To do so we would need to know whether firms' inventions were significant departures from past inventions, and whether firms' inventions were qualitatively different from their network ties' past inventions. There also is a lack of solid comparative evidence to support the claim that network structures are more efficient than other forms of organizing located in the contexts of markets and hierarchies (Podolny and Page, 1998). Addressing this question is important in light of understanding the best contexts for entrepreneurs to gain access to resources and to learn the ropes of entrepreneurial processes. Evidence suggests that overly embedded firms decrease their survival prospects in a sample of small, privately owned garment manufacturers (Uzzi, 1996). Building on this work, an important question is whether the same result would hold in a population of small and large firms (Aldrich, 1999) in which resource dependencies may hold different meanings and consequences (Thornton, 2001).

Research on networks in relation to management teams, the key asset of new venture formation, is under developed, but promises to produce interesting policy and scholarly payoff. For example, anecdotal evidence stemming from public policy groups, such as the Councils for Entrepreneurial Development and the National Commission on Entrepreneurship, indicates that the quality of management teams is not evenly distributed across incubator regions or more generally in the economy. Moreover, some incubator regions are resource-dependent in the sense that they can spawn significant innovations from their universities, but cannot create the firms needed to develop those innovations. For example, some incubator regions lack the level of management talent and human capital needed to develop the rate of innovations from their nearby, world-class universities. Under such conditions, local innovations can be creamed-off by other firm-rich regions such as Silicon Valley, creating a resource-dependent "third-world country" effect among incubator regions.

It may be that this disparity in management team resources explains why some incubator regions do better than others in terms of having the ability to grow large firms – and hence in the centralization and accumulation of wealth. Management teams are groups of individuals that are both trainable and mobile – they are the human capital of incubator regions. As Florida (2000) argues, regions are now in the position of having to "compete in the age of talent." Given Freeman's (1986) argument that firms are an important mechanism to create, train, and spin-off entrepreneurs, then in incubator regions without large firms, who will train entrepreneurs? Moreover, how will new ventures recruit management teams in regions where the local norms of the venture capital business support the practice of "flipping deals" rather than encouraging the organic growth of firms?

Future research also should build on status-based arguments (Podolny, 1993, 2001) by applying them to an earlier stage of the entrepreneurial process in order to better understand how individuals and firms discover entrepreneurial opportunities – augmenting the Austrian school of theorizing (Shane, 2000). The concept of status also could be applied to more macro levels of analysis and to testing in different cultural contexts. Venture capitalists are especially attuned to the importance of status in lowering the risks of investing in intangible assets. Given this, it would be fruitful to follow the trend in the practitioner community for cross-national syndication to examine if status effects may be culturally contingent.

An important question is how new firms that emerge from within-firm networks may differ from those that emerge from outside of pre-existing firms. More generally, Thornton (1999, pp. 38–39) raised the question of which context is most effective for the founding of firms – markets or hierarchies. In a review of the literature on entrepreneurship, Shane and Venkataraman (2000) argue that whether new ventures are developed within pre-existing firms or new firms are created expressly to pursue such ventures depends upon the type of environment and the opportunity in question. It could be that ventures formed within a pre-existing firm have an edge, in that hierarchical networks have an advantage in more quickly and easily transmitting information and fostering the learning of entrepreneurship (Burt, 2000; Teece, 1999). On the other hand, it may be that networks within firms do not provide enough incentive for innovation to be realized, so entrepreneurship is not fostered as much in networks within firms as in markets. It could also be the alternative case that hierarchical systems limit in certain ways the transfer of routines and knowledge between subunits of the system (Ocasio and Thornton, 2002). Some of these ideas date back to empirical observations from classic case studies (Frankel, 1955), but beg for theoretically motivated inquiry using large sample research methods.

The controversies that surround incubators generate a number of questions for future research. Given their observed failure rate since the rise of the dot.com phenomenon, is the incubator concept as a viable economic and organizational form flawed? How do incubators differentiate themselves from competing organizational forms with proven track records, such as venture capital firms, and more informal arrangements, such as bands of angels? What is their performance record? Who are the stakeholders? Venture capitalists, for example, argue that the success or failure of a new company comes down to the people, but do incubators attract the real entrepreneur? Are experienced entrepreneurs attracted to and funded by venture capitalists and only inexperienced entrepreneurs attracted to incubators? Given these arguments, will incubators be counterproductive in giving entrepreneurs a false and sheltered sense of success? Last, the international prevalence and the astonishing rise of incubators stimulate theoretical questions that beg for large sample research on the role of organizations and the state in attempting to "level the playing field" for entrepreneurs (Eshun, 2002).

REVIEW OF GEOGRAPHIES AND ENTREPRENEURSHIP

There is abundant theoretical and empirical literature suggesting that geography may significantly impact rates and patterns of entrepreneurship. Krugman ([1991] 2000) argues that an understanding of geography is essential to a well-developed economic perspective. Howells (1996, p. 18) argues that, "geographical distance, accessibility, agglomeration, and the presence of externalities provide a powerful influence on knowledge flows, learning, and innovation" (cited in Asheim and Cooke, 1998, p. 200). Acs and Armington (2002) suggest that theories of entrepreneurship should examine regions as the unit of analysis to understand how knowledge spillovers operate. We review work on geography and the clustering of firms, venture capitalists and their role in the entrepreneurial process, and the "ideal" type of geography for fostering entrepreneurship.

Geographical Clustering and Entrepreneurship

Cooper and Folta (2000) define clusters as groups of similar companies who may interact with one another and draw from the same resource pool. Clustering occurs around the world, in both low-tech and high-tech fields. They further describe the inequality among regions, calling attention to certain geographical regions that are especially rich in entrepreneurship. There are a number of explanations for why and where clustering occurs.

Krugman ([1991] 2000, p. 5) points out that individuals, firms, and industries are concentrated in particular regions of the United States. Such clustering tends to remain true over long periods of time. He discredits equilibrium-based explanations in explaining why firms are not evenly distributed across space. Alternately, Krugman replaces this traditional economic argument with another, costs and benefits, which he argues leads to industrial clustering. He argues that the reason such clustering occurs is that it is expensive to produce items across large tracts of space, and economies of scale, or benefits, can be realized by locating where other firms which supply, buy from, or even compete with, a given firm are located.

Acs et al. (1999) and Anselin et al. (2000) illustrate that research universities play a key role in the formation of clustering. Acs et al. (1999) argue that two related hypotheses explain the development of high-technology clusters in the vicinity of major university R&D activity. First, university research is a source of knowledge and innovation which diffuses through personal contacts to adjacent firms usually located in science parks. The second highlights the role of the university in producing human capital such as science and engineering graduates. Their analysis shows that academic research produces a positive, local, high-technology employment spillover at the city level. This indicates that personal contact and face-to-face communication are important mechanisms in explaining the transfer and clustering of scientific innovation into jobs and products.

Feldman (1993) argues that firms cluster to mitigate the uncertainty of innovation: proximity enhances the ability of firms to exchange ideas, discuss solutions to problems, and be cognizant of other important information, hence reducing uncertainty for firms that work in new fields. Feldman (1993) further argues that firms producing innovations tend to locate in areas where there are necessary resources and that resources accumulate due to a region's past success with innovations. Analyzing data from the Small Business Administration, she shows how innovations in several different industries are highly concentrated in particular states within the United States. Following Feldman's (1993) ideas, new computer hardware firms, for example, are expected to locate in areas where old computer hardware firms, suppliers, and universities with good departments of computer science, electrical engineering, and mechanical engineering are located.

Other authors writing about geographic clusters, however, implicitly or explicitly challenge agglomeration theory – arguing that it is too simple an explanation for the geographic clustering that can be observed in many industries. Some argue that resource-rich clusters do not always benefit firms. Others argue that resources develop later in a cluster's lifecycle, and thus cannot be the only reason that early entrepreneurial ventures locate in a given cluster.

Sorenson and Audia (2000) show that shoe producers in the U.S. were highly concentrated in a few regions in 1940, and essentially remained so over the next fifty years. They argue that this pattern occurred because many of the resources and inputs new shoe firms need, such as know-how and networks, come from firms already producing shoes. They argue that locations of current shoe producers play a large role in determining locations of new shoe producers, thus creating clusters that tend to sustain themselves over time. Though new shoe producers receive needed inputs from pre-existing shoe manufacturers in clusters, the picture Sorenson and Audia paint is not entirely perfect. Shoe manufacturers who opted to locate in places where there were already many shoe producers failed more often than those who located in places where the concentration of shoe producers was lower (Sorenson and Audia, 2000, p. 440). They present a revised version of agglomeration theory – forms tend to cluster geographically not because economic resources are locally clustered. In fact, shoe firms suffered increased mortality from clustering. In sum, Sorenson and Audia (2000) argue that clustering occurs because more social-type resources, such as know-how, are locally clustered. It remains to be seen whether their arguments will hold in the contemporary context of offshore manufacturing.

Feldman (2001) and Feldman and Francis (2001) elaborate on the agglomeration argument of Feldman (1993) by explaining the early part of cluster formation, the period before many resources are available in a given region.Using previous work on entrepreneurship and interviews with entrepreneurs to explore the development of an Internet and biotechnology cluster around Washington, D.C., Feldman (2001) and Feldman and Francis (2001) argue that clusters form not because resources are initially located in a particular region, but rather through the work of entrepreneurs. Early entrepreneurs locate their businesses in a region and adapt to the particularities of the location. As their businesses begin to thrive, resources such as money, networks, experts, and services arise in, and are attracted to, the region. With this infrastructure in place, more entrepreneurial ventures locate and thrive in the region, which ultimately may create a thriving cluster where none previously existed.

Stuart and Sorenson (1999) found that clustering occurs in the biotechnology industry and benefits firms at different lifecycle stages. Clustering occurs because ties between entrepreneurs and those who control the resources necessary to an entrepreneur's new venture tend to be geographically concentrated. From 1978 to 1996, Stuart and Sorenson (1999) analyzed the impact of proximity to certain types of resources on the likelihood of a region gaining another biotechnology company after the first one was established in the region. The resources explored are developers of the technology used, competitors and other firms in the industry, venture capitalists, and technical experts. Stuart and Sorenson (1999) found that when the effects of the four resource types are modeled separately, each resource has a significant, positive effect on the biotechnology firm founding rate in the area. When the effects of all four types of resources are modeled together, however, only the effects of having other, similar firms in the area remain positive and significant. They find that this effect declines because there are more biotechnology firms across the nation, i.e., as the biotechnology industry ages. In terms of new biotechnology firm success, when all four resource location measures are modeled separately, only the developer measure has a positive and significant effect on time to IPO. When the four resource types are modeled together, however, competitor firms and venture capitalists have a significantly negative effect on time to IPO, while developers retain their positive, significant effect on the IPO rates of nearby firms. Thus, Stuart and Sorenson (1999) show that resources such as expertise and money lead new firms to be founded in certain areas and contribute to the success of new firms in the biotechnology industry. However, their findings also show that the resources that lead to new firm foundings are not the same ones that lead a new firm to thrive. They create a model to predict the locations most likely to spawn a new biotechnology firm, and to have a new firm succeed. The model shows that San Diego and South San Francisco are the most likely to have a new biotechnology firm founded, while firms have the worst chance of going public in the San Francisco Bay Area, and the best chance at the intersection of Pennsylvania, New York, and New Jersey. Stuart and Sorenson (1999) claim that this finding challenges the traditional economic explanation of clustering, agglomeration theory, which argued that similar firms are founded in particular regions because those regions were where firms of that type would be most likely to succeed. Thus, they find evidence that clustering occurs near important resources in the biotechnology industry, but complicate arguments about economic clustering by suggesting that firms may not be formed in the geographical locations that will most allow them to thrive.

Geography, Venture Capital, and Entrepreneurship

Research shows geography affects venture capital. Thompson (1989) states that venture capital is not evenly spread across space. He provides evidence that both the givers and receivers of venture capital are highly concentrated in certain areas of the United States – showing California, New York, and New

England as the major players in the giving of venture capital funds, and the West and Southwest to be major receivers of funds. Thompson (1989) shows that venture capital has diffused geographically over time – arguing that it is a complex phenomenon whose role in economic development cannot be understood using an equilibrium model predicting the equal spread of venture capital across space over time.

Sorenson and Stuart (2001) show the value of proximity in venture capital investing, exploring the determinants of venture capital investment in the United States between 1986 and 1998. Generally, they find that the likelihood of a venture capitalist investing in a given target declines with increasing geographical distance between the venture capitalist and the company. This pattern is explicable given the hands-on commitment which venture capitalists make to finding and evaluating a target, and then aiding a new company. They find several factors that can attenuate this main effect of geographical distance. Venture capital firms that are older and have more general experience in investment are more likely to invest in companies that are more distant. Age loses significance when experience is added to the model, and experience loses significance when network-type effects are added. They find that those venture capitalists who are central in the venture capital network are more likely to invest in companies which are farther away. Additionally, venture capitalists are more likely to invest in a distant company if another venture capitalist with whom they have previously invested is also investing in that company, especially if the other venture capitalist is located close to the target company. Thus both networks and experience can lead venture capitalists to invest in companies farther away geographically than their typical investments.

Ideal Geographies for Entrepreneurship

As Storey (in this volume) shows in his analysis of the question of whether governments should support programs to develop small firms, considerable differences exist in the policies of developed countries. Another area of work with policy implications focuses on ideal geographies for entrepreneurship. The ideal geographies work highlights the characteristics that make a location a fertile ground for entrepreneurial ventures – exploring locations ranging from the level of cities or regions to that of nation-states. In particular, Woolcock (1998) has argued that the subject of networks should be added to policymaking agendas for national development, theorizing that the underdeveloped nations that thrive are those that have trustworthy ties within networks and between nations.

Asheim and Cooke (1998) divide industrial regions around the world into two major types: planned and unplanned. The planned include some United States science parks, such as Research Triangle Park, as well as the scientific city of Villeneuve d'Ascq, near Lille, France, where a large number of universities, research institutes, and incubators have been created to foster technical research and inventions. Among the unplanned regions, Asheim and Cooke

(1998) include the industrial district of Emilia-Romagna in Italy, where pre-existing concentrations of tile artisans have formed a district of more technologically advanced tile makers. Though both models of technical regions have some proven success, they find flaws with each. They claim that in the unplanned regions there is little innovation, while in planned regions firms do not network very well. Given the strengths and weaknesses of each model, Asheim and Cooke (1998) then create a new model for technical regions which combines the strengths of planned and unplanned regions while eliminating the weaknesses of each. The ideal technical region for Asheim and Cooke (1998, p. 235) would include structures linking people and technologies, incubators to foster new businesses, universities to add expertise, and larger businesses that could work with, and buy from, small, young companies. In a region like this, one would expect to see entrepreneurship flourishing. Asheim and Cooke (1998, p. 235) note that this ideal model is already being realized in some Nordic countries.

Florida (2000, 2002) writes about ideal regions for high-technology development, focusing on lifestyle issues – the relationships between people and places. The rise of entrepreneurship has taken place in those areas that are rich in intellectual and cultural capital – which in turn draws human capital. Based upon quantitative and qualitative research on American technology regions and workers, including several case studies, he discusses ways for American regions to recruit high-technology industries and high-technology workers. He argues that it is not enough for a region merely to boast many technology jobs. Rather, the "creative class" is attracted to cities and regions that are generally pleasant places to live. He argues that cities and regions that wish to succeed in the high-technology economy must invest in a clean environment, a good infrastructure, and sustainable growth. High-technology businesses and workers, he argues, favor locating in areas where the environment is less polluted and the regional infrastructure is strong – perhaps boasting good transportation, top-quality universities, and an outdoor lifestyle. As Florida states (2000, p. 7), "Quality-of-place is the missing piece of the puzzle. To compete successfully in the age of talent, regions must make quality-of-place a central element of their economic development efforts."

Other authors focus on geography at the level of the model state. Through the use of historical case studies, Campbell and Lindberg (1990) develop the argument that the state is an actor that makes various types of changes in property rights laws, creating new opportunities for innovation and entrepreneurship. They argue that one mechanism through which the American government has shaped the economy is its power over property rights. For political and economic reasons, the American state can – and does – change the rules about property rights. In response to these legal changes, businesses change their structures, new opportunities open up, and old ones shut down. Campbell and Lindberg (1990, pp. 639–640) give examples of the state intervening in the economy via property rights legislation, including the de-monopolization of the American telecommunications industry and the governmental acquisition of private railroad companies to save the railroad sector.

Evans (1995, 1996) delineates the characteristics of the model state for industrial development. For Evans (1996, p. 263), the ideal state would exhibit what he terms *"embedded autonomy."* Such a state would be strong internally and connected to private outside resources. Such a state, argues Evans (1996), existed in Korea, and was able to bring the national technology industry to the forefront of the international economy in the 1970s and 1980s. According to Evans (1996), other states, for example, India and Brazil, lacked either the internal state cohesiveness or the external connections to make their technology sectors as internationally competitive as those of Korea. Though the embeddedly autonomous state sounds like a perfect model for development, Evans (1996) notes that when strong states combine with private actors and actually succeed in developing technology sectors, the balance of power can swing away from the state, even though the state, perhaps in a somewhat different form, may still be necessary for the new technology sector to survive and thrive. Evans (1996, pp. 275–277) argues that this moving of the power away from the state is what happened in Korea, and it ultimately hurt the technology sector. Applying Evans's (1996) line of reasoning, then, entrepreneurs would be best served by location in a state which is strong internally and connected externally, but flexible enough to adapt as the balance of power shifts with the creation of new markets.

Going Beyond Geography

Several authors suggest that locating in the correct geography is helpful for a new venture, but is not in and of itself sufficient to guarantee success for the new enterprise. Asheim and Cooke (1998) and Evans (1996) suggest that, within the correct location, networking must take place in order for new firms to thrive. In addition, corporate and regional culture are necessary elements for entrepreneurship to be successful in the right geography.

Saxenian (1994), in comparing the high-technology regions of California's Silicon Valley and Boston's Route 128, argues that geography contributed to the success of Silicon Valley's high-technology sector, and was aided by personal characteristics of the individuals and the differences in organizational structure and culture. In Silicon Valley, individuals with similar backgrounds came together to found technology businesses in a small area where the rules were not clearly established. They formed a culture of pioneering and entrepreneurship where everyone helped one another, regardless of firm affiliations. This communal spirit, facilitated by the network structure of firms, small geography, and employee mobility, ensured that individuals frequently encountered one another. In contrast, New England had a history of innovation and an established way of doing business which involved keeping ideas strictly within the hierarchical boundaries of the firm. Additionally, New England's Route 128 corridor was geographically larger than Silicon Valley, which may have reduced the possibility for frequent interaction among individuals. In sum, Saxenian (1994) argues, it was the combination of people, culture, and geography that allowed Silicon Valley to surpass Route 128 in America's high-technology race.

Feldman and Desrochers (2001) echo the importance of culture to entrepreneurial success even within a promising geography. They claim that, though universities such as Stanford and the Massachusetts Institute of Technology have been central to the development of high-technology regions, universities have different cultures, some of which do not promote the kinds of activities helpful in developing a technology cluster. Feldman and Desrochers (2001) studied one Washington, D.C., area university and found that, although interesting research was conducted, the university's culture discouraged technology transfer. This culture inhibited the progress of the university until recently when it started to make small inroads in contributing to the development of local industry.

QUESTIONS FOR FURTHER RESEARCH

The research on geography and entrepreneurship reviewed above represents a wide range of theoretical perspectives on where entrepreneurship occurs and how entrepreneurial environments differ from other environments. This literature is both consistent with and challenging of classic perspectives in geography, such as regional density and proximity. Clustering remains a prevalent phenomenon around the world. Many of the questions that have traditionally confronted economists, regional developers, geographers, and sociologists in reference to economic geography remain unresolved. Traditionally, economists have argued that clustering occurs because entrepreneurs are attracted to resource-dense locations. However, much of the research reviewed refutes this economic explanation of clustering, doing so in many cases with strong empirical evidence from large sample studies on populations of organizations. Future research should continue to address the conundrums of agglomeration with respect to why entrepreneurs and industries tend to cluster, but in particular should advance to questions on whether clustering enhances economic success, and why one region or cluster may have a competitive advantage over another.

Another traditional economic question that presents possibilities for future research on geography and entrepreneurship is the issue of density. Positions on the effects of density range from a high density of competing firms leading to entrepreneurship (Porter, 1980; Feldman, 1993), to density leading to the death of competing firms (Carroll and Hannan, 1989a, b), to positions arguing that a high density of competing firms is both beneficial and detrimental (Sorenson and Audia, 2000; Stuart and Sorenson, 1999). The question thus remains to be clarified via further research: What are the effects on entrepreneurship of locating in a resource-rich or firm-dense location? Additional issues to be clarified via such research would include what sorts of density benefit firms, and what sorts might be detrimental to firms. Stuart and Sorenson (1999) show that the lifecycle stage of a firm is an important variable intervening in how density affects the success of entrepreneurial ventures. They note that the national density of biotechnology firms attenuates the effects of local resources upon founding rates of biotechnology firms in a given local area. This suggests that the effects of locally rich resources (local density) may depend on national resource pools (national density). Moreover, the work of Smith and Powell (2002) implies that local density and the lifecycle stage of a network are related to levels of innovation in geographies.

One phenomenon whose impact cannot be ignored is the growth of the Internet. An interesting line of research could explore how this invention, and the spread of Internet access around the world, affects the interplay of geography and entrepreneurship. It has been demonstrated that entrepreneurship occurs as a result of local forces such as clustering and proximity; might the development of Web-based technologies and resources foster global effects? However, it could be counter argued that the Internet is incapable of transmitting information in the same way as person-to-person interactions (Howells, 1990; Nohria and Eccles, 1992; Feldman, forthcoming), and thus is not as viable a networking resource in creating entrepreneurial ventures. While it may seem logical that the importance of geography would fade away in favor of the influence of a global Web, Sorenson and Stuart (2001) remind us that regionalism plays an important role, even in the global economy. Feldman (forthcoming) argues in a review paper that the Internet may actually increase regionalism and the power of geography in several ways. First, the spread of the Internet may create a divide between those who can afford access to the infrastructure and those who cannot. Feldman further suggests that as Internet access spreads and workers can choose to live anywhere and still access the information they need, they may choose to live in desirable locations, with others similar to them, and thus the world may become even more clustered as a result of the Internet than it was before information was electronically accessible. The advent and spread of the Internet provides a fruitful arena for research into the roles that proximity and geography may play in the entrepreneurship of the next millennium.

CONCLUSION

This chapter has explored literatures on two contexts that impact various aspects of entrepreneurship: networks and geography. We have drawn upon economic and organization theories from different levels of analysis to highlight issues and questions for further research. This chapter concludes with a few final sections that discuss the possible interconnections between networks, geography, and entrepreneurship.

Networks and Entrepreneurship

The literature reviewed has shown that networks with cohesion in which trust is fostered are contexts in which information flows easily, characteristics that are central to reducing the risk of investment in innovation. Whether networks connect individuals, groups, or firms to one another, or tie together actors from two or more of these categories, they are contexts that provide the social, financial, and human capital that fosters entrepreneurship. Research is needed that considers issues of power and status in exploring how different groups of actors construct and access their networks and purposely use networks for entrepreneurial gains, and how these differences may impact entrepreneurial outcomes. Research beyond anecdotal case studies is needed that shows how networks led to the discovery of opportunities and introduced would-be entrepreneurs to management teams and to the venture capital marketplace. Future research should examine these person–place questions with respect to identifying the supply- and demand-side and the local and global forces. For example, capital is mobile in global equities markets, however venture capital is local and less mobile because it is constrained by the relational and spatial aspects of reputational and cultural capital. When cultural capital is tied to geography, it is a demand-side or pull chararacteristic. When cultural capital operates at the individual-level, as in the "entrepreneurial spirit," and is a result of cognition and socialization, it is mobile and is a supply-side or push force in the development of entrepreneurship (Redding, 1990). A better understanding of these theoretical mechanisms is need in developing educational and policy programs in entrepreneurship.

Networks are governance structures that include a variety of organizational, as distinct from market, contexts. Research is needed that compares the outcomes of various organizational forms for commercializing certain types of innovations, such as public versus private incubators, incubators versus bands of angels, and others. More generally, this question can be asked about organization versus market contexts – both for the training and creation of entrepreneurs and for the founding of new firms. The variety of organizational alternatives for entrepreneurs to found new ventures has been increasing; they represent a continuum that varies in the degree of structural centralization, from licensing contracts to intrapreneurship in a formal hierarchy. Research on these structural alternatives has not kept pace with their development in the growth of both numbers and varieties. Hence, knowledge is limited on how such structural alternatives may be solutions to the problems that entrepreneurs face in exploiting entrepreneurial opportunities.

The incubator firm in its various incarnations is a relatively new creature on the entrepreneurial landscape and as a result it is understudied. We have only descriptive data, yet this important phenomenon presents an opportunity to explore research hypotheses at the cusp of firm and market boundaries (Williamson, 1975). Teece (1999, p. 146) argues specifically that research is needed on the relationship between innovation and the boundaries of firms. Moreover, as an organizational form propelling the rate of entrepreneurship, incubators have grown rapidly and have witnessed a high rate of mortality with the post-dot.com market cycle. The rapid dynamics of this population of firms make it an appropriate context of analysis for a population ecology study.

University and government sponsored incubators make sense, in that they provide shelter from market forces for teaching purposes to train scientists to be a part of an entrepreneurial management team, to commercialize technologies that do not have self-evident market applications, and to develop technologies with huge start-up costs. However, the publicly owned, profit-making variant of the incubator firm is an economic anomaly because one could argue that it should attract inexperienced entrepreneurs and hence raise, rather than lower, the learning curve. Research needs to address whether its incentive structure and set of stakeholders may not be competitive with corporate or venture capital alternatives.

Geography and Entrepreneurship

The work on geography and entrepreneurship has demonstrated that geographical concentrations are found in many industries and in nations around the world. Geographical proximity and geographical clustering provide the resources necessary to the flourishing of entrepreneurial ventures including knowledge, services, and money. Furthermore, some geographies have been theorized or found to be more conducive to entrepreneurship than others.

Despite the work on geography and entrepreneurship, work remains to be done, especially on some of the basic questions about clustering and the impact of the Internet on geography. Agglomeration has been the traditional economic explanation of geographical clustering. Though much of the work presented here has refuted the agglomeration explanation, a new theory for geographical clustering remains to be found. Similarly, the positive and negative effects of density, another concept popular in explanations of industrial clustering from both economic and sociological perspectives, needs to be researched to adjudicate the inconsistencies and define the contingencies. Finally, the Internet and its spread across the world may have far-reaching effects on entrepreneurship. Whether, and how, the Internet affects the geography of entrepreneurship will be a question of the utmost importance for scholars of entrepreneurship in the coming years.

Putting it All Together: Networks, Geography, and Entrepreneurship

We have reviewed the literatures on networks and entrepreneurship in separate sections from those on geography and entrepreneurship. However, this distinction is an analytical one, not an actual one, as these differences are not likely to be clear-cut. It may be that geographical proximity leads to networking, which aids in entrepreneurial ventures. This certainly seems to be the idea behind Saxenian's (1994) argument on the advantages that catapulted Silicon Valley ahead of Route 128 in America's high-technology sector. In a theoretical piece, Johannisson (2000, p. 380) implies that geographical clusters of industry lead to networking, and the combination of physical closeness and networking can lead to entrepreneurial ventures. On the other hand, it could be that networking leads to geographical closeness. Shane and Cable (1999, pp. 35–36) suggest that the connections between entrepreneurs and venture capitalists which make financing easier to obtain may lead entrepreneurs to locate to, or stay in, regions where venture capitalists are located, thus leading to geographical concentration. One classic theorist, Macaulay (1963), argued that close connections to other people tend to be located within a close geographic distance of the individual actor. Thus, it may be that geography leads to networks, which in turn create opportunities for entrepreneurship. Conversely, it may be that networks lead to geography, which then creates spaces for entrepreneurial ventures. Networks, geography, and entrepreneurship are intertwined in complex ways which are difficult to parse and to understand, but which provide rich motivations and opportunities for future research.

REFERENCES

Abell, P. (1996). Self-employment and entrepreneurship: A study of entry and exit. In Jan Clark (ed.), James S. Coleman: *Consensus and Controversy*, Routledge: Falmer, NY, pp. 175–205.

Acs, Z. and C. Armington (2003). Endogenous Growth and Entrepreneurial Activity in Cities. Center for Economic Studies, working paper, CES 2003 January.

Acs, Z., L. Anselin and A. Varga (2001). Patents and innovation counts as measures of regional production of new knowledge. *Research Policy*, 1–17.

Acs, Z. and D. Audretsch (1988). Innovation in large and small firms. *American Economic Review*, 78, 678–690.

Acs, Z., D. Audretsch and M. Feldman (1994). R&D spillovers and recipient firm size. *Review of Economics and Statistics*, 76(2), 336–340.

Acs, Z., F. Fitzroy and I. Smith (1999). High technology employment, wages and R&D spillover: Evidence from U.S. cities. *Economic Innovation and New Technology*, 8, 57–78.

Ahuja, G. (2000). Collaboration networks, structural holes, and innovation: A longitudinal study. *Administrative Science Quarterly*, 45(3), 425–455.

Aldrich, H. (1999). *Organizations Evolving*. Beverly Hills, CA: Sage.

Aldrich, H. and Wiedenmayer, G. (1993). From traits to rates: An ecological perspective on organizational foundings. *Advances in Entrepreneurship, Firm Emergence and Growth*, 1, 145–195.

Anselin, L., A. Varga and Z. Acs (2000). Geographical spillovers and university research: A spatial econometric perspective. *Growth and Change*, 31, fall, 501–515.

Asheim, B.T. and P. Cooke (1998). Localized innovation networks in a global economy: A comparative analysis of endogenous and exogenous regional development approaches. *Comparative Social Research*, 17, 199–240.

Audretsch, D.B. and M.P. Feldman (1996). R&D spillovers and the geography of innovation and production. *American Economic Review*, 86, 630–640.

Audretsch, D.B. and P.E. Stephan (1996). Company–scientist locational links: The case of biotechnology. *American Economic Review*, 86, 641–652.

Birley, S. and S. Stockley (2000). Entrepreneurial teams and venture growth. In D.L. Sexton and H. Landstrom (eds.), *The Blackwell Handbook of Entrepreneurship*, pp. 287–307. Malden, MA; Oxford: Blackwell Business.

Block, Z. and I.C. Macmillan (1995). *Corporate Venturing*. Cambridge, MA: Harvard Business School Press.

Brown, S.L. and K.M. Eisenhardt (1995). Product development: Past research, present findings, and future directions. *Academy of Management Review*, 20(2), 343–378.

Burt, R.S. (1992). *Structural Holes*. Cambridge, MA: Harvard University Press.

Burt, R.S. (1998). The gender of social capital. *Rationality and Society*, 10(1), 5–46.

Burt, R.S. (2000). The network structure of social capital. Pre-print for a chapter in *Research on Organizational Behavior*, 22, 345–423.

Campbell, J.L. and L.N. Lindberg (1990). Property rights and the organization of economic activity by the state. *American Sociological Review*, 55, 634–647.

Carroll, G.R. and M.T. Hannan (1989a). Density delay in the evolution of organizational populations: A model and five empirical tests. *Administrative Science Quarterly*, 34(3), 411–430.

Carroll, G.R. and M.T. Hannan (1989b). Density dependence in the evolution of populations of newspaper oganizations. *American Sociological Review*, 54(4), 524–541.

Chesbrough, H.W. and D.J. Teece (1996). When is virtual virtuous?: Organizing for innovation. *Harvard Business Review*, 96103, 65–73.

Coleman, J. (1988). Social capital in the creation of human capital. *American Journal of Sociology*, 94, S95–S121.

Cooper, A. and C. Daily (1997). Entrepreneurial teams. In D.L. Sexton and R.W. Smilor (eds.), *Entrepreneurship 2000*. Chicago: Upstart.

Cooper, A. and T. Folta (2000). Entrepreneurship and high-technology clusters. In D.L. Sexton and H. Landstrom (eds.), *The Blackwell Handbook of Entrepreneurship*, pp. 348–367. Malden, MA; Oxford: Blackwell Business.

Dacin, T., M.J. Ventresca and B.D. Beal (1999). The embeddedness of organizations: Dialogue and directions. *Journal of Management*, 25(3), 317–356.

D'Arbeloff, A. (2000). Do incubators work? In T. Hurtwitz and L.L.P. Thibeault (eds.), *Venture Update: A Publication for Venture and Private Equity Investors*. 1, Summer, 9–11.

Davis, G.F. (1991). Agents without principles? The spread of the poison pill through the intercorporate network. *Administrative Science Quarterly*, 36, 583–613.

Davis, G.F. and H.R. Greve (1997). Corporate elite networks and governance changes in the 1980s. *American Journal of Sociology*, 103(1), 1–37.

Desrochers, P. and M.P. Feldman (forthcoming). *The University and the Region: Spin-Off Firms and Organizational Evolution*. Industry and Innovation, Baltimore, MD: Johns Hopkins University Press.

DiMaggio, P.J. (1992). Nadel's paradox revisited: Relational and cultural aspects of organization structure. In N. Nitin and R. Eccles (eds.), *Networks and Organizations: Structure, Form, and Action*, pp. 118–139. Cambridge, MA: Harvard Business School Press.

DiMaggio, P.J. (1994). Culture and economy. In S.J. Smelzer and R. Swedberg (eds.), *Handbook of Economic Sociology*. Thousand Oaks, CA: Sage.

DiMaggio, P.J. (1997). Culture and cognition. *Annual Review of Sociology*, 23, 263–287.

Dore, R. (1983). Goodwill and the spirit of market capitalism. *British Journal of Sociology*, 34, 459–482.

Eshun, J.P. (2002). *Leveling the Playing Field: How Business Incubators Lower the Market Entry Barriers for Entrepreneurs and Business Start-ups*. Academy of Management, Denver, CO.

Evans, P.B. (1995). *Embedded Autonomy: States and Industrial Transformation*. Princeton, NJ: Princeton University Press.

Evans, P. (1996). Embedded autonomy and industrial transformation. *Political Power and Social Theory*, 10, 259–282.

Feldman, M.P. (1993). An examination of the geography of innovation. *Industrial and Corporate Change*, 2, 451–470.

Feldman, M.P. (2001). The Entrepreneurial event revisited: Firm formation in a regional context. *Industrial and Corporate Change*, 861–891.

Feldman, M.P. (2000). The Internet revolution and the geography of innovation. *International Social Science Journal*, Summer.

Feldman, M.P. and P. Desrochers (2001). *University Culture and Technology Transfer at Johns Hopkins University*. Mimeo.

Feldman, M.P. and J. Francis (2001). The entrepreneurial spark: Individual agents and the formation of innovative clusters. Paper prepared for the Conference on *Complexity and Industrial Clusters – Dynamics, Models, National Cases*, organized by the Fondazione Montedison under the aegis of the Accadèmia Nazionale dei Lincei, Milan, Italy, June 19–20.

Finlay, W. and J.E. Coverdill (2000). Risk, opportunism, and structural holes: How headhunters manage clients and earn fees. *Work and Occupations,* 27(3), 377–405.

Fligstein, N. (2001). *The Architecture of Markets: An Economic Sociology for the 21st Century.* Princeton, NJ: Princeton University Press.

Florida, R.L. (2000). Competing in the age of talent: Quality of place and the new economy. A Report Prepared for the R.K. Mellon Foundation, Heinz Endowments, and Sustainable, Pittsburgh.

Florida, R.L. (2002). *The Rise of the Creative Class: And How it's Transforming Work, Leisure, Community and Everyday Life.* New York: Basic Books.

Florida, R.L. and W.M. Cohen (1999). Engine or infrastructure? The university role in economic development. In L.M. Branscomb, F. Kodama and R. Florida (eds.), *Industrializing Knowledge: University-Industry Linkages in Japan and the United States,* pp. 589–610. Cambridge, MA: The MIT Press.

Florida, R.L. and M. Kenney (1988). Venture capital, high technology and regional development. *Regional Studies,* 22(1), 33–48.

Frank, D.J. and J.W. Meyer (2001). The profusion of individual roles and identities in the postwar period. *Sociological Theory,* 20(1), 86–105.

Frankel, M. (1955). Obsolescence and technological change in a maturing economy. *American Economic Review,* 45(3), 296–319.

Freeman, J. (1986). Entrepreneurs as organizational products: Semiconductor firms and venture capital firms. *Advances in the Study of Entrepreneurship, Innovation, and Economic Growth,* Vol. 1, pp. 33–52. Greenwich, CT: JAI Press Inc.

Friedland, R. and R.R. Alford (1991). Bringing society back in: Symbols, practices, and institutional contradictions. In W.W. Powell and P.J. DiMaggio (eds.), *The New Institutionalism in Organizational Analysis,* Chicago: University of Chicago Press, pp. 267–292.

Gereffi, G. (1994). The organization of buyer-driven global commodity chains. In G. Gereffi and M. Korzeniewicz (eds.), *Commodity Chains and Global Capitalism,* pp. 95–122. Westport, CT: Greenwood.

Gifford, S. (1998). *The Allocation of Limited Entrepreneurial Attention.* Boston, MA: Kluwer Academic Publishers.

Glushik, J. (2001). Personal Communication, March, 6.

Gompers, P. and J. Lerner (2000). Does the venture capital structure matter? In P. Gompers and J. Lerner (eds.), *The Venture Capital Cycle,* 4th printing, pp. 95–123. Cambridge: The MIT Press.

Granovetter, M.S. (1985). Economic action and social structure: The problem of embeddedness. *American Journal of Sociology,* 91, 481–510.

Greiner, L. (1972). Evolution and revolution as organizations grow. *Harvard Business Review,* July–August, 37–46.

Guillen, M. (2001). Is globalization civilizing, destructive or feeble? A critique of six key debates in the social science literature. *Annual Review of Sociology,* 27, 235–260.

Gulati, R. and M. Gargiulo (1999). Where do networks come from? *American Journal of Sociology,* 104(5), 1439–1493.

Hamel, G. (1991). Competition for competence and interpartner learning within international strategic alliances. *Strategic Management Journal,* 12(Supplement), 83–103.

Hannan, M.T., J.N. Baron, G. Hsu and O. Kocak (2000). Staying the course: Early organization building and the success of high-technology firms. Paper prepared for Harvard Business School 2000 Entrepreneurship Conference, "The Entrepreneurial Process: Research Perspectives." Harvard Business School, Dec., 7–8, Oct. 20.

Hannan, M.T. and G.R. Carroll (1992). *Dynamics of Organizational Populations: Density, Legitimation, and Competition.* New York: Oxford University Press.

Hannan, M.T., G.R. Carroll, E.A. Dundon and J.C. Torres (1995). Organization evolution in multinational context: Entries of automobile manufacturers in Belgium, Britain, France, Germany, and Italy. *American Sociological Review,* 60, 509–528.

Hansen, M.T., N. Nohria and J.B. Berger (2000). *The State of the Incubator Marketplace.* Boston, MA: Harvard Business School, June, pp. 1–40.

Higgins, M. and R. Gulati (2001). Getting off to a good start: The effects of upper echelon affiliations on interorganizational endorsements and IPO success. *Organization Science*.

Howells, J. (1990). The location and organization of research and development: New horizons. *Research Policy*, **19**, 133–146.

Howells, J. (1996). Regional Systems of Innovation? Paper presented at HCM conference on "National Systems of Innovation or the Globalisation of Technology? Lessons for the public and business sector." ISRDS-CNR, Rome, April.

Jang, Y.S. and M. Rhee (2002). *The State of Business Incubation: The Korean Case*. Academy of Management, Denver, CO.

Jepperson, R.L. (2001). Political modernities: Disentangling two underlying dimensions of institutional differentiation. *Sociological Theory*, **20**(1), 61–85.

Johannisson, B. (2000). Networking and entrepreneurial growth. In D.L. Sexton and H. Landstrom (eds.), *The Blackwell Handbook of Entrepreneurship*, pp. 368–386. Malden, MA: and Oxford, UK: Blackwell Business.

Karim, S. and W. Mitchell (2000). Path-dependent and path-breaking change: Reconfiguring business resources following acquisitions in the U.S. medical sector 1978–1995. *Strategic Management Journal*, **21**, 1061–1081.

Kogut, B. (1988). Joint ventures: Theoretical and empirical perspectives. *Strategic Management Journal*, **9**, 319–332.

Krugman, P. (1991). *Geography and Trade*, 8th printing, 2000. Cambridge, MA: The MIT Press.

Laumann, E.O. (1991). Comment on "The future of bureaucracy and hierarchy in organization theory": A report from the field. In Bourdieu and Coleman (eds.), *Social Theory for a Changing Society*, pp. 90–93. Boulder, CO: Westview Press.

Leonard, D. and W. Swap (2000). Gurus in the garage. *Harvard Business Review*, Nov./Dec. 71–73, 76–80, 82.

Lin, N., K.S. Cook and R.S. Burt (eds.) (2001). *Social Capital: Theory and Research*. New York: Aldine de Gruyter.

Low, M.R. and E. Abrahamson (1997). Movements, bandwagons, and clones: Industry evolution and the entrepreneurial process. *Journal of Business Venturing*, **12**, 435–457.

McClelland, D.C. (1961). *The Achieving Society*. Princeton, NJ: Van Nostrand.

McGrath, R.G., I.C. MacMillan and S. Scheinber (1992). Elitists, risk-takers and rugged individualists? An exploratory analysis of cultural differences between entrepreneurs and non-entrepreneurs. *Journal of Business Venturing*, **7**, 115–135.

Macaulay, S. (1963). Noncontractual relations in business: A preliminary study. *American Sociological Review*, **28**, 55–67.

Malecki, E.J. (1997). Entrepreneurs, networks, and economic development: A review of recent research. *Advances in Entrepreneurship, Firm Emergence and Growth*, Vol. 3, pp. 57–118. Greenwich, CT: JAI Press.

Marshall, A. [1890] (1916). *Principles of Economics: An Introductory Volume*. London: Macmillan.

Martin, J.M. (1992). *Cultures in Organizations: Three Perspectives*. Oxford University Press.

Meyer, G.W. (1994). Social information processing and social networks: A test of social influence mechanisms. *Human Relations*, **47**(9), 1013–1047.

Meyer, J.W. (1994). Rationalized evironments. In W.R. Scott and J.W. Meyer (eds.), *Institutional Environments and Organizations: Structural Complexity and Individualism*. Thousand Oaks, CA: Sage.

Meyer, J. and B. Rowan (1977). Institutionalized organization: Formal structure as myth and ceremony. *American Sociological Review*, **48**, 147–160.

National Commission on Entrepreneurship (2001). *Building Entrepreneurial Networks*. Washington DC: Kauffman Center for Entrepreneurial Leadership.

Nelson, R.R. (1993). *National Innovation Systems*. New York: Oxford University Press.

Nohria, Nitin and R.G. Eccles (1992). *Networks and Organizations: Structure, Form, and Action*. Boston, MA: Harvard Business School Press.

Ocasio, W. and P. Thornton (2002). Markets with hierarchies: The effects of alternative strategies and structures on organizational survival, Kellogg Graduate School of Management working paper.

Organization for Economic Cooperation and Development (1986). *Venture Capital: Context, Development and Policies.* Paris: Organization for Economic Cooperation and Development.

Phillips, D. (2001). A genealogical approach to organizational life chances: The parent-progeny transfer and Silicon Valley Law Firms 1946–1956. *American Sociological Association, Regular Session on Organizations,* August.

Podolny, J.M. (1993). A status-based model of market competition. *American Journal of Sociology,* **98,** 829–872.

Podolny, J.M. (2001). Networks as pipes and prisms of the market. *American Journal of Sociology,* **107**(1), 33–60.

Podolny, J.M. and K.L. Page (1998). Network forms of organization. *Annual Review of Sociology,* **24**(1), 57–77.

Porter, M.E. (1980). *Competitive Strategy: Techniques for Analyzing Industries and Competitors.* New York: Free Press.

Porter, M.E. (1990). *The Competitive Advantage of Nations.* New York: Free Press.

Powell, W.W. (1990). *Neither Market Nor Hierarchy: Network Forms of Organization in Research in Organizational Behavior,* Vol. 12, pp. 295–336. Greenwich, CT: JAI Press.

Powell, W.W. and P. Brantley (1992). Competitive cooperation in biotechnology: Learning through networks? In N. Nitin and R. Eccles (eds.), *Networks and Organization Structure, Form and Action,* pp. 366–394. Boston, MA: Harvard Business School Press.

Powell, W., K.W. Koput and L. Smith-Doerr (1996). Interorganizational collaboration and the locus of innovation: Networks of learning in biotechnology. *Administrative Science Quarterly,* **42**(1), 116–145.

Ranger-Moore, J., J. Banaszak-Holl and M.T. Hannan (1991). Density-Dependent Dynamics in Regulated Industries: Founding Rates of Banks and Life Insurance Companies. *Administrative Science Quarterly,* **36**(1), 36-6.

Redding, S.G. (1990). *The Spirit of Capitalism,* Berlin; New York: W. de Gruyter.

Roure, J.B. and M.A. Maidique (1986). Linking prefunding factors and high-technology venture success: An exploratory study. *Journal of Business Venturing,* **1,** 295–306.

Saks, M. (2002). *The Social Structure of New Venture Funding: Stratification and the Differential Liability of Newness.* In M. Lounsbury and M. Ventresca (eds.), *Social Structure and Organizations Revisited,* Vol. 19, pp. 263–294. Oxford, UK: Elsevier Science.

Saxenian, A. (1994). *Regional Advantage: Culture and Competition in Silicon Valley and Route 128.* Cambridge, MA: Harvard University Press.

Schoonhoven, C.B. and K.M. Eisenhardt (1992). Regions as industrial incubators of technology-based ventures. In E. Mills and J. McDonald (eds.), *Sources of Metropolitan Growth.* New Brunswick, NJ: Center for Urban Policy Research.

Scott, A.J. (1999). The geographic foundations of industrial performance. In A.D. Chandler, P. Hagstrom and O. Solvell (eds.), *The Dynamic Firm: The Role of Technology, Strategy, Organization, and Regions,* pp. 384–401. London: Oxford University Press.

Scott, W.R., R. Meyer and J.W. Meyer (1994). *Institutional Environments and Organizations: Structural Complexity and Individualism.* Thousand Oaks, CA: Sage.

Scott, W.R. [1995] 2001. *Institutions and Organizations.* Thousand Oaks, CA: Sage. 2nd ed.

Selznick, P. (1957). *Leadership in Administration.* Berkeley, CA: University of California Press.

Sewell, W.H. Jr. (1992). A theory of structure: Duality, agency, and transformation. *American Journal of Sociology,* **98**(1), 1–29.

Shane, S. (1993). Cultural differences on national innovation rates. *Journal of Business Venturing,* **8,** 59–73.

Shane, S. (2000). Prior knowledge and the discovery of entrepreneurial opportunities. *Organization Science,* **11**(4), 448–469.

Shane, S. and D. Cable (2002). Network ties, reputation, and the financing of new ventures. *Management Science,* **48**(3), 364–381.

Shane, S. and S. Venkatarama (2000). The promise of entrepreneurship as a field of research. *Academy of Management Review,* **25**(1), 217–226.

Shaver, K.G. and L.R. Scott (1991). Person, process, choice: The psychology of new venture creation. *Entrepreneurship: Theory and Practice*, 16(2), 23–45.

Simon, H.A. (1997). *Administrative Behavior*, 4th edition. New York: Macmillan.

Smith, J.O. and W. Powell (2002). Knowledge Networks in the Boston Biotechnology Community. Paper presented at the conference on "Science as an Institution and the Institutions of Science." University of Siena, January.

Sorenson, O. and P.G. Audia (2000). The social structure of entrepreneurial activity: Geographic concentration of footwear production in the United States, 1940–1989. *American Journal of Sociology*, 106(2), 424–462.

Sorenson, O. and T. Stuart (2001). Syndication networks and the spatial distribution of venture capital investments. *American Journal of Sociology*, 106(6), 1546–1588.

Staber, U. and H. Aldrich (1995). Cross-national similarities in the personal networks of small-business owners: A comparison of two regions in North America. *Canadian Journal of Sociology*, 20(4), 441–467.

Stark, D. (1996). Recombinant property in East European capitalism. *American Journal of Sociology*, 101, 993–1027.

Stinchcombe, A. (1965). Social structure and organizations. In J.G. March (ed.), *Handbook of Organizations*, pp. 142–193. Chicago, IL: Rand McNally & Company.

Stinchcombe, A. (2002). New sociological microfoundations for organizational theory: A postscript. In M. Lounsbury and M. Ventresca (eds.), *Social Structure and Organizations Revisited*, Vol. 19, pp. 415–433. Oxford, UK: Elsevier Science.

Strang, D. and J.W. Meyer (1994). Institutional conditions for diffusion. In W.R. Scott and J.W. Meyer (eds.), *Institutional Environments and Organizations: Structural Complexity and Individualism*. Thousand Oaks, CA: Sage.

Stuart, T., H. Hoang and R.C. Hybels (1999). Interorganizational endorsements and the performance of entrepreneurial ventures. *Administrative Science Quarterly*, 44(2), 315–349.

Stuart, T. and O. Sorenson (1999). *The Geography of Opportunity: Spatial Heterogeneity in Founding Rates and the Performance of Biotechnology Firms*. Elsevier journal, Research Policy.

Suchman, M.C., D.J. Steward and C.A. Westfall (2001). The legal environment of entrepreneurship: Observations on the legitimation of venture finance in Silicon Valley. In C.B. Schoonhoven and E. Romanelli (eds.), *The Entrepreneurship Dynamic: Origins of Entrepreneurship and the Evolution of Industries*, pp. 349–382. Stanford, CA: Stanford University Press.

Teece, D.J. (1999). Design issues for innovative firms: Bureaucratic incentives and industrial structure. In A.D. Chandler, P. Hagstrom and O. Solvell (eds.), *The Dynamic Firm: The Role of Technology, Strategy, Organization, and Regions*. London: Oxford University Press.

Thornton, P.H. (1999). The sociology of entrepreneurship. *Annual Review of Sociology*, 25, 19–46.

Thornton, P.H. (2001). Personal versus market logics of control: A historically contingent theory of acquisition. *Organization Science*, 12(3), 294–311.

Thornton, P.H. (2002). The rise of the corporation in a craft industry: Conflict and conformity in institutional logics. *Academy of Management Journal*, 45(1), 81–101.

Turk, H. (1970). Interorganizational networks in uban society: Initial perspectives and comparative research. *American Sociological Review*, 34, 1–19.

Uzzi, B. (1996). The sources and consequences of embeddedness for the economic performance of organizations: The network effect. *American Sociological Review*, 61, 674–698.

Veblen, T. (1972). Professor Clark's economics. In E.K. Hunt and J. Schwartz (eds.), *A Critique of Economic Theory*. Harmondsworth, UK: Penguin.

Warren, R. (1967). The interorganizational field as a focus of investigation. *Administrative Science Quarterly*, 12, 396–419.

Weber, M. (1904). *The Protestant Ethic and the Spirit of Capitalism*. Berkeley, CA: University of California Press.

Weber, A. (1929). *A Theory of the Location of Industries*. Chicago: University of Chicago Press.

White, H.C. (2002). *Markets from networks: Socioeconomic models of production*. Princeton University Press.

Williamson, O.E. (1975). *Markets and Hierarchies*. New York: Free Press.

Williamson, O.E. (1991). Comparative economic organization: The analysis of discrete structural alternatives. *Administrative Science Quarterly*, **36**, 269–296.

Winterbottom, M.R. (1958). The relation of need for achievement to learning experiences in independence and mastery. In J.W. Atkinson (ed.), *Motives in Fantasies, Action, and Society*, pp. 453–478. Princeton, NJ: Van Nostrand

Woolcock, M. (1998). Social capital and economic development: Toward a theoretical synthesis and policy framework. *Theory and Society*, **27**, 151–208.

Zajac, E. and J. Westphal (2001). Explaining institutional decoupling: The case of the stock repurchase programs. *Administrative Science Quarterly*, **46**(2), 202–228.

PART SEVEN

Entrepreneurship, Economic Growth and Policy

Much of the first six sections of the Handbook are devoted towards understanding what actually constitutes entrepreneurship and what shapes and influences entrepreneurial activity. In Part VII the impact of entrepreneurship on economic performance is analyzed. Chapter 17, "The Impact of Entrepreneurship on Economic Growth," by Martin Carree and Roy Thurik synthesizes both theoretical models as well as empirical studies linking different measures of entrepreneurial activity to measures of actual economic performance, most typically employment growth. The actual unit of observation or analysis varies considerably across the spatial dimension. Some of the studies are at the unit of analysis of the country, while others are for regions. Still, Carree and Thurik integrate these disparate studies and present them in a coherent manner suggesting a fairly robust and compelling positive relationship between entrepreneurial activity and growth.

While Carree and Thurik provide an overview of the studies pointing to a positive link between entrepreneurship and economic development, in Chapter 18, "Entrepreneurship, Small and Medium Sized Enterprises and Public Policies," David Storey addresses the role that public policy has played and should potentially play. From his chapter it becomes clear that public policy can influence entrepreneurship, both positively and negatively.

MARTIN A. CARREE[1,2,3] and A. ROY THURIK[1,2]

[1]*Centre for Advanced Small Business Economics (CASBEC) at Erasmus University, Rotterdam,*
[2]*EIM Business and Policy Research, Zoetermeer,*
[3]*Faculty of Economics and Business Administration, University of Maastricht*

17.   The Impact of Entrepreneurship on Economic Growth

INTRODUCTION

The last two decades have witnessed a wealth of studies analyzing the *determinants* of entrepreneurship. While some of these studies are theoretical (e.g. Holmes and Schmitz, 1990), others are empirical (e.g. Evans and Leighton, 1990). The *consequences* of entrepreneurship, in terms of economic performance, have also generated an extensive literature. However, this literature has generally been restricted to two units of observations – that of the establishment or firm, and that of the region. Noticeably absent are studies linking the impact of entrepreneurship on performance for the unit of observation of the country. A large literature has emerged analyzing the impact of entrepreneurship on economic performance at the level of the firm or establishment. These studies typically measure economic performance in terms of firm growth and survival (Audretsch, 1995; Caves, 1998; Sutton, 1997).

The compelling stylized facts that have emerged from this literature are that entrepreneurial activity, measured in terms of firm size and age, is positively related to growth.[1] New firms and (very) small firms grow systematically larger than large and established incumbents. These findings hold across modern Western economies and across time periods. The link between entrepreneurship and performance has also been extended beyond the unit of observation of the firm to include geographic regions. A small literature exists linking measures of entrepreneurial activity for regions to the economic performance of those regions (e.g. Audretsch and Fritsch, 2002; Acs and Armington, 2003).

However, when it comes to linking entrepreneurship to growth at the national level, there is a relative void despite recent efforts of the Global Entrepreneurship Monitor (GEM) research program (Reynolds et al., 2001). The purpose of this chapter is to provide a survey of what is known about the links between entrepreneurial activity and macro-economic growth. Despite

---

[1] See Audretsch, Klomp and Thurik (2002) for a recent survey of studies dealing with Gibrat's Law.

Z.J. Acs and D.B. Audretsch (eds.), Handbook of Entrepreneurship Research, 437–471
© *2003 Kluwer Academic Publishers. Printed in Great Britain.*

the numerous studies claiming a link of entrepreneurship to economic growth the relative void may be attributable to a paucity of theoretical frameworks linking entrepreneurship to growth, as well as severe constraints in measuring entrepreneurship in a cross-national context. Furthermore, there is the reversed causality of economic development influencing entrepreneurial activities. In this chapter we provide five short overviews of the relevant literature and complement them with some new material.

Explanations for economic growth have generally been restricted to the realm of macro-economics (Romer, 1990). However, a different scholarly tradition linking growth to industrial organization dates back at least to Schumpeter (1934). According to this tradition, performance, measured in terms of economic growth, is shaped by the degree to which the industry *structure* utilizes scarce resources most efficiently. This (most efficient) industrial structure does not alter in case its underlying determinants are stable. However, as Chandler (1990), Scherer and Ross (1990) and Dosi (1988) emphasize, a change in the underlying determinants would be expected to result in a change in the industry structure most conducive to growth. Certainly, Chandler (1990) and Scherer and Ross (1990) identified a shift in industry structure towards increased centralization and concentration throughout the first two-thirds of the previous century as a result of changes in the underlying technology along with other factors.

More recently, a series of studies has identified a change in the determinants underlying the industry structure that has reversed this trend. The most salient point of this change is that technological change, globalization, deregulation, shifts in the labor supply, variety in demand, and the resulting higher levels of uncertainty have rendered a shift in the industry structure away from greater concentration and centralization towards less concentration and decentralization. A series of empirical studies have uncovered two systematic findings regarding the response of industry structure to changes in the underlying determinants. The *first* is that the industry structure is generally shifting towards an increased role for small firms. The *second* is that the extent and timing of this shift is anything but identical across countries. Apparently, institutions and policies in certain countries have facilitated a greater and more rapid response to technological change and globalization, along with the other underlying factors, by shifting to a less centralized and more dispersed industry structure than has been the case in other countries. The question of whether countries that have shifted towards a greater role for entrepreneurship enjoy stronger growth is of large importance to policy makers.

Entrepreneurship is "at the heart of national advantage" (Porter, 1990, p. 125). Concerning the role of entrepreneurship in stimulating economic growth, many links have been discussed. It is of eminent importance for carrying out innovations and for enhancing rivalry. This directs our attention to two related phenomena of the 1980s and 1990s: The resurgence of small business and the revival of entrepreneurship. There is ample evidence that economic activity moved away from large firms to small firms in the 1970s and 1980s.

The most impressive and also the most cited is the share of the 500 largest American firms, the so-called Fortune 500. Their employment share dropped from 20 percent in 1970 to 8.5 percent in 1996 (Carlsson, 1992, 1999).

Acs and Audretsch (1993) and Carlsson (1992) provide evidence concerning manufacturing industries in countries in varying stages of economic development. Carlsson advances two explanations for the shift toward smallness. The *first* deals with fundamental changes in the world economy from the 1970s onwards. These changes relate to the intensification of global competition, the increase in the degree of uncertainty and the growth in market fragmentation. The *second* deals with changes in the character of technological progress. He shows that flexible automation has various effects resulting in a shift from large to smaller firms. Also Piore and Sabel (1984) argue that the instability of markets in the 1970s resulted in the demise of mass production and promoted flexible specialization. This fundamental change in the path of technological development led to the occurrence of vast diseconomies of scale.

Brock and Evans (1989) argue that the shift away from large firms is not confined to manufacturing industries and provide four more reasons why this shift has occurred: The increase of labor supply leading to lower real wages and coinciding with an increasing level of education; changes in consumer tastes; relaxation of (entry) regulations and the fact that we are in a period of creative destruction. Loveman and Sengenberger (1991) stress the influence of two trends of industrial restructuring: That of decentralization and vertical disintegration and that of the formation of new business communities. These intermediate forms of market coordination flourish owing to declining costs of transaction. Furthermore, they emphasize the role of public and private policies promoting the small business sector. Audretsch and Thurik (2000) point at the necessary shift towards the knowledge-based economy being the driving force behind the move from large to smaller businesses. In their view globalization and technological advancements are the major determinants of this challenge of the Western countries.

The causes of this shift are one aspect. Its consequences cover a different area of research. Acs (1992) was among the first to discuss them. He distinguishes four consequences of the increased importance of small firms: Entrepreneurship, routes of innovation, industry dynamics and job generation. His claims are that small firms play an important role in the economy serving as agents of change by their entrepreneurial activity, being the source of considerable innovative activity, stimulating industry evolution and creating an important share of the newly generated jobs. Acs and Audretsch (1990) and Audretsch (1995) are key references on the role of smallness in the process of innovative activities. See also Cohen and Klepper (1992) discussing the role of firm size and diversity for obtaining technological progress. The role of small firms in the job creation process remains controversial.[2]

---

[2] See Carree and Klomp (1996) and Davis, Haltiwanger and Schuh (1996) for a discussion.

The reevaluation of the role of small firms is related to a renewed attention to the role of entrepreneurship in firms. In case the size class distribution has an influence on growth, it must be differences in organization that matter. The major difference between the organization of a large firm and a small one is the role of ownership and management. In a small firm usually there is one person or a very small group of persons, who are in control and who shapes the firm and its future. The role of such a person is often described with the term "entrepreneurship". Also, attention has been given to the role of entrepreneurship in economic development, i.e., for the functioning of markets. Many economists and politicians now have an intuition that there is a positive impact of entrepreneurship on the growth of GDP and employment. Furthermore, many stress the role of the entrepreneur in implementing innovations. This renewed interest of politicians and economists coincides with a revival of business ownership rates in most Western economies.

In the remainder of this introductory section some remarks will be made about conceptualizing entrepreneurship. In section 2 we will deal with the influence of economic development on entrepreneurship. In section 3 types of entrepreneurship and their relation to economic growth are discussed. The effect of the choice between entrepreneurship and employment is dealt with in section 4. Sections 5 and 6 deal with entrepreneurship in endogenous growth models and with empirical evidence, respectively. Section 7 concludes. The general emphasis will be on the role of entrepreneurship for economic development at the macro-economic level. Sections 3, 4 and 5 contain some new material. Readers not interested in the sometimes rigorous approach of the economic sciences can skip the mathematical expositions of these sections.

Conceptualizing Entrepreneurship

Entrepreneurship is an ill-defined, multidimensional, concept. The difficulties in defining and measuring the extent of entrepreneurial activities complicate the measurement of their impact on economic performance. Understanding their role in the process of growth requires a framework because there are various intermediate variables or linkages to explain how entrepreneurship influences economic growth. Examples of these intermediate variables are innovation, variety of supply, entry and exit of firms (competition), specific efforts and energy of entrepreneurs, etc. See Figure 1 where also some conditions for entrepreneurship are provided. These conditions include personal traits that lie at the origin of entrepreneurship and cultural and institutional elements.[3]

Entrepreneurship has to do with activities of individual persons. The concept of economic growth is relevant at levels of firms, regions, industries and nations. Hence, linking entrepreneurship to economic growth means linking the individual level to aggregate levels. In order to consider this link we first pay attention

---

[3] See also Audretsch, Verheul, Thurik and Wennekers (2002) and Wennekers, Uhlaner and Thurik (2002).

Conditions (personal, cultural, institutional)
↓
Entrepreneurship (multidimensional)
↓
Intermediate linkages (innovation, variety, competition, entrepreneurial efforts, etc)
↓
Economic growth

Figure 1. Introductory framework

Source: Wennekers and Thurik (1999).

to a definition of "entrepreneurship". Inspired by Hébert and Link (1989), Bull and Willard (1993) and Lumpkin and Dess (1996), the following definition of entrepreneurship can be proposed: Entrepreneurship is the manifest ability and willingness of individuals, on their own, in teams, within and outside existing organizations to perceive and create new economic opportunities (new products, new production methods, new organizational schemes and new product–market combinations), and to introduce their ideas in the market, in the face of uncertainty and other obstacles, by making decisions on location, form and the use of resources and institutions (Wennekers and Thurik, 1999). Essentially, entrepreneurship is a behavioral characteristic of persons. It should be noted that entrepreneurship is not an occupation and that entrepreneurs are not a well-defined occupational class of persons. Even obvious entrepreneurs may exhibit their entrepreneurship only during a certain phase of their career and/or concerning a certain part of their activities.[4]

Entrepreneurship is not synonymous with small business. Certainly, small firms are an outstanding vehicle for individuals to channel their entrepreneurial ambitions. The small firm is an extension of the individual in charge (Lumpkin and Dess, 1996, p. 138). However, entrepreneurship is not restricted to persons starting or operating an (innovative) small firm. Enterprising individuals in large firms, the so-called "intrapreneurs" or "corporate entrepreneurs", undertake entrepreneurial actions as well. In these environments there is a tendency of "mimicking smallness," for instance using business units, subsidiaries or joint ventures.

Because in colloquial speech many terms like entrepreneurs, self-employed and businessmen are used indiscriminately, its operationalization and measurement are far from obvious. However, one can make some pragmatic distinctions. *First*, between the concepts *entrepreneurial*, and *managerial* in the sense of

---

[4] See also Gartner (1989, p. 64) who asserts that "The entrepreneur is not a fixed state of existence, rather entrepreneurship is a role that individuals undertake to create organizations"; and Schumpeter (1934, p. 78) who states that "Because being an entrepreneur is not a profession and as a rule not a lasting condition, entrepreneurs do not form a social class in the technical sense as, for example, landowners or capitalists or workmen do."

organizing and coordinating. *Second*, between business-owners or *self-employed* (including owner-managers of incorporated firms)[5] and *employees*. Based on this double dichotomy of self-employed versus employee and entrepreneurial versus managerial, three types of entrepreneurs may be distinguished. These three types are the Schumpeterian entrepreneurs, the intrapreneurs and the managerial business owners who are entrepreneurs in a formal sense only. This is illustrated in Table 1.

Schumpeterian entrepreneurs are found mostly in small firms. They own and direct independent firms that are innovative and creatively destroy existing market structures. After realizing their goals Schumpeterians often develop into managerial business owners, but some may again start new ventures. Intrapreneurs or entrepreneurial managers also belong to the core of entrepreneurship. By taking commercial initiatives on behalf of their employer, and by risking their time, reputation and sometimes their job in doing so, they are the embodiment of leadership resulting in entrepreneurial ventures in larger firms. Sometimes these entrepreneurial employees, either in teams or on their own, spin off, start new enterprises and become Schumpeterian entrepreneurs. Managerial business owners (entrepreneurs in a formal sense) are to be found in the large majority of small firms. They include many franchisees, shopkeepers and people in professional occupations. They belong to what Kirchhoff (1994) calls 'the economic core' and are the seedbed for some of the entrepreneurial ventures.

THE INFLUENCE OF ECONOMIC DEVELOPMENT ON ENTREPRENEURSHIP

The relationship between unemployment and entrepreneurship has been shrouded with ambiguity. On the one hand, one strand in the literature has found that unemployment stimulates entrepreneurial activity, which has been termed as a "refugee effect." On the other hand, a very different strand in the literature has identified that higher levels of entrepreneurship reduce unemployment, or what has been termed as a "Schumpeter effect." Taken together, these two relationships result in considerable ambiguities about the relationship between rates of unemployment and self-employment (Audretsch, Carree and Thurik, 2001). Similarly, there exist ambiguities about the interrelationship of

Table 1. Three types of entrepreneurs

	Self-employed	Employees
Entrepreneurial	Schumpeterian entrepreneurs	Intrapreneurs
Managerial	Managerial business owners	Executive managers

Source: Wennekers and Thurik (1999).

[5]The terms self-employed and business owners will be used interchangeably throughout this chapter.

entrepreneurship and economic growth. In this section we will discuss how business ownership rates are influenced by economic development. We will pay attention to the role the "Schumpeterian regime switch" has played in this relationship. We discuss the pre-1970s era of declining business ownership rates and the period thereafter in which the rates have risen in most Western economies. The emphasis of the succeeding sections will be on how the business ownership rate at the economy-wide level influences the extent of structural transformation and subsequent economic growth.

Joseph Schumpeter's contribution to our understanding of the mechanisms of technological progress and economic development is widely recognized. In *The Theory of Economic Development* he emphasizes the role of the entrepreneur as prime cause of economic development. He describes how the innovating entrepreneur challenges incumbent firms by introducing new inventions that make current technologies and products obsolete. This process of creative destruction is the main characteristic of what has been called the Schumpeter Mark I regime. In *Capitalism, Socialism and Democracy*, Schumpeter focuses on innovative activities by large and established firms. He describes how large firms outperform their smaller counterparts in the innovation and appropriation process through a strong positive feedback loop from innovation to increased R&D activities. This process of creative accumulation is the main characteristic of the Schumpeter Mark II regime.

The extent to which either of the two Schumpeterian technological regimes prevails in a certain period and industry varies. It may depend upon the nature of knowledge required to innovate, the opportunities of appropriability, the degree of scale (dis)economies, the institutional environment, the importance of absorptive capacity, demand variety, etc. Industries in a Schumpeter Mark II regime are likely to develop a more concentrated market structure in contrast to industries in a Schumpeter Mark I regime where small firms will proliferate.

Decline of Business Ownership

The first three-quarters of the 20th century can be described as a period of accumulation. From the Second Industrial Revolution till the 1970s the large firm share has risen in most industries and the economy as a whole. It was the period of "scale and scope" (Chandler, 1990). It was the era of the hierarchical industrial firm growing progressively larger by exploiting economies of scale and scope in areas like production, distribution, marketing and R&D. The conglomerate merger wave of the late 1960s seemed to have set the case. The period has the characteristics of the Schumpeter Mark II regime with a declining small firm presence in most industries. The policies of (European) governments also contributed to this decline by promoting large business. The proportion of the labor force that is self-employed has decreased in most Western countries until the mid-1970s. Several authors (Blau, 1987; Kuznets, 1971; Schultz, 1990; Yamada, 1996) have reported a negative relationship between economic development and the business ownership (self-employment) rate.[6] In many Western countries and industries this decline has ended and even reversed. Many old and large firms have been losing ground to their small, new and more entrepreneurial counterparts. We label this as a regime switch (reversal of the trend) from Schumpeter Mark II to Schumpeter Mark I. Audretsch and Thurik (2001a) label this as a regime switch from a managed to an entrepreneurial economy.

Reversal of the Trend

Since the mid-1970s the self-employment rate has started to rise again in most modern economies. Blau (1987) observes that, while the proportion of self-employed in the nonagricultural U.S. labor force declined during most of this century, this decline bottomed out in the early 1970s and started to rise until at least 1982.[7] More recently business ownership increased in several other countries as well. Audretsch and Thurik (2001a) show that the business ownership growth rate was higher in the period of 1998–1986 than in the period 1986–1974 for 16 of 23 OECD countries. Also other authors have provided evidence of a reversal of the trend towards less self-employment. Acs, Audretsch and Evans (1994) report that of 23 OECD-countries, 15 experienced an increase in the self-employment rate during the 1970s and 1980s. They show that the weighted average of the self-employment rate in OECD-countries rose slightly from 8.4% in 1978 to 8.9% in 1987. Audretsch and Thurik (2001a) show that this growth accelerates in the 1990s. Large firms have been downsizing and restructuring in order to concentrate on "core business" again. In the meantime the entrepreneur has risen from the dead. High-technology innovative small firms have come at the forefront of technological development in many (new) industries.

There are several well-documented reasons for the revival of small business and self-employment in Western economies.[8] *First,* the last 25 years of the 20th century may be seen as a period of creative destruction. Piore and Sabel (1984) use the term "Industrial Divide", Jensen (1993) prefers the term "Third Industrial Revolution", and Freeman and Perez (1988) interpret it as the

---

[6]There are a couple of theoretical models proposed to explain the decline of self-employment, and of small business presence in general. Lucas (1978) shows how rising real wages may raise the opportunity cost of self-employment relative to the return. Given an underlying "managerial" talent distribution this induces marginal entrepreneurs (in this context Lucas refers to managers) to become employees. This pushes up the average size of firms. Iyigun and Owen (1998) develop a model implying that economic development is associated with a decline in the number of entrepreneurs relative to the total number of employees. They argue that fewer individuals are willing to run the risk associated with becoming an entrepreneur as the "safe" professional earnings rise with economic development. See also Schaffner (1993).

[7]Other sources showing that the growing importance of large business has come to a halt in Western countries are Carlsson (1989), Loveman and Sengenberger (1991), Acs and Audretsch (1993), Acs (1996) and Thurik (1999).

[8]Brock and Evans (1986) were the first to provide an elaborate overview.

transition from the fourth to the fifth Kondratiev wave. The most obvious evidence is the emergence of new industries like the software and biotechnology industries. Small firms play an important role in these new industries. Acs and Audretsch (1987) provide empirical evidence that small firms have a relative innovative advantage over their larger counterparts in such highly innovative industries. Evidence for the comparative advantage of small firms in inventing radically new products is also given in Prusa and Schmitz (1991) and Rothwell (1983, 1984).

Second, new technologies have reduced the importance of scale economies in many sectors. Small technology-based firms started to challenge large companies that still had every confidence in mass production techniques (Meredith, 1987; Carlsson, 1989). Jensen argues that "It is far less valuable for people to be in the same geographical location to work together effectively, and this is encouraging smaller, more efficient, entrepreneurial organizing units that cooperate through technology" (Jensen, 1993, p. 842). This is supported by Jovanovic claiming that: "recent advances in information technology have made market-based coordination cheaper relative to internal coordination and have partially caused the recent decline in firm size and diversification" (Jovanovic, 1993, p. 221).

Third, deregulation and privatization movements have swept the world. In many Western countries there have been strong tendencies to deregulate and privatize (OECD, 1995, pp. 39–49). Phillips (1985) reports that small firms have been dominant in the creation of new businesses and new jobs in deregulated industry sectors in the U.S. in the early 1980s.[9] In addition, governments acknowledge and promote the role of small (start-up) firms in establishing economic growth and development (OECD, 1998).

Fourth, there has been a tendency of large firms to concentrate on their "core competences" (Carlsson, 1989). Jovanovic (1993) reports that, as a consequence, the 1980s were characterized by corporate spin-offs and divestment. Aiginger and Tichy (1991) blame the opportunistic conglomerate merger wave of the late 1960s for much of the "back-to-basics" and downsizing (or rightsizing) tendencies.

Fifth, increasing incomes and wealth have led to an increase in the demand for variety (Jackson, 1984). Cross-cultural influences have also enlarged the demand for variety. Small firms are often the most obvious suppliers of new and specialized products. The decrease in diversification as reported by Jovanovic (1993) suggests that large firms have not been capable of entering into such market niches.

Sixth, self-employment is more highly valued as an occupational choice than before. Roughly one out of four young U.S. workers pursue self-employment according to Schiller and Crewson (1997). Kirchhoff (1996) argues that self-

---

[9] See Berkowitz and Holland (2001) for the effects of privatization on small enterprise formation in Russia.

employment is not characterized anymore as under-employment or as mom-and-pop establishments, but as a way to achieve a variety of personal goals.

Finally, the employment share of the services sector has been well documented to increase with per capita income (Inman, 1985). Given the relatively small average firm size of most services (barring airlines, shipping and some business and financial services) this creates additional opportunities for business ownership.

Obviously, some of these factors may have a temporary effect only. For example, it is not unlikely for the outsourcing and deregulation waves to dry up. In addition, many of the start-ups in the newly emerged industries fail to survive (for instance, Internet-based start-ups from the late 1990s). On the other hand, there are more permanent effects like the impact of new technologies. We refer again to Freeman and Perez (1988). They claim that in the new techno-economic paradigm (fifth Kondratiev wave) the organization of firms will be "networks" of large and small firms. Moreover, the introduction of these new technologies is also positively related to the stage of economic development because they cannot be made effective without the necessary skills and other investments. This structural influence of economic development is reinforced by the increasing variety of demand for specialized goods and services and the enhanced valuation of self-realization, both dependent on the level of prosperity.

Types of Entrepreneurship and their Relation to Economic Growth

Throughout intellectual history, the entrepreneur has worn many faces and fulfilled many roles (Hébert and Link, 1989). In this section we focus on three entrepreneurial roles, emphasized by Schumpeter, Kirzner and Knight, respectively. A *first* is the role of innovator. Schumpeter was the economist who has most prominently drawn attention to the "innovating entrepreneur".[10] He or she carries out "new combinations we call enterprise; the individuals whose function it is to carry them out we call entrepreneurs" (Schumpeter, 1934, p. 74). A *second* is the role of perceiving profit opportunities. We label this role as Kirznerian (or neo-Austrian) entrepreneurship (see for instance Kirzner, 1997). A *third* is the role of assuming the risk associated with uncertainty. We label this role as Knightian entrepreneurship.[11] When an individual introduces a new product or starts a new firm, this can be interpreted as an entrepreneurial act in terms of each of the three types of entrepreneurship. The individual is an innovator, he (assumes that he) has perceived a hitherto unnoticed profit

---

[10]Schumpeter's *Theory of Economic Development* was published in German in 1911, and in English in 1934.

[11]The Knightian entrepreneur has also been interpreted as the "neo-classical entrepreneur" (see for instance Shane, 2000). In the neo-classical (equilibrium) framework, entrepreneurship is explained by fundamental attributes of people (like "taste" for uncertainty).

opportunity and he takes the risk that the product or venture may turn out to be a failure.

Based on their study of the history of economic thought about entrepreneurship, Hébert and Link (1989, p. 47) propose the following "synthetic" definition of who an entrepreneur is and what he does: "the entrepreneur is someone who specializes in taking responsibility for and making judgemental decisions that affect the location, form, and the use of goods, resources, or institutions". When searching for links between entrepreneurship and growth, this definition does not suffice. The dynamics of perceiving and creating new economic opportunities and the competitive dimensions of entrepreneurship need more attention. The key contribution of entrepreneurship to economic growth might be singled out as being "newness". This includes the start-up of new firms but also the transformation of "inventions and ideas into economically viable entities, whether or not, in the course of doing so they create or operate a firm" (Baumol, 1993, p. 198).

The management literature has a broad view upon entry. In surveying this literature, Lumpkin and Dess (1996) integrate the renewing aspects of entrepreneurship. "New entry can be accomplished by entering new or established markets with new or existing goods or services. New entry is the act of launching a new venture, either by a start-up firm, through an existing firm or via internal corporate venturing" (Lumpkin and Dess, 1996, p. 136). In their view, the essential act of entrepreneurship is more than new entry as we see it. Entrepreneurial activities, "new entry" in existing, large firms often takes place by mimicking smallness. Newness through start-ups and innovations as well as competition are the most relevant factors linking entrepreneurship to economic growth. While managerial business owners fulfill many useful functions in the economy such as the organization and coordination of production and distribution, they cannot be viewed as the engine of innovation and creative destruction. This is the major function of Schumpeterian entrepreneurs and intrapreneurs.

Different Types of Entrepreneurship

In the following model we give an example of the economic impact of (the lack) of Kirznerian (neo-Austrian) and Knightian entrepreneurship (for the latter see also Kihlstrom and Laffont, 1979) using the example of the retail sector. A more Schumpeterian approach will be dealt with in section 5. The model is a simplified version of the carrying capacity model by Carree and Thurik (1999b). The model is used to indicate how a lack of entrepreneurship may affect economic performance. The non-mathematically interested reader may want to proceed with the last paragraph of this section.

Assume that there are two local markets, labeled i and j, in which retailers sell a homogeneous good. Retailers can only be in one market or the other. The total demand by consumers in the two local markets is assumed to have price elasticity equal to unity:

$$Q_x = a_x/p_x \qquad x \in \{i, j\}. \tag{1}$$

Each retailer k in market x maximizes profit $\pi_k = (p_x - \beta)q_k - \alpha$ where α are fixed costs and β are variable costs, both of which are identical across firms. Assume that the retailers form a Cournot oligopoly, hence not taking into account the reactions by competitors when changing the level of output q_k. Because the cost function of each retailer is assumed to be identical, also the output levels are identical to $q_k + Q_x/N_x$. In case there are N_x firms in market x, the equilibrium market price is easily derived to be

$$p_x = \beta \frac{N_x}{N_x - 1} \qquad x \in \{i, j\}. \tag{2}$$

Hence, in Cournot equilibrium total output within market x equals

$$Q_x = \frac{a_x}{\beta} \frac{N_x - 1}{N_x}. \tag{3}$$

By inserting equation (3) into the profit function we derive that in equilibrium

$$\pi_k = \frac{\beta Q_x}{N_x(N_x - 1)} - \alpha = \frac{a_x}{N_x^2} - \alpha. \tag{4}$$

There is an equilibrium across regions in case entrepreneurs in one region earn as much as entrepreneurs in the other region. This implies that

$$\frac{N_i}{N_j} = \sqrt{\frac{a_i}{a_j}}. \tag{5}$$

This equilibrium condition assures maximum total output for the two markets combined given a certain fixed number of entrepreneurs, N. To derive this, note that $N_j = N - N_i$ and that, therefore, the sum of outputs is

$$Q_i + Q_j = \left(a_i \frac{N_i - 1}{N_i} + a_j \frac{N - N_i - 1}{N - N_i} \right) \bigg/ \beta. \tag{6}$$

Maximizing equation (6) with respect to N_i gives us the exact same outcome as given in equation (5). Now we come to the final issue of how many entrepreneurs there will be. Following Carree and Thurik (1999b), we assume there exists a critical profit level π^* that entrepreneurs seek to receive as compensation for their efforts. In case profit falls short of the critical level, entrepreneurs will exit until the profit level increases to the critical level. In case profits exceed the critical level (new) entrepreneurs will enter until the profit level decreases to the critical level. An important determinant of the critical profit level is the extent to which entrepreneurs want to be compensated for the risk they face.

We give a numerical example to indicate the impact of a lack of either Kirznerian or Knightian entrepreneurship. Assume that the two markets are identical in size, $a_i = a_j = 50$, and that the fixed costs parameter α and critical profit level π^* both equal one. The variable costs parameter β is assumed to be 0.1. The total number of retailers in each of the two markets is then derived from $a_x/N_x^2 - \alpha = \pi^*$ and is found to equal five after inserting the numerical values. The total output of the two markets is derived from (3) to equal 800.

Now assume that instead of both markets having five firms that there is one market with six and one market with four firms. Total output then equals 792 instead of the maximum output of 800. Hence, the consequence of at least one of the six retailers not being alert to the prevailing disequilibrium entails a output loss of one percent. The lack of Kirznerian entrepreneurship that would otherwise have alerted one retailer to change location (market) leads to lower output.[12] Now assume instead that entrepreneurs want to have a (50%) higher compensation for the uncertainty they are confronted with and that the critical profit level π^* equals 1.5 instead of 1. The number of firms is each market then reduces to 4.47 and total output drops to 776. Hence, the consequence of entrepreneurs being more averse to risk is a drop in total output. A decrease in the number of individuals prepared to take risks in the marketplace (Knightian entrepreneurs) leads to an output loss.[13] The next section will elaborate on this issue: Choosing between entrepreneurship and employment.

THE EFFECTS OF THE CHOICE BETWEEN ENTREPRENEURSHIP AND EMPLOYMENT

In this section we present a simple model of occupational choice in which the impact of entrepreneurial activities is analyzed by considering the consequence of not allowing firms to enter (or exit) or of not allowing firms to expand (or to limit) their activities. We distinguish between three possible economic "systems" labeled "market economy", "semi-planned economy" and "planned economy". Before presenting the details of the occupational choice model, we will first discuss important recent papers concerning the intertemporal relation between occupational choice and economic development.

We will briefly discuss the contributions made in three articles: Banerjee and Newman (1993), Iyigun and Owen (1999) and Lloyd-Ellis and Bernhardt

---

[12] Yu (1998) provides an interesting analysis of the importance of Kirznerian (adaptive) entrepreneurship in explaining Hong Kong's economic development. He finds that the small Hong Kong firms are usually the first groups to get out of a declining sector and move into new markets. He claims that the diversification of Hong Kong's economy into the service sector "can be explained consistently by the dynamic operations of adaptive entrepreneurship" (pp. 902–903).

[13] Ilmakunnas and Kanniainen (2001) find empirical evidence for OECD countries to support the Knightian view that economic risks shape equilibrium entrepreneurship in an occupational choice model. They find evidence of both "national economic risk" (changes in GDP) and social insurance for labor risks (unemployment compensation), assumed not to be available to self-employed, to negatively impact the rate of self-employment.

(2000). The papers deal with the complicated issue of the two-way interaction between occupational choice and economic development. On the one hand, both the number of individuals choosing to become self-employed and their entrepreneurial skills affect economic development. On the other hand, the process of development affects the returns to occupations. It transforms the nature of risks and the possibilities for innovation.

Banerjee and Newman (1993) develop a model in which the distribution of wealth plays a central role. They assume that occupational decisions are dependent upon the distribution of wealth because of capital market imperfections, due to which poor agents can only choose working for a wage and wealthy agents become entrepreneurs. The initial distribution of wealth determines whether in the long run an economy converges to a case of only self-employment in small-scale production ("stagnation") or to one where an active labor market and both large- and small-scale production prevail ("prosperity"). Banerjee and Newman stress that the model implies that the initial existence of a population of dispossessed, whose best choice is to work for a wage, is the condition needed for an economy to achieve the stage of prosperous capitalism.

Whereas Banerjee and Newman focus on financial requirements as the defining characteristic of entrepreneurship, Iyigun and Owen (1999) focus on the element of risk. Iyigun and Owen distinguish between two types of human capital: Entrepreneurial and professional. Entrepreneurial activities are assumed to be more risky than professional activities.[14] Entrepreneurs in the model accumulate human capital through a work-experience intensive process, whereas professionals' human capital accumulation is education-intensive. The models predicts that, as technology improves, individuals devote less time to the accumulation of human capital through work experience and more to the accumulation of human capital through professional training. The allocation of an increasing share of time to formal education continues until a steady state is reached (see Iyigun and Owen, p. 224). Hence, entrepreneurs would play a relatively more important role in intermediate-income countries and professionals are relatively more abundant in rich countries. However, both entrepreneurship and professional activities are important and those countries that initially have too little of either entrepreneurial or professional human capital may end up in a development trap. Iyigun and Owen point at former communist countries as an example of economies that have a highly educated labor force but that still not achieve the high-income steady state due to a shortage of entrepreneurs (p. 225).

Lloyd-Ellis and Bernhardt (2000) also derive how the scarcity or abundance of entrepreneurial skills is the defining variable behind the equilibrium development process. In their model, individuals may choose between working as

---

[14]The uncertainty in the return to entrepreneurial ventures is that with probability q an individual achieves an income of λ_t, the endogenously determined technology level, times his entrepreneurial capital and with probability $1 - q$ he receives no income. There is no uncertainty assumed in the return to education, being λ_t times their professional capital (see Iyigun and Owen, p. 220).

entrepreneurs, wage laborers in industry or in subsistence agriculture. Just like in the Banerjee and Newman model entrepreneurs are faced with a limited capital market and (inherited) wealth is needed to permit entrepreneurial activity to expand. The economy in the model goes through four separate stages. An interesting outcome of the model is that the average firm size rises quickly in the first stages of the development process, but then falls in the later stages of the development process. The number of entrepreneurs (outside agriculture) as a fraction of population may rise in each of the stages (Lloyd-Ellis and Bernhardt, p. 157).

We will present a simple new model of occupational choice in which the impact of entrepreneurial activities is analyzed by considering the consequence of not allowing firms to enter (or exit) or of not allowing firms to expand (or to limit) their activities. We distinguish between three possible economic "systems". In the *first* system, labeled "market economy", there is complete freedom of entry and exit and of firms adjusting their inputs to maximize profits. In this system there is complete entrepreneurial and managerial freedom. In the *second* system, labeled "semi-planned economy", there is no freedom of entry or exit. However, firms are free to adjust their input quantities so as to achieve maximum profits. In such an economic system the large incumbent firms are considered as the engines of economic progress. Starting new enterprises is hampered by regulations and by relatively low esteem of business ownership. The *third* economic system, labeled "planned economy", has also lost its managerial freedom of adjusting inputs to maximize profits. Firms are assigned to produce output using a certain fixed amount of labor even though it may lead some firms to be unprofitable.

Clearly, the three economic "systems" are extremes. However, comparing the economic performance of such virtual systems may enhance our understanding of the total contribution of entrepreneurial activity on the long and short term on economic performance. In addition, the conditions in the three systems may approximate actual conditions in existing economic systems. For example, the market economy of the United States grants (potential) entrepreneurs considerable freedom with little government intervention. In contrast, the economies of Continental Europe, like France and Germany and the Scandinavian countries, have a much larger role for government. In these countries government has actively intervened to support large enterprises in the recent past. The Soviet type of economic systems is the prime example of the planned economy system. The model described below is used to compare the relative performance of the three "systems".[15] The non-mathematically interested reader may want to proceed with the last paragraph of this section in which we discuss the main results.

Consider a population of N individuals that can choose between being an employee and being a manager (business owner). Each person i is assigned a

---

[15]The model is only concerned with occupational choice, not with the (dis)incentives present in economic "systems" to pursue product or process innovation.

certain managerial ability e_{it} in period t. This ability can be used in combination with an input of L_{it} employees earning an equal wage w_t to produce a total output of some (homogeneous) good $Q_{it} = e_{it} L_{it}^{\beta}$ with β in between zero and one. Assuming the price of the good to be unity total profit for manager i in period t will be $\pi_{it} = e_{it} L_{it}^{\beta} - w_t L_{it}$. From the first order condition $(\partial \pi_{it}/\partial L_{it} = 0)$ we find the optimal levels of labor input and profit:

$$L_{it}^* = (\beta e_{it}/w)^{1/(1-\beta)} \tag{7}$$

and

$$\pi_{it}^* = (1-\beta) e_{it} (\beta e_{it}/w)^{\beta/(1-\beta)}. \tag{8}$$

From equation (8) it is clear that individuals with higher levels of managerial ability will have higher profits $(\partial \pi_{it}^*/\partial e_{it} > 0)$. In case individuals are free to enter and/or exit we would see incumbents exiting the market (and becoming employee) in case their optimal level of profits is less than the wage level, while employees would start enterprises in case their optimal level of profit would exceed their wage level. In conformity with Lucas (1978) an equilibrium is reached where individuals become managers if and only if

$$e_{it} > \frac{w_t}{\beta^{\beta}(1-\beta)^{1-\beta}}. \tag{9}$$

In each of the three economic systems it is assumed that the wage level is determined by the equilibrium condition of demand and supply of labor to be identical. If we denote the number of managers/entrepreneurs by M_t and their set by Θ_t, then this condition reads

$$N - M_t = \sum_{i \in \Theta_t} L_{it}^* \Leftrightarrow w_t = \beta \left(\sum_{i \in \Theta_t} e_{it}^{1/(1-\beta)}/(N-M_t) \right)^{1-\beta}. \tag{10}$$

From equations (9) and (10) the equilibrium structure given free entry and exit can be determined. Given the distribution of the abilities e_{it} the equilibrium occupational choice and (maximum) total output can be derived. In case of changes in the ability distribution the manner in which equilibrium on the labor market is restored differs across the economic systems. In case of the "market economy" system there will be entry of managers with increased ability and exit of managers with decreased ability, changes in firm sizes and changes in the wage level. In case of the "semi-planned economy" system there will be changes in firm sizes of incumbents and changes in the wage level. The one variable that restores equilibrium in the "planned economy" system is the wage level because of the absence of managerial discretion to adapt labor demand. It is obvious that due to larger "degrees of freedom" the total output after changes in the ability distribution will be highest for the "market economy" and smallest for the "planned economy". The differences between the performances will be larger, the more the ability distribution changes over time. Hence, in periods of important changes in technological regimes and on the longer term the differences are likely to be largest. This finding is related to that presented by Eliasson (1995) that lack of new entry of firms will adversely impact economic performance not so much on the short term but *in the long term.*

ENTREPRENEURSHIP IN ENDOGENOUS GROWTH MODELS

One of the reasons that entrepreneurship disappeared from economic theory is that it played no role in the neoclassical growth model as developed by Solow (1970). An important characteristic of this growth model is that technological improvements are exogenous and therefore independent of economic incentives. Economic growth in the traditional growth models is achieved by capital accumulation and exogenous technological progress, both of which leave little room for any entrepreneurial role whatsoever (see also Baumol, 1968). The more recently developed endogenous growth models also support the idea that improvements in technology have been the key force behind perpetually rising standards of living. However, this long-term growth process is assumed in many endogenous growth models to be determined by purposive, profit-seeking investment in knowledge (Grossman and Helpman, 1994, p. 24). The act of seeking profits by shifting resources to achieve improvements in technology can be seen as an entrepreneurial act because the outcome of the investments is uncertain. However, it is not common for endogenous growth models to explicitly address the issue of entrepreneurship as driving force of technological and economic development. We will discuss three exceptions in this section. The *first* exception is the Aghion and Howitt's (1992) model of creative destruction (see also Aghion and Howitt, 1997; Howitt and Aghion, 1998). The *second* exception is the endogenous market structure model by Peretto (1998, 1999a, 1999b), and the *third* exception is the imitation model developed by Schmitz (1989). Of these three exceptions the model by Aghion and Howitt has been the most influential and we will discuss it in some detail.

Aghion and Howitt introduce the notion of Schumpeterian "creative destruction" into a growth model by having firms investing resources in research to achieve a new product that renders the previous product obsolete.[16] Capital is excluded from the basic model and growth results from technological progress, being a result from competition among firms that generate innovations. Firms are motivated by the prospect of (temporary) monopoly rents after a successful innovation is patented. A next innovation will again destroy these rents as the existing good is being made obsolete by the Schumpeterian entrepreneur. We will discuss a simple version of the basic model as presented by Aghion and

---

[16] It may be argued that Schumpeterian entrepreneurship cannot be modelled using the standard assumptions of the neo-classical model like profit maximization. It is evident that the Aghion and Howitt models fail to do complete justice to Schumpeter's discussions of the motivations that underlie entrepreneurial behaviour. We are grateful to the referee of this chapter for pointing this out.

Howitt in their section 2. The non-mathematically interested reader may want to proceed below equation (5.8).

Assume that there are four different kinds of units: A final consumption good y, an intermediate good x, unskilled labor used to produce the final good and skilled labor that can be used to produce the intermediate good or that can be used in research. The total amount of unskilled labor is fixed at M. The total amount of skilled labor is fixed at N and the amount used to do research is denoted by n, leaving $N - n$ units for production of the intermediate good. The final good is assumed to be produced using a Cobb-Douglas type of production function (with input factors unskilled labor and intermediate goods) and, since M is fixed, it can be written as

$$y_t = A_t x_t^\alpha \qquad 0 < \alpha < 1 \tag{11}$$

where t is the index of period. The parameter A_t denotes the productivity of the intermediate input in period t. The intermediate good is produced using skilled labor, not used for research, and linear technology:

$$x_t = N - n_t. \tag{12}$$

Innovations arrive in a random sequence, with the Poisson arrival rate of innovations in the economy equal to λn_t (see also Howitt and Aghion, 1998, equation (6)). The arrival rate depends only upon the current flow of input to research. Hence, there is no memory in the technology of research. The index t of period increases by one each time a new innovation has arrived, hence it is not a time index. The length of the time interval from t to $t + 1$ is random and has an exponential distribution with parameter λn_t. During this time interval prices and quantities are assumed to be constant. Each innovation (the invention of a new intermediate good) makes the previous intermediate good obsolete because it allows the production of the final good y_t to become more efficient. The increase in efficiency is determined by the factor γ:

$$A_t = A_0 \gamma^t \qquad \gamma > 1. \tag{13}$$

The model is a "winner takes it all"-model in the sense that a successful innovator is assumed to obtain a patent used to monopolize the intermediate sector. The patent lifespan is assumed to be infinite but the monopoly lasts only till the next innovation when the intermediate good is replaced by the next vintage. Each market is assumed to be perfectly competitive with the exception of the monopolized intermediate sector.

The successful innovator has a temporary monopoly and seeks to maximize its profit during this interval. The final good sector will choose the amount of intermediate goods, x_t, so as to maximize $y_t - p_t x_t$ with the price of the final good as the "numéraire" and p_t being the price charged by the monopolist. The first order condition is

$$p_t = \alpha A_t x_t^{\alpha - 1}. \tag{14}$$

The monopolist takes this condition into account and maximizes its own profit $(\alpha A_t x_t^{\alpha-1} - w_t)x_t$ with w_t being the wage level of skilled labor. The optimization gives as outcomes for profit, price and output of the intermediate good:

$$\pi_t = \left(\frac{1-\alpha}{\alpha}\right) w_t x_t, \qquad p_t = w_t/\alpha \qquad \text{and} \qquad x_t = \left(\frac{w_t}{\alpha^2 A_t}\right)^{1/(\alpha-1)}. \qquad (15)$$

We now turn to the amount of resources devoted to research, n_t. Because of constant returns to scale in the technology of research, the number of firms performing research is indeterminate. The firm(s) that employ(s) n_t units of skilled labor performing research activities to achieve monopoly in period $t+1$ will have an instantaneous probability λn_t of having a successful innovation with instantaneous value V_{t+1} (which does not depend upon n_t). The expected flow of profits equals $\lambda n_t V_{t+1} - w_t n_t$ which is maximized for $n_t \geq 0$. Because the research sector is perfectly competitive λV_{t+1} equals the wage level w_t.[17]

The value V_{t+1} is the expected present value of the flow of monopoly profits π_{t+1}, or

$$V_{t+1} = \frac{\pi_{t+1}}{r + \lambda n_{t+1}} \qquad r > 0 \qquad (16)$$

with r being the constant rate of time preference. Equation (16) reveals the important characteristic of the Aghion and Howitt model that current research negatively depends upon future research: Creative destruction discourages current research because the prospect of monopoly rents is diminished.

The intertemporal relation between n_t and n_{t+1} is determined by substituting equations (12), (15) and (16) into the condition $w_t = \lambda V_{t+1}$. This results in

$$1 = \lambda \frac{\left(\dfrac{1-\alpha}{\alpha}\right) \gamma \left(\dfrac{N - n_{t+1}}{N - n_t}\right)^{\alpha-1} (N - n_{t+1})}{r + \lambda n_{t+1}}. \qquad (17)$$

We now concentrate upon the (unique) stationary equilibrium in which $n_t = n_{t+1} = \hat{n}$. From equation (17) we then derive the stationary equilibrium value

$$\hat{n} = \frac{\gamma(1-\alpha)/\alpha}{1 + \gamma(1-\alpha)/\alpha} N - \frac{r}{\lambda(1 + \gamma(1-\alpha)/\alpha)}. \qquad (18)$$

Equation (18) shows a direct connection between research in stationary equilibrium $\hat{n}$ and the degree of market power. The higher the value of α the lower is the degree of market power. Specifically, $1 - \alpha$ is the Lerner index (price minus marginal costs divided by price). Hence, some extent of market power to achieve rents is needed for Schumpeterian entrepreneurs to engage into research. Aghion and Howitt (1992, p. 336) derive the average growth rate of real output to be $\lambda \hat{n} \ln(\gamma)$. The effect of market power attracting entrepreneur-

---

[17] We do not discuss the possibility of the wage level being less than λV_{t+1}.

ial energy shows the importance of imperfect competition for the growth process.

Competition and growth are inversely related in this Schumpeterian model, something usually not supported by empirical evidence (for instance, see Nickell, 1996). Aghion and Howitt (1997), therefore, extend their model to show that a more competitive market structure may contribute to economic growth. In Howitt and Aghion (1998), the authors add capital to their model of creative destruction. They show that capital accumulation and innovation are complementary processes and equal partners in the growth process. Aghion and Howitt have contributed to the endogenous growth literature by connecting purposive, profit-seeking investment in knowledge to the persons performing this task: Entrepreneurs.

In a series of papers Peretto introduces a different kind of endogenous growth model where an endogenous market structure is incorporated. His model has a key role for the number of firms, again in the intermediate sector, determining the returns to investment and R&D. An important difference between his model and the model by Aghion and Howitt is the assumption that monopolistic firms in the intermediate sector set up in-house R&D facilities to produce a continuous flow of cost-reducing innovations. This differs from the independent research firms in Aghion and Howitt (1992). The relation between the number of firms and returns to investment and R&D in the Peretto (1999b) model is determined by a trade-off between external and internal economies of scale. External economies of scale are a result of complementarities across firms because aggregate output is increasing in the number of intermediate goods.[18] A large number of firms in the model therefore leads to high specialization, large investment and R&D programs, and fast growth. On the other hand, the fragmentation of the market due to a large number of firms leads to small investment and R&D programs, and slow growth. An increase in the number of firms increases the market size through the specialization effect whereas each firm's market share is reduced through the fragmentation effect. As a consequence there is a hump-shaped relation between the number of firms and economic growth.

In Peretto (1998) entrepreneurs play a more visible role. His model seeks to explain a shift in the locus of innovation from R&D undertaken by inventor-entrepreneurs ("competitive capitalism") to R&D undertaken within established firms in close proximity to the production line ("trustified capitalism"). In the model the economy converges to a stable industrial structure where entrepreneurial R&D and the formation of new firms peter out, while growth is driven while corporate R&D undertaken by established oligopolists drives growth.[19]

---

[18] Peretto uses a Dixit-Stiglitz type of production function, exhibiting economies of specialization, with the homogeneous final good y determined by the N intermediate goods x_i as: $y = (\int_0^N x_i^{(\varepsilon-1)/\varepsilon} \, di)^{\varepsilon/(\varepsilon-1)}$.

[19] This is an *escalation effect*: The fall in the number of firms is due to technological opportunities leading firms to invest in R&D which is characterized by sunk costs that make entry and incumbency more costly and labor more scarce for production.

While it is true that from about 1870 till 1970 the corporate laboratories affiliated with large manufacturing firms have been increasingly responsible for commercial R&D, the disappearance of entrepreneurial energy as important determinant of economic growth is an unrealistic feature of the model. In Peretto's setup entrepreneurs must develop new differentiated products since entering an existing product line in Bertrand competition with the incumbent is bound to lead to losses because of sunk entry costs. Entrants are net creators of knowledge, as "they create a new product and the knowledge necessary to run manufacturing operations" (p. 58). Although in more developed stages the economy in Peretto's model experiences a transition from entrepreneurial to corporate R&D, entrepreneurship plays a vital role in economic development: Only when a critical number of firms have entered the market, established firms begin investing in R&D. A key result of Peretto's models is that "there is an inverted-U relationship between the number of firms and steady-state growth" (Peretto, 1999a, p. 1762).

Schmitz (1989) was the first to present an endogenous growth model that relates entrepreneurial activity and economic growth. However, his entrepreneurs are more "passive" than in the other models because their role is restricted to that of "imitation". This may have contributed to the Schmitz model being less influential than the Aghion and Howitt model. His model implies that the equilibrium fraction of entrepreneurs in an economy is lower than the social optimal level, providing a rationale for policies stimulating entrepreneurial activity. We end this section stressing that one may also set up endogenous growth models in which (a specific notion of) entrepreneurship may not be beneficial to growth. Peng (2000) constructs such a model in which entrepreneurs do not carry out research, but choose between research projects. He finds a negative relationship because of the rent-seeking element in the exercise of entrepreneurship.[20]

EMPIRICAL EVIDENCE

There are various strands in the empirical literature showing the effect of entrepreneurship on economic growth. We will concentrate on four strands of empirical research.[21] The *first* deals with the question of the effect of turbulence on economic growth. Turbulence, viz., the sum of entry and exit in industries or regions, can be interpreted as an indicator of entrepreneurial activity. The

---

[20]The idea that entrepreneurial energy as such may not suffice for economic progress was also expressed by Baumol (1990) stressing the importance of entrepreneurship being led into productive channels.

[21]The Global Entrepreneurship Monitor (GEM) research program (Reynolds et al., 2001) is yet a different approach. It seeks to assess the level of national entrepreneurial activity and to relate this to the rate of economic growth. Entrepreneurial activity is measured through questionnaires in 29 countries in 2001, 21 countries in 2000 and 10 countries in the first year of assessment, 1999. The research program shows some preliminary evidence of the level of entrepreneurial activity to be associated with economic growth.

second strand concentrates on the effect of (changes in) the size-distribution in regions on subsequent economic growth. In case a region has a larger share of small firms when compared to another region this could indicate a higher level of entrepreneurial activity. The *third* strand investigates the effect of the number of market participants in an industry on economic growth. An increase in the number of competitors is usually related to more intensive entrepreneurial activity. The *fourth* strand of empirical literature concentrates on the effect of the number of self-employed (business owners) on subsequent growth. In developed economies the rate of self-employment will be related to the extent of entrepreneurial activity. New firms usually start with a phase of self-employment *sensu stricto*, viz., with no paid employees. A *fifth* and last source of evidence on the relation between self-employment and progress is the economic history of the formerly centralized planned economies. A characteristic of these economies was the almost complete absence of small firms (and private ownership of the means of production), and this extreme monopolization constituted one of the major factors leading to the collapse of state socialism (Acs, 1996). The development of small enterprises is considered a vital part of the current transition process in Eastern Europe. This last source of evidence will not be discussed in the present chapter.[22]

The empirical evidence of the effect of turbulence on subsequent economic growth is mixed. Caves (1998, p. 1973) concludes that in the short run, turnover from entry and exit appears to make only a very small contribution to an industry's productivity growth. However, he adds that in the long run, the entry–exit turnover makes a more important contribution. Bosma and Nieuwenhuijsen (2000) use data for 40 Dutch regions for the 1988–96 period and find that turbulence positively affects total factor productivity growth in the service sector but not so in manufacturing.

A different literature has focused on the impact of entrepreneurship on subsequent economic performance, at the regional level. The unit of observation for these studies is at the spatial level, either a city, region, or state. The most common and most exclusive measure of performance is growth, typically measured in terms of employment growth. These studies have tried to link various measures of entrepreneurial activity, most typically startup rates, to economic growth. Other measures sometimes used include the relative share of SMEs, and self-employment rates.

Reynolds (1999) finds some evidence for turbulence to be related to economic growth using American Labor Market Area data for the 1980–92 period. Labor Market Areas generally include a metropolitan area and the surrounding rural area from which it draws both employees and consumers. Acs and Armington (2002) link a measure of entrepreneurship to growth at the Labor Market Area level. Their measure of entrepreneurial activity is the new firm birth rate in each of these local economies. They test the hypothesis that increased entrepre-

---

[22]The role of entrepreneurship in transition economies is discussed in e.g. Nolan (1995) and McMillan and Woodruff (2002).

neurial activity leads to higher growth rates of local economies. They find that the higher levels of entrepreneurial activity are strongly positively associated with higher growth rates, even after controlling for establishment size, and agglomeration effects.

Audretsch and Fritsch (1996) analyzed a database identifying new business startups and exits from the social insurance statistics in Germany to examine whether a greater degree of turbulence leads to greater economic growth. Each record in the database identifies the establishment at which an individual is employed. The startup of a new firm is recorded when a new establishment identification appears in the database, which generally indicates the birth of a new enterprise. While there is some evidence for the United States linking a greater degree of turbulence at the regional level to higher rates of growth for regions (Reynolds, 1999), Audretsch and Fritsch (1996) find that the opposite was true for Germany during the 1980s. In both the manufacturing and the service sectors, a high rate of turbulence in a region tends to lead to a lower and not a higher rate of growth. They attribute this negative relationship to the fact that the underlying components – the startup and death rates – are both negatively related to subsequent economic growth. Similar evidence for Germany is found by Fritsch (1997).

Audretsch and Fritsch (1996) conjectured that one possible explanation for the disparity in results between the United States and Germany may be the extent of innovative activity in terms of new-firm startups and the ability of new firms to ultimately displace the incumbent enterprises. It may be that innovative activity did not play the same role for the German *Mittelstand* as it does for SMEs in the United States. To the degree that this was true, it may hold that regional growth emanates from SMEs only when they serve as agents of change through innovative activity.

Divergent findings from the 1980s about the relationship between the degree of entrepreneurial activity and economic growth in the United States and Germany posed something of a puzzle. On the one hand, these different results suggested that the relationship between entrepreneurship and growth lacks a general pattern across developed countries. On the other hand, it also provided evidence for the existence of distinct and different national systems capable of supporting economic growth. Convergence in growth rates seemed to be attainable even when maintaining differences in underlying institutions and structures.

However, in a more recent study, Audretsch and Fritsch (2002) find that different results emerge for the 1990s. Those regions with a higher startup rate exhibit higher growth rates. This would suggest that, in fact, Germany is changing over time, where the engine of growth is shifting towards entrepreneurship as a source of growth.The results of their 2002 paper suggest a somewhat different interpretation. Based on the empirical evidence that the source of growth in Germany has shifted away from the established incumbent firms during the 1980s to entrepreneurial firms in the 1990s, it would appear that a process of convergence is taking place between Germany and the United

States, where entrepreneurship provides the engine of growth in both countries. Despite remaining institutional differences, the relationship between entrepreneurship and growth is apparently converging in both countries.

Audretsch and Keilbach (2002) include a measure of entrepreneurship capital in estimating a production function model for Germany. They find that the degree of entrepreneurship capital has a positive impact on growth in Germany.

The positive relationship between entrepreneurship and growth at the regional level is not limited to Germany in the 1990. For example, Foelster (2000) examines not just the employment impact within new and small firms, but the overall link between increases in self-employment and total employment in Sweden between 1976 and 1995. By using a Layard-Nickell framework, he provides a link between micro behavior and macroeconomic performance, and shows that increases in self-employment rates have had a positive impact on regional employment rates in Sweden.

Hart and Harvey (1995) link measures of new and small firms to employment generation in the late 1980s for three regions in the United Kingdom. While they find that employment creation came largely from SMEs, they also identify that most of the job losses also came from SMEs. Callejon and Segarra (1999) use a data set of Spanish manufacturing industries between 1980 and 1992 to link new-firm birth rates and death rates, which taken together constitute a measure of turbulence, to total factor productivity growth in industries and regions. They adopt a model based on a vintage capital framework in which new entrants embody the edge technologies available and exiting businesses represent marginal obsolete plants. Using a Hall type of production function, which controls for imperfect competition and the extent of scale economies, they find that both new-firm startup rates and exit rates contribute positively to the growth of total factor productivity in regions as well as industries.

The empirical evidence of the effect of (changes in) the size distribution of firms on subsequent growth performance appears more clear-cut, at least for data of the late 1980s and early 1990s. Carree and Thurik (1998, 1999a) show that the share of small firms in manufacturing industries in European countries in 1990 has had a positive effect on the industry output growth in the subsequent four years. Thurik (1996) reports that the excess growth of small firms[23] has had a positive influence on percentage change in gross national product for a sample of 16 European countries in the period 1988 through 1993. Robbins, Pantuosco, Parker and Fuller (2000) perform an analysis of 48 U.S. states for the 1986–95 period and find that states with a higher proportion of (very) small business employment experience higher level of productivity growth and Gross State Product growth. Audretsch, Carree, van Stel and Thurik (2002) find evidence for 17 European countries that the consequences for economic growth of not shifting the industry structure away from large business towards small business have been rather large. Likewise, Carree (2002) shows evidence for

---

[23] The excess growth of small firms in that study is defined as the percentage change in the value-of-shipments accounted for by small firms minus that accounted for by large firms.

the five largest economies (France, Germany, Japan, U.K. and U.S.) that manufacturing industries that underwent only little downsizing in the 1977–90 period experienced less subsequent growth when compared internationally.

Nickell (1996), Nickell, Nicolitsas and Dryden (1997) and Lever and Nieuwenhuijsen (1999) present evidence that competition, as measured by increased number of competitors, has a positive effect on the rate of total factor productivity growth. This positive effect is in line with Geroski's (1989) finding of overall productivity growth in 79 U.K. manufacturing industries to increase with the lagged rate of gross entry of new firms. One reason for these findings is that an increased number of market participants and increased entrepreneurial activity often go hand in hand. There have been some studies on the impact of the number of market participants on *regional* economic growth as well. Glaeser, Kallal, Scheinkman and Shleifer (1992) examine three determinants of regional sectoral growth: Specialization, diversity and competition. They find that local competition, measured as the relative number of businesses per worker, encourages employment growth in industries. Fritsch (1997) and Audretsch and Fritsch (2002) relate start-up activity in German regions to subsequent growth. They find that for Germany the impact of start-up activity on economic growth was absent in the 1980s but became positive in the 1990s.

A fourth strand of literature has started to focus upon the effect of self-employment on growth. Blanchflower (2000, p. 497) finds no evidence for a panel of OECD countries of increases in the self-employment rate to increase economic growth. However, he uses uncorrected OECD Labor Force Statistics data suffering from lack in comparability across countries and, in a list of additional cases, lack in comparability over time due to changes in counting procedures. In a recent paper Carree, van Stel, Thurik and Wennekers (2002) investigate whether countries that deviate from an "equilibrium" business ownership rate for comparable levels of economic development suffer in terms of economic growth. In their view deviations between the actual and the "equilibrium" rate of business ownership will diminish the growth potential of an economy in the medium term. A shortage of business owners is likely to diminish competition with detrimental effects for static efficiency and competitiveness of the national economy. It will also diminish variety, learning and selection and thereby harm dynamic efficiency (innovation). On the other hand, a glut of self-employment will cause the average scale of operations to remain below optimum. It will result in large numbers of marginal businesses, absorbing capital and human energy that could have been allocated more productively elsewhere. They develop an error-correction model to determine the "equilibrium" rate of business ownership as a function of GDP per capita.[24] Their estimated "equilibrium" relationship, using corrected OECD Labor Force Statistics data, is presented in Figure 2 together with the actual (corrected)

---

[24]Carree, van Stel, Thurik and Wennekers hypothesize an "equilibrium" relationship between the rate of business ownership and per capita income that is U-shaped, but in fact find it to be impossible to statistically discriminate U-shaped "equilibrium" functions from L-shaped functions.

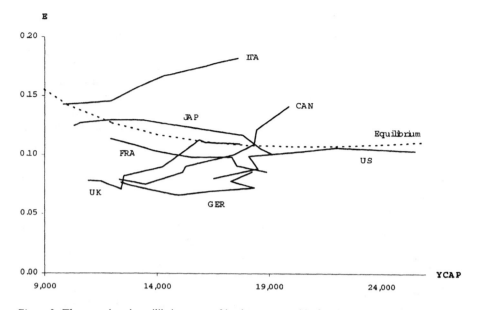

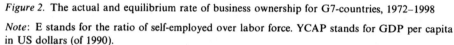

Figure 2. The actual and equilibrium rate of business ownership for G7-countries, 1972–1998

Note: E stands for the ratio of self-employed over labor force. YCAP stands for GDP per capita in US dollars (of 1990).

Source: Carree, van Stel, Thurik and Wennekers (2002).

data of the G7-countries. The estimation results show that a deviation of the actual number of business owners from the "equilibrium" rate has a significantly negative impact on economic growth.

Figure 2 shows that most countries had too few self-employed relative to the equilibrium value. An obvious exception is Italy. It indicates that the high level of self-employment in Italy is not efficient: It has a relatively large negative impact on economic growth.[25] Countries with a low business ownership rate compared to the equilibrium include the Scandinavian countries. These economies are characterized by a large public sector, relatively low entry and exit rates and high taxes. Eliasson (1995) and Braunerhjelm and Carlsson (1999) blame part of Sweden's relatively bad economic performance in the 1980s on limited private initiative and a lack of structural adjustment. Another country with a relatively low business ownership rate is Germany. Figure 2 also shows that, at least until recently, Germany has failed to restructure where for example the United Kingdom has. Klodt (1990) blames (West) German industrial policy for repressing structural change in supporting large-scale industries with subsidies. An important reason for the lack of a vibrant sector of new firms and

---

[25] In Italy, research and development expenditures are by far the lowest among the largest OECD countries as a percentage of gross national product. This is in line with the idea that when there are too many business owners, the scale advantages in research and development are not utilized. See Cohen and Klepper (1996).

industries in Germany up till the mid 1990s has been the high barriers to innovative activity (Audretsch, 2000).

It should be stressed that the number of self-employed is a possible yardstick of entrepreneurship as statistical information is often available along the ownership dimension. However, this yardstick can be misleading. For instance, it is unknown whether the relatively high number of self-employed in Italy as compared to Germany expresses a high level of Schumpeterian entrepreneurship or merely a time lag in economic development influencing the number of marginal establishments or merely differences in sectoral composition. In recent empirical studies other approximations are brought forward. Audretsch (1995) uses the employment share of surviving young firms as a proxy for entrepreneurial activity in manufacturing industries. This variable may well express the comparative entrepreneurial positions of these industries. Outside the manufacturing sector this variable may be biased due to the occurrence of franchising firms and marginal or part-time start-ups. Moreover, the rate of intrapreneurship, both in new and incumbent firms, is lacking.

FUTURE ANALYSIS AND POLICY ISSUES

We expect a framework relating entrepreneurial activity to economic growth to hinge on at least four elements. *First*, on the literature identifying the microeconomic foundations of growth emphasizing the role of knowledge externalities in the growth process (Romer, 1986 and 1994). *Second*, it should identify intermediate linkages like the ones mentioned in Figure 1. *Third*, it should deal with dual causality in the relation between entrepreneurial activity and growth. And *finally*, it should take into account the multidisciplinary character while linking together different levels of analysis.[26] Before discussing some policy issues we will first present such a framework derived from Wennekers and Thurik (1999).

A Framework for Future Analysis

Figure 3 presents a framework inspired by the many insights reaped from the various strands of the literature. Three levels of analysis are distinguished since linking entrepreneurship to economic growth also means linking the individual level to the firm and the macro level.

Entrepreneurial action happens at the firm level. Entrepreneurs need a vehicle transforming their personal qualities and ambitions into actions. Small firms where the entrepreneur has a controlling stake provide such a vehicle. Larger firms often mimic smallness (using organizational forms like business units, subsidiaries and joint ventures) to introduce corporate entrepreneurship

---

[26] See Audretsch, Thurik, Verheul and Wennekers (2002) for such a framework concerning the determinants of entrepreneurship.

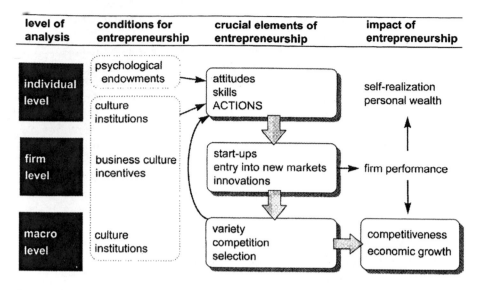

level of analysis	conditions for entrepreneurship	crucial elements of entrepreneurship	impact of entrepreneurship

Figure 3. Framework for linking entrepreneurship to economic growth

Source: Wennekers and Thurik (1999).

or intrapreneurship. The outcomes of these entrepreneurial manifestations at the firm level generally have to do with "newness". This can be newness through product, process and organizational innovation, entry of new markets and innovative business start-ups.

At the aggregate level of industries, regions and national economies the many individual entrepreneurial actions compose a mosaic of new experiments. In evolutionary terms this can be termed variety. A process of competition between these various new ideas and initiatives takes place continuously leading to the selection of the most viable firms and industries. Variety, competition, selection and also imitation expand and transform the productive potential of a regional or national economy (by replacement or displacement of obsolete firms, by higher productivity and by expansion of new niches and industries).

In this process, Schumpeterian entrepreneurs, intrapreneurs and managerial business owners all play their part (see Table 1). Next to the linkages from the individual level to the aggregate level, there are important feedback mechanisms. Competition and selection amidst variety undoubtedly enable individuals (and firms) to learn from both their own and other's successes and failures. These learning processes enable individuals to increase their skills and adapt their attitudes. The outcome of these so-called spillovers will be new entrepreneurial actions, creating a recurrent chain of linkages.

Clearly, the outcome of these dynamic processes depends on a set of conditions like the ones referred to in Figure 3. *First,* this refers to the national (or regional) cultural environment, and to the internal culture of corporations. The linkages between culture and entrepreneurship are by no means simple and straightforward, and much is still unknown about these processes. The history of the rise and fall of nations has shown that cultural vitality, thriving sciences and high tide in entrepreneurship often coincide (Wennekers and Thurik, 1999). *Second*, the institutional framework, both on the national level and within firms, defines the incentives for individuals to turn their ambitions into actions, and determines to what extent unnecessary barriers will hamper them. The importance of institutions for the development of entrepreneurship is paramount and deserves further study.

Some Policy Issues

One of the central goals of public policy common among all modern economies is the generation of growth and the creation of employment. Much of the policy debate to generate growth and jobs has relied on a macro-economic framework and focused on the traditional macro-economic policy instruments. The survey of the present chapter suggests that a different, less traditional instrument for generating growth and employment plays an important role – policies that generate and promote entrepreneurship (OECD, 1998). Empirical evidence surveyed in this chapter suggests that those countries that have experienced an increase in entrepreneurial activity have also enjoyed higher rates of growth. However, the actual mechanisms, i.e., the intermediate linkages, why entrepreneurship generates growth are less obvious. The present chapter relies on a rich body of literature, both theoretical and empirical, analyzing the micro foundations of entrepreneurship. Entrepreneurship generates growth because it serves as a vehicle for innovation and change, and therefore as a conduit for knowledge spillovers. Thus, in a regime of increased globalization, where the comparative advantage of modern economies is shifting towards knowledge-based economic activity, not only does entrepreneurship play a more important role, but also the impact of that entrepreneurship is to generate growth. This has led Yu to argue that "any policy recommendation on economic development should be based on an analysis that incorporates entrepreneurship, the engine of economic growth" (Yu, 1998, p. 906). Similarly, Holcombe claims that "the incorporation of entrepreneurship into the framework of economic growth not only fills in the institutional details to help make the growth process more understandable, but also points toward more promising economic policy recommendations for fostering economic growth" (Holcombe, 1998, p. 60).

As the comparative advantage in Western Europe and North America has become increasingly based on new knowledge, public policy towards business has responded in two fundamental ways. The *first* has been to shift the policy focus away from the traditional triad of policy instruments essentially constraining the freedom of firms to contract – regulation, competition policy or antitrust, and public ownership of business. The policy approach of constraint was sensible as long as the major issue was how to restrain footloose multinational corporations in possession of considerable market power. Instead, a new policy approach is emerging which focuses on enabling the creation and commercialization of knowledge (Audretsch and Thurik, 2001a). Examples of such policies include encouraging R&D, venture capital and new-firm startups. The shift from constraining to enabling policies goes together with the shift from the Schumpeter Mark II regime to the Schumpeter Mark I regime. The *second* fundamental shift involves the locus of such enabling policies, which are increasingly at the regional or even local level. The last decade has seen the emergence of a broad spectrum of enabling policy initiatives that fall outside of the jurisdiction of the traditional regulatory agencies. See, for instance, the issues of the *European Observatory for SMEs* (EIM/ENSR, 1993 through 1997 and European Commission, 2000).[27] The current decade will witness many more such enabling policies.

Acknowledgement

The authors are grateful to Zoltan Acs, David Audretsch, Bruce Kirchhoff, Boris Lokshin and André van Stel for comments. The present chapter draws on a range of earlier research, viz. Carree and Thurik (1999b), Carree, van Stel, Thurik and Wennekers (2002), Wennekers and Thurik (1999), Audretsch, Verheul, Thurik and Wennekers (2002) and Audretsch and Thurik (2000, 2001a and 2001b). Martin Carree is grateful to the Royal Netherlands Academy of Arts and Sciences (KNAW) for financial support. Finally, the present paper is part of the SNS project on Entrepreneurship and Growth financed by the Marcus and Marianne Wallenberg's Foundation.

References

Acs, Z.J. (1992). Small business economics: A global perspective. *Challenge*, **35**, November/December, pp. 38–44.

Acs, Z.J. (1996). Small firms and economic growth. In P.H. Admiraal (ed.), *Small Business in the Modern Economy*. De Vries Lectures in Economics, Oxford, U.K.: Blackwell Publishers.

Acs, Z.J. and D.B. Audretsch (1987). Innovation, market structure, and firm size. *Review of Economics and Statistics*, **69**, 567–574.

Acs, Z.J. and D.B. Audretsch (1990). *Innovation and Small Firms*. Cambridge, MA: MIT Press.

Acs, Z.J. and D.B. Audretsch (1993). Conclusion. In Z.J. Acs and D.B. Audretsch (eds.), *Small Firms and Entrepreneurship: An East-West Perspective*. Cambridge, U.K.: Cambridge University Press.

Acs, Z.J., D.B. Audretsch and D.S. Evans (1994). The determinants of variation in the self-employment rates across countries and over time, mimeo (fourth draft).

Acs, Z.J. and C. Armington (2003). Endogenous Growth and Entrepreneurial Activity in Cities. Center for Economic Studies, CES 2003 January.

Aghion, P. and P. Howitt (1992). A model of growth through creative destruction. *Econometrica*, **60**, 323–351.

---

[27]Sternberg (1996) documents how the success of a number of different high-technology clusters spanning a number of developed countries is the direct result of enabling policies, such as the provision of venture capital or research support.

Aghion, P. and P. Howitt (1997). A Schumpeterian perspective on growth and competition. In D.M. Kreps and K.F. Wallis (eds.), *Advances in Economics and Econometrics: Theory and Applications*, Vol. 2, pp. 279–317. Cambridge, UK: Cambridge University Press.

Aiginger, K. and G. Tichy (1991). Small firms and the merger mania. *Small Business Economics*, 3, 83–101.

Audretsch, D.B. (1995). *Innovation and Industry Evolution.* Cambridge, MA: MIT Press.

Audretsch, D.B. (2000). Entrepreneurship in Germany. In D.L. Sexton and H. Landström (eds.), *The Blackwell Handbook of Entrepreneurship.* Oxford, UK: Blackwell Publishers.

Audretsch, D.B. and M. Fritsch (1996). Creative destruction: Turbulence and economic growth in Germany. In E. Helmstadter and M. Perlman (eds.), *Behavioral Norms, Technological Progress, and Economic Dynamics: Studies in Schumpeterian Economics*, Ann Arbor: University of Michigan Press, pp. 137–150.

Audretsch, D.B. and M. Fritsch (2002). Growth regimes over time and space. *Regional Studies*, 36, 113–124.

Audretsch, D.B. and M. Keilbach (2003). *Entrepreneurship capital and economic performance.* Centre for Economic Policy Research (CEPR) discussion paper No. 3678.

Audretsch, D.B. and A.R. Thurik (2000). Capitalism and democracy in the 21st century: From the managed to the entrepreneurial economy. *Journal of Evolutionary Economics*, 10, 17–34.

Audretsch, D.B. and A.R. Thurik (2001a). What is new about the new economy?: Sources of growth in the managed and entrepreneurial economies. *Industrial and Corporate Change*, 10, 267–315.

Audretsch, D.B. and A.R. Thurik (2001b). Linking entrepreneurship to growth, STI working paper 2001/2. Paris: OECD.

Audretsch, D.B., M.A. Carree and A.R. Thurik (2001). Does entrepreneurship reduce unemployment? Discussion paper TI01-074/3. Tinbergen Institute, Erasmus University, Rotterdam.

Audretsch, D.B., M.A. Carree, A.J. van Stel and A.R. Thurik (2002). Impeded industrial restructuring: The growth penalty. *Kyklos*, 55, 81–98.

Audretsch, D.B., L. Klomp and A.R. Thurik (2002). Gibrat's Law: Are the services different? Report ERS-2002-04-STR, Erasmus Research Institute for Management, Erasmus University Rotterdam.

Audretsch, D.B., I. Verheul, A.R. Thurik and S. Wennekers (eds.) (2002). *Entrepreneurship: Determinants and Policy in a European-US Comparison.* Boston/Dordrecht: Kluwer Academic Publishers.

Banerjee, A.V. and A.F. Newman (1993). Occupational choice and the process of development. *Journal of Political Economy*, 101, 274–298.

Baumol, W.J. (1968). Entrepreneurship and economic theory. *American Economic Review*, 58, 64–71.

Baumol, W.J. (1990). Entrepreneurship: Productive, unproductive and destructive. *Journal of Political Economy*, 98, 893–921.

Baumol, W.J. (1993). Formal entrepreneurship theory in economics: Existence and bounds. *Journal of Business Venturing*, 8, 197–210.

Berkowitz, D. and J. Holland (2001). Does privatization enhance or deter small enterprise formation? *Economics Letters*, 74, 53–60.

Blanchflower, D.G. (2000). Self-employment in OECD countries. *Labour Economics*, 7, 471–505.

Blau, D. (1987). A time series analysis of self-employment. *Journal of Political Economy*, 95, 445–467.

Bosma, N. and H. Nieuwenhuijsen (2000). Turbulence and productivity in the Netherlands, EIM research report 9909/E, EIM Small Business Research and Consultancy, Zoetermeer, the Netherlands.

Braunerhjelm, P. and B. Carlsson (1999). Industry structure, entrepreneurship and the macroeconomy: A comparison of Ohio and Sweden, 1975–1995. In Z.J. Acs, B. Carlsson and C. Karlsson (eds.), *Entrepreneurship, Small and Medium-Sized Enterprises and the Macroeconomy.* Cambridge, UK: Cambridge University Press, pp. 137–158.

Brock, W.A. and D.S. Evans (1986). *The Economics of Small Businesses: Their Role and Regulation in the U.S. Economy.* New York: Holmes and Meier.

Brock, W.A. and D.S. Evans (1989). Small business economics. *Small Business Economics*, 1, 7–20.

Bull, I. and G.E. Willard (1993). Towards a theory of entrepreneurship. *Journal of Business Venturing*, **8**, 183–195.

Callejon, M. and A. Segarra (2000). Business dynamics and efficiency in industries and regions: The case of Spain. *Small Business Economics*, **13**(4), 253–271.

Carlsson, B. (1989). The evolution of manufacturing technology and its impact on industrial structure: An international study. *Small Business Economics*, **1**, 21–37.

Carlsson, B. (1992). The rise of small business: Causes and consequences. In W.J. Adams (ed.), *Singular Europe, Economy and Policy of the European Community after 1992.* Ann Arbor, MI: University of Michigan Press, pp. 145–169.

Carlsson, B. (1996). Differing patterns of industrial dynamics: New Zealand, Ohio and Sweden, 1978–1994. *Small Business Economics*, **8**, 219–234.

Carlsson, B. (1999). Small business, entrepreneurship, and industrial dynamics, In Z. Acs (ed.), *Are Small Firms Important?* Boston/Dordrecht: Kluwer Academic Publishers, pp. 99–110.

Carree, M.A. (2002). Industrial restructuring and economic growth. *Small Business Economics*, **18**, 243–255.

Carree, M.A. and L. Klomp (1996). Small business and job creation: A comment. *Small Business Economics*, **8**, 317–322.

Carree, M., A. van Stel, R. Thurik and S. Wennekers (2002). Economic development and business ownership: An analysis using data of 23 OECD countries in the period 1976–1996. *Small Business Economics*, **19**, 271–290.

Carree, M.A. and A.R. Thurik (1998). Small firms and economic growth in Europe. *Atlantic Economic Journal*, **26**(2), 137–146.

Carree, M.A. and A.R. Thurik (1999a). Industrial structure and economic growth. In D.B. Audretsch and A.R. Thurik (eds.). *Innovation, Industry Evolution and Employment.* Cambridge, UK: Cambridge University Press, pp. 86–110.

Carree, M.A. and A.R. Thurik (1999b). The carrying capacity and entry and exit flows in retailing. *International Journal of Industrial Organization*, **17**, 985–1007.

Caves, R.E. (1998). Industrial organization and new findings on the turnover and mobility of firms. *Journal of Economic Literature*, **36**, 1947–1982.

Chandler, A.D. Jr. (1990). *Scale and Scope: The Dynamics of Industrial Capitalism.* Cambridge, MA: Harvard University Press.

Cohen, W.M. and S. Klepper (1992). The trade-off between firm size and diversity in the pursuit of technological progress. *Small Business Economics*, **4**, 1–14.

Cohen, W.M. and S. Klepper (1996). A reprise of size and R&D. *Economic Journal*, **106**, 925–951.

Davis, S.J., J. Haltiwanger and S. Schuh (1996). Small business and job creation: Dissecting the myth and reassessing the facts. *Small Business Economics*, **8**, 297–315.

Dosi, G. (1988). Sources, procedures and microeconomic effects of innovations. *Journal of Economic Literature*, **26**, 1120–1171.

EIM/ENSR (1997). *The European Observatory: Fifth Annual Report.* Zoetermeer: EIM Business and Policy Research.

Eliasson, G.E. (1995). Economic growth through competitive selection. Paper presented at 22nd Annual E.A.R.I.E. Conference 3–6 September 1995, mimeo.

European Commission (2000). *The European Observatory for SME: Sixth Report*, submitted to the Enterprise Directorate General, Luxembourg: KPMG Consulting, EIM Business and Policy Research, and ENSR.

Eurostat (1994). *Enterprises in Europe*, third edition. Luxembourg.

Evans, D.S. and L.S. Leighton (1989). Some empirical aspects of entrepreneurship. *American Economic Review*, **79**, 519–535.

Foelster, S. (2000). Do entrepreneurs create jobs? *Small Business Economics*, **14**(2), 137–148.

Freeman, C. and C. Perez (1988). Structural crises of adjustment: Business cycles and investment behavior. In G. Dosi, C. Freeman, R. Nelson, G. Silverberg and L. Soete (eds.), *Technical Change and Economic Theory.* London: Pinter Publishers.

Fritsch, M. (1997). New firms and regional employment change. *Small Business Economics*, **9**, 437–448.

Galbraith, J.K. (1967). *The New Industrial State*. London: Routledge.

Gartner, W.B. (1989). "Who is an entrepreneur?" Is the wrong question. *Entrepreneurship Theory and Practice*, **13**, 47–68.

Glaeser, E.L., H.D. Kallal, J.A. Scheinkman and A. Shleifer (1992). Growth in cities. *Journal of Political Economy*, **100**, 1126–1152.

Grossman, G.M. and E. Helpman (1994). Endogenous innovation in the theory of growth. *Journal of Economic Perspectives*, **8**(1), 23–44.

Hart, M. and E. Harvey (1995). Job generation and new and small firms: Some evidence from the late 1980s. *Small Business Economics*, **7**, 97–109.

Hébert, R.F. and A.N. Link (1982). *The Entrepreneur*. New York: Praeger.

Hébert, R.F. and A.N. Link (1989). In search of the meaning of entrepreneurship. *Small Business Economics*, **1**, 39–49.

Holcombe, R.G. (1998). Entrepreneurship and economic growth. *Quarterly Journal of Austrian Economics*, **1**(2), 45–62.

Holmes, T.J. and J.A. Schmitz Jr. (1990). A theory of entrepreneurship and its application to the study of business transfers. *Journal of Political Economy*, **98**, 265–294.

Howitt, P. and P. Aghion (1998). Capital accumulation and innovation as complementary factors in long-run growth. *Journal of Economic Growth*, **3**, 111–130.

Ilmakunnas, P. and V. Kanniainen (2001). Entrepreneurship, economic risks, and risk insurance in the welfare state: Results with OECD data 1978–93. *German Economic Review*, **2**, 195–218.

Inman, R.P. (ed.) (1985). *Managing the Service Economy*. Cambridge, UK: Cambridge University Press.

Iyigun, M.F. and A.L. Owen (1998). Risk, entrepreneurship, and human capital accumulation. *American Economic Review, Papers and Proceedings*, **88**, 454–457.

Iyigun, M.F. and A.L. Owen (1999). Entrepreneurs, professionals, and growth. *Journal of Economic Growth*, **4**, 213–232.

Jackson, L.F. (1984). Hierarchic demand and the Engle curve for variety. *Review of Economics and Statistics*, **66**, 8–15.

Jensen, M.C. (1993). The modern industrial revolution, exit, and the failure of internal control systems. *Journal of Finance*, **68**, 831–880.

Jovanovic, B. (1993). The diversification of production. *Brookings Papers: Microeconomics*, 1993, 197–235.

Kihlstrom, R.E. and J.J. Laffont (1979). A general equilibrium entrepreneurial theory of firm formation based on risk aversion. *Journal of Political Economy*, **87**, 719–748.

Kirchhoff, B.A. (1994). *Entrepreneurship and Dynamic Capitalism*. Westport, CT: Praeger.

Kirchhoff, B.A. (1996). Self-employment and dynamic capitalism. *Journal of Labor Research*, **17**, 627–643.

Kirzner, I.M. (1997). Entrepreneurial discovery and the competitive market process: An Austrian approach. *Journal of Economic Literature*, **35**, 60–85.

Klodt, H. (1990). Industrial policy and repressed structural change in West Germany. *Jahrbücher für Nationalökonomie und Statistik*, **207**, 25–35.

Krugman, P. (1991). *Geography and Trade*. Cambridge, MA: MIT Press.

Kuznets, S. (1971). *Economic Growth of Nations, Total Output and Production Structure*. Cambridge, MA: Harvard University Press/Belknapp Press.

Lever, M.H.C. and H.R. Nieuwenhuijsen (1999). The impact of competition on productivity in Dutch manufacturing. In D.B. Audretsch and A.R. Thurik (eds.), *Innovation, Industry Evolution and Employment*. Cambridge, UK: Cambridge University Press, pp. 111–128.

Lloyd-Ellis, H. and D. Bernhardt (2000). Enterprise, inequality and economic development. *Review of Economic Studies*, **67**, 147–168.

Loveman, G. and W. Sengenberger (1991). The re-emergence of small-scale production: An international comparison. *Small Business Economics*, **3**, 1–37.

Lucas, R.E. (1978). On the size distribution of firms. *BELL Journal of Economics*, **9**, 508–523.

Lucas, R.E. (1988). On the mechanics of economic development. *Journal of Monetary Economics*, **22**, 3–42.

Lumpkin, G.T. and G.G. Dess (1996). Clarifying the entrepreneurial orientation construct and linking it to performance. *Academy of Management Review,* 21, 135–172.

McMillan, J. and C. Woodruff (2002). The central role of entrepreneurs in transition economies. *Journal of Economic Perspectives,* 16(3), 153–170.

Meredith, J. (1987). The strategic advantages of new manufacturing technologies for small firms. *Strategic Management Journal,* 8, 249–258.

Nickell, S.J. (1996). Competition and corporate performance. *Journal of Political Economy,* 104, 724–746.

Nickell, S., P. Nicolitsas and N. Dryden (1997). What makes firms perform well? *European Economic Review,* 41, 783–796.

Nolan, P. (1995). *China's Rise, Russia's Fall: Politics, Economics and Planning in the Transition from Stalinism.* New York: St Martin's Press.

OECD (1995). *Competition Policy in OECD Countries, 1992–1993.* Paris.

OECD (1998). *Fostering Entrepreneurship.* Paris.

Peng, B. (2000). Is entrepreneurship always good for growth? CRIEFF Discussion Paper 0024, University of St. Andrews.

Peretto, P.F. (1998). Technological change, market rivalry, and the evolution of the capitalist engine of growth. *Journal of Economic Growth,* 3, 53–80.

Peretto, P.F. (1999a). Firm size, rivalry and the extent of the market in endogenous technological change. *European Economic Review,* 43, 1747–1773.

Peretto, P.F. (1999b). Industrial development, technological change, and long-run growth. *Journal of Development Economics,* 59, 389–417.

Phillips, B.D. (1985). The effect of industry deregulation on the small business sector. *Business Economics,* 20, 28–37.

Piore, M.J. and C.F. Sabel (1984). *The Second Industrial Divide: Possibilities for Prosperity.* New York: Basic Books.

Porter, M.E. (1990). *The Competitive Advantage of Nations.* New York: Free Press.

Prusa, T.J. and J.A. Schmitz Jr. (1991). Are new firms an important source of innovation? Evidence from the software industry. *Economics Letters,* 35, 339–342.

Reynolds, P.D. (1999). Creative destruction: Source or symptom of economic growth? In Z.J. Acs, B. Carlsson and C. Karlsson (eds.), *Entrepreneurship, Small and Medium-Sized Enterprises and the Macroeconomy.* Cambridge, UK: Cambridge University Press, pp. 97–136.

Reynolds, P.D., S.M. Camp, W.D. Bygrave, E. Autio and M. Hay (2001). *Global Entrepreneurship Monitor – 2001 Executive Report* [online]. Babson College, IBM, Kauffman Center for Entrepreneurial Leadership and London Business School. Available: http://www.gemconsortium.org, accessed December 2002.

Reynolds, P.D. (1999). Creative destruction: Source or symptom of economic growth? In Zoltan J. Acs, Bo Carlsson and Charlie Karlsson (eds.), *Entrepreneurship, Small and Medium-sized Enterprises and the Macroeconomy.* Cambridge: Cambridge University Press, pp. 97–136.

Robbins, D.K., L.J. Pantuosco, D.F. Parker and B.K. Fuller (2000). An empirical assessment of the contribution of small business employment to U.S. state economic performance. *Small Business Economics,* 15, 293–302.

Romer, P.M. (1986). Increasing return and long-run growth. *Journal of Political Economy,* 94, 1002–1037.

Romer, P.M. (1990). Endogenous technological change. *Journal of Political Economy,* 98, 71–101.

Romer, P.M. (1994). The origins of endogenous growth. *Journal of Economic Perspectives,* 8, 3–22.

Rothwell, R. (1983). Innovation and firm size: A case for dynamic complementarity; or, is small really so beautiful? *Journal of General Management,* 8, 5–25.

Rothwell, R. (1984). The role of small firms in the emergence of new technologies. *OMEGA,* 12, 19–29.

Schaffner, J.A. (1993). Rising incomes and the shift from self-employment to firm-based production. *Economics Letters,* 41, 435–440.

Scherer, F.M. and D. Ross (1990). *Industrial Market Structure and Economic Performance.* Boston, MA: Houghton Mifflin Company.

The Impact of Entrepreneurship on Economic Growth 471

Schiller, B.R. and P.E. Crewson (1997). Entrepreneurial origins: A longitudinal inquiry. *Economic Inquiry*, 35, 523–531.

Schmitz, Jr. J.A. (1989). Imitation, entrepreneurship, and long-run growth. *Journal of Political Economy*, 97, 721–739.

Schultz, T.P. (1990). Women's changing participation in the labor force: A world perspective. *Economic Development and Cultural Change*, 38, 457–488.

Schumpeter, J.A. (1934). *The Theory of Economic Development*. Cambridge, MA: Harvard University Press.

Schumpeter, J.A. (1950). *Capitalism, Socialism and Democracy*. New York: Harper and Row.

Shane, S. (2000). Prior knowledge and the discovery of entrepreneurial opportunities. *Organization Science*, 11, 448–469.

Solow, R.M. (1970). *Growth Theory: An Exposition*. Oxford, UK: Oxford University Press.

Sternberg, R. (1996). Technology policies and the growth of regions. *Small Business Economics*, 8, 75–86.

Storey, D.J. and B.S. Tether (1998). Public policy measures to support new technology-based firms in the European Union. *Research Policy*, 26, 1037–1057.

Sutton, J. (1997). Gibrat's legacy. *Journal of Economic Literature*, 35, 40–59.

Thurik, A.R. (1996). Small firms, entrepreneurship and economic growth. In P.H. Admiraal (ed.), *Small Business in the Modern Economy*. De Vries Lectures in Economics, Oxford, UK: Blackwell Publishers.

Thurik, A.R. (1999). Entrepreneurship, industrial transformation and growth. In G.D. Libecap (ed.), *The Sources of Entrepreneurial Activity*, Vol. 11, *Advances in the Study of Entrepreneurship, Innovation, and Economic Growth*, pp. 29–65. Stamford, CT: JAI Press.

Wennekers, A.R.M. and A.R. Thurik (1999). Linking entrepreneurship and economic growth. *Small Business Economics*, 13, 27–55.

Wennekers, S., L.H. Uhlaner and R. Thurik (2002). Entrepreneurship and its conditions: A macro perspective. *International Journal of Entrepreneurship Education*, 1, forthcoming.

Yamada, G. (1996). Urban informal employment and self-employment in developing countries: Theory and evidence. *Economic Development and Cultural Change*, 44, 289–314.

Yu, T.F. (1998). Adaptive entrepreneurship and the economic development of Hong Kong. *World Development*, 26, 897–911.

DAVID J. STOREY

University of Warwick

18.   Entrepreneurship, Small and Medium Sized Enterprises and Public Policies*

Introduction

Governments throughout the world now recognise the important role in economic and social welfare played by smaller enterprises. In countries such as the United States and the United Kingdom there has been a striking change over the past forty years: In the 1960s small scale enterprise was equated with technological backwardness, managerial conservatism and modest economic contributions. This contrasts with the current view that, whilst many small firms do fit the 1960s stereotype, the sector also contains dynamic and innovative enterprises that collectively make a considerable contribution to economic well being (Acs, Carlsson and Karlsson, 1999). The magnitude and nature of this contribution continues to be a subject of discussion amongst scholars (Storey, 1994), but governmental awareness of the role of small enterprises has risen sharply.[1]

Governments can facilitate or impede this contribution and this paper reviews public policies towards SMEs in developed – OECD – countries. It seeks to review the contribution that such policies and programmes have made in those countries. A key focus is on methodologies for assessing the impact of policies.

*This paper has benefited from comments received from many individuals. Fundes/IADB financed a version of this paper. Albert Berry, Emilio Zavalos and Maria Vega provided important insights. Presentations were also made to Rotterdam School of Management in the Netherlands, Department of Economics, University of Cork, Ireland, NUTEK in Stockholm and HM Treasury in London. I also valued the comments from Andrew Burke, Denny Dennis and Anders Lundstrom who read and commented upon the paper. However, my initial debt is to the OECD SME Best Practice Working Party and its secretary Marie-Florence Estimé. In my role as Expert to that Committee, I was confronted with these issues on many occasions and the paper clearly stems from that experience.

[1] For example European governments such as Sweden and the Netherlands have produced policy documents on this subject for the first time. Ministry of Economic Affairs (2000). Another illustration, this time from the US, is Audretsch's (2002) observation that policy to promote SMEs became politically bi-partisan in recognising that small businesses were the major source of new job creation in that country.

Z.J. Acs and D.B. Audretsch (eds.), Handbook of Entrepreneurship Research, 473–511
© 2003 *Kluwer Academic Publishers. Printed in Great Britain.*

Section 2 discusses the rationale for the existence of such policies. Section 3 then provides examples of a wide range of such policies. Here a distinction is made between policies that address directly the problems identified by small businesses themselves, and policies that are more closely aligned to the concerns of the public policy makers themselves. Section 4 provides a context for reaching a judgement on the effectiveness of the policies by addressing the issue of policy evaluation. Section 5 reaches some general conclusions on policy effectiveness in the developed economies. Section 6 then widens that discussion to cover not only the technicalities of the evaluation, but also the wider political and economic framework in which it takes place. Section 7 provides an overall conclusion.

However, before beginning any discussion of the rationale for SME policies it is necessary to clarify the definition of SME policies that will be used. Our focus is on public policies; by this we mean those which use taxpayers' funds to directly or indirectly target primarily or exclusively SMEs. Using this definition excludes the wide range of assistance/services provided for SMEs by the private sector. Specifically we exclude services to SMEs provided by banks, accountants, lawyers and private sector consultants. The definition also excludes public policies that, although they strongly influence SMEs, do not have such firms as their prime focus. Examples of such policies are macroeconomic policies designed to achieve a benign trading environment of stable growth with low inflation. These are excluded from consideration on the grounds that such a framework seeks to benefit all sizes of firms and not primarily or exclusively SMEs. Other similar examples of excluded policies include banking regulatory policy, except where the specific focus is SMEs.

It is also necessary to emphasise that the prime focus of the review is on SME policies, rather than entrepreneurship policies. Lundstrom and Stevenson (2001) make this distinction. They view SME policies as focused upon existing enterprises, whereas entrepreneurship policies are directed towards individuals. These individuals are considering, are about to, or have recently started a new business. But, since they currently play only a modest role in the policy armoury of developed economies, it is SME policies that will receive the bulk of the coverage in this chapter.

Finally, it has to be emphasised that the review uses the term SME. The term itself is not common parlance in all countries. Most notably the United States continues to use the phrase "small business" rather than SME. Furthermore the precise definition of an SME/small business also varies between countries. Until fairly recently the EU definition of an SME corresponded to the US definition of a small business – as one having less than 500 employees. However, in 1996 the EU changed its SME definition so that today an SME is (broadly) defined as having less than 250 workers. Within the SME category the EU also specifically defines Medium sized firms as having 50–249 employees, small firms as having 10–49 employees and Micro-firms as having less than 10 workers. The fact that a small firm in the EU is defined as having a maximum of 49 workers, whereas a small business in the United States has less than 500 employees clearly provides the basis for confusion and difficulties of cross country comparison.

These problems are accentuated when further definitional differences from countries such as Japan and Australia are included.[2]

Table 1 makes the important contextual point that, even using identical definitions, the economic contribution of small firms varies widely across OECD countries. Using employment as the measure, it is clear that large firms are considerably more important in the North American countries of Canada and the US, than in the European countries of France and Sweden. This is by no means simply explained by differences in income per head since rich Switzerland has the lowest proportion of employment in large firms. In short, developed economies are not characterised by uniformity in the size distribution of enterprises, but North America has a higher proportion of its employment in large firms than Europe.

Despite the differences in definition of SMEs, and their different economic contribution within the OECD countries, such enterprises exhibit some common characteristics:

- They are generally owned and managed by the same individual or group of individuals.
- They lack market power, having only a small share of markets – or more unusually a bigger share of a tiny or localised market.
- They are legally independent in the sense of not being owned by a larger group of firms.

In some respects such firms may be considered to be at a disadvantage, compared with large firms and it is the efforts by public policy to offset this "disadvantage" which is at the heart of SME policy in developed economies. It is to this issue that we now turn.

Table 1. Percentage shares of employees by size of enterprise: whole economy

	0–19	*20–49*	*50–99*	*100–499*	*500+*
Canada	20	10	8	16	45
France	31	13	—— 25 ——		30
Sweden	31	11	—— 25 ——		33
Switzerland	39	12	—— 25 ——		24
USA	20	—— 18 ——		15	48

Note: Canada data are 1–19 employees, i.e. do not include self-employed without employees.
Source: OECD (2000): table A2, p. 211.

[2] In Australia a small business in manufacturing is defined as having less than 100 employees, whereas in services the upper limit is 20 employees. In Japan an upper limit of 250 employees is used.

Why Should Government Intervene to Help Small Firms?

"Government intervention is justified only where the private and social costs and benefits (of new firm formation) diverge, or where the existing distribution of income significantly distorts the extent to which willingness to pay reflects an individual or groups demand for a good or service" (Storey, 1982, p. 205).

It is well established that, subject to certain key assumptions, goods and services are allocated efficiently through the price mechanism (Rowley and Peacock, 1974). The key assumptions are competition in the goods market, informed consumers, an absence of externalities and willingness to pay reflecting demand.

In the context of small firm public policy intervention the key assumptions most likely to be contravened are those of perfect information and the absence of externalities.

Three types of information imperfection can occur.

(a) Individuals do not realise (are ignorant of) the private benefits of starting a business.
(b) Small business owners do not realise the private benefits of obtaining expert advice from "outside" specialists.
(c) Financial institutions are unable to assess accurately the viability of small firms and (on balance) overestimate the risks of lending to this group. Lack of access to finance, in comparison with larger firms, makes it difficult for small (new) firms to develop/start.

In addition, policy intervention can be justified where there is a divergence between private and social returns. Where social returns exceed private returns, positive externalities or spillovers exist. Here firms may not undertake projects which, whilst in the interests of society as a whole, yield the firm insufficient returns. The role of a public subsidy is to make it privately worthwhile for the firm to undertake the project, enabling society as a whole to benefit. In practice, as will be shown, it is difficult to ensure that public programmes succeed in ensuring that *only* those projects with positive externalities are implemented, and that public funds are not used to subsidise projects that would have been undertaken without the subsidy (Lerner, 1999; Wallsten, 2000).

So how does government respond to these information imperfections? This section discusses responses to each of the three information imperfections, and to the presence of externalities, in turn.

(a) Raising the Awareness of Individuals to the Private Benefits of Starting a Business

Governments, in many countries, have sought to raise the awareness of individuals – or groups of individuals – to the private benefits of starting a business.

In some instances the focus has been on raising the overall rate of new business formation in an economy.

A prime example of this was the efforts of the Thatcher government which came to power in the UK in 1979 with a clear objective to create an "Enterprise Culture" (Burrows, 1991). The clear message of this administration was to seek to change social attitudes of the UK population. The objective was to shift the UK away from what it perceived to be a "dependency culture" – in which workers relied on large organisations and the state to provide them with employment. Instead the UK was to become a country in which people went out and created their own jobs by starting their own businesses. The dependency culture would be transformed into an "enterprise culture".

Whilst the Thatcher "enterprise culture" was aimed at almost all individuals in the UK, this is the exception rather than the rule. Instead, government initiatives seeking to make certain individuals or groups more enterprising/ entrepreneurial are more typical. In Europe much of the focus has been on young people – the young unemployed in Southern Italy (Law 44), young graduates and young people more generally in the UK (STEP, PYBT and LIVEWIRE).[3] In the US, on the other hand, enterprise policy is currently focused upon minorities and females. Implicitly this assumes either the spirit of enterprise is insufficiently endemic within some US citizens and needs encouragement, or it assumes the presence of prejudice/discrimination against such groups.

Countries with governments seeking to encourage "enterprise", whether in the population as a whole or amongst specific groups, assume there are barriers to the transition of some groups into self-employment/business ownership. One important barrier is lack of awareness. For example, young people may not even consider small business/self-employment as a source of employment for themselves. This is particularly true in "transition" economies, but may also be the case in countries where entrepreneurs have comparatively low social esteem – such as Sweden (Boter et al., 1999). Even in moderately entrepreneurial economies such as the UK, some groups – such as graduates – have traditionally viewed self-employment as inappropriate or insufficiently prestigious (well paid).[4]

One example of a UK-based programme designed to influence the attitudes of young people to self-employment and small business is the Shell Technology Enterprise Programme [STEP]. This seeks to enhance the awareness of college students of the benefits of working in a small business through short-term

---

[3] STEP is the Shell Technology Enterprise Programme. This is a work experience programme in a small firm undertaken by undergraduate students. PYBT is the Prince's Youth Business Trust (now Prince's Trust); it provides finance and advice to young people seeking to establish/develop small enterprises. LIVEWIRE is a signposting and advisory service for young entrepreneurs.

[4] Belfield (1999) finds undergraduate students are keenly aware that small firms pay less well than large and are less likely to provide training opportunities. Westhead (1997) in a survey of UK undergraduates, finds 90 percent view employment in a multinational as highly prestigious, whereas only 20% view self-employment/employment in a small firm as prestigious.

placements during their summer vacation. A second example of enterprise support to young people is Law 44 which provides a wide range of financial and advisory support to individuals aged 18 to 30 wishing to establish a new business in Southern Italy.

Policies to raise awareness constitute the response of government to what is perceived to be a market failure caused by information imperfections. The more tricky question is whether, from an ethical point of view, this differs from "brain washing/social engineering", since it is a deliberate and conscious act by the State to change the attitudes and aspirations of its people. It is surprising that this question seems to have received little consideration amongst those proposing such policies.

(b) Raising the Awareness of Small Business Owners to the Private Benefits of Obtaining Information from Outside Sources

In almost all developed economies the state provides some forms of subsidised information and advice for smaller businesses. For example, Personal Business Advisors in the UK, the ALMI services in Sweden or SCORE in the United States are all, to different degrees, part-funded by the taxpayer in order to provide advisory services to small firms at below market rates.

The prime market failure being rectified by these subsidised small firm advisory services is imperfect information. The subsidy implies small firm owners are unaware of the private benefits such advice can provide. They therefore tend to purchase a socially sub-optimal quantity of advice, meaning their business is either more likely to fail, or to perform less well than it would do if the subsidised advice were unavailable.

As an illustration, successive UK governments for thirty years[5] have been prepared to subsidise small firms "tasting" of the benefits from advice provided by "external" advisors. This is because it is assumed that, once the firm has obtained the advice, the private benefits to the firm can be more accurately assessed. Given this more informed position, it is assumed that those businesses expecting to gain will be prepared to purchase, without the need for the subsidy.

The second market failure-based justification for subsidising small business advisory services is that the enhanced performance of such businesses yields social benefits (positive externalities). These are discussed in more detail in section (d), below, but, in the current context, externalities occur in the following way. Small businesses which use the advice may be less likely to fail, and/or

---

[5]Following the recommendations of the Bolton Committee (1971), the UK government established the Small Firms Information Centres. It said, "We should like to see the signposting and information function vested in a single, easily identifiable organisation with a network of local offices in all the most important centres of industry and commerce". In making this recommendation the Committee clearly had in mind an important distinction. This is between subsidising/enhancing the awareness of the availability of advice – which they viewed as acceptable – and subsidising the direct provision of the advice – which they did not. As they say, "Businessmen must be left to accept for good or ill, the consequences of their own judgement", p. 138.

likely to grow more rapidly. This yields social as well as private benefits – most notably those of additional job creation and the enhancement of the long-term competitiveness of the economy as a whole (Birch, 1979; Department of Trade and Industry, 1998).

In practice, it is often unclear whether it is the "information-imperfections" or the "externality" arguments that underlie the provision of publicly subsidised advice for small firms. It is however important to be clear on the rationale for policy since the two justifications have very different policy implications. Where the case is made for the long-term divergence between social and private benefits there is, in principle, a case for a continuing public subsidy and low charges to be paid by the small firm. But, where the case is based on the assumption of ignorance of the small firm owner of the private benefits of external advice, the case can only be made for a once-off "taster" subsidy.[6]

It is frequently observed that small firm owners are notoriously reluctant to pay for advice from outsiders. Curran, Berney and Kuusisto (1999), in their discussion of the ability of the UK's Personal Business Advisors to charge fees for their advice, say:

> "It is unlikely that substantial additional resources will come from fees since resistance amongst SME owners to paying fees is well-entrenched".

As illustrations of these theoretical issues, two very different approaches to the provision of publicly subsidised information and advice for small firms are now reviewed. The first, defined as the ALMI model, is predicated on the notion that there are positive externalities associated with subsidising small firms to acquire external advice. The second is the Enterprise Initiative (EI) model, which assumes market failure as one where small firms under-estimate the private benefits of external advice.

In presenting these models we reiterate that the different diagnoses of market failure lead to very different "solutions". However, we also show that these attempts to rectify market failure present politicians with important decisions on pricing and the introduction of an appropriate regulatory framework.

(i) The ALMI Model

Under the ALMI model, in Sweden, business advice is provided directly to small firms by a public sector organisation, with the cost being covered wholly or primarily by the taxpayer. Hence it implicitly assumes that there are social benefits to the economy as a whole, as well as private benefits to the small enterprise, from the provision of subsidised advisory services. To obtain these social benefits requires a continuing subsidy; otherwise small firms will purchase less information than is socially optimal.

---

[6] Bolton (1971) was very clear in this matter. It viewed government expenditure to overcome lack of awareness as acceptable. It did not accept the case for subsidising "missionary services designed to overcome prejudice or to persuade businessmen of the value of advisory services against their better judgement".

Whilst conceptually simple, the ALMI approach makes it very difficult to assess the "free" market demand for small firm advisory services for the following reasons. First, because provision by a public organisation can lead to "crowding out" of private consultants by the public suppliers who are "cheaper" because they have the benefit of the subsidy. Second, because the public provider has, effectively a monopoly position, suppliers have a reduced incentive to generate satisfied clients in order either to stay in business or to develop their own consultancy business. In short, the public sector is less incentivised. Thirdly, the small business sector may be unwilling to buy services, designed to help them run their own businesses better, from public servants – after all, what do they know about running a business? Whilst this may be a rational or an irrational act, it causes the demand for small firms advisory services to be lower – in an ALMI model – than under full information.

(ii) The Enterprise Initiative (EI) Model

An alternative approach is not to have the advisory services delivered by a public organisation such as ALMI, but rather to subsidise the use of private sector advisors/consultants. The classic example was the UK Enterprise Initiative (EI) which operated between 1988 and 1994. Here the use of approved private sector consultants by small firms to provide information was subsidised from public funds. A maximum of 15 days' use of consultants was permitted per firm. It is therefore an example of a "taster" initiative, based on the view that small firms without the subsidy will purchase a privately sub-optimal quantity of external advice. In EI there is no case for a continuing subsidy – as with ALMI – since the only purpose is a once-off demonstration to the individual small firm of the private benefits of the external advice.

Some of the problems with the ALMI approach are overcome in the EI model because the advisory services are provided by private firms which compete with one another, and which, if they under-perform, will fail. Hence the small firm customer is likely to obtain a better service under EI than ALMI because, in the former case, the advisors/consultants are incentivised.

The EI model, however, also has its problems. First, there needs to be some additional state regulations to ensure that the advisors/consultants who undertake the work for small firms are both suitable and bona fide. Without such regulation of the external consultants, there is limited value in the Initiative since small firms would be purchasing advisory services with the same level of ignorance as in the "free" market. Hence the state checks the bona fides of the consultant, and may also operate a "matching" or "introduction/brokering" service to combine small firms with appropriate consultants/advisors. The problem is that this service is trying to second guess the marketplace and, when matters go wrong – as they inevitably do – the EI is held responsible. This requirement to second guess the marketplace stems from a recognition that markets are at their most effective when the consumer is experienced through repeat purchasing, and least effective when the consumer is purchasing for the first time. As the latter is the case here, the consumer is assumed to benefit from the guidance provided by regulating the consultants.

A second regulatory problem is that of setting the appropriate charging/allocation policy, and here it is vital to be clear on objectives. Is the objective to ensure that the maximum possible numbers of firms obtain a "taste" of the benefits of utilising the services of a consultant? Is the object to ensure that those firms that participate in the Initiative demonstrate enhanced performance? Is the object to ensure that, once the subsidy is removed, that small firms are significantly more likely to use an external consultant than prior to participation in the Initiative?

A variety of charging/allocation options are available. The first is that no charge is made to the small firm for the use of the advisor/consultant. This, however, risks the Initiative having a politically unacceptably high budget; more likely is that resources are allocated on an arbitrary basis such as "first come, first served", or providing only a very limited amount of time per firm, neither of which are guaranteed to maximise welfare. Allocating on a "first come, first served" basis, for example, means that take-up will be more heavily concentrated amongst those firms that are most aware or well networked, yet these may not be those most likely to benefit from the provision of information. Indeed, since they are, by definition, currently comparatively well informed, they may be deemed less likely to benefit than those who are currently poorly informed.

Allocating advisory services in very small quantities may ultimately be self-defeating. This is because the firms know they will not obtain enough advice either to make it worthwhile them applying, or for them to reach an informed judgement about whether the advice was of value. It also makes it difficult for the state to be able to judge whether the provision of the advice has influenced the performance of the firm.

An alternative approach is to restrict use of the Initiative to certain types of firms. These restrictions might eliminate firms in certain sectors, certain regions, or those beyond a specified size or age. Multiple or sequential use of the Initiative might also be prohibited. However, this type of non-price rationing risks being arbitrary and bureaucratic. For example, two firms which are identical in almost all respects may find one excluded from access to advisory services if it has slightly more employees than the other, or is located outside the location boundary or has a slightly different industrial classification. These factors are not necessarily good indicators of whether the firms (or the economy more widely) would benefit from the information services.

In principle, it is desirable for those using information/advice services to pay a charge since this, in part, avoids the problem of non-price rationing discussed above. The EI approach was to require some of the cost of the advisor/consultant to be paid for by the small firm with the remainder being covered by the state. The effective state subsidy rate may be varied so that certain types of small firms, which are thought likely to benefit most from use of the advice, would be more heavily subsidised. The advantage of a charging scheme is that it lowers the cost to the state of the Initiative, but it also "simulates" the market for small firm advisory services. By varying the subsidy the state can make some estimate of the demand for advice. The key disadvantage of charging for such services is that the firms which may benefit from them most may be the least able to pay – because of their precarious financial position.

Relating this then to the objectives of the Initiative, if the objective is to maximise the number of small firms that obtain a "taste" of the benefits of having an advisor/consultant, then it is not appropriate to charge. To ensure the budget for the Initiative is politically acceptable a tight restriction would be placed on the amount of time the advisor/consultant provided. In this case, the "jam" would be spread very thinly across many firms. It is not to be expected that there would be any resulting observable change in their performance because the amount of "jam" received by an individual firm is so modest. The use of charges is therefore not compatible with this objective.

However, as noted earlier, a key objective could be to ensure the Initiative leads to an enhanced performance on the part of assisted firms. In this case, it may be appropriate to charge on the grounds that only those firms who themselves believe they will benefit from the Initiative will pay the charge, and that the firm's own judgement is the best indicator of potential benefit. The use of a charge means access to the Initiative is restricted, so that more "jam" is allocated per small firm. For this reason, it is more likely that an observable impact upon firm performance could both be present and be identified by the firm. Charging is therefore compatible with achieving this objective.

A third objective may be to ensure more extensive use of advisors/consultants once the subsidy is removed. Again, the use of charging is compatible with this objective on the grounds that those firms most likely to subsequently use the advisor/consultant will be those perceiving themselves as having benefited from the advice received. This, as argued above, is compatible with a charging strategy.

In summary, the market failure-based rationale for EI is that small firms under-estimate the private benefits of obtaining external advice/consultancy. The role of EI was to provide a "once-off" public subsidy to enable the small firm to "taste" the benefits of external advice. Having tasted, the firm would then be an informed consumer, hence overcoming the market failure.

(c) Financial Institutions are Unable to Assess Accurately the Viability of Small Firms

In a fully informed, efficient capital market, good projects are funded and bad projects are not, irrespective of the resources of the borrower.

What then happens where the financial institution knows some borrowers are more risky than are others, but has imperfect and asymmetric information? This realistically describes three key characteristics of the market for small firm loans. First, financial institutions know that, as a group, small firms are more risky than large. Second, the information available to financial institutions about small firms is less than that available about large firms. Third, the borrower is better informed about the risk of the project than the lender.[7]

If finance markets behaved in a manner similar to conventional markets, then high-risk borrowers would be prepared to pay a price premium over low-risk borrowers to obtain access to funds. For its part, financial institutions would be prepared to lend at this higher, market-clearing, rate.

Yet markets supplying finance to small firms do not behave in this manner. Allocation of funds does not take place through the price mechanism, but instead through rationing (Stiglitz and Weiss, 1981). Thus the high-risk project/business is not able to obtain funds by offering to pay the price premium; instead the financial institution is more likely to be influenced by the borrower's access to collateral. Hence there may be good projects/businesses, which are prepared to pay a risk premium market rate, but which are denied access to funds because of their own lack of access to collateral. This is referred to as a "funding gap".

The practical significance of the "funding gap" is that if viable (small) businesses are unable to obtain access to funds, because of imperfect information, this leads to welfare losses to society. It therefore provides an, in principle, justification for government intervention.

There are, however, two reasons why evidence of the presence of collateral-based lending to small firms, of itself, may not justify state intervention. The first is that, as Bester (1985) argues, the pledging of collateral can be interpreted as signalling the viability of the project. Thus the low expected return project will have low pledged collateral, and so collateral is viewed as a satisfactory device for signalling the expected value of the project. The problem here is that collateral signals access to wealth, as well as project valuation. Collateral-based lending risks discriminating in favour of the rich and against the poor in a manner unrelated to project valuation. It therefore strengthens rather than reduces the case for intervention.

A second reason why a "gap" does not necessarily justify government intervention is that the inability to borrow from financial institutions may merely reflect a difference between the objective risk assessment of the bank and the consistently (over-) optimistic views of entrepreneurs. De Meza (2002) develops this reasoning in several papers (De Meza and Webb, 1987; De Meza and Southey, 1996). He argues that asymmetric information results in too many low-quality projects being funded. Social welfare would therefore be more enhanced by discouraging entry into entrepreneurship than by government intervention to eliminate "funding gaps".

---

[7] In practice, particularly for start-up businesses, this assumption is not necessarily valid. It seems more plausible to argue that the bank, with many years of codified experience in lending (or not lending) to new firms is a better judge of the risk of a new venture than a prospective borrower with no prior business experience. Nevertheless, even in this case, information is asymmetric.

Nevertheless, the presence of identified funding gaps has been used to justify government intervention in the provision of loans for small businesses. As will be shown later, a frequent form of that intervention is a Loan Guarantee Scheme, examples of which are found in France, Canada, USA, UK, Netherlands, as well as many less developed economies (Llisteri, 1997; Riding and Haines, 1999).

Loan Guarantee Schemes seek to overcome market imperfections in the provision of debt finance for small firms. They focus on ensuring that good projects are not precluded from access to finance through lack of access to collateral. Whilst the details of such schemes vary between countries, the basic principle is that if private banks judge a project to be viable, but only when collateralised, a loan may be made on the LGS. Interest on this loan will be charged at a premium rate but, in the event of default, government generally covers somewhere between 70% and 85% of the loss (KPMG, 1999).

The perception that information imperfections/asymmetry generates "funding gaps" is, of course, not restricted to loan capital. Similar issues apply in the market for private equity. Here the high fixed costs of due diligence can mean that modest sums of seed capital are not provided by financial institutions, or are provided on a socially sub-optimal scale. Public programmes to address these "gaps" exist in a number of countries. Mason and Harrison (2000) review these programmes and make important distinctions between different types of programme. The first is where public money is supplied to formal venture capital funds to encourage them to make investments that would not normally have been made on strict commercial criteria. The second is the provision of tax incentives to wealthy individuals to encourage them to become business angels. A third type of programme uses public money to subsidise the greater awareness of angels and businesses of one another.

(d) Un-Priced External Benefits May Be Present

Many governments have programmes to provide public subsidies to new and small firms in the science and technology sectors. Such programmes are justified on two grounds: The first is that financial institutions, because of information imperfections, are particularly poor at assessing risk in technology-based ventures.

The second ground is that of the presence of spillovers generated by new technology-based firms. The arguments are closely linked to the case for subsidies for Research and Development (Klette et al., 2000). It is that innovating firms, because they cannot fully exclude other firms from modifying or copying their innovation, will be less likely to innovate than is socially optimal. Society is therefore denied the benefits of this innovation, which could be considerable for firms developing new products or services. The role of the public subsidy is therefore to make the innovation more privately worthwhile for the firm, encouraging its introduction, and so enhancing welfare.

The best-known example of such a programme is the Small Business Innovation Research (SBIR) Program (Lerner, 1999; Wallsten, 2000). It began in 1982 and, by 1997, its annual budget exceeded $1 billion. Monies are allocated on the basis of open competition in two phases. In Phase I funds of up to $100,000 can be allocated to the successful firm to "determine the scientific and technical merit of an idea". Up to $750,000 is available to successful firms in Phase II to "develop the idea".[8]

HOW DOES GOVERNMENT INTERVENE?

Section 2 discussed the rationale for government intervention in support of small and medium-sized enterprises. In order to anchor that rationale in reality, examples of interventions have been presented where appropriate. That approach, however, fails to provide a "big picture" of the considerable variety of approaches and specific initiatives implemented in developed countries. It also ignored the reality that government intervention on behalf of SMEs frequently has a powerful political momentum. This section aims to provide a "big picture" of the nature of intervention. The political discussion is covered in section 4.

A key theme of section 2 was the stark differences in the attitudes of governments in developed countries to the question of public intervention in support of small firms. At one extreme, and clearly different from virtually all other countries in the world,[9] is the United States, where Dennis (1999) can say: *"the United States has no small business or entrepreneurship policy."*

According to Dennis, the United States, has a competition policy in which Entrepreneurship and small business play a key role, with government acting to ensure neutrality amongst competitors, irrespective of size. He points to the opening sentences of the Small Business Act 1953 and comments

> "Small business is not mentioned in its own policy outline until the eightieth word. Three references to competition precede it. Even security is a forerunner. Competition, and implicitly the consumer, is the overriding concern of the law, not entrepreneurial or small business per se."

Yet, even he admits that, whilst the concept is clear, in practice these economic principles become entwined with social objectives. It is also the case that the US has specific SME policies – such as SBDCs and SBIR. Nevertheless, the key philosophical standpoint of the United States is that the role of government is to hold, rather than enter, the ring.

---

[8] A similar programme operates in the UK. SMART Awards are made to firms undertaking development projects in innovative technologies. In exceptional cases, the amount awarded to a firm could be up to £450,000.

[9] Switzerland is probably the only country, to this author's knowledge, which comes close to the United States in this regard.

Country members of the European Union, however, broadly take a different view.[10] Here both national governments, and the European Union itself, view small firms as key sources of job creation and competitiveness. They also view themselves as playing a role in promoting economic development by having specific policies to support small firms. They therefore, implicitly or explicitly, view the positive externalities associated with support for SMEs – most notably job creation – as their justification for intervention.

EU countries have therefore introduced an almost bewildering range of policies to assist smaller enterprises. It is certainly not appropriate here to seek to itemise these policy interventions. For this, the interested reader should consult ENSR (1997) for a review of EU policies or OECD (1996, 1997, 1998) for countries outside the EU.

Table 2 provides a structure for examining such interventions without assuming, of course, that they necessarily constitute "best practice". The Table distinguishes between those interventions that respond to the problems articulated by small firms, and the interventions that reflect more closely the agenda of government. The former is shown in the top half of the table and the latter in the lower half. A distinction is also made between generic problems identified on the left-hand side and specific policy interventions on the right.

Table 3 develops this by taking the main areas in table 2 and identifying specific programmes that seek to overcome the problems identified. Table 3 seeks to be illustrative rather than comprehensive, so only some of the topics identified in Table 2 are covered in Table 3. Table 3 is structured similarly to Table 2, with policies relating to the SME Agenda in the top half of the table and those more closely linked to the agenda of government in the lower half of the table.

In selecting the items for inclusion in Table 3 efforts have been made to provide a wide geographical coverage of countries of different sizes and economic philosophies. Even so, there is better coverage of policies in English-speaking countries simply because this material was more accessible to this author.

Despite these biases the table provides a description of programmes that seek to address items of concern to SMEs and to government. It also reaches a broad judgement of the extent to which the programme has been successful, where this judgement about based on factors such as whether, following an evaluation, the programmes life/scale was extended. However, as will be shown in sections 4 and 5 of this chapter, some evaluations are more rigorous than are others. For this reason, judgements on programme success are not based on a set of consistent criteria or appraisal methods.

---

[10]Within the EU there is a wide spectrum of opinion with the US position being, on balance, comparatively favoured by the UK and least favoured by France and the Scandinavian countries. Canada may also be taken as an example of a country with some interventionist policies to support SMEs.

Table 2. Policy areas and illustrations

SME's agenda	Policies
1. Finance	Loan Guarantee Schemes (USA, Canada & UK) Sabatani Act (Italy)
2. Markets/Demand	Europartinairt (EU) Trade Fairs (Greece) Public Procurement (USA)
3. Admin Burdens	Enterprise & De-Regulation Unit (UK) Business Entry Point (Australia) Business Administration Courses (Portugal)
4. Premises	Science Parks (Italy, Germany) Managed Work Space Incubators (Finland)
5. New Tech	Business Innovation Centres (EU) SBIR (USA)
6. Skilled Labour	Small Firms Training Loan (UK)
Government's agenda	
1. Entrepreneurial Skills	Advice (ALMI, Sweden) SBDCs (USA) Training (Japan)
2. Entrepreneurial Awareness	LiveWIRE (UK) Atlantic Canada (Canada)
3. Competitiveness	SBIR (USA)
4. Special Groups	Young People (Law 44 – Italy) Micro loans to Women (Sweden) American Indians (USA)
5. Regional/Spatial Issues	Business Birth Rate (Scotland)

The budgets of these programmes are often considerable. Despite its protestations, the US government expenditure on small firm programmes is, in absolute terms massive, with the SBIR programme alone having an annual budget of more than 1 billion US$. Details of such budgets are provided later in section 5.

ASSESSING THE EFFECTIVENESS OF INTERVENTION: CLARIFICATION OF OBJECTIVES

The above section demonstrated that governments intervene in a wide variety of ways in order to assist SMEs. The central question of interest to taxpayers and policy-makers is whether such intervention is effective.

It is not possible to even begin to make such an assessment unless the objectives of the policy are clearly specified. This means they have to be

Table 3. Illustrations of public programmes to assist SMEs and enhance entrepreneurship

SMEs AGENDA

Problem	Programme	Description	Country	Evaluation	Success
1. Access to Loan Finance	Loan Guarantee Scheme	SMEs without access to own collateral obtain access to bank loans by state acting as guarantor	UK, USA, Canada, France, Netherlands	OECD (1997) KPMG (1999) Riding and Haines (2001)	Yes, generally viewed as helpful, but small scale impact on the overall financing of SMEs in most countries
2. Access to Equity Capital	Enterprise Investment Scheme	Tax breaks for wealthy individuals to become business angels	UK	Not of current scheme	Unknown
3. Access to Markets	Europartenariat	Organisation of Trade Fairs to encourage cross-border trade between SMEs	EU	The Sweden Europartenariat was assessed by NUTEK (1998)	General satisfaction amongst firms that participated
4. Administrative Burdens	Units established within government to seek to minimise administrative burdens on smaller firms	Sunsetting Legislation, Deregulation Units	Netherlands, Portugal, UK	No formal evaluations	The view of small firms themselves is that bureaucratic burdens have increased markedly in recent years
5. Science Parks	Property based developments adjacent to universities	Seek to promote clusters of new technology based firms	UK, France, Italy and Sweden	DTI (1994)	Conflicting findings on impact of SPs on performance of firms
6. Managed Workspace	Property provision to assist new and very small firms	Often called business incubators, these provide premises for new and small firms on "easy-terms"	World-wide	United Nations (2000)	General recognition that such initiatives are of value
7. Stimulating Innovation and R&D in small firms	Small Business Innovation Research Program	$1 billion per year is allocated via a competition to small firms to stimulate additional R&D activity	USA	Lerner (1999) Wallsten (2000)	Lerner implies SBIR enhances small firm performance, but Wallsten is unable to show it leads to additional R&D

8. Stimulating Training in small firms	Japan Small Business Corporation (JSBC)	JSBC and local governments provide training for owners and managers of small firms. The training programme began in 1963	Japan	None	Unknown

GOVERNMENT'S AGENDA

1. Entrepreneurial Skills	Small Business Development Corporations (SBDCs)	Counselling is provided by SBDC mentors to small business clients who may be starting a business or be already trading	USA	Chrisman and McMullan (1996)	This study finds SBDC clients have higher rates of survival and growth than might be expected. Reservations over these findings are found in this text
2. Entrepreneurial Awareness	Entrepreneurship Education	To develop an awareness of enterprise and/or an entrepreneurial spirit in society by incorporating enterprise into the school and college curriculum	Australia, Netherlands, but leading area was Atlantic Canada	Lundstrom and Stevenson (2001)	Conventional assessments are particularly difficult here because of the long "lead times"
3. Special Groups	Law 44	Provides finance and mentoring advice to young people in Southern Italy, where enterprise creation rates were very low	Southern Italy	Del Monte and Scalera (2001) OECD (1997) Maggioni et al. (1999)	This is an expensive programme, but most studies show the survival rates of assisted firms to be well above those of "spontaneous" firms

formulated in a manner that is, in principle, capable of measurement. Unfortunately, this is rarely the case.

Instead, objectives are specified in very general terms, such as "creating a more enterprising society", or "making this country the most enterprise-friendly country in the world in which to do business". Only if there were tangible measures that underpin these objectives – such as international league tables providing an agreed set of criteria to measure the "enterprise-friendly" nature of a country – would such objectives be "clearly specified". To our knowledge, no such league tables exist.

A second problem is that, even where SME policies are clearly specified, they frequently have multiple objectives, some of which may even compete with one another. Finally, in many cases, the objectives have to be inferred from politicians' statements, rather than being specified in official documents.

Table 4 illustrates some of the above issues. It shows SME policies may have several, and possibly conflicting, objectives.

The table makes an important distinction between "intermediate" and "final" objectives. The purpose of the distinction is that policy-makers frequently infer the two are identical, whereas in practice they differ sharply. Row 1 of Table 4 illustrates the point. SME policy in developed economies is normally emphasised most strongly during periods of recession and high unemployment, because small firms are believed to be important sources of job creation. Clearly, in times of high unemployment, job creation is more highly valued by politicians than in conditions of full employment. In this sense, the link is made that if smaller enterprises generate jobs this will lead to the desirable "final" objective of reducing unemployment.

In practice, this link between job creation and unemployment is, in fact, quite complex. For example, even if small enterprises do generate additional jobs, these are more likely to be low paid, and part-time than such jobs created

Table 4. Objectives of small firm policy

Intermediate	Final
1. Increase employment	– Increase employment
	– Reduce unemployment
2. Increase number of start-ups	– Increase number of start-ups
	– Increased stock of firms
3. Promote use of consultants	– Promote use of consultants
	– Faster growth of firms
4. Increase competition	– Increase competition
	– Increase wealth
5. Promote "efficient" markets	– Promote "efficient" markets
	– Increase wealth
6. Promote technology diffusion	– Promote technology diffusion
	– Increase wealth
7. Increase wealth	– Votes

Source: Storey (1994).

by larger firms. Small firm owners may also seek different types of workers in terms of skills and motivation from larger firms (Cowling and Storey, 1998). For all these reasons, individuals who are unemployed may not fill the jobs generated by small firms. Instead, small employers may favour individuals from outside the labour force, but who only work part-time. They may also favour individuals who travel into the area/country from outside. So, if for example, the "final" objective of policy is to lower unemployment for young males, then this may not be best achieved by stimulating small enterprises which may employ females or formerly retired workers. It is therefore critical that evaluators are clear whether it is the "intermediate" or the "final" objective that is the ultimate aim of policy.

The remainder of Table 4 provides other examples of possible confusion between "intermediate" and "final" objectives of enterprise policy. Row 2 illustrates that there can be a lack of clarity about whether the objective is to increase the number of start ups or whether it is to increase the total number of firms in the economy. If it is the latter, this, in principle, could be achieved by seeking to lower the death rate of firms. However, the policies to achieve this would be radically different from those designed to raise the birth rate of firms. Similar levels of confusion are apparent from the other "intermediate" and "final" objectives. The interested reader can review these at length in Storey (1994).

The final row of the table emphasises that public policies towards small enterprises have a clear political dimension. They are formulated by politicians who need to take account, not only of the interests of small enterprise owners and their workers but also the wider political agenda, in their efforts to become elected and re-elected. It is therefore naïve to believe that politicians will voluntarily favour the specification of a single target upon which they will be judged, even if that single target could be agreed.

So what may reasonably be expected? The first reasonable expectation is that a broad framework for SME policy could be specified, reflecting political priorities. Such a framework could include commitments to facilitating the access to resources of those wishing to start businesses; to minimising the disadvantages of small scale in dealing with government; to eliminating evidence of discrimination against groups in society, etc.

Within this broad context it is then appropriate to introduce legislation which reflects these broad principles. The critical issue is that the legislation has to have clearly specified objectives or targets which are capable of measurement. It should not be the task of the evaluators to have to infer the objectives of the legislation. That is the responsibility of the legislators.

It is also necessary to set aside funds to enable an assessment of the impact of the legislation to be conducted. Where, for example, substantial public funds are committed there should be a budget of perhaps 0.5% set-aside for evaluation. The legislation should also specify the methodology for the conduct of the assessment. We return to these issues at the end of the following section.

Assessing the Effectiveness of Intervention: The Six Steps

This section will identify, as examples, several major policy interventions, in a number of different countries, which have been the subject of recent scrutiny by academic researchers. Many have already been described in section 2 when the rationale for intervention was outlined.

These examples are intended to reflect a diversity of philosophies and approaches to small firm support. Hence they are drawn from the United States, Canada and from the European Union. The interventions seek to address market failures in policy areas such as "start-ups", "finance", "information" and in "research and development".

Our use only of those evaluations conducted by academics is for two reasons; firstly, as Curran et al. (1999) note, these tend to be more critical than those undertaken either by the sponsoring organisation itself or by private sector consultants.[11] The second reason is that, because of the refereeing process, the academic research is expected to ensure all relevant information is in the public domain.

The choice of these programmes is determined exclusively by the availability of academic evaluations, conducted very recently, and which are published in reputable academic journals. As we note in the next section, we cannot necessarily assume that the impact of these programmes is necessarily typical of the small business support programmes either in these countries or elsewhere. Indeed we make a case that, if anything, these are likely to be amongst the more effective programmes on the grounds that the bureaucrats have allowed (external) evaluations to take place and for the findings to enter the public domain.

Table 5 identifies the programmes, the evaluation of which will be reviewed. It shows that, as well as covering several countries, they are directed towards very different sub-sets of the population of SMEs. For example, as noted in section 3, the SBIR programme is concerned with high-tech small firms, whereas Law 44 is concerned with encouraging the start up of new firms by young people. Some programmes, such as SBLA or SBIR provide finance only, whereas GI and Law 44 provide finance and advice. In contrast, SBDC and EI only subsidise access to expert advice. Taken as a group, however, the evaluations cover many of the generic forms of small business support provided by governments as shown in Tables 2 and 3.

Table 5 also shows that expenditure on such programmes can be substantial. Clearly it is difficult to compare, for example, small firm programme expenditures in a small country such as Ireland with those in the vastly larger United States. Nevertheless, the expenditure on a programme such as SBIR is clearly substantial in absolute terms. It was noted earlier that Wallsten (2000) reports

---

[11]Curran et al. say, in their review of research on UK Business Links (BLs), "As in evaluations of other SME policies, independent evaluations of BLs by academic researchers have been less favourable than those sponsored by central government or BLs themselves", p. 65.

Table 5. Six examples of programme evaluation

Country	Programme	Functions of programme	Approximate annual expenditure	Currently operating?	Source of evaluation
1. United States	Small Business Innovation Research (SBIR)	Grants to High Technology businesses for Research and Development	1.1 billion $US in 1997	YES	Lerner (1999) Wallsten (2000)
2. United States	Small Business Development Centres (SBDCs)	Training and Counselling services	139 million $US	YES	Chrisman and McMullan (1996)
3. United Kingdom	Enterprise Initiative Marketing (EI)	Subsidised use of External Marketing Consultants	45 million GBP per annum	NO: ended in 1994	Wren and Storey (2002)
4. Northern Ireland/ Republic of Ireland	Grant Assistance in Ireland (GI)	Marketing, Training and Investment Grants	20 million GBP in NI approx. similar in Republic	YES	Roper and Hewitt-Dundas (2001)
5. Canada	Small Business Loan Act (SBLA)	Guaranteeing Loans to Small Businesses	42.5 million $C	YES	Riding et al. (1999)
6. Italy	Law 44	Subsidising new businesses established by young people in S. Italy	Not known	YES	Maggioni et al. (1999) Del Monte and Scalera (2001)

the SBIR total budget in 1998 exceeded 1 billion USDs. The budget is also substantial on a per-enterprise basis, with awards of up to 100,000 USD for Phase I winners and up to 750,000 USD for Phase II winners under the SBIR programme.

SME Enterprise support programmes are also substantial in other countries. For example, Wren and Storey (2002) report the scale of budgets associated with several of the programmes in Table 5. For example, the ALMI service in Sweden absorbed 7–8% of that country's net industrial costs; the Law 44 programme in Italy has cost in excess of 300 million ECUs. Finally, the latest estimate of "soft" support to SMEs from the UK government is 650 million GBPs.

Given the substantial sums of public money devoted to SMEs it is surprising that Lerner (1999) can say, with some justification:

"Despite economists' interest in interactions between governments and firms, the public subsidisation of small firms has attracted virtually no scrutiny."

To review evaluations of these programmes, which clearly exhibit considerable diversity, requires some common framework. This is provided in the current author's earlier work on this topic (Storey, 1999). That paper identified six generic types of evaluation of small business policies in developed countries, shown as Table 6.

The generic types of evaluation are referred to as "Steps" with the least sophisticated being Step 1, and the most sophisticated as Step 6. In this review, since we are only concerned with "best practice", we will only concern ourselves with examples of Steps 4, 5 and 6 evaluations.

Two keys to successful evaluations are:

(i) To ensure that the firms which respond in the evaluation are representative of all "treatment" clients, given that inevitably only a sample of clients will be included. This problem is overcome partly by absolute sample size and partly by statistical testing for sampling bias.
(ii) To accurately estimate what would have happened to the "treatment" firms if they had not been treated.

It is the latter that distinguishes the Evaluations referred to as Steps 4, 5, and

Table 6. The six steps: monitoring and evaluation

Monitoring	
Step I	– Take up of Scheme
Step II	– Recipients' Opinions
Step III	– Recipients' views of the differences made by the Assistance
Evaluation	
Step IV	– Comparison of the Performance of "Assisted" with "Typical" Firms
Step V	– Comparison with "Match" Firms
Step VI	– Taking account of selection bias

6 from those in Steps 1, 2 and 3. The former group explicitly tries to attribute performance change in the SME to the provision of the assistance. The latter merely seek to ensure the policy-maker can track the public funds were spent in an appropriate manner and, at best, obtain feedback on whether the recipient felt the contribution was helpful.

(i) Step 4 Evaluations:

Two examples of Step 4 evaluations are presented in this section. The first is the evaluation of the economic impact of Small Business Development Centres (SBDCs) in the United States. The second is the appraisal of the Canadian Small Firms Loan Act (SFLA).

Chrisman and colleagues have undertaken assessments of the impact of SBDCs (Chrisman and Katrishen, 1994; Chrisman and McMullan, 1996) using a methodology first developed in Chrisman et al. (1985). SBDCs provide free, comprehensive, counselling, training and technical assistance services to small businesses. Training is viewed as a "group" activity, in the sense of being provided to classes of either potential or new business owners. Counselling, on the other hand, is the provision of "one-to-one" advice by specialists. SBDCs are generally a partnership between the Small Business Administration (SBA), local and state government, the private sector and educational institutions. Public money for SBDCs, coming from the Small Business Administration, is currently about 150 million USDs annually.

The Chrisman studies only examine counselling services, and so are not concerned with the training role of SBDCs. They take a (representative) sample of SBDC counselling[12] clients – the "treatment" firms. For established firms Chrisman et al. examine changes in sales and employment in "treatment" firms in 1990 – before they received the counselling – with their sales and employment in 1991 after "treatment". For those firms who reported that they felt they had benefited from the Counselling [80%], a comparison is made with the "weighted average growth rates for US businesses on each measure". The assumption is that the difference between the performance of the "treatment" group and the weighted average is a good measure of the impact of the counselling.

However, this assumption is open to question for two reasons. First, because the "treatment" firms may differ from the "weighted average" firms in observable respects which influence performance. For example, the two groups of firms may differ in terms of age, size, sector or geography. Failure to account for these "observables" risks rendering invalid the assumption that, in the absence of treatment, these "treatment" firms would have performed in a manner similar to the "weighted average".

---

[12] Note that Training clients are not included. In 1977 there were 15 times as many training as counselling clients in SBDCs. By the mid-1980s this ratio had fallen to 3 : 1 and by the late 1990s it had fallen further to 1.5 : 1.

It is therefore necessary to take observable firm characteristic differences into account, where there is evidence that these may influence performance.[13] This is undertaken in the Step 5 analyses in which "treatment" firms are compared with another group of firms from which they do not differ in terms of key observables. The latter are often referred to as "match" firms on the grounds that they are selected to match with the "treatment" firms in terms of observables such as size, sector, geography and age.

The second doubt is that, even if there were no significant differences between the "match" and the "treatment" firms in terms of observable characteristics, the two groups could differ in terms of "unobservables". The Step 6 evaluations seek to control for these.

Even bigger challenges are posed by attempts to estimate the contribution of Loan Guarantee Schemes such as the Canadian Small Business Loan Act (SBLA). The challenges are bigger because, as Riding and Haines point out, a key function of the Act is to facilitate the establishment of enterprises that would not otherwise have started in business. This type of calculation is probably best undertaken using time-series data in the format analysed by Barlow and Robson (1999) rather than by seeking responses from loan recipients because of the difficulties of interpreting replies.[14]

But, setting aside the question of new firms, Riding and Haines (1999) use two indicators of the additionality provided by the SBLA to established firms. First, they compare the age profile of SBLA firms with the lending profile of the Commercial banks. They find 14% of the portfolio of the SFLS is to firms that are less than one year old, compared with 5% for the banks. They infer that, without the SFLA, 9% of firms would have been un-funded.

A second group of established businesses benefiting from the SFLA are those who believe they would not have been funded without the Act. Riding and Haines then compare the jobs created in the SBLA firms in 1995 with the national population. They then attribute the difference between the two to the SBLA.

---

[13] As an illustration, assume the counselling clients were primarily high-tech firms that, as a group, exhibit faster growth than were firms in more conventional sectors. Hence comparing SBDC clients with a weighted average of firms would be expected to yield differences in performance, but not necessarily because of the advice received, but because of the markets served by the clients. Similar arguments apply to factors such as size and age, where (surviving) younger and smaller firms would be expected to grow faster than larger and older small firms.

[14] The difficulty of using loan respondents is that only firms which are in business, and which received a loan, can be asked about whether they would have been in business without the loan. Even for those attempting to answer as truthfully as possible, this is a difficult question since there are so many factors involved. We also suspect that many respondents do not answer truthfully: Some will underestimate the impact of the loan on the grounds that it is their foresight and determination that lead to the establishment of the business, rather than government funding. Conversely, some respondents may overestimate the impact – some may simply wish to please the interviewer. Others may think it is in their future interests to have such facilities available, even if they were not influential in starting their business. Clearly the researcher has little idea about the impact of these conflicting motivations.

This raises the same issues as the Chrisman et al. evaluations, by comparing the "treatment" group with the national population. It is that the "treatment" firms may differ from the national population in terms of both "observables" and "unobservables". Step 5 evaluations, to be discussed in the next sub-section, are examples of where explicit account is taken of "observables".

(ii) Step 5 Evaluations:

An example of a Step 5 evaluation is that by Lerner (1999) of the Small Business Innovation Research Program (SBIR) in the United States. This programme allocated 1.1 billion USDs (in 1997) to small businesses seeking to undertake Research and Development. Phase I awards are now up to 100,000 USDs. At a later stage firms may re-apply for Phase II awards of up to 750,000 USDs.

In his evaluation Lerner hypothesises that "subsidy recipients should perform at least slightly better than their peers". He then takes a sample of firms in receipt of SBIR Phase I awards and identifies two matching samples. The first set of matches do not differ from the awardees ("treatment" firms) in terms of industry and firm size at the time of the award. The second matching sample is matched on geographic location and firm size.

This careful process ensures that, taking account of the "observables" of firm size, sector and geography the two groups of firms do not differ. Lerner then compares the changes in sales and employment over time of the two groups and finds the SBIR ("treatment") firms significantly out-perform the matches. He also finds that mean differences between the groups are not a reflection of the presence of extreme values (outliers).

A second example of a Step 5 evaluation is that by Maggioni et al. of the Italian Law 44. This Law provides government funding of up to 90% for capital investment in businesses started by young people under the age of 35 in the South of Italy. 30% of the government funding is in the form of low interest loans and the remainder is grant. In addition, young entrepreneurs are mandated to use the services of "mentors" for advice; no charge is made to the business for this. Finally, 30%–40% of the operating costs of the business during its first two years is also subsidised.

Maggioni et al. (1999) examines the effectiveness of the Law. The two year survival rate of these new firms is almost 80%, which is impressive for any economy, but particularly for businesses established by young people.[15] To test this, Maggioni et al. take a sample of 45 Law 44 firms in the Naples area and match these with 45 new firms from the local Chamber of Commerce. Matching

---

[15] As illustrations, Cressy and Storey (1996) find that about 60% of new firms survived for a two-year period. For UK firms registered for VAT the survival rate after 2 years is 70%. In Germany, Bruderl et al. (1992) find a two-year survival rate of 75%. Cressy and Storey find that businesses established by young people, under the age of 25, have a survival rate, over four years, of 30%, whereas those started by individuals between the ages of 55–65 have a 70% survival rate.

takes place on the grounds that the two samples do not differ in terms of geography (all in Naples area), age (all new starts) and sector.

Maggioni et al. find the "treatment" firms are more "resistant to exit"[16] despite their debt levels being higher. However, they find no evidence of significantly faster sales or employment growth in the "treatment" group.

Whilst Step 5 evaluations, such as those by Lerner, and by Maggioni et al.,[17] take explicit account of "observables", we noted above that they do not seek to take account of "unobservables". In the case of small firms' policy initiatives, the key unobservable is that of selection.

There are two types of selection: Self-selection and Committee selection. Self-selection takes place when firms can choose whether or not to participate in a programme. If the programme is aimed at, for example, enterprises seeking to grow, then it is likely that the firms who apply to participate will be, on balance, more growth-orientated than those that do not apply This is particularly the case where not all applicants are likely to be successful. The more growth-oriented applicants are therefore "self selecting" into the programme. This has potentially serious implications when comparing "treatments" with matches. It is that, even if the "treatments" actually received no funding/assistance, they would have been expected to perform better (grow faster) than the matches because they were more growth-oriented. Hence, when the performance of the two groups is compared over time, it is not clear whether any observed differences are attributable to initial differences in growth orientation (self-selection) or to the impact of the programme.

What independent evidence is there for self-selection into public programmes? KPMG (1999) in their examination of the UK Loan Guarantee Scheme (SFLGS) say:

> "86% of firms in our Survey reported that they were growth orientated. This suggests that the SFLGS appealed to firms who were more growth orientated than the general SME population" (p. 4).

What is more difficult to demonstrate is whether they were more growth-oriented than a group of SMEs matched with SFLGS applicants on "observables" such as sector, size and geography. In the case of either SBIR or Law 44, is there any intuitive reason for suspecting the presence of self-selection, after taking account of matching?

It might be argued that all government programmes, especially those focusing on encouraging growth, are likely to attract better-networked (informed) and more motivated firms. Bennett and Robson (1999) provide some partial evidence for this. They show that for UK Business Links, which focused their advisory services on small businesses seeking to grow, that receiving a site visit

---

[16]This is the term used by Maggioni et al. to capture barriers to exit as assessed by the business owners.

[17]Other examples of Step 5 evaluations include those conducted in Atlantic Canada such as those of Thomas and Landry (2001).

and having a written brief/contract was correlated with historic employment growth. After taking account of "matching", however, it is more difficult to make a strong intuitive case for self-selection. It therefore becomes an empirical question as to whether self-selection is actually present within programmes.

A more powerful intuitive case can be made for the presence of Committee selection. This applies when not all applicants to a Programme/Scheme are successful. This is clearly the case in the SBIR Program, where typically about 10 Phase I applications are made for every award made, and only half of those progress to a Phase II award. Although it is not discussed by Maggioni et al., there is also Committee Selection present in Law 44, since under one quarter of all applicants are successful.[18]

As Lerner discusses, Committee Selection could also be subject to political influence but, in principle, the merits of the proposal in terms of the policy objectives should be the prime consideration. Hence, for SBIR, selection should be based on the technical merits of the proposal, whereas for Law 44 selection should be on the basis of the commercial strength of the business plan.

If the Committee is a good selector – that is, it can identify the good from the less good project – then comparing the performance of awardees with the matches will mean the awardees will always perform better – irrespective of whether they received the award or not. Observed differences in the performance of the awardees and the matches may therefore reflect the skill of the Committee in its selection. It does not necessarily reflect the impact of the programme.

To summarise, when the awardees are compared with the matches, in the presence of Committee Selection, it is not clear to what extent differences in performance reflect the benefits of the programme or the extent to which it reflects the ability of the Committee to select.

In principle, it is expected that there will be a positive impact of Committee selection – otherwise allocation could be random and the Committee would serve no useful function. It is plausible, however, to argue that Committees could exercise a "negative" or political influence in the manner implied by Lerner. He suggests that, whilst there is no concept of "geographical equity" in the SBIR provisions, it is noteworthy that all states have received at least one award in recent years. He implies this may reflect early SBIR awards, which were heavily concentrated amongst states with many high tech firms. In this sense the Committee impact could be negative because the "best" firms do not necessarily obtain the awards, which are given to less good firms in more favoured geographical areas.

Overall, Step 5 evaluations risk suffering from both self-selection and Committee-selection bias. The expected overall effect of this is to over-estimate the impact of programmes by underestimating how the "treatment" group would have performed in the absence of the treatment. This occurs because

---

[18] OECD (1997) p. 101 reports that 4500 business plans were evaluated and 1000 were approved. In practice this may deflate the approval rate since decisions on the some of the applicants were still pending.

the controls/matches are an imperfect proxy for the treatment group because of both sample selection and committee-selection.

(iii) Step 6 Evaluations:

Step 6 evaluations seek to overcome these limitations. Several address the issue of self-selection, but none, to this author's knowledge, fully address Committee selection.

Analytically we can consider that our task as evaluators is to assess the impact of policy (I). However, observed impact may be considered to comprise both Selection (S) and Actual impact (A). Selection (S) comprises both Self-Selection (SS) and Committee-Selection (CS). Stage 5 evaluations measure I rather than A whereas Stage 6 evaluations seek to quantify S in both its forms (SS and CS).

This section provides four examples of Step 6 evaluations. The first are more advanced analyses of both the SBIR and Law 44 programmes discussed in the above section. The third is an assessment of the UK Enterprise Initiative (EI) (Wren and Storey, 2002). Finally, we examine grants to small businesses in Northern Ireland and the Republic of Ireland (GI) (Roper and Hewitt-Dundas, 2001; Wallsten, 2000) in his evaluation of SBIR is concerned with somewhat different issues from Lerner. Wallsten examines whether SBIR leads to additional private sector R&D expenditure, but is concerned that prior work may have encountered the problem of endogeneity. In this case, although there is clearly a correlation between firms receiving awards and R&D, this may be because firms doing more R&D win more awards. This, in principle, is therefore a selection issue. Wallsten's findings are that firms with more employees and more patents win more awards, but the grants themselves do not appear to affect employment. Taking more robust account of selection therefore questions the real impact of this $1 billion programme.

Del Monte and Scalera (2001) have also recently reviewed the impact of Law 44. They argue that it is not appropriate to examine the success of a "start up" programme by comparing the survival rates of "assisted" and "natural" firms and expecting the former to exceed the latter. This is because the objective of the programme is to encourage individuals, who otherwise would not have done so, to start a firm. This emphasises the importance of clarity in specifying the objectives of policy (Storey, 1999). The key, and surprising, empirical finding from Del Monte and Scalera (2001) is that it is the larger Law 44 firms that are the least likely to survive. This suggests policy-makers need to encourage firms, in their own interest, to reduce the scale of their grant application.

We now turn to examine two examples of Step 6 evaluations. Section 2 of this chapter described the UK Enterprise Initiative (EI) in which small firms were able to obtain subsidised access to advice from vetted external consultants. The subsidy was available for up to 15 days' assistance at a rate of 50%. Wren and Storey (2002) examine the element of the Enterprise Initiative devoted to

Marketing.[19] The programme operated between 1988 and 1994 incurring a total public subsidy of 275 million GBP.

The GI programmes reviewed by Roper and Hewitt-Dundas are currently in operation in both Northern Ireland and the Republic of Ireland. These grants are for both fixed capital and for "soft" services such as marketing or export assistance or workforce training.

Wren and Storey (2002) specifically address (self-) selection by estimating impact through a two-stage procedure originally outlined by Heckman (1979). It is able to achieve this since records are available both of all enquirers – in the geographical area studied – and all those who decided to proceed and obtain the subsidised advice. The key policy result is that participation in EI does enhance the probability of survival and growth of a sub-group of middle-sized small firms. However, the key methodological result is that a failure to take explicit account of (self-) selection bias leads to this impact being over-estimated by a factor of more than three in the longer run.[20]

Roper and Hewitt-Dundas (2001) review the impact of grants in Northern Ireland and the Republic of Ireland. They recognise the potential impact on the evaluation of Committee-Selection, if the objective of policy-makers is to target assistance towards small firms most likely to grow – the so-called "picking winners" policy. They find the selection and impact indicators to be non-significant for Republic of Ireland firms. Three conclusions are compatible with this finding: First, that a "picking winners" policy does not exist; second that, whilst it is the objective of policy, it is not being implemented. Finally, whilst such a policy might have existed, it did not influence performance. For Northern Ireland, the significant selection term implies assistance is directed towards slower growing firms, by inducing faster employment (but not sales) growth after "treatment".

To conclude therefore, there is a very strong case for Step 6 evaluations that take account of both self- and committee selection. The empirical case is that, where they have been undertaken, self-selection is generally present and failure to account for it leads to over-estimation of programme impact. Perhaps even more disconcerting is that there are no studies which explicitly take account of committee selection, yet it is this type of selection which, for certain programmes, is most likely to influence perceived outcomes. Expressed baldly, failure to take account of committee selection is likely to significantly over-estimate the impact of some programmes.

LEARNING THE LESSONS

We have seen above that Lerner is certainly correct that substantial sums of public money are devoted, throughout the world, to policies designed to assist

---

[19] Other elements were product and service quality, manufacturing and service systems, design, business planning, financial and management information systems. Marketing, however, was the most popular of the Initiatives, accounting for almost one quarter of the 114,000 projects.

[20] Taking no account of self-selection EI appeared to raise the survival rate of firms by up to 16% over an eight-year period. However, this fell to 5% when self-selection was incorporated.

small firms. It may be the case that, within the US, sophisticated policy evaluation has been rare, but this is at least partly because of that country's avowed philosophy of having "no policy" in this area. This is much less true for other parts of the world. In countries such as Canada, Sweden and the UK more evaluations are taking place, and the evaluations themselves are better, in the sense of being more sophisticated. In short, the science exists.

Given the ease and applicability of the science, two troubling issues remain. The first is why, even within the same country, some items of policy are more likely to be evaluated. The second is why best practice methods are not always implemented.

The greater frequency of evaluations of some small enterprise policy instruments/areas than others is apparent in the UK and a plausible case may be made that evaluations are only undertaken, and made public, of "successful" programmes. For example, its Loan Guarantee Scheme has been externally evaluated on four occasions since its inception in 1981 (Robson Rhodes, 1984; NERA, 1990; PEIDA, 1992; KPMG, 1999). Broadly, on all occasions it has been given "a clean bill of health". Perhaps not surprisingly, Kuusisto et al. (1999) in their Delphi study of "experts" report "the most commonly cited successful intervention" in the UK policy arena to be the Loan Guarantee Scheme.

The converse is the case for the Business Expansion Scheme (BES) and its successor the Enterprise Investment Scheme (EIS). Both of these Schemes provided tax breaks for individuals or groups of individuals purchasing equity in small enterprises. In their Delphi review, Kuusisto et al. report the view of "experts" that the least successful intervention in the SME policy area was BES. This was introduced in 1983, abolished in 1993, reintroduced as the Enterprise Investment Scheme in 1994 and continues today. Despite this "chequered history", it has only been evaluated once – by KPMG – shortly before its abolition in 1993. No external evaluation of EIS has been undertaken.

This variation in frequency of evaluation is shown in Table 7. It shows that some items of policy have never been evaluated,[21,22] whereas others, such as the LGS are periodically assessed. The items that appear never to be assessed in some cases appear to be ones where the small business community appears most exercised.[23,24]

[21] This is not to imply there have been no studies of the impact of bureaucratic burdens on SMEs. Rather, to the author's knowledge, there have been no studies of the effectiveness of these policies on SMEs. For example, an Enterprise and Deregulation Task Force existed for many years yet no external evaluation was conducted of its impact upon SMEs.

[22] It is also not to imply that there have been no "external" evaluations/assessments. For example, the Enterprise Investment Scheme has recently been "evaluated" by BDO Stoy Hayward (1999) but only to make recommendations as to improving take-up, not to evaluate whether the Scheme should exist, or what its benefits are.

[23] This appears similar to the point made by Hoy (1997). He, however, compared the topics within small business and entrepreneurship upon which academics published articles in leading journals with the stated agenda of small business owners at the White House Conference. He found that overlap of "interest" to be modest, but markedly more than a decade earlier.

[24] Surveys of small business owners in the UK, such as those by SBRT and FSB, generally indicate that "the state of demand" is their key concern. After that, depending on the state of the

Table 7. SME policy items in the UK

1. Reduction of Bureaucratic Burdens	No external evaluation
2. Tax Incentives	No external evaluation
3. Legislative Exemptions	No external evaluation
4. Late Payment legislation	No external evaluation
5. Loan Guarantee Scheme	4 external evaluations
6. Enterprise Investment/Business Expansion Scheme	1 external evaluation

Five key public policy issues therefore arise and each will be dealt with in turn:

(i)   Which items of policy are evaluated?
(ii) What factors influence whether evaluations are conducted internally or externally?
(iii) Who should conduct external evaluation?
(iv) How can evaluation be undertaken to the highest possible standards?
(v)   What should happen as a result of the evaluation?

(i) Which items of policy are evaluated?

UK experience suggests SME policy evaluation is more likely to take place where the policy will obtain a "clean bill of health" than where the outcome is less certain. This is particularly true for policies where the objectives are "fuzzy", examples of which are policies to minimise bureaucratic burdens or late payment legislation.

The simple answer to the question is that ALL items of policy, once they have been in place for a short period of time – say, three years – should automatically be subject to some form of evaluation.

(ii) What factors influence whether evaluations are conducted internally or externally?

Those evaluations undertaken by external organisations are – on balance – more likely to enter the public domain than those conducted "in-house". Almost by definition, it is difficult to know whether those items of policy above have been the subject of "internal" evaluation. Nevertheless, we do know that governments have a much greater opportunity to ensure the evaluation is favourable (if that is what is required) when it is undertaken "in-house". It was precisely this which the House of Commons Trade and Industry Select Committee (1999)

macro-economy, the issues of access to labour, access to finance and recently the growth of bureaucratic burdens are high on the list.

accused the UK government of in its "massaging" of the findings from the internal evaluation of the SMART[25] programme.

The above experience suggests that *all* items of policy should be evaluated externally, so there is no opportunity for selecting internal evaluation where there is a greater likelihood that the results will not enter the public domain if they are unpalatable.

(iii) Who should conduct external evaluations?

The central conceptual issue here is that of "regulatory capture", initially articulated by Stigler (1971). The key values of the external assessment are that the results are more likely to enter the public domain where the analysis is prepared by an independent organisation, likely to take a dispassionate and objective view. It is appropriate here to repeat the point made by Kuusisto et al. (1999) that, on balance, official external evaluations have been more favourable than those evaluations that were undertaken independently.

The problem of regulatory capture is that even an "independent" or external organisation that undertakes considerable work for government risks being "captured". Such organisations may be influenced to be "reasonable" by the risk of losing the goodwill of an important client, with the clear implication of not obtaining future work. This is most likely to influence the behaviour of private commercial organisations – and particularly small ones that are seeking to develop a reputation in the market. It is less likely for academic organisations to be less driven by the need for "repeat" business. Nevertheless, even this distinction between private consultancies and academic organisations is becoming increasingly blurred, so some risk of "capture" is present, irrespective of the type of organisation undertaking the evaluation.

"Capture" takes two forms. The first is that the bureaucrat whose programme is being evaluated, and whose Department is financing the evaluation, exercises a strong influence upon those organisations invited to tender, and ultimately upon the chosen evaluator. In this situation there is a powerful incentive to employ a "tame" evaluator. The second form of "capture" is to seek to influence the outcome of the evaluation during its progress.

There is, however, a key dilemma in this area. It is that evaluators build up expertise by working in a particular subject area, so that working on several evaluations, for example of SME policy, is likely to enhance the skills of the evaluator. This advantage has to be set against the increasing risk of "capture".

---

[25] Small Firms Merit Award Scheme for Research and Technology. This is modelled on the United States SBIR Program and was introduced in 1986. No official external evaluation has been funded. The Select Committee said: "We have no grounds for serious criticism of the SMART programme; far from it. ... We do however have grounds for complaint at the apparently scant regard the department pays to its evaluation of its own schemes and the use of evidently selective and unattributed evidence to inform Parliament through the Annual Department Report of the proven outcome of schemes."

There is no simple solution to this problem. The introduction of "quotas" for consultants would clearly be both unwieldy and lose the benefit of learning on the part of the evaluator. However if evaluation were to be "built in" to policy, as will be recommended in the next two sections, then responsibility for the letting of external contracts should move to a specialist part of government, unrelated to the Department responsible for that programme. Ideally, that should be in the Finance or Audit departments that would obtain the funding from central earmarked sources.

(iii) How can evaluation be undertaken to the highest possible standards?

Given the findings of the paper the following constitute characteristics of good practice:

- Objectives have to be clearly specified in the legislation and "converted" into targets that make it clear when the legislation is deemed to be a success and when it is deemed to have failed.
- A budget for evaluation is set aside in the legislation to conduct the evaluation, together with a statement on the methodology to be used to conduct the evaluation. This has to be prepared by the Ministry of Finance (see below) who would be consulted on the extent to which the "targets" in the legislation were amenable to evaluation. It may be necessary to begin the monitoring for estimating the impact of the legislation prior to the legislation being implemented.
- All items of policy, once they have been in place for about three years, should automatically be subject to evaluation.
- All policy items should be evaluated externally approximately every six years.
- All external evaluations are to be managed by an independent Audit Office, reporting to the Ministry of Finance, but conducted by non-governmental organisations.[26]
- The (anonymised) data collected in the evaluations to be made available to bona fide researchers.
- The methodology for the evaluations will vary but it is to be expected that it will be conducted over a significant period of time – say, five years – and begin, ideally, before the legislation is implemented. It would be expected to combine both leading edge quantitative (statistical) as well as qualitative approaches.
- Copies of all evaluations would automatically be published and be distributed to politicians of all parties and the media.

(iv) What should happen as the result of evaluation?

The key theme of the above recommendations is that evaluation is *not* "the end of the line". Instead it has to become better integrated into the process of

---

[26]In the United States the General Accounting Office (GAO) is probably the nearest example.

policy making, rather than being grudgingly conducted to find out, many years after the policy was implemented, whether or not it worked. Using evaluation as an "end of the line" tool risks it being seen as a threat to all those engaged in the policy process – those designing legislation and those implementing programmes.

The task of those promoting evaluation is to move from evaluation being seen as a threat, to engaging the support of all personnel implementing programmes. Their support is crucial since successful evaluation requires good data being collected by staff implementing programmes. The problem is that such staff – perhaps understandably – regard their prime responsibility as delivering a service to their clients rather than "filling in forms". Given they are not pre-disposed to help, if they view the data collected as being used to undermine the programme, it makes them much more reluctant to collaborate.

The key point therefore is that evaluation should not be "the end of the line", but part of the process by which programmes and policies are modified and improved in the light of experience. Achieving this requires changes in the behaviour of several groups. The first are the legislators. They need to be made aware that new legislation on programmes will be assessed, and that the specification of clear objectives and targets is central to that assessment. Programmes need clear criteria for assessing whether they are judged successful or unsuccessful and it is the responsibility of the legislators to ensure that clarity is present. The legislators also have a responsibility for ensuring there is an appropriate budget and an agreed approach to conducting the evaluation.

Once enshrined in legislation, this sends a powerful signal to those managing and implementing programmes that evaluation is taken seriously. It emphasises that collecting information on customers/clients it not "clerical box-ticking", but rather a vital ingredient to ensure programme improvement.

However, it is after the evaluation is completed that the real change is needed. Too frequently the evaluation is either "parked" or is the subject of acrimonious debate between the evaluators and the sponsoring/managing organisation. Neither outcome is desirable, yet frequently occur when the sponsoring/managing organisation feels it has had the evaluation imposed upon it. This emphasises the need, yet again, for the evaluation to be part of the programme when is begins and not viewed as an add-on.

Where evaluations are successful, in the sense of changing policy, is where the objectives of programmes become revised in the light of the evaluation evidence. For example, programmes may have several objectives/targets and the evaluation may show that some targets are clearly met, whereas others are not. The evaluation provides the unique opportunity for a dialogue about objectives and targets between the sponsoring and the managing departments. Failure to meet some targets may, in the light of experience, be viewed as of little importance, whereas the achievement of others may imply that it has been set too low.

In short, the evaluation provides the basis for a dialogue between the sponsoring and management organisation, which is intended to lead to the setting of more appropriate targets for the future. Far from being the "end of the line", the evaluation provides the basis for setting future objectives and targets for policy. In other cases, of course, because of changed circumstances or because programmes are poorly managed, their closure could be recommended, but this happens relatively infrequently.

CONCLUSIONS

This paper has reviewed the rationale for public policy in support of SMEs in developed countries. It begins with the assumption that public policy is justified by evidence of market failure and that the test of success is whether the intervention is beneficial to the economy.

The two most frequently cited reflections of market failure are information imperfections and the presence of externalities or spillovers. Programmes for subsidised training, education, information provision and finance are justified on the grounds that small, and particularly new or nascent firms, are poorly informed consumers of advisory services. This leads to such services being under-used, leading to the subsequent under-performance of the ventures. The case for public subsidy is further strengthened by the existence of positive externalities – such as enhanced job creation and competitiveness – associated with enhanced performance. This chapter, however, has pointed out that justifying public programmes on the grounds of information imperfections infers subsidies should only be "once-off", so as to encourage learning. In contrast, justifying public programmes on the grounds of spillovers implies a more continuing public commitment.

Within developed countries there is a wide range of philosophical approaches in public policy towards small business and Entrepreneurship. At one end of the spectrum is the United States, which views small business policy as almost synonymous with competition and the interests of the consumer – although, in practice, having major programmes such as SBIR in place. There is a clear contrast with EU countries, historically motivated by a desire for job creation, which seem to have an almost bewildering range of small firm support programmes.

This chapter has reviewed these programmes and concludes that there is a striking absence of clear objectives and targets in the legislation. This makes the conduct of evaluation extremely difficult. Despite these problems, the chapter reviews SME programmes in four countries – USA, UK/Ireland, Canada and Italy – and the techniques used by academic researchers to estimate impact. All the evaluations are examples of good practice, but the level of sophistication does vary sharply. The central task for the researcher is to adequately compare the performance of the firms that participate in public programmes with a relevant group of firms that do not participate, so being legitimately able to attribute the difference in the performance of the two groups to programme participation. Whilst identification of the participants [the treatment group] is not always easy, in most instances this is handled satisfactorily by researchers. Unfortunately, the non-treatment group, in most studies, is frequently inadequately derived. Too few studies take account of the selection bias endemic in such groups, so placing a major question mark over such research. In terms of the classification provided in this chapter, only evaluations that reach Step VI should be viewed as reliable. This is the challenge for researchers and journal editors!

The audience for this study is not only the research community, but also those formulating and implementing public programmes for SMEs. The chapter concludes by making eight recommendations for this audience. These range from the clear specification of Targets and Objectives to the procedures to be used for evaluating policy. It emphasises that evaluation is not "the end of the line" in the policy-making process. Instead evaluation needs to be built-in to policy making when legislation is being formulated and it needs to engage all those involved in delivering public policies to small enterprises. Once conducted, evaluations are the ideal vehicle for re-assessing the objectives and targets of small firm policies in the light of evidence, making them more strongly focused on the market failure they are designed to overcome. There is the suggestion that public programmes to assist SMEs are subject to "regulatory capture" in the sense that they focus more heavily upon the interests of politicians and bureaucrats, than upon the small firms they are intended to assist. The task of those responsible for such programmes is to be transparent in formulating objectives and in facilitating studies that accurately assess whether such objectives have been met.

Overall the key message is that, throughout developed economies, there are a wide range of publicly funded programmes to assist small firms. Whilst the espoused philosophy underpinning these programmes varies, the presence of presumed market failure is a common theme. This review concludes that a combination of a reluctance of bureaucrats to submit their programmes to careful scrutiny, and the application of much weak science where this has taken place, means this continues to be a very fruitful area for research. It is this author's hope that this opportunity will be exploited in the coming years.

References

Acs, Z. and D. Audretsch (1988). Innovation in large and small firms. *American Economic Review,* **78**, 678–690.

Acs, Z., B. Carlsson and C. Karlsson (1999). *Entrepreneurship, Small and Medium Enterprises and the Macro-economy.* Cambridge University Press, London.

Audretsch, D.B. (2002). The dynamic role of small firms: Evidence from the US. *Small Business Economics,* **18**, 13–40.

Barlow, D. and M.T. Robson (1999). Have unincorporated businesses in the UK been constrained in their ability to obtain bank lending? Paper presented at "Funding Gaps Controversies" Conference, University of Warwick, UK, 12–13 April.

BDO Stoy Hayward (1999). *The Enterprise Investment Scheme: Why Investors and Companies do not use the Scheme.* Confederation of British Industry, London.

Belfield, C.R. (1999). The behaviour of graduates in the SME labour market: Evidence and perception. *Small Business Economics,* 12(3), 249–259.

Bennett, R. and P. Robson (1999). Intensity of interaction in supply of business advice and client impact: A comparison of consultancy, business associations and government support initiatives for SMEs. ESRC Centre for Business Research, WP.142, University of Cambridge.

Bester, H. (1985). Screening versus rationing in credit markets with imperfect information. *American Economic Review,* 75, 850–855.

Birch, D.L. (1979). *The Job Generation Process.* MIT Program on Neighborhood and Regional Change.

Bolton, J.E. (1971). *Small Firms: Report of the Committee of Inquiry on Small Firms.* Cmnd 4811. London: HMSO.

Boter, H., D. Hjalmarsson and A. Lundstrom (1999). *Outline of a Contemporary Small Business Policy.* Swedish Foundation for Small Business Research, FSF, Stockholm.

Bruderl, J., P. Preisendorfer and R. Ziegler (1992). Survival chances of newly founded business organisations. *American Sociological Review,* 57, April, 227–242.

Burrows, R. (ed.) (1991). *Deciphering the Enterprise Culture.* London: Routledge.

Chrisman, J.J. (1995). The small business development center program in the USA: A statistical analysis of its impact on economic development. *Entrepreneurship and Regional Development,* 7, 143–155.

Chrisman, J.J. and F. Katrishen (1994). The economic impact of small business development center counselling activities in the United States: 1990–91. *Journal of Business Venturing,* 9, 271–280.

Chrisman, J.J. and W.E. McMullan (1996). Static economic theory, empirical evidence and the evaluation of small business assistance programme: A reply to Wood. *Journal of Small Business Management,* 34(2), 56–66.

Chrisman, J.J., R.R. Nelson, F. Hoy and R.B. Robinson Jr. (1985). The impact of SBDC consulting activities. *Journal of Small Business Management,* 23(3), 1–11.

Cowling, M. and D.J. Storey (1998). *Job Quality in SMEs.* European Foundation for the Improvement of Living and Working Conditions, Dublin.

Cressy, R. and D.J. Storey (1996). *New Firms and their Banks.* National Westminster Bank, London.

Curran, J., R. Berney and J. Kuusisto (1999). *A Critical Evaluation of Industry SME Support Policies in the United Kingdom and the Republic of Ireland – Introduction to SME Support Policies and their Evaluation.* Ministry of Trade and Industry, Finland, Studies and Reports 5/1999.

De Meza, D. (1999). SME Policy in Europe. In D.L. Sexton and H. Landstrom (eds.), *Handbook of Entrepreneurship.* Oxford, UK: Blackwells, pp. 87–106.

De Meza, D. (2002). Overlending?. *Economic Journal,* 112(477), F17–F31.

De Meza, D. and C. Southey (1996). The borrowers curse: Optimism, finance and entrepreneurship. *Economic Journal,* 106, 375–386.

De Meza, D. and D.C. Webb (1987). Too much investment: A problem of asymmetric information. *Quarterly Journal of Economics,* 102, 281–292.

Del Monte, A. and D. Scalera (2001). The life-duration of small firms born within a start-up programme: Evidence from Italy. *Regional Studies,* 35(1), 11–21.

Dennis, W. (1999). Research mimicking policy: Entrepreneurship/small business policy in the United States. In D.L. Sexton and H. Landstrom (eds.), *Handbook of Entrepreneurship.* Oxford, UK: Blackwells, pp. 64–82.

Department of Trade and Industry (1994). *Science Parks and the Growth of High Technology Firms.* London: HMSO.

Department of Trade and Industry (1998). *Our Competitive Future: Building the Knowledge Driven Economy.* London: HMSO.

ENSR (1997). *The European Observatory for SMEs.* Fifth Annual Report, EIM, Zoetermeer, Netherlands.

Heckman, J.J. (1979). Sample selection bias as a specification error. *Econometrica,* 47, 153–161.

House of Commons Trade and Industry Committee (1998). *Small and Medium Sized Enterprises*, 6th Report. London: HMSO.

House of Commons Trade and Industry Committee (1999). *Small Business and Enterprise*, 13th Report. London: HMSO.

Hoy, F. (1997). Relevance in entrepreneurship research. In D.L. Sexton and R.W. Smilor (eds.), *Entrepreneurship 2000*. Chicago: Upstart Publishing Company, pp. 361–376.

Klette, T.J., J. Moen and Z. Grilliches (2000). Do subsidies to commercial R&D reduce market failure? Microeconometric evaluation studies. *Research Policy*, 29(4–5), 471–495.

KPMG (1999). *An Evaluation of the Small Firms Loan Guarantee Scheme*. London: Department of Trade and Industry.

Kuusisto, J., R. Berney and R. Blackburn (1999). *A Critical Evaluation of SME Support Policies in the United Kingdom and the Republic of Ireland – an In Depth Delphi Study of Selected SME Support Policies and their Evaluation*. Ministry of Trade and Industry, Finland, Studies and Reports 6/1999.

Lerner, J. (1999). The government as venture capitalist: The long-run impact of the SBIR program. *Journal of Business*, 72(3), 285–318.

Llisteri, J.J. (1997). Credit guarantee schemes: Preliminary conclusions. *Financier*, 4, 95–112.

Lundstrom, A. and L. Stevenson (2001). *Entrepreneurship Policy for the Future*. Stockholm: Elanders Gotab.

Maggioni, V., M. Sorrentino and M. Williams (1999). Mixed consequences of government aid in the new venture process: Evidence from Italy. *Journal of Management and Governance*.

Mason, C.M. and R.T. Harrison (2000). Venture capital: Rationale, aims and scope. *Venture Capital*, 1(1), 1–47.

Ministry of Economic Affairs (2000). *The Entrepreneurial Society: More Opportunities and Fewer Obstacles for Entrepreneurship*. The Hague, Holland.

National Economic Research Associates (1990). *An Evaluation of the Loan Guarantee Scheme*. Department of Employment, Research Paper No. 74.

National Federation of Independent Businesses (2001). *Small Business Policy Guide*. Washington DC.

NUTEK (1998). *Europartinariat Northern Scandinavia 1996: Effects and Experience*. Swedish National Board for Industrial and Technical Development, Stockholm.

OECD (1996). *Best Practice Policies for Small and Medium Sized Enterprises*. Paris.

OECD (1997). *Best Practice Policies for Small and Medium Sized Enterprises*. Paris.

OECD (1998). *Best Practice Policies for Small and Medium Sized Enterprises*. Paris.

OECD (2000). *OECD Small and Medium Enterprise Outlook*. Paris.

PEIDA (1992). *Evaluation of the Loan Guarantee Scheme*. London: Department of Employment.

Riding, A.L. and G. Haines Jr. (2001). Loan guarantees: Costs of default and benefits to small firms. *Journal of Business Venturing*, 16(6), November, 595–612.

Robson R. (1984). *A Study of Small Businesses Financed under the Loan Guarantee Scheme*. London: Department of Trade and Industry.

Roper, S. and N. Hewitt-Dundas (2001). Grant assistance and small firm development in Northern Ireland and the Republic of Ireland. *Scottish Journal of Political Economy*, 48(1), February, 99–117.

Rowley, C. and A. Peacock (1974). *Welfare Economics: A Liberal Restatement*. Oxford, UK: Martin Robertson.

Stigler, G.J. (1971). The economic theory of regulation. *Bell Journal of Economics*, 2, 3–21.

Stiglitz, J.E. and A. Weiss (1981). Credit rationing in markets with imperfect information. *American Economic Review*, 73, 393–409.

Storey. D.J. (1994). *Understanding the Small Business Sector*. London: Routledge/ITP.

Storey, D.J. (1999). Six steps to heaven: Evaluating the impact of public policies to support small businesses in developed economies. In D.L. Sexton and H. Landstrom (eds.), *Handbook of Entrepreneurship*. Oxford, UK: Blackwells, pp. 176–194.

Thomas, T. and B. Landry (2001). Evaluating Policy Outcomes in Federal Economic Development Programs in Atlantic Canada. ACOA, New Brunswick.

United Nations (2000). *Best Practice in Business Incubation*. Geneva: UN/ECE.

Wallsten, S.J. (2000). The effects of government-industry R&D programs on private R&D: The case of the Small Business Innovation Program. *RAND Journal of Economics*, **31**(1), Spring, 82–100.

Westhead, P. (1997). *Students in Small Business: An Assessment of the 1994 STEP Student Placement Scheme*. Small Business Research Trust, Milton Keynes, UK.

Wren, C. and D.J. Storey (2002). Evaluating the effect of "soft" business support upon small firm performance. *Oxford Economic Papers*, **54**, 334–365.

PART EIGHT

Epilogue

RITA GUNTHER McGRATH

Colombia University Graduate School of Business

19.   Connecting the Study of Entrepreneurship and Theories of Capitalist Progress

An Epilogue

INTRODUCTION

In the beginning was the corporation. Or so it seems, as Acs and Audretsch have pointed out in the Editors' Introduction to this Handbook. However, the "modern industrial corporation" is a relatively recent invention in historical terms. Chandler (1990) dates its emergence to the last half of the nineteenth century, when advances in transportation and communications both enabled and demanded the formation of large corporations managed by professionals. Such corporations came to represent the engines of national economic growth and of individual wealth creation in countries whose very membership in the group of industrialized nations speaks to the success of this organizational form (Acs and Audretsch, Introduction, this volume; Baumol, 2002).

Prior to the rise of the large multi-national corporation (MNC), owner-managed firms were taken utterly for granted as the *primary* vehicle through which business was conducted. Founders started companies. If things went well, these firms grew, under the direct management of owner-entrepreneurs. The class of professional managers was extremely small. It is a testament to the success of the large industrial firm and the institutions that developed as it did that business founding came to be seen as exceptional rather than the rule by the latter half of the twentieth century, at least in developed economies. Interestingly, we seem to have now come full circle, with new firms as a major research focus and an interest in innovation more broadly attracting both scholarly and practitioner attention.

As this handbook comes to a close, it is worthwhile to reflect on the core contributions entrepreneurship research might make. Researchers and practitioners seem to have taken for granted that entrepreneurial firms play a starring role in the process of economic growth and technological change. Recent research, however, suggests that the key drivers are in fact larger collectivities – collections of firms in regions, for instance, or global oligopolies (Baumol, 2002; Schoonhoven and Romanelli, 2001). New firms certainly have a role to play, but when one thinks about it, it is the larger firm or industry collective

Z.J. Acs and D.B. Audretsch (eds.), Handbook of Entrepreneurship Research, 515–531
© 2003 *Kluwer Academic Publishers. Printed in Great Britain.*

that facilitates a new firm's impact. Most founders of new firms come from older ones. Most customers of new firms are established ones (or consumers). Most technologies used by new firms are derived from knowledge created by established ones. Even Microsoft would not have succeeded in establishing so dominant a position in personal computer operating systems had the company not built on IBM's credibility. This leads to the question of what we can expect from entrepreneurship research as a distinct point of departure for future scholars.

This epilogue does not purport to synthesize all the fascinating future questions that the 19 chapters in the handbook have raised. Rather, I would like to use this opportunity to focus readers' attention on a role for entrepreneurship research that has not been reflected in the other essays. I believe that entrepreneurship scholars are well positioned to consider big questions with respect to the future of capitalist economies, even though these may lie outside its normal "small young firm" focus. It is worthwhile to raise our sights and take advantage of the creative possibilities of a nascent "field" without a particular doctrine to our advantage.

Large organizations almost certainly will continue to represent a disproportionately influential source of economic growth (Harrison, 1994a; Harrison, 1994b; Baumol, 2002). They also almost certainly will be subject to frequent, unpredictable, challenges. A possible advantage scholars studying entrepreneurial phenomena have is that they have traditionally been more interested in change, disruption and novelty than in the status quo. A second possible advantage such scholars have is that the research methodologies and points of reference among those working in the area have been diverse (although some might say diverse to the point of incoherence). In this diversity lies opportunity. As the chapters in this book make clear, entrepreneurship scholars have grappled with issues of researching outliers rather than central tendencies, of problems arising when the phenomenon of interest is the exception rather than the rule and of studying phenomena that defy aggregation (MacMillan and Katz, 1992).

Building on this history might allow the entrepreneurship community to make a contribution to a dialogue on the nature of capitalist systems that is gaining in urgency. At the center of this dialogue is a paradox. The innovative investments of large organizations are recognized as critical to economic growth and development. Yet, the disruptive effects of innovative investments are a de-stabilizing force. Thus, on the one hand large firms and the institutions surrounding them are the main drivers of capitalist economic development, while on the other hand they are its most visible victims.

Entrepreneurship as an Engine of Change in Capitalist Economies

Without taking sides in the vibrant "what is entrepreneurship" debate, I believe that the study of entrepreneurship is interesting to a broad scholarly community because it has fundamentally to do with the study of mechanisms of economic change. Entrepreneurship scholars are always concerned with how old ways of doing things disappear and new ways come into being, and with the actors, technologies and organizations influencing and influenced by these changes (Venkataraman, 1997; Shane and Venkataraman, 2000; Schoonhoven and Romanelli, 2001). In capitalist systems, to study entrepreneurship is to study its fundamental workings, a point emphasized by Schumpeter (1942) many years ago. The study of entrepreneurship is fundamentally about the process of economic change.

In this essay, I suggest three issues that are illustrative of topics that would constitute substantive research opportunities for those interested in change in capitalist economies. The first concerns investment incentives for innovation. The second concerns the 'destruction' aspects of Schumpeter's "creative destruction" formulation. The related third issue involves the legitimacy of capitalist competition and the dark sides of entrepreneurial progress.

INCENTIVES TO INVEST IN INNOVATION

A taken for granted assumption in the entrepreneurship literature is that the structure of payoffs (to use Baumol's 1993 term) to innovative activity influences both its prevalence and its direction. Business founders are guided by the profit motive, because they have the chance to take advantage of an opportunity not obvious to others. Others who invest in businesses, similarly, are guided by the profit motive, and will tend to invest where they anticipate earning the greatest returns. Risk, in the sense of variability of returns, influences the return on investment that would be considered adequate. Understanding how investors perceive the attractiveness of investments in innovation is critical for the effective functioning of capitalist economies, because if investors perceive no returns for investing in innovation, presumably they will not bother to fund it.

The formulae most popularly used in the field of finance to allocate capital, however, take little account of innovation, entrepreneurship, or idiosyncratic firm behavior (Bettis, 1983). Instead, standard formulations in finance suggest that capital should be allocated on the basis of systemic, not unsystemic (firm-specific) risk profiles. The resulting paradox is this: Although many (Foster, 1986; Baumol, 2002) argue that large corporations compete on the basis of their ability to innovate, entrepreneurial activities are not central to standard methods for calculating investment attractiveness. Indeed, conventional tools have been linked with under-investment in innovation (Kester, 1981). The pressing question is thus how should the incentive to innovate be reflected in the tools used to allocate capital? The opportunity seems ripe to consider this question.

Risk and Option Value: Investing in "Long Shots"

In the field of strategy, Chatterjee, Lubatkin and Schulze (1999) have proposed a "post-CAPM" world, in which unsystematic (or firm-specific) risk is taken into account in capital asset allocation. They argue that many attributes of a firm have an option-like component to them which would yield a better understanding of a firm's true risk profile than a conventional assessment, and which would re-introduce a role for strategy and management into the calculation of financial incentives. For new firms, the proportion of its value that is amenable to present value analysis is relatively small, relative to the proportion represented by its option potential.

Treating organizational assets as options is an approach that has come to be called "real options reasoning" (Bowman and Hurry, 1993; Dixit and Pindyck, 1994). Real options represent a preferential right to select a course of action at some point in the future, ideally when more information is available. This right is created by choices regarding investments today. Investments in R&D, for instance, are often characterized as real options because they convey the right, but not the obligation, for a firm to commercialize any resulting discovery (Dixit and Pindyck, 1994; McGrath, 1997; McGrath and Nerkar, 2001).

The value of a real option depends on an asymmetry between potential gains and losses. The larger the upside opportunity and the more any downside losses can be contained, the more valuable a real option becomes. One interesting implication is that investors in real options should be more concerned with the magnitude of possible losses than with their frequency. Ventures, it has been argued, can thus be considered real options, providing that exit is a possibility. They will be more promising to the extent that their downside exposure is contained, and their upside opportunity is substantial (McGrath, 1996).

Options logic does appear to fit observed investment behavior in new ventures. Failure rates in ventures are high, and the potential for success (on average) is small. The President's Report on the State of Small Business (1997) indicates that six hundred thousand businesses are started annually in the United States. Of these, few grow substantially. Aldrich (1999, pp. 108–109), for example, notes that throughout the 1980s, only 3,186 firms went public in the United States. Of this high-potential population, only 58 percent were still listed on any exchange as of the end of 1989 (see Welbourne and Andrews, 1996). Yet, there seem to be large numbers of investors willing to take a chance on such a "long shot." For instance, the venture capital industry raised $130 billion between the third quarter of 1999 and the end of 2000 (Norton, 2001, citing data provided by Venture Economics and the National Venture Capital Association).

Implicit in the investment logic for new ventures is a contrarian perspective on mean-enhancing versus variance-enhancing activities. The options-oriented investor is most interested in those factors that extend the right-hand tail of the potential performance distribution. They might well prefer an investment in a high-variance (risky) venture, other things being equal, because it has the potential to dominate low-variance ventures (a point made by March, 1991; see also Morris, Teisberg and Kolbe, 1991). Further, an options perspective is consistent with the boom-and-bust cycle of internet investment, suggesting that many investors took out options on the potential for growth of Internet firms, but allowed these options to expire when the potential appeared to be less than anticipated.

One implication of using an options lens to inform valuation is that the whole concept of success and failure in venturing may need to be revisited. As I have argued elsewhere (McGrath, 1999), research tends to have a pro-success preoccupation, with the result that insight into failure's influences on economic value is lost. If failures can be discarded at low cost, the net effect may be to increase value because greater variety can be created for the same level of investment than if every new initiative had to be followed through to completion. Similarly, low-cost failures facilitate discovery processes by highlighting dead ends and closing off unpromising alternatives.

What Can Entrepreneurship Offer to a Better Theory of the Structure of Incentives for Investment in Innovation?

This discussion has centered on a paradox. Although investments in innovation are seen as crucial to both firm-level success and the growth of the economy overall, innovation considerations are not central to the most widely-used capital allocation methods. Instead, investors seem to use a logic that more closely resembles investment in options, where the primary incentive is a substantial upside. What contribution can an entrepreneurial perspective make to this issue? I suggest three.

The first involves the perception of incentives. If the allocation of entrepreneurial talent in a society reflects the structure of payoffs, how are the incentives perceived? The opportunity for entrepreneurship scholars is to use their insight into individual and collective cognitive processes to ascertain how these payoff structures are actually perceived and to what extent these perceptions translate into individual and collective behaviors. For instance, Pindyck (1982) identified several ways in which managerial behavior departs from the expectations of conventional theory, suggesting that managers intuit the value due to options and behave accordingly. Understanding how payoff structures are cognitively represented might even lead to better financial theory. Indeed, there is considerable excitement in the fields of finance and economics today as scholars in a new behavioral finance stream of work begin to explore the implications of human psychology for how economic systems work in practice (see Thaler, 1992 for one of the seminal initial pieces in this research tradition). This is a possible point of intersection with entrepreneurship research.

Ideally, research would inform investment theory as well as those aspects of the payoff structure that are amenable to policy influence. A nice exemplar of the kinds of insight entrepreneurship research can provide is Busenitz and Barney's (1997) study of differences in risk perception between company founders and managerial employees, in which they learned that the two groups have systematically different heuristics for considering risky situations. At a more macro-level, Kortum and Lerner's (1999) study suggests how a policy-level shift (a change in regulations allowing pension funds to invest in venture firms) translated into increases in funds available for investment and productive patenting, thus changing the structure of payoffs to investors in pension funds and thereby changing their behavior.

A second opportunity for entrepreneurship scholars is to develop a construct that anticipates the value created by investments in innovation. A point of departure might be Rumelt's concept of "entrepreneurial rents." Rumelt (1987) distinguishes among the classic concept of rents, representing a firm's ability to take advantage of a scarce resource it possesses (such as proprietary access to raw materials), and entrepreneurial rents, which result from the discovery of new combinations of resources that are to some extent proprietary to their discoverers. He defines entrepreneurial rent as follows:

> "... the difference between a venture's *ex post* value (or payment stream) and the *ex ante* cost (or value) of the resources combined to form the venture. If we posit expectational equilibrium (*ex ante* cost equals expected *ex post* value) then expected entrepreneurial rents are zero. The basic thrust of this definition is to identify those elements of profit that are the result of *ex ante* uncertainty" (p. 143).

One of the most useful aspects of Rumelt's argument is that he goes on to specify a parsimonious set of three necessary preconditions for the presence of entrepreneurial rents. The first is that an innovation must be a "socially efficient" replacement for an existing combination of resources. The second is that the innovator must be able to avoid having its rents appropriated (for instance, by powerful suppliers). The third is that the innovation must be able to take advantage of isolating mechanisms which deter rapid competitive imitation or matching. Rumelt's formulation is admirable for its parsimony and thus lends itself to operationalization.

A third investment-relevant topic for entrepreneurship scholars concerns spillovers. Spillovers, broadly defined, consist of benefits to third parties from a firm's investments in innovation that are not realized by the party making the investment. Because the originating firm is not compensated, the conventional argument is that firms should seek to avoid spillovers, and that policies (such as patenting and trademark legislation) should be put in place to guarantee property rights for the outcome of investments in innovation. This conventional view is being challenged.

For one thing, in increasingly information-intensive environments, preventing spillovers is extremely difficult (Boisot, 1995). For another, there are many occasions when spillovers are beneficial to firms (McGrath and McGrath, 2001; Baumol, 2002; Saxenian, 1994). The difficulty is that conventional theory still does make a valid point: Absent a clear mechanism to capture a portion of the benefit from investments in innovation, entrepreneurs and firms are unlikely to invest in it.

The question comes down to better understanding when one should hoard information and when one should share it. Entrepreneurship scholars have a good opportunity to define such improved boundary conditions for the theory of spillovers by pursuing a traditional strength of scholars working in the area – namely an individual and firm-level focus on activities over time and in context (for instance, Gatewood, Shaver and Gartner, 1995). Two areas in which the spillover issue is central are in the literature on regional development (see Acs, de Groot and Nijkamp, 2002; Schoonhoven and Romanelli, 2001) and a small, but growing literature on the nature of Schumpeterian change (for instance, Tripsas, 1997).

WHATEVER HAPPENED TO THE DESTRUCTION IN "CREATIVE DESTRUCTION"?

Schumpeter's famous phrase "gales of creative destruction" certainly captures the imagination (Schumpter, 1942). The scholarly community, however, has been so fascinated with the "creative" part of the Schumpeterian formulation that we give relatively little emphasis to the "destruction" part. This is a huge oversight. Until we understand how old combinations of factors of production are dis-assembled, we cannot understand the process of creating and implementing new combinations of factors of production.

Baumol (2002) proposes that innovation has become a life-or-death matter for established corporations in free-market economies. Other scholars have observed that when a firm's assets consist not of physical things, but of information and individual skills and knowledge, swift change in their constitution is not only possible, but far more likely (Boisot, 1995). The result would seem to be short organizational life-cycles and a greater prevalence of discontinuation, or at least of volatility in performance for large organizations. The destruction aspect of Schumpeter's concept is thus increasingly with us.

The normative literature seems to offer corroborating evidence. In the first few years of the 2000s, bear market conditions revealed immense vulnerability for even well-established organizations. Charan and Useem reported that 257 public companies with $258 billion in assets declared bankruptcy in 2001 alone, while 26 of America's largest corporations lost over two-thirds of their market value, including such premier names as Hewlett-Packard and Charles Schwab. A similar pattern could be seen in Europe, in which well-regarded leading firms such as Ericsson, Nokia and ABB wrestled with collapsing share prices. Even in Japan, large firm bankruptcies were becoming more common (Porter, Takeuchi and Sakakibara, 2001).

Firms seem caught between increasingly difficult competitive circumstances and increasingly elevated shareholder expectations. Hamel (2000) reports that in 1999 31% of S&P 500 outperformed the average, while 58% did so in 1992. Repercussions include increased churn among executive ranks. A recent study concluded that nearly half of the CEOs of the world's very largest companies have been in office three years or less (Drake, Beam and Morin, 2001). Another, which examined CEO turnover from 1995 to 2001, reported that turnover of CEOs increased by 53 percent, while average tenure declined from 9.5 years to 7.3 years (Lucier, Spiegel and Schuyt, 2002).

Thus, despite evidence that the period of time during which a corporation can enjoy a period of dominance is shrinking, the premise that a large corporation will be relatively enduring persists in our theorizing (see Foster and Kaplan, 2001). Arguments premised on historical scale and scope advantages for diversified firms have persisted (Goold, Campbell and Alexander, 1994; Prahalad and Hamel, 1990). It seems clear, however, that the "good corporation" of Whitman's 50's style benchmark is less and less the norm (Whitman, 1999).

Schumpeter, of course, posited such destruction as essential to capitalist progress. Because of this, he anticipated capitalist organizational structures to be inherently fragile and self-obsoleting. Witness the following passage from his *Capitalism, Socialism and Democracy* (1942):

> Since capitalist enterprise, by its very achievements, tends to automatize progress, we conclude that it tends to make itself superfluous – to break to pieces under the pressure of its own success. The perfectly bureaucratized giant industrial unit not only ousts the small or medium-sized firm and "expropriates" its owners, but in the end it also ousts the entrepreneurs and expropriates the bourgeoisie as a class which in the process stands to lose not only its income but also what is infinitely more important, its function.

To adopt Schumpeter's view of capitalist progress implies that we need to take into account the essential fragility of an organization in a capitalist system. Yet, the entrepreneurship literature by and large ignores half of his process. Instead, it has elected to focus primarily on how new combinations come into being, rather than to take a more balanced look at how old ones vanish.

This can lead to oversights in understanding. To take a regional example: Many of the technologies that later created enormous wealth in Silicon Valley were invented and commercialized in the Northeastern United States, in states such as New Jersey. Why, then, did the digital revolution create such growth in California and not on the East Coast? The taken for granted explanation is that enlightened individuals such as Stanford's Frederick Terman sparked a wave of innovation by transferring university technology to small firms, which were able to create a self-renewing network-based ecosystem (Saxenian, 1994). Silicon Valley's success has sparked a virtual cottage industry seeking to transfer university technology to startup firms (Miner, Eesley, Devaughn and Rura-Polley, 2001). Results have been decidedly mixed. In fact, Terman himself was unsuccessful in two subsequent attempts he personally undertook to re-create Silicon Valley (Leslie and Kargon, 1996).

Accepted explanations for the success of Silicon Valley thus do little to help us understand why the revolution occurred there and not elsewhere (Acs, 2000). If we look at what would have to be destroyed elsewhere for something like Silicon Valley to emerge, a much richer picture of the process can be developed.

Consider the constraining effects of resource dependence in more developed communities at the time Silicon Valley was formed (Pfeffer and Salancik, 1978). In the case of New Jersey, for instance, people and corporations were dependent on resources generated by an existing technological and economic regime. They had great jobs with bright futures, their corporations (such at AT&T and RCA) were stable and secure, and the existing economic pattern seemed powerful enough to deliver results for a long time to come.

Jim Carnes, former CEO of the Sarnoff Center (a subsidiary of SRI International which originated as the research arm of RCA, the Radio Corporation of America) captures this sense:

"We were the first high-tech state. We've had Edison, RCA Labs, Bell Labs. In the 1930's, RCA was the Microsoft of the United States. It was in Camden, Harrison, later in Princeton. It was a New Jersey company ... Let's face it. The Silicon Valley, starting in the second half of the 70's, 80's and 90's took over that cachet [of being a high tech region] based initially on the semiconductor business. ... General Electric, RCA – the large companies – had a vested interest in earlier technologies. RCA, for example, made tremendous money with vacuum tubes. RCA failed to make the appropriate kind of investments because they were protecting their previous investments. ... The guys in California didn't have any previous interest, and they took over." (interview in *Business News*, New Jersey, 2001).

It is of course a purely theoretical question to ask whether New Jersey could have become Silicon Valley were its inhabitants prepared to destroy what they had to take a chance on, a new technological regime. My point is merely to suggest that the entrepreneurship field has an opportunity to address an important, and neglected aspect of the process of change by incorporating both creation and destruction as twin parts of the entrepreneurship phenomenon.

What Can Entrepreneurship Offer to a Better Understanding of the Nature of Creative Destruction?

Entrepreneurship scholars are well placed to contribute to an understanding of the nature of creative destruction. I propose two paths forward.

First, in studying startups and growing businesses, entrepreneurship scholars have the opportunity to look, in parallel, at the businesses and activities these displace. This suggests a slight shift in emphasis: Rather than focusing on the entrepreneurial venture only, scholars would need to understand its activities in context. Exemplary work along these lines is Henderson and Clark's (1990) investigation of architectural innovation and its effects on a population of firms. Absent a careful look at the firms that were not successful, in addition to those that were, the underlying pattern of change would have been impossible to detect. At a minimum, entrepreneurship scholars should wean themselves from the temptation to select their samples on the basis of a dependent variable, such as some aspect of success, and to ignore attempts that failed in developing theories of entrepreneurial success.

Related to this first opportunity is a second, namely, to re-examine the work that has been done on organizational discontinuance, with the objective of better understanding the causes for growth and decline. Consider, for instance, the considerable work that has been done on organizational mortality in the population ecology tradition (see Baum, 1996 for an overview). This literature is admirable for its theoretical coherence and the consistency with which data are gathered on the changes in composition of organizational populations. It is typically silent, however, on the activities of different population members, on the interactions between differing populations and on the welfare outcomes for the economic areas in which population change occurs. Moreover, the way in which data are gathered for most of these studies does not allow a particularly nuanced view of organizational mortality, as they are typically captured through the presence or absence of a firm in an archival record.

An outstanding example of research that re-visited taken for granted assumptions with respect to organizational mortality is Gimeno, Folta, Cooper and Woo's (1997) study of the selection process in a sample of small businesses. In contrast to the presumption in the ecological literature that selection acts through resource deprivation to cause firms to fail, Gimeno et al. observed a different and far more subtle process. The business owners in their sample established highly individual thresholds for acceptable performance of their ventures. Performance below the threshold, even if acceptable from a purely economic point of view, triggered closure. Interestingly, performance above the threshold, even if unacceptable from a purely economic point of view, did not. Their work suggests a much larger role for entrepreneurial choice and the weighing of alternatives than is commonly depicted in the ecological literature.

The Institutional Legitimacy of Capitalism and the Dark Sides of Entrepreneurship

If one accepts that the idea that entrepreneurship is interesting because it has to do with change in capitalist economies, then it stands to reason that some changes will be for the better (for some) while other changes will be for the worse (for some). Scholars have disproportionately focused on creation of the new, presumably superior, markets and technologies rather than seeking to understand their negative consequences. Economic decline, social adjustment costs, huge income disparities, business closures, loss of community and the funneling of vast resources to people who are sometimes simply lucky can result from the entrepreneurial process.

Aghion and Howitt (1998) observe that capitalist progress does not take into account the losses from creative destruction in allocating its rewards. Innovations that make older resource combinations obsolete may well pay off for their champions. At a societal level, however, the benefit may be harder to ascertain. Baumol (2002, p. 23) illustrates the problem: "An innovation with an expected market value of $10 million will be an attractive proposition to the innovator if its expected private cost is $7 million. But it will be a net loss to society if the process also makes $8 million in older assets obsolete." Moreover, those who reap the rewards from innovation are typically not the same people who pay its price. Taking place across nations and industries, the process can generate extremes in income and appear unfair to those on the losing end.

As Stinchcombe (1997) points out, it is remarkable that the potential for massive redistribution of benefits is considered legitimate, given that much of human history has been devoted to humans seeking to thwart or avoid competition. Absent the legitimacy of competition and appropriate supporting institutional norms, market capitalism cannot work effectively. An increasingly important question is whether processes that make some firms and populations of firms obsolete will continue to be legitimate. If so, will institutional actors be able to effectively cope with the negative consequences?

We are already witnessing a backlash against the institutional rules for cross-border economic activity, and increasing concern for issues such as preservation of heterogeneous lifestyles amidst pressures for global homogenization and sensible treatment of environmental risks. If we continue to give short shrift to the dark sides of entrepreneurship, the legitimacy that makes free-market contracting work can easily be compromised.

Let us consider some of the underpinnings of a working free market economy. Stinchcombe (1997), building on the work of Commons (1950), makes the point that market contracting can only exist when parties agree on future performances. Institutions are essential to the existence of markets because they represent the working rules that define how power may be used in making and enforcing such contracts. Absent an agreed-upon system of rules, parties to transactions are unlikely to make commitments for the future, and as Commons puts it, there can be "little or no present value, present enterprise, present transactions or present employment" (p. 104) absent such rules (see also Van de Ven, 1993). The legitimacy of the working rules and of the parties subject to them is thus an essential pre-requisite to the functioning of a free market economy.

Stinchcombe further argues that markets cannot exist unless parties predict both that transaction partners are likely to be competent to act as they say they will and are morally committed to act as they say they will. In the entrepreneurship literature, this consideration has been well represented in Stinchcombe's (1965) concept of the "liability of smallness and newness" that causes parties to future transactions to question a new firm's competence and commitment to future actions.

A basic assumption about governance is also descended from Commons's concept of the working rules of capitalist organizing (Commons, 1974 [1924]). The premise of these working rules is that only the Board of Directors of a corporation can allocate the property of that corporation. In other words, although shareholders have a property interest in the corporation, they cannot simply march in and take the office copier to satisfy this interest. Enforcing such working rules in the case of a corporation with primarily physical assets is a far more straightforward affair than enforcing them when the assets are intangible. This creates a real question with respect to the legitimacy of taken for granted ways of governing corporations.

As increasing proportions of the assets of large organizations are intangible, controlling their use becomes extraordinarily problematic. Further, knowledge about their true worth is unlikely to be available to those who are at the "top" of the organization in a hierarchical sense. Most theories of corporate governance presume that the best information about what is going on in a corporation can be found at the hierarchically highest levels. In an intangible-based business, this assumption may not hold (Child and McGrath, 2001). If governance is challenged, the question of who can legitimately contract on the part of a firm becomes a crucial issue. When parties to future transactions feel that their contracting partners cannot actually control the competencies forming the basis for an agreement, agreements are unlikely. When contracting is widely seen to be illegitimate, it is apt to be slow and incomplete.

Capitalist systems are unusual in their acceptance of the dark sides of entrepreneurship. In other forms of economic organization, preventing such dark sides is deemed more worthwhile than pursuing its upsides. Citing Finley (1965), Baumol reproduces the following story (1993, p. 31):

> There is a story, repeated by a number of Roman writers, that a man – characteristically unnamed – invented unbreakable glass and demonstrated it to Tiberius in anticipation of a great reward. The emperor asked the inventor whether anyone shared his secret and was assured that there was no one else; whereupon his head was promptly removed, lest, said Tiberius, gold be reduced to the value of mud.

Without rules to drive productive entrepreneurship, an entire society can forfeit the benefits to public-good and productivity creation stemming from innovative behavior. Witness Japan's long struggle throughout the 1990s – a struggle often attributed to the lack of legitimacy and incentives for entrepreneurial activity (Porter, Takeuchi and Sakakibara, 2001).

The challenge is clear: We need to develop a better sense of how capitalist gains and losses are distributed and what kinds of institutions will be necessary to mediate this process.

What Can Entrepreneurship Offer to a Better Understanding of the Dark Sides of the Entrepreneurial Process and its Continued Legitimacy?

Entrepreneurship scholars are well-placed to offer a point of view on what the institutions of capitalism should be. Doing so, however, requires that scholars temper the tendency for unabashed enthusiasm over the entrepreneurial process. We already have some good examples for how a richer perspective might be developed.

At the individual level, Kets de Vries (Kets de Vries, 1985; Kets de Vries and Miller, 1984) has suggested that we pay too little attention to the pathological aspects of entrepreneurial personalities. Egotistical, neglectful, and dangerous to themselves and others, people who start businesses can use their talents for socially negative ends. At the worst, greed and ruthlessness can come to take over entirely. The corporate scandals of the 2001–2002 period, which saw revelations of malfeasance on a grand scale in seemingly reputable organizations, serve to reinforce the point that absent institutional controls, greedy individuals can get away with self-serving rent-seeking.

Further consistent with a more balanced view of the entrepreneur, Baumol (1993) articulated the idea that the process can be productive, unproductive, or destructive. Entrepreneurial talent is not automatically dedicated to socially desirable ends – it requires institutions to accomplish this. Baumol reminds us that entrepreneurship as we know it cannot exist without institutional legitimacy, and that the form entrepreneurial activities take is fundamentally shaped by institutional rules.

Institutional development is increasingly important not only at the level of public policy, but also within firms. If information about what is really going on is located at the line level, away from the "top" of a corporate hierarchy, then governance processes need to be developed to extend to that line level. Institutional rules need to be developed that can usefully cope with decentralized market contracting. Entrepreneurship, with its work on how young and new businesses overcome problems of moral hazard and information asymmetry might have some interesting models to offer (Cable and Shane, 1997). Entrepreneurship scholars have also spent considerable time understanding how liabilities stemming from a lack of legitimacy can be counter-acted (for instance, Venkataraman and Van de Ven, 1993; see also Aldrich, 1999).

The field of entrepreneurship would do well to pay attention to research done in other fields that looks at institutional rules that can mitigate some of these dark sides. Of particular interest is work on emerging institutions in post-communist countries (for instance, Spicer, McDermott and Kogut, 2000). This research suggests that it takes time for appropriate institutions to support and control the entrepreneurial process to emerge, and that prior to the creation of an appropriate institutional environment a society is highly vulnerable to thuggery on the part of its entrepreneurs.

The message very clearly is that if we are to grapple with issues of the institutional context for entrepreneurship, we ignore the dark sides at our peril (see Aldrich and Martinez, this volume).

New Theories and Capitalist Progress: A Role For Entrepreneurship?

In organizational scholarship, what Stinchcombe (1997, p. 6) calls "narrow" conceptions that are mathematically tractable seem to be valued more highly than what he calls detail about the "guts of the causal process." Challenges to prevalent assumptions, however, call such narrow research into question and create interesting opportunities for scholars who study entrepreneurship. In this chapter, I have identified three themes that represent opportunities for entrepreneurship scholars to weigh in with new, even provocative ideas: The nature of incentives to innovation; the process of destruction as well as creation; and the challenges to institutional legitimacy created by the dark sides of the entrepreneurial process. My hope is that these questions are sufficiently intriguing to broaden the kinds of phenomena that entrepreneurship researchers examine, while sustaining its core focus on change in capitalist economies.

Those of us working in entrepreneurship today have an advantage over the area's pioneers. By now, we have the benefit of several decades of entrepreneurship research, from the annual compilations published by Babson College to the 15 + years of focused journals such as the *Journal of Business Venturing* to several good handbooks and guides.[1] In this essay, I have tried to suggest that the field of entrepreneurship may offer a useful vantage point from which to tackle some of the more pressing issues of today's business organizations and the institutions in which they exist. The insight gained by entrepreneurship scholars through their study of often-small, fragile, new entities can, I believe, be powerfully leveraged to improve our understanding of the workings of the capitalist system. Large established firms that were presumed to be far less vulnerable to challenge can be seen to struggle with the very kinds of issue that entrepreneurship scholars have thought about for a long time.

If entrepreneurship scholars are to make such a contribution, I believe we also need to be asking different questions as part of our future research agenda. We need to seat our questions in terms of what is known and not known about processes of change, rather than trying to validate previously held assumptions. We should be looking for anomalies and weak signals that may suggest when a new set of boundary conditions or relationships is present (Christensen, Carlile and Sundahl, 2002). Throughout, building bridges with scholars looking at similar problems in other disciplines will continue to be important. Entrepreneurship, as it begins to leave its adolescence behind, has a compelling opportunity to start to make a difference in the way scholars think about economic organization.

References

Acs, Z. (ed.) (2000). *Regional Innovation, Knowledge and Global Change*. London: Pinter.

Acs, Z., H.F.L. de Groot and P. Nijkamp (2002). Knowledge, innovation and regional development. In Acs, de Groot and Nijkamp (eds.), *The Emergence of the Knowledge Economy: A Regional Perspective*, pp. 1–14. Berlin: Springer.

[1] For those just getting started, let me draw attention to several solid texts that build on this body of literature to create a context for learning what territory has already been covered and where new thinking might be welcome. In addition to this excellent volume, I would also direct readers' attention to Schoonhoven and Romanelli (2001), Bhide (2000), and for those interested in corporate entrepreneurship, Hitt, Ireland, Camp and Sexton (2002).

Aghion, P. and P. Howitt (1998). *Endogenous Growth Theory*, Cambridge, MA: The MIT Press.

Aldrich, H. (1999). *Organizations Evolving*. Thousand Oaks, CA: Sage Publications.

Baum, J.A.C. (1996). Organizational ecology. Chapter 13. In Clegg, S.R., Hardy, C., and Nord, W.R. (eds.), *Handbook of Organization Studies*, pp. 77–114. Thousand Oaks, CA: Sage Publications.

Baumol, W.J. (1993). *Entrepreneurship, Management and the Structure of Payoffs*, Cambridge, MA: MIT Press.

Baumol, W.J (2002). *The Free-Market Innovation Machine: Analyzing the Growth Miracle of Capitalism*. Princeton, NJ: Princeton University Press.

Bettis, R. (1983). Modern financial theory, corporate strategy and public policy: Three conundrums. *Academy of Management Review*, 8, 406–414.

Bhide, A. (2000). *The Origin and Evolution of New Businesses*. New York: Oxford University Press.

Boisot, M. (1995). *Information Space: A Framework for Learning in Organizations, Institutions and Culture*. New York: Routledge.

Bowman, E.H. and D. Hurry (1993). Strategy through the option lens: An integrated view of resource investments and the incremental-choice process. *Academy of Management Review*, 18, 760–782.

Busenitz, L.W. and J.B. Barney (1997). Differences between entrepreneurs and managers in large organizations: Biases and heuristics in strategic decision making. *Journal of Business Venturing*, 12, 9–30.

Business News, New Jersey (2001). Jim Carnes, on being, and remaining, a high-tech state. *Business News, New Jersey*, 23, October, 13.

Cable, D.M. and S. Shane (1997). A "prisoners" dilemma approach to entrepreneur-venture capitalist relationships. *Academy of Management Review*, 22, 142–176.

Chandler, A.D. (1990). *Scale and Scope: The Dynamics of Industrial Capitalism*. Cambridge, MA: Belknap Press.

Charan, R. and J. Useem (2002). Why companies fail. *Fortune*, 27, May.

Chatterjee, S., M. Lubatkin and W.S. Schulze (1999). Toward a strategic theory of risk premium: Moving beyond CAPM. *Academy of Management Review*, 24, 556–567.

Child, J. and R.G. McGrath (2001). Organizations unfettered: Organizational form in an information-intensive eonomy. *Academy of Management Journal*, 44, 1135–1148.

Christensen, C.M., P. Carlile and D.M. Sundahl (2002). The process of theory building. Working paper, Harvard Business School, presented at the 2002 Academy of Management Meetings.

Clayton, M.C., P. Carlile and D.M. Sundahl (2002). The Process of Theory Building. Working paper, presented at the 2002 Academy of Management Meetings, Denver, CO. August 9, 2002.

Commons, J.R. (1974). *Legal Foundations of Capitalism*. Reprinted by Univ. Wisc. Press and Arno Press; originally published by Macmillan, 1924.

Commons, J.R. (1950). *The Economics of Collective Action*. Madison, WI: University of Wisconsin Press.

Dixit, A.K. and R.S. Pindyck (1994). *Investment under Uncertainty*. Princeton, NJ: Princeton University Press.

Drake, Beam and Morin (2001). CEO Turnover and Job Security. Special Report, 2001 [online]. Available: http:// www.dbm.com.

Foster, R. (1986). *Innovation: The Attackers' Advantage*. New York: Summit Books.

Foster, R. and S. Kaplan (2001). *Creative Destruction: Why Companies that are Built to Last Underperform the Market – and How to Successfully Transform Them*. New York: Doubleday.

Gatewood, E.J., K.G. Shaver and W.B. Gartner (1995). A longitudinal study of cognitive factors influencing start-up behaviors and success at venture creation. *Journal of Business Venturing*, 10, 371–391.

Gimeno, J., T.B. Folta, A.C. Cooper and C.Y. Woo (1997). Survival of the fittest? Entrepreneurial human capital and the persistence of underperforming firms. *Administrative Science Quarterly*, 42, 750–783.

Goold, M., A. Campbel and M. Alexander (1994). *Corporate Level Strategy: Creating Value in the Multibusiness Company*. New York: John Wiley & Sons.

Hamel, G. (2000). *Leading the Revolution*. Boston, MA: Harvard Business School Press.

Harrison, B. (1994a). The myth of the small firm as the predominant job creators. *Economic Development Quarterly,* **8,** 3–18.

Harrison, B. (1994b). *Lean and Mean: Why Large Corporations will Continue to Dominate the Global Economy.* New York: Guilford Press.

Henderson, R.M. and K.B. Clark (1990). Architectural innovation: The reconfiguration of existing product technologies and the failure of established firms. *Administrative Science Quarterly,* **35,** 9–30.

Hitt, M.A., R.D. Ireland, S.M. Camp and D.L. Sexton (2002). *Strategic Entrepreneurship: Creating a New Mindset.* Malden, MA: Blackwell Publishers.

Kester, W.C. (1981). Growth options and investment: A dynamic perspective on the firm's allocation of resources. Unpublished Ph.D. dissertation, Harvard University, Cambridge, MA.

Kets de Vries, M.F.R. and D. Miller (1984). Neurotic styles and organizational pathology. *Strategic Management Journal,* **5,** 35–55.

Kortum, S. and J. Lerner (1999). What is behind the recent surge in patenting? *Research Policy,* **28,** 1–22.

Leslie, S.W. and R.H. Kargon (1996). Selling Silicon Valley: Frederick Terman's model for regional advantage. *Business History Review,* **70,** 435–472.

Lucier, C., E. Spiegel and R. Schuyt (2002). Why CEO's fail: The causes and consequences of turnover at the top. *Strategy + Business,* 28 Special Report [online]. Available from Booz/Allen/Hamilton: http://www.bah.com, September 29, 2002.

McGrath, B. and R.G. McGrath (2001). Spillovers and Strategy: Implications of the Network Economy. Working paper, Columbia Business School, New York, NY.

McGrath, R.G. (1996). Options and the entrepreneur: Towards a strategic theory of entrepreneurial wealth creation. *Best Papers Proceedings Academy of Management Annual Meetings, Cincinnati, Ohio, August 1996.* Published in the Academy Proceedings. The meeting was held in Cincinnati, Ohio, published by the Academy of Management, pp. 101–105.

McGrath, R.G. (1997). A real options logic for initiating technology positioning investments. *Academy of Management Review,* **22,** 974–996.

McGrath, R.G. (1999). Falling forward: Real options reasoning and entrepreneurial failure. *Academy of Management Review,* **24,** 13–30.

McGrath, R.G. and A. Nerkar (2001). Real Options Reasoning and a new look at the R&D Investment Strategies of Pharmaceutical Firms. Paper presented at the 2001 Strategic Management Society Meetings in San Francisco, California. October, 2001.

MacMillan, I.C. and J.A. Katz (1992). Idiosyncratic milieus of entrepreneurial research: The need for comprehensive theories. *Journal of Business Venturing,* 7(1), 1–8.

March, J.G. (1991). Exploration and exploitation in organizational learning. *Organization Science,* 2(1), 71–87.

Miner, A.S., D.T. Eesley, M. Devaughn and T. Rura-Polley (2001). The magic beanstalk vision: Commercializing university inventions and research. In Schoonhoven and Romanelli (eds.), *The Entrepreneurship Dynamic,* pp. 109–146, Chapter 5. Stanford, CA: Stanford University Press.

Morris, P.A, E.O. Teisberg and A.L. Kolbe (1991). When Choosing R&D projects, go with long shots. *Research-Technology Management,* Jan–Feb, pp. 35–40.

Norton, R. (2001). The decline (but trust us on this, not the fall) of the American venture capitalist. *Business,* 20, October, 81–86.

Porter, M.E., H. Takeuchi and M. Sakakibara (2001). *Can Japan Compete?* New York: Macmillan.

Pfeffer J. and G. Salancik (1978). *The External Control of Organizations: A Resource Dependence Perspective.* New York: Harper & Row Publishers.

Prahalad, C.K. and G. Hamel (1990). The core competence of the corporation. *Harvard Business Review,* **68,** 79–91.

Rumelt, R.P. (1987). Theory, Strategy and Entrepreneurship. In D.J. Teece (ed.), *The competitive challenge: Strategies for industrial innovation and renewal.* New York: Harper and Row, pp. 137–158.

Saxenian, A. (1994). *Regional Advantage: Culture and Competition in Silicon Valley and Route 128.* Cambridge, MA: Harvard Business School Publishing.

Schoonhoven, C.B. and E. Romanelli (2001). *The Entrepreneurship Dynamic: Origins of Entrepreneurship and the Evolution of Industries.* Stanford, CA: Stanford University Press.

Schumpeter, J.A. (1942). *Capitalism, Socialism and Democracy.* New York, NY: McGraw-Hill.

Shane, Scott and S. Venkataraman (2000). The promise of entrepreneurship as a field of research. *Academy of Management Review,* 25, 217–226.

Spicer, A., G.A. McDermott and B. Kogut (2000). Entrepreneurship and privatization in central Europe. The tenuous balance between destruction and creation. *Academy of Managment Review,* 25(3), 630–649.

Stinchcombe, A. (1997).On the virtues of the old institutionalism. *Annual Review of Sociology,* 23, 1–18.

Stinchcombe, A.L. (1965). Organizations and social structure. In J.G. March (ed.), *Handbook of Organizations.* Chicago: Rand McNally.

Tripsas, M. (1997). Unraveling the process of creative destruction: Complementary assets and incumbent survival in the typesetter industry. *Strategic Management Journal,* 18 (special issue), 119–142.

Van de Ven, A. (1993). The development of an infrastructure for entrepreneurship. *Journal of Business Venturing,* 8(3), 211–230.

Van de Ven, A. (1993). The institutional theory of John R. Commons: A review and commentary. *Academy of Management Review,* 18, 139–152.

Venkataraman, S. (1997). The distinctive domain of entrepreneurship research. In J. Katz and R. Brockhaus (eds.), *Advances in Entrepreneurship, Firm Emergence, and Growth.* Greenwich, CT: JAI Press, III, pp. 119–138.

Venkataraman, S. and A.H. Van de Ven (1993). Hostile environmental jolts, transaction set, and new business. *Journal of Business Venturing,* 13, 231–255.

Welbourne, T.M. and A.O. Andrews (1996). Predicting the performance of initial public offerings: Should human resource management be in the equation? *Academy of Management Journal,* 39, 891–919.

Whitman, M.N. (1999). *New World, New Rules: The Changing Role of the American Corporation.* Boston, MA: Harvard Business School Press.

Index

International Handbook Series on Entrepreneurship

1. Zoltan J. Acs and David B. Audretsch (eds.): *Handbook of Entrepreneurship Research*. 2003.   ISBN 1-4020-7358-5